SCHOOL AND SOCIETY

READINGS IN

School

THE SOCIAL AND PHILOSOPHICAL

and

FOUNDATIONS OF EDUCATION

Society

CARL H. GROSS

STANLEY P. WRONSKI

JOHN W. HANSON

MICHIGAN STATE UNIVERSITY

D. C. HEATH AND COMPANY BOSTON

Preface

THIS is a book for a particular time, a particular society, and a particular purpose. While many of the selections do come from works that have made their mark in the history of ideas, they are included here because they shed light on important dimensions of the contemporary scene. The total import of the collection lies with the many readings that are especially relevant to the present.

There are always advantages and potential dangers in any such emphasis on contemporaneity. Among the advantages are immediate relevance to the lives of readers, the possibility of sloughing off portions of the past which are of historical interest only, and the likelihood of providing more precise focus. Chief among the potential dangers of contemporaneity is the tendency to balance precariously on the knife-edge of the present, and to lose that perspective which time alone provides. We sincerely believe that the sense of present we have tried to maintain is not such a contemporaneity out of context; rather, it is grounded in a sound understanding of the development of society and of education. This book remains, however, a book for today and tomorrow, a book for the period immediately ahead.

As an aid to the classroom teacher in meeting both anticipated and unanticipated situations, this book is intended to be unabashedly *practical* in the most meaningful sense of the word. It attempts to provide the reader with a useful conceptual framework for making commitments and formulating action. It aims not so much

at providing the teacher with a ready made philosophy of education as at enabling him to develop for himself a defensible and consistent point of view toward the profession to which his life is to be devoted. In a real sense, then, this book is designed as a *tool* — a tool to be used in the difficult tasks of reflection and decision.

While the editors have attempted to leave the final decisions to the student, we do not pretend that this volume does not reflect our own judgments and points of view. Any volume covering a broad field must be selective. The selection of topics, problems, and viewpoints included reflects our system of values and our judgments. We have tried to make this system of values explicit to alert the student. Probably nowhere is our value system more significant than in determining which topics are to be treated as issues and which are to be treated as relatively fixed and stable. No sound decisions can be reached by viewing everything as being in a state of flux and uncertainty. Where we have viewed some matters as relatively determined, we have done so in the belief that these fixities reflect the composite judgment of competent experts and that they will, in part, provide the stable background which may be used in resolving many of the crucial issues facing teachers today.

Basically the philosophic viewpoint which has influenced our selections is that of a democratic pragmatism, a reasoned belief that the democratic way of life and the moral and intellectual processes requisite to that life provide us with the surest guidelines for effective teaching. Inevitably there will be a variety of reactions to this basis for editorial selection. But no one will find this collection altogether reassuring to his favorite viewpoint, since the book's primary aim is clarification of issues, often through opposing viewpoints, to the end that decisions may be reached. If this volume in some measure provides the intellectual resources for creative teaching, and if it provides the intellectual foils against which the student may test himself in the creative process of serious learning, it will have served a far more useful purpose than that of *comfortable* reading.

In one particular way this volume is the debtor of the democratic tradition it espouses. Such a collection as this is possible only because of *the democratic allegiance to the wide accessibility and the free exchange of ideas.* The wide range of divergent views here presented and analyzed was made possible only by the generosity of many publishers and authors who, firm in this belief, have permitted their ideas to be used. With less specific acknowledgment, we must also express our deep sense of gratitude to our colleagues who, both through specific suggestions while this volume was being compiled and through the free exchange of ideas during our many years of teaching together in this field, have in fact contributed many of the ideas we now cherish as our own.

Carl H. Gross
East Lansing, Michigan

John W. Hanson
Nsukka, Nigeria

Stanley P. Wronski
South Weymouth, Massachusetts

Contents

SCHOOL AND SOCIETY

I

Prologue

SECTION 1. The nature of teaching

To be a teacher in our time and our society is to engage in one of the most challenging and demanding occupations to which man has yet addressed himself. Successful teaching involves a degree of practical intelligence and moral judgment required in few other occupations. Thus teaching is not an occupation for which candidates can be routinely trained, that is, for which they can be drilled in a set of specific techniques which, once mastered, will provide them with a comprehensive set of tools adequate to the trade. The tools of the trade in teaching are more complex, more fundamental, than any set of techniques which can be acquired by rote memory or purely repetitive practice; for teaching is a calling which constantly involves *the act of choice* — a calling which imposes upon those who accept its challenge the requirement that they make decisions and solve problems in a multitude of unresolved and continually developing situations. It is this quality which gives to teaching its fundamentally professional status.

As teaching inevitably requires the teacher to exercise the art of choice, good teaching is distinguished from poor teaching or mis-teaching largely in terms of the *quality* of the choices made. The good teacher is thus the one who makes wise decisions or who solves his problems intelligently; that is, the good teacher is one who, in a given set of circumstances, is able to determine what is on the whole best to do and proceeds to do it. The poor teacher, on the other hand, is most frequently the one who is unaware of the choices which confront him, blind to the wider factors involved in the situation, or lacking in the ability to make an effective decision or the courage to carry out that decision. Thus the teacher who blindly assumes that a given body of content is to be taught under any and all circumstances, the one who views any specific teaching technique as always applicable, the one who seeks to treat all students or all signs of undesirable behavior in the same manner — in short, the teacher who is uninformed about the broader context within which his specific teaching is occurring — can never be considered the good teacher.

If one is to equip himself to be a good teacher, then it follows that he must prepare himself to choose wisely and well. In the myriad of complex situations which confront teachers this is, of course, not easy, and no truly great teacher feels that he has been universally successful in meeting the challenge of all situations. But there are certain fundamental ingredients for making wise choices. When these ingredients are lacking, choices become shallow or arbitrary at best, undeliberate or unrecognized at worst. The first requirement, then, is to assure the presence of these ingredients. What are these essential ingredients for choosing wisely?

First of all, the teacher who would choose wisely must *recognize* or be aware of the situations in which he has the possibility and the obligation to make deliberate choices. Actually, we make deliberate or reflective choices only in situations which we *recognize* as problematical. Problematical situations may be of different orders, but they regularly fall into one of several types. We usually recognize that we have a decision to make when we confront a situation in which (1) we are confused about the ends or purposes which should guide our action, (2) we recognize such ends or purposes but find them to be in conflict with one another, or (3) we are uncertain as to the best means of achieving whatever ends we have in mind. Whenever a teacher determines reflectively whether or not he should send Johnny to the office, whether he should take his class on a given field trip, whether he should request a conference with a given parent, whether he should teach a unit on the United Nations or a unit on the Soviet Union, he is facing one or the other of these problematical situations. He is facing the fundamental task of the teacher: trying to relate the best available means to reflectively chosen ends. He is engaged in *purposive* activity in the most meaningful sense of the word: he is giving attention to both the *purposes* he has in mind and to the *means* which alone can realize these purposes.

Thus the first essential ingredient in choosing wisely is that the person making the choice must be aware of the purposes for acting or the goals to be achieved. Without some concept of what is to be accomplished, choices are meaningless. To choose a course of action without knowing what to accomplish would be like choosing an automobile route without knowing where one wanted to go. But it is never enough merely to have goals: one is constantly confronted with the additional requirement that he have *worthy* goals. We all possess a myriad of goals or purposes. Some have been acquired without prior judgment as to their worth (*prejudices,* if you will);

some have been acquired only after temperate and reflective thought. Good teachers are those who are willing to engage in the difficult task of sorting out worthy goals from the unworthy, significant goals from the insignificant, urgent or central goals from the luxurious or peripheral goals. In this way they determine hierarchies of objectives or values which guide them in their actions.

How does the good teacher make this judgment of worth, of significance, of centrality of goals? This is neither an easy task nor a task which, once accomplished, can be conveniently forgotten. As situations vary and evolve, new ingredients alter the structure, and new goals, once unrecognized or inappropriate, assume commanding importance. Two reasonably certain criteria present themselves for judging the appropriateness of choices. First, those choices of goals which look only to the immediate situation tend to be shortsighted and inadequate; those which are made after careful evaluative analysis of the wider context within which teaching occurs are customarily more appropriate and worthy. Second, those choices of goals and values which are made with a full awareness of the various alternatives available tend to be more appropriate and worthy. American education rests upon choice; it will be a sound education if teachers are fully aware of the wider context within which they work and of the alternative values which are available for choice.

Although both the awareness of problems and the clarification and evaluation of goals are essential to the successful practice of teaching, good teaching is always more than this. Goals which are not or cannot be translated into practice are too often the enemy rather than the friend of good teaching. This has occurred all too often as goals have become slogans or rallying cries which, voiced loudly and often, seem to have expended the energy and potential of their adherents. Having uttered the slogans or rallied to the cry, too many teachers are wont to believe their work is done. They fail to recognize that slogans and achievement may be very different things. Whenever this is the case, goals or purposes become substitutes for, rather than ingredients in effective teaching; they become moral sops for teachers who fail to achieve in actual practice. Thus no goal is worthy of the loyalty expended upon it if it is not capable of directing or modifying the action of its adherents.

The good teacher is always an active searcher after those means by which his considered goals may be actualized or brought into being. This requires that he give constant attention to *what is;* it requires more urgently that he be continually aware of *what can be.* He is a student of *what is,* for only then can he recognize the extent to which worthy goals are not being met or recognize the unrealized potential of the situation. He is a student of *what can be,* for only then can he realistically seek out the paths of professional activity which will help him achieve worthy goals. But whether he is studying *what is* or *what can be,* he must recognize that these are studies which are subservient to his ultimate responsibility; for the teacher is essentially an adherent of *what ought to be,* and his fundamental commit-

ment as teacher is to modify *what is* so that it may in actuality develop into what *ought to be.* He is not a passive witness to each and every existing teacher situation; he is an active, responsible, courageous agent deeply devoted to intelligent change.

The study of the philosophical and social foundations of education can readily enable you to discover what teaching is and what teaching can be. It can only help you to discover for yourself what teaching ought to be. This must be a process of discovery on your part, for in a democratic society it would be presumptuous to present the final answers to you. Your lot is to share in shaping the future of teaching. In accepting the role of teacher you assume the responsibility of helping determine what constitutes a better life; you join with others in helping your society, especially through its young members, to realize its full potential in acquiring such a life. In broadest outlines, this is the course that each teacher sets forth upon; its successful completion calls for a full measure of creative intelligence, constantly renewed by a study of fact and ideal, on the part of each teacher. The creative transformation, by a process of reflective choice, of what *is* into what *can be* and what *ought to be* is what makes the great teacher.

SECTION **2. The areas of choice**

Throughout your teaching career you will be confronted by choices which must be made. Your ability to recognize the choices to be made and your ability to make them deliberately, intelligently, and consistently will be basic to your success as a teacher. Although the specific choices facing you will be many and varied, these will tend to fall into line once certain fundamental or underlying choices have been made. It is important, consequently, to think through first the basic decisions confronting all members of the teaching profession, for in making

these decisions deliberately you will secure guidelines which will prove invaluable in making subsequent specific teaching decisions. Many of the most important issues confronted by the profession of teaching, and by the individual teacher, fall in the following areas of decision.

Responsibility for education. The American educational system is characterized by pluralism or diversity. At each of the levels of instruction — elementary grades, secondary grades, and college — there are institutions which represent quite different conceptions of the appropriate locus of responsibility for education. Undoubtedly the largest building blocks in the edifice of American education are the public schools. Such schools represent the belief that education is essentially a state function — a function to be carried on in public, by the public, for the benefit of both the individual and the public. But familiar as this portion of the edifice is to all of us, our educational system contains other important building blocks as well. Some four million youngsters annually attend school in the largest of our religious school systems. This system, while recognizing the civic responsibility of education, represents the view that education is more than a civic affair; that basically and legitimately it resides in the hands of the Church and family. This school system, then, reveals a different point of view of the relative claims of Church and State on the time of the young.

Still other important blocks in the school edifice are provided by the non-public, non-church-affiliated schools. These schools represent the belief that education at its best is a private affair in which parents select for their child the particular educational milieu in which they feel he can best develop. Americans conceive of private education as an option. Thus parents have the *privilege* of sending their young to private schools, but must then assume the corresponding *obligation* to carry the financial burden of this education if they select the option.

All three systems share much that is common in the American scheme of values. Yet each of them tends to have a different clientele, a different set of emphases, a different central orientation. A teacher can clearly be most effective if he enters a school system which is in keeping with his own commitment on the fundamental issue: Is education centrally a religious, a public, or a private function?

Cultural scope of the educational function. Education is inevitably concerned with helping the young take their places in society. But what is the nature of the society into which these young are to be initiated? This is a particularly urgent problem for American society, since the historical development of American education has usually placed the legal control over our schools in the state and local community. At the same time the historical development of world civilization has moved inescapably toward the interdependence of social units throughout the world. Careful students of the social scene are almost universally agreed that events or developments happening anywhere in the world have repercussions throughout human society. When this extended interdependence exists alongside various forms of local and regional traditions — unfortunately often replete with biases, prejudices, and blindspots — dangerous frictions and inadequacies often appear. In this situation the teaching profession must take a stand. As yet the profession is uncertain of its course. Some within it maintain that schools must be designed to serve the particular local communities in which they are rooted. This is one extreme of the grass roots philosophy of American social life — the faith in small face-to-face relations and the fear of larger social units. A second group maintains that education is essentially a regional function. This group looks to the long-standing regional traditions and calls attention to the cultural richness that has come to our country out of the spectrum of regional variations. Education, this group believes, should be designed to perpetuate and develop the " way of life " of the particular region. A third group looks upon education as essentially national in scope and function. Believing that a central fact of our present social system is the participation of the individual in the total national society, and recognizing the extreme mobility of our people, this group sees need for placing increased emphasis upon national control and scope in education.

Finally, some persons view even this national scope as being too confining: to them the international community of all human kind is the true social group to which the individual belongs. Such persons are seeking to assure us that this realization is fostered through education. Each of these groups has laid strong claims to the allegiance of some persons within the profession, but each teacher must decide upon the worthiness of the respective claims. He must stand ready with his own commitments as the interests and allegiances of adherents to these different social perspectives come into conflict with one another.

The aims and content of education. Perhaps there is nowhere any greater confusion on the American intellectual scene than that which exists in respect to the aims and content of education. The confusion revealed by the American public is shared within the profession of teachers. Yet teachers, individually and collectively, must reach conclusions as to what their aims are and what content will best achieve these aims. There are some who view education as quite exclusively the training of the intellect. Such persons propose leaving other functions to other institutions and devoting the school to the one purpose they judge it to be uniquely capable of performing — intellectual training. There are some who view education as helping individuals adjust to the existing order — to helping them solve the problems which our society poses. These persons look to the *problems* that individuals have in growing up in our society as determining the aims and content of instruction and would not have the school overly concerned about the " academic respectability " of the materials and instruction implied. There are others who would view education as centering in and growing out of the *interests* of children and youth. Education to them should become the handmaiden of interests. Still others would see the schools as deliberate agents of social change. On the basis of the findings of the human sciences, the schools would select those social changes which need to be made and would educate the young to recognize the need for bringing these changes to pass.

These fundamental orientations toward education ordinarily do not present themselves to the teacher or the school in this abstract form. Rather they crop up in specifics: With a given amount of money to spend, should our high school put in fourth year French or add a course in driver training? Should the required English course include a study of modern television, or should it devote the extra time to a more exacting study of the classics? Should vocational education be taught in the public schools or left to labor and industry? Should the elementary teacher attempt to lead her children to respect each other regardless of nationality, color of skin, or religion, even if their parents do not hold such tolerant beliefs? Such questions are illustrations of the general problem of function in education. Each of them rests for its solution upon the determination of appropriate criteria of worth. Such criteria can only be derived from answering the basic question: What are the aims of education?

The student body. With limited financial resources available for expanding educational functions, it seems probable that questions concerning the recipients of education will continue to be important for years to come. The American faith in *universal education* has enjoyed a long and hallowed tradition. But the meaning of universal education is still far from clear. *How much* education should everyone receive? What are our obligations when the individual appears uninterested or incapable of benefiting from the education we are providing? These problems are always with us. Their difficulty is compounded when the question of standards of excellence is raised. Some would judge schools by their ability to capitalize on the potential of the intellectual elite. Others would judge the excellence of schools by their ability to bring all, or a high percentage, of their students at least up to certain predetermined standards. Others would judge the excellence of the schools by the diversification of their programs to meet the demands of differing groups. Acceptance of any one of these orientations would affect the distribution of our resources among the differing individuals and groups attending our schools. The distribution of these resources — teachers, facilities, and money — will inevitably affect both the quantity and the quality of education which different persons receive. This distribution will determine the real meaning we are going to give to universal education.

Organization and discipline. Both organization and discipline essentially deal with the structure of human relations. Closely related to the question of *whom* we should educate is the problem of *how* to group or organize whatever students we seek to educate. Both the pattern of organization and the pattern of human relations practiced by teacher and school will affect the kind of students we retain, the kinds of learning which students acquire, the kind of product we turn out. A host of questions immediately arises when we face the problem of organizing the student body for learning: should we group students according to ability, should we separate students into different tracks or programs, or should we organize students so they have some experiences in common? Not one of these questions can be answered until we have first answered the prior question of what purposes are to be served. One organization will be most conducive to achieving one set of results; another organization will give best promise of producing another set of results. Similarly, each teacher is confronted with the problem of the nature of discipline and the methods of achieving it. As with organization, so discipline is always related to a concept of what is desired. Few teachers would disagree that they wish students to be " disciplined individuals." Basic disagreement arises, however, as to what constitutes a disciplined individual capable of contributing maximally in today's society.

Educational authority. The problem of determining *who* should decide *what* with respect to education is a particularly difficult one in a democratic society. It is commonplace in American educational thought that " the schools belong to the people." As with most educational slogans, however, this one tends to be vague. To *what people* do the schools belong? To what extent is their authority delegated to the professional persons they certify and select as qualified instructors? The problem of educational authority is, however, part of the larger issue of the role of authority and expert knowledge in any democracy. No society can long endure which does not capitalize upon its resources of expert knowledge. At the same time, no democratic society can abdicate broad public control over the basic policies which guide that society. This poses a dilemma which is particularly acute in the intellectual realm. Witness the current confusion in education. On the one hand, teachers proclaim their professional competence and authority to educate the young. They support this with claims to academic freedom as the necessary safeguard for intellectual development and human progress. On the other hand, parents express a legitimate and essential concern for the welfare of their youngsters *as they see this welfare.* They buttress this by pointing to the rights of parents and to their democratic faith that " the schools belong to the people." The careful delimitation of the appropriate roles of lay and professional authority in determining the educational program remains an unresolved challenge to new teachers.

Professional role. The teacher, upon entering his profession, finds himself immediately involved in carrying on roles within various spheres of activity. For example, he serves as a director of learning of young people in the classroom, as a colleague among faculty members in a particular school, as both a member and an employee of a given community. In each of these spheres he is called upon or expected to play various roles. Sometimes these roles complement and support each other while at other times they are contradictory. In each of these spheres his effectiveness depends upon his ability to act in the light of the best available knowledge and in accordance with the highest ethical standards of his profession. Moreover, the true measure of his success will be determined by his ability to resolve the conflicts between the various demands and expectations in such a manner that his primary educational function is not imperilled. Any such resolution can only occur if inherent problems are clearly recognized, if the respective roles and expectations are not only seen but evaluated, and if a consistent set of principles capable of directing practice is thoughtfully formulated and scrupulously employed.

Professionalization. We clearly live in a society in which the organized group has become the effective means of achieving political and social action. In such a society, it is urgent that the teaching profession so organize itself that the social and professional objectives which it espouses can best be advanced. What form of organization and self-discipline will achieve this is an issue in education. This issue is complicated by the uncertain status of teaching as a profession. Thus the teaching group is faced with the problems inherent in maintaining high standards for admission to and retention in the profession. At the same time, it is faced with the problems inherent in helping the public recognize the professional quality of its service and its own areas of expert knowledge. Any professional organization of teachers must face these two problems. Any such organization must likewise face the more pervasive challenge of operating so as to enhance the performance of the educational function — to advance the cause of education, broadly conceived, in a democratic society. Some have sought to advance toward these objectives through affiliating with other groups deeply devoted to public education — for example, with organized labor. Others have sought to achieve these objectives through the formation of independent, all-inclusive teacher organizations. No clear answer exists within the profession as to how it can best organize to achieve its full potential. It will be a continuing task of the oncoming generation of teachers to seek out and find increasingly effective ways of resolving these problems and to organize in such a way as to realize the full potential which resides in education.

No final resolution of these issues is yet available. The reading which you will be doing will not resolve them directly. This reading can at best only help you recognize the issues and reach your own considered decisions in respect to each of them. Once you have clearly delineated and tentatively resolved these broad issues, the legions of specific problems you will confront as a teacher will begin to fall into place and the direction to be taken for their successful solution will become clear.

One further caution is in order. Although a careful study of the social and philosophical foundations of education is necessary in order to form your initial teaching commitments, such a study cannot give you the final answers to the problems of the profession you are entering. As a matter of fact, if such a study is successful, it will help you come to view your answers as tentative and open to subsequent revision as your background of study and experience grows. Principles are no less useful as guides to action because they are viewed as mutable and subject to subsequent revision. Rather, it is only when they are so viewed that a genuinely professional approach to teaching will be acquired; for, in a very real sense, the great teacher is himself always a willing learner, capitalizing on experience as it comes along to refine and clarify the professional operation in which he has been engaged.

SECTION 3. Some underlying assumptions

In a volume such as this, consisting of varied readings representing a wide spectrum of points of view, the reader may justifiably inquire about the particular points of view, preferences, assumptions and persuasions that are subscribed to by the editors. The editors, in turn, feel that the reader is entitled to such information. An explicit statement of such underlying assumptions has the basic advantage of facilitating communication between the editors and the reader. Clear channels of communication tend in turn to facilitate learning.

In the following section of this chapter, therefore, we identify and elaborate upon some of the significant points of view that underlie the thinking of the editors. The reader should be forewarned, however, that not all of the selected readings in this volume reflect this same pattern of thinking. On the contrary, we have included selections that start from quite different — and sometimes diametrically opposite — assumptions.

Relationship of school, society, and culture. One of our key assumptions in compiling this volume is that education ought to be functionally related to the society and the culture in which it operates. Education is not apart from the culture; it is a part of it. As an illustration of this relationship, consider the following excerpts from Ruth Benedict's *Patterns of Culture,* in which the cultural pattern of the Plains Indians is contrasted with that of the Pueblo-dwelling Zuni Indians.

" This self-reliance and personal initiative on the plains were expressed not only in shamanism but in their passionate enthusiasm for the guerrilla warfare that occupied them. Their war parties were ordinarily less than a dozen strong, and the individual acted alone in their simple engagements in a way that stands at the other pole from the rigid discipline and subordination of modern warfare. Their war was a game in which each individual amassed counts. These counts were for cutting loose a picketed horse, or touching an enemy, or taking a scalp. The individual, usually by personal dare-deviltry, acquired as many as he could, and used them for joining societies, giving feasts, qualifying as a chief. Without initiative and the ability to act alone, an Indian of the plains was not recognized in his society. The testimony of early explorers, the rise of outstanding individuals in their conflicts with the whites, the contrast with the Pueblos, all go to show how their institutions fostered personality, almost in the Nietzschean sense of the superman. They saw life as the drama of the individual progressing upward through grades of men's societies, through acquisitions of supernatural power, through feasts and victories. The initiative rested always with him. His deeds of prowess were counted for him personally, and it was his prerogative to boast of them on ritual occasions, and to use them in every way to further his personal ambitions." [1]

[1] Ruth Benedict, *Patterns of Culture* (Boston, 1934), p. 98. Quoted by permission of Houghton Mifflin Company.

The "ideal man" of the mild-mannered Zunis, on the other hand, is almost directly the opposite to that of the Plains Indians.

". . . Personal authority is perhaps the most vigorously disparaged trait in Zuni. 'A man who thirsts for power or knowledge, who wishes to be as they scornfully phrase it "a leader of his people," receives nothing but censure and will very likely be persecuted for sorcery,' and he often has been. Native authority of manner is a liability in Zuni, and witchcraft is the ready charge against a person who possesses it. He is hung by the thumbs until he 'confesses.' It is all Zuni can do with a man of strong personality. The ideal man in Zuni is a person of dignity and affability who has never tried to lead, and who has never called forth comment from his neighbors. Any conflict, even though all right is on his side, is held against him. Even in contests of skill like their foot races, if a man wins habitually he is debarred from running. They are interested in a game that a number can play with even chances, and an outstanding runner spoils the game: they will have none of him." [2]

It would seem obvious, even to the most inexperienced observer, that the type of education — both formal and informal — that is carried on in these two societies is markedly different. The Plains Indians are *not* taught, either at home or in schools, to be submissive, agreeable, and charitable. The Zuni Indians, on the other hand, are *not* taught to be aggressive, contentious, and selfish.

So it is in any society. In the long run there must be some kind of harmonious relationship between the educative experiences of the members of that society and the major characteristics of the social patterns, customs, and norms of the society. To the extent that there are discrepancies in this relationship there is also a lack of integration within the total society. This is not to argue, of course, that the schools must always reflect and indoctrinate for all dominant social patterns. Sometimes certain customary ways of doing things *ought* to be changed, and the school is one of the most useful social agencies for effecting such changes.

Before any teacher or prospective teacher begins to have his pupils either conform to or modify the existing social pattern, he ought to know something about the dominant characteristics of the society in which both he and his pupils are immersed. He should know about the societal facts of life. It is for this reason that any good teacher preparation program includes a substantial amount of what is termed general education. The areas dealt with in most general education programs typically include the following: natural sciences, social sciences, humanities, and communication arts. Within these academic areas the student deals with one or more of the social institutions that so vitally influence behavior within any society. The major social institutions found in all societies are those relating to the family, government, economy, religion, and education. Without in any way attempting to review the dominant attributes of these social institutions, let us use them as convenient points of departure to illustrate the importance of relating the school to society and culture.

The changing nature of the family in American society has been verified by the sociologists, feared by some moralists, analyzed by governmental researchers, and condemned by some preachers. Approximately one in every four marriages in the United States ends in divorce. More married women are working or actively seeking employment now than in any other period of peace. Undesirable home and family conditions are considered to be a major causative factor in juvenile delinquency. What do these social phenomena mean to the

[2] *Ibid.*, pp. 98–99.

teacher? First of all, he must be aware of these and similar conditions, particularly as they apply to the local community in which he teaches. Being aware of them should enable him to deal more objectively and effectively with the child who is emotionally upset because his parents are in the process of getting a divorce, the child who "doesn't mix" with neighborhood peers because she has to take care of the baby while her mother is working the afternoon shift, or the child who is a "white collar delinquent" because he finds no means at home for satisfying a need for distinctive achievement.

As for significant contemporary developments in governmental institutions, among the most important is the all-pervasive role of government in the lives of all citizens. Whether we like it or not, some agency of government is vitally concerned with the fact that we are born, are enrolled in school, are applying for a marriage license, are submitting an income tax form, and are buried. We have practically reached the stage in which government, whether benevolent or not, is concerned about our welfare from womb to tomb. These social realities about government impose a dual obligation upon the teacher. In the first place they indicate a need to make pupils aware of the increased interdependence of man in a complex society. They also indicate that the scope of public education, as one of the major arms of government, is increasing in about the same proportion as other governmental functions.

Similar observations could be made about the other key social institutions in our society. There are continuing decisions to be made, for example, about the allocation of resources within our economic system of private enterprise and government regulation. What should be the proportion of our productive goods and services allocated for education compared with the amount for national defense, highways, private capital investments,

consumer goods, and the like? As for the matter of religion, where do we draw the fine line separating church from state or the line that separates teaching *about* religion from indoctrination *in* a religion? And finally, since the schools are a social agency both for retaining the culture and modifying it, what should be the relative emphasis on these two conflicting aims, and on what philosophic bases does the teacher make judgments to retain or modify?

This matter of making judgments brings us to another important consideration about the relationship between school and society. The professionally-minded teacher is not only aware of objective factual data about social realities, but he also is obligated to make some kind of normative judgment of them. By normative judgment we mean that the teacher is involved in the process of evaluation or making value judgments, that is, determining what *ought* to be. The kinds of normative decisions that the teacher is called upon to make practically every day puts him in a unique category among professional people. The mechanical engineer or the biologist, for example, will probably not make as many normative decisions involving other human beings during his entire professional life as the typical teacher will make in one school year. These decisions impose a tremendous responsibility on the teacher. They emphasize again that the accumulation of factual information about the society and culture in which we live, while indispensable to the teacher, is still not sufficient in itself; it must be synthesized within a process of decision-making which involves judgments about social institutions, social customs, individual patterns of behavior, and individual beliefs. This process of decision-making, in turn, rests upon one's philosophical commitments.

The foregoing discussion involving the school, society, value judgments, and philosophy may perhaps be crystallized by considering a specific situation. The Soviet Union, for example, has achieved remarkable success in recent years in the area of launching man-made satellites. As a result of this success and other achievements in Soviet science, many people have asked whether the Russian system of education is better than that in the United States. This question, or some variation of it, is particularly asked of those who have studied Russian education. The reply of George Counts, one of the foremost students of Russian society and education, is simply that the question doesn't make sense. It is as if we were to try to solve a mathematical problem by indiscriminately using two different numbering systems. In order for the question to be meaningful we must first ask what the goals, aspirations, and basic values are in each society. Then we must inquire as to whether the system of education is tending to achieve these goals and re-inforce these basic values. Without arguing for the case of cultural relativism, one may very well say that the Russian system is doing an adequate job of promoting the goals and values of a *communistic society*. But such a system may well be — and probably is — unsuited to a democratic society. Much of the recent public discussion of Russian versus American education, however pointless it may be, does serve to emphasize the overriding consideration that the educational system in *any* society should be functionally related to its culture.

Commitment to democracy. The editors of this volume believe that the democratic way of life not only expresses a fundamental commitment of this society but is the most humane set of goals and social conditions yet worked out by man. The principles of democracy are not completely understood, practiced, or subscribed to by all citizens in our society. Equal treatment under the law is not a reality in every section of the land. The right to vote is often limited. Minorities frequently find their rights restricted or denied. Yet for all our shortcomings, our people as a whole claim loyalty to the democratic ideal. Our Declaration of Independence and our Constitution with its Bill of Rights are historic landmarks in the growth of democracy. Our young men have given their lives in war in order to "make the world safe for democracy." The history of our country is replete with such instances of national policies and actions taken in the name of this ideal.

The roots of democracy as a way of life in the United States are varied and deep. In Chapter 5 these roots are examined in some detail; here our purpose is merely to identify them as underlying presuppositions of the editors — presuppositions which have inevitably influenced their selection of materials and their very identification of significant issues. The major roots of our democratic belief draw sustenance from rich soil: from the *philosophical* conviction that the greatest self-realization of each individual is possible only in a democracy; from the *religious* conviction that the individual is of infinite, hence equal, worth; from the *historical* conviction that man's progress through time can best be charted in terms of his acquisition of human rights. These roots have nourished a tree of many branches. Democracy as a way of life has economic, political, religious, social, and educational implications. The first four of these deserve brief mention here; the last is the main concern of this book.

Economic democracy. What are the implications of this democratic way of life for the individual citizen? Perhaps one of the ways in which democracy has been most seriously misunderstood is that its ramifications within the many and varied facets of living have not received the attention they have deserved. Sometimes we act as if we believed that as long as we have prevented starvation, democracy as a way of life has been realized. The prevention of starvation is important to any society, but the true selfhood upon which democracy is predicated is not realized by merely being kept alive. True selfhood is achieved only when the individual has the opportunity to function as a *productive* member of society. This requires that each individual have an opportunity to engage in work that is socially useful and individually rewarding; that he live out his life free from the onus of charity. Being wholly dependent upon other individuals for survival rather than sharing with them in providing the requisites for a good life may, in fact, be as enslaving as slavery or as deadening as death. Dignity is gone. Freedom vanishes. Individuality is lost. Self-respect dies. Democracy rather seeks to help each individual find that place in society where he can produce most effectively for himself and his fellow men.

If we aspire to this goal, far more can be achieved than we have ever dreamed of accomplishing. The story is told of the mentally retarded individual who worked for years on a box-making machine. His job had been taught to persons of normal intelligence in less than an hour. Yet the foreman was always harassed by the fact that " normal " individuals were not challenged by the job. After a few weeks, they asked to be transferred. Their abilities had to be used in other, more demanding spots. It took the foreman a day to teach this mentally retarded individual the job of tripping the machine, keeping his hands away from danger, and producing the box. Yet after several years, he still retained his job. He went home from work facing his neighbors and the world with the satisfaction that he, too, was producing. He had a niche in the world. Productively, in terms of material goods, his services were not as valuable as those of the skilled mechanic, the experimental worker, the toolmaker; but he had acquired a sense of his own dignity and worth. Similarly, productive democracy requires that there must

always be a place for the man of vision. Such a man does not achieve selfhood when his work does not challenge him, when his abilities are not used as effectively as they might be. The engineer who is doing the work of a technician loses respect for himself; the teacher who finds himself entangled in endless clerical work despairs. Democracy demands that we help all persons find those fields of work where their abilities can be put to the most productive use. Only then can they take pride in their achievements. Only then can they sense their own true dignity and worth. A society so dedicated, with each doing that which he is best qualified to do, is a truly productive democracy.

But the implications of democracy for economic life are not limited to the *production* of goods and services. A democratic society is equally concerned with the *distribution* of goods — with the right of the individual to share in the goods which the society provides. Every economic system must answer not only the questions of *who* shall produce goods and *how* they shall be produced, but the equally urgent questions of *what* goods shall be produced and *to whom* they shall be provided. A democratic society cannot be concerned only with the production of goods *for survival*. Food, shelter, protection, and clothing are important; but a democracy posited on a faith in the worth of the individual must likewise be concerned with providing those goods and services which lead to the enrichment and expansion of human life. The democratic society places its faith in the resources of man's imagination to find means which will ultimately provide all men with the cultural wealth which will allow them to realize their full creative capacities. In the words of a noted analyst of democracy, the democratic criterion for the distribution of goods and services can be simply stated: no one to have superfluity until everyone has enough for healthy life and wholesome growth. The means of achieving this end — the legal requirements, the educational provisions, the social arrangements — are part of the unfinished business of democracy. But the abiding faith of the democratic society is that the creative intelligence of man is capable of translating material values into human values of enduring worth. Our faith is that things shall be made to serve people; people shall never serve things.

Political democracy. The implications of democracy as a way of life for the political realm have been most frequently identified and defined. The individual has a right to share in making laws that affect him and in profiting from the application of the public effort. One extension of this basic principle is the right of each individual to participate in politics to the full extent of his capabilities. This is encompassed in the concept of government by the people. There are specialized functions in government which require special abilities, talents, and training. Democracy does not imply that all individuals are qualified for all jobs in government, but rather that all shall have the opportunity to be judged fairly for positions. Interest, ideology, ability, and training should be the determining factors for choosing the men who make our laws, execute them, or make legal judgments in accordance with them. Economic status, religious affiliation, nationality, race, or social class should never bar the qualified individual from office. A second extension of the basic political principle is that government shall be *in the public interest*, not the private interest of any group or individual. This is encompassed in the concept of government *for* the people. But determining the public interest, acquiring the public philosophy, is not assured by the process of election. People must *learn* how to govern themselves. They must come to understand the great domestic and international issues of their day, to analyze them, and to

make intelligent decisions concerning them. They must be able to choose wisely among the candidates who wish to represent them. Preparation for such decisions and such choices is the indispensable province of education for political democracy. Only free teachers can provide this preparation.

The implications of political democracy for the effective freedom of the teacher in our society are too often overlooked. Partisan political affiliation ought never to be the basis for jeopardizing the fundamental civil rights of the individual — whether that individual be Republican, Democrat, doctor, mechanic, or *teacher*. A competent and qualified teacher should not be dismissed because of political affiliation. As a good citizen a teacher should stand ready to take an active part in government as the need becomes apparent. In order to do this, he must often be active in party politics. As long as he does not neglect his responsibilities as teacher and does not use his classroom as a political rostrum to further partisan political views, he should be encouraged to demonstrate political concern and action, not penalized for so doing. Often teachers are better qualified to hold local political office than other available individuals. Yet in some communities holding office is not possible because local public opinion expects the teacher to be neutral. Such neutrality robs society of competence. Yet more fundamental, it makes of teachers — those to whom we entrust the future — second-class citizens, persons of less than equal dignity and worth.

Freedom of religion. The freedom to believe the truth which one beholds is often held to be the cornerstone of democracy. But despite the centrality of intellectual freedom, it and other single values must respect the wider constellation of humane values which guide a democratic society. Thus while democracy grants each individual the right to choose the form of religion he would practice, or even to choose no religion if he will, democratic freedom does not include his right to deprive others of comparable privileges. The practice of a religion which would demean another's dignity or work cannot be condoned in the name of religious freedom. Furthermore, the faith of democracy is that religious belief is a private matter, susceptible to a minimum of legal persuasion or coercion. In the words of the Supreme Court of our land, " we have staked the very existence of our country on the faith that complete separation between the state and religion is best for the state and best for religion." Thus each individual in a democratic society has the right to develop his selfhood through his religious activities and life without let or hindrance. The teacher, as a democratic citizen, enjoys the *right* to participate freely in the full activities of his church according to interest, ability, and time. He has the *obligation* to help maintain the same right for others.

Freedom of thought. The freedom to believe, or to question, is not limited to beliefs which touch upon the relationship of man to God; the same freedom of the mind must also extend to the relationships of man to man, of fact to fact, of value to value. Only in a society in which man is free to seek the truth where he may find it, to follow the argument wherever it may lead, is he able to realize his full potential as an individual or is he able to contribute fully to the well-being of his fellow man. In democracy there is no truth so certain that it is not amenable to challenge. Democracy places its faith in the strength of truth to down falsehood on the battleground of ideas. We do not provide freedom of thought to protect error, but to discover truth; for the student of history knows well that yesterday's error is today's truth, and the truth of yesterday is often today's folly. It is among the legions devoted to this quest for truth through freedom that democratic education inevitably enlists itself.

Social democracy. In a genuinely democratic society, advancement is based upon achievement, not upon inherited position. Whenever a society employs invidious standards which distinguish between persons, not in terms of their individual potential or contribution, but in terms of the accident of their birth — where they were born, to whom they were born, or with what color skin they were born — that society robs itself. Two illustrations will suffice to demonstrate the significance of this in education.

The first illustration is in reference to the " drop-out " problem. The " drop-out " is the youngster who leaves school prior to the completion of the public high school. The causes of " dropping out " are many and varied, but the effect of the social class origin of youngsters on their remaining in school or leaving school is amply attested to by the weight of statistical evidence. The vast majority of early school leavers come from homes low on the social class scale. In part this can be explained by the paucity of refinement in lower class homes when compared with the richness of the environment of the upper classes — a paucity which reflects itself in the meager background of experience which youngsters bring to school. In part it can be explained by the lack of educational motivation provided within this meager home environment. But in part it must also be explained by the unintentional barriers which the school and teachers place in the path of youngsters from such environments. The educational aspirations of these young people are stultified by the combined effect on their personality of home environment, school failure, and rejection. It would appear that social classes carry with them, and persons operating within a social class system readily reveal, feelings of inferiority and superiority which are inconsistent with our commitment to the dignity and worth of each individual.

The second illustration takes as its

reference point our patterns of thought about race and ethnic groups, patterns of thought which have led to segregation in schools. It is fundamentally inconsistent with democratic principles for a person's race or nationality to be used as a criterion to set limits upon his rights and privileges. A democratic principle requires that each shall be judged as an individual, not as a member of the group into which he was born. A person can never achieve complete selfhood as long as he is made to feel inferior by being classified according to his skin pigmentation or native language. Such classification, least of all appropriate in intellectual and educational matters, has led to just such a sense of inferiority. A person may be well on the way to the achievement of significant selfhood, however, once he is accepted in his own right as a fellow man and as a human being with dignity and worth. It is to the goal of creating such an atmosphere of respect that education should aspire.

No society can survive unless it criticizes itself, locates its weaknesses, marks the ways in which it falls short of its ideals — and then proceeds resolutely to overcome these. Adherents of the democratic faith believe that democratic freedom, the freedom to develop ideas and implement them through a free political machinery, is the best assurance man has developed that this self-correction will take place. Our society must actively work for improvement in each of the four areas just described. Perhaps this demand for renewal through action has been expressed as forcibly as anywhere in Bailey's *Festus:*

> We live in deeds, not years; in
>   thoughts, not breaths;
> In feeling, not figures on a dial.
> We should count time by heart
>   throbs. He lives most
> Who thinks most — feels the noblest
>   — acts the best.

Education in a society committed to democracy as a way of life is now given more definite direction. It can be expressed by the goal of *developing each individual to the fullest extent of his capabilities as a cooperative member of democratic society.* This objective represents a harmonious balance between the claims of the individual and the claims of society. If the first part of this goal is accepted without the second, individualism reigns supreme and the social cement of common concern vanishes. If the second part of this goal is emphasized at the expense of the first, individual creativity may go unnurtured and society will pale into sameness.

Our statement of the goal demands more than lip service to the cause of individual differences. It takes into account the fact that some children will attain different goals and reveal different strengths from others. If we recognize the dignity and worth of each individual, we will want to have each child develop his talents and abilities to the ultimate — an ultimate measured in terms of personal development and social worth. Society would be drab indeed if mediocrity and conformity were to become our goal. It is our individual differences that give richness and color to our society.

That these guideposts can give us direction as to the immediate objectives, functions, curricula, and methodologies of the school is clear. In terms of public policy they imply that schools shall be publicly supported. The base of support must be sufficiently broad to assure that children in all geographical sections have equal educational opportunities. They require that the child not be discriminated against because he lives in an economically deprived school district, state, or region. They require that all school buildings and equipment be adequate to the task of developing each student to his full potential. At times this will necessitate changes in long-standing educational and political traditions. In order to achieve genuine equality of educational opportunity, additional federal support may be necessary, and small schools may have to be consolidated. Furthermore, no child should have his educational development thwarted by reason of inferior teachers. This means that improved standards for the accreditation of teachers will be required. It means further that salaries will have to be improved in order to attract competent teachers into all areas of the land. The full rights of citizenship and the right to reasonable privacy in out-of-school life must be provided to the teacher. Only then can the steady flow of qualified individuals into the profession be assured.

Although these brief considerations have touched upon some of the broad directions which we hold that educational policy should follow, the specifics must always be worked out by the individual teacher. In a dynamic civilization the specifics can never be worked out for all future generations or for each locality. The teacher has a right and a responsibility to develop a philosophy of education based on careful reflection and sound knowledge, and also to work out, in cooperation with his fellow teachers, a curriculum and a methodology both appropriate to the particular school in which he serves and in harmony with the democratic commitment of our society.

The method of intelligence. The reactions by individuals to the Kinsey reports on sexual behavior in the human male and female were quite varied. Some people objected vigorously even to the idea of a scientific study on such behavior. Some openly ridiculed the reports. Some condescendingly took the attitude that there was really nothing new that they could learn about the subject; on the contrary they could tell Dr. Kinsey a thing or two. One prominent newspaper columnist indignantly retorted that the whole project was worse than useless, and if he were asked to be interviewed by Dr. Kinsey or his associates, he would tell them in no uncertain terms where to go.

These reactions to the Kinsey reports reflect varying ways in which people respond to the matter of truth-seeking by scientific investigation. It is true that the subject of Dr. Kinsey's investigations is one about which people are highly emotional. It is also true that some of Dr. Kinsey's methodological procedures are open to serious question by objective critics. The fact remains that a substantial number of people living in our supposedly scientific twentieth century still have serious misgivings about the possibility of gaining knowledge of some aspect of human relations through a scientific and systematic approach. Without arguing the merits or the demerits of the Kinsey reports, we can see that when their interests or emotions are involved people apparently appeal to quite different criteria for arriving at their conception of truth. Some place almost exclusive reliance on their own personal experiences. Some rely on intuition or hunches. Some rely on acknowledged sources of authority such as a religious creed, political party, or presumed economic law. Some rely unknowingly on bias and prejudice. Some rely on a method of intelligence. Some employ a mixture of the above.

A basic assumption of the editors of this volume is that the method of intelligence provides us with the most effective way of meeting the kinds of problems that arise in teaching. These problems may range from the day-by-day human situations that confront the teacher to the long-range decisions involving the role of the school in a democratic society. What is here referred to as the method of intelligence encompasses the gist of what you may have encountered elsewhere in literature under the term " the scientific method," " reflective thinking," " critical thinking," or " problem-solving," The major elements of this method are the following:

First, a problem is perceived. What is considered to be a problem in a given society will be an indication of what the members of that society regard to be among their basic goods and values. It may involve the question of whether an elementary school should adopt a no-failing policy for all pupils or whether a secondary school should emphasize science or mathematics and de-emphasize athletics. An essential characteristic of any problem is that there is a perplexing situation or tension, and a plausible or cogent case can be made for two or more alternative solutions.

Second, the problem is clearly defined, delimited, and stated. This is not as simple a matter as it might appear. For example, the problem involving the no-failing policy may be delimited by applying it to only the primary grades, or to only one school, or to one entire school system. To state a problem so that it will be without ambiguity or vagueness is about as difficult as giving oral or written directions that are clearly understood by all. Furthermore, if a group of people are to be working on the problem, not all are likely to agree as to what facets of it merit the greatest emphasis. What would appear to be a slight change in wording may in fact alter the essential issue or problem fundamentally. A typical statement of the problem, using the above example, may be: "What is the most desirable promotion policy for School X to follow in order to provide optimum emotional and intellectual growth in the child? "

Third is the process of formulating hypotheses which represent possible solutions to the problem and determining the verifiable implications of these hypotheses. One possible hypothesis to the problem above could be the following: " A no-failure policy in School X is likely to result in less emotional insecurity on the part of children." Once the hypothesis has been formulated, it is necessary to reason out its logical implications. This usually involves " if-then " thinking. For example, such thinking in this instance might lead to the proposition, " If this is the most desirable policy to follow, then we would expect to find less

emotional insecurity in borderline students who have been promoted than in those who have been retained in grade." It is now possible to obtain data which would test the adequacy of the hypothesis by seeing if the then condition has in fact been the case. These data need to be screened for reliability, relevance, and validity. It is during the data-gathering process that the investigator is obligated to exercise the most rigorous standards of intellectual honesty if he is to sift fact from unvalidated opinion and weigh the merits of competing hypotheses. If the extant information on the subject is still inadequate for reaching a conclusion, the investigator may have to initiate his own search for information by such means as surveys of professional judgment, interviews, direct observations, or longer-range classroom experimentation.

Fourth is the drawing of conclusions based upon the preceding analysis of data as these data are related logically to hypotheses. These data may refute or support previously stated hypotheses. The hypothesis mentioned above, for example, may possibly be refuted by analyzing data from personal interviews, sociograms, personality inventories, or direct observations. It should be kept in mind, however, that conclusions are to take into account not only factual data but also the extent to which the actual data relate conclusions to educational objectives which are themselves consistent with the underlying goals and values of the society.

The final step in the method of intelligence is taking action. In a democratic society this has especial significance. One of the key concepts of democracy is that a good citizen is one who acts as well as knows. He has not only the right to influence public policy, but the obligation to do so. Of course, not all action need necessarily be overt. A change in attitude, opinion, or understanding qualifies psychologically as change in behavior and thus indicates that learning has presumably taken place. Unless overt action is taken however, it may not be possible for others to ascertain that learning has indeed taken place. If overt action is to be taken, it too should meet certain criteria:

.It should be consistent with the conclusions reached.

It should take into consideration the peculiarities of the place and time.

It should be capable of modification as the situation changes.

It should be feasible.

It should be in harmony with the basic value commitments of a democratic society.

These criteria are, of course, most apt to be met in those cases where the problem has been initially identified with care and then properly narrowed and defined.

Several observations and precautions should be made about the foregoing scheme. Although the various elements of the method of intelligence are presented as if they always occur in the sequence indicated, such is not the case. Some steps may be telescoped into one, others may be broken down into sub-categories, still others may be transposed. For example, if a given situation is recognized by all concerned to be a problem, the process of gathering data may be begun immediately after a quickly acceptable statement of the problem. Another less obvious observation is that flashes of insight by individuals working on the problem may lead to an uneven pace of progress. Such insights, of course, are to be encouraged, even though occasionally some may lead to digressive paths. A still less obvious consideration is that the method of intelligence, like the method of science, is *not* exclusively inductive. In general the path of progress is from the unknown to the known. But within the total process there are instances in which sub-steps are verified by reference to deductive reasoning. Finally, there is no intent on the part of the editors to argue that the method of intelligence is the *only* way by which all truths are arrived at. Religious dogma, intuition, even extra-sensory perception — these and other as yet unknown paths to knowledge may possibly result in deeply penetrating perceptions. In the area of secular educational problems, however, our predominant approach is the method of intelligence.

CHAPTER ONE BIBLIOGRAPHY

BRUNER, JEROME S., *The Process of Education*. Cambridge: Harvard University Press, 1960.

> This book is primarily concerned with the learning and teaching process. It stresses the belief that we have underestimated the capacities of most learners, thus contributing to the gap between what society demands of the young and what they are taught in school. Bruner argues for more teaching about " the fundamental structure " of subject matter areas.

FRASIER, GEORGE W., *An Introduction to the Study of Education*. Rev. ed. New York: Harper and Brothers, 1956.

> This is a textbook for students of education with Part II devoted to " Foundations Fields in Teacher Education." Within this part is a section on democracy and education with discussions based primarily on appropriate quotations from John Dewey.

GOULD, GEORGE and YOAKAM, GERALD A., *The Teacher and His Work*. Second ed. New York: The Ronald Press Company, 1954.

The relationship of the school to the culture is described. Chapter nine, " Social Trends and Education," and Chapter twelve, " Control and Organization of Education in the United States," deal with issues raised in this prologue.

HANSEN, KENNETH H., *Philosophy for American Education*. Englewood Cliffs: Prentice-Hall, Inc., 1960.

Chapter one deals with several everyday concerns in education (finance, discipline, what to teach), emphasizing that in answering questions about these concerns, one needs and uses some kind of philosophy.

HOPKINS, L. THOMAS, *Interaction, The Democratic Process*. Boston: D. C. Heath and Company, 1941.

In Chapter V entitled " How Does Philosophy Affect the Curriculum? " the author builds his answer upon three examples. The different philosophies of two counselors and a principal provide answers to important questions with which each must deal, making the illustrations practical and interesting.

THAYER, V. T., *The Role of the School in American Society*. New York: Dodd, Mead and Company, 1960.

Thayer has two especially good chapters (6 and 7) on the changing economic and social status of youth in American society. He also deals with such critical issues as church-state relations in education, academic freedom, segregation, and federal aid.

2

Educative Agencies in Society

One of the persistent criticisms that foreigners make about American education — and for that matter, about our entire society — is its undue emphasis on the present and its corresponding lack of concern with the past. Some historians have disparagingly referred to this phenomenon as the disease of " presentitis." If the criticism is at all warranted, it is probably more valid for educators than it is for those concerned with other social institutions in our society. In general the professional political scientist, for example, has engaged in a more extensive study of the history of political institutions than has the professional educator engaged in a study of the history of education. Similarly the proverbial man in the street is probably somewhat more aware of the historical backgrounds of our political institutions than he is of our educational institutions. One professional educator has characterized our lack of concern with the historical antecedents of formal education as the " besetting sin of pedagogy."

This chapter is an attempt to provide some degree of that elusive quality called perspective to the study of American education. The perspective, however, is not merely that of time depth. In fact, except for some rather incidental allusions to educative agencies or factors in past societies, the readings are more concerned with providing breadth in one neglected dimension of education — the informal educative processes. Especially significant in informal education are the family and other primary groups in any society. The types of societies in which family and other primary group influences are most visible are present and

past primitive societies. In such cultures the impact and pervasive influence of informal education is more clearly, and sometimes dramatically, visible.

The study of informal education has especial relevance for those entering the teaching profession. In the first place the nature of the child's learning experiences within the family and peer group give us a good clue as to the predominant values and beliefs held by the members of that society. Such education demonstrates the relationship of school and society. In any society the schools — or their counterpart in informal educational experiences — tend to reinforce the dominant societal values. Secondly, the study of informal education demonstrates in a negative way the relationship between goals of education and the reflective decision-making that results in progress toward these goals. Even the casual student of education in primitive societies is struck by the fact that there is very little conscious, deliberate, and reflective examination of the society's educative processes. They are almost all accepted on an unexamined a priori basis. The primitive warrior-father, for example, sternly insists that his son demonstrate bravery in battle and utter contempt for his enemies " because that is as it should be."

The positive counterpart to such an unreflective acceptance of traditional ways of doing things is the method of intelligence. It is comparatively easy for an " outsider " to use a detached, objective approach in analyzing some remote primitive society. The difficulty arises in trying to see ourselves as others see us. And yet it is precisely this detached, objective approach that is so often needed in analyzing our own educational goals and procedures. As professional persons, teachers ought to be able to step back out of this world as it were, to view with detachment this complex social institution called education. Having done this they are in a better position to apply the method of intelligence to resolve the various issues confronting the profession.

The evolution of complex formal educative agencies, such as the schools, roughly parallels the development of other social institutions as, for example, the economy. Just as our contemporary economic system is infinitely more complex than a barter economy, so also our schools are so interwoven with other strands of our social fabric as to constitute an incredibly complex pattern. This chapter is intended to give some indication of the breadth of this complex, from the simple informal teaching of primitive mother and child to the institutionalized formal education carried on within a school " system."

SECTION 1. Informal education

There was a time when anthropological monographs — especially those about exotic, primitive societies — had an almost intrinsic appeal to the reading public. The people described were so quaint, their customs so odd, their beliefs so amusing. It was easy for those living in so-called civilized societies to regard such primitive people either with amused toleration, condescension, or puzzlement. In fact, such essentially smug reactions have been distinct impediments to the realization of the potential learning that may be gained from many anthropological studies. For the anthropologist is concerned, among other things, with providing vicarious examples of human behavior that are unknown to us or different from our own, and also with providing evidence of the wide variability in behavior and beliefs among mankind. Such is the case with the following selection by Todd, taken from his book, *The Primitive Family as an Educational Agency.*

It is interesting to note some of the insights demonstrated by Todd in this book, which was published in 1913. For example, his twofold breakdown of primitive education into vocational and moral ("including custom, tradition and religion") closely parallels a prevalent modern division. And some of his descriptions of laxity and permissiveness toward primitive children would make even a parody of progressive education appear mild by comparison. He provides one of the best reasons for the study of primitive education in the preface, where he writes:

" Because a thing is primitive does not mean that it is to be overlooked or despised. Its sympathetic study may reveal unsuspected treasure. Witness only the revival of dancing in our most modern schools: as I have herein shown, dancing was not only one of the chief subjects in the primitive curriculum but was one of the most effective agencies for social control. . . ." [1]

Perhaps a concluding word should be said about another element of the selection by Todd. It is the phenomenon known as " cultural shock," and is a frequent trademark of the anthropologist. Of course, the extent to which this phenomenon is impressed upon the reader will be dependent to a large extent on the experiential background — both direct and vicarious — that the reader brings to the written page. Suffice it to say that, so far as the editors of this volume are concerned, cultural shock is in much the same category as the " quaintness " of ethnological literature: it has no justification *per se,* but only to the extent that it en-

---

[1] Preface, p. vii.

ables the reader to gain a greater understanding of human behavior. If the excerpts from Todd's volume do nothing else, they should make each of us especially wary of any statement beginning, " After all, it's only human nature for children to — ." Regardless of what is said to complete this sentence, the entire statement will be very difficult to verify in most cases, and impossible to verify when socially conditioned behavior is involved.

ARTHUR J. TODD
Education in primitive societies

AIMS AND CONTENT OF PRIMITIVE EDUCATION

In the following discussion we have attempted to study primitive education under several aspects, viz., its Aims, Content, Methods, and Organization. But it will soon become apparent how unavoidably the several topics overlap, this in simple consequence of their lack of differentiation in practice. Perhaps we should remind ourselves at the outset that savages are educable, not only according to their own systems, but also to a considerable extent according to ours. Furthermore, we are to recognize that savage habits, traits, customs, and crafts are not, and never have been, innate instincts, but are the products of real learning. Eastman, for instance, writes on behalf of his Indian tribe mates:

> It seems to be a popular idea that all the characteristic skill of the Indian is instinctive and hereditary. This is a mistake. All the stoicism and patience of the Indian are acquired traits, and continued practice alone makes him master of the art of woodcraft.

AIMS

Habit and Adjustment its Aims. — If we define the purpose of education as " fitting for life," we may say that the aims of savage education and modern education are identical. But if we add the Aristotelian notion that education is for the *good* life, then it is true that modern rises above savage education to just the degree of this qualification. At its lower extreme, savage education touches the nurture methods of the higher animals. Indeed, as we have already shown, children among certain peoples fare little better, so far as education is concerned, than if they were offspring of the beasts. Igorot children, for example, are said to learn the tribal industries " quite as a young fowl learns to scratch and get its food." And Itau Eskimo " wachsen auf wie die Schosshunde." [1] But at its best the aim of savage education was the formation of a body of habits; it was adjustment to pres-

From Arthur J. Todd, *The Primitive Family as an Educational Agency*, pp. 142–150, 153–155, 159–160, 163–166, 171–172, 175–176, 166, 168, 171. New York, G. P. Putnam's Sons, 1913. Reprinted by permission.

[1] " grow up like lap dogs." — Ed.

ent environment, actual or imagined, rather than the progressive adjust-ment to a changing environment which is the aim of modern teaching. The distinction appears best when we say that modern education seeks to de-velop flexibility, the conscious ability to vary, to meet new situations; in other words, that it tends to shift the center of " selection " from without to within consciousness. Those moralists and educators who believe that the perfect human type is a perfect automatism of wonderful range and ac-curacy, err according to our notions, but would have been eminently at home in savagery. They neglect the dynamic element, the fact that the set of conditions we call the " world " or the " environment " is not fixed once for all, but is inconstant, moves, changes, is in perpetual flux, as Heraclitus observed. Hence the mere habit of acting will not suffice. There must be as well the power of not acting. And however small we leave this *margin of refusal*, it must be there; indeed, it is the vital element in the whole scheme of adaptation. The most important habit of all is the habit of thinking; and this is *per se* the habit of flexibility, of deliberation, of negation of other habits. An automatic spring lock is not only valueless, but dangerous as well, without the key to unlock it. This key is the way of escape, the cor-rective to fixity, the safeguard of life and liberty. Savage instruction almost wholly neglected the key, being concerned only with habitual response to present conditions and the solving of present problems. Yet there must have been some element of variation in primitive life, else we should still be chip-ping stone axes and grubbing for roots. The variation came not so much from conscious teaching, as from exterior forces, war, migration, exogamy, etc., and in later times, trade and political organization.

Savage Education " Practical." — Savage education as habit-forming ex-pressed itself in the twofold aim of vocational and moral fitness. Since the emphasis, especially in the beginning, lay on the vocational, and the moral contained little or no ethical element as such, but was concerned only with custom and ritualistic religion, we might say that savage education was *practical*, limited to the arts of self-maintenance. Religion, we repeat, was in aim, content, and method, almost wholly unethical, and applied to wringing a larger livelihood from the earth or the unwilling powers that controlled it, or to preventing by exorcism and propitiation unfriendly powers from cutting off the means of life, or life itself. If we say that edu-cation is the teaching of " values," then primitive man reflected in his edu-cation his notions of certain crude industrial arts and peace with the unseen powers as the things most worth while in life. Hence he placed the premium upon doing, and belief as an aid to doing, rather than upon thinking. Fur-thermore, his doing focused upon the satisfaction of immediate wants. Only when higher barbarism is reached do we find much attempt to control the future, though it is evident that no progress would have been possible with-out some discounting of the present in favor of the future. Yet speaking by and large, food, and defense from enemies either of this world or more particularly of that terribly real and dangerous other-world, are primitive man's first aims in his learning, whether it be unconscious and self-acquired or the result of combined self, familial, and group instruction.

At an age when civilized children would just be commencing to learn to read books, the savage child is busy, though he scarcely knows it himself, in learning to read nature, and in acquiring the knowledge which will enable him not only to obtain his own supply of food, but to guard himself against the attacks of enemies.

From the subordination of the individual to the group, it is evident that savage education was designed, especially when it became conscious, to secure the solidarity of the group, rather than to convey a body of exact knowledge. *In general we may say, then, that primitive education [is] aimed chiefly, whether consciously or not, at securing and developing keen perceptive powers, physical endurance, and discipline.*

CONTENT

Evolution of the Curriculum. — The Curriculum of savage education, as already indicated in its Aims, includes two general groups of " subjects," vocational and moral, the latter including custom, tradition, and religion. Yet in practice the two groups are constantly associated. Tradition or taboo may rigidly prescribe the technique of industry, and religion constantly breaks over into the economic régime, not only to determine the forms of industry, but even to proscribe and interrupt their normal course of operation; as, for example, where mortuary customs require the destruction of property or suspension of labor or the lying fallow of land. Among the lowest nature-peoples, where the range of ideas is narrowest, the arts few and simple, social organization the loosest, the curriculum reduces to its lowest terms. Yet even here learning is not an easy process; for under such conditions each generation must go back to the beginning, as there is no storing up of capital, of tools, or even of methods. On the contrary, the practice of destroying the property of the dead left to the survivors the difficult task of creating *ab ovo* their means of production. Only with the rise of intelligence, the settlement in a more or less permanent abode, the accumulation of property, the division of labor, the formation and transmission of tradition, and the organization of conscious education, could there be any short cut, any recapitulation in brief of racial experience. This stage once reached, the " course of studies " becomes immediately more varied and more precise. The development of trade and political organization, together with the increasing complexity of social and religious concepts, brings a corresponding extension and depth to the content of education. Ordeals, drill, initiatory rites, instruction in tribal traditions, religious beliefs, laws, and customs, begin to occupy the larger part of the curriculum, which still includes occasional definite lessons in the tribal arts of self-maintenance. But, far from being delivered *en bloc* by some primitive educational expert, their whole system of instruction was developed out of the very heart of savagery itself by the slow zigzag method of trial and failure in the struggle for existence.

Classification of Primitive Peoples. — Several attempts have been made to classify primitive peoples according to their attitude toward education. Steinmetz makes a threefold grouping: (1) Those absolutely without training of any sort. (2) Those where education is beginning, without or almost without discipline. (3) Those where hard treatment and strict training prevail. Such a classification rests obviously on the notion of education as *formal* training closely correlated with discipline. Another writer uses consideration of the child's interests as the basis of classification, but arrives at substantially the same result: (1) Those peoples in which there is no attempt to discipline the child *for his own sake.* (2) Where the child is disciplined primarily *to make him useful to his parents.* (3) Where he is educated and provided for primarily *for his own sake.* In neither of these schemes, however, are the stages mutually exclusive; as in the case of types of marital organization, so here, the stages overlap, or may exist concurrently. Spencer's dictum that warlike peoples are strict in training their children, and peaceable peoples lax, offers us little help; for such a generalization sprang rather from his espousal of a favorite antithesis between the military and the industrial types of society than from a thorough examination of the facts themselves. We have been unable to arrive at any hard and fast classification that will hold good in every case. The following scheme, however, is offered as a working guide: (1) Cases where there is little or absolutely no formal instruction or discipline, where whatever is learned is "picked up" much after the animal fashion, where the economic, political, and familial organization is still loose, and where the forces of "selection" are still largely exterior and unconscious. (2) Where a developing social organization has stretched the range of interest, where a reservoir of experience begins to appear and brings with it a conscious demand for the preservation and perpetuation of this body of experience, and hence the beginnings of organized instruction. (3) Where the notion of education as a paramount selective agency holds sway. The first two classes alone pertain to our subject. It will be found that this classification applies to both the content and the organization of primitive education, and perhaps to its methods and results as well. A few typical cases will illustrate this general course of development.

"Soft Pedagogy." — First, then, come the cases in which there is neither conscious education nor formulated discipline. The Lower California Indians perfectly illustrate both points. We have already noted their resentment toward discipline. Father Baegert is no less explicit as to their neglect of learning.

Nothing, [he says,] causes the Californians less trouble and care than the education of their children, which is merely confined to a short period, and ceases as soon as the latter are capable of making a living for themselves — that is, to catch mice and to kill snakes. If the young Californians have once acquired sufficient skill and strength to follow these pursuits, it is all the same to them whether they have parents or not. Nothing is done by these in the way of admonition or instruction, nor do they set an example worthy to be imitated by their offspring. . . . The consequence is, that the children follow their own inclinations without any restraint, and imitate all the bad habits and practices of their equals, or still older persons, without the slightest apprehension of being blamed by their fathers and mothers, even if these should happen to detect them in the act of committing the most disgraceful deeds. The young Californians who live in the missions commence roaming about as soon as the mass is over, and those that spend their time in the fields go wherever, and with whomsoever, they please, not seeing for many days the faces of their parents, who, in their turn, do not manifest the slightest concern about their children, nor make any inquiries after them. . . .

Sparing the Rod. — A wise old German used to say that " wenn gleich ein Kind ein Engel wäre so bedürfe es doch der Ruthe." [2] But the birch of our forefathers was sadly neglected in savagery. It is a gross error to assert that corporal punishment is a return to savagery or a survival of it. Only as we approximate civilization does the discipline of the rod cut much of a figure; it was not a barbarian, but a Greek poet who said, " the man who has not been flogged, did not get any education." At times, for example during the Middle Ages, when asceticism held sway, this symbol of control received such worship as never did Astarte in the days of her glory. But no savages were ever ascetics by choice, and in general their attitude toward children was marked by sentimentalism rather than by correction and guidance.

Steinmetz cites a list of thirty-two peoples among whom no parental discipline exists. It includes the Ainos, Loyalty, Marshall, and Pelew Islanders, New Hebrideans, Dyaks, Warraus, Patagonians, Kubu, Bechuana, Ama-Xosa, Bakuba, Toba-Battaks, etc. Ploss adds the Dengas of the Upper Nile and the Farafrahs of the Libyan Desert. It is pretty generally true that but little family discipline exists among peoples whose children acquire maturity and independence at an early age. A curious little cameo illustrative of this condition has been preserved for us by an eighteenth century traveler to the Loango: " A missionary one day heard a mother giving a small commission to her son. The child was only about eight years old, but he answered gravely, " Do you think then that I am a boy? " Wuttke notes the absolute lack of discipline amongst the Kamtchdales. Crantz wrote of the Greenlanders over a century and a half ago, and the observation still holds good:

[2] " Even if a child were an angel it would still need a switch." — Ed.

The children are brought up without any discipline, or any severity of reprimand or chastisement by their parents. But indeed severe treatment of the Greenlander's children is on the one hand not very needful, because they run about as quiet as lambs, and fall into very few extravagancies; and on the other hand it would be fruitless, because if a Greenlander cannot be influenced to do a thing by gentle entreaty, or by rational arguments, he will sooner be killed than compelled to it. Whether this is the effect of a natural self-will in their complexion, or whether it proceeds from the long habit of unrestrained education, I am not able to determine. . . .

Unformulated Group Discipline. — It must not be supposed that if savage children failed to receive correction it was because they never needed it. On the contrary, the savage child needed trimming and pruning no less than our modern young hopeful; and what is more to the point, he got it, though not exactly through well formulated means. But in all ages " youth and crabbed age " have been judged by their peers and had their rough edges taken off by that subtle process of attrition which is the first requisite to association. So that when we say no discipline exists among a given people, we mean merely that there is no formulated discipline, institutionalized, as it were, and located in the hands of parent, schoolmaster, etc. Among the Seri Indians, for example, there is no formal discipline, but this informal rubbing down goes on just the same.

The boys are at once the most restless and the most lawless members of the tribe — indeed, the striplings seem often to ignore the maternal injunctions and even to evade the rarely uttered avuncular orders, so that their movements are practically free, except in so far as they are themselves regimented and graded by strength and fleetness or success in hunting.

Aggressiveness Fostered. — Another word might be added regarding the deliberate cultivation of youthful aggressiveness. Lewis and Clarke state that among the Shoshones, a warlike Indian tribe, the children were seldom corrected;

. . . the boys, particularly, soon become their own masters; they are never whipped, for they say that it breaks their spirit, and that after being flogged, they never recover their independence of mind, even when they grow to manhood.

A recent writer on the Indians lays down a generalization which is substantially accurate.

In contrast to Pueblo ideas of parental authority, it is worthy of notice that, in many parts of aboriginal America, obedience has not been considered an essentially commendable characteristic of social life. Among some of the wilder tribes, a rebellious, quarrelsome disposition on the part of the sons has been encouraged rather than opposed. Chastisement for obstinacy has been considered detrimental to the growth of courage, and hence obstructive in the making of a warrior. With many savages, quarrels are of almost daily occurrence, and brawls among the youths are constantly going on. . . .

Beginnings of Conscious Education. — Into the second group, according to the classification we have adopted, fall those peoples who, while recognizing to a certain degree the value of education to the individual and to the group, do not perceive its full significance; whose educational technique is obviously limited and uneven; or who fail properly to balance instruction and discipline. In a certain sense, modern civilized nations, almost without exception, might well be included within this group; it is merely a question of more or less. But here we are concerned rather with the " less," and the limits of the group will be easily enough described if we place at one end, say the Australians, where the education of the youth really begins only at his initiation; and at the other, the Russians of the fifteenth or sixteenth century, where to break a child's ribs with the stick of correction was considered of vastly more educative value than any attempt to cultivate his mind.

Vocational Training. — First in importance comes vocational training. It is here that familial instruction appears at its best, for most of the savage arts of self-maintenance are domestic, and not sufficiently differentiated to require skilled teaching. The father usually assumed the duty of introducing his son into the manly arts and carried him along on fishing or hunting expeditions, the first years of infancy past. To the mother naturally fell the business of acquainting her daughter with whatever details of housewifery or agriculture her own life compassed. Such instruction had the advantage of being actually in the art itself or in miniature playful imitations of the art. To prepare himself for shooting reindeer, the Eskimo lad is given a tiny bow and arrows, and a little reindeer fœtus set up for him to aim at. The Dakota girl had her little work-bag with its awl and sinew, and learned to make diminutive moccasins as her mother made large ones. Education in these simple arts is comparatively easy, for the problems are vivid, specific, and directly anticipatory to real life, with the further advantage that they admit of constant repetition and drill. To the savage child the technical processes of his elders, warfare, the chase, the medicine dance, agriculture, and hearthside industries, were vastly more accessible than are our own more highly complex systems of industry. To be sure, our modern boy may still mimic in play certain social functions; he may whip off the tops of weed enemies, or metamorphose himself into a battleship, turn a flip, or execute a buck and wing dance. Yet these plays can hardly be called definite anticipations of his future life. The contrast is all the more striking if we turn to his industrial games. What sort of play, or what sort of work in miniature will prepare him to build a modern steam-heated house, steer an armored cruiser, weave a blanket, carve a gunstock, or prepare the mold for a steel casting? Modern industry has grown remote from child-hood, and is only accessible by a careful formal educational introduction. The industrial revolution brings with it an inevitable demand for inten-sive education. However it may have bred a generation of laissez-faireists in political economy, it cannot tolerate them in education and live. But primitive societies faced no such complexities. In a community of fisher-men practically all were fishers; among herdsmen all were herders; and the son, if his father did not teach him the art, learned in spite of himself from his fellows in the group.

It is not unfair to say that the beginnings of savage education closely resemble the apprentice system, and that the employments of the family and of the group as a whole are static and hereditary. That Chinese cob-bler who carried a sign on his back reading, " I have been a cobbler for 400 years," summarized primitive vocational education. It will suffice to enumerate the chief savage occupations figuring on their " course of studies." Hunting, fishing, canoeing, sledding, trapping, and crude build-ing predominate. Warlike peoples specialize with the spear or bow. In agricultural communities the hoe and the yam stick, amongst herders the care of cattle, are the chief solicitudes. It is almost universally true that the domestic education of girls precedes that of boys. In many tribes where little home training is bestowed upon the boys, their sisters early become miniature housewives. And where both sexes are formally taught, the girls usually come first. Furthermore, domestic education has nearly always played a much larger part in the girl's life. . . .

Moral Education. — Primitive industrial education, as we have seen, was largely domestic, but not altogether so; and both the family and the group shared in physical training. But in moral instruction the rôle of the group seems to overshadow that of the family. This is not surprising if, as we believe, the *mores* are a group product. We have already pointed out that even among peoples supposedly without any sort of formal educa-tion there always went on a more or less unconscious process of regiment-ing, springing out of the very nature of association itself. But among peo-ples of higher culture status, moral instruction takes on a more definite and deliberate character. To be sure, such moral instruction is largely unethical, and consists rather in the What, the content of the social code, and only rarely the Why. Unreasoned acquiescence is the most becoming attitude in the savage disciple. If it ever occurs to the learner to question, more What is invented to explain the difficulty. This is why custom per-sists and why from time to time new myths must be invented to explain age-old practices. Hence the importance of tradition and folklore in primi-tive life. Count Okuma is inclined to refer the very beginnings of con-scious education in old Japan to the poems, songs, and legends incident to the ancestor cult. It is undeniable that family ancestor worship was an exceedingly important factor in moral discipline. But it was insufficient, nay, even deleterious; for vigorous group life requires a broader, more flexible moral content. When social differentiation has gone far enough to permit the emergence of a definitely organized priesthood, a considerable share of distinctively moral teaching falls to it. But long before the constitution of ecclesiasticism, the priest or medicine man coöperates with the tribal elders in the inculcating and perpetuation of tribal lore and custom (in which we include the whole vast system of ghostism and dæmonology, the whole theory and practice of keeping peace with "the unseen powers"). Indeed, this is the typical moral engine in savagery. . . .

Specific Group-Interest in Moral Education. — Vastly more important than domestic moral training seem to have been the puberty rites and initiatory ceremonies widely practiced among primitive peoples. Whether conducted by tribal elders or under the auspices of some secret society, these rites comprised not only a considerable amount of industrial technique, but nearly all of what we should call training for citizenship. The secret society was a school for social solidarity, as well as a sort of tribal guild of arts and crafts. These points are well brought out by Professor Haddon in an observation on the natives of Mer, an island in the Torres Straits. The lads, he says, "were instructed in all that related to their daily life, in the most approved methods of fishing, fighting, or housebuilding, and in all the duties which are classed as man's work, in addition to rules of conduct, the customs of the tribe, and the traditions of the elders." The same writer found the initiation ceremonies at Tud

very good discipline. The self-restraint acquired during the period of complete isolation was of great value, and being cut off from all the interests of the outer world, the lads had an opportunity for quiet meditation, which must have tended to mature their minds, especially as they were at the same time instructed in a good code of morals. It is not easy to conceive of a more effectual means for a rapid training.

The training was furthermore exceedingly definite and concrete; it inculcated honesty, generosity, filial respect, and the putting away of childish things. This citation will suffice for the present to show that *the primitive group as a whole was concerned with the subject of morals in its curriculum.* . . .

Physical Training. — Perhaps only secondary to purely vocational instruction comes physical training in the primitive curriculum. It ranges from the Pentathlon of the Greeks to practices rivaling the Samurai-code of mediæval Japan. Many savage children have astonished European travelers by their precocity in swimming. The Polynesians and Sea Dyaks, for example, swim almost before they can walk. Nimbleness of limb and endurance are the commonest ideals.

The Apache boy had for pedagogue his father and grandfather, who began early to teach him counting, to run on level ground, then up and down hill, to break branches from trees, to jump into cold water, and to race, the whole training tending to make him skilful, strong, and fearless. . . .

The Bedouin method of " hardening " is typical. The boy is

accustomed from his earliest youth to the fatigues and dangers of a pastoral life, and his constitution is steeled to endurance, hardships, and privations. Fathers desire to see their sons possessed, at an early age, of a manly spirit of independence and of a prudent assurance of self-confidence.

The Caraib youth received a peculiarly brutal training.

In the Antilles the father invited his most intimate friends, and on admonishing his son to be valiant in the fight and take vengeance on his enemies, he killed a bird of prey called oūashi, by striking it against the forehead of his son, who was made to devour the heart, that by this act of barbarism he would be steeled to commit the more barbarous deed of devouring the heart of the enemies of his nation.

The Fiji Islanders accustom their children early to regard the murder of a man as slight and commonplace.

One of the first lessons taught the infant is to strike its mother, a neglect of which would beget a fear lest the child should grow up to be a coward. Thus these people are nurtured " without natural affection," and trained to be " implacable, unmerciful." Several proofs of this, I have witnessed at Somosomo; mothers leading their children to kick and tread upon the dead bodies of enemies. . . .

Here is a consummate example in proof of the theory that traits of character lie rather in social than physical heredity. It is also an apt denial of the notion that " ferocity " is an innate instinct. It affirms with savage distinctness the power of education over nature. . . .

SECTION **2. Formal education**

As society became more complex it was inevitable that systems of formal education would emerge to supplement and sometimes supplant informal education carried on by the family. One of the factors accounting for the growth of formal education was the principle of the division of labor among members of a society. Just as some members of a social group were trained to be warriors and some priests, so also some were especially trained to carry on prescribed educational functions. As Brubacher points out in the following selection, the mere establishment of some kind of formal schooling implies that direct experience alone is not sufficient as a teacher. Indeed, as Benjamin Franklin once pointed out, experience " keeps a dear school."

But the mere establishment of systems of formal education has created more problems than it has solved. One of the most persistent of these concerns the balance between " real-life " experiences and " book learning " in the total education of the individual.

The history of education has recorded times when the pendulum has swung from one extreme to the other on these two elements. As with the old hackneyed argument of heredity versus environment, much of the disputation on this matter has been pointless; both elements are a part of the educational makeup of all individuals in a civilized society. The capacity of the individual and his function in society largely influence the extent to which one of those elements predominates over the other.

Adult education, as an aspect of formal education that is only lightly touched on in this selection by Brubacher, deserves further mention here. At no other time in the history of education has adult education been so vigorously promoted and so extensively engaged in. One of the reasons for this is the blunt and frightening realization that contemporary mankind may not have a " second chance " to redeem itself should it blunder its way into a nuclear holocaust. For the first time in the history of man we cannot dejectedly wring our hands over the mess this present generation has gotten us into and then placidly assume that the next generation will have to straighten things out again. As Robert Maynard Hutchins has pointed out, we cannot afford the risk of *not* educating our adults. For the most part such education will be formal or at least rest mainly on vicarious experience. This may well be the most demanding test to which formal education has yet been subjected.

JOHN S. BRUBACHER
The development of formal education

THE TRANSITION FROM INFORMAL EDUCATION TO FORMAL SCHOOLING

In early primitive times, education was little differentiated from the daily activities of the adult generation. It was something that occurred at odd moments during these activities and incidental to them. The young learned such life activities as hunting, making artifacts, and worshiping tribal divinities by participating directly and informally in these activities along with older and more experienced people. Even the play of children was in large measure an imitation of adult activities, their toys diminutive models of the implements of their parents.

But even as early as the culture of primitive society, education was already losing its informality. This decrease in informality came about through the primitive initiation ceremony. It is common to stress this ceremony as a milestone in the life of the young. Occurring about the period of adolescence this ceremony marked the transition from childhood with its immaturity and irresponsibility to adulthood with its privileges and duties. As a matter of fact, however, initiation was more than a ceremony to mark the passing of a milestone. It was, in addition, a period of intensified education. Often it lasted several days or even weeks during which the candidate for adulthood was both instructed and tested. He was instructed in the special secrets and lore of his tribe and tested in his

From John S. Brubacher, A *History of the Problems of Education,* 1947, pp. 357–364. Copyright McGraw-Hill Book Company, Inc. Reprinted by permission.

ability to endure pain, hunger, and fear. If he survived this ordeal, the event was celebrated with feasting and dancing.

It is easy to see how the semi-informal education of initiation passed over into the more formal education of the school. The educational experiences of initiation were barely one step removed from the daily life experiences of adults. Although the adult members of the tribe took time off to administer the rites and although they often went away to some particular place to hold them, the experiences prepared were as nearly like life as they could be made. Certainly, the youth had no difficulty in perceiving their relevancy. In the course of time, however, these consciously designed educational experiences became two, three, and even more steps removed from the life experiences for which they prepared. As this time approached, the institution we have come to call " school " came more and more into view.

Several factors tended to produce this situation. One of the earliest appeared with the increase of the cultural heritage. As this heritage accumulated, it became so great in extent that there was no longer time to transmit it informally. There was even danger that parts of it might become lost or forgotten. As a result, a special institution, the school, was gradually evolved where such parts of the culture might be perpetuated. As thus evolved, the school was not directly concerned with life. Rather was it, as the sociologists have described it, a residual institution. Like a residuary legatee, it caught and perpetuated the odds and ends of the social culture that otherwise might have been transmitted through daily life experiences.

Even more significant in broadening the gap between life and education and necessitating the school was the increase in the complexity of the cultural heritage. The culture transmitted at the time of initiation was never so intricate that the youth could not understand it by direct and immediate participation in the adult activities prescribed. At a later time, however, the culture became so much more complex and difficult that an increasing number of adult activities lay beyond their comprehension. Youth's level of meanings was distinctly below that of the mature members of his group. Educational experiences had to be arranged in stages, therefore, like a system of locks in a canal, to lift the youth up to a level where they could participate in adult activities with the same meanings that adults attached to them. In other words, the intricacies of culture had to be simplified for them into a series of graduated steps. But each of these steps placed education that much further away from the life activities for which they were preparatory. Educational experiences were still selected and pointed toward life, but obviously education had progressed far from the incidental informality of life toward the conscious formality of school.

Probably no single item of the complexity of culture made school more necessary than did the reduction of the social culture to written form.

When this occurred in very ancient times, the youth had first to learn the symbols of a written language, to say nothing of its grammar, before he could partake of the adult culture. Naturally, this required a preparatory state, a stage apart from life itself. Moreover, it required that some adults make an adult activity of instructing youth in reading and writing and later on in the mysteries locked in the recorded culture itself. Thus the complexity imposed on the social culture by writing led not only to a formal school but to a group of formal or professional teachers as well.

Under the conditions of informal education, adults became *ad hoc* teachers as occasion might demand. Parents in their daily occupations continually stepped in and out of the role of teacher. In so advanced a culture as that of the Spartans every adult was responsible for the instruction of the young, regardless of blood relation. But as culture became more complex and especially as this complexity was due in part to recording the culture in written symbols, a division of labor gradually occurred in society so that some adults made it their special business to be teachers of the young. Naturally, they specialized in teaching the recorded culture of the past; but as this changed relatively slowly, teachers tended to get out of touch with active life, the culture of the present, which was constantly being reshaped on the anvil of daily experience. Thus again formal education became differentiated from informal, and school became differentiated from life.

The relation of education to life in an advanced state of culture is further revealed by the etymological origin of the word for school. Our word " school " derives from the Greek $\sigma\chi o\lambda\acute{\eta}$, whose root meaning is " leisure." Evidently the Greeks so consistently devoted their leisure to educational pursuits that custom gave the word for " leisure " an added meaning. For one thing this bit of etymology reinforces the conclusion that formal education, or school, had by this time long since ceased to be identical with life and was now definitely several steps removed. It indicates that the social culture had become so vast and so complex that one had to have leisure from ordinary activities in order to master it.

For another thing, the identification of school with leisure marked the achievement of the basic economic conditions that later permitted the pursuit of education as an end in itself, as something more than just the means of entering the adult group and maintaining its continuity. At first, leisure was the indispensable prop for any education whatever. The quantity of leisure and education at this stage was just enough to cover the minimum necessary to ensure the continuance of society. Later, notably in the commercial culture of the Greeks, when peace and the arts and sciences produced a superabundance of leisure, education could be pursued, not merely as a means, but as an end as well. As an end it became the object of pursuit by adults as well as by the younger generation.

The point was a very critical one for the subsequent relation of education and life. When reached by various civilizations, it was, all too often, the last step in the separation of education and life. While education was pursued as a means of entering the adult group and preserving its social continuity, there was a constant check on the effectiveness with which one was achieving this end of life. But once a leisure class made education its own end, education constantly ran the risk of becoming esoteric and out of touch with life. This, however, was a late development. Yet, in spite of this risk, it remains to say that the pursuit of education as an end in itself also paradoxically led to a new identity of education and life. Reaching the stage of indulging in education for its own sake implied that leisure pursuits had become regularly accepted as adult activities. In other words, education took its place along with politics, religion, and the like, in its demands on adult time and attention.

It would be a mistake to think that the evolution of a formal school with a curriculum largely of written materials and later with a staff of professional teachers entirely supplanted the earlier process of informal education. As a matter of fact, informal education paralleled formal schooling right down through the ages into modern times. In quantity, if not in quality, informal education predominated in this long period. A boy developed into a hunter or fisher, a farmer or merchant, an artisan or priest by what he learned on the job. From earliest times right down to and beyond the period of the guilds of the Middle Ages, a more or less formal sort of apprenticeship education existed. In fact, it was the only kind of education that the great mass of mankind ever knew. Until the nineteenth and twentieth centuries only a very small percentage of the population had either need or inclination for the formal literary education of the schools. Even with the coming in the past century of compulsory schooling for all, shrewd educators did not forget that children spent more hours out of school than in and that the informal education of those hours was often more effective than the formal education of schooling.

RELATIVE VALUE OF FORMAL AND INFORMAL EDUCATION

The question whether formal or informal education is superior has long been a favorite topic of debate among educational theorists. The Greeks, for instance, raised the question whether one could formally teach virtue — in their estimation the highest qualification of a citizen. In the old Greek education the young had learned virtue as a matter of habituation while informally engaged in the everyday duties of citizen. The norm of virtue was embodied in great men, past and present. Admiration for the ideal qualities of these men prompted emulation and imitation. In later Greek education a group of teachers known as " Sophists " claimed to teach virtue by reading and talking about it. They discussed the norm of virtue as an idea or ideal.

Naturally, these two views of education clashed. The advantage that lay with the older, more informal education was that virtue was ingrained or habituated in and through conduct. The advantage that lay with the Sophists, the "progressives" of their day, was that they were able to reconstruct the ideal or norm of virtue to meet the new and changing demands of their time. In a formal school, teachers could abstract the idea of virtue from the concrete context of its practice. In the abstract form of idea they could be critical of it and reshape it in the light of criticism. The limitation of the old informal education was that it suffered from the conservatism of routine, from the inhospitality of habit to innovation. The limitation of the new formal education was that it was too intellectual. It lacked the motivation to be found in the informal education of life.

If the Greeks doubted that a satisfactory education could be obtained apart from life, Roger Ascham (1515–1568), the great English educator of the sixteenth century, seriously doubted that a good education could be had apart from school. He took little stock in the adage that experience is the best teacher. Rather he contended that "Learning teacheth more in one year than experience in twenty; and learning teacheth safely when experience maketh more miserable than wise." This statement will indicate how far the formal conception of education had gained in prestige in the twenty centuries intervening between the sixteenth century and the golden age of Greece.

Yet it is statements such as this which mark the crest of the historical movement from life to informal education and from informal education to formal schooling. In fact, in the very act of teaching "safely" the crest of the wave of formal education overarched itself and came tumbling down. Formal education had been safe because it was identified with the written culture where were recorded the tried and true experience of the social group. But the experience was always past experience. Formal and book education was concerned particularly with the past. The greater the book, the longer the past seemed to dominate men's minds and the more the social culture represented by contemporary living was put at a discount. Because of this, one might say that the social culture recorded in books tended to be more inelastic than that which was grounded in the habits of daily living. Habits may change ever so slowly; but they are alive, and they do grow. The written culture should be able to criticize and renew itself too, every time a new book is published. But, alas, instead of progressing with the slow changes in the daily course of living, the recorded culture fell behind. Cultural lag developed. Safety predicated on the past was gained at the risk of maladaptation to the present and future.

It was such periods of cultural lag that gave rise to the recurrent demand for "realism" in the schools. The demand for realism was the demand that the steps which formal education has taken away from actual life be retraced. The twentieth century excepted, perhaps at no period was this demand for realism greater than in the centuries preceding and following the one in which Ascham lived. The Renaissance had been the heyday of bookish education. But it overreached itself in nominating the books of just one author, Cicero, the great Roman stylist, as the ones that could be most safely imitated for thought and form. The time came, however, when teachers were recommending Cicero to a generation whose thought and action could no longer find adequate expression in his idiom. Aware they were out of touch with life, a few tried to be more realistic. The so-called " Humanistic realists " kept to the ideal of education through the written culture, but they attempted to make a selection of classical authors whose ideas were contemporary with the later day and age. Other reformers, sometimes called " sense realists," tried to introduce the new sciences into the schools. These sciences were growing apace outside the school walls and represented one of the most vital life activities of the time. Still other reformers, often known as " social realists," retraced their steps all the way back to life and, like the great Frenchman Montaigne (1533–1592), urged travel and mixing in society as a better sort of education than was to be had in the schools.

Instead of trying to determine the relative superiority of life or school as an educator, many recognized that each had its appropriate and distinct role to perform, that an education without the contribution of both was deficient. As far back as Biblical times the Jews made the formal education of words parallel the informal education of deeds. In Deuteronomy, Jehovah enjoined, " And these words, which I command thee this day, shall be in thine heart: And thou shalt teach them diligently unto thy children, and shalt talk of them when thou sittest in thine house, and when thou walkest by the way, and when thou liest down, and when thou risest up." This injunction was still being repeated in a time and place as remote as nineteenth-century America. There, when he was trying to stir Connecticut out of its educational lethargy, Henry Barnard (1811–1900) urged fathers to give an educational turn to conversation with their sons while at table and even while plowing their fields.

The same idea is evident in the writings of John Locke (1632–1704), the educational mouthpiece of seventeenth-century England. In his essay *Some Thoughts Concerning Education* he showed a high regard for the education to be had from books and gave careful attention to the fields to be studied. But he did not, on this account, neglect the informal education of out-of-school experience. On the contrary, he recommended that a father should talk to his son about important matters as soon as his son's maturity and experience would permit. His underlying idea was that only as a boy is treated like a man will he become a man. And, vice versa, a father must treat a son no less like a man when the boy was the one to propose his boyish concerns for mutual discussion.

In eighteenth-century prerevolutionary France, LaChalotais (1701–1785) made an even more striking balance between the contributions of formal and informal education, school and life. In his *Essay on National Education* he frankly stated, " All that needs to be known is not contained in books. There are a thousand things about which it is possible to learn by conversation, by usage, and by practice; but," he went on to point out,

" only minds that are already somewhat trained can profit by this sort of instruction. . . . In society, the spirit of study and of business seem opposed to each other; but a man will not understand business well if he has not studied. The important thing is to acquire the main principles of the more uncommon kinds of knowledge; experience — which is the best teacher — will accomplish the rest."

By the twentieth century the extent and complexity of civilization had increased to so great an extent that "uncommon" kinds of experience markedly outstripped the range of direct common experience. The environment to which the individual had to react became enlarged far beyond the immediate time and place in which he found himself. Consequently, the American William C. Bagley (1874–1946) was inclined to reverse the relative emphasis of LaChalotais on school and experience. He did not think raw experience so good a teacher as the school, for the school could provide a unique type of experience — vicarious experience. From his point of view the unique function of the school was that it enabled the pupil to transcend the limitations of raw or common experience. Through school studies like history and geography, the pupil was able to transcend the limitations of the time and place in which he lived and thus vicariously absorb experiences otherwise quite uncommon to daily experience.

In the writings of America's most eminent educational philosopher, John Dewey (1859–1952), neither school nor life was favored over the other, neither was one thought of as supplemental to the other. Instead, Dewey enunciated the doctrine that education and life were one. This was not, however, an exclusive return to the informal education of life experience. The theory of the oneness of education and life sought rather to tear down any barrier between the two without destroying the identity of either. Thus, instead of confining itself to its four walls, the school was urged to avail itself of varied community resources for whatever educational value they might have. The school's getting outside its own skin might extend all the way from excursions into the community to making the school an adjunct of the farm and the factory. And to the extent that the school stayed within its four walls it was demanded that the curriculum pursued there be a form of living that is immediately significant. . . .

CHAPTER TWO BIBLIOGRAPHY

DEWEY, JOHN, *The School and Society*. Chicago: University of Chicago Press, 1900.

> Dewey notes the cleavage between formal and informal education. He contends that the school should evolve into an agency which is reflective of the best of the larger community, promoting those activities which are included within the purposes of the community. A good school will do for a youngster what a good informal education would attempt to do.

HAMBLY, W. D., *Origins of Education Among Primitive Peoples*. London: Macmillan and Company, 1926.

A British anthropologist summarizes aspects of informal education among primitive peoples. Special attention is given to " moral, religious, physical and social education," especially among societies that have had little or no influence from Europeans.

MILLER, NATHAN, *The Child in Primitive Society.* London: Kegan Paul, Trench, Trubner & Co., 1928.

Chapters VIII through X deal with education in primitive societies. Miller stresses that such education is not " wholly unreflective, or casually imitative." Rather, there is purposeful transmission of cultural values. He cites many of the same anthropological studies referred to by Todd.

READ, MARGARET, *Children of Their Fathers.* London: Methuen & Co., 1959.

Unlike much of the literature on primitive education which deals with practices in many varied societies, this is a study in depth of natives in the Ngoni villages in Nyasaland, Central Africa. It is an excellent account of how an anthropologist approaches the study of education.

SPINDLER, GEORGE D., editor, *Education and Anthropology.* Stanford: Stanford University Press, 1955.

The deliberations of a pioneering conference of anthropologists and educators are presented in this volume. Each group presents insights that contribute to a further understanding of education as a social institution. In general, the anthropologists question the value-laden assumptions of the educators; the educators question whether the anthropologists can, or should, be as objective as they profess.

3

The Responsibility for Formal Education:
Public and Private

As societies become increasingly complex, as the concerns of children become more remote from the activities of adults, and as the problem of preparation for participation in the society becomes more pressing, formal education comes into being. The institution of formal education, or schooling, has certain inherent problems, which in various societies have been differently resolved. In our time most of these problems still appear open for final resolution. We are still confronted by puzzling dilemmas posed by competing claims. Fundamentally, three interrelated issues arise and must be answered in determining the appropriate locus of responsibility for conducting formal education.

The first of these is the problem of *function*. Whenever schools are established, they are established to serve some purpose, or function, which is itself an outgrowth of some kind of world-view or philosophy. For example, if one believes that this formal schooling is necessary in order that the individual may be of service to the society and contribute to the life of the group, it is clear that the function is *social*. This function may still be variously interpreted: it may be judged to be social in the sense that effective participation in a society is the only way of maximizing individual potentiality. This is the democratic presupposition, and it rests upon a faith in the worth and integrity of the individual as realized through social means. On the other hand, this function may be social in the sense that the individual is viewed exclusively as a means to serve the society or to promote progress toward some social goal. This is the totalitarian presupposition and rests upon a belief in the supremacy of the state or society as end in itself. Similarly it may be argued that the function of education is *individual* — that is, that education is designed to promote the welfare or interests of the individual. This is the point of view held by many Americans who see education for their children primarily in terms of helping their children " get ahead." Or it may be argued that the function of education is largely *religious* — that it is a means of providing induction into a religious community which exceeds or encompasses the civil community or society. These concepts of function ordinarily, but not necessarily, are closely tied to the other two issues which must be faced.

The second issue is that of *support*. Unlike informal education, which exists in every society and which is often carried on incidentally in the very process of fulfilling other social functions, formal education requires that special means of support be found. The more complex the social system into which the young are to be inducted or in which they are to make their way, the more elaborate and expensive the support required. Early conceptions of the teacher on one end of the log and the pupil on the other have given way to highly complex learning arrangements. Libraries, gymnasia, science laboratories, professional instructors, and flexible classrooms all require expenditures, so that today it is estimated that the educational expenses in the United

States alone for all public elementary and secondary schools exceed $17 billion. The resolution of the problem of support is generally associated closely with the issue of function. Those people who have viewed education as rendering primarily a private function, as basically serving to help the individual achieve or maintain his place, have seen educational support as being primarily a private responsibility. Those who have seen education as being chiefly designed to assure that an individual can take a useful place in society, and can fulfill himself through service in that society, have generally looked to society for the support of education. Those who have seen education as being primarily designed to assure that an individual acquire the full dimensions of his religious character have generally believed that religious groups should furnish the major financial support. Inasmuch as education is often viewed as serving a variety of these functions, however, the question of the appropriate source of support is generally not as clear-cut as here implied; and with the increasing burden of educational costs, the desire of private and religious schools for public assistance is developing.

The third issue is that of *control*. This issue is closely related to each of the others. If there is to be assurance that a function is adequately performed, it is important that control rest in the hands of those centrally concerned with the performance of this function. Thus, those who have viewed education as being primarily a public function have assumed that public schools should not only be publicly supported, but that they should be publicly controlled as well. Similarly, those favoring religious-oriented education want its control in religious hands, as those supporting private schools want them privately controlled. There is, however, a second

reason why the problem of control is practically implicated. It is a fact of political and economic life that complete divorce between support and control can seldom be maintained. Thus, support given various enterprises by governments generally leads to government regulation or control to insure that the monies are employed for the purposes or functions recognized as public concern; support given by private individuals is only forthcoming as long as these individuals view the enterprise supported as serving their purposes or program. The power of the purse strings is strong in education as in other areas.

One further factor complicates the total question of responsibility in any society dedicated to respect for the worth and integrity of the individual. Any society dedicated to humane propositions must inevitably devote scrupulous care to the *welfare* of each recipient of education. In our society it is our policy to see that youngsters in all schools are equally assured of the health and welfare benefits of fire protection, public health services, hot lunch programs, and the like. But if education *itself* is recognized as central to human welfare, the ultimate question involves what kinds of control and support over this central function must be exercised by a society committed to respect for the dignity and welfare of the individual. This question has not yet been squarely faced or answered.

The readings which follow present four competing conceptions of the appropriate locus of responsibility for education. Three of them represent theories which have flourished, or do flourish, in the free world. The other represents an alternative posited in a society committed to a radically different world-view. Each claims to define or delimit the appropriate relationship between school and society; not all can be equally correct.

SECTION **1. The responsibility for education: the case for private responsibility**

An interesting indication of the way we are all trapped by our own culture to the extent that we fail even to recognize its most basic presuppositions is the assurance with which most teachers assume the propriety of the public school system. Recent threats in some states to do away with the public schools have generally been viewed by the profession and the public as either idle or incredible. In other cultures and other times the very concept of a public school system has seemed as wrong or as incredible as the idea of a contemporary culture without a public school system seems to us. It is only our complementary concept of educational diversity — a concept which has permitted or welcomed the growth of private and parochial schools *alongside* our public schools — which has kept Americans from being blinded to alternative approaches to education which are available.

Our private school system today has strong advocates. Such advocates differ from many in the past, however, for they base their advocacy not on the position of *replacing* public education by private education but rather by pointing to complementary or auxiliary functions which they believe private education can best perform. It is sometimes argued, for example, that private schools have a freedom to experiment which the public schools, bound by public controls, do not have. Such experiments, it is argued, can redound to the advantage of public as well as private schools. Similarly it is sometimes argued that the " competition " between public and private schools is healthy for both; by being forced to compete, each strives to excel, and educational progress is the inevitable result. At other times it is argued that for a particular clientele, the private school is better able to render certain special services. All too frequently this latter orientation has been associated with a kind of social elitism, a view that persons should be educated to fill certain pre-established social ranks in life, in which case these schools tend to inculcate the modes and manners of a particular social class. Although each of these arguments is offered as a justification for private schools today, a more basic rationale for the essentially private character of education has traditionally served as a foundation for the private school. This rationale implies a general theory of government — its domain and its limitations; and perhaps the general rationale for private schools within this wider context has never been more explicitly formulated than by Herbert Spencer, a nineteenth century British philosopher and social theorist.

Herbert Spencer's position on education can best be understood in the framework of his over-all orientation and the task he set himself. Spencer devoted his life to an attempt to formulate a systematic social philosophy which would translate the meaning of nineteenth century science — stirred to the depths by the concept of evolution — into social theory. He looked to evolution as providing a natural key to human problems. His *Social Statics,* from which his views on education are taken, was published in 1850, nine years before Darwin's *Origin of the Species,* but it clearly reveals the effect of pre-Darwinian evolutionary thought. The stamp of early evolutionism is upon it: the belief that human progress must be gradual, that attempts at hasty planned reformation can only interrupt the natural order and upset progress; that individuals must learn to adapt to changing situations; that we must rely upon the unameliorated natural consequences of action as necessary ingredients in progress; that individualism and laissez-faire are the best approach to politics and social policy. But Spencer's work not only reflects the findings of such nineteenth century thinkers as Lamarck, Malthus, and Darwin; it equally reflects his devotion to marshaling the empirical evidence necessary to support his theories. In his constant reference to facts he foreshadows much contemporary educational investigation.

His argument for private education is significant in that it touches upon many of the great issues of both political and educational theory and reveals the close relationship between the two. He faces the issue of whether a government should be limited to the performance of one essential function or concerned with all aspects of welfare. He faces the issue of whether an educational system controlled by government can serve the purpose of critic or reformer of that social system — or whether publicly controlled education must, perforce, be throughly static, that is, designed to preserve the *status quo*. He challenges the ready assertion that education can be justified in terms of its social increments — the reduction of crime and other forms of social disorder, pointing out that often we merely alter the particular form of social disorder. He faces the issue of whether public education, if it is to alter its character in any fundamental way, can be anything but propagandistic. Finally, and most significantly, he faces the fundamental issue of the nature of *freedom*, an issue which in the final analysis is found to underlie almost any democratic theory of education. His analysis, startling as it is to those who accept without question many of the presuppositions of the present social order, is worthy of careful study.

HERBERT SPENCER
A criticism of governmental activities in education

NATIONAL EDUCATION

1. In the same way that our definition of state-duty forbids the state to administer religion or charity, so likewise does it forbid the state to administer education. Inasmuch as the taking away, by government, of more of a man's property than is needful for maintaining his rights, is an infringement of his rights, and therefore a reversal of the government's function toward him; and inasmuch as the taking away of his property to educate his own or other people's children is not needful for the maintaining of his rights; the taking away of his property for such a purpose is wrong.

Should it be said that the rights of the children are involved, and that state interposition is required to maintain these, the reply is that no cause for such interposition can be shown until the children's rights have been violated, and that their rights are not violated by a neglect of their education. For, as repeatedly explained, what we call rights are merely arbitrary subdivisions of the general liberty to exercise the faculties; and that only can be called an infringement of rights which actually diminishes this liberty — cuts off a previously existing power to pursue the objects of desire.

From Herbert Spencer, *Social Statics* (New York: D. Appleton and Company, 1873), pp. 360–363, 389–390.

Now the parent who is careless of a child's education does not do this. The liberty to exercise the faculties is left intact. Omitting instruction in no way takes from a child's freedom to do whatsoever it wills in the best way it can; and this freedom is all that equity demands. Every aggression, be it remembered — every infraction of rights, is necessarily *active*; whilst every neglect, carelessness, omission, is as necessarily *passive*. Consequently, however wrong the non-performance of a parental duty may be — however much it is condemned by that secondary morality — the morality of beneficence — it does not amount to a breach of the law of equal freedom, and cannot therefore be taken cognizance of by the state.

2. Were there no direct disproof of the frequently alleged right to education at the hands of the state, the absurdities in which it entangles its assertors would sufficiently show its invalidity. Conceding for a moment that the government is bound to educate a man's children, then, what kind of logic will demonstrate that it is not bound to feed and clothe them? If there should be an act-of-parliament provision for the development of their minds, why should there not be an act-of-parliament provision for the development of their bodies? If the mental wants of the rising generation ought to be satisfied by the state, why not their physical ones? The reasoning which is held to establish the right to intellectual food, will equally well establish the right to material food: nay, will do more — will prove that children should be altogether cared for by government. For if the benefit, importance, or necessity of education be assigned as a sufficient reason why government should educate, then may the benefit, importance, or necessity of food, clothing, shelter, and warmth be assigned as a sufficient reason why government should administer these also. So that the alleged right cannot be established without annulling all parental responsibility whatever.

Should further refutation be thought needful, there is the ordeal of a definition. We lately found this ordeal fatal to the assumed right to a maintenance; we shall find it equally fatal to this assumed right to education. For what is an education? Where, between the teaching of a dameschool, and the most comprehensive university *curriculum*, can be drawn the line separating that portion of mental culture which may be justly claimed of the state, from that which may not be so claimed? What peculiar quality is there in reading, writing, and arithmetic, which gives the embryo citizen a right to have them imparted to him, but which quality is not shared in by geography, and history, and drawing, and the natural sciences? Must calculation be taught because it is useful? why so is geometry, as the carpenter and mason will tell us; so is chemistry, as we may gather from dyers and bleachers; so is physiology, as is abundantly proved by the ill-health written in so many faces. Astronomy, mechanics, geology, and the various connate sciences — should not these be taught, too? they are all useful. Where is the unit of measure by which we may determine the respective values of different kinds of knowledge? Or, assuming them determined, how can it be shown that a child may claim from the civil power knowledge of such and such values, but not knowledge of certain less values? When those who demand a state-education can say exactly how much is due — can agree upon what the young have a right to, and what not — it will be time to listen. But until they accomplish this impossibility, their plea cannot be entertained. . . .

11. Thus, in the present, as in other cases, we find the dictate of the abstract law enforced by secondary considerations. The alleged right to education at the hands of the state proves to be untenable; first, as logically committing its supporters to other claims too absurd for consideration; and again, as being incapable of definition. Moreover, could the claim be established, it would imply the duty of government despotically to enforce its system of discipline, and the duty of the subject to submit. That education ought not to be dealt in after the same manner as other things, because in its case " the interest and judgment of the consumer are not sufficient security for the goodness of the commodity," is a plea with most suspicious antecedents; having been many times employed in other instances, and many times disproved. Neither is the implied assumption that the " interest and judgment " of a government *would* constitute a sufficient security admissible. On the contrary, experience proves that the interests of a government, and of all the institutions it may set up, are directly opposed to education of the most important kind. Again, to say that legislative teaching is needful, because other teaching has failed, presupposes a pitiably narrow view of human progress; and further, involves the strange scepticism that, though natural agencies have brought the enlightenment of mankind to its present height, and are even now increasing it at an unparalleled rate, they will no longer answer. The belief that education is a preventive of crime, having no foundation either in theory or fact, cannot be held an excuse for interference. And, to crown all, it turns out that the institution so much longed for is a mere dead machine, which can only give out in one form the power it absorbs in another, minus the friction — a thing which cannot stir toward effecting this kind of education without abstracting the force now accomplishing that — a thing, therefore, which cannot educate at all. . . .

SECTION 2. **Education as a public responsibility: The case in a democratic society**

Perhaps no more explicit reply to Spencer's thesis could be presented than that made by the American educator Thomas H. Briggs in his now classic lecture, *The Great Investment*. Presented some eighty years after Spencer's treatise and in a cultural milieu more familiar to us, Briggs' lecture develops an argument to justify a sharply different conception of the role of education in a free society. Although each sees the need for the state to protect and perpetuate itself, these two social theorists differ sharply on the appropriateness of using education as a state agency in meeting this need. Briggs' argument, one all too often overlooked by the American public, rests less upon the role of education in individual advancement than upon the role of education in the perpetuation and improvement of the State. Such an argument inevitably comes up against the very challenges which Spencer had early propounded: the threat that education will become conservative and not render a corrective function if under state control; the alleged threat of the ever-expanding functions of government; the danger inherent in placing too great a reliance on a single easy " solution " to a social ill which has long prevailed. In part the differences in the positions of these two men reflect fundamentally different political theories and world-views; in part their differences arise out of the assessment of the evidence available in their respective times and cultures. Operating within the empirical tradition, however, each would have been willing to put his position to the test of the facts. We owe it to them to do no less. No serious student of education can fail to ask himself the question of whether the weight of evidence since Spencer's time has in effect rendered his position on the social outcomes of public education invalid, or whether the accumulated evidence of the last three generations has vindicated Briggs' optimistic faith in education as a public enterprise.

To view Briggs' lecture as an uncritical apologia for public education in a democratic society, however, would be to overlook its penetration. Much of his lecture is devoted to providing answers to the basic question of *function* and its correlative questions of *control* and *support*. But it does more than this. In a very real sense this lecture raises and attempts to answer further crucial issues always resident in education in a democratic society: the issue of the appropriate roles for public and professional authority in such education; the possibility of developing independent thought in any school controlled by the State; the place of education in improving the quality of community living; the conflicting claims made upon education by individual interests and social goals. No defense of public education which fails to come to terms with such issues as these can face the challenge of the contemporary scene. The enduring virtue of Briggs' lecture is that in it he has faced and attempted to resolve just such issues.

THOMAS H. BRIGGS
The function of the State in educational matters

After considering all the answers that have been proposed, by laymen on various levels and by the few professional educators who apparently have thought of the important matter, one on reflection finds that the reason why the State institutes schools, enforces attendance through the elementary stages, and makes no charge for tuition is absurdly simple. The State supports free public schools to perpetuate itself and to promote its own interests. Education is, then, a long-term investment that the State may be a better place in which to live and a better place in which to make a living.

From Thomas H. Briggs, *The Great Investment: Secondary Education in a Democracy*, 1930, pp. 8–13, 40–48, 52–59. Reprinted by permission of the Harvard University Press.

This reason is so obviously sound and so obviously superior to all others that have been proposed that it apparently needs only understanding to gain approval. It would seem that some such reason must from early days have been in the popular mind, certainly that it must clearly be there now, to explain the practically unanimous support of public schools. Often there is disagreement in a community as to how much money shall be voted for their support, but it has been a long time since any one raised a voice against them as a justifiable institution. Every year to support free schools the State takes money from the purses of all of its citizens — from childless spinsters and bachelors, from retired farmers and bankers, and from " soulless corporations " as well as from parents. It never asks if the taxpayer "loves little children "; it never asks if he is willing to contribute; and strangely enough he never protests the principle. The question of public support for schools is settled and, whether understandingly or not, settled in the right way.

The reason is not only sound, it is also important. Already we are aware of a reaction to the rapid increase in the costs of public schools, a reaction which unless checked promises more seriously to cripple progress than it has already done in some communities. The only reliable way of insuring the continuance of generous support and of increasing it to an extent commensurate with estimated needs is to place it on a sound basis of reason. Free education is a business investment and not a benevolence. Philanthropy, charitableness, and good will are welcomed as enriching educational support and opportunities; but reason is essential to insure justice and wise development. If education is seen as a necessity for preserving and for bettering the State, opposition to adequate appropriations takes on the tone of treason. The thesis that is being presented is no mere academic justification of the marvelous phenomenon of free public education in our country. It has many important implications, some of which will presently be discussed. To the extent to which it is understood and accepted it will give direction to reforms in education which in their perfection would be revolutionary.

Other forms of government may maintain themselves and even temporarily prosper with education limited to the few who direct and drive a vulgar populace; but in a democracy, where one vote counts for as much as another, where success is dependent upon unit citizens all sufficiently intelligent and informed and trained to evaluate and act wisely on their information, popular education is imperative. This statement needs no defense, so generally is it accepted.

A widespread righteousness is in a republic a matter of necessity. Where all rule all, each man who falls into evil courses infects his neighbor, corrupting the law and corrupting still more its enforcement. The question of manufacturing moral men becomes, accordingly, in a democracy, urgent to

*a degree unknown in a country where but a few selected persons guide the
state.*[1]

In other forms of government a leader is strong in proportion to the ignorance and the faith of his followers; democratic leadership is strong in
proportion to the educated intelligence of the people. Carlyle once said,
" Invent the printing press and democracy is inevitable." The printing press
has long been invented — and many other causes of democracy; they have
had their inevitable results, which are not likely for a long time to come,
if ever, to be directed backward. Those who decry democracy and rejoice
to point out its failures have not yet been able to propose anything approaching a satisfactory substitute. " The very ignorance, bias, frivolity,
jealousy, instability, which are alleged to incapacitate them (the masses)
from share in political affairs," says Dewey,[2] " unfit them still more for
passive submission to rule by intellectuals." Whether democracy is in any
degrees whatever good or bad, it is our accepted principle of government,
and it can be made better only by an intelligently and purposefully directed
education. The cure for democracy is truly more democracy — of a real
kind. We are as a people fond of declaiming of liberty, but it is possible
and can exist only through an education appropriate to each so that all
have a chance to develop toward that element of equality without which
the apotheosis of liberty can not exist.

The open questions are what kinds of education shall be provided and
how far shall it extend. Fundamentally it must provide for such training
as will perpetuate the State and promote its interests; and in wisdom it
should continue until the law of diminishing returns begins to operate for
each individual. Democracy is not " a utopia of escape," but a concatena-
tion of opportunities for service. It can succeed only as this fact is perceived
and as education is provided that sets up the proper attitude in young citizens and prepares them for such services to the State, indirect as well as
direct, as each is competent to perform. De Tocqueville long ago pointed
out " that popular government is educative as other modes of political
regulation are not." Preparation of all for this type of higher assured and
continuous education is more important in State supported schools than
is preparation for the higher and for the great majority of secondary school
students not sincerely desired college education, to which so much effort
is now devoted. An appreciation of the imperative need of this kind of
" preparatory schooling " will come only if the true function of State support of free schools is understood. Lest there be a misunderstanding, it
should be clearly stated here that preparation for higher education, academic and technical, and provision of such education for those who have
proved their competence for it are also an obligation of the State,[3] for

[1] Palmer, G. H.: *The Teacher*, page 32.   [2] *The Public and Its Problems*, page 205.
[3] Throughout this discussion the term *State*, when capitalized, is used to indicate not
political units of government, like Massachusetts or Arizona or North Carolina, but

such students thus trained will pay large dividends. But this preparation will, by the criterion implied, be limited and also supplementary to the preparation for the higher education that democracy demands and to an extent insures. . . .

But as " progress does not depend upon the similarity which we *find* but upon the similarity which we *achieve*," [4] education carries the responsibility for the largest part of the increase of desirable integration. A State is sovereign, wrote Viscount Haldane, " in so far as its members in unity direct themselves in the expression of the common purposes they are evolving. . . . It gives rise to the power of a great group unified by common ends."

The educated furnish stimulus to growth, which is the most satisfying of all man's activities, because the truly educated never cease themselves to grow. They are fecund of a variety of means to meet the problems of life, proposing this means and that until a solution is found that profits all the members of the larger social group. This ability in even a single individual makes a community a better place in which to live; when possessed by all, or even by many, it becomes a tremendously profitable social asset. The educated, too, are in varying degrees rich in resources for avocational and for vocational successes. As time never hangs heavy on their hands, they escape many of the temptations of less fortunate people to meddle and to interfere with the affairs of others; instead, they are ready to share their wealth of ideas and tastes with those who have a measure of appreciation. They furnish to others desires and emulations to increase their intellectual, æsthetic, and moral resources, that life may be more abundant and that they may share it more generously with others in their social groups.

The educated make a community a better place in which to live, further, because their own appetites, desires, and demands have brought together the means of satisfying numerous and various wants. Among them are libraries, museums, exhibits of art in its many forms, from painting and sculpture through architecture and a well-planned city, parks for recreation, places of entertainment on the levels sufficiently high that they demand effort for enjoyment and result in a satisfying consciousness of growth, conveniences of every kind, skilled service for all needs. The variety and richness of such assets, all of which have come because of educated needs, attract new citizens and make all comfortable to whatever extent they are used. The poorest inhabitant of such a community has an actual as well as

---

rather, the societal organization that has assumed responsibility for education. It may be a local school district, a municipality, a county, a political state, the entire population of the country, or any combination of these. The tendency properly seems to be units of support of increasing extent, which is a recognition of the break-down with the developments in modern civilization of isolation and independence. This arbitrary definition must be kept continuously in mind when considering the arguments for the thesis herein defended.   4 Follett, *The New State*.

a potential wealth greater than any one can possess in a community which has not been built up by demands of those made competent by education.

Partly because of education, partly because of its results, and partly, perhaps, because of other reasons, communities rank as to poverty and crime inversely on the whole as they rank in education. There is strong reason for believing that the negative correlation would be even larger still if the machinery of education were directed more consistently and more intelligently toward achieving economic comforts and respect for law, whether common or statute, objectives that are generally proclaimed and commonly neglected in practice. Similarly, education contributes somewhat and indubitably could contribute much more to making communities better in which to live by raising the levels on which intelligence commonly operates, especially regarding matters of wide social concern and specifically of political action. Obviously a democratic government is not successful unless the voices of the people are raised for and against proposals according to social values; and obviously the more informed the citizens are, the more skilfully they use native intellectual gifts in perceiving the better among the worse, just so much more successful democracy will be. If education can not, when it seriously wills to do so, affect such matters, what agency, pray, can be trusted to influence the people consistently for the common good? When ignorance, prejudices, and short-sightedness — and it is these far more often than malevolence — commonly lead to votes that negate those supported by the opposite characteristics, no government is on a sound foundation; it can not continue to make its territory a better place in which to live. Any one who permits himself to think on this matter must realize the direct dependence of democracy on education — not an education that is merely memoriter fact accumulations, but one that is seriously concerned with preserving the State and with bettering it in every way possible.

And finally to be mentioned, though doubtless there are other contributions, education tends to make any community a better place in which to live by raising the standards of living. This in many ways it assuredly does. It affords some direct instruction, which it might easily increase in amount and in effectiveness; it reveals both in its plant and through instruction higher types than many pupils know; it employs teachers who by various means have learned what higher standards are and also the advantages of following them. A low standard of living by one family is degrading to a neighborhood; seldom concealed, it is infectious. A high standard, on the other hand, is an example, an encouragement, and a stimulus to emulation. It can not be doubted that education has greatly affected standards of living or that it can be made to do more. The extent to which education helps to a higher standard is an important contribution to making the whole community a better place in which all may live.

It is argued, too, that education makes a community better in which to earn a living. Of course a very small part of the curriculum has been formulated with the intent of directly contributing to economic effectiveness; and on the higher levels liberal and cultural courses may so divert interests and ambitions from economic accumulation that, after a comfortable living is assured, powers are directed to an enriched life with the result that earnings are below those which are possible. By all ideal standards this is entirely as it should be. As any one who has studied the various attempts to prove the economic values of education will realize, the problem is very complex. Often cause and effect are confused and a common cause for both education and prosperity is ignored. But the evidence, which there is no space to review here, seems unmistakable. There is a close relationship between such education as is provided and economic prosperity. The ability to read, to figure, to apply acquired knowledge, and to learn new processes more economically has contributed to make men better able to make a living. That the contribution of education to earning power could be considerably greater if curricula were made more directly vocational is so obvious as to need no argument.

The effect of general education on the ability to make a living, whatever its scientific explanation, is too commonly recognized to be entirely fallacious. The following quotation from Macaulay is illustrative:

But by far the most important event of this short session was the passing of the Act for the settling of schools. By this memorable law it was, in the Scotch phrase, statuted and ordained that every parish in the realm should provide a commodious school house and should pay a moderate stipend to a schoolmaster. The effect could not be immediately felt. But, before one generation had passed away, it began to be evident that the common people of Scotland were superior in intelligence to the common people of any other country in Europe. To whatever land the Scotchman might wander, to whatever calling he might betake himself, in America or in India, in trade or in war, the advantage which he derived from his early training raised him above his competitors. If he was taken into a warehouse as a porter, he soon became foreman. If he enlisted in the army, he soon became a sergeant. Scotland, meanwhile, in spite of the barrenness of her soil and the severity of her climate, made such progress in agriculture, in manufactures, in commerce, in letters, in science, in all that constitutes civilization, as the Old World had never seen equalled, and as even the New World has scarcely seen surpassed.[5]

In our devotion to cultural education, the importance of which is not only conceded but emphasized, we often lose sight of the fact that it contributes to only one phase of the perfect man. No person can ideally be a good citizen unless he is equipped by nature and by training to make a living, and the more adequate that is, the better in many ways for his neighbors as well as for himself and his family. The ship of state can not

[5] Macaulay, *History of England*, Chapter XXII.

move steadily or comfortably forward with a cargo of inactive and non-contributory passengers. Hence for the perpetuation and also for the promotion of the State, education should insure that every citizen be better prepared to make a better living for himself and for his dependents. As a matter of fact, almost every person does learn in some way to make a living. It is only reasonable to assume that by special instruction every one can be trained so that he can be made more quickly productive and also efficient on a higher level — both for making a living and for making a life. If such training, during the twelve to fifteen year period, could increase the annual earning power by only ten per cent, which seems a modest expectancy, the increment of income would pay the entire cost of the public school system.

But it is not merely by increasing productiveness that education contributes to making the State a better place in which to make a living. Education of the consumer increases demands and thus furnishes work for others. Many shortsighted economists in their enthusiasm for the development of foreign markets for our goods lose sight of the fact that the best market, and ultimately the only one that can continue to pay for what it buys without disturbing exchange, is here at home. So as education has revealed the higher necessities of life, or the necessities of higher life, and has created a keen appetite for them, it has tended to make the State a better place in which to make a living. Where there are large demands there are opportunities for work, which in part explains the migration in our country from the rural to urban communities, for in spite of improved transportation it is in the cities that greater demands usually afford greater opportunities.

There is sufficient evidence to warrant our believing that education reduces crime and even more reason to make us confident that it could tremendously increase its influence in this respect if it seriously undertook the responsibility. The same evidence makes us believe that education has had no inconsiderable part in reducing poverty, in increasing the saving of what has been earned, not for hoarding but for intelligent investment for larger production. Certainly it would not be hard to prove that popular education has reduced disease, both by making every one aware of laws of health which he must follow and also hospitable to the advice and services of the expert, whom education has made an asset to the State. If education does decrease crime, poverty, and disease, it has very materially contributed to making the State a better place in which to make a living. . . .

One objection is sure to be voiced when the thesis is presented that education is an investment by the State for the promotion of its own interests. That objection is based on concern for the rights of the individual and a fear that he may be prostituted by corporate society. Fortunately there is in reality little conflict. The interests of the State can be best served only if the individual is at the same time carefully developed in a way that is best for him. The State needs citizens effective in all sorts of ways — in

commerce and in chemistry, in agriculture and in astronomy, in manu-
facture and in mathematics. The natural laws of competition and of demand ultimately thwart individual aspirations and hopes, which are usually
confused with the so-called rights, far more than the State is likely to do.

The State can not be bettered unless the individual is first bettered himself, and so he is not likely to suffer under the principle that is being defended. But unfortunately it often appears to a short-sighted vision that
the individual can be profited with no obvious or probable benefit to the
supporting State. In such a situation there will be conflict. Let us suppose,
for illustration, that a pupil has a desire to enter some college not for its
academic training but for the pleasure that is possible in its social life or the
prestige of being an alumnus. Let us suppose, further, that because of in-
dolence or of inability he has shown during his introductory courses in
mathematics no promise of even a reasonable success in pursuing the advanced courses necessary for admission. Which interests shall be dominant
in a decision as to whether he shall be permitted to pursue advanced
courses in the public secondary school? Shall those in authority, representing the State, use public funds for the further presentation of a subject that
the pupil could not or would not in the past reasonably master so that
it promised any material values to him? Does the objective that he seeks,
a period of carefree comraderie, promise enough of value to him to make
it reasonable to expect him thereby to be a better citizen? If a case can not
be made for the further expenditure of public funds with a reasonable expectancy of profitable returns, responsibility rests with the pupil and his
parents to secure at their own expense preparation for the desired end.

It may be objected further that the school authorities may be in error
in their judgment or that the pupil may turn over a new leaf and manifest better results or that when he gets into college he may be awakened
to keen academic interests. Such arguments would be considered absurd
everywhere else in the world. School authorities may err in judgment,
though naturally they should exercise every care possible not to do so and
always are likely to give an individual the benefit of a doubt; but they have
a responsibility to follow such judgments as they are able to make on the
basis of accumulated evidence. If they err frequently and seriously, they
are of course incompetent and should be replaced. It is the most patent
dishonesty, of course, for one set in a position of trust by the State to shirk
responsibility merely because it is personally unpleasant. It is possible that
the pupil may make a new start and do better work; but if every reasonable
effort has been unsuccessfully made to get good work in the preliminary
courses, the responsibility now shifts to the pupil. If he manifests his ability
and his willingness to work in other similar courses, which may be provided,
or in the subject which he pursued under private instruction, the school
authorities may properly reinstate him as a good investment, reasonably
expecting profitable returns to the State that provides the funds. But the
responsibility after failure is his. (There is, of course, some essential learn-

ing that must be imparted at any cost whatever, precisely because it is essential; but in the illustration that is being developed, this is not the case.) And, finally, it is possible that a student may after going to college with an unworthy motive awaken to the value of its courses and profit materially from them. It is possible, but what is the probability? Decision should be made here as in any other investment. If all knowledge of this student and of former students who have gone forward under similar circumstances makes the risk a reasonable one, the school authorities will take it — primarily, however, because success will make the investment profitable to the State through the betterment of the individual. If the risk does not seem reasonable, it can not with honesty be taken.

Not infrequently a man who has been placed by the State as its representative in charge of an educational unit is confronted by an individual who says, " As a taxpayer, I demand thus and so for my child." Unsupported by any philosophy of public education, the school authority can argue only by meeting the challenge with the same weapons that are threatened. Of course the criterion to be used on such a demand is that evolving from our thesis. If what the taxpayer wants contains a reasonable promise of a dividend to the supporting State, it should be done, not as a concession but as a matter of policy; if it does not, the demand should be shown to be what it really is, a raid on the public treasury for a fancied private profit. In any other department of public works the true issue would be much more readily seen.

So much has been made of the individual and his rights that it is high time for emphasis to be given to the rights of collections of individuals. " Both words, individual and social," writes John Dewey,[6] " are hopelessly ambiguous, and the ambiguity will never cease so long as we think in terms of an antithesis. The human being whom we fasten upon as individual *par excellence* is moved and regulated by his associations with others; what he does and what the consequences of his behavior are, what his experience consists of, can not even be described, much less accounted for, in isolation." In only a mistaken and short-sighted view can any individual be said to have rights that are opposed to the interests of one or more of the groups with which he is associated. In no instance can his rights transcend those collective rights of the individuals that compose his group; otherwise the rights or interests of the many yield to those of the one. A social philosophy centers attention on the welfare of the group, in which each individual may find opportunities for such development as will contribute his best for their betterment. A restricted view may see conflict, but in reality it simply does not exist.

There may be, and indeed there often is, conflict, however, because each individual is a member of several groups — his family, his gang, his class, his school, his community, and his State, for instances. Ideally each is or

---

[6] *The Public and Its Problems*, page 186.

should be related to the larger and enveloping group as an individual is to it. And in no case would a long vision reveal conflict; but actually such idealism does not always prevail: gang may weaken class, and a selfish class intent upon immediate and selfish pleasure may undermine the structure of the school as a whole. It is only natural that an immature youth should magnify the importance of his immediate desires or that he should feel a greater loyalty to those members of the smaller groups with whom he is in continual and intimate contact; but it is a function, and an important function, of education to reveal to him the superior claims and the greater importance of the larger and more remote groups with which he as well as each of the smaller groups likewise is identified. With divided and seemingly conflicting loyalties he lacks the integration that makes for real character and for effective citizenship. If the number who fail of this appreciation is large and the conflicts are important, the integrity of the State is materially weakened. That this distressing result actually exists one can hardly deny, and it exists for the precise reason that education, not being generally and practically conceived as an investment for the perpetuation and betterment of the State, has failed to attempt seriously and with the skills of which it is capable, to seek an integration through showing the obligations to the supporting social group. The emphasis has been too much on privileges, which have come to be conceived as " rights," and too little on responsibilities and obligations.

" The notion that intellect," writes the same distinguished philosopher previously quoted, " is a personal endowment or personal attainment is a great conceit of the intellectual class." It is quite a natural conceit, however, and will persist unless intelligently planned education effectually inculcates ideas of service. Such education, though seemingly altruistic, is really and ultimately a contribution to personal as well as to social prosperity and happiness. Whatever case can be made for the selfish development of intellect fails utterly when that development is at the expense of the social group. Certainly it can not be successfully maintained that the public at its own sacrifice appropriates money to educate an individual for the development of powers which will be used selfishly to the detriment of the State. From this negative concept it is only a logical step to the positive statement: the appropriation is made that the individual may be developed so as to be better able and better disposed to contribute to the betterment of the supporting State. . . .

SECTION 3. Education as a public responsibility: The case in an authoritarian society

One of the clearest ways to recognize the crucial importance of education in perpetuating and developing a way of life is to note the educational system, not of one's own society, but of a markedly different and competing society. In our time the educational system of the Soviet Union is uniquely appropriate for such a purpose. Clearly dedicated to the proposition that education is the servant of the state, the Soviet school system presents in the sharpest outlines the close functional relationship possible between the school and society. Recent pronouncements by Khrushchev and the Central Committee of the Communist Party which outline a new course for Soviet education indicate in striking tones the place of education in perpetuating and perfecting the communist state. Here there is no question that the educational system is to serve a chosen social *function* — namely, the preparation of all children to take part in building the communist state and in producing the material values for that state; here there is no question of *support* for such a crucial enterprise; here there is no question of *control,* national policy being established by the state within rigidly prescriptive limits.

Meeting the challenge of Soviet education does not, of course, imply duplicating Soviet educational efforts; rather it implies an equally intelligent and dedicated approach to our own educational problems in order that American education may be as effective in providing for the needs of our social system as Soviet education may be in meeting the needs of theirs. This is not to say, of course, that in some respects the endeavor may not be similar. Any divorcement between education and life can be equally destruc-

tive to a democratic or a totalitarian society; any lack of concern for improving the quality of community life can be equally stagnating; any failure to develop a deep sense of concern and commitment for the welfare of society can be equally enervating. But while there are such similarities, there are overriding differences. The root problems of democratic education which Briggs recognized are transformed beyond recognition in the totalitarian framework. The democratic problem of developing the capacity for independent thought is replaced by the problem of building unequivocal devotion to communism and a spirit of implacability toward competing doctrines; the democratic problem of resolving potential conflict between individual interests and social goals is peremptorily resolved by viewing individuals solely as means to social ends; the problem of educational authority vanishes when basic educational decisions flow inevitably down from constituted political authorities, unquestioned and unquestionable. The real challenge to our education is not the challenge of Soviet education: it is rather the challenge to find suitable democratic answers to our inherently democratic educational problems. The usefulness of any study of the Soviet theses on education, of any authoritarian statement on the responsibility for and function of education, depends upon the reader's clear recognition that this is the real challenge.

COMMUNIST PARTY CENTRAL COMMITTEE
Theses on education in the USSR

ON THE STRENGTHENING OF THE RELATIONSHIP OF THE SCHOOL WITH LIFE AND ON THE FURTHER DEVELOPMENT OF THE SYSTEM OF PUBLIC EDUCATION IN THE COUNTRY

1. The Soviet country is living through a period of extraordinary growth. The economy of the state is developing at a tempestuous rate. Science and culture are flourishing as never before. The well-being of the workers is rising constantly. The outstanding victories in all spheres of economic and

cultural construction gained by the Soviet people — true masters of their life and creators of history — are an object of their legitimate pride. They fill with happiness and hope the hearts of millions of friends of peace and socialism throughout the world. They plunge into fear and gloom the enemies of the working class.

As a result of the wise domestic and foreign policy of the Communist Party and the Soviet State, the Soviet people have successfully achieved great things. During the years following the historic Twentieth Congress of the Communist Party of the Soviet Union, Soviet society has taken a new and great step forward on the road to the gradual transition from socialism to communism. These have been years of tremendous acceleration in the rate of communist construction and in the development of workers' initiative in the political life of the country and in the realm of economic and cultural activity. Guided consistently by the great legacy of Lenin the Party has rallied ever closer about itself the wide popular masses.

The Soviet country is confronted with the resolution of new grandiose tasks. The Twenty-First Congress of the Communist Party of the Soviet Union will consider and confirm the control figures on the development of the national economy during the years 1959–1965. The Seven-Year Plan will embrace a great program of Communist construction. The fulfillment of this program will make the Soviet land even more rich and powerful. It will be of decisive importance in the triumph in peaceful competition of the socialist over the capitalist system. The Soviet people are fully confident of their ability to fulfill the outlined plans.

2. The decisive role in the fulfillment of the plans of construction belongs to the Soviet people. Their dedication to the cause of Communism, their will to work, their ability to translate into life the great design of the Communist Party are the foundation of our victories. The reservoir of the talents of the people of the Soviet land is inexhaustible. Ever new millions of builders of Communism join the ranks of conscious and active workers of Soviet society. V. I. Lenin taught us that the rearing and the instruction of the younger generation, the training of highly qualified specialists for all branches of economy, science, and culture must always be a subject of special concern to the Communist Party and the Soviet State.

The Soviet school has prepared millions of educated, cultured citizens, active participants in socialist construction. It has reared remarkable contingents of outstanding scientists, engineers, and builders whose researches and creative work are embodied in such historic scientific and technological triumphs as the artificial earth satellites, atomic electric power stations, atomic icebreakers, and swift jet passenger planes. But the Soviet people

The Central Committee of the Communist Party, " Draft of theses on the Question of Strengthening the Relationship of the School with Life and on the Further Development of the System of Public Education in the Country," in George S. Counts (editor), *Khrushchev and the Central Committee Speak on Education*, 1959, pp. 30–33, 37–39, 41–43, 44–47, 64–66. Reprinted by permission of the University of Pittsburgh Press.

cannot rest on their laurels. Life places new tasks before the school. Our schools of general and higher education lag behind the demands of Communist construction. They have serious shortcomings. Chief among these shortcomings is the well-known separation of teaching from life. At the contemporary stage of Communist construction this defect in the system of public education is peculiarly intolerable.

"Every young boy, every young girl," said Comrade N. S. Khrushchev at the Thirteenth Congress of the Young Communist League, "must know that while studying in school he or she must prepare for work in order to create values useful to man and society. Everyone, regardless of the economic status of his parents, must follow the same road — to learn, and having learned, to work."

We must reconstruct public education so that Soviet secondary and higher schools may play a more active role in the entire creative activity of the Soviet people. The ways for such a reconstruction are outlined by the First Secretary of the Central Committee of the Communist Party of the Soviet Union, Comrade N. S. Khrushchev, in his memorandum, "On the strengthening of the relationship of the school with life and on the further development of the system of public education in the country." The proposals contained in the memorandum have been approved by the Presidium of the Central Committee of the Communist Party of the Soviet Union and find passionate support on the part of the Soviet people who regard the reconstruction of the school as an urgent task. These proposals are directed toward raising still higher the cause of the Communist rearing of the younger generation and the training of specialists for all branches of economy, science, and culture.

THE SCHOOL AND THE BUILDING OF COMMUNISM

3. The Communist transformation of society is indissolubly linked with the rearing of a new man in whom spiritual wealth, moral purity, and physical perfection will be harmoniously combined. The man of the Communist tomorrow will be free of unworthy traits, bred by the exploiting regime, such as private-ownership egoism, desire to live at the expense of another's labor, Philistinism, individualism, et cetera.

One of the chief vices of the old social order was the gulf between physical and mental labor. The separation of mental from physical work was associated with the appearance of private ownership of the tools of production and the separation of society into hostile, antagonistic classes. The growth of the contradictions of capitalism further deepened the antithesis between mental and physical work. Marxist teaching dissipated the bourgeois legend of the inevitable and everlasting existence, on the one hand, of the drab mass of people, whose lot is subordination and heavy physical toil, and, on the other, a handful of people who allegedly are destined by nature itself to think, to govern, and to develop science, literature, and art. The experience of the Soviet Union, the experience of the Chinese people, and the experience of the peoples of the other socialist countries have demonstrated beyond doubt that the toilers, freed from the chains of exploitation, irrespective of racial, national, and other differences, can govern a state, not worse, but better, than the exploiters, and that they can develop the economy, science, literature, and art at unprecedented rates. . . .

8. . . . The Soviet Union has advanced to one of the first places in the world with respect to the development of science and technology. In the quantity and the quality of the training of specialists it has surpassed all other countries. When the first Soviet artificial earth satellite burst into the expanses of the cosmos, many sober and thoughtful people in the capitalist world acknowledged that the broad development and the high level of secondary and higher education in the USSR were among the primary causes responsible for the brilliant victory of Soviet science and technology. The American press wrote in alarm that the Soviet secondary school devotes much more time and attention to the study of mathematics, physics, chemistry, and biology than the American. The United States of America, whose ruling circles had boasted of their leading position (in science and technology), now declare that the USA must overtake the Soviet Union in the training of specialists of all kinds. This is an achievement about which one can only be proud.

In Soviet society a remarkable generation of young people has been reared. They devote all their knowledge and energy, all their abilities and talents to the building of Communism. The high moral qualities of Soviet youth were brilliantly demonstrated on the labor fronts of socialist construction during the years of the first five-year plans, in the Great Patriotic War, in the heroic deeds involved in the cultivation of virgin and idle lands, in the construction of huge electric power stations, mines, and blast furnaces, in the building of new industrial centers in the east and the north of our country, and in many other labor exploits of these days.

9. The progressive development of productive forces in the process of building a Communist society, the perfecting of socialist relations, and the further advance of Soviet democracy create favorable conditions for moving ahead and successfully solving the new problems of the Communist rearing and education of our youth.

The Twentieth Congress of the Communist Party of the Soviet Union pointed out that a serious shortcoming of our schools is a recognized separation of instruction from life and poor preparation of the graduates for practical activity. In its current report to the Congress the Central Committee of the Communist Party of the Soviet Union declared that " In order to strengthen the relationship of the school with life we must not only introduce into schools the teaching of new subjects which give the foundations of knowledge on questions of technology and production, but also arrange for the systematic participation of students in work in enterprises, on collective farms and state farms, on experimental plots, and in school workshops. We must reconstruct the teaching program of the middle school with an emphasis on greater specialization in production in order that boys and girls who graduate from the ten-year school may have a good general education which will open the way to higher education and at the same time prepare them for practical work, inasmuch as the majority of the graduates will be drawn immediately into work in various branches of the national economy.

Following the Congress, some work has been accomplished in bringing the school closer to life. The results already obtained from initial experiments to combine instruction with productive work in a number of schools of the Russian Republic, the Ukraine and other Union republics are undoubtedly of value. In the Stavropol region, for example, the brilliant idea was conceived of organizing student brigades on collective farms. Brigades are formed from students in the eighth and ninth grades. The collective farms reserve plots of land to such brigades. Students carry out such tasks in agriculture as are within their strength and in accordance with the work program outlined by the school. These tasks are performed without detriment to the curriculum of the school. In winter and spring definite hours are assigned for work, and in the summer time students are for the most part engaged in work on the farms. Young boys and girls are reared in labor, are being accustomed to discipline, and are being prepared to become competent skilled workers in agriculture.

A thorough study of experience in a number of schools which combine education with productive work will be of help in reconstructing public education.

However, the situation in the secondary and higher schools as a whole remains practically unchanged, and the relationship of the school with life is altogether inadequate, as heretofore. The Central Committee of the Party and the Council of Ministers of the USSR, therefore, think it urgent to review thoroughly the question of practical measures to strengthen the relationship of the school with life and to develop further the system of public education in the country. . . .

11. . . . In organizing the education and the rearing of the younger generation on the foundation of relating instruction to life and work within their strength, the age of the school children should be taken into consideration. It is desirable that all of our young people, from the ages of fifteen or sixteen, be drawn into socially useful work. Therefore secondary education should be divided into two stages.

12. *The first stage* of secondary education should be a *compulsory eight-year school*, to replace the present seven-year school. Compared with the seven-year school the compulsory eight-year school will be a considerable step forward in the development of public education. The eight-year school will graduate young people with a greater fund of general knowledge. They will be psychologically and practically better prepared to participate in socially useful activity. A school of this type will resolve more successfully the

tasks of Communist education and of labor and polytechnical instruction. It will offer the students a wider range of knowledge, will eliminate the overloading of studies now present in the seven-year school, will make possible a more serious treatment of the physical education of the children, and will develop in them good artistic taste. In the preparation of girls for labor in the eight-year school the peculiar features of women's work should be taken into consideration.

In the process of educating for work the school is called upon to acquaint the students with the diverse forms of work in our society, help school children to express their interests, and assist them in choosing intelligently their future professions.

The eight-year school will be an incomplete secondary general-education labor polytechnical school. In sparsely populated localities primary schools of four grades should be retained. Graduates from these schools will enter the fifth grade of the nearest school.

Upon graduation from the eight-year school all of the young people must be drawn into socially useful work in enterprises, on farms, etc. This will create more equal conditions with regard to labor and education for all citizens. And this will be a good means of rearing the young people in the spirit of the heroic traditions of the working class and the collective farm peasantry.

13. Youth will receive a complete secondary education at the *second stage of instruction*. The completion of secondary education on the basis of a union of instruction with productive work may be accomplished in the following ways.

The first, basic way. Youth who go into productive work on completing the eight-year school first receive preliminary vocational training, then while working they study in the *school for working or rural youth*. This school should give the students a complete secondary education and help them raise their vocational qualifications.

The second way provides training for youth, who have completed the eight-year course, *in the secondary general-education labor polytechnical school with training in production* (similar to the schools of factory-mill and agricultural apprenticeship) which, with the assistance of the neighbouring industrial enterprises, collective farms, state farms, repair-technical stations, etc., will realize the union of instruction with productive labor and give the students a complete secondary education and vocational training for work in one of the branches of the national economy or culture.

The third way provides instruction for a part of the youth *in technicums* which operate on the basis of an eight-year school, where students will receive a full secondary education, work specialization, and the rank of specialist of middle qualification.

The new system of public education will enable every boy and girl to prepare better for life, to acquire a definite vocation, and to choose the most appropriate means of getting a complete secondary education. . . .

17. In addition to the above mentioned schools of the second stage of secondary education, it is desirable to preserve schools for the most gifted children in the field of music, choreography, and the fine arts. In case of need dormitories are established in connection with these schools for out-of-town children and for children of large families. The parents' share in bearing the living expenses of the children should be determined by the same considerations as in the case of boarding schools.

Schools for the most gifted children and youth in the field of art give their students a general secondary education, labor training, and special preparation in the field of a specific art. Graduates of these schools may enter directly the appropriate higher institutions of learning.

Schools and agencies of public education should devote more attention to the development of the abilities and inclinations of all children in the field of the arts, as well as in mathematics, physics, biology, and other branches of science. The organization in schools and higher institutions of learning of circles, studios, and special lectures should be widely practiced. Also societies of young mathematicians, physicists, chemists, naturalists, and technicians should be formed, and youthful talents should be sought out and carefully nurtured. Thought should be given to the question of creating special schools for youth with unusual inclinations and abilities for mathematics, physics, chemistry, and biology. It goes without saying that after organizing these schools admission of boys and girls will be on the recommendation of a school's pedagogical council and on the successful passing of special examinations.

18. In schools of the second stage of secondary education the level of general and polytechnical education, now prescribed for the ten-year school, would have to be raised. Special attention should be paid to the teaching of physics, mathematics, chemistry, drawing, and biology. The study of foreign languages in all schools of the country should be drastically improved. The network of schools in which instruction in a number of subjects is conducted in foreign languages should be expanded.

The reconstruction of the school should by no means result in neglecting the study of the humanities which play a very important role in the formation of the Communist world outlook of the students.

We must overcome the underestimation of the physical and aesthetic training of school children. The various forms of amateur activity on the part of the young in the spheres of technology, art, nature study, physical education, and sport, also tourism, should be encouraged even more than they are now.

The reconstruction of school education will require a change not only in the content but also in the methods of teaching to foster the greatest possible development of the independence and initiative of students. Visual aids in teaching should be improved by an extensive use of motion pictures, television, and so forth. Abstractness in teaching the basic sciences and production must be overcome. It is particularly important to encourage in schools technical inventiveness, work of students in designing new apparatus and models, technical organization, and agricultural experimentation. . . .

20. Serious improvement is needed in the field of character education in the school. It must foster in the students a love of knowledge, a love of labor, and respect for working people. It must form in them a Communist world outlook, nurture them in the essence of Communist morality, supreme loyalty to their Motherland and to the people in the spirit of proletarian internationalism. . . .

21. The reconstruction of public education raises anew the question of the work of Pioneer [1] and Komsomol [2] organizations in the school. Children and adolescents of Pioneer age will be attending the eight-year school. This means that the role of the Pioneer organization in the school assumes great importance. In schools of the second stage of instruction the Komsomols may have their own organization or may unite with the Komsomol organization in production. All this will require significant changes in the work of the school Pioneer and Komsomol organizations and in the leadership over them of the Komsomol and Party organs. . . .

46. The importance of the higher schools in the field of moral and ideological training is great. They must graduate individuals who are masters of their chosen specialties, who are active and ardent champions of Leninist ideas and the policy of the Communist Party, who are daring, cheerful, and profoundly convinced of the victory of our cause.

In the cultivation of these qualities study of the social sciences plays a large role. A knowledge of the foundations of Marxism-Leninism is indispensable for specialists in all areas. They must study Lenin and know how to apply his enormous theoretical heritage in life, to build our life in a Communist fashion. The study of Marxism-Leninism must bear a creative, aggressive, and militant character. We must rear our youth in the spirit of irreconcilability with bourgeois ideology and all manifestations of revisionism. The teaching of the social sciences must be connected indissolubly with the study of the natural sciences; it must help the students to develop a scientific method of thought. The high demands made upon the teaching of Marxist-Leninist theory in the higher schools obligate every teacher constantly and stubbornly to deepen his knowledge and to relate his work closely to practice, to the tasks of today.

The moral and ideological education of youth in higher institutions of learning is the business of all professors and instructors, as well as of the Party, the trade union, and the Komsomol organization. It is their duty to cultivate in students a Marxian-Leninist world outlook, love of labor, Communist morality, and habits of social activity.

[1] The Society of Young Pioneers (children ten to sixteen years).
[2] The League of Young Communists (youth sixteen to twenty-six years).

The higher school must develop in students a responsible attitude toward their studies, a creative approach to the mastery of the sciences, and a capacity for independent work. The overloading of students with required assignments should be eliminated and students in advanced courses should be encouraged to engage in scientific research work.

47. A large amount of work must be undertaken for the purpose of bringing the network of the higher schools of the country closer to production. The number of these institutions should be increased in new industrial centers, particularly in the regions of Siberia, the Far East, and the republics of Middle Asia. The unwarranted concentration of higher educational institutions in Moscow, Leningrad, Kiev, and certain other cities should be abolished.

48. The reconstruction of the system of higher education in the direction of combining instruction with work in production must be so planned and organized that the number of annually graduating specialists needed for the national economy, science, and culture should increase. It would be desirable to achieve the reorganization in a considerable number of the higher schools gradually during the next three to five years, beginning in 1959. Heads of economic councils, enterprises, scientific research and other organizations should make available to the higher schools regular paid jobs for workers and technicians to be filled by students. They should also organize the production training of students, give them housing accommodations, provide them with work clothes, et cetera.

All measures for the reconstruction of the higher schools are designed to help these institutions perform still better the important state tasks confronting them.

The reconstruction of the secondary and the higher school touches the interests of millions of people, all of the Soviet people. The correct resolution of this task will be of tremendous importance for the further material and spiritual development of Soviet society, particularly in the light of those great plans which the Twenty-First Congress of the Communist Party of the Soviet Union will discuss and adopt. Bringing the school closer to life will create the truly essential conditions for a better education of the younger generation who will live and work under Communism.

There is not a single family in our country which is not keenly interested in the questions of school reconstruction. Therefore the Central Committee of the Communist Party of the Soviet Union and the Council of Ministers of the USSR deem it necessary to submit the present theses to a nationwide discussion. This will make it possible in finally determining the specific ways of reconstructing the system of public education to utilize more fully the practice of outstanding secondary and higher schools which have already made some progress in the labor education of youth, as well as to profit from suggestions coming from wide circles of the Soviet public. And of course in this work the national characteristics of each Union republic must be taken into consideration.

The contemplated reconstruction will enhance the role of the school in the education and rearing of youth, will raise considerably their general educational level and their practical qualifications, will serve as a better guaranty of training highly qualified personnel for all branches of national economy, science, and culture, and will contribute in even greater degree to the growing might of the Soviet Union which marches with a firm step on the road to the building of Communism.

SECTION **4. The religious responsibility for education**

The three positions regarding the responsibility for education which have thus far been presented are all essentially *secular* in nature. Their authors view the function of the schools as preparing youngsters to participate in contemporary society. The position that responsibility for education is primarily secular is not a view held by all Americans. Adherents of several major religious denominations have taken the position that education is more appropriately a function of the Church than of the State, and these denominations have correspondingly established parochial school systems for the education of their young members. Illustrative of such parochial school systems is that of the Catholic Church. It is the position of the Catholic Church that, wherever feasible, each well-regulated parish should provide a parochial school for the education of the children of that parish. The rationale for this position is clearly stated in the Encyclical Letter of Pope Pius XI on *Christian Education of Youth*. The presence of parochial education as a viable alternative to public education in America is clearly attested to by the ten percent of our young persons who receive their education in religious schools.

The presence of these schools in America is one illustration of the tradition of educational diversity which we have developed. The relation of these schools to social control has been most clearly defined by our fundamental principle of the separation of Church and State. The First Amendment to the Constitution enjoins that

" Congress shall make no law respecting the establishment of religion, or prohibiting the free exercise thereof . . ." The Supreme Court of the United States has further amplified this constitutional provision in an opinion in which it stated that " The First Amendment has erected a wall between church and state. The wall must be kept high and impregnable." The principle of separation of Church and State, originally limiting only the federal government, has, furthermore, been extended to apply to state and local governments by the passage of the Fourteenth Amendment. The First Amendment, as thus extended by the Fourteenth Amendment, constitutes the central tradition on the relation between religion and government in our society. It is a tradition which guarantees the freedom to worship and practice the religion of one's choice, on the one hand, and prohibits governmental aid or support for religion, on the other. Thus the Supreme Court has ruled that churches possess the right to establish their own schools and that, " The fundamental theory of liberty upon which all governments in this Union repose excludes any general power of the State to standardize its children by forcing them to accept instruction from public teachers only." But the fact that churches have a *right* to establish such schools has not carried with it the expectation that public funds would be forthcoming for their support. As a matter of fact, the First and Fourteenth Amendments, as interpreted by the Court, have expressly prohibited our civil governments from passing laws or providing monies "which aid one religion, aid all religions, or prefer one religion over another." It is within this legal context that the parochial schools operate on the American scene.

The arguments for religious responsibility in education which are advanced in the Papal Encyclical and the proposed implementation of such responsibility present many challenging problems when applied in a pluralistic democracy. One such question is the question of *support:* Does or does not a valid concept of *justice* require that public monies be provided to support parochial as well as public schools? A second such question is related to providing integrated, balanced lives for individuals: Does secular education necessarily result in individuals whose lives are bifurcated or compart-mentalized into religious and non-religious elements — persons whose religion comes into play only on special occasions or within special contexts — and does parochial education avoid this? A third such question is the question of independent thought: Can a society which posits its faith on the right and responsibility of individuals to face issues and make up their own minds accept the concepts of correct thought and carefully controlled access to ideas implied in the Encyclical? But perhaps the ultimate question which is besetting our time is the moral question: Is it really true that an embracing and humane morality cannot be naturally grounded but must rest upon sectarian religious foundations? It is in response to such issues as these that the ultimate assessment of the claim to religious responsibility for education will have to be made.

POPE PIUS XI
The Christian education of youth

A *social activity*. Education is essentially a social and not a mere individual activity. Now there are three necessary societies distinct from one another and yet harmoniously combined by God, into which man is born: two, namely the family and civil society, belong to the natural order; the third, the Church, to the supernatural order.

In the first place comes the family, instituted directly by God for its peculiar purpose, the generation and formation of offspring; for this reason it has priority of nature and therefore of rights over civil society. Nevertheless, the family is an imperfect society, since it has not in itself all the means for its own complete development; whereas civil society is a perfect society, having in itself all the means for its peculiar end, which is the temporal well-being of the community; and so, in this respect, that is, in view of the common good, it has pre-eminence over the family, which finds its own suitable temporal perfection precisely in civil society.

The third society, into which man is born when through baptism he receives the divine life of grace, is the Church; a society of the supernatural order and of universal extent; a perfect society, because it has in itself all

Pope Pius XI, "Christian Education of Youth," in *Five Great Encyclicals*, pp. 39–45, 48, 50–51, 53–57, 61–62, 65–68. Reprinted by permission of the Paulist Press. Notes have been omitted.

the means required for its own end, which is the eternal salvation of mankind; hence it is supreme in its own domain.

Consequently, education which is concerned with man as a whole, individually and socially, in the order of nature and in the order of grace, necessarily belongs to all these three societies, in due proportion, corresponding, according to the disposition of Divine Providence, to the coordination of their respective ends.

The Church. And first of all education belongs pre-eminently to the Church, by reason of a double title in the supernatural order, conferred exclusively upon her by God Himself: absolutely superior therefore to any other title in the natural order.

The first title is founded upon the express mission and supreme authority to teach given her by her Divine Founder: " All power is given to Me in heaven and in earth. Going therefore, teach ye all nations, baptizing them in the Name of the Father, and of the Son, and of the Holy Ghost, teaching them to observe all things whatsoever I have commanded you, and behold I am with you all days, even to the consummation of the world." Upon this magisterial office Christ conferred infallibility, together with the command to teach His doctrine. Hence the Church " was set by her Divine Author as the pillar and ground of truth, in order to teach the divine faith to men, and keep whole and inviolate the deposit confided to her; to direct and fashion men, in all their actions individually and socially, to purity of morals and integrity of life, in accordance with revealed doctrine."

Supernatural motherhood. The second title is the supernatural motherhood, in virtue of which the Church, spotless spouse of Christ, generates, nurtures and educates souls in the divine life of grace, with her Sacraments and her doctrine. With good reason then does St. Augustine maintain: " He has not God for father who refuses to have the Church as mother."

Hence it is that in this proper object of her mission, that is, " in faith and morals, God Himself has made the Church sharer in the divine magisterium and, by a special privilege, granted her immunity from error; hence she is the mistress of men, supreme and absolutely sure, and she has inherent in herself an inviolable right to freedom in teaching." By necessary consequence the Church is independent of any sort of earthly power as well in the origin as in exercise of her mission as educator, not merely in regard to her proper end and object, but also in regard to the means necessary and suitable to attain that end. Hence with regard to every other kind of human learning and instruction, which is the common patrimony of individuals and society, the Church has an independent right to make use of it, and above all to decide what may help or harm Christian education. And this must be so, because the Church as a perfect society has an independent right to the means conducive to its end, and because every form of instruction, no less than every human action, has a necessary connection with man's last end, and therefore cannot be withdrawn from the dictates of the divine law, of which the Church is guardian, interpreter and infallible mistress.

This truth is clearly set forth by Pius X of saintly memory: " Whatever a Christian does even in the order of things of earth, he may not overlook the supernatural; indeed, he must, according to the teaching of Christian wisdom, direct all things towards the supreme good as to his last end; all his actions, besides, in so far as good or evil in the order of morality, that is, in keeping or not with natural and divine law, fall under the judgment and jurisdiction of the Church."

It is worthy of note how a layman, an excellent writer and at the same time a profound and conscientious thinker, has been able to understand well and express exactly this fundamental Catholic doctrine! " The Church does not say that morality belongs purely, in the sense of exclusively, to her; but that it belongs wholly to her. She has never maintained that outside her fold and apart from her teaching, man cannot arrive at any moral truth; she has on the contrary more than once condemned this opinion because it has appeared under more forms than one. She does however say, has said, and will ever say, that because of her institution by Jesus Christ, because of the Holy Ghost sent her in His Name by the Father, she alone possesses what she has had immediately from God and can never lose, the whole of moral truth, *omnem veritatem*, in which all individual moral truths are included, as well those which man may learn by the help of reason, as those which form part of revelation or which may be deduced from it."

The rights of the Church. Therefore with full right the Church promotes letters, science, art, in so far as necessary or helpful to Christian education, in addition to her work for the salvation of souls; founding and maintaining schools and institutions adapted to every branch of learning and degree of culture. Nor may even physical culture, as it is called, be considered outside the range of her maternal supervision, for the reason that it also is a means which may help or harm Christian education.

And this work of the Church in every branch of culture is of immense benefit to families and nations which without Christ are lost, as St. Hilary points out correctly: " What can be more fraught with danger for the world than the rejection of Christ? " Nor does it interfere in the least with the regulations of the State, because the Church in her motherly prudence is not unwilling that her schools and institutions for the education of the laity be in keeping with the legitimate dispositions of civil authority; she is in every way ready to co-operate with this authority and to make provision for a mutual understanding, should difficulties arise.

Again it is the inalienable right as well as the indispensable duty of the Church, to watch over the entire education of her children, in all institutions, public or private, not merely in regard to the religious instruction there given, but in regard to every other branch of learning and every regulation in so far as religion and morality are concerned.

Nor should the exercise of this right be considered undue interference, but rather maternal care on the part of the Church in protecting her children from the grave danger of all kinds of doctrinal and moral evil. Moreover, this watchfulness of the Church not merely can create no real inconvenience, but must on the contrary confer valuable assistance in the right ordering and well-being of families and of civil society; for it keeps far away from youth the moral poison which at that inexperienced and changeable age more easily penetrates the mind and more rapidly spreads its baneful effects. For it is true, as Leo XIII has wisely pointed out, that without proper religious and moral instruction " every form of intellectual culture will be injurious; for young people not accustomed to respect God, will be unable to bear the restraint of a virtuous life, and never having learned to deny themselves anything, they will easily be incited to disturb the public order."

The Church's mission. The extent of the Church's mission in the field of education is such as to embrace every nation, without exception, according to the command of Christ: " Teach ye all nations "; and there is no power on earth that may lawfully oppose her or stand in her way. In the first place, it extends over all the Faithful, of whom she has anxious care as a tender mother. For these she has throughout the centuries created and conducted an immense number of schools and institutions in every branch of learning. . . .

The family and the State. This is the more true because the rights of the family and of the State, even the rights of individuals regarding a just liberty in the pursuit of science, of methods of science and all sorts of profane culture, not only are not opposed to this pre-eminence of the Church, but are in complete harmony with it. The fundamental reason for this harmony is that the supernatural order, to which the Church owes her rights, not only does not in the least destroy the natural order, to which pertain the other rights mentioned, but elevates the natural and perfects it, each affording mutual aid to the other, and completing it in a manner proportioned to its respective nature and dignity. The reason is because both come from God, who cannot contradict Himself: " The works of God are perfect and all His ways are judgment."

This becomes clearer when we consider more closely and in detail the mission of education proper to the family and to the State.

The family. In the first place the Church's mission of education is in wonderful agreement with that of the family, for both proceed from God, and in a remarkably similar manner. God directly communicates to the family, in the natural order, fecundity, which is the principle of life, and hence also the principle of education to life, together with authority, the principle of order.

The Angelic Doctor with his wonted clearness of thought and precision of style, says: " The father according to the flesh has in a particular way

a share in that principle which in a manner universal is found in God. . . .
The father is the principle of generation, of education and discipline and
of everything that bears upon the perfecting of human life."

The family therefore holds directly from the Creator the mission and
hence the right to educate the offspring, a right inalienable because inseparably joined to the strict obligation, a right anterior to any right whatever of civil society and of the State, and therefore inviolable on the part
of any power on earth. . . .

We have therefore two facts of supreme importance, as We said in Our
discourse cited above: The Church placing at the disposal of families her
office of mistress and educator, and the families eager to profit by the offer,
and entrusting their children to the Church in hundreds and thousands.
These two facts recall and proclaim a striking truth of the greatest significance in the moral and social order. They declare that the mission of education regards before all, above all, primarily the Church and the family,
and this by natural and divine law, and that therefore it cannot be slighted,
cannot be evaded, cannot be supplanted.

State rights. From such priority of rights on the part of the Church and
of the family in the field of education, most important advantages, as we
have seen, accrue to the whole of society. Moreover in accordance with the
divinely established order of things, no damage can follow from it to the
true and just rights of the State in regard to the education of its citizens.

These rights have been conferred upon civil society by the Author of Nature Himself, not by title of fatherhood, as in the case of the Church and
of the family, but in virtue of the authority which it possesses to promote
the common temporal welfare, which is precisely the purpose of its existence. Consequently education cannot pertain to civil society in the same
way in which it pertains to the Church and to the family, but in a different way corresponding to its own particular end and object.

Now this end and object, the common welfare in the temporal order,
consists in that peace and security in which families and individual citizens
have the free exercise of their rights, and at the same time enjoy the greatest spiritual and temporal prosperity possible in this life, by the mutual
union and co-ordination of the work of all. The function therefore of the
civil authority residing in the State is twofold, to protect and to foster, but
by no means to absorb the family and the individual, or to substitute itself
for them.

Accordingly in the matter of education, it is the right, or to speak more
correctly, it is the duty of the State to protect in its legislation, the prior
rights, already described, of the family as regards the Christian education
of its offspring, and consequently also to respect the supernatural rights
of the Church in this same realm of Christian education. . . .

Church and State. All that We have said so far regarding the activity of
the State in educational matters, rests on the solid and immovable founda-

tion of the Catholic doctrine of The Christian Constitution of States set forth in such masterly fashion by Our Predecessor Leo XIII, notably in the Encyclicals *Immortale Dei* and *Sapientiae Christianae*. He writes as follows: " God has divided the government of the human race between two authorities, ecclesiastical and civil, establishing one over things divine, the other over things human. Both are supreme, each in its own domain; each has its own fixed boundaries which limit its activities. These boundaries are determined by the peculiar nature and the proximate end of each, and describe as it were a sphere within which, with exclusive right, each may develop its influence. As however the same subjects are under the two authorities, it may happen that the same matter, though from a different point of view, may come under the competence and jurisdiction of each of them. It follows that Divine Providence, whence both authorities have their origin, must have traced with due order the proper line of action for each. The powers that are, are ordained of God."

Now the education of youth is precisely one of those matters that belong both to the Church and to the State, " though in different ways," as explained above. " Therefore," continues Leo XIII, " between the two powers there must reign a well-ordered harmony. Not without reason may this mutual agreement be compared to the union of body and soul in man. Its nature and extent can only be determined by considering, as we have said, the nature of each of the two powers, and in particular the excellence and nobility of the respective ends. One is committed directly and specifically the charge of what is helpful in worldly matters; while the other is to concern itself with the things that pertain to heaven and eternity. Everything therefore in human affairs that is in any way sacred, or has reference to the salvation of souls and the worship of God, whether by its nature or by its end, is subject to the jurisdiction and discipline of the Church. Whatever else is comprised in the civil and political order, rightly comes under the authority of the State; for Christ commanded us to give to Caesar the things that are Caesar's, and to God the things that are God's."

What is true of the State, is true also of science, scientific methods and scientific research; they have nothing to fear from the full and perfect mandate which the Church holds in the field of education. Our Catholic institutions, whatever their grade in the educational and scientific world, have no need of apology. The esteem they enjoy, the praise they receive, the learned works which they promote and produce in such abundance, and above all, the men, fully and splendidly equipped, whom they provide for the magistracy, for the professions, for the teaching career, in fact for every walk of life, more than sufficiently testify in their favor.

These facts moreover present a most striking confirmation of the Catholic doctrine defined by the Vatican Council: " Not only is it impossible for faith and reason to be at variance with each other, they are on the contrary of mutual help. For while right reason establishes the foundations of faith, and, by the help of its light, develops a knowledge of the things of God, faith on the other hand frees and preserves reason from error and enriches it with varied knowledge. The Church therefore, far from hindering the pursuit of the arts and sciences, fosters and promotes them in many ways. For she is neither ignorant nor un-appreciative of the many advantages which flow from them to mankind. On the contrary she admits that just as they come from God, Lord of all knowledge, so too if rightly used, with the help of His grace they lead to God. Nor does she prevent sciences, each in its own sphere, from making use of principles and methods of their own. Only while acknowledging the freedom due to them, she takes every precaution to prevent them from falling into error by opposition to divine doctrine, or from overstepping their proper limits, and thus invading and disturbing the domain of faith."

This norm of a just freedom in things scientific, serves also as an inviolable norm of a just freedom in things didactic, or for rightly understood liberty in teaching; it should be observed therefore in whatever instruction is imparted to others. Its obligation is all the more binding in justice when there is question of instructing youth. For in this work the teacher, whether public or private, has no absolute right of his own, but only such as has been communicated to him by others. Besides every Christian child or youth has a strict right to instruction in harmony with the teaching of the Church, the pillar and ground of truth. And whoever disturbs the pupil's faith in any way, does him grave wrong, inasmuch as he abuses the trust which children place in their teachers, and takes unfair advantage of their inexperience and of their natural craving for unrestrained liberty, at once illusory and false. . . .

False naturalism. Hence every form of pedagogic naturalism which in any way excludes or weakens supernatural Christian formation in the teaching of youth, is false. Every method of education founded, wholly or in part, on the denial or forgetfulness of original sin and of grace, and relying on the sole powers of human nature, is unsound. Such, generally speaking, are those modern systems bearing various names which appeal to a pretended self-government and unrestrained freedom on the part of the child, and which diminish or even suppress the teacher's authority and action, attributing to the child an exclusive primacy of initiative, and an activity independent of any higher law, natural or divine, in the work of his education. . . .

Sex instruction. Another grave danger is that naturalism which nowadays invades the field of education in that most delicate matter of purity of morals. Far too common is the error of those who with dangerous assurance and under an ugly term propagate a so-called sex-education, falsely imagining they can forearm youth against the dangers of sensuality by means purely natural, such as a foolhardy initiation and precautionary instruction for all indiscriminately, even in public, and, worse still, by exposing them at an early age to the occasions, in order to accustom them, so it is argued, and as it were to harden them against such dangers.

Such persons grievously err in refusing to recognize the inborn weakness of human nature, and the law of which the Apostle speaks, fighting against the law of mind; and also in ignoring the experience of facts, from which it is clear that, particularly in young people, evil practices are the effect not so much of ignorance of intellect as of weakness of a will exposed to dangerous occasions, and unsupported by the means of grace. . . .

Co-education. False also and harmful to Christian education is the so-called method of " co-education." This too, by many of its supporters, is founded upon naturalism and the denial of original sin; but by all, upon a deplorable confusion of ideas that mistakes a leveling promiscuity and equality, for the legitimate association of the sexes. The Creator has ordained and disposed perfect union of the sexes only in matrimony, and, with varying degrees of contact, in the family and in society. Besides there is not in nature itself, which fashions the two quite different in organism, in temperament, in abilities, anything to suggest that there can be or ought to be promiscuity, and much less equality, in the training of the two sexes. These in keeping with the wonderful designs of the Creator are destined to complement each other in the family and in society, precisely because of their differences, which therefore ought to be maintained and encouraged during their years of formation, with the necessary distinction and corresponding separation, according to age and circumstances. These principles, with due regard to time and place, must in accordance with Christian prudence, be applied to all schools, particularly in the most delicate and decisive period of formation, that, namely, of adolescence; and in gymnastic exercises and deportment, special care must be had of Christian modesty in young women and girls, which is so gravely impaired by any kind of exhibition in public. . . .

And let no one say that in a nation where there are different religious beliefs, it is impossible to provide for public instruction otherwise than by neutral or mixed schools. In such a case it becomes the duty of the State, indeed it is the easier and more reasonable method of procedure, to leave free scope to the initiative of the Church and family, while giving them such assistance as justice demands. That this can be done to the full satisfaction of families, and to the advantage of education and of public peace and tranquillity, is clear from the actual experience of some countries comprising different religious denominations. There the school legislation respects the rights of the family, and Catholics are free to follow their own system of teaching in schools that are entirely Catholic. Nor is distributive justice lost sight of, as is evidenced by the financial aid granted by the State to the several schools demanded by the families.

In other countries of mixed creeds, things are otherwise, and a heavy burden weighs upon Catholics, who under the guidance of their Bishops and with the indefatigable co-operation of the clergy, secular and regular, support Catholic schools for their children entirely at their own expense; to this they feel obliged in conscience, and with a generosity and constancy worthy of all praise, they are firmly determined to make adequate provision for what they openly profess as their motto: " Catholic education in Catholic schools for all the Catholic youth." If such education is not aided from public funds, as distributive justice requires, certainly it may not be opposed by any civil authority ready to recognize the rights of the family, and the irreducible claims of legitimate liberty. . . .

Let it be loudly proclaimed and well understood and recognized by all, that Catholics, no matter what their nationality, in agitating for Catholic schools for their children, are not mixing in party politics, but are engaged in a religious enterprise demanded by conscience. They do not intend to separate their children either from the body of the nation or its spirit, but to educate them in a perfect manner, most conducive to the prosperity of the nation. Indeed a good Catholic, precisely because of his Catholic principles, makes the better citizen, attached to his country, and loyally submissive to constituted civil authority in every legitimate form of government. . . .

The true Christian. Hence the true Christian, product of Christian education, is the supernatural man who thinks, judges and acts constantly and consistently in accordance with right reason illumined by the supernatural light of the example and teaching of Christ; in other words, to use the current term, the true and finished man of character. For, it is not every kind of consistency and firmness of conduct based on subjective principles that makes true character, but only constancy in following the eternal principles of justice, as is admitted even by the pagan poet when he praises as one and the same " the man who is just and firm of purpose." And on the other hand, there cannot be full justice except in giving to God what is due to God, as the true Christian does.

The scope and aim of Christian education as here described, appears to the worldly as an abstraction, or rather as something that cannot be attained without the suppression or dwarfing of the natural faculties, and without a renunciation of the activities of the present life, and hence inimical to social life and temporal prosperity, and contrary to all progress in letters, arts and sciences, and all the other elements of civilization. To a like objection raised by the ignorance and the prejudice of even cultured pagans of a former day, and repeated with greater frequency and insistence in modern times, Tertullian has replied as follows: " We are not strangers to life. We are fully aware of the gratitude we owe to God, Our Lord and Creator. We reject none of the fruits of His handiwork; we only abstain from their immoderate or unlawful use. We are living in the world with you; we do not shun your forum, your markets, your baths, your shops, your factories, your stables, your places of business and traffic. We take ship with you and we serve in your armies, we are farmers and merchants with you; we interchange skilled labor and display our works in public for your service. How we can seem unprofitable to you with whom we live and of whom we are, I know not."

The true Christian does not renounce the activities of this life, he does not stunt his natural faculties; but he develops and perfects them, by coordinating them with the supernatural. He thus ennobles what is merely natural in life and secures for it new strength in the material and temporal order, no less than in the spiritual and eternal. . . .

Conclusion. Now all this array of priceless educational treasures which We have barely touched upon, is so truly a property of the Church as to form her very substance, since she is the mystical body of Christ, the immaculate spouse of Christ, and consequently a most admirable mother and an incomparable and perfect teacher. This thought inspired St. Augustine, the great genius of whose blessed death we are about to celebrate the fifteenth centenary, with accents of tenderest love for so glorious a mother: " O Catholic Church, true Mother of Christians! Not only dost thou preach to us, as is meet, how purely and chastely we are to worship God Himself, whom to possess is life most blessed; thou dost moreover so cherish neighborly love and charity, that all the infirmities to which sinful souls are subject, find their most potent remedy in thee. Childlike thou art in molding the child, strong with the young man, gentle with the aged, dealing with each according to his needs of mind and of body. Thou dost subject child to parent in a sort of free servitude, and settest parent over child in a jurisdiction of love. Thou bindest brethren to brethren by the bond of religion, stronger and closer than the bond of blood. . . . Thou unitest citizen to citizen, nation to nation, yea, all men, in a union not of companionship only, but of brotherhood, reminding them of their common origin. Thou teachest kings to care for their people, and biddest people to be subject to their kings. Thou teachest assiduously to whom honor is due, to whom love, to whom reverence, to whom fear, to whom comfort, to whom rebuke, to whom punishment; showing us that whilst not all things nor the same things are due to all, charity is due to all and offense to none."

Let us then, Venerable Brethren, raise our hands and our hearts in supplication to heaven, " to the Shepherd and Bishop of our souls," to the divine King " Who gives laws to rulers," that in His almighty power He may cause these splendid fruits of Christian education to be gathered in ever greater abundance " in the whole world," for the lasting benefit of individuals and of nations. . . .

Given at Rome, at St. Peter's, the thirty-first day of December, in the year 1929, the eighth of Our Pontificate.

Pius Pp. XI.

CHAPTER THREE BIBLIOGRAPHY

CHAMBERLAIN, ERNEST B., *Our Independent Schools*. New York: American Book Company, 1944.

> A study of the role of private schools especially written to illuminate the distinctive character, problems, and contributions of such schools in the American culture.

DUNN, WILLIAM KAILER, *What Happened to Religious Education?* Baltimore: Johns Hopkins Press, 1958.

> This is a study of the decline of religious instruction in American public schools from 1776 to 1861. " The struggle over sectarianism, then, and not hostility or indifference to religion as such mainly caused the decline of religious teaching." This is the central idea for which the author provides evidence and arguments.

GILKES, A. N., *Independent Education*. London: Victor Gollanez Ltd., 1957.

> The High Master of St. Paul's puts forth convincing reasons for private education (called public) in a Great Britain leaning toward more state control of education.

HEELY, ALLAN V., *Why the Private School?* New York: Harper and Brothers, 1951.

> A well written account of the purposes and arguments for the private educational institutions of the United States. It is an expression of the opinions of the author, headmaster of Lawrenceville School.

Journal of Educational Sociology, 30:337–384, April, 1957.

> Three short articles (pp. 337–342) contribute to an understanding of the role of private schools in the United States. Following this are articles by various staff members of the Ethical Culture Schools, New York City, designed to illustrate what may take place in the school to fulfill its role on the American scene. Among the topics dealt with are experimentation, mathematics, social awareness, quality, and teacher education.

MANN, HORACE, *Lectures and Annual Reports on Education*. Cambridge: Published for the Editor (not identified), undated. Pp. 39–86 and 143–188.

> The writings of this deservedly renowned educator are perennially interesting. His logic, humor and apt illustrations draw our attention to the basic problems which education must always face and which it is the responsibility of our citizens to understand and help resolve. Lecture I is his well spoken appeal for public interest and support of education. Lecture III is entitled " The Necessity of Education in a Republican Government."

PFEFFER, LEO, *Church, State, and Freedom*. Boston: Beacon Press, 1953.

> A comprehensive and analytical treatment of the relationship between church and state. Deals with such topics as the principle of church-state separation in the United States, state aid to religious groups, religious education in the public schools, and federal aid to education.

VanDUSEN, HENRY P., *God in Education*. New York, Charles Scribner's Sons, 1951.

A vigorous statement on behalf of religious education in the public schools, particularly at the college level. VanDusen questions recent Supreme Court decisions upholding the separation of church and state. The Court " has been wrong more than once before "; it is now the duty of " every religiously minded American " to challenge these decisions.

4

The Responsibility for Education: Geographic Dimensions

The very act of educating is the process of inducting or initiating someone into a special group. Alexander Meiklejohn, in discussing this process in one of the selections which follows, says, ". . . the fundamental question with regard to any system of education is, 'By what social group is it given; what are the purposes of that group; why does it will that its members be educated?'" In a world fraught with tension and misunderstanding, with actual or potential conflict not only between social groups but between different levels of social institutions or government, this question takes on frightening dimensions. Into what groups should we attempt to induct our young? What basic orientations and understandings are their birthright as human beings? How can we reconcile the conflicting claims of local and cosmopolitan groups upon their loyalties and understandings?

These are root questions; the answers provided to them will ultimately shape our entire educational endeavor. When states or local communities forbid mention of the aims of UNESCO, when regions of the country claim immunity from the guarantees provided by the national state, when nations abandon the common moral principles upon which cooperative action might be based, these problems push ruthlessly to the surface. The way we answer them will undoubtedly determine the kind of a world in which we will live; the wisdom with which we answer them may well determine whether we will have *any* world in which to live. The answers are not clear, and the claims of the past lay strong hold upon us. The challenge of our time is to alter or abandon that which is inadequate to the present and the future while holding fast to that of the past which is good.

SECTION 1. The local community as the locus of educational responsibility

America has always cherished a belief that face-to-face democracy, the democracy of the small town, the democracy of the town meeting, is a cornerstone of the good life. Such a faith has had as its ready counterpart a moral suspiciousness of big government — a fear that any government which is removed in space easily becomes unresponsive to the *will* of the people and yet more easily becomes negligent of the *rights* of the people.

Nowhere has this social philosophy revealed itself more clearly than in our faith in the local public school and the local school district. In the words of one group of educational authorities, the guiding principle must be, "Keep the schools and the government of the schools close to the people so that the citizens generally, including parents and taxpayers, may know what their schools are doing, may have an effective voice in the school program . . . " This is the *grass roots philosophy* of American education; and thus while legal control of education has been vested in the states, almost without exception the local community, with the local school board as its agent, has been the chief instrumentality entrusted with exercising this control.

This philosophy of the local control and function of education which grew and matured as part of our social heritage has, in the twentieth century, been strengthened by the prevailing winds of psychology and philosophy. Modern psychology has pointed to the necessity of experience if words and symbols are to be clothed with meaning; to the urgency of out-of-school reinforcement if in-school learnings are to be retained; to the necessity of concrete application if abstract principles are to affect character. The modern community, to modern psychology, is the ideal learning laboratory. At the same time, contemporary social philosophy, bearing the imprint of pragmatism, has asked itself the question, " education to what ends? " — and has answered the question, " education for social ends." To John Dewey " learning by doing " and " shared activity for shared goals " became the key concepts; and two generations of educators have followed in this tradition.

The natural outgrowth of the confluence of these traditions, the psychological and the philosophical, has been the development of the concept of the *community school* — a concept which embodies, on the one hand, the principle that the community should be a living laboratory for school learning and, on the other hand, the idea that the school should serve the community and should contribute to the democratic resolution of its problems. This concept would attempt to bridge the gap between formal instruction and daily living, between the individual profit of the student and the social welfare of the community, between the immaturity of the young and the maturity of the adult population. But the educational concept and the educational reality have frequently seemed to diverge so widely that today, for perhaps the first time, the concept itself is being seriously questioned by many educators. Does local control mean genuine *community* control — or control by a powerful segment of the community devoted to its own private ends? Is preparation for and practice of effective living in the local community really an adequate preparation for effective living in vastly different communities or in the wider society? With a highly mobile population which does not settle where it is educated, is control really vested at that point in the social structure which is most vitally concerned about the educational product? What are the obligations of the school and the teacher when narrow parochial beliefs run contrary to the commitments of the wider society? Such questions as these have led educators to re-examine more carefully the concept of the *community school,* less with the prospect of abandoning it than with the prospect of determining more accurately the appropriate residence and limits of educational authority and the appropriate balance between social functions. With these issues in mind, one should analyze the concepts of community control and community function in the following selections.

ASSOCIATION OF SCHOOL ADMINISTRATORS
Strengthening community life through the school

The improvement of American life begins by strengthening it at the community level. The most hopeful signs today of the ultimate well-being of our society are the trends that are in evidence in this direction. Sociologists are studying local communities as never before. Progressive churches are thinking in terms of health and recreation, housing, wages, and interdenominational cooperation for community betterment. Social agencies are organizing community councils on which every socially minded agency and organization has representation for the purpose of coordinating effort. City planners are developing master plans for breaking up large communities into smaller natural communities which are functionally complete. Significantly, the school is conceived by these planners as the center of community activities. These developments are typical of many. They give the schools a new meaning. They suggest community readiness. They also suggest areas of opportunity and responsibility.

Schools are beginning to stir in their acceptance of community responsibilities. Here and there a new type of school has come into being. It is known as the community school. In a real sense it is a social institution. It concerns itself not only with traditional functions but with the life activities of the men, women, and children of its community. Its principal purpose is the improvement of community life. It is the forerunner of a trend. These schools, in their efforts to strengthen and improve American life at the local community level are recognizing and accepting responsibility for the discharge of four distinct functions:

1. To nurture within the orbit of the school's influence the primary conditions and requirements of social health which are prerequisite to the growth of wholesome personalities and the happy, useful adjustment of individuals to their social environment.

2. To provide for and direct the participation in and contribution to the organized life of the immediate community of individual pupils and school groups.

3. To assume responsibility and furnish competent leadership (a) in developing community consciousness of the needs of children and youth, and (b) in coordinating the work of the community's youth agencies.

4. To serve to the limit of its resources the cultural, recreational, and communal needs of the adults of its community.

Establishing the conditions and requirements of social health. The school is a *community-moving* agency. Its function in this respect is to move the

From American Association of School Administrators, *Schools for a New World,* Twenty-fifth Yearbook, 1947, pp. 50–55. Reprinted by permission.

community through every influence it can muster to improve the conditions of community life from which its pupils come. These conditions affect greatly the social health of the community and of its individual members. The conditioning factors of social health in community life are many. Among the most important are recreation, public health, community cleanliness, cultural opportunity, churches, home life, conditions of employment, and community pride. With all of these the school is concerned. When these conditions are good, or when the community is consciously and earnestly working for their improvement, it is possible for the school successfully to develop socially healthy and socially well-adjusted individuals. When these conditions are bad the efforts of the school are largely negated. Thus it is the school's responsibility to seek earnestly to improve these conditions, especially the conditions of home life. The relationship here is very close. Preparing students for, and helping adults achieve, wholesome family living, in particular giving insight into the problems of love and marriage, is one of the school's most important tasks.

The school is also a *community treatment* agency. Its function here is to provide in the school and release into the community the therapies of social health. The specific requirements of social health, fortunately, because of their importance, are becoming better known. They are the authentic conclusions of studies in the fields of psychology, sociology, anthropology, and mental hygiene. They apply equally to the relations of individuals with each other in local communities and of individual nations and peoples with others in the world community. They are:

a. That each individual have *a sense of security* within his environment.

b. That each individual have *a sense of enjoyment* of his environment.

c. That each individual have *a sense of belonging* to a group within the school or community environment, and of living within the lives of others.

d. That each individual have *a sense of responsibility* for the welfare of his group and participate in determining the decisions of his group.

e. That each individual have *a sense of fellow feeling* toward all members of his group that is a composite of such primary feelings as love, respect, goodwill, mutuality, and fair play.

f. That each individual have *a sense of confidence* in his adequacy and ability to participate in active group situations.

In the interdependencies of all human relationships at whatever level, local, national, or international, these are the primary requirements under which individuals and peoples must have their being in a healthy, free society. These are the essentials of peace. It remains for our society to give them reality. To this end the schools are a chief instrumentality. It is their function to acquire the understandings which are necessary and develop and administer technics and processes appropriate to their development. There is much here to be done, in the training of teachers, in organizing the school, and in the selection and direction of pupil activities. Fortunately, many organized groups of teachers and administrators have established workshops for the development of these processes.

Participating in the organized life of the community. The school is a *community-building* agency. A community is of course built by its citizens. By curious anomaly and peculiar connotation, in most states a citizen of a community is considered to be a person who is twenty-one years of age and over. The rest are children and youths not yet ready for the privileges and obligations of citizenship. Nothing could be more fallacious. Children and youths are just as truly citizens of their community as their elders. They differ in this respect from their parents and teachers only in maturity, degree of independence, and possession of the right of suffrage. But they, too, have community obligations and community tasks.

In every community there are large fields of community action which are closely related to the interests and activities of youths. Students frequently exercise more influence, even more constructive influence, upon the thinking of the community in these areas than adults. Most annual reports of superintendents of schools have given considerable space, in recent years, to reporting a multitude of community activities of organized school groups under the supervision of the schools in support and promotion of the community's war efforts. The unity of peace is as important at least as the unity of war. The contributions of youths to the peaceful pursuits of community life can be as valuable as their contributions in wartime. In many communities school groups participate in community chest campaigns and the like, and in numerous public observances; they represent their schools on community councils, establish and promote community projects of their own; and perform many necessary and useful community services. For the children and youths of the community these are the vestibule activities of community life. They should be recognized as such, not, as often is the case, as community chores " wished off " on the schools. Their scope and range are vast. They can and should be made a principal medium of induction of youths into responsible participation in the strengthening and improvement of American life.

The universal phase of American life at the community level is work. Vocational schools, for a quarter of a century, have recognized that guiding and supervising youths in work experience in the community is an important part of their principal function, and have developed their school programs accordingly, with excellent educational results. Much more recently, nonvocational schools have accepted work experience under the school's direction and supervision as a valuable part of their pupils' general education. But their acceptance has been largely in theory. So far, these schools in the main have lacked the imagination to put their theory of this activity to work. Here again the schools can profit from the exigencies of wartime, when manpower shortages forced upon secondary schools emergency released time programs. But the great educational opportunity offered by these programs must not be overlooked. If they serve merely to impart a firsthand knowledge of industrial and business processes, and to improve the work attitudes and habits of future workers and nothing more, they will have missed their real opportunity. Better communities will not be built by inducting youths into a community *status quo*. The purpose of this activity is the strengthening and improving of American life. The problems of American life here to be laid hold of and constructively dealt with by the schools are the problems of management and of labor, problems of industrial human relations.

Developing community consciousness of the needs of youth. The school is a *community leadership* agency. Its vigorous leadership should be in evidence at the community level in all activities that have educational significance. But its most important responsibility in this field is leading the community to an understanding and awareness of the needs of its children and youths. Traditionally, schools have " washed their hands " of responsibility for youth outside of school hours, and many still do so. If and when their purpose becomes the improvement of American life, they may do so no longer. They become, instead, the principal community agency for the organization and development of all of the community's resources that can serve youth's needs. They assume initiative. They convince the community that its school plant should be used in the late afternoons and evenings, on Saturdays, and during the summer months. They teach the community what it needs to know about its youths.

The needs of youth in modern community life, especially in cities, are legion. Homes are not what they were. Too many movies emphasize sex, thrills, or unnatural human relationships — they stimulate and sophisticate, too seldom wholesomely educate; radio, reasonably clean, grinds out whatever will catch the ear, though there is steady improvement; pulp magazines purvey the sordid and the improbable. Hollywood dress and morals set patterns and influence standards; moral values depreciate. Such are the typical examples of what youth contends with on the way to adulthood. It is poor soil, if untended, in which to sprout moral responsibility, in which to develop the ability of putting community before self. Communities cry for leadership in this area of responsibility. The school is the strategic community agency to supply this leadership.

In the discharge of this responsibility the school is the logical agency for coordinating the activities of all of the community's youth agencies. This leadership, to the extent it has been exercised, has gone by default usually to one of the community's social agencies. It has resulted in the spasmodic development, here and there, of crudely functioning youth councils. But they have done little to break down the long-established rivalries, the duplications of effort, and the cross purposes that too frequently have characterized youth agency relationships. In some instances schools have not been represented on these councils. They should be operating at the heart of such activities, in active pursuit of a purpose to strengthen and improve community life.

Serving the needs of the adult community. The school is a *community service* agency. When it accepts as its principal purpose the strengthening and improving of community life, it becomes the center of the community's civic, cultural, and recreational activities. It is lighted every night. Here parents discuss and study their personal problems, the problems and needs of their community, and what goes on in the world about them; they try to read behind the news of the day; mothers study child care and home management; fathers use tools in the shops or compete with each other in the gymnasium; in many activities young people mingle with their elders. Here is the meeting place of community councils, special committees, and social and civic clubs. Here are formed the plans for community action on a dozen fronts. Here the community discovers itself and forges its identity. Here the roots of community life are watered, and the delicate plant nourished. Already there are a few such schools. There will be more as schools increasingly accept their function of serving not alone the educational and recreational needs of the adults but their communal needs as well. . . .

SECTION 2. The geographic region as the locus of educational responsibility

America has long prided itself on its philosophy of diversity: its basic belief that the structure of a democratic society provided the soil in which widely divergent patterns of life, human aspirations, and human orientations could flourish in harmony, and in which their adherents could live in mutual respect. That it has not always been possible to harmonize or reconcile divergent value schemes has been amply revealed by such periods of tragedy as the Civil War. But the hope and the belief are still with us. There are still those who would plead to see " cultural differences respected, and not thwarted or obliterated." Such a belief is in keeping with the American tradition; but the basic question must be asked. Should this freedom to differ be permitted to flourish unrestricted, or are there limits to the right to differ? Is there some wider national or moral framework within which differences may flourish, but outside of which such differences become intolerable?

This problem has most vehemently and forcibly come to the fore in our own times in the struggle for equal rights by members of oppressed groups. Thus some advocates of Southern regionalism have pleaded they be permitted to retain their cherished Southern way of life — a way of life rich in tradition and supported by social customs arching the centuries. The plea to respect a cherished way of life can never fall upon deaf ears in a democracy; but it is a plea, which like all causes, must be evaluated for its ultimate worth and reasonableness. Is this a way of life which is cherished by all who would be affected by it — or only by some? Is it a way of life rooted in the traditions of the dignity and respect of the human individual — or degrading to some individuals? Upon the answer to such questions must its claim to reasonableness be judged. But the argument that regionalism is a worthy focus for education need not rest its case on the tenets of segregation: it has further and more profound foundations. Through analysis of its other ramifications, more worthy of democratic consideration, one can deter-

mine the appropriate claims of the region to the allegiance of educational
institutions. Such a claim, quite divorced from the arena of racial dispute, is effectively advanced by Donald Davidson in *The Attack on Leviathan*.

DONALD DAVIDSON
A Southerner defends regionalism

Although regionalism is sometimes called a theory, and sometimes a literary
movement, it could better be taken as the new name for a process of differentiation within geographic limits that is as old as the American republic
and perhaps was predestined in the settlement of our continental area. The
regionalists are those who wish to see the cultural differences respected, and
not thwarted or obliterated. No matter from what field they draw their
data — whether historical, scientific, or artistic — the regionalists agree that
America, far from being perfectly homogeneous and standardized, is amaz-
ingly heterogeneous and diverse. They do not, of course, agree as to the
exact outlines of the regional map. But in general they hold that New England, the metropolitan East, the South, and the Middle West, are well-
developed and self-conscious regions that have already attained a high degree of differentiation; and that the younger regions of the Southwest, the
Northwest, and the Pacific Coast are building up regional traditions as
clearly marked as in the older parts of the country.

It is therefore dangerous to talk glibly about American education or
American culture, as if there were no regional differences. The person who
generalizes thus freely, on the assumption that some quite uniform national
tradition is floating in the air and can be apprehended and applied as the
pure American thing, is sure to be met, sooner or later, with the assertion,
"That won't do in the South," or "We don't do things that way in the
East." Sometimes the challenge is crude and direct, and then we have such
violent phenomena as anti-evolution laws. More often the rebellion is so
passive and gradual that we hardly realize that it is taking place. But presently it is discovered that education is having no effect; it is being dissipated in an indifferent or quietly hostile atmosphere. Such resistance, far
less spectacular but more general than anti-evolution laws, is a hidden factor in much of our educational confusion today.

The principles of regionalism supply an element of realism which has
been lacking in the diagnosis of our educational leaders. While we must
grant that the body of educational knowledge is, or ought to be, universal
rather than parochial and narrow, we must also acknowledge, if we be honest and realistic, that there is no central authority with power to decide,
for the United States at large, what is universal and what is narrow. But

From Donald Davidson, *The Attack on Leviathan* (Chapel Hill: University of North
Carolina Press, 1938), pp. 243–250, 254–257. Reprinted by permission of the author.

it is in our educational and intellectual bill of rights that any section or region or state or city has the full liberty of making that critical decision on its own responsibility.

Nevertheless, students of regionalism well know that such a central authority has often been assumed or aspired to by a process familiar in American history. Whenever a given region, East, South, or West, has at stake some profound regional interest, it is very likely to present its peculiar regional interest in the light of a national interest, and to argue for its general acceptance.

Let us be plain about the matter. In education, it now happens to be the metropolitan East, and especially metropolitan New York, which is offering its ideas in the disguise of national ideas, and so is tending to assume a central authority that does not properly belong to it. The ideas of New York and its metropolitan province may of course have great excellence for the region where they are generated. But they do not necessarily and invariably confer a benefit upon other regions. In fact, the dissemination of these ideas, through the channels which New York possesses and other regions lack, may sometimes be resented as a hostile invasion, and may indeed often be an actual subversion of good and fruitful regional patterns that ought to be preserved and not destroyed. We would not desire a conquest by New York so complete as to impoverish the national life by robbing it of diversity; or a retaliation from some regional quarter so fierce as to introduce disorder and irritation.

On the contrary, a good regional theory of education would call for our institutions to exercise a dual function. In so far as they can introduce the student to a body of learning that is clearly universal and timeless, they must necessarily abstract the student to some extent from his regional background. At the same time, it would be a mistake to try to make the complete Southerner over into the complete New Yorker, or vice versa. An education cannot divorce itself wholly from its background. It has a clear duty to make its learning or its technique adaptable to the background where it is expected to function. Besides, the institution ought to draw something from the life of its own region and so make its unique and independent contribution to the general, or national, tradition. To emphasize the abstracting function unduly will lead to servility — to an aggregation of satellites revolving humbly around the master orb. But an exaggeration of the purely local would be just as undesirable; it would lead to provincialism or sectionalism in the bad sense. Ideally, we should desire an easy give and take, out of which would grow a rough composite, a national tradition including the regional traditions and having no existence apart from them. This national American tradition might be a little vague and hard to define, like the European tradition; but it would not present the false and vicious simplification under which we wince when a Frenchman or an Englishman fails to appreciate the rich complexity of American traditions.

It is clear that we are in more danger, at the moment, of taking up a false nationalism than of dropping into the opposite error of sterile provincialism. For the metropolitan idea is well advertised, and the regional idea poorly advertised.

In the new kind of Freshman composition texts, for example, the editors do not carry out their announced purpose of orienting the student. He is introduced, to be sure, to a certain range of " conflicting opinions and attitudes." But in the books I have examined, there is far less conflict of opinion than the editors claim. With a unanimity that is striking, our anthologists have favored selections that represent, on the whole, the range of opinion in the metropolitan East alone. They apparently propose to orient the Freshman by giving him as large a dose of metropolitanism as they can get between the covers of a book. They thrust him into contact with the minds of the professional contributors to New York magazines: the men and women who have outdone all previous metropolitan generations in their studied disregard for the country west and south of the Hudson River.

Who these people are, every teacher of Freshman English knows. The average book of " provocative " models is almost certain to contain the inevitable essay on the machine age by Stuart Chase; a bit of socialistic economics from Henry Pratt Fairchild; one of Will Durant's lectures for women's clubs; a few pleasantries by H. L. Mencken; an article on American architecture by Lewis Mumford; a slice of autobiography by Ludwig Lewisohn; an article on religion by John Haynes Holmes or Harry Emerson Fosdick; something about politics or scholarship from Walter Lippmann; and a few literary teasers by Heywood Broun, Henry Hazlitt, or Joseph Wood Krutch.

It is not the inclusion of such writers that I object to. As a teacher of Freshman English, I envy the intellectual attainments of Freshman classes in those fortunate institutions where, without disturbance or bewilderment, the Jew, the Catholic, the Methodist, and the Baptist can receive their common lessons in religion from Lewis Browne, Herbert Asbury, and Harry Emerson Fosdick, to say nothing of Dean Inge and Bertrand Russell. I do not hold that the Freshman should be insulated from contact with such minds; but I find it exceedingly strange that he should be allowed to discover these, the favorites of the metropolis, and no other minds. It cannot be a very sound orientation which subjects the Freshman to only one kind of stimulating ideas. We cannot all live in New York, or in a place that is like New York. It is an odd way to begin an education, if the student is to be encouraged to put aside at once, as unworthy of appreciative loyalty, the ideas of the region where he will have to live, and to take on, no matter what his environment, the habits of the big-city mind.

Yet if the Freshman must accept the evidence of his book of models, he is driven, however reluctantly, in that direction. Of the life of the great outlying regions, the books give almost no hint. This state of affairs is surprising, when we recall how greatly American literature and social criticism have been enriched in recent years by the growth of strong regional movements in the South and West, led by alert and productive writers, who are fully represented in the current anthologies of poetry, drama, or short stories. But these writers are not to be found in the Freshman orientation texts. André Siegfried or Bertrand Russell may possibly be called in to make pronouncement on Fundamentalism in the South, but not John Donald Wade of Georgia or John Crowe Ransom of Tennessee, who can tell that story from the inside. The New York critics are invited to deliver their gloomy harangues on literature and art, but Vernon Louis Parrington of the Northwest is nowhere to be discovered. We may get something on politics from Harold Laski or Walter Lippmann, but nothing whatever from the great group of regional historians and biographers who have rebuilt, in bold and lively terms, the image of the diverse American tradition that our iconoclasts have been engaged in repudiating: nothing, that is to say, from Beveridge, Dodd, Bowers, Phillips, Owsley, Milton, Webb, Freeman, Eckenrode, Tate, Lytle, and a host of other able writers. The historians, in fact, have suffered from as great a neglect as the creative writers; but the regionalists who have made it their particular business to explore the traditions of South and West are given no consideration at all.

In the world of print the ascendancy of New York is so much taken for granted that I am sure the editors of these texts were not conscious of yielding to a bias when they chose their selections. They have only followed the New York magazines where these have led, without realizing that most of the New York magazines are hardly any longer national magazines, but are tending to become sectional and propagandist organs. But the bias is there, and it is too remarkable to go unrecorded.

For example, in one new text I find 31 American authors included. Of these 20 were born in the East; 10 in the Middle West; 1 in the South; none in the Far West. Of the 20 Easterners, all have remained in their native region, and nearly all are now in New York City. Of the 10 Middle Westerners, 5 are now identified with New York colleges or periodicals, and 2 are elsewhere in the East. The lone Southern-born man, Mr. Abraham Flexner, also has long since moved to New York. If these regional immigrants may be counted as metropolitan converts, as in all probability they should be, we then have a total of 28 Easterners to 3 non-Easterners. The book is practically an all-Eastern text. The only reference to regional culture that I find in it is contained in an essay by Will Durant, and is as follows: " Why is it that, broadly speaking, tolerance and freedom of the mind flourish more easily in the North than in the South? "

This is an extreme example, of course. The preponderance of Easterners over non-Easterners is hardly ever as great as 9 to 1 in other textbooks. It is more likely to be 5 to 1 or 4 to 1. It is sure to be as much as 3 to 1. What would be a just proportion, I do not know. Merely to count noses is a deceptive and probably a meaningless kind of analysis. I cite the figures only to dramatize in a rather bald way a tendency that seems worth noting. It would be fairer to rest the case on subject matter alone. By and large, I

think I am safe in claiming that the overwhelming majority of the contributors, regardless of their place of origin or residence, and regardless, too,
of the intrinsic merit of their contributions (which I do not here question),
represent America of the Eastern metropolis rather than America of the
Western and Southern hinterland. If the editors of the orientation texts
are to be as impartial as they invariably protest themselves to be, it is time
to alter this bias and to show some regard for the agrarian culture of the
South, the town culture of upper New England, the mixed culture of the
Middle West, and the culture of the plains, the mountains, or the coast,
or other regions.

Among the new texts I have looked into, only one, a collection entitled
These United States, and edited by Professors Jones, Huse, and Eagleson
of California, makes any attempt to suggest the regional diversity of
America. The opening essay, by William B. Munro, is a persuasive exposition of the views held by contemporary regionalists as to the mixed and
pluralistic tendencies of American life. In the national motto, *E pluribus
unum*, Professor Munro argues that " the accent is on the *pluribus*." But
the ensuing essays hardly carry out this theme. The contributors are largely
the old familiar crowd of defeated artists and newspaper columnists.

Yet it is something to have even a beginning. I should like to think that
the appearance of one book is a sign that others are on the way. Out of
regard for the sanity of teachers and the self-respect of students, if not for
the good of the Republic, some person or persons ought to break through
the conventional pattern and give us texts with a little more life and diversity in them than is afforded by these cullings from last year's New York
magazines. And surely, if we are to have an orientation course, dealing
frankly with issues contemporary and historical, it is impossible to keep the
regional text out of the reckoning. . . .

Nevertheless we can escape some of our difficulties by recognizing regionalism as a natural function of our educational body politic. If it is good
pedagogy to proceed from the familiar to the strange, then the regional
text has its place in some courses; and especially in any courses which propose to guide the student toward some more stable and gracious conception
of civilization than now prevails. Perhaps it is desirable for the Georgia
Freshman to know something about modern physics or the skepticism of
Bertrand Russell; but it is no paradox to argue that his critical approach to
such subjects will not be hampered, and may be improved, if he is first allowed to get some respect and understanding for the plantation culture of
which he is a rooted part. We need to halt the uprooting process in modern education and to give our students the sense of belonging somewhere
and being somebody that modern thought in the abstract seems incapable
of providing. The regional text will also harmonize with the new and reasonable tendency to break through the strict barriers of course-subjects;
and the Freshman English course will join hands with the courses in his-

tory or political science. Sophistication will come soon enough, anyway; and often enough too cheaply, too superficially. The regional text ought to carry the most difficult lesson that moderns have to learn: that the kingdom of God is within you, or at least around you, and is not a far-off dazzle of towers that may not, after all, really exist.

The advent of regionalism in the Freshman work — if such should come about — would be only one phase of its penetration into English departments, or, for that matter, into all college activities that touch the foundations and tendencies of American life. Since the publication of Parrington's *Main Currents in American Thought* and similar works, it is no longer possible for the subject of American literature, whether in graduate or undergraduate courses, to be treated as an Eastern product, a little diluted by barbarian infusions from South and West. The new tendency is to view American literature as the expression of regional cultures which blend into the composite national culture. In undergraduate courses this means that a form of regionalism is actually being taught as a basic condition for understanding our literary past and present. In the graduate work it leads to studies of the regional material near at hand, whether it be the collection of ballads, the study of a cultural pattern, or the biography of a regional figure. By this process the graduate student and his professor find themselves in the surprising new role of interpreters of a region and conservers of a regional tradition.

From this role it is an easy step to the role of regional spokesman. Into many English departments there has recently come a new type of professor, who is a creative writer or critic, and maybe the author of a novel or of a topical essay as often as a contributor to PMLA.[1] Such professors, and with them, the eminent and non-acàdemic poets or dramatists whom universities are beginning to call into residence, tend often to become outspoken regionalists, who gather students of similar minds around them and become in time the nucleus for active regional groups. They publish magazines and anthologies, they write and direct plays and manage theatres, they edit book-review pages. Sometimes the magazines are ephemeral; but the substantial success of *The Virginia Quarterly Review, The Southern Review, The Midland, The Sewanee Review, The Frontier,* and various others augurs well for the future of the magazine that originates in the literary interest of an English department working in a particular region.

Behind such unmistakable expressions of the regional trend of English departments lies the new tendency of colleges and universities — and eventually, we may suppose, of high schools and common schools — to adapt themselves anew to their regional environment. The sociologist is to be found adventuring in the slums, the court-rooms, the farm lands of his contiguous territory; his adventure is already convincing him, in many cases, that the regional approach has merit. The economist, going about the

---

[1] Publications of the Modern Language Association — Ed.

market-place, is having a similar experience; and the political scientist and the historian are struggling as never before with the definition and instrumentation of regional factors. Then, too, the widespread activities of the New Deal, in such enterprises as the TVA and in the work of state planning commissions as well as in private business, are calling into the service of regional communities the geologist, the professor of medicine, the engineer. Such activities take away the colleges and universities from academic isolation and bind them close to regional life, with powerful consequences for their own inner order as well as their external influence. Regionalism takes on more and more of an official and lively status as this process gains way; it becomes more definitely a counter-tendency, working through educational institutions, to the national regimentation into which we seemed about to slip. As it gains in strength, it will lead to changes, both in higher and in lower systems of education, of a sort not now predictable. But certainly we shall have fewer of those missionary institutions which conceive that their duty consists in the uncritical and servile transmission of the standards of a supposedly cultured region to a supposedly uncultured and barren one. We have had enough of this one-way traffic of educational and social ideas. We need a two-way system, which allows ideas not only to come in but to go out. A right principle of cultural diffusion would hold that our colleges ought to become true cultural centres, receiving at least as much cultural vitality from their environing regions as from more distant ones. For such centres, regional but not in any sense parochial, the region becomes laboratory, audience, and judge. Their educational direction may be toward the universal, but it will then be a universal that is wrapped up with a particular way of life.

SECTION 3. The nation as the locus of educational responsibility

Although education in America has generally been thought of as a matter for state and local control (especially in the light of the Tenth Amendment, which reserves powers not specifically delegated the national government to the states and the people), it is of concern to the national government. This less dominant, but nonetheless pervasive, thread of national concern is woven through the fabric of our history. Even prior to the formation of our present government, the Northwest Ordinance indicated our national concern for education by providing for the support of education in each township. The tradition of national concern and support thus initiated has

continued until the present. Important milestones in the history of federal aid have been the Morrill Act creating the land-grant colleges, the establishment of the United States Office of Education, the Smith-Hughes Act providing financial support for vocational education, and the National Defense Education Act. Despite these evidences of national interest, however, the popular tradition has continued to be that education could best serve its functions if the fundamental locus of responsibility, authority and program remain in the state and local community.

The strength of the tradition against national control of education gained its initial support from a suspicion of centralized government and a belief that local governments were " close to the people," " democratic," and " champions of human rights." This tradition flowered in a country which had thrown off the yoke of foreign control. It thrived in a climate of laissez-faire freedom during the nineteenth century. But the accuracy of the social interpretation upon which it rested has not always gone unchallenged. Critics have asked, for example, whether it is true that local governments have been the real champions of human rights. Has, for example, the federal government been more inclined to deprive individuals of their basic rights than have state and local governments? At the same time critics have called attention to the fact that it is no longer true that individuals live out their lives within the confines of the local community into which they are born. There has, in effect, been an increased willingness to view the national government as a champion rather than a potential enemy of the welfare of the people, even as a protector of the oppressed. There has been an accompanying tendency to view the national society as the society which most fully encompasses the life of the individual. Without decrying many of the benefits of local, state, and regional participation, there has been a growing belief that their very parochialism may ultimately make them an inappropriate locus for such exclusive educational authority as they have enjoyed in the past.

The particular issue which has brought the question of education and the national community to the fore in our times has been the question of the financial support for education. In facing the problem of finding adequate financial support to provide for equality of educational opportunity, professional educators have had to face, once again, the question of the most appropriate locus of control of the public schools. One competent observer has marked the alternative posi-

tions which educators have assumed, and the fundamental issue they must face, in the following words:

" One position, which seems to be the one most widely held among educators, is that federal control is bad because any centralized control of education is bad, but it is nevertheless imperative that educational opportunity be equalized by the use of federal funds. Therefore, federal funds should be granted to the states on the basis of need but with the specific provision that there be no federal control. . . .

" A second general position is that federal control is bad and it is impossible to have federal aid without federal control . . . However greatly the funds are needed, the danger of centralized control is so great, and it will be so bad in its effects, that it is better to dispense with the funds than to run the risk of federal control.

" The third position is that the demands of education in a democratic nation make it imperative for the federal government to provide funds for equalizing education, and it is not only inevitable that federal regulation accompany the funds but it is desirable that it do so. It is desirable not only in order to safeguard public funds but also to insure that both the kind and quality of education necessary to meet national needs be provided on a nation-wide basis. . . .

" The current controversy over federal control of education is only the immediate manifestation of a much broader and much more fundamental issue. Schools as social institutions are eventually subject to social control of some kind. In a democracy ultimate authority over education is grounded in the will of the people, as is the authority of political institutions. Even in a democracy however, that authority must be wielded in accordance with some principle and through some kind of administrative structure. The controversy over federal control of education is a controversy over the form of the institutional structure through which society will exercise its control over education." [1]

It is to this fundamental issue that each member of the profession, as indeed each citizen of a democracy, should address himself.

The two articles which follow reflect the view that education has a national function to serve, yet they reveal three differing conceptions of the appropriate way to assure that this function is served. The first, by Benjamin Rush, signer of the Declaration of Independence and intellectual leader in the early days of the Republic, is an interesting early formulation of the center of attention in education. His concept of education and his scheme for a national university are detailed enough to reveal in striking

[1] Archibald Anderson, *Social Aspects of Education*, Stipes, 1948, pp. 191–192. Quoted by permission.

terms the changes which have occurred in educational thought since his time. The second, by Myron Lieberman, challenges the entire grass-roots philosophy of educational control in the light of our changing times and keener recognition of the locus of effective action. Before being too willing to sacrifice well-established tradition to new insights, we must, however, face two practical problems: Can greater national direction be provided without sacrificing the mainsprings of local interest and professional creativity which have characterized American education at its best in the past? Can greater national direction be provided without sacrificing the concern for building good human communities and utilizing the unique learning opportunities provided in the concrete context of local community living? It is in the light of such questions as these that new proposals must be assessed.

BENJAMIN RUSH
The views of a founding father on education

OF THE MODE OF EDUCATION PROPER IN A REPUBLIC

The business of education has acquired a new complexion by the independence of our country. The form of government we have assumed, has created a new class of duties to every American. It becomes us, therefore, to examine our former habits upon this subject, and in laying the foundations for nurseries of wise and good men, to adapt our modes of teaching to the peculiar form of our government.

The first remark that I shall make upon this subject is, that an education in our own, is to be preferred to an education in a foreign country. The principle of patriotism stands in need of the reinforcement of prejudice, and it is well known that our strongest prejudices in favour of our country are formed in the first one and twenty years of our lives. The policy of the Lacedemonians is well worthy of our imitation. When Antipater demanded fifty of their children as hostages for the fulfillment of a distant engagement, those wise republicans refused to comply with his demand, but readily offered him double the number of their adult citizens, whose

From Dagobert D. Runes (editor), *Selected Writings of Benjamin Rush*, 1947, pp. 87–96, 101, 104–105. Reprinted by permission of the Philosophical Library, New York.

habits and prejudices could not be shaken by residing in a foreign country. Passing by, in this place, the advantages to the community from the early attachment of youth to the laws and constitution of their country, I shall only remark, that young men who have trodden the paths of science together, or have joined in the same sports, whether of swimming, skating, fishing, or hunting, generally feel, thro' life, such ties to each other, as add greatly to the obligations of mutual benevolence.

I conceive the education of our youth in this country to be peculiarly necessary in Pennsylvania, while our citizens are composed of the natives of so many different kingdoms in Europe. Our schools of learning, by producing one general, and uniform system of education, will render the mass of the people more homogeneous, and thereby fit them more easily for uniform and peaceable government. . . .

Next to the duty which young men owe to their Creator, I wish to see a regard to their country, inculcated upon them. When the Duke of Sully became prime minister to Henry the IVth of France, the first thing he did, he tells us, " Was to subdue and forget his own heart." The same duty is incumbent upon every citizen of a republic. Our country includes family, friends and property, and should be preferred to them all. Let our pupil be taught that he does not belong to himself, but that he is public property. Let him be taught to love his family, but let him be taught, at the same time, that he must forsake, and even forget them, when the welfare of his country requires it. He must watch for the state, as if its liberties depended upon his vigilance alone, but he must do this in such a manner as not to defraud his creditors, or neglect his family. He must love private life, but he must decline no station, however public or responsible it may be, when called to it by the suffrages of his fellow citizens. He must love popularity, but he must despise it when set in competition with the dictates of his judgment, or the real interest of his country. He must love character, and have a due sense of injuries, but he must be taught to appeal only to the laws of the state, to defend the one, and punish the other. He must love family honor, but he must be taught that neither the rank nor antiquity of his ancestors, can command respect, without personal merit. He must avoid neutrality in all questions that divide the state, but he must shun the rage, and acrimony of party spirit. He must be taught to love his fellow creatures in every part of the world, but he must cherish with a more intense and peculiar affection, the citizens of Pennsylvania and of the United States. I do not wish to see our youth educated with a single prejudice against any nation or country; but we impose a task upon human nature, repugnant alike to reason, revelation and the ordinary dimensions of the human heart, when we require him to embrace, with equal affection, the whole family of mankind. He must be taught to amass wealth, but it must be only to encrease his power of contributing to the wants and demands of the state. He must be indulged occasionally in amusements, but he must be taught that study and business should be his principal pursuits in life. Above all he must love life, and endeavour to acquire as many of its conveniences as possible by industry and economy, but he must be taught that this life " is not his own," when the safety of his country requires it. These are practicable lessons, and the history of the commonwealths of Greece and Rome show, that human nature, without the aids of Christianity, has attained these degrees of perfection.

While we inculcate these republican duties upon our pupil, we must not neglect, at the same time, to inspire him with republican principles. He must be taught that there can be no durable liberty but in a republic, and that government, like all other sciences, is of a progressive nature. The chains which have bound this science in Europe are happily unloosed in America. Here it is open to investigation and improvement. While philosophy has protected us by its discoveries from a thousand natural evils, government has unhappily followed with an unequal pace. It would be to dishonor human genius, only to name the many defects which still exist in the best systems of legislation. We daily see matter of a perishable nature rendered durable by certain chemical operations. In like manner, I conceive, that it is possible to combine power in such a way as not only to encrease the happiness, but to promote the duration of republican forms of government far beyond the terms limited for them by history, or the common opinions of mankind. . . .

From the observations that have been made it is plain, that I consider it is possible to convert men into republican machines. This must be done, if we expect them to perform their parts properly, in the great machine of the government of the state. That republic is sophisticated with monarchy or aristocracy that does not revolve upon the wills of the people, and these must be fitted to each other by means of education before they can be made to produce regularity and unison in government.

Having pointed out those general principles, which should be inculcated alike in all the schools of the state, I proceed now to make a few remarks upon the method of conducting, what is commonly called, a liberal or learned education in a republic.

I shall begin this part of my subject, by bearing a testimony against the common practice of attempting to teach boys the learned languages, and the arts and sciences too early in life. The first twelve years of life are barely sufficient to instruct a boy in reading, writing and arithmetic. With these, he may be taught those modern languages which are necessary for him to speak. The state of the memory, in early life, is favorable to the acquisition of languages, especially when they are conveyed to the mind, through the ear. It is, moreover, in early life only, that the organs of speech yield in such a manner as to favour the just pronunciation of foreign languages.

Too much pains cannot be taken to teach our youth to read and write our American language with propriety and elegance. The study of the

Greek language constituted a material part of the literature of the Athenians, hence the sublimity, purity and immortality of so many of their writings. The advantages of a perfect knowledge of our language to young men intended for the professions of law, physic, or divinity are too obvious to be mentioned, but in a state which boasts of the first commercial city in America, I wish to see it cultivated by young men, who are intended for the compting house, for many such, I hope, will be educated in our colleges. The time is past when an academical education was thought to be unnecessary to qualify a young man for merchandize. I conceive no profession is capable of receiving more embellishments from it. The French and German languages should likewise be carefully taught in all our colleges. They abound with useful books upon all subjects. So important and necessary are those languages, that a degree should never be conferred upon a young man who cannot speak or translate them.

Connected with the study of languages is the study of eloquence. It is well known how great a part it constituted of the Roman education. It is the first accomplishment in a republic, and often sets the whole machine of government in motion. Let our youth, therefore, be instructed in this art. We do not extol it too highly when we attribute as much to the power of eloquence as to the sword, in bringing about the American Revolution.

With the usual arts and sciences that are taught in our American colleges, I wish to see a regular course of lectures given upon History and Chronology. The science of government, whether it relates to constitutions or laws, can only be advanced by a careful selection of facts, and these are to be found chiefly in history. Above all, let our youth be instructed in the history of the ancient republics, and the progress of liberty and tyranny in the different states of Europe. I wish likewise to see the numerous facts that relate to the origin and present state of commerce, together with the nature and principles of money, reduced to such a system, as to be intelligible and agreeable to a young man. If we consider the commerce of our metropolis only as the avenue of the wealth of the state, the study of it merits a place in a young man's education; but, I consider commerce in a much higher light when I recommend the study of it in republican seminaries. I view it as the best security against the influence of hereditary monopolies of land, and, therefore, the surest protection against aristocracy. I consider its effects as next to those of religion in humanizing mankind, and lastly, I view it as the means of uniting the different nations of the world together by the ties of mutual wants and obligations.

Chemistry by unfolding to us the effects of heat and mixture, enlarges our acquaintance with the wonders of nature and the mysteries of art; hence it has become, in most of the universities of Europe, a necessary branch of a gentleman's education. In a young country, where improvements in agriculture and manufactures are so much to be desired, the cultivation of this science, which explains the principles of both of them, should be considered as an object of the utmost importance.

Again, let your youth be instructed in all the means of promoting national prosperity and independence, whether they refer to improvements in agriculture, manufactures, or inland navigation. Let him be instructed further in the general principles of legislation, whether they relate to revenue, or to the preservation of life, liberty or property. Let him be directed frequently to attend the courts of justice, where he will have the best opportunities of acquiring habits of comparing, and arranging his ideas by observing the discovery of truth, in the examination of witnesses, and where he will hear the laws of the state explained, with all the advantages of that species of eloquence which belongs to the bar. Of so much importance do I conceive it to be, to a young man, to attend occasionally to the decisions of our courts of law, that I wish to see our colleges established, only in country towns.

But further, considering the nature of our connection with the United States, it will be necessary to make our pupil acquainted with all the prerogatives of the national government. He must be instructed in the nature and variety of treaties. He must know the difference in the powers and duties of the several species of ambassadors. He must be taught wherein the obligations of individuals and of states are the same, and wherein they differ. In short, he must acquire a general knowledge of all those laws and forms, which unite the sovereigns of the earth, or separate them from each other.

I beg pardon for having delayed so long to say any thing of the separate and peculiar mode of education proper for women in a republic. I am sensible that they must concur in all our plans of education for young men, or no laws will ever render them effectual. To qualify our women for this purpose, they should not only be instructed in the usual branches of female education, but they should be taught the principles of liberty and government; and the obligations of patriotism should be inculcated upon them. The opinions and conduct of men are often regulated by the women in the most arduous enterprizes of life; and their approbation is frequently the principal reward of the hero's dangers, and the patriot's toils. Besides, the first impressions upon the minds of children are generally derived from the women. Of how much consequence, therefore, is it in a republic, that they should think justly upon the great subject of liberty and government!

The complaints that have been made against religion, liberty and learning, have been, against each of them in a separate state. Perhaps like certain liquors, they should only be used in a state of mixture. They mutually assist in correcting the abuses, and in improving the good effects of each other. From the combined and reciprocal influence of religion, liberty and learning upon the morals, manners and knowledge of individuals, of these, upon government, and of government, upon individuals, it is impossible to measure the degrees of happiness and perfection to which mankind may be raised. For my part, I can form no ideas of the golden age, so much celebrated by the poets, more delightful, than the contemplation of that happiness which it is now in the power of the legislature of Pennsylvania to confer upon her citizens, by establishing proper modes and places of education in every part of the state. . . .

* * *

PLAN OF A FEDERAL UNIVERSITY

" Your government cannot be executed. It is too expensive for a republic. It is contrary to the habits of the people," say the enemies of the Constitution of the United States. — However opposite to the opinions and wishes of a majority of the citizens of the United States, these declarations and predictions may be, they will certainly come to pass, unless the people are prepared for our new form of government by an education adapted to the new and peculiar situation of our country. To effect this great and necessary work, let one of the first acts of the new Congress be, to establish within the district to be allotted for them, a federal university, into which the youth of the United States shall be received after they have finished their studies, and taken their degrees in the colleges of their respective states. In this University, let those branches of literature only be taught, which are calculated to prepare our youth for civil and public life. . . .

Let the Congress allow a liberal salary to the Principal of this university. Let it be his business to govern the students, and to inspire them by his conversation, and by occasional public discourses, with federal and patriotic sentiments. Let this Principal be a man of extensive education, liberal manners and dignified deportment.

Let the Professors of each of the branches that have been mentioned, have a moderate salary of 150l. or 200l. a year, and let them depend upon the number of their pupils to supply the deficiency of their maintenance from their salaries. Let each pupil pay for each course of lectures two or three guineas.

Let the degrees conferred in this university receive a new name, that shall designate the design of an education for civil and public life.

In thirty years after this university is established, let an act of Congress be passed to prevent any person being chosen or appointed into power or office, who has not taken a degree in the federal university. We require certain qualifications in lawyers, physicians and clergymen, before we commit our property, our lives or our souls to their care. We even refuse to commit the charge of a ship to a pilot, who cannot produce a certificate of his education and knowledge in his business. Why then should we commit our country, which includes liberty, property, life, wives and children, to men who cannot produce vouchers of their qualifications for the important trust? We are restrained from injuring ourselves by employing quacks in law; why should we not be restrained in like manner, by law, from employing quacks in government?

Should this plan of a federal university or one like it be adopted, then will begin the golden age of the United States. While the business of education in Europe consists in lectures upon the ruins of Palmyra and the antiquities of Herculaneum, or in disputes about Hebrew points, Greek particles, or the accent and quantity of the Roman language, the youth of America will be employed in acquiring those branches of knowledge which increase the conveniences of life, lessen human misery, improve our country, promote population, exalt the human understanding, and establish domestic, social and political happiness.

Let it not be said, " that this is not the *time* for such a literary and political establishment. Let us first restore public credit, by funding or paying our debts, let us regulate our militia, let us build a navy, and let us protect and extend our commerce. After this, we shall have leisure and money to establish a University for the purposes that have been mentioned." This is false reasoning. We shall never restore public credit, regulate our militia, build a navy, or revive our commerce, until we remove the ignorance and prejudices, and change the habits of our citizens, and this can never be done 'till we inspire them with federal principles, which can only be effected by our young men meeting and spending two or three years together in a national University, and afterwards disseminating their knowledge and principles through every county, township and village of the United States. 'Till this is done — Senators and Representatives of the United States, you will undertake to make bricks without straw. Your supposed union in Congress will be a rope of sand. The inhabitants of Massachusetts began the business of government by establishing the University of Cambridge, and the wisest Kings in Europe have always found their literary institutions the surest means of establishing their power as well as of promoting the prosperity of their people.

These hints for establishing the Constitution and happiness of the United States upon a permanent foundation, are submitted to the friends of the federal government in each of the states, by a private
Citizen of Pennsylvania.

MYRON LIEBERMAN
The myth of local control

One of the most important educational trends in the next few decades is likely to be the decline of local control of education. Such a development is long overdue. Local control of education has clearly outlived its usefulness on the American scene. Practically, it must give way to a system of educational controls in which local communities play ceremonial rather than policy-making roles. *Intellectually*, it is already a corpse. At least, I

From Myron Lieberman, *The Future of Public Education*, 1960, pp. 34–42, 51–55. Reprinted by permission of the University of Chicago Press.

propose to treat it as such in this book. The proper way to treat a corpse is to conduct an autopsy upon it and then bury it promptly. Having done this, we can better understand the rationale for the school system which will emerge from the present chaos in education.

An autopsy of local control reveals several reasons for its demise. In the first place, mobility and interdependence have completely undermined the notion that local communities ought to have a free hand in educating their children. Second, national survival now requires educational policies and programs which are not subject to local veto. Third, it is becoming increasingly clear that local control cannot in practice be reconciled with the ideals of a democratic society. Finally, local control is a major cause of the dull parochialism and attenuated totalitarianism that characterizes public education in operation.

Let us analyze these reasons briefly. In order to do so, consider carefully the following question: *Who* should decide whether the children in a given community should be required to learn to read and write?

Some persons would undoubtedly argue that parents should have the right to raise their children as illiterates if they wish to do so. Most people would probably feel that the public ought to have the right of final decision in this matter. Still, there are many publics: local, state, regional, national, international, and even publics which are not defined geographically. Which of these publics should be authorized to have the last word in the matter?

Until a short time ago, every state had a compulsory education law. These laws took the power to decide our hypothetical question out of the hands of parents and local communities. Recently, however, some states have passed standby legislation which would enable them to abolish compulsory education in order to avoid racial integration in their public schools. States cannot be prevented by the federal government from abolishing public education. There is no way that the federal government can force a state legislature or local community to appropriate money to operate public schools. But what about our basic question — should the decision as to whether children shall learn to read and write be properly regarded as one for local communities or even state governments to make?

The reasons why the power to make this decision was taken away from parents and later from local communities will help us to answer this question. One reason was based upon the concept of fair play for the individual child. There was growing acceptance of the belief that a child's chances in life should not depend upon whether his parents or his local community were willing and able to educate him.

Should a child's chances depend upon whether he lives in a state which is willing to educate him? Certainly not as long as we adhere to the concept of an open society, one in which the individual's chances are not determined by fortuitous factors. As far as the individual child is concerned, the extent to which his state government is willing to provide him with an education is as much a fortuitous matter as the socioeconomic status of his parents or the educational values of his local community.

Consider the problem from a social standpoint instead of an individual one. We are an extremely mobile people. Most of us eventually move away from the community in which we received our education. In the year ending in April, 1958, 30,800,000 Americans changed their residence. Over 11,000,000 moved from one county to another; about half this number moved to a different state. Thus, on the average, every American moves to a different state two times during his life. Under these circumstances, does it make sense to insist that the citizens of one state have no right to insist upon literacy for the children of other states? Today, we plead for federal aid to education in order to equalize opportunities between states. Tomorrow, we could hardly contend that the federal government must stand by idly while a state legislature compounded the inequity by depriving children of an education altogether.[1]

As an abstract proposition, it has always been clear that it is undemocratic to permit educational opportunity to be determined by circumstances of race, geographical location, or economic status. It has also been clear that our national welfare was dependent upon the extent to which individual talents were able to flourish, regardless of their social, economic, racial, or geographical origins. Neither the ideal of equality of opportunity nor the fact of our interdependence is new. What is new is the urgency of these things. Proposals for federal aid to education in order to equalize educational opportunities between states have been ignored by Congress for generations. The same proposals, advanced as a counterpoise to Russian scientific progress, are now regarded as insufficient by panic-stricken congressmen who never supported them on equalitarian grounds.

Some idea of the bankruptcy of local control of education may be seen in the statistics concerning selective service registrants disqualified for failure to pass mental tests. In 1956 the lowest rate of rejection for failure was in Montana, where 2.5 per cent of the registrants failed these tests. The highest rate was in Mississippi, where 44.9 per cent of the registrants failed the tests. In ten states, fewer than one out of every twenty registrants failed to pass; in eleven other states, one or more out of every four registrants failed to pass.[2]

The vast differences among the states in the rate of disqualification are not due solely to the differences in the quality of their school systems. A

[1] My argument treats control of education by the states as local control of education. Fundamentally, this identification is sound although people do not now think of control at the state level as local control. It is only a matter of time before they do so, and then the control of education at the state level will go the way of control at the parental and community levels. In point of time, the decline of community control over broad educational policy will precede the decline of state control over it, but the same forces that undermine the one will eventually undermine the other.

[2] NEA Research Division, *Research Bulletin*, XXXVI, No. 1 (February, 1958), 29.

registrant educated in Montana might take his selective service tests in Mississippi or vice versa. The statistics on rejection include the failures to pass because of inherited mental deficiency, and there are other causes for such failure over which the schools have no control. Nevertheless, the differences between the states cannot be explained solely by non-educational causes. Because some states and communities provide a decent minimum education for only a small minority of their children, we must, in all states, draft persons who, for family or occupational reasons, ought not to be in the armed services at all. This is only a small part of the exorbitant price we are paying for local control of education. The intellectual smog that has obscured our grasp of this fact is being cleared away once and for all by such dramatic events as the riots in Little Rock and the Russian conquests of space.

LOCAL CONTROL AND TOTALITARIAN CONTROL

The prevailing point of view is that anything but local control of education, with perhaps a few concessions made to control at the state level, would be a step toward totalitarianism. This view is profoundly mistaken. Our present system of local control is far more conducive to totalitarianism than a national system of schools would be. I know that this statement is not acceptable to the overwhelming majority of the American people, including the teachers, but I am willing to stand on it.

The assertion that our educational system tends toward totalitarianism seems absurd on its face. A totalitarian system is one which develops a massive uniformity of outlook. It is based upon a policy of intellectual protection for a point of view that cannot stand the test of free discussion. We have a multitude of schools of all denominations or no denomination at all. Among the teachers and students in our public schools, there are adherents to every major political, economic, and religious point of view. What could be further from totalitarianism than this?

In most states the purposes and the content of education are left to local school boards to determine. Undoubtedly, there are some constitutional limits to the purposes for which communities may operate public schools. However, these limits have never been spelled out, and there is great latitude in what a community might require of its schools. Since the purposes of education are set forth locally, the predominant groups in the community tend to establish purposes which accord with their particular religious, political, economic, or social points of view. As a practical matter, therefore, local control results in the same kind of intellectual protectionism that characterizes schools in totalitarian countries.

The basic problem is not that communities define the purpose of education to be the acceptance of the Protestant faith or unswerving devotion to the single tax or the inculcation of the tenets of the Democratic party. Some communities have not blinked at adopting purposes as sectarian as these, but this is not where the problem lies. Even where a community accepts the most liberal educational purposes for its public schools, its interpretation of what intermediate objectives and what educational programs fulfill these purposes may have the same stultifying effect as outright adherence to a sectarian purpose. Every pressure group is for the general welfare, but each has its own version of what measures do in fact promote the general welfare. Similarly, every pressure group is for a liberal or a democratic education, but has a special version of what intermediate objectives and what educational programs lead to this result.

What is crucial is that, at the local level, it is relatively easy for a preponderant group to enforce a policy of intellectual protectionism for its sacred cows. Thus the white majorities in Southern communities in which fundamentalist sects predominate exclude instruction . . . [involving] . . . evolution. Some communities have prohibited the study of the United Nations or of UNESCO. Ours is a heterogeneous country, but in most communities the predominant racial, religious, economic, or political groups are able to veto whatever in the school program displeases them.

Looking at our system as a whole and seeing the existence of public schools teaching diverse doctrines, one might infer that our schools are free. We do not readily recognize the totalitarianism implicit in our situation because not all schools protect the same dogmas. Nonetheless, a diversity of schools based upon intellectual protectionism for different dogmas does not constitute a " democratic school system." At least, it does not do so if " democratic " refers to the education actually provided in these schools instead of to the legal structure which encourages a variety of one-sided programs.

The diversity of our undemocratic schools is not the only factor which maintains the fiction that we have a democratic school system. No matter how successful a group may be in excluding certain facts and ideas from the public schools, television, radio, and other mass media are almost certain to expose students to these facts and ideas. The power structure of American society is such that no single group is able to enforce or to indoctrinate its dogmas on the population as a whole. People look at this situation and say, " Our schools have kept us free." They should say, " Our freedoms have survived our schools."

THE MYTHOLOGY OF LOCAL CONTROL

Many persons believe that public education was not made a federal responsibility in the Constitution because the founding fathers feared the potentialities for dictatorship in a federal school system. Actually, education was not included as a federal function in the Constitution because the idea of free public education had not even occurred to the founding fathers. At the time of the American Revolution, the concept of universal public education was receiving attention for the first time and then only from a few frontier thinkers. Our decentralized school system was not an inspired stroke of genius but a historical accident, resulting from the fact that the ideal of free public education for all became widely accepted only long after the American Revolution.

Our schools have never been an important foundation of our free society. Our freedom is partly due to a separation of powers which enable us to transact public business reasonably well while avoiding excessive subjection to government officials. Perhaps for this reason we tend to regard the diffusion of power over our schools as an essential element of our free society. But adherence to the general principle that we must avoid excessive concentration of power does not automatically justify every separation or diffusion of it. Everything depends upon the circumstances — what powers are involved, who is to wield them, and so on. It is preposterous to think that merely because their political genius was expressed through a constitution embodying a remarkably successful separation of powers, the founding fathers would align themselves today with the supporters of local control of education.

People are seldom aware of the non-public character of public education. They tend to regard it as a legal concept and to neglect it as an educational concept. However, the ideal of public education means more than having some governmental unit — local, state, or federal — provide the funds to operate schools. Public education has a referent in the quality of education as well as in its financial basis. The qualitative referent is an education in which the search for truth is carried on regardless of what empires topple, interests collapse, or heads roll. Without this, public education is a delusion, as dangerous as the notion that mere government ownership of the means of production will automatically result in their operation for the public welfare instead of for private interests. The socialization of a service at any level of government is no automatic guarantee that the service will be performed in the public interest. The " new class " should have ended all of our illusions on this score.

Public schools, then, are not necessarily infused with a public spirit. Likewise, the fact that a school is privately controlled does not mean that its program is necessarily sectarian in character. The programs of some privately controlled institutions such as Harvard are more free of parochial limitations than the programs in most publicly controlled institutions. In short, we cannot assume anything about the educational program of a school merely from a knowledge of whether the school is publicly or privately controlled.[3] Nor can we infer that the educational program of a school is undemocratic merely because the school is locally controlled or that it is democratic merely because the schools are part of a national sys-

---

[3] The notion that private education *per se* is superior to public education is assiduously cultivated by private school interests at all levels. It is a myth insofar as it pretends to be a generalization or even a statement of probable tendency. This myth results in outright tragedy at the elementary and secondary levels if parents assume that exorbitant fees automatically purchase educational advantages not available in the public schools.

tem. The relationship between the legal status of a school and the quality of its educational program is never one of strict logical implication.

The system of legal controls under which schools operate is only one factor which serves to shape their educational programs. However, it is an extremely important factor. Because a national system of controls is more likely to broaden the purposes of education and to preserve the professional autonomy of teachers, it is much more likely to provide a truly liberal education than a multitude of totalitarian systems under local control. It is a striking fact that in England, which has a national system of education, the teachers are on record as being opposed to local control of education precisely because they fear that it would undermine their professional autonomy.[4] Meanwhile, teachers in the United States, who lack any substantial measure of professional autonomy, continue to act as if local control must be maintained inviolate lest academic freedom (which they do not possess) be imperiled.

The decentralization of our schools is often justified by an appeal to the experimental nature of this situation. We supposedly have fifty state school systems, each of which is free to try something different from the others. Each state has delegated considerable power to local school boards, which supposedly multiplies the experimental possibilities. This is thought to make for progress, since each state and each system is not only free to try something new but is free to benefit from the experience of other systems.

There is no doubt that some change for the better occurs in this way. Nevertheless, such enormous decentralization cannot be justified on the grounds that the different school systems constitute a vast pool of educational experimentation. The different schools do not constitute experiments except in the loosest sense of the word. They do not operate under conditions carefully controlled for purposes of analysis and comparison. They just operate. . . .

Somehow, we might just muddle through the last half of the twentieth century with an eighteenth-century educational system. The chances are, however, that the practical sense of the American people will be forced to assert itself and that they will develop a centralized school system while simultaneously reaffirming their faith that any such system is un-American.

It is difficult to predict the form which centralization will take. It is possible that centralization may take place while much of our present educational structure is formally left intact. To understand this, bear in mind that a national system of education is not necessarily the same thing as a

[4] Educational leaders in England are very outspoken in their view that any trend toward giving local boards of education increased control over the financing of education would be a threat to the freedom of the teaching profession. See Sir Ronald Gould, "The Teaching Profession," *The Concept of Professional Status* (London: College of Preceptors, 1957), p. 42.

federal system of education. A federal system would be one in which the schools were operated by the federal government. However, education might continue to be the legal responsibility of states and local communities, while it also became substantially similar over the country as a result of non-governmental pressures.

The point can be illustrated by the situation in medicine. Legally, medical education and licensure are controlled by the various state medical boards. In actuality, these state boards are so dominated by the American Medical Association that we have a national system of medical education. There are some variations from state to state, but nothing compared to the chaos in teacher education and licensure. There are other occupations wherein the legal control of professional training and entry is a state function but wherein the activities of national professional organizations and accrediting agencies have brought about a national system of professional training and licensure.

The same possibility exists for elementary and secondary education. That is, even though education at these levels may continue to be the legal responsibility of state and local governments, various organizations and social pressures may force the different states and communities to adopt the same basic educational program. Under these circumstances, it would make sense to speak of an educational system that was national but not federal.

It is unlikely that in the next few decades we shall have a federal school system covering the entire country. Such a development would occur only if the failures of states and communities to carry out their educational responsibilities were to be brought home dramatically to the American people by some such event as the abolition of public education in the South. I am convinced, however, that we are about to move rapidly toward a national system of education. What is certain is not the form but the fact that we shall have a much more centralized system of education in the future than we have had in the past. The idea that the present chaos in education is the price one has to pay for living in a democracy, or the even more nonsensical notion that the prevailing educational chaos is one of the foundations of democracy, will linger on but without any real force in our society.

Unquestionably, the most important barrier to a centralized system of public education is the notion that any such system would be "totalitarian" or "undemocratic." We are warned that a centralized system would provide an opportunity for one particular group, say a political party, to seize control of the schools, and by indoctrinating its point of view, maintain itself in power. Since this line of reasoning is undoubtedly the basis of our fear of a centralized school system, I wish to consider it at some length.

Those who think along these lines usually point to Soviet Russia to illustrate the dangers of a centralized system of education. But it should be obvious that one cannot assume that a centralized system *per se* is more likely to be totalitarian than our own. England, France, and the Scandinavian countries all have national systems. In all of these, there is less political interference with teachers than there is in the United States. Put positively, there is more freedom to teach and to learn in all of these national school systems than there is in the overwhelming majority of schools in the United States.

In the United States, how would any particular group, be it political, religious, or economic, achieve such complete control of all schools that it could produce a generation of unthinking disciples? To develop such a generation would require complete control of our mass media. This in turn would presuppose fairly complete control of the government. Any pressure group which could achieve such controls would have no need to control the schools. Indeed, it could safely permit schools to operate as they do now, preparing generations of civic illiterates who firmly believe they have fulfilled the highest obligations of citizenship when they have flipped a lever in a voting booth.

We already have many schools supported by the federal government. What evidence is available indicates that the teachers in these federal schools have more, not less, freedom than teachers elsewhere. For example, there is as much or more academic freedom at Howard University, which is supported by federal funds, than there is at the overwhelming majority of institutions of higher education.

People are opposed to a centralized system of schools for many reasons, not all of them noble ones. Some of the opposition comes from private school interests which would not share in the federal funds which will undergird such a system. We need private schools, but the arguments which some private school spokesmen make against federal aid or a federal school system are unrealistic. Private educational institutions whose *raison d'être* is to keep the faithful from being exposed to heretical points of view oppose federal aid to education on the grounds that such aid would mean mass conformity and indoctrination. The free and independent mind which these institutions claim to nurture is what some of them fear above everything else.

Nonetheless, it must be conceded that many people have a gnawing fear of a centralized school system which is quite unrelated to any thought that their particular points of view might not survive in such a system. These people do not fear for their points of view in an atmosphere of intellectual freedom. They would not exclude a fair presentation of other points of view in the schools even if they had the power to do so. Their fear is for the integrity of the system, not for the fate of their particular views on political, economic, religious, racial, or other controversial issues.

Ironically, these fears often are based upon experiences with local control. Every inadequacy of a local board reinforces rather than weakens the fear of a federal system. Under the present system, the worst blunders are confined to a limited area. What would happen, people ask, if a national school board or federal school administrator were to engage in the educational follies which characterize some local school boards?

The answer is that it would be a calamity, but the more we centralize our school system (up to a point, of course), the less likely it is that such a calamity will occur. The crucial point is that at the national level, no one group has the kind of power to interfere with the educational program that one sees every day under a system of local control. The rabble rousers who can successfully frighten a large city school system like that of Los Angeles into dropping an essay contest on the United Nations would not have a chance in a federal school system. Nor would the more powerful pressure groups be able to shape the educational program to their own ends. None has sufficient power by itself to do this. Each would be watched and checked if necessary by all the others if it attempted any massive interference with the educational program or with educational personnel. Since no non-professional group would have the power to dictate the educational program or personnel policies, and since teachers would not be subject to local censorship, the teachers would be free to discuss points of view which are now proscribed by local boards of education.

The fact, if it be a fact, that no pressure group would be able to dominate a centralized system might not sound very appealing. Would the integrity of such a system rest upon a balance of power among large national pressure groups, all of whom would subvert the school program to their own ends if they could? If so, what assurance is there that tomorrow, or the day after, the balance of power will not change so as to provide one of these groups, or a combination of them, with the opportunity they seek?

If by "assurance" is meant an ironclad guarantee, of course there is none. We are choosing between practical alternatives, not between mathematical solutions, one of which is the perfect answer. It is local control of education which provides a greater opportunity for national pressure groups to dominate the educational programs of the public schools, on a *national* basis. The reason is that local school boards are unable to withstand the pressures which can be generated by powerful national organizations which know what they want from our schools. However, there is another factor which seems to me to clinch the case for a centralized school system, at least insofar as the criterion of academic freedom is concerned. This factor is the impact which centralization is likely to have upon teachers' organizations and the role which they would play in protecting the integrity of a centralized public school system. . . .

SECTION **4. Education as an international function and responsibility**

It has become a commonplace in our time to refer to the fact that we live in a world characterized by interde-pendency. Intellectually, few persons in our society would deny this. Such expressions as "one world," "the shrinking globe," and "the international economy" are accepted by most Americans as commonplace estimations of the world situation. Isolationism, the belief that Americans can be indifferent to what goes on elsewhere in the world, has died a hard but nonetheless decisive death. Pearl Harbor, the atomic bomb, intercontinental air transportation, missiles, and the conquest of space have all underlined this recognition. Ours is, thus far, an internationalism built largely around self-concern. Space projects, race problems, and legal practices are frequently viewed in terms of their impact on our relations with other peoples and governments. We have cultivated the friendship of other nations because they are essential to our survival. But in spite of our intellectual recognition that our welfare and destiny are inextricably bound up with those of the rest of the world, our emotional commitments, our enduring loyalties, our parochialisms do not appear to have been fundamentally altered. There is no reason to believe that the problem of discrepancy between intellectual recognition and fundamental values and orientation is uniquely American. A characteristic of our times is the intellectual recognition of problems for which emotional commitments are not yet ready. It is to this problem of preparing the total man for actual participation in a genuinely international community that an increasing number of educational leaders are today addressing themselves.

The chief international organ which has been established to bring into focus the educational components of an international community has been the United Nations Educational, Scientific and Cultural Organization, better known as UNESCO. The preamble to its Constitution is a delineation of the basic problems of the world order: it poses the challenge that education must become broad enough in scope and profound enough in function to encompass the whole human race if war is to be avoided and peace is to be sustained. This preamble to its Constitution, which came into force on November 4, 1946, reads as follows:

" The Governments of the States parties to this Constitution on behalf of their peoples declare,

" that since wars begin in the minds of men, it is in the minds of men that the defences of peace must be constructed;

" that ignorance of each other's ways and lives has been a common cause, throughout the history of mankind, of that suspicion and mistrust between the peoples of the world through which their differences have all too often broken into war;

" that the great and terrible war which has now ended was a war made possible by the denial of the democratic principles of the dignity, equality and mutual respect of men, and by the propagation, in their place, through ignorance and prejudice, of the doctrine of the inequality of men and races;

" that the wide diffusion of culture, and the education of humanity for justice and liberty and peace are indispensable to the dignity of man and constitute a sacred duty which all the nations must fulfil in a spirit of mutual assistance and concern;

" that a peace based exclusively upon the political and economic arrangements of governments would not be a peace which could secure the unanimous, lasting and sincere support of the peoples of the world, and that the peace must therefore be founded, if it is not to fail, upon the intellectual and moral solidarity of mankind.

" For these reasons, the States parties to this Constitution, believing in full and equal opportunities for education for all, in the unrestricted pursuit of objective truth, and in the free exchange of ideas and knowledge, are agreed and determined to develop and to increase the means of communication between their peoples and to employ these means for the purposes of mutual understanding and a truer and more perfect knowledge of each other's lives;

"In consequence whereof they do hereby create the United Nations Educational, Scientific and Cultural Organization for the purpose of advancing, through educational and scientific and cultural relations of the peoples of the world, the objectives of international peace and of the common welfare of mankind for which the United Nations Organization was established and which its Charter proclaims."

This is the charter and the challenge for international education.

If this challenge to see education as genuine initiation into an international society is accepted, the same two problems of *control* and *content* inevitably arise. Perhaps no clearer plea for the international scope and control of education has been made than that advanced, in the middle of the

Second World War, by the American philosopher and educator, Alexander Meiklejohn. The extent to which UNESCO, as an organ of the United Nations, can achieve this dream of a genuinely international education is one which is as yet unanswered. The translation of the dream into the reality of an educational program is one which will require many years of arduous work, if it is to be realized at all. It seems appropriate that a member of the professional staff of UNESCO, Pedro Orata, should be allowed to speak as to the necessary content of education for an international community. An outstanding Philippine educator who received part of his education in the United States, Orata has devoted himself to providing meaning to the UNESCO commitment. In the second of the selections which follow, he faces the brutally demanding question, as every thinking person must: What is the education which is fundamental that all receive if we are to survive and prosper in one world?

ALEXANDER MEIKLEJOHN
Education for world citizenship

The human road, we have said, leads from barbarism to civilization. So far as they are intelligent, men seek to establish reasonable relations with their fellows. Such relations are not possible with mosquitoes or tornadoes or trees. But they are possible with normal human beings. And the human task, so far as men are moral and intellectual, is that of extending the scope of reasonable co-operation to its widest and deepest limits. The final goal of that attempt would be the creation of a world-state, in which the appeal to reason would have replaced the resort to violence in the relations of all men to one another.

1

If we accept for humanity the goal which our argument has suggested, the ruling motive of education becomes clear. Learning is not merely the acquiring of mastery over intellectual subject matter. It is, first of all, initia-

From Alexander Meiklejohn, *Education Between Two Worlds*, 1942, pp. 277–291. Reprinted by permission of Harper & Brothers.

tion into many social groups and, ultimately, into one social group. The teacher leads his pupil into active membership in a fraternity to which he himself belongs. The motive force of that fraternity is found in a common devotion to a common, co-operative enterprise. Just as, in the home, each child learns, or should learn, to play his part in the family circle, so, in our schools and colleges, every citizen of the world should become " at home " in the human " state." He should acquire a sense of what humanity is try- ing to do, and a will to join in doing it.

The calling of the teacher, as so defined, is one of infinite difficulty. But it's also infinitely significant. He is commissioned to form and fashion both human society as a whole and the individuals of whom that society con- sists. He acts for the state with a completeness of responsibility which is equaled by no other official.

As he engages in his task, the teacher needs two kinds of equipment. He must acquire command, both of method and of content. On the one hand, he must be expert in the technique of his art. To this end he must know human nature just as any artist knows his materials. He must have con- sidered the principles and practices which are propounded in Rousseau's *Emile*. He must understand how intelligence grows and is kept from growing. In each specific case he must assess capacities and incapacities, powers and impediments. He must discover how to cultivate powers and to remove impediments. Like Comenius he must seek to provide for the plants which he is cultivating, good soil in which to grow, a sunny place whose warmth will stimulate their powers to action. Unlike Comenius, the modern teacher will find his sun, not in the mind and will of God, but in the human fellowship which, against frightful odds, mankind is trying to establish.

2

We have said that a teacher should read Rousseau's *Emile*. But it is far more important that he read, and study, and read again, the *Social Con- tract*. One of the greatest failures of our contemporary training of teachers is that they become mere technicians. They learn the tricks and devices of the classroom. But they do not learn the beliefs and motives and values of the human fellowship for the sake of which the classroom exists. The primary question of teaching theory and practice is one of purpose. Why do we teach? What should we teach? For whom do we teach? What is our goal, and what is the source of its authority over us? Those are the ques- tions which must be answered if our teachers are to be themselves mem- bers of the fraternity into which they seek to initiate their pupils. Only as those questions find solution do our schools and colleges understand what they are doing.

3

The argument of this book has centered around the contention suggested by Rousseau that education is, and must be, carried on under the authority of some social group. It is an expression of the will of some social " organism, instinct with one life, moved by one mind." Teacher and pupil are not isolated individuals. They are both agents of the state. They are called upon to go about the business of learning. And, as they do so, the truth, beauty, and goodness with which they deal, come to them, not from some foreign source, not from their own separate experiences, but from the " state " of which they are members. The content of teaching is found in the modes of behavior, the " patterns of culture," which are approved, and criticized, by the fellowship for which the teaching is done. And, that being true, it is clear that the fundamental question with regard to any system of education is, " By what social group is it given; what are the purposes of that group; why does it will that its members be educated? "

4

In the course of our argument we have touched upon four different answers to this basic question. And these four answers give as many " general theories of education."

First, the answer which Comenius gave to the question of authority and purpose was direct and unequivocal. His pupils were the children of God. His teachers were servants of God. Schools and colleges were, therefore, commissioned to follow after the mind and will of God. The Divine purpose was directed toward the making of a human community. It required peace rather than violence, reasonableness rather than selfishness, intelligence rather than stupidity. The " world-state " was established by the Divine will. And a common citizenship in that state prescribed a common curriculum of wisdom and piety for all·mankind.

But, with the weakening of theological beliefs and sanctions our culture has faced the task of providing a " secular " authorization for the purposes of teaching. We moderns have, therefore, tried to describe, in " scientific " terms, the relation between an individual, whether pupil or teacher, and a social consciousness which is wider and deeper than his own. These scientific accounts of human behavior have followed three lines. They suggest, therefore, three different types of educational theory which are now competing for our acceptance.

5

The disorganic theory, in its most extreme form, finds an individual life to be related to the conscious life around it as a drop of water in a stream is related to the current which carries it along. In this figurative description, the total stream of consciousness, as it flows, has no intention of doing so. It does not choose its course. It may, at points, become aware of its own process. But that awareness is merely cognitive. It is a recognition of conditions and their consequences as mere facts. Each individual drop of consciousness, therefore, as it is swept along, may feel what is happening to itself and to others. It may even recognize the influence of this set of conditions or that as determining the course of events. But it cannot participate in the purpose of controlling that course, for the simple reason that there is no such purpose in which to participate.

When we say that this " scientific " account of human relations can never provide a basis for a theory of education, we are not denying its validity as " science." We are saying that knowledge, as such, does not express purpose. It describes happenings. Knowledge of conditions and consequence is necessary for the directing of education. But it is not sufficient. It is only as knowledge, being used for the purposes of human brotherhood, becomes intelligence, that it serves the purposes of the teacher. Pupils must learn, not only what they are and how they act, but also what they have to do and be. They must see themselves as participating in enterprises which have a right to their allegiance.

6

A second, less extreme form of disorganic theory, does not exclude purposes from the stream of events. But it finds them to be scattered, multifarious, episodic. They occur on specific occasions. They appear and disappear as individuals and groups are stirred to " adjust " themselves to their situation, to adjust their situation to themselves. This is the point of view which Dewey expresses when he describes the " conscious " activities of men as dealing with a " plurality of problematic situations." Each of these situations requires purposive action. But each is dealt with separately as the specific conditions may require. They do not fuse into a single situation. It is true that a number of individuals may become a social group, that their many enterprises may become one enterprise. But these groupings also, are separate and episodic. At the best, they give us only a multiplicity of conflicting pressure groups, each going its own way. The stream of events is marked here and there by eddies or currents of conscious purpose. But, in its general flow, it remains merely a stream which rushes along with no conscious control of what it is doing.

This view of human behavior is, likewise, inadequate as a basis for a theory of education. As already noted, it gives us, not one human education, but a vast multiplicity of separate and unrelated educations. It finds in the circumstances and interests of each individual life the materials and the needs which prescribe a peculiar and distinctive plan of teaching. But it does not express that general will of the state, that devotion to the common good, which is required if the members of a social group are to be properly prepared for reasonable co-operation in the life of the community.

7

As against extreme naturalism or partial pluralism, this book has insisted upon a continuous purpose which runs through the course of human experience. We have not said that that purpose dominates the total course of events. But we have said that it seeks such domination, so far as it is humanly possible. The race of man has before it the possibility of being civilized. And it is that possibility which defines the course of education.

All women and children and men may become intelligent, loyal members of a single social group. And it is for that group that teaching should be done. Teaching itself should be intelligent and loyal. It should recognize that the will to reasonableness has critical authority over all individuals and all groups which are found in the ranks of humanity.

It follows from what has been said that all human beings should have the same essential education. This assertion does not deny that they should have different educations as well. The drummer and the violinist have different techniques to acquire. But they must also learn to play together. It would be disastrous if, in the midst of a symphony, either drummer or violinist were found unable to make his instrument play. But it would be at least equally disastrous if either of them should play with vigor and efficiency but with no regard for the score which had been placed before his eyes.

Humanity has, I insist, one intelligence. That intelligence, it is true, is only " in the making." Its making is a difficult and precarious venture. It may at any time collapse. And yet, the statement that all men may share in a common enterprise is both true and significant. It tells us, in part, what the world is. It tells us, in part, what men are. And it is upon that basis of fact that any proper plan of human education must be based. It is the lack of that basis of fact which has made our current theories of teaching so negative, so lacking in positive direction. There is a fellowship of civilizing intelligence into which every human being, so far as he is capable of it, must be initiated. Each of us must have loyalty to that company. As pupils, we must turn aside from the resort to violence. We must acquire skill in the appeal to reason. We must become citizens of the world. Education is the fitting of people, young and old, for the responsibilities and opportunities of that citizenship.

8

If we accept the belief that the whole world of human behavior can be dealt with as a single enterprise which a single co-operative human intelligence is trying to direct, and if we regard all lesser enterprises as finding their basic justification and criticism as participants in this all-inclusive attempt, some general conclusions concerning education seem to follow.

First, governments, local, provincial, national, and super-national, are equipped to teach. The handing over of the control of education from the church to the state has not been a fatal blunder. The state is not Moloch. It is not " nothing but your worst, nothing but the worst of us, lifted up." On the contrary, the state is the best of us, trying to control and to elevate the worst of us. It is ourselves seeking to be reasonable, to live in justice and freedom with one another. Man, at his best, is a political animal. His wisdom creates manners and morals. The same wisdom, when institutionalized, creates laws, roads, hospitals, parks, pensions, peace, schools. But these two expressions of wisdom are not hostile to one another. They are one in purpose, one in idea and value. And since that is true, education by the government is radically sound in principle. As our culture now stands, no other institution can equal the state as the representative of those purposes and beliefs which are the fruits of human reasonableness. We do not understand what a state is unless we see that it is both a student and a teacher. We belie its essential nature when we regard it as a policeman.

The statement just made does not mean that "private schools" may not do good teaching. After all, the thinking of the race is done by individuals. And groups of individuals who are disinterested, who are moved to teach, not by private interest or party bias, but by zeal for public intelligence — such groups may teach successfully. On the whole, however, the drift of circumstances is against them. Under current economic conditions private schools and colleges are, almost inevitably, agencies of special privilege. They give to a few advantages which are denied to the many. And that very inequality is destructive of education in reasonableness. It is hard to teach justice when the selection of the students must be recognized as unjust. Inequality of educational opportunity does not conduce to the inculcation of a zest for equality. Actions teach more effectively than words. And for this reason the role of private education seems sure to be a dwindling one.

At this point it may be objected that schools, when conducted by a government, are, of necessity, "plunged into politics," that they are used by "the party in power" for the furthering of its own selfish purposes. And that objection will hold good so long, and so far, as we Americans can see in political life, only the strife of contending pressure groups. That prevailing social philosophy has done enormous damage to our schools. But, on the other hand, that philosophy is false. And our actual social practice rises, at some points, far above it. In the organization of the state university, for example, our governments have devised a system of administration which combines, with amazing success, the independence of the teacher, and the responsibility of the institution to the public as a whole. The essence of that system of administration is found in the belief that men who are qualified to study and teach can be trusted to do so in the public interest. As against this, in other fields of political action, we Americans have dealt with our public servants on the theory that they cannot be trusted. We have assumed that they need to be watched, to be kept under constant pressure by us. And the inevitable result is that we have had as public officials the kind of person who needs to be watched, who responds to pressure. Every teacher knows, that suspicion breeds trickiness and guile. Persons who are not trusted become unworthy of being trusted. That "pressure" philosophy will never give us a democracy. It must be abandoned. Mutual confidence is the prerequisite of freedom. Unless men can trust each other, there is no hope of reasonableness between them. I do not mean that a democracy should give up control over its representatives. But I do mean that such control should not be degrading and hence self-defeating. Our national state legislatures give constant illustration of that degradation and self-defeat. They represent, not democracy, but a crude and stupid individualistic falsification of it which, while keeping the forms of freedom, has made men themselves unfit to be free.

As we attempt the sadly needed revision of our processes of government, we may find valuable suggestions in the structure and procedure of our state universities. We have, in those institutions, men who, in the public interest, are seeking for the truth. They are, in the best sense of the term, " responsible public servants." And yet, it would, on the whole, be meaningless to " subject them to pressure," to send telegrams telling them what truth to find, as we do with the members of our legislatures. The public servant of a free society must himself be free. That fact our pressure-group philosophy has disastrously obscured.

9

Our first conclusion has been that teaching should be a government activity. But, second, which of our governments shall take charge of it? Shall it be the village or the town or the county or the state or the nation or the world-nation? Each of these " states " represents a level of reasonableness. Each of them has its own " pattern of culture." And the choice among them is, in effect, the choice of the subject matter of our teaching. Shall we teach young people to live in a village or in a nation or in the world? The answer to that question must not be oversimplified. Every human being needs to learn how to live in all the social groupings to which he " belongs." And yet, if our argument is valid, one principle emerges from it which is of primary importance. Fundamentally education belongs to the world-state. The reasonableness of that institution includes and criticizes all the lesser reasonablenesses of our experience. Every human being, young or old, should be taught, first of all, to be a citizen of the world, a member of the human fellowship. All other lessons are derivatives of that primary lesson.

The statement just made branches out in two different directions. It tells us, first, that all education should be given " for " the world-state. It tells us, second, that all education should be given " by " the world-state. If we can explain those two assertions, our attempt at a theory of teaching will have reached its goal.

10

The need of so transforming our plans of education that our pupils will learn to participate in the total human enterprise is thrust upon us as we see the dictatorships of Germany, Italy, and Japan at work in the field of teaching. They have built and are running educational machines which torture and twist the minds of their people out of all resemblance to the forms of human reasonableness. Those nations are guilty of many crimes. But the deepest and blackest of all their offenses are committed against their schools. It is not true, however, that they are the only sinners. The democracies, too, in more subtle ways are likewise guilty. Our localisms and provincialisms do not so obviously and brutally undertake to root out of our minds the appeal to reason. But they are, nevertheless, effective in doing so. It is not enough today to teach a young person to play his part in the life of Indiana or Boston or the South. It is not enough to make him a loyal Pole or Japanese or Canadian or Brazilian. The world is in crisis. There has come upon us all the necessity, as well as the opportunity, of creating a world-state, of making reasonableness prevail for all humanity. And we must have schools which will serve that purpose.

As I write these words my mind goes back to Comenius and to the Christian faith which was for him the basis of education. He saw *all* young people as the children of God. He saw them all, therefore, as having the same life to live. He, therefore, wished to provide for all alike, rich and poor, girls and boys, noble and ignoble, the same lessons in the same scheme of instruction. And that insight, in the new setting which the advance of secularism has brought upon us, still holds good. If we are to have an effective human fellowship, the pupils in every corner of the earth will have the same basic lessons to learn. They need to know each other. They must become aware of the humanity of which they are members. They must become acquainted with that whole human undertaking which we sum up under the phrase, "the attempt at civilization." Only by having that common knowledge, can they become reasonable in their relations to one another. "The proper study of mankind is Man."

11

The second implication of our principle is that the control of education, its planning and basic administration should be in the hands of the world-state. It is, I think, obvious as we plan for the future, that the nation which is to include all the nations and rule over them must have military force sufficient to give it mastery over its members. It must have a legislature and an executive. It must have courts of justice. It must have an equitable and stable system of finance and trade. But more pressing than any of these is the need for a universal scheme of instruction, whose driving force shall be the purpose that all men shall live together in peace and freedom, with reasonable regard for one another. First of all, the world-state like any other state must be a teacher. If it cannot teach, it will do nothing else successfully.

I have spoken of the desperate urgency of the need that people be educated as citizens of the world. But not even that urgency must be allowed to lead us into the illusion that changes have been made when they have been written on paper or even when they have been voted by legislatures. No teaching can go far beyond the actual living, the prevailing pattern of culture of the group by which it is given. Schools, like churches, are too often used as mechanisms of compensation. We live by one code which, in our hearts, we condemn. And we try to restore the balance by having another code taught to our children. But that procedure in education is just as futile and disastrous as was, in an earlier day, Sunday preaching which was balanced by Monday practice. We cannot teach world fellowship unless we believe in it, unless we put it into action by the creation of a political organization which shall take charge of the fortunes and the virtues of humanity. To attempt it would be like trying to teach Shakespeare to young people in whose homes the only reading is found in the pulp magazines. It is not easy to teach children to despise their parents. Nor is it, perhaps, desirable.

12

At this point, our argument returns to the principle from which, at the suggestion of Rousseau, it took its start. Education is, and must be, an activity carried on by a social group. It is initiation into an existing " pattern of culture." And, as such, it depends upon the support and the authority of the group to which both the pattern and the pupil belong. But that means that we cannot teach world reasonableness unless there is a reasonable world. We cannot teach citizenship in a world-state unless a world-state exists. Are we Anglo-Saxons willing to recognize that implication and to act accordingly? Are we willing to put aside the hypocritical superiorities of the " White Man's Burden "? Are we able to stop the brutal pretense of giving " justice " to the " lesser breeds without the law," and to join with them as fellows in creating a law which shall be equal for all mankind? There is a curiously vital connection between teaching and the truth. If we practice justice and freedom we can teach them. If we do not practice them our words are like " the crackling of thorns under a pot."

13

If we are to have a world-state and to teach its lessons it is clear that the most difficult, as well as the most essential, education must be given, not to children but to men and women. As the new world takes form, the minds of children of every race and country will accept it as easily, more easily, than the chaotic, confusing, self-contradictory scheme of behavior which we now present to them. But that is not true of the grownups. We elders are caught in fear, in habit, in custom, in prejudice, in prudence, in common sense. It is we, therefore, who resist the education or re-education which we need. If we are to have the moral and intellectual reconstruction which are implied in the making of a world-state, the prime essential is an adequate process of adult education. Our minds will have to be refashioned. And we ourselves must do it. There is no one else to teach us. We, members of a common humanity, acting together as one sovereign people, must teach ourselves to do and to be what our common citizenship offers us to do and be. We must learn to so know and care for all of our fellow men that we can participate with them in the one common cause. That task of human self-education our generation is called upon to begin. But it will be only a beginning. The road to reasonableness goes on and on.

14

From church to state! From myth to fact! — Can our culture make that transition? There can be little doubt, as Matthew Arnold has told us, that an old world is " dead." And for a long time now the new world has seemed " powerless to be born." And the essential guilt of " the three great democracies," Britain, France, and the United States, as well as of lesser democracies, has been their holding back in the face of the vast and terrifying possibility of a new birth. All over the world the new expression of the human spirit has been striving to break loose, to enter upon its career.

In China, so long abused and mistreated and contemned, there is new hope, new resolution, new achievement. The ancient wisdom is making contact with the modern world. In Russia, a new and relatively untried wisdom has come into action. And the magnificent loyalty and endurance and efficiency of the Russian people, in the face of overwhelming odds, give some suggestion of the power and majesty which a creative program might bring to us. India, too, is stirring. Her demand for justice and freedom will not be denied. She will not remain a subject people. Even the hysterical madness of the Germans and Italians and Japanese springs from the conviction that, the present chaos being intolerable, something better can be devised to take its place. The words of Adolf Hitler are madness. And yet that madness, as a power which threatens the peace and freedom of the modern world, does not spring primarily from the mind of Hitler. It is the madness of a civilization which has denied its own faith, which has been untrue to its own principles. If we believe in democracy we must practice it between nations as well as within our own nation. If we believe in freedom we cannot be content that other peoples shall be enslaved. If we believe in law and order we must join in establishing them for all mankind. If we believe in equality we cannot defend so desperately our own " higher standard of living." If we believe in reasonableness we must follow wherever reason may lead.

In the midst of all our agonies and uncertainties the new world is being born. It is that new world which gives meaning to education. Every pupil must be learning for it. Every teacher must be teaching for it. Every scholar must be thinking for it. Humanity is reasonable as well as unreasonable. It is the struggle between these two which defines the course of education. We know what teaching is only as we see and feel what the free spirit of man is trying to do and to be.

PEDRO T. ORATA
Fundamental education as a world-wide necessity

Fundamentally, fundamental education is not a new idea. It is as old as education itself — it is education for life. Neither is it only for the three-fourths of the world's population who are living substandard lives in so-called under-developed areas and in the slums of industrially advanced cities, but for the entire human race. It is not poverty, disease and ignorance alone that we must fight if civilization is to be preserved and improved, but power, greed and exploitation. Reduced to its lowest terms, the present state of affairs in the world is not the result of the lack of education — if by education we mean knowledge about peoples and the world in which we live, the ability to control resources for human ends, the possession of scientific method or of a high degree of culture — but because education has become the monopoly of a fraction of the earth's two billion population who have taken advantage of it to exploit the rest.

As recently as during the time of Abraham Lincoln, it was said: " Peace eternal in a nation united." No nation could be half slave and half free. A few years ago, President Truman suggested a change in the inscription in the peace monument at Gettysburg to read, instead: " Peace eternal in a world united." The world cannot be united when three-fourths of mankind live in conditions of want and the remaining one-fourth want more than they already have.

Fundamental education as originally used by UNESCO is a new name for an old idea, in the sense that it aims to provide a " common ground for all peoples " so that the whole of mankind may live together in peace — free from want, poverty, ignorance, fear, exploitation and discrimination. It is a movement, a democratic movement, to free man from himself. Both the illiterates of the East and the highly literates of the West need fundamental education — the former to improve their health and economic well-being through literacy, the latter to improve their attitudes in order to free themselves from prejudice, selfishness and other complexes. The last world wars, if not all wars in the past, were not caused by illiterates, but by so-called leaders of thought and culture who talked peace, but meant war and got it.

The problem of fundamental education is two-fold: First, for the vast majority of peoples living in the dark ages in Asia, Africa, South America and Southern Europe — one and a half billion of them — education for economic self-sufficiency, for health, and for functional literacy; and second, for the rest of mankind, educational re-orientation or, more specifically, education for love of all men and for international understanding and peace.

Pedro T. Orata, " What Is Fundamental Education? " *Educational Theory*, 3:276–280, July, 1953. Reprinted by permission.

Education for better living. Fundamental education may, then, be defined briefly as education for better living. With this warning, however, that better living for the under-developed and under-privileged groups will not be possible without a simultaneous re-direction of education in the more privileged countries. Unless improvement takes place in these countries which supply the initial leadership for the first group, their effectiveness as leaders will be minimized, indeed jeopardized and even neutralized by the lack of confidence in them by those whom they are supposed to guide. Until such time, the leading nations could be told: " Physician, heal thyself." In some countries there is a widespread suspicion that technical assistance from whatever source is a new form of exploitation. Unless evidence is shown to the contrary, there will always be a fear of this on the part of the assisted group.

Literacy plus. After centuries of fumbling in formal education — meaning education for literacy and the acquisition of knowledge of subject matter — leading educators throughout the world are coming to realize that what the learner needs is more than a command of the three R's — reading, 'riting and 'rithmetic — and even the fourth R — religion — but command of living in a world which is changing and shrinking so fast. This includes the command of a certain amount and type of subject matter — that which is pertinent to the problems of living — but not the whole of it. To live abundantly and safely one must profit from the experience of the race, recorded in archives and in books and other literature. To be able to learn and apply technical skills in industry and agriculture, one must be able to understand and interpret written instructions, maps, graphs, and the like. One must learn to read with understanding and to be able to evaluate reading matter.

As Dr. Frank C. Lauback says, illiterate people " are disqualified for skilled labour because they cannot take notes of what they hear, neither can they refer to printed sources. They must depend upon what they hear or see for themselves. They cannot even understand the purposes of pictures or diagrams unless they can read the explanations." He continues: [1]

Technical industries are nearly impossible unless workers can read instructions and blueprints. Technological progress in every country depends first upon the ability of the people to read. Illiterates must engage nearly entirely in unskilled or semi-skilled occupations and so are unable to earn high wages. The average wage of illiterates in lower India was given by Indian leaders as five cents a day. In the tea fields in Java it was quoted at seven cents a day. This probably fairly well represents the average wage of illiterates the world over. Millions get no wage, only food and a little clothing. They are virtual slaves.

[1] Frank C. Lauback. "Adult Literacy as a Means of Social Reorganization." A paper submitted to the Preparatory Fundamental Education Commission of UNESCO, 1946. P. 1. (Mimeographed)

But literacy is not enough. Skill in reading, like all skills, is only a means to an end. Time and again, it has been shown that literacy without competence is useless, and without character, often dangerous. In many countries today there are thousands upon thousands of high-school and college graduates who are good only for certain types of white-collar jobs, which are over-crowded. Their literacy does them no good, in fact, it tends to unfit them for life in their community. Many of them, having acquired from their books high standards of wishful living and failing to attain those standards, contrive all kinds of ways — fair or foul — to get cash quickly.

To attain better living standards one must learn not only to read, but also to improve one's health, earn more to sustain self and family, provide better housing facilities, enjoy life and work with others, conserve and use wisely one's resources and exercise intelligence.

The conditions of living among three-fourths of the world inhabitants are often lacking in those factors that would enable them to do this. In many places life is so reduced to bare subsistence level that it is impossible to make it worth while. Children die prematurely, pestilence and famine strike, disease is rampant, food is insufficient and inadequate, superstition rules and the people live constantly in fear and want. And yet it often happens that poverty and disease are worst where nature seems kindest, and that where it seems harsh the people are progressive and enlightened.

The paradox of ignorance. One of the greatest ironies of our time is the fact that we were saved in the last two world wars by ignorance. Had Germany and Japan possessed the atomic bomb before the Allies did, the outcome of the last conflict might have been different. Now that Russia has it, we are not certain even that we can survive or what kind of life we are going to live, if we do. If the next war is going to be the dog fight that the previous wars were, there will be little left of what we call Western civilization. Mankind will not likely be entirely wiped out, but little will be left of Europe and America, all because of science misapplied, meaning without ethical and moral principles to stand on. We have always naively accepted the platitude that truth will make us free, only to find out rather late that whether it does or not depends upon who has it and how it is used.

This is no brief for ignorance, but the time is coming when ignorance is bliss and is twice blessed — it blesseth those that have it and those that have it not. It is true that a little knowledge is a dangerous thing. It may be added that the more the knowledge which is only half-baked, the greater the danger. Besides, if we can believe the Director-General of the World Health Organization that it takes only seven ounces of a known substance and a favourable wind to kill all the people of this planet, what a blessing it would be if we did not know that substance at all. Knowing is no insurance against misapplication which is far more dangerous than ignorance.

Does this mean that we would stop educating? Probably not — but it means educating differently and for different ends. For one thing, we must disabuse ourselves of the still prevailing notion that education is synonymous with the imparting of information, that literacy is salvation necessarily, but that it is a good tool depending upon the use made of it. This means that we should no longer teach boys and girls and men and women merely to read, write and do their sums, without relating these skills during the learning period to desirable ends to be achieved. This means that geography, history, civics and economics should be taught, not as subjects, but as disciplines and tools for developing a way of life which will make for co-operation and understanding among peoples of all races and national origins. This means that science — chemistry, physics and mathematics — should be taught alongside ethics and morality. This means that the technological subjects — engineering, agriculture, architecture — should be made to fit in with a social pattern that will unify instead of divide the populations of the earth.

In brief, the present conception of literacy, as if it were a miracle that will free people from ignorance, poverty and disease, will have to be re-examined and revised. The mass literacy movement in many parts of the world needs to have a sense of direction that will lead to the ideal of inter-dependence among men and nations and not to the strengthening of jingoistic nationalism and shallow patriotism. Nothing can enslave people to false leaders and gods easier than the ability to read material in print that is false and narrow. Nothing is a more effective instrument of demagoguery than the ability to speak and write convincingly. The more literate a person is, if he is without moral character, the more dangerous he is to society. The more he knows, if he is incompetent, and unwilling to translate what he knows to appropriate action, the more is he a parasite or can become so to his illiterate relatives and to society. A fool that is also "wise" is a greater menace than a plain ignoramus.

Literacy, competence, character. To repeat, this is no brief for ignorance. The one billion and a half illiterates in the under-developed areas must be assisted to lift themselves up from their present condition of ignorance, poverty and disease. I maintain, however, that mere literacy — unaccompanied in the process of its acquisition by training to learn to be understanding and critical of what they are made to read — is no way to the salvation of these people. And, unless reading leads to or is the outcome of some useful activity that will enable the learners to improve the conditions of their living, it will not help them very much. Three weeks, three months or even three years is too short a period to accomplish these objectives. The fact of the matter is that really good education, particularly fundamental education, requires more careful planning in relation to objectives, more time to do it, better guidance and supervision, better prepared teachers, and more complicated procedures than is claimed by persons who may be efficient administrators, but who do not always see the forest for the trees. In our hurry to achieve results, let us not cause the adult illiterates in under-developed countries merely to learn to read and in that way give them only the veneer of education without its real substance — functional knowledge, competence and character.

Fundamental education for all. In this sense, as used by UNESCO, fundamental education — a "common ground for all peoples" — has to do with the entire human race. A world half with and the other half without fundamental education cannot be united, for they lack the "common ground" that should bind them together, consisting of those moral and spiritual qualities and the economic and physical stability that alone will enable them to survive and progress together.

Fundamental education is democratic education at its best, beginning with those people who do not have any kind of education and continuing with those who have much formal training who are physically well-built and highly developed intellectually but who live with frustrated hopes and jittery existence, always wanting more of the world's goods but obtaining less and less satisfaction and enjoyment from living.

In this wider sense, fundamental education is orientation in right living. It is a kind of education which gives one a sound philosophy of life, the competence and training necessary to live it, and the character and courage to let and help others live on the basis of true equality. Such an education should combine the best elements of Eastern culture as exemplified in Christ, Confucius and Buddha, and those of the West as embodied in scientific and technological discoveries and inventions and in political and legal philosophies and administration, which have made Europe and America the leaders of modern society. This blending of East and West alone will make possible a unified and stable world.

What are the elements of these cultures the blending of which will make possible "the intellectual and moral solidarity of mankind"? What did Christ, Confucius and Buddha teach which we have not learned? The simple command "Do unto others as thou wouldst be done by," which forms the core of the teaching of Christ, should be followed today more than ever before when the have's want more and the have-not's get less and less of the materials of life. The teachings of Confucius on "filial piety" are needed nowadays to strengthen home and family life, which is being torn asunder by divorce and illegitimacy. Buddha's ideal of self-abnegation if applied should put an end to exploitation and promote greater satisfaction in living in all people, who will find that the greatest happiness in life is in the attainment of things that money cannot buy — service to one's fellow men and self-sacrifice.

The wise men of the East have taught us that we cannot live by bread alone. But our Western brothers have shown that we cannot live without bread either. The spirit must have life just as necessarily as life must have spirit. The two elements must be united if the world is to be saved from poverty, ignorance, fear and disease on one hand, and exploitation and prejudice on the other. Man must learn to control nature (East) and himself (West), or nature (atomic bomb and biological warfare) will put an end to man. This is no longer a threat. The atom bomb can be considered obsolete as a weapon of war. Biologists have discovered something more powerful than physicists have invented, which will make armies superfluous, and planes and navies of no avail. What the world needs most urgently today is a type of education and leadership which will teach us how to make proper use of atomic energy and all other scientific discoveries and inventions — for the good of man and not for his destruction.

Returning to the original question raised in this paper: " What is fundamental education? " the answer which I propose is: " It is education in *right* and *efficient* living."

Who needs this kind of education? My answer is: Who doesn't?

CHAPTER FOUR BIBLIOGRAPHY

AMERICAN ASSOCIATION OF SCHOOL ADMINISTRATORS, *Educational Administration in a Changing Community*. Washington: The Association, 1959.

> The blending of responsibility for public education between the nation, region and local community is illustrated. The responsibilities and controls exercised by governments and groups is the subject of chapter four.

HALES, DAWSON, *Federal Control of Public Education*. New York: Columbia University Press, 1954.

> A review of local and federal participation in education during specific periods of time. The arguments concerning both are reviewed and a conclusion for a rational policy for today is presented. Contains a good bibliography.

HANNA, PAUL R., " Design for a National Curriculum," *Nation's Schools*. 62:43–45, September, 1958.

> Hanna makes specific proposals for the formulation of a national curriculum by efforts of non-political and voluntary agencies, for evaluation of this idea, and for continuous study and revision of such a curriculum. He feels that the curriculum should incorporate up-to-date national needs but does not favor federal control.

HUXLEY, JULIAN, *UNESCO: Its Purpose and Its Philosophy*. Washington: Public Affairs Press, 1948.

> This brief account of the aims of the United Nations Educational, Scientific, and Cultural Organization reflects Huxley's regard for " scientific humanism." He argues that the highest product of evolution to date is " the well-developed individual." This provides the support for the democratic principle of the dignity of man to which UNESCO is committed.

KNAPP, ROYCE H., *American Regionalism and Social Education*. Cambridge: Harvard University Press, 1947.

> Recognizing many problems as being of importance to a group of states which form a geographic region, this study attempts to formulate recommendations for the social studies curriculum which will promote under-

standing and cooperation for solving them on a regional basis. The study is of the New England region.

LIEBERMAN, MYRON, "Four Myths Cripple Our Schools," *Nation.* 188:179–183, Feb. 2, 1959.

Lieberman makes a blunt assault on the idea that local control of education is good for the education of our people. He supports his view by attacking " four myths " which he believes Americans have uncritically accepted as fundamental in their support of local control of education.

NATIONAL SOCIETY FOR THE STUDY OF EDUCATION, *Community Education, Principles and Practices from World Wide Experience.* Chicago: The Society, 1959.

This volume deals with the topic of community education in an international setting. Aspects of several current programs of international educational endeavors are described and evaluated.

TUNNARD, CHRISTOPHER, " America's Super Cities," *Harper's Magazine.* 217:59–65. August, 1958.

The great sprawling urban regions which contain the greatest numbers of our people are described. This description is of value particularly as a stimulant to further thinking concerning the proper locus of responsibility for education in our society, the population of which is moving frequently, and becoming increasingly concentrated and interdependent.

WARING, THOMAS R., " The Southern Case Against Desegregation." *Harper's.* 212:39–45. January, 1956.

The editor of the Charleston, South Carolina, *News and Courier* presents an outspoken defense of segregation, particularly in the schools. He warns the Northern reader that " he may be infuriated long before he reaches the end of the article."

5

Democracy as a Way of Life

Democracy is often equated solely with political theory. The term *democracy* as used in this chapter will refer to a philosophy — a way of life. As has been noted previously, democracy in this respect carries with it implications for all realms of human activity — economic, political, religious, intellectual, and social. Thus, it is a frame of reference as well as a process or way of living. It is more than a formalized school of philosophy with a distinctive metaphysics, epistemology, logic, and axiology. If it is to be worthy of loyalty it must be consistent, inclusive, achievable, and practical.

The question may now be asked: what are the elements of democracy as a philosophic principle? Probably the most essential elements are respect for the dignity and worth of each individual, social sensitivity, devotion to equality of opportunity, and reliance on the free play of intelligence. Each individual, regardless of political affiliation, economic status, creed, nationality, race or social class, has integrity and value, and has the right to expect treatment which reflects this integrity and value. He is not merely a man, but a human being with tremendous potentiality. He has the right to realize his maximum potentiality as long as his development does not prevent other individuals from similarly realizing theirs. Thus, he must continually try to understand other human beings, to respect and be sensitive to their interests alongside his own. He ought not to step on another individual in order to advance his own well-being. He must guide his actions by the Golden Rule and Kant's practical imperative: " So act as to treat humanity, whether in thine own person or in that of any other, in every case as an end withal, never as a means only." [1] His actions and decisions must always take into account their anticipated effect upon others. He must realize that no action is entirely personal, but always has an effect upon his neighbors, whether in close proximity or separated by oceans.

Since *all* the people of the world have dignity and worth, social sensitivity requires that our area of concern must be ever widening, that our thoughts and actions must not be judged good or bad in themselves, but only in reference to their effects upon all concerned. Social sensitivity thus becomes a corollary to the principles of the integrity of each individual. Similarly, democracy does not imply that each individual is equal or identical in ability and talents, but it does recognize the principle that all persons should have equal opportunity to promote their abilities and talents. This is particularly important at a time when costs for education are mounting and an increasing number of children need formal education. It is imperative that our children have the opportunity to continue their education as long as they will profit therefrom.

Finally, democracy as a way of life rests upon the faith that human beings have the ability to promote the greatest welfare for all through group action. If we feel that one individual or a small group must do the thinking or make the fundamental decisions for all the people, we have lost faith in the

[1] Immanuel Kant, *Theory of Ethics* (trans. Abbott: 4th ed.), p. 47.

free play of human intelligence. Whenever this occurs, human worth has become a relative term in the worst sense, and some people are being judged to have more value than others, rather than different worth from others. In such situations, certain individuals, due to birth, wealth, social status, religious position, or intellectual ability, are judged to have more value than others and are accorded special status. It is true that group action will sometimes result in failure, but history is replete with illustrations of the failures and errors of dictators, kings, experts, and status individuals. Democracy represents the historical conviction that as education develops the full capabilities of each human, and as each one becomes socially sensitive, the free play of human intelligence will justify itself. The history of civilization has not brought us to the stage where this conviction is universally shared. Even now voices are heard challenging the proposition that democracy can work and that man has enough intelligence to govern himself through group action. Any social system must always be judged in comparison with available alternatives. The current alternatives to democracy are not acceptable, as they eventually lead to enslavement.

Two excerpts follow which deal with democracy as a philosophic principle. The first is written by Boyd H. Bode, a leading educational philosopher of the twentieth century, who spent much of his life working out the implications of democracy as a way of life. He saw a refinement of these implications as the fundamental problem facing America, and believed that the school's prime responsibility was to be the agent which put democracy into operation. As he viewed it, ". . . the school is peculiarly the institution in which democracy becomes conscious of itself." [2] The selection by Bode also

[2] Boyd H. Bode, *Democracy as a Way of Life,* New York: Macmillan Company, 1950, p. 95.

indicates his deep concern for the need of widening the concept of democracy.

In the other excerpt we find that Gordon C. Lee has broken down the principles of American democracy into a more extended list of elements than has just been enumerated. Other writers have used other classifications, but the reading presented by Lee will give the prospective and practicing teacher a framework within which he can understand the philosophic principle, build his own philosophy in harmony with the points mentioned, and develop practices for life and teaching which will give him consistency. It should also dispel the prevalent complaint that *democracy* cannot be defined, and is, therefore, an unacceptable term or an unachievable concept. It is not an immutable concept, but will continually be refined as men and women analyze democracy and practice it. This will be all the more marked in a civilization where flux and change are the only constants.

Despite the changing nature of society, there are some elements in civilization which have given us an historical basis for a democratic scheme of values. Equality, fraternity, and liberty have been either the implied or expressed goals of nearly all of those who have attempted to improve the lot of mankind individually or collectively. It has sometimes been stated that these words too, like democracy, have been used so loosely that they mean as many things as there are individuals using them. This chapter analyzes these concepts and presents readings showing their meaning. The reader should develop a workable definition of them and see how they are part of the basic fabric of democracy. He will ask himself some of the following questions: Are these concepts compatible? Or does freedom for one individual inhibit the freedom of another and thereby promote inequality? Is equality synonymous with sameness? Does it promote mediocrity? Do equality and fraternity limit freedom and stifle individuality? Does fraternity thwart those types of eccentricity which at times lead to great discoveries, inventions, or visionary theories, which later have great practical value to society? Does freedom lead to license and, eventually, to anarchy? Does freedom produce a type of individuality which is antithetical to social sensitivity and group action? Are freedom, equality, and fraternity merely idealistic terms which can never be realized in the practical world of the twentieth century?

Subsequent sections of this chapter deal with such issues as whether individualism and community can be reconciled in a democratic scheme of values, whether there is any authority or discipline in a democracy, whether such authority tends to become absolute, and whether experimental inquiry may be used as a basis for revising our democratic scheme of values. Solutions to these problems are not simple. However difficult it may be to resolve them,

we cannot avoid them or retreat from them.

Finally, the editors have also presented two important readings criticizing democracy. Although the editors are themselves committed to the democratic way of life, they are convinced that an informed person must be aware of the arguments raised here. Most probably one of the reasons we are too often unable to make a good defense of democracy is that we have taken too much for granted. The concept may be nebulous to us because we have heard it so often and have often seen only lip-service given to it. Frequently anything distasteful has been labeled " undemocratic " and everything pleasant " democratic." Thus through misuse and carelessness words can become vague and ambiguous. Not only must teachers clearly understand what is meant by democracy, but they must be able to interpret it to their students.

BOYD H. BODE
The democratic frame of reference

Whether a person acts as a citizen, or as a producer, or as a consumer, he is conscious of an overarching purpose, which provides new meanings and new incentives for what he is doing. In other words, it provides a comprehensive plan for the organization of both individual and collective conduct, which is essentially what is meant when we speak of a *way of life*. Such a way of life often has a surprising power in making life more meaningful and releasing latent energies. It is precisely the increment of meaning, with its concomitants of appreciations, which raises the routine life of human beings above that of the brutes. Life must be made meaningful if it is to become satisfying, if it is to serve as an outlet for our enthusiasms. It is no accident that the backbone of each of these movements is furnished by the enthusiasm of the young people to whom they make their appeal.

In terms of our present discussion the common element in communism and Hitlerism is that each provides its adherents with a distinctive way of life. Can the same be said of democracy? Rule by the majority is a method

From Boyd H. Bode, *Democracy as a Way of Life*, 1950, pp. 7–9, 39–50. Reprinted by permission of The Macmillan Company.

of settling conflicts of opinion; it does not provide opinions. When policies are needed for dealing with problems, the principle of majority rule gives no indication as to what kind of policies are needed. Even if we make the idea of democracy include the doctrine that men are " free and equal " we are not much better off. When are men " free " and when are they " equal "? If freedom means absence of restraint, then the demand for freedom means that there should be no legislation or control of any kind. If equality means that all differences among men should be ignored, then musicians may be put in charge of surgical operations and presidents may be chosen by drawing slips of paper out of a hat. Freedom must be achieved inside of a system of social control and not outside of it; and equality must mean the appropriate recognition of individual differences within the framework of social life. But what kind of social control and framework does this require? In other language, what is the distinctively democratic way of life? As compared with these other points of view, democracy is lacking in definiteness of purpose. It tends to substitute sentimentalities about freedom and equality and the brotherhood of man for a clear-cut program of action. . . .

In some way or other we must make our peace with the notion of " free and equal." It lies too near the heart of what we mean by democracy to be ignored or slurred over. As was said a moment ago, this phrase had a reasonably satisfactory meaning in its day. This meaning, unfortunately, is not adequate for us. Community life in its earlier form is on its way out. Moreover, there is room for the suspicion that it was really based on dictatorship — not of an autocrat, or of the proletariat, but of the community. There was freedom and equality, if you will, inside the basic pattern or way of life maintained by the particular community. But the pattern itself had a certain fixity or immutability, which characterizes dictatorships of whatever kind and which is not easily reconciled with the idea of a genuine democracy. How, then, did it happen, if our early democracy was founded on dictatorship, that this fact was so successfully kept out of sight? In our tradition of democracy there seems to be no recognition of any such thing. We hold that all men are created free and equal and that all are entitled to life, liberty and the pursuit of happiness; with no strings attached. In the ordinary dictatorship the mailed fist is constantly in evidence. In our own case we seem to have been unable to see it, even when it was thrust into our faces. In other words, we have succeeded in playing up one element in the situation and playing down the other so as to emerge with the conviction that our democracy is a complete antithesis to dictatorship.

This conviction is too much diluted with error to warrant the self-complacency which is exhibited by the average American, yet it contains an element of truth. Since there was no single pattern for belief and conduct to which all the people were required to conform, the idea of freedom and equality became dissociated from all connection with patterns and so was cultivated as an absolute value, even though it was not thus dissociated in fact. Moreover, the diversity of patterns created both the need and the disposition to accept something less than the rigid conformity which is ordinarily demanded by dictatorships. Consequently, there was a genuine difference in psychology. Lastly, the multiplicity of communities and the mobility of the American people tended to locate individuals in communities that were congenial to them, so that the restriction was scarcely felt. The limitation on belief and conduct was there, but its yoke was easy and its burden was light. By comparison it is only when diversities of belief are considerable that the demand for conformity to a common scheme of living is felt as an extraneous compulsion and an invasion of liberty. Moreover, a like-minded community does not ordinarily find it necessary to maintain special officials and special agencies to take care of occasional lapses from community standards. That is to say, the average citizen does not find himself constantly in the presence of the visible symbols of an external authority, as in the case of the ordinary dictatorship. In such circumstances the whole psychological quality of the situation is different from what it would otherwise be.

The standards for the conduct of ladies and gentlemen in the *ante bellum* South are a case in point. These standards were certainly rigid, and they could not be violated with impunity, even when good sense would have so decreed. Ladies had to faint, duels had to be fought, extravagant standards of hospitality had to be maintained. There was no easy escape from these standards; but what made their authority so final was the fact that the average person whom they concerned did not want to escape. They were bred into the bone, and social pressure was likely to have the inward assent of the person to whom it was applied. A tradition may be hidebound to almost any degree without necessarily creating a feeling of tyranny on the part of those who are victimized by it. Since the tradition belongs to the way of life that has been accepted, conformity to it and active assistance in maintaining it is experienced, not as domination, but as freedom. Like the atmosphere we breathe, it creates no feeling of pressure but a sense of liberation.

With this background we can easily understand both the fear of governmental interference and the curious insensitiveness, in this land of vaunted freedom, to acts of coercion and violence in the suppression of nonconformists. In a dim and unformulated way the community patterns were not regarded as limitations of personal freedom but as instrumentalities for achieving freedom. The essence of freedom lay, not in the lack of restraint, but in the character or quality of the restraint. A person became free by accepting the patterns and acting accordingly; by making restraint self-imposed and internal, instead of being a prescription by an external authority. Consequently, the violation of these patterns was not regarded as an assertion of personal freedom, but as an attack on the whole basis of freedom. To use a term that has been made familiar during recent years, such violation was deemed " subversive," and to tolerate it was regarded not as a virtue but as a vice.

This attitude has a certain undeniable logic. Philosophers tell us that a person is not free merely because there is no restraining influence to keep him from acting on any stray suggestion or impulse. As William James remarked, a baby is not free, but is owned and controlled by his environment. He becomes free in proportion as he can hold in abeyance his immediate reactions and modify them in the light of relevant considerations. A man who feels that he has been insulted, for example, may strike the offending person, or challenge him to a duel, or seek to avenge himself through business channels; or he may decide to ignore the insult, or even to turn the other cheek. In so far as the final action is the outcome of reflection, it is obviously an expression of his standards of value or his " way of life." The act is then a free act, in the only intelligible meaning of the word " free." But freedom is made possible by the fact that there is a " frame of reference " or " way of life " in terms of which the matter in hand can be judged. Otherwise there is nothing to go by and our reactions become random and blind. This helps us to understand the paradox that dictatorships claim to be roads to freedom. It also indicates why people are reluctant to give up old and familiar patterns. To revise basic patterns is no easy task. It is much more tempting to complain that we don't know what the world is coming to, and to regard innovators as persons who from ignorance or malice take a delight in disturbing the peace.

In brief, there is a world of difference between conformity to a standard because there is in the background the menace of a club and conformity because the thing to which we conform belongs to a frame of reference which we accept and use as a means for the organization of thought and conduct. In Bobby Burns' language:

> The fear o' hell's a hangman's whip
> To haud the wretch in order;
> But where ye feel your honour grip,
> Let that aye be your border.

An unsympathetic critic might reply that the difference is the difference between a wretch who is motivated by fear and a wretch who has been taught to kiss the rod. But it is more than that. We may concede without reservation that tradition and ignorance and thickheadedness may constitute a fearsome bondage. Nevertheless, we have here a clew as to how freedom may be acquired. If we start with the premise that our " frame of reference " or " way of life " furnishes the tools for the application of intelligence to conduct, then the problem of making conduct increasingly intelligent becomes the problem of escaping from the limitations which are imposed by our " way of life " the moment we insist or take for granted that this way of life must not be subjected to any change. The refusal of Charles I to accept any limitation of the divine right of kings; the obedience to orders by the Light Brigade, even though it was obvious that " someone had blundered "; the acceptance of the dictum that a man must not marry, in any circumstances, outside of his " class "; the insistence that " debts of honor " must be paid ahead of the debts owing to the butcher and the grocer; the obligation to carry on a senseless family feud; the resistance to economic changes because these are not in line with the " American System "; the refusal to pay any heed to the deliverances of science where these conflict with theological creed — all these are instances of an unquestioning, and sometimes even heroic, submission to a sacrosanct scheme of things when a wider sensitiveness to human values would seem to be more in accordance with good sense.

Even if this be conceded, however, we are not out of the woods. What constitutes proper sensitiveness to human values? Some guiding principle is needed. The extreme opposite to domination by a fixed scheme of things is blind revolt, the disposition to regard all change as inherently good, which is perhaps even less intelligent. How are we to differentiate between changes which are good and changes which are bad?

The issue can now be sharply drawn. If judgments of good and bad, of right and wrong, must be made in terms of an antecedent " frame of reference," in the sense of a fixed scheme or creed, then the principle of dictatorship is vindicated, and democracy is plausible only because its basic absolutism is kept from view. The only liberty that is then permitted is liberty within the law, as laid down by absolutism. On the other hand, if there is no absolute standard of judgment, then our judgments must be made in terms of participation in common interests, regardless of other considerations. Conduct on the part of communities or of individuals must be evaluated with reference to its effect on promoting common interests among men. Liberty grows as the area of common interests is widened. Democracy then becomes identified with this principle of relativity, as contrasted with the absolutism of dictatorships. There is no middle ground.

From the standpoint of democracy the fact that a community is a community of interests and purposes is the most important thing about it. This sharing of interests is the indispensable condition for achieving a level of development above that of the brutes. Eighteenth-century writers sometimes talked as though a life apart from the corrupting influences of our fellow men and directed entirely by the benign forces of " nature " would insure ideal human development. Sociologists tell us, however, that children who, through some quirk of circumstance, grow up without human companionship remain permanently on a subhuman level. As far as the development of capacity is concerned, any form of human association, no matter how degraded, is better than none. Such association inevitably means development of capacity, even if this development is lopsided or misdirected. Degradation occurs if certain possible forms of sharing are left unutilized, with the result that the corresponding capacities become atrophied. Habit and custom may prevent the development of shared interests, as among savages; the deliberate imposition of fixed credos may destroy what has already been achieved, as in the case of dictatorships of whatever kind. Any such imposition means that individual men and women are being used as a means to some extraneous end; that, in short, they are being started on the road toward degradation. The end that is set up may be the glory of God or the glory of race or the glory of empire or the glory of a tradition or what not; the final result is the same. No such end has any value except in so far as it increases our capacity for sharing in common concerns and thus contributes to human freedom. All creeds and social organizations are means to an end, and this end lies inside the process of living together and working together; it is not located on a far-off mountaintop created by an iridescent dream. The kingdom of heaven is within us, within the everyday lives of a toiling, sweating humanity. A democracy which fails to recognize this fact cannot hope to escape a certain degree of unconscious hypocrisy, of a holier-than-thou attitude toward other forms of social organization. It is at this point that the issue is joined. . . .

GORDON C. LEE
Abiding principles of American democracy

It has been said that democracy will die if it is ever conclusively defined. This must not deter us from striving to understand its meanings and its underlying values. Democracy is not tangible, not concrete, and certainly not stable in its meanings. Nonetheless, we must endeavor ceaselessly to capture its essence. For if a society's institutions must be built, tested, and judged in terms of the values which that society cherishes, those values must be constantly in the forefront. This study of American education takes as its basic premise, therefore, the conviction that the schools, indeed the entire educational process, are established and maintained ultimately to perpetuate, foster, and strengthen the basic principles of democracy. We cannot proceed on such a basis without an examination of the principles themselves.

The discussion which follows is an attempt to state and define those elements in the American value system which are essential, those principles by which we live and which condition and govern (or *should*) our every action, if we in truth accept the democratic ethic as our standard. What, then, are these principles and what do they mean? What are the essential ingredients of American democracy, within which American schools operate and which the schools exist to perfect and enhance? In all humility, twelve such elements are presented. They are conceived as mutually indis-

From Gordon C. Lee, *An Introduction to Education in Modern America,* revised edition, 1957, pp. 39–51. Reprinted by permission of Holt, Rinehart and Winston, Inc.

pensable, and no inference is intended to suggest that some are more important or more crucial than others.[1]

Cultural pluralism. Contemporary social anthropologists have suggested a term which admirably expresses one of the primary facets of American democracy. Noting, as we did earlier, the heterogeneous racial, national, and cultural origins of the American people, these social scientists see the United States as " culturally pluralistic." Whatever the American people are, it is because of the contributions of countless diverse cultural groups: Germans, English, Swedes, Chinese, Negroes, Jews, and many more. But cultural pluralism as a democratic principle is more than the statement of the fact; it refers more basically to the climate of opinion which *accepts and honors* these cultural tributaries. History records examples without number of the rejection by a national or racial group of the advantages of cultural exchange. In all such cases, even down to our own day, such unintelligent inhumanity has been the product of nondemocratic regimes. Conversely, therefore, one of the essential elements in the American democratic creed is the spirit of respect for and acceptance of the contributions of all cultures, races, nationalities, religions, *on their own merits.* Out of the blending and the reformulation of these culturally unique elements emerges a stronger, more virile, and more humane whole. This is democracy in America.

Respect for the dignity of the individual. An eminent student of the contemporary Russian scene tells us that the Soviet Union is democratic with regard to all cultures and undemocratic with regard to all people. He refers here to the fact that, in the Soviet Union, the central government affords considerable freedom for the expression of cultural uniqueness to the several member nations, allowing them to use the local language, enjoy local literature, art, music, and the like. At least externally, here is an example of cultural pluralism in operation. But the individual member of each cultural minority is regarded as of small consequence: his aims and aspirations, his likes and dislikes, his *individuality* are ignored. Within the relatively superficial framework of freedom to participate in the expression of certain harmless cultural patterns, the individual loses his identity completely. This, too, has been the general result with tyranny all through the ages.

Such a condition is the antithesis of democracy. Central to the democratic faith is respect for human personality and the dignity of the individual. It was to this that Jefferson addressed himself when he wrote of " Life, liberty, and the pursuit of happiness." And it was to this that Franklin Roosevelt and Winston Churchill were attending when they drafted the Atlantic Charter, with its concern that the individual should be enabled to live free from fear and want, free to express himself and worship as con-

[1] What follows is adapted in large part from a syllabus prepared for the basic course in Foundations of Education by the Division of Foundations of Education, Teachers College, Columbia University.

science and reason dictate. The individual human being has a right to live his own life, uncoerced and unoppressed, so long as he in turn does not imperil or impair the welfare and happiness of others, so long as he respects the rights of others to that to which he considers himself entitled. This, too, is essential to American democracy.

The pre-eminence of individual welfare. It must follow from the preceding that the welfare of the individual is a democratic society's primary concern. Again, for nondemocratic cultures in antiquity and in the mid-twentieth century, the welfare of the state or the monarchy or the party has been elevated while concern for individual well-being has been depressed, ignored, or indeed condemned as evil. Democracy in the United States, however, holds that the only justification for governments, states, social institutions of any description must ultimately be found in their effective contribution to *individual* welfare, happiness, and dignity. This means, of course, that the individual is superior to any agency created in his interest or for his service and that ultimately, again, the appropriate role of such institutions must be defined in terms of their relation to individuals. To cite but a single example: a man is accused of offense against the laws which society has enacted for its protection. It would be much more efficient, expeditious, and inexpensive if, when the court of original jurisdiction finds him guilty, sentence were immediately imposed. But the concern of a democracy for individual welfare allows for the right of appeal and retrial. The rights of the individual take precedence even over the institutions established to protect those rights. American democracy would be a very different thing were this element disavowed or denied.

Civil liberties. And what are these rights which democratic institutions are designed to guarantee, protect, and promote? Essentially, they are found most consummately expressed in the Bill of Rights, those first ten amendments to the Constitution the promise of which was a condition of ratification. Jefferson had described it as self-evident that " all men are created equal; that they are endowed by their Creator with certain unalienable rights. . . ." Of what do these rights consist, these liberties which we call civil because they accompany and are indispensable to the nature of citizenship itself?

All are declarations of freedom; freedom to think and express oneself without restriction save only as the laws of treason or libel constitute limitations; freedom to worship, or not to worship, without social or juridical interference of any kind; freedom to stand secure in the possession of property, protected by the requirement that " due process of law " be exercised; freedom from " unreasonable searches and seizures " and the guarantee of the right to receive just compensation for private property appropriated for public use; and the freedom which is implicit in the requirement of trial by jury. To these basic liberties proclaimed in the Bill of Rights have been added others: freedom from " involuntary servitude "; the right to vote, guaranteed against restrictions of race or sex; and the further guarantee that rights proclaimed in the federal constitution are equally the responsibility of the several states.

And these rights are "unalienable." They are beyond the power or province of governments, parties, courts, or legislatures to restrict or abridge. They may not be abrogated or denied even by popular majorities, save only as the extensively safeguarded amendment procedure provides. Only thus could they be in truth secure and only thus can a democracy exist. American democracy required such a principle.

Separation of church and state. From among the freedoms enumerated above, many would point to one as the linchpin of democracy in America. This one is the freedom of religious expression. The original settlements on these shores were in large measure the direct result of an absence of religious tolerance in Europe. The chief instruments of our beginnings as a nation — the Declaration of Independence, the Constitution, and the Bill of Rights — testify to an intense commitment to the proposition that (to use the memorable words of Madison) "religion, or the duty which we owe to our Creator, and the manner of discharging it, can be directed only by reason and conviction . . . according to the free dictates of conscience."

It was believed essential, therefore, that religion be freed from any dependence upon the support of the civil state, save as the state strove to uphold the principle of freedom itself. True spiritual independence was seen to be impossible of realization if churches were to be subject to the dictates or controls of the state. Equally, full freedom in the secular political sphere was felt to be jeopardized as particular churches or sects exercised controls over civil affairs. At the same time, as the number and variety of religious denominations in America multiplied ever more rapidly, it became obvious that the traditional alliance of the civil government with particular churches was incompatible with the idea of freedom for *all* forms of belief. The only possible position open to a state, in a society committed to complete freedom of religious expression and convinced that preferential treatment of certain faiths frustrated the achievement of that freedom, was absolute neutrality. The only means of maintaining that neutrality was to separate the churches from the state, to prohibit state interference in matters of religion, and to insist upon scrupulous regard for the essentially private, individualistic character of religious experience. If freedom of religion is indeed at the heart of the democratic ethic in the United States, then the principle of church-state separation is perhaps the pillar on which all our liberties rest.

Majority rule — minority rights. An earlier paragraph suggests that it is the majority in the final analysis which has the primary responsibility for the preservation of the civil rights. This is so in a democracy because there the majority rules; the majority has the power. Thus, as we have noted, it was a fear of the "tyranny of the majority" which motivated the urge for rights which are inalienable, for a judicial system with powers of appeal and review, for the doctrine of states' rights, for the principle of separation of powers or " checks and balances." These, which constitute restraints in the American system of government, operate to encourage if not demand that majority responsibility accompany majority power.

The majority rules, to be sure. The 51 percent can and often do elect a government against the opposition of the 49 percent. There is, inevitably, the danger that "King Numbers" will hold sway and that the verdict of the majority will be taken as synonymous with the popular will. But today's minority is likely to be tomorrow's majority, and both are equal before the law. Both are charged with responsibility for acting consistently with the *general* welfare in the context of the freedoms and rights which are the inalienable possession of all. Democracy could not exist otherwise.

Duty and privilege. We have spoken at some length of rights — can democracy subsist on rights alone? Carl Becker gives us the answer as he titles his noble essays on the American political philosophy *Freedom and Responsibility in the American Way of Life.* Freedom *and* responsibility — rights *and* duties. Clearly all that has been discussed so far implicitly assumes a component of individual responsibility. The rights are held to be inalienable, true enough. But the very fact means that the individual has a responsibility to conduct himself in such a way that the rights will in fact be honored, respected, and preserved.

We speak then of duty. The individual has a duty to participate actively and intelligently in the management of society's affairs. He has a duty to respect the civil liberties of others as he demands that they be respected for himself. His duty, nay, his privilege is to conduct his life — private, social, economic, political, or religious — in such fashion that the rights he respects are enhanced and made ever more meaningful. This privilege, accorded only to the select few in non-democratic systems, of sharing in the making of decisions and the formulation of policy in matters affecting the general welfare, is perhaps the highest of human functions. In a system dedicated to the improvement and enhancement of the free individual, the principle of responsibility is fundamental.

Human progress. The basic principles of American democracy were forged in the atmosphere of the Age of Reason, that period in the history of Western thought when science and philosophy seemed clearly to have established the priority of man over forces natural or supernatural. Central to the idealism which this seventeenth- and eighteenth-century " enlightenment " evoked was the conception that rational man, master of his own fate, was indeed a creature of potentially limitless perfectibility. Man, through the operation of his reason, had the power and the capacity to progress indefinitely — indeed, man could not withstand the inevitability, the inexorability of such progress. He and his institutions were destined for infinite perfection if only the human mind were allowed full freedom. Here was optimism of the highest order, especially when viewed in contrast to the fatalism of medieval Catholic theology or Reformation Protestant dogma, which had condemned man through the doctrine of original sin to eternal damnation.

The Declaration of Independence and the Constitution, then, were drafted by men who were the inheritors or apostles of the new status of human reason. Faith in mankind and in the inevitability of his perfection was the underlying premise for the promulgation of the doctrine of inalienable, natural rights. That faith required an increasing place for human reason in the management of temporal matters; its certain corollary was a government democratic in form and spirit.

There are those who find this dream totally irrelevant to the conduct of contemporary affairs. They tell us that recent history has conclusively proved that human progress is *not* inevitable and that to base a system of government or a philosophy of life upon any such outmoded concept is folly indeed. But democracy cannot shed its heritage so easily or so glibly. After more than a century and a half of experience it is perhaps legitimate to speak of the mellowing of the democratic ideal, in the sense of coming into closer contact with the facts of human existence. Democracy may not now represent commitment to the principle of inevitable human perfectibility. It is equally clearly *not* committed on the other hand to a disavowal of the *possibility* of human progress. As we noted at the outset of this discussion, democracy escapes exact definition precisely because of this quality of belief in change for the better. Democracy, dedicated as we have seen to the improvement of the conditions of human life and the enhancement of individual happiness, is never content with a status quo; it is constantly and inherently dissatisfied with conditions as they are. It seeks after progress because *it believes in progress*. Here, again, is evidence of the oppositeness of democratic and totalitarian attitudes, for the latter can survive only as circumstances grow ever more static. Democracy must advance or it ceases to be democracy. This too is of the essence of America.

Freedom of enterprise. We have noted our fundamental commitment to the dignity and welfare of the individual and have stressed our belief in the possibility of human progress. These principles are joined as attention is focused on still another central ingredient, perhaps best listed as freedom of enterprise. The underlying traditions of all cultures reflect certain social, political, and religious views; they also reflect subscription to some conception of economic life. For the United States, the economy, the business of making a living, has always been regarded as an area in which opportunity for individual initiative and creativity must be protected and encouraged. Perhaps in no other sphere has philosophical and political controversy been so acute, but the nation has never departed from the principle that, with due regard for the general welfare, freedom for economic endeavor is essential.

It is quite true that economic activity today is far more closely regulated, by government and by business itself, than in earlier times. This condition leads some to insist that true freedom of enterprise is no more, that it vanished with the laissez-faire theories and the " rugged individualism " of the nineteenth century. But it is well to remember that at no period in our history has the economy been totally free; we have always insisted upon some elements of control in the social interest. We have come to speak, with pride, of the American " mixed " economy, signifying an acceptance of and a belief in the operation, side by side, of private and public (that is, governmental) enterprise.

The fact remains, however, that the core of the American democratic tradition as applied to economic affairs is the belief in the freedom of the individual — merchant, manufacturer, farmer, or landlord — to conduct his business at the highest possible level of independence consistent with the general good. His status as an individual and his potential contribution to the social progress for which America stands are fully realized only as this freedom of enterprise is protected and promoted.

Peaceful change. The Age of Reason was revolutionary in the strongest sense of the term. With a few notable exceptions, such as Athenian democracy at certain periods, the kind of change or progress to which democracy is dedicated had always been accompanied previously by strife and bloodshed. Such movements were regarded by some as mutinies, by others as revolutions; to paraphrase Jawaharlal Nehru, the mutiny which succeeded was hailed as a revolution, while the revolution that failed was damned as a mutiny. So it had always been in Western history. But the men of the enlightenment demanded consideration for the power of the mind over the brute force of authority. The founders of the United States government, steeped in the new tradition, were the prime movers of a successful mutiny, a revolution. They were dedicated to the protection of human rights and the promotion of human happiness. The kind of society they sought to establish was committed to change, to progress, even of a revolutionary character, but it was also committed to the advancement of human well-being. Were the two forever irreconcilable? No! was the enlightenment's answer. Human progress *can* be achieved peacefully, if human reason is given full freedom to operate. Social institutions must be so organized as to encourage and guarantee that freedom.

The American government from its inception provided for what has very appropriately been called the " institutionalization of revolution." The Constitution recognizes the inevitability of change and provides for the orderly, nonviolent consummation of basic reorganization, indeed reconstitution of American institutions. Recognizing, as Jefferson had noted, that one of man's natural rights was the right to revolt against oppressive authority, the founders attempted to prevent such revolt from resulting in war and chaos. The fifth article of the Constitution, which outlines the procedures whereby the document may be amended, is the guarantee to the people that they shall have the last word, that with them rests the ultimate authority. But it charges the people with the responsibility for modifying basic institutions through *peaceful* means, through the respect of the rights and the dignity of all persons. *Peaceful* change — the appeal to reason, to intelligence, a government by persuasion rather than coercion. This principle, novel and unique as it may have been at the time of the adoption of the Constitution, (" A constitutional mode of altering the Constitution is, perhaps, what has never been known among mankind before." So spoke James Iredell in the North Carolina ratification convention in July 1788) has surely become at once a foundation stone and a buttress to the democratic way.

Free public education. What assurance is there that human reason is equal to the charge here laid upon it? The answer would seem to be, perhaps, that there is no incontestable assurance but that human reason is, to use Lincoln's words, " the last best hope of earth." Can a government which is based upon the assumption that human intelligence is capable of ordering human affairs neglect any measures which might increase the capacities and potentialities of that intelligence? The answer, it seems clear, is an unequivocal no.

" If a nation expects to be ignorant and free in a state of civilization," wrote Jefferson, " it expects what never was and what never will be." The entire history of the American people has demonstrated the unfailing national belief in the essentiality to democracy of education. Public education has been sponsored and maintained on the most extensive scale known to man. Private and parochial schools have been protected, occasionally subsidized, by a government expressing the popular conviction that education must be encouraged.

The present status of American public education has not been achieved without a struggle. But two fundamental conditions for education in the United States seem to have been conclusively established, conditions essential to education in and for democracy. Briefly stated these two essentials are: (1) there should be a publicly supported, publicly controlled system of schools, not under the authority of any private or special segment of society. This does not mean that nonpublic schools are incompatible with this ideal. On the contrary [an] inevitable corollary to the principles of cultural pluralism and freedom of expression is the right to establish schools for the effective representation of different points of view. But democracy also requires schools beyond the control of any fractional group or minority interest. (2) These public schools should be freely available. Free public education means education which is conducted by the public for its own service and must not be denied to anyone on account of its cost. Supported by general taxation, freed from the necessity of tuition charges, education is truly public when it is available to all, regardless of wealth, social position, geographical location, race, or other conditions. It is all too clear that subscription to the principle of free public education has not guaranteed equal educational opportunity. But with an educational program restricted to those who could afford to pay for it, democracy's obligations would be impossible of fulfillment. If integral to democracy are such elements as respect for human dignity and individual welfare, freedom of expression, and the reliance upon human intelligence, surely essential to their realization is a free public educational system.

Social mobility. All the foregoing may well be said to come together and to contribute to the implementation of still another essential element. The frontier conditions immediately began to weaken the hold of the class structure of society typical of European cultures. In the face of the boundless opportunities which awaited the diligent or the ambitious, the Old World criteria of birth, lineage, or previous social position steadily lost their influence. To be sure, on these shores as in Europe, a social structure was visible almost from the start. But (and it is a large and highly significant "but") there was not then nor is there now anything inherent in the system operating to rigidify, to establish enduring social stratification. Of course, the United States today can show plenty of examples of social disparity and class stratification, with wealth, property, political or economic influence, and occasionally talent or professional position serving as the criteria in place of blood and noble connections. These social levels are obvious and altogether real. Nevertheless, the collection of democratic principles rejects any suggestion that these levels become permanent and immutable. Freedom demands for everyone the opportunity to advance as far as his talents will permit. The crux of the matter here lies with the word "enduring." American democracy, as is inevitable for any culture, must live with and in a social framework. American democracy insists that the framework shall not become a strait jacket, a mold, a hierarchy which negates democracy. This too seems essential to the democratic way of life.

Two statements from the opening lines of this . . . [discussion] . . . require reiteration. That this recital of principles represents the ideal rather than the reality is, or should be, obvious to everyone. For each of the twelve essential ingredients, the gap between the actual and the ideal is extremely wide; indeed, there is sharp difference of opinion as to whether for some of them the gap is wider or narrower than it was in Washington's day. For each, a long list of examples could be presented to show how far we are from complete realization of the faith we preach and hold dear. Again we address those who, scoffingly or cynically, denounce the principles as meaningless. To this denunciation we cannot subscribe; as motive forces in our society (an international society now) these principles, these ideals are surely more powerful than ever. But we have far to go.

A reminder is entered, too, that these twelve essentials should not, indeed cannot, be considered independently. None of them operate in a vacuum; all must be viewed and analyzed in their relations to and their effects upon the others. That which we call American democracy is not merely a sort of sum of items added together. It is rather more like the basic themes of a great symphony, whose harmonies depend upon orchestration and whose beauties are the products of reverent and dedicated cooperation.

Finally, a word about the relation of all this to American education. It would be possible to present, following each of the twelve principles, illustrations without end of the role of the schools in making democracy work. As the real is farther from the ideal, so then is the job of the schools more clearly demonstrable and more vital. Surely, more than any other social institution, the schools of America, both public and private, have the obligation and the high privilege of striving to meet this challenge. As we examine philosophies of education, curricula, teaching methods, administrative procedures, and some of the countless cultural influences which impinge upon the work of the schools, it behooves us to consider them all in the light of the purposes, the ideals, the essential morality of democracy. There can be no more crucial call to Americans of the mid-twentieth century than this. . . .

SECTION 1. **Equality**

Liberty, equality, fraternity were the words to inspire the lower classes of France and to inflame the French Revolution. Although these words seemed clear enough to thousands who then and since have fought and died for the principles espoused, we have seen from the previous section that even the word *liberty* has different connotations to different people. What is equality? We use the word frequently, and most people would assure us they know what it means. Is it sameness? When we think of equality of humans, we immediately recognize that individuals differ as to size, shape, abilities, and also potentialities. What then do the writers mean when they use this term? Two of the selections which follow, written by Henry A. Myers and Nicholas Murray Butler, indicate somewhat divergent points of view. Does equality only refer to " equality under the law," or do human beings actually have equal worth? If they have equal worth, does this negate individuality or even liberty? If individuals have equal worth, does this promote mediocrity and retard progress and individual ability and initiative? Are these concepts compatible?

In order to answer some of these questions, we must go back to the basis of the principle of equality. Is this just a matter of definition, or is there actual evidence that equality exists? The answer lies in the underlying principle of this chapter — democracy as a way of life. If we accept the principle that each individual has integrity and worth, then in this respect there is equality. Then there is not only " equality under the law," but equality in the sense that each individual has a right to achieve his complete potential as long as he is a cooperative member of society. Different individuals will vary as to their potential, and they will have the freedom and liberty to excel, but there will be no incompatibility between liberty, equality, and fraternity.

There is only one alternative to equality, namely, inequality. If people are unequal, then some are superior to others, and the inferior individuals would be subservient to the superior persons. Though individuals may differ as to ability, size, and beauty, yet basically we must accept their equality as to their individual integrity and worth. A society based upon the principle of inequality inevitably leads to a class society with privileges for the few, whether it be based upon wealth, religion, race, nationality, or intellect. Totalitarianism flourishes in this environment.

The readings in this section are introduced by the *Universal Declaration of Human Rights* approved by the General Assembly of the United Nations at its plenary meeting on December 6, 1948. The principle of equality is clearly enunciated in this document subscribed to by the major nations of the world. The title of the charter indicates that it contains the basic principles to which most human beings subscribe.

Myers has analyzed the question of equality in his book, *Are Men Equal?* The following selection will help the reader to clarify the concept, see the alternatives to accepting inequality, and understand equality with its seeming limitations. Butler's article presents a more limited view of equality and raises some of the classical arguments in favor of inequality.

UNITED NATIONS GENERAL ASSEMBLY
Universal declaration of human rights

PREAMBLE

Whereas recognition of the inherent dignity and of the equal and inalienable rights of all members of the human family is the foundation of freedom, justice and peace in the world,

Whereas disregard and contempt for human rights have resulted in barbarous acts which have outraged the conscience of mankind, and the advent of a world in which human beings shall enjoy freedom of speech and belief and freedom from fear and want has been proclaimed as the highest aspiration of the common people,

Whereas it is essential, if man is not to be compelled to have recourse, as a last resort, to rebellion against tyranny and oppression, that human rights should be protected by the rule of law,

Whereas it is essential to promote the development of friendly relations between nations,

Whereas the peoples of the United Nations have in the Charter reaffirmed their faith in fundamental human rights, in the dignity and worth of the human person and in the equal rights of men and women and have determined to promote social progress and better standards of life in larger freedom,

Whereas Member States have pledged themselves to achieve, in cooperation with the United Nations, the promotion of universal respect for and observance of human rights and fundamental freedoms,

Whereas a common understanding of these rights and freedoms is of the greatest importance for the full realisation of this pledge,

Now therefore

United Nations, General Assembly, *Universal Declaration of Human Rights*, Document A/811 (16 December 1948).

THE GENERAL ASSEMBLY PROCLAIMS

This universal declaration of human rights as a common standard of achievement for all peoples and all nations, to the end that every individual and every organ of society, keeping this Declaration constantly in mind, shall strive by teaching and education to promote respect for these rights and freedoms and by progressive measures, national and international, to secure their universal and effective recognition and observance, both among the peoples of Member States themselves and among the peoples of territories under their jurisdiction.

Article 1 All human beings are born free and equal in dignity and rights. They are endowed with reason and conscience and should act towards one another in a spirit of brotherhood.

Article 2 Everyone is entitled to all the rights and freedoms set forth in this Declaration, without distinction of any kind, such as race, colour, sex, language, religion, political or other opinion, national or social origin, property, birth or other status. Furthermore, no distinction shall be made on the basis of the political, jurisdictional or international status of the country or territory to which a person belongs, whether it be independent, trust, non-self-governing or under any other limitation of sovereignty.

Article 3 Everyone has the right to life, liberty and security of person.

Article 4 No one shall be held in slavery or servitude; slavery and the slave trade shall be prohibited in all their forms.

Article 5 No one shall be subjected to torture or to cruel, inhuman or degrading treatment or punishment.

Article 6 Everyone has the right to recognition everywhere as a person before the law.

Article 7 All are equal before the law and are entitled without any discrimination to equal protection of the law. All are entitled to equal protection against any discrimination in violation of this Declaration and against any incitement to such discrimination.

Article 8 Everyone has the right to an effective remedy by the competent national tribunals for acts violating the fundamental rights granted him by the constitution or by law.

Article 9 No one shall be subjected to arbitrary arrest, detention or exile.

Article 10 Everyone is entitled in full equality to a fair and public hearing by an independent and impartial tribunal, in the determination of his rights and obligations and of any criminal charge against him.

Article 11 (1) Everyone charged with a penal offence has the right to be presumed innocent until proved guilty according to law in a public trial at which he has had all the guarantees necessary for his defence.

(2) No one shall be held guilty of any penal offence on account of any act or omission which did not constitute a penal offence, under national or international law, at the time when it was committed. Nor shall a heavier penalty be imposed than the one that was applicable at the time the penal offence was committed.

Article 12 No one shall be subjected to arbitrary interference with his privacy, family, home or correspondence, nor to attacks upon his honour and reputation. Everyone has the right to the protection of the law against such interference or attacks.

Article 13 (1) Everyone has the right to freedom of movement and residence within the borders of each state.

(2) Everyone has the right to leave any country, including his own, and return to his country.

Article 14 (1) Everyone has the right to seek and to enjoy in other countries asylum from persecution.

(2) This right may not be invoked in the case of prosecutions genuinely arising from non-political crimes or from acts contrary to the purposes and principles of the United Nations.

Article 15 (1) Everyone has the right to a nationality.

(2) No one shall be arbitrarily deprived of his nationality nor denied the right to change his nationality.

Article 16 (1) Men and women of full age, without any limitation due to race, nationality or religion, have the right to marry and to found a family. They are entitled to equal rights as to marriage, during marriage and at its dissolution.

(2) Marriage shall be entered into only with the free and full consent of the intending spouses.

(3) The family is the natural and fundamental group unit of society and is entitled to protection by society and the State.

Article 17 (1) Everyone has the right to own property alone as well as in association with others.

(2) No one shall be arbitrarily deprived of his property.

Article 18 Everyone has the right to freedom of thought, conscience and religion; this right includes freedom to change his religion or belief, and freedom, either alone or in community with others and in public or private, to manifest his religion or belief in teaching, practice, worship and observance.

Article 19 Everyone has the right to freedom of opinion and expression; this right includes freedom to hold opinions without interference and to seek, receive and impart information and ideas through any media and regardless of frontiers.

Article 20 (1) Everyone has the right to freedom of peaceful assembly and association.

(2) No one may be compelled to belong to an association.

Article 21 (1) Everyone has the right to take part in the government of his country, directly or through freely chosen representatives.

(2) Everyone has the right of equal access to public service in his country.

(3) The will of the people shall be the basis of the authority of government; this will shall be expressed in periodic and genuine elections which

shall be by universal and equal suffrage and shall be held by secret vote or by equivalent free voting procedures.

Article 22 Everyone, as a member of society, has the right to social security and is entitled to realisation, through national effort and international co-operation and in accordance with the organisation and resources of each State, of the economic, social and cultural rights indispensable for his dignity and the free development of his personality.

Article 23 (1) Everyone has the right to work, to free choice of employment, to just and favourable conditions of work and to protection against unemployment.

(2) Everyone, without any discrimination, has the right to equal pay for equal work.

(3) Everyone who works has the right to just and favourable remuneration insuring for himself and his family an existence worthy of human dignity, and supplemented, if necessary, by other means of social protection.

(4) Everyone has the right to form and to join trade unions for the protection of his interests.

Article 24 Everyone has the right to rest and leisure, including reasonable limitation of working hours and periodic holidays with pay.

Article 25 (1) Everyone has the right to a standard of living adequate for the health and well-being of himself and of his family, including food, clothing, housing and medical care and necessary social services, and the right to security in the event of unemployment, sickness, disability, widowhood, old age or other lack of livelihood in circumstances beyond his control.

(2) Motherhood and childhood are entitled to special care and assistance. All children, whether born in or out of wedlock, shall enjoy the same social protection.

Article 26 (1) Everyone has the right to education. Education shall be free, at least in the elementary and fundamental stages. Elementary education shall be compulsory. Technical and professional education shall be made generally available and higher education shall be equally accessible to all on the basis of merit.

(2) Education shall be directed to the full development of the human personality and to the strengthening of respect for human rights and fundamental freedoms. It shall promote understanding, tolerance and friendship among all nations, racial or religious groups, and shall further the activities of the United Nations for the maintenance of peace.

(3) Parents have a prior right to choose the kind of education that shall be given to their children.

Article 27 (1) Everyone has the right freely to participate in the cultural life of the community, to enjoy the arts and to share in scientific advancement and its benefits.

(2) Everyone has the right to the protection of the moral and material

interests resulting from any scientific, literary or artistic production of which he is the author.

Article 28 Everyone is entitled to a social and international order in which the rights and freedoms set forth in this Declaration can be fully realised.

Article 29 (1) Everyone has duties to the community in which alone the free and full development of his personality is possible.

(2) In the exercise of his rights and freedoms, everyone shall be subject only to such limitations as are determined by law solely for the purpose of securing due recognition and respect for the rights and freedoms of others and of meeting the just requirements of morality, public order and the general welfare in a democratic society.

(3) These rights and freedoms may in no case be exercised contrary to the purposes and principles of the United Nations.

Article 30 Nothing in this Declaration may be interpreted as implying for any State, group or person any right to engage in any activity or to perform any act aimed at the destruction of any of the rights and freedoms set forth herein.

HENRY A. MYERS
Are men equal?

Are men in fact equal? In any sense of the word which leaves out the question of final worth, they are not. If we measure men with the eye, we find a variety of sizes, shapes, and colors; these are apparent at a glance, and closer inspection reveals variations within variations and differences upon differences. If we set men to lifting weights or performing any feat of strength, the results are the same; a dead heat between two is rare, among three almost impossible. Set them at a task, and if we are patient, we shall see them drop out one by one; if the goal is far enough away, it is almost inevitable that at some point only one will remain. Measure their thinking by any known method; at once we find a great range in ability. If we stop with a single test, many may reach a given score, but if we persist, in time we may be able to assign to each his proper standing, which will be higher or lower than that of any of his fellows. Finally, if we choose a virtue and could devise some cunning scale of temptation and resistance, we should, judging by all that we know of human nature, find the same range of differences among our fellows. Physically, mentally, and morally, men are not equal.

Since life is always weighing men against each other in every possible manner, these results are known to every one; they are the basis of the

From Henry A. Myers, *Are Men Equal?* 1945, pp. 17–24, 153–163. Reprinted by permission of G. P. Putnam's Sons.

doctrine of true or natural superiority, which is almost always presented, or appealed to, as an obvious fact. Yet probably no man has ever lived who has not at some time or other discovered meaning in the idea of equality. This likelihood is not so much at odds with the other facts of experience as it may seem at first to be. The shortcoming of measurement is that it never settles the question of ultimate worth. It is hard to put a man in his place with a tape measure. Weigh him and find him wanting: he will insist that others are no better than he. Bigger, stronger, cleverer, more determined they may be; better they are not. Our fellow, by measurement small in one way or another, simply rejects the standards used against him. Without knowledge of philosophical terms, he denies their validity, as easily as a baby breathes or cries without words to describe its actions.

If a man finds measurement used to assign privilege to another and privation to himself, he at once doubts the quality measured as a proper standard. According to the conventions of his time and place, he may find it easy to reject some standards, hard to reject others. Any American will hoot if his worth is measured by the number of his known ancestors; he will very likely resist the claims of wealth to distinction. He is awed by intelligence tests and quails before moral judgments, but if they are used to drive him into a corner, he will at last turn against the kind of intelligence or virtue which he lacks.

Take any man, anywhere, any time, who in spite of all the facts of measurement says that he is as good as others — what does he mean? He means, most certainly, that the quality which has been measured is not the standard by which his place in society should be determined. He means that the immensely complex relations of men to each other should not be determined by a standard which puts him at a disadvantage. He cannot deny the obvious facts of measurement; he can see for himself where he stands. He denies, however, that this particular standing should serve as the price tag of his final worth.

We have been considering a man who, in some test, finds himself nearer the bottom than the top. If all men were losers, or if all humbly gave thought daily to the number of standards which might be used against them, faith in equality would everywhere prevail. But there are winners as well as losers, and most winners are satisfied with the doctrine of inequality, particularly if the standard by which they have been judged brings with it honors and privileges.

It is easy to be broad-minded about other men's possessions. It is easy for the learned man to see the social injustice which brings special privileges to wealth. He has no money, and he is sure the rich man is no better than he. Reflecting on the evils of plutocracy, he dreams of a time when philosophers shall be kings, when the rulers of men shall prove themselves fit by the particular test for intelligence which he has himself devised. His dreams are undisturbed by the thought that the intelligence required to make a king may be only craft, a skill no more suitable to determine final worth than the craft required to make money. As an intellectual he is a man of knowledge, who hungers for more; he naturally ascribes to the learned all those virtues which the man who has a little money and longs for more finds, without fail, in the wealthy.

Here we have the central problem of society. No man wishes to have his place determined by a quality which he lacks or by a kind of activity in which he does not excel. On the other hand, too many will fight for a social order in which men are placed by the skill in which they themselves are found superior. No wonder both equality and inequality have been presented as obvious facts.

II

Societies have been organized by many standards of inequality. In simple societies the powerful defend, as the true order of nature, the standard — birth, warlike skill, wealth, morality, or wiliness — which is their basis for the relations of men. In complex societies, founded on an interrelated and ever-changing constellation of superiorities, they defend a more abstract and generalized notion of inequality. The order of nature, they may say, can be described as the survival of the fittest. Those who agree, we may be sure, possess some skill which makes them powerful in society; they are the fit who survive. Thus the powerful become lovers of " natural law." They can view the dispossessed as they shift for themselves with the calm interest of the scientist who inspects an anthill, and they may even come to view the sterilization and " liquidation " of the unfit — the criminal, feebleminded, and infirm who have failed in the Great Test — as procedures even more in harmony with nature's laws. These are, after all, the culls in life's basket, stamped with disapproval by nature herself, and there are many ways, in societies organized on the principle of inequality, of exposing the unfit infant on the hillside.

And yet we must not suppose that the doctrine of inequality, which seems to spring from the smug assumption of men that their little skills are the final standards of value in the universe, leads only to adroitly concealed brutality. Inequality has a fatal beauty, which may be described in one word: *order*. Plato reveals this beauty in *The Republic* by unveiling the idea of justice in the form of perfect order, an ideal state with each man in his place. This same beauty, based on order, delights us in romantic accounts of the Old South, or in stories of the *ancienne noblesse*, or in novels based on medieval and feudal pomp and circumstance. As we drift in fancy from plantation to manor house, through castle halls and stately ceremonies, or feast with philosophers and artists, we are never concerned with the cost to men long dead of these witches' realms of beauty. In fancy we choose our own place, at the top, in the company of wit and wisdom, of brave knights and gentlemen and kings. The lowly whom we meet are quaint and humorous, loyal and devoted; above all, they know their place, and have never thought of challenging the standards which determine it.

And if they aspire to anything which might upset the perfect order of beauty, they do so, like Bottom in A *Midsummer Night's Dream*, only to provide that touch of incongruity which reminds us lightly that among superior beings, in a social order that cannot be threatened, a man out of place is a perfect ass.

Sentiment and romance are escapes from the realities of life, particularly from the fixed conditions of human experience. In life itself societies based on inequality have always had an undeniable charm for those who were able to contemplate their structural beauties from a favorable position, but this charm has had its fearful price — namely, that all members of the society, willingly or unwillingly, must accept the standard which has determined place. Only readers of romances may choose freely, without meeting the test.

No wonder, then, that conservatives have always viewed liberal ideas as a prelude to disorder and charged democratic societies with chaos and ugliness. The charge is hard to meet. Equality has a short history, and much of its own proper beauty is locked in the hearts of unborn artists; inequality stretches into the long past of enchantment. Henry Adams, learned historian, walking sedately through the great cathedrals of France, was able to choose his own company in the Middle Ages. He chose saints, philosophers, mystics, poets, architects, and kings. At home, in the hurly-burly of post-Civil War America, he could find no congenial place. We can understand the pessimism to which he finally succumbed. How could mediocrity and confusion have triumphed over structural beauty in society unless aided by the malignant will of the universe itself? So it is with past-minded lovers of beauty and order, who find the thread of human unity in a cathedral across the centuries only to lose it in the multiplicity of their own times.

III

When we see the close tie between beauty and order, and admit that much of our treasured literature and art comes to us from old orders of inequality, we must ask whether beauty or perfection of any kind could be found in a society based on the surly contention of losers that the winners are no better than they. Is it not true that the idea of equality is merely a device whereby underlings and failures contrive at times, by mere weight of numbers, to drag every kind of human excellence down into the swamp of mediocrity?

Enemies of equality have always found pleasure in pointing out that even its friends desert it when it touches upon their own interests. The sick equalitarian, they say, does not argue that one doctor is as good as another; he sends for the best. If a voter, he does not admit that one candidate is as good as another. If a father, he does not believe that another child can replace his own. And so in all his dealings with men: in judging his own interests, he has no recourse to the abstract idea of equality. With doctors, lawyers, merchants, and thieves, with sweethearts, wives, and children, he uses all possible degrees in the scale of good, better, and best. This is certainly true. If it were not, he would be guilty of an insane denial of all differences among men.

Although many a democrat has foolishly denied, with great damage to his cause, that there are important differences of ability among men, these differences exist in every kind of human activity, and in a marked degree. Some superior abilities are native; others are acquired. We now know that the same environment for all will not equalize them. A common diet will not produce men of equal strength or courage. No classroom or teacher can send forth a group of students all equally bright or diligent. The friend of equality cannot deny these facts; they are not matters of possible dispute.

Of all the men who, after losing in a test of skill, have denied the superiority of others, few have meant thus to deny their own specific and proved weakness, failure, or deficiency. They have meant to deny only that it should be used as a criterion for more than its worth — to brand them as altogether inferior to their fellows. Behind this denial lies the deep conviction that the social compact, whatever else it may involve, is between men, and not between warriors, or property owners, or doctors, or politicians. It is as a man that the equalitarian asks to be judged by those who fix his place in relation to others. In this sense only must his contention that the others are no better than he be understood, a contention which has nothing to do with sending for a doctor, or casting a vote, or indeed with duly respecting excellence in any skill.

He wishes to be judged as a man. Long ago Walt Whitman, pondering on this problem, exclaimed: " What is a man anyhow? What am I? What are you? " That is indeed the fundamental question in determining man's place in society. We enrich human life with dignity and meaning precisely in so far as we progress toward an answer. And when we begin to see others as we see ourselves, the dignity and meaning of life unite in a beauty proper to faith in equality.

Inequality is made beautiful only by the trick of concealing its cost: we condone it in the romantic past, in which, as readers, we freely place ourselves at the top of society; we enjoy it in the utopian dreams of the future, in which we share imaginatively the advantages of privilege and power; we may even find it beautiful in the present, if the present is for us a picture framed by otherworldliness.

Reassured by faith in a Creator who will sometime turn all inequalities into justice, Thomas Aquinas, saint and philosopher, can delight in the " admirable intellectual order " of the universe, which appeared to him as a strict hierarchy, a ladder of perfection extending step by step from the least rational of beings to the Great Intelligence. To men like Saint Francis of Assisi and Walt Whitman, who feel that equality is the final meaning of experience, the pride in reason which leads us through orders of superiority into the past and the future, and into eternity itself, is a poor, and even dangerous, substitute for beauty here and now. The world of Saint Francis is familial, not intellectual. Brothers, brothers, he urges men, remember your Father, and his love for you. And seeing the true center of all things both great and small, he does not stop with men. He preaches to the birds, addressing them as his sisters; he composes a chant of thankfulness for brother sun and sister moon, for brother wind and sister water, for brother fire and mother earth. This spirit can turn the present moment, in any century, into poetry and beauty. Under its spell Whitman gave the world two great chants on living and dying; one was inspired by the death of Abraham Lincoln, the other by a bird that flew out to sea, never to return. . . .

* * *

THE MEANING OF AMERICAN DEMOCRACY

The surrender of Cornwallis at Yorktown established the fact of American independence. Twenty years before the event few had considered it probable or even possible. Even Franklin had argued that the thirteen colonies would never unite against a mother nation " which 'tis well known they all love much more than they love one another." In the Revolution he had labored in many ways to discredit his own prophecy, but never more effectively than in the hours he devoted to improving Jefferson's first draft of the Declaration of Independence. In the stern conditions of war the Declaration had met Franklin's own favorite test for truth. It had worked. Its central proposition had united the colonists, in spite of their little love for one another, into a people strong enough to throw off the yoke of British rule. In return for these services the Declaration held a first mortgage on the new nation's future. Victory under the banner of Jefferson's proposition meant more than political independence: it gave the new American people a national existence forever identified with faith in human equality.

A nation established in the name of equality must keep the faith or lose its best excuse for being. After Yorktown the American people were free from political interference from abroad, but they were bound by the conditions of a faith which they had openly and proudly proclaimed. They were committed to a great experiment. Henceforth, under the eyes of the world, they must either live in a manner befitting equals or lose the national unity and identity which they had achieved. If in their hour of need they had hastily subscribed to a proposition which they did not fully understand, victory sentenced them to the hard school of experience, there to live with the proposition of equality until they learned its " lesson complete."

The lesson of equality begins, as we have seen, with the general agreement of men that in a just society the standing of every member is determined by his true worth. If we call the roll of the political thinkers whom we have considered — Aristotle, Plato, Cicero, Jefferson, Lincoln, Calhoun, Sumner, Hitler, and many others — we find that without exception all agree that social justice depends upon the correct appraisal of men. But if we ask what standard is to be used in appraising men, and call the roll again, we find the same thinkers divided into opposed camps, one proclaiming equality and the justice of equal rights, the other professing superiority and insisting upon the justice of " every man in his place."

The doctrine of superiority separates man from man by inspiring an anarchy of conflicting claims. The pretender to superiority always insists that the quality which he possesses and which others lack is the true standard of human worth. In ancient times every people claimed superiority over its neighbors. Only Greeks (according to Greeks) were fit for mastery; other peoples (called " barbarians " by the Greeks) were designed by nature for slavery. In modern times every nation has spokesmen who boast that its way of life is superior to the primitive and backward ways of foreign peoples. Plato and Aristotle found in reason and virtue new standards of superiority, but like all later philosophers of the school of inequality, each naïvely offered for universal acceptance the definitions of reason and virtue which best suited his own temperament and abilities. Calhoun found in the slaveholder's intensified love of his own liberty a natural proof of superiority. The list of standards of superiority is endless: the hard worker proposes to judge men by industrial virtue; the fighter uses his tribal military code; the white man claims supremacy over his little brown brother; the self-righteous call upon God to place the damned under the heels of the elect. Since every human being has some trait which no other man can match, the doctrine of superiority disintegrates into an anarchy of conflicting claims. If there were no alternative, if there were no truly just standard of human worth, men might well reconcile themselves to political atomism and to a state of warfare that could be interrupted only by the brief intervals when ruling tyrants were too strong to challenge.

Realizing that all men are possible contenders for the place at the top of the social order, the pretender to superiority always claims the backing of nature in his own bid for power. He takes advantage of the failure of most men to distinguish between facts and values. He first points to the natural differences among men which every sensible observer accepts as matters of fact. These differences, he argues, prove that the idea of human equality is inherently absurd. Once he has established the inherent absurdity of the idea of equality by falsely presenting it as an insane denial of facts, he quickly translates the admitted differences among men into superior and inferior values. Different men, he insists, are stamped by nature as higher or lower. One more step: higher men are better men, who have a just right to put every inferior in his place. The highest man? The pretender takes one last look at the reflection of his values in the clear pool of nature, and discovers his own image on the top rung of the ladder.

Although he insists that his standard of values is derived from nature, he is never willing to let nature take its course. His fear that nature may fail to place the " best " men on top exposes the fallacy in his doctrine. At times he is fearful of losing the power which he enjoys: the slaveholder dreaded the day when abolitionists would gain control of the Federal government; the economic libertarian feared that the American people might use their power to limit the rewards of industrial virtue. At other times he fears that he will never enjoy the power which he craves: the philosophers who dreamed of being kings were in fact regarded by many of their fellow Athenians as little better than rogues; the Hitler who dreamed of ruling mankind addressed his plans from prison to a defeated and almost powerless Germany. Obviously, if the " best " men may be treated as rogues, if superman may be imprisoned and the master nation defeated in battle, if slaveholders and captains of industry may lose their social and economic supremacy, the pretenders to superiority are not backed by nature. Their appeal to nature is merely a device whereby they seek to endow their personal preferences and prejudices with universality and authority. That every pretender honestly believes in his own superiority is a circumstance which adds little charm to a false and pernicious doctrine.

An anarchy of conflicting claims, each supported only by the self-esteem of individuals, can never provide society with a standard of values. Our hopes of finding a universally acceptable standard of human worth rest, therefore, on the arguments for equality.

1. *The proposition of equality is true because it is useful.* The contention that the truth of a proposition may be judged by its practical consequences has always favorably impressed the American mind. If Franklin did not invent the pragmatic view of knowledge, he at least presented its first principle vividly in the *Autobiography.* As a young man, he tells us, he argued so persuasively against revealed religion that he succeeded in perverting his friends Collins and Ralph. When he later discovered that his friends, freed from a sense of moral responsibility, had wronged him greatly without the least compunction, and when he remembered that Keith, another skeptic, had also injured him, and that he had himself, as a skeptic, treated Vernon and Miss Read badly, he judged the principles of skepticism by their apparent consequences. " I began to suspect," he says, " that this doctrine, tho' it might be true, was not very useful." William James added a second principle to pragmatism: if some ideas should be rejected because they lead to bad consequences, others should be accepted on faith alone if they are certain to lead to good consequences. " In such a case," James writes in *The Will to Believe,* " the part of wisdom as well as of courage is to *believe what is in the line of your needs,* for only by such belief is the need fulfilled." Justice Oliver Wendell Holmes stressed the praiseworthy side of the pragmatic attitude — its tolerant search for

wisdom through free trade in ideas — when he declared that "the best test of truth is the power of the thought to get itself accepted in the competition of the market."

Critics of pragmatism maintain that although the pragmatic view reveals the fundamentals of knowledge, it reveals them in the wrong order. Propositions, they say, are not true because they are useful, but useful because they are true. We need not take part in this controversy. Since we have other reasons for our faith, it is enough for us to know that the proposition of equality meets the pragmatic tests with flying colors.

To put the fundamental social problem in its simplest and most practical terms: how can men do business with one another unless they have common standards? Since even the simplest statements of fact require objective standards of reference, confusion would reign supreme in a community which lacked impersonal devices for telling time and for measuring and weighing objects. In such a community strong men would call a certain stone light, and their weaker companions would call it heavy; tall men would call an obstacle low, and their shorter neighbors would call it high; late risers would call a certain moment in the day early, and early risers would call it late. And if the community lacked even the simplest kind of monetary standard, a fair exchange of goods would be difficult, if not impossible.

Without standards men cannot live together. If the world is divided into isolated communities, however, the standards used by different peoples need not be universally acceptable. In a divided world every tribe or neighborhood may have its local system of measurement and evaluation. Every tribe may take the distance from the chief's nose to the tip of his middle finger as a unit of measurement, and it will matter little that other tribes have chiefs with longer or shorter arms. Every tribe may balance objects against the weight of the chief's fist, and it will matter little that other tribes have chiefs with heavier or lighter fists. Every neighborhood may tell time by sunrise, high noon, and sunset, untroubled by the fact that the sun rises earlier or later in other places. Each tribe may use some favorite food, like the yam, or a locally prized kind of wampum, as a standard of value in exchanging goods, untroubled by the fact that its standard might be considered worthless by faraway peoples.

If one man lived alone in the world, he could indeed be the measure of all things — of facts as well as of values. In a world inhabited by isolated peoples, each community may choose its own standards of measurement and value. But in a world in which traders and travelers go freely to and fro, standard time, standard weights and measures, and a standard system of exchange are necessities. Such a world will not be possible, however, until men agree upon the most important standard of all, upon the final standard of all human values, the standard to be used in appraising men and determining standard justice.

Since the idea of equality affects every aspect of our lives, it is perfectly intelligible on the level of ordinary business dealings. If a man approaches me, and tells me that all dollar bills are equal in every respect, or that the dollar bill in one of his hands is equal in every respect to the silver dollar in the other, I rightly conclude that his idea of equality is inherently absurd. But if he tells me that all dollar bills and all silver dollars are equal in value, I readily agree. His proposition is neither metaphysical nonsense nor a vague figure of speech; it is literally and precisely true. If we wish to do so, my friend with the dollars and I can go on to discuss human equality on the same sensible and utilitarian level. We understand that equality means equality of value, not equality in every respect. We can agree that in a society where all dollars are equal in value, men have laid the indispensable foundation for the free exchange of goods and services. And we can also agree that when all men have equal purchasing power in the market of human rights, the foundations of standard justice are secure.

History, regardless of the personal views of historians, reveals on endless pages the bad consequences of the doctrine of superiority. It stands exposed as the ruling principle of a divided world. In the divisive moral codes of tyrants, in the specious but equally dangerous pretensions of the self-righteous and the intellectually presumptuous, men can never find the formula for one world, the universally acceptable standard which is needed to establish standard justice. The anarchy of conflicting claims inspired by the doctrine of natural inequality and the sorrows of a world in which natural might is right are enough to turn all men toward the standard of equality. And men who have every reason to believe that good consequences will follow their acceptance of a principle can easily find the will to believe that the principle is true.

The history of the United States shows conclusively that the proposition of equality works. It unites men, making society possible. The history of mankind shows that inequality, injustice, and war are one and inseparable. The present moment in world affairs seems favorable to our dream of universal democracy. In presenting our national faith once again for consideration by other peoples, we address ourselves to men who say they are as eager as we to secure the blessings of liberty, tranquillity, and justice for all mankind. Once, we remember, thirteen suspicious and jealous colonies, separated from one another by distances and natural barriers more formidable at the time than any that now separate man from man, were fused into one nation and one people by a common faith in human equality. From the Declaration of 1776 to the ratification of the Constitution in 1789 — only thirteen years from the acceptance of a common standard of justice to the fact of union! The miracle can be repeated, and on a larger scale, if all men realize that agreement upon a common standard is foundational to agreement upon the mechanics of union.

The moment seems favorable, but our long experience as a nation warns us against false optimism. Many generations may live and die before all men accept as final the verdict of history that the standard justice of equal rights is the highest and only enduring form of expediency. Democrats must steel themselves to face bitter disappointments in the days of reaction which seem to follow every great war. Many who have learned the lesson of equality through suffering will forget it in the first carefree hour. Old pretenders to superiority who have saved themselves from the bad consequences of their doctrine by falsely professing conversion to democracy will throw off the mask as soon as their smaller tyrannies are no longer endangered by the greater tyrannies of Hitlerism, Fascism, and Bushido. But the possibility of failure, or of many failures, cannot free us from the moral responsibilities of a nation dedicated to the proposition that all men are equal. This is such a moment as comes only a few times to a nation in the course of its destiny. In a moment similarly charged with possibilities of success or failure George Washington stood firm, and we can do no better now than to remember his words and honor his example. " Let us raise a standard to which the wise and honest can repair. The event is in the hand of God."

2. *The idea of equality has its source in the private man's sense of his own infinite worth.* (All immortal souls are equally precious in the eyes of God.)

The Federal government may employ a bureau of scientists to protect its standards of weight and measure from heat and cold and from every change which time imposes upon things. It may keep the gold which makes all dollars equal in an underground vault of impenetrable steel and concrete, sealed with the masterpiece of its ablest locksmith and guarded in time of danger by a division of armed men. It may unfurl the flag symbolizing the perpetual union of forty-eight states on every public building, in every fort and military reservation, and on every armored ship at sea. It may keep the Liberty Bell in Independence Hall and display the engrossed parchment copy of the Declaration of Independence in the Library of Congress so that young boys and girls and pilgrims of every age and from every corner of the land may see with their own eyes the hallowed mementoes of the birth of the Republic. But the supreme standard which determines its justice and which is the germinal principle of the democratic way of life it must leave at all times in the keeping of the private man.

In churches and schools, in factories and on farms, on crowded city streets and on country byways, or in the quiet rooms of birth and creation and death — whenever or wherever we see another as we see ourselves, we meet the measure of social rights and wrongs. The private man carries it with him in his sense of infinite worth, which is nearer and dearer to him, in his best and worst hours, than his personal distinction and glory.

When the private man insists that others are no better than he, no matter how many times they may have surpassed him in tests of strength, he is using his individuality, the self-contained circle of his experience, the personal world which begins and ends with his awareness, as the final standard of all human values. From the relative standards which others have used to brand him as less than a man and to place him beneath them in the social order — from the partial decisions which favor heavy fists, sharp wits, and busy fingers — he appeals to an absolute, to the sense of infinite worth which is the primal fact of his being.

The logic of equality, as he presents it, is simple and unassailable, once we understand that human equality means equality in ultimate value: since one infinite can be neither more nor less than another, all men, as persons, as individuals, are equal in worth. The wording of his proposition of equality is simple and to the point. In spite of all differences in strength, one man, he says, is as good as another. Whole schools of philosophers and other knowing ones could not say it better.

In our worst and best hours we cling to the standard of infinite worth. In our worst hours, after we have failed to meet the tests which the strong have cunningly devised to keep us in our place, we defend it as the true standard of social justice. In our best hours, after we have broken the spell of loneliness by sharing joy and sorrow with comrades and loved ones, we find in it the promise of a society of equals. But since our worst and best hours are few and far between, we often sacrifice the wisdom of equality to the sense of personal distinction and glory which rewards every victor in a trial of strength.

We must not underestimate the craving of every human being for personal distinction. The love of glory is so deeply implanted in our nature that the mere recital of an heroic deed is enough to quicken our heartbeats, even though the deed may have happened long ago, and far away, and in a cause to which we are indifferent.

The bright gesture of the minstrel Taillefer at the battle of Hastings will serve as an illustration. When William of Normandy crossed the channel to invade England, he took Taillefer with him, and on the eve of battle, charged the minstrel with the duty of arousing the will to win or die in every Norman knight and man-at-arms. But Taillefer was not content to urge others on to victory. He exacted from William a promise to reward him with a title of nobility if he should himself strike the first blow. In the first charge on Senlac hill, Taillefer rode in front, tossing his sword in the air and catching it again while he chanted the heroic song of Roland.

He struck the first blow, and he was the first to fall. Other men enjoyed the fruits of the victory at Hastings, and the world has forgotten most of them, but Taillefer's shining bid for glory lives on, and will live as long as there are human hearts to respond to the wild music of his deed.

The difference between the sense of infinite worth and the sense of personal distinction is that while the first may be transformed into a universal idea applicable to all and into a standard of values acceptable to all, the second may not. When we try to universalize our sense of distinction, we cannot get beyond ourselves; when we try to turn pride in victory into a social creed, we end up in the doctrine of superiority with its anarchy of claimants, each cloaking his pretensions under the threadbare dogma of natural inequality.

In the flush of victory we are tempted to claim superiority. The heady sense of personal distinction begets an appetite for more, and we read into our triumphs a significance which they lack. When we come out on top in a trial of strength, or in many trials of strength, we have truly proved that we are better than other men in one respect, or in many respects, but we have not proved that we are better men than they. That point we can never prove. The life of any man is anchored in a deep ocean of awareness, and no other man is strong enough to cut him adrift from the sense of his own worth. To make him a truthful witness to our superiority, we may kill him, and stand exulting over his body, only to find that he has eluded us, and will never testify.

3. *A tragic sense of the common fate of man arises in hearts united by shared joys and sorrows.* (Divine justice prevails either here and now or in the hereafter.)

The sense of sharing a common fate, which is the basis of enduring comradeship and love, is also the firmest foundation for a free society. This sense prevents our momentary passions of pity and envy from hardening into the antisocial attitudes of condescension and discontent. When we are bound to another human being in triumph and disaster, we are lifted above the passions of pity and envy: his grief is our grief; his joy is our joy; we are as one in a union of hearts. Similarly, when men have the vision of an inevitable justice, divine or natural, which equalizes all individual destinies, they are prepared to welcome the sharers of a common fate into one society. . . .

NICHOLAS MURRAY BUTLER
Limitations on equality

Finally, I will speak for a moment of the effect of some tendencies that are world-wide, and which America shares with every other country in the world. Two thousand five hundred years ago the philosophers of Elea said that the fundamental problem of human thought was the problem of the One and the Many. Nothing has happened in two thousand five hundred years to make it necessary to alter that statement. The relation between the One and the Many is the fundamental question of logic, of ethics, of religion, of practical politics. In practical politics it takes the form of the relation between the individual and the multitude, the mass of the people harnessed in society or in the political state. It is now more than a hundred years — about a hundred and fifty years — since the

From Nicholas Murray Butler, *Faith of a Liberal*, 1924, pp. 53–55, 65–67. Reprinted by permission of Charles Scribner's Sons.

philosophers of France, and then the leaders of the great French Revolution, gave to the world the phrase Liberté, Égalité, Fraternité. From that
day to this, mankind everywhere has been discovering that Liberté and
Égalité are incompatible. Liberty and equality of influence, equality of
economic conditions, are impossible for the reason that the deepest law
of nature is that all progress is the result of inequality, or difference. And
unless you mean merely equality before the law, which is simply part of
liberty, you have entered upon a hopeless sea of contradiction. Set a thousand men free at this moment and make them all absolutely equal, and
to-morrow at sundown no two of them would be alike. Nature forbids. In
America and in other nations we are face to face with the question " Do
you prefer liberty, or will you seek equality at the expense of liberty? "
That is the ruling political problem in this world to-day and in every part
of the world. If one wants equality he can have it. Equality is very easy to
gain, but the penalty of equality is social, political, and economic death.
Liberty is life. Take the Continent of Europe with its beautiful valleys and
its rolling hills, its magnificent mountains. It supports in comfort and
satisfaction a great population. All the world comes to see its great cities,
its noble monuments, its beautiful landscapes, its wealth of human tradition and accomplishment. Take the Continent of Europe and level it,
make it equal, cut down all the high mountains, fill up all the low places.
You would have a continent about three hundred metres above sea level,
absolutely flat, where no green thing would grow, where no river would
run, where no city could be built, where no human being could live. But
you would have established equality. You can do precisely that in social
and political life if you choose, because that is in the power of man. But,
believe me, if you do, you deny liberty, you deny life, and you compel
death of civilization, of art, of letters, of industry, and, finally, of humanity
itself. We, in the United States, interpret equality to mean equality before the law, equality of rights, of opportunity, but we do not interpret it
to mean an equality which can only be reached by the denial or restriction
of liberty. We choose liberty, and our aim is so intelligently to inspire our
people that they will use liberty to extend fraternity. Believe me, the last
of those three great words is in many ways the most important, although it
has received the least attention. Fraternity will solve many human problems, both between individuals and between nations. Make all men equal
before the law, strip away privilege and special opportunity, and, as
Manzoni said so long ago, set every man free to do his best under the
leadership of the wisest and best, give him liberty, teach him fraternity,
and in return you will get a real equality worth having, an equality that is
consistent with liberty and with life. American public opinion is clear and
definite on that fundamental point: We choose liberty, we seek fraternity,
and we insist upon equality before the law. But we do not propose to give
to that term an interpretation that would deny liberty and make fraternity
impossible. Fraternity between men within a nation, fraternity between

nations, fraternity between France and the United States is our hope and our goal. . . .

Perhaps an explanation, if found, will be manifold rather than single and complex rather than simple. It will probably have to take account of the clash in men's minds between the results of liberty and the desire for equality; of the steadily growing incapacity of representative government and the steadily increasing lack of confidence in it; of the unwillingness to subordinate an immediate advantage to a future gain; of the dissatisfaction with any principle or rule of conduct, however noble or however hoary with age and honorable with service, that stands in the way of individual or group interest; and finally of the breakdown of the doctrine of a common citizenship in a democratic Republic before the increasingly sharp division of citizens into classes or groups, with accompanying class or group interest, class or group ambition, and class or group power.

The clash between liberty and equality is as old as human society itself. The only possible way of escape from this clash appears to be to cultivate that fraternity or sense of brotherhood which is indicated in the third and last term of the famous formula of the French Revolution. Liberty leads to an inequality and compels it. Equality makes liberty, and therefore progress, impossible. Liberty is the principle of life. Equality is a characteristic of death. There are no justifiable restraints upon liberty save those which grow out of the equal right of every other human being to liberty and to protection and security in the enjoyment of liberty. Some few forms of that inequality which follows upon liberty are generally accepted without resentment; but other forms are bitterly contested and quickly give rise to feelings of envy, hatred, and malice. Our modern democracies have not yet progressed to a point where they are ready to defer to knowledge or capacity if that knowledge or capacity exerts an influence which has any relation to their immediate political or social interests. These democracies are perfectly willing to acclaim excellence in the dead, but they greatly dislike yielding to its leadership in the living.

This attitude is still more clearly and more constantly in evidence in all that relates to property. It is quite forgotten that property has an ethical basis, and is nothing more or less than that which the individual has produced or acquired by his own capacity and thrift. So far from understanding that all individual property is the result of thrift, there are in increasing number those who cry out ecstatically with Proudhon that all property is theft. Property is an attribute of personality, and individual property is essential to liberty. It is the name given to that which belongs to an individual because by his own effort he has produced or acquired it. The differences between individuals which underlie liberty and which make all human progress possible, speedily bring it about that individuals of varying opportunity, varying capacity, and varying temperament possess varying and widely different amounts of property. If these differences result from the fair and just use of opportunity and capacity, well and good; no public or general interest is at stake unless this property be acquired through injustice or by reason of privilege. Justly acquired property is, in a free state, freely exchanged, granted, or bequeathed. A public interest is involved only when the amount or character of individual property is such as necessarily to carry with it a power over the lives of others which is inconsistent with that very liberty and equality of opportunity out of which the institution of property has itself arisen. This may be described as the antinomy of liberty, and it must be resolved from the standpoint of liberty and not from that of the destruction of liberty. . . .

SECTION 2. Fraternity

Certainly one of the most difficult of the great democratic concepts to define or elucidate is the concept of brotherhood. No mere intellectual analysis seems to do justice to the freight of feeling attached to this ideal. Fraternity is an emotional tie that seems to bind together all democratic ideals into the humane person and the humane society. It finds its model in the harmonious and loving relationships within the family. But it would expand these relationships far beyond this intimate circle. It represents the attempt to encompass mankind as a whole. It is, at heart, a belief that the self — far from being narrowly *selfish* — is capable of enlargement so that its concerns encompass the welfare of all mankind. This encompassing quality is reflected in Edwin Markham's quatrain: [1]

He drew a circle that shut me out —
Heretic, rebel, a thing to flout.
But Love and I had the wit to win:
We drew a circle that took him in!

Clearly the development of such a sense, the establishment of such a value, is paramount in an age when persons seem lost, when the world seems to have gone awry, when we must constantly ask ourselves how we can overcome our differences, our bitternesses, our hatreds. The importance of the school as an agency in expanding this quality of brotherly love beyond the narrow confines of the immediate family is obvious. How we are to expand this concern for others, this feeling of identity with their welfare, to encompass the wide scope of human kind, is the challenge that lies before us.

The four selections which follow stand as milestones in the literature of fraternity. The first, from the Bible, emphasizes that thread of fraternity which stresses man's obligation to his neighbor. The second, selected from the great poet of democracy, Walt Whitman, emphasizes that thread in fraternity which enables man to identify with his fellow man, to rejoice with another's success, to feel another's pain. The third, selected from a modern classic on democracy, illustrates how this value is consistent with our very nature and with the perennial aspirations of man. The fourth is a brief excerpt on the idea of brotherly love as seen by a modern behavioral scientist. It is perhaps these four threads which unite to form the composite quality we know as fraternity.

[1] Edwin Markham, "Outwitted." Quoted by permission of Doubleday & Company, Inc.

LUKE 10:25–37
The good Samaritan

Then one of the experts in the Law stood up to test him and said,

"Master, what must I do to be sure of eternal life?"

"What does the Law say and what has your reading taught you?" said Jesus.

"The Law says, 'Thou shalt love the Lord thy God with all thy heart and with all thy soul and with all thy strength and with all thy mind — and thy neighbor as thyself,'" he replied.

"Quite right," said Jesus. "Do that and you will live."

But the man, wanting to justify himself, continued,

"But who is my 'neighbor'?"

And Jesus gave him the following reply:

"A man was once on his way down from Jerusalem to Jericho. He fell into the hands of bandits who stripped off his clothes, beat him up, and left him half dead. It so happened that a priest was going down that road, and when he saw him he passed by on the other side. A Levite also came on the scene, and when he saw him he too passed by on the other side. But then a Samaritan traveler came along to the place where the man was lying, and at the sight of him he was touched with pity. He went across to him and bandaged his wounds, pouring on oil and wine. Then he put him on his own mule, brought him to an inn and did what he could for him. Next day he took out two silver coins and gave them to the innkeeper with the words: 'Look after him, will you? I will pay you back whatever more you spend, when I come through here on my return.' Which of these three seems to you to have been a neighbor to the bandits' victim?"

"The man who gave him practical sympathy," he replied.

"Then you go and give the same," returned Jesus.

WALT WHITMAN
A poetic expression of fraternity

SONG OF MYSELF

10

The runaway slave came to my house and stopt outside,
I heard his motions crackling the twigs of the woodpile,
Through the swung half-door of the kitchen I saw him limpsy and weak,

Luke 10:25–37: From *The Gospels*. Translated into modern English by J. B. Phillips, © 1958, p. 151. Reprinted by permission of The Macmillan Company.

Walt Whitman: From "Song of Myself," in *Leaves of Grass*, 1891–92 edition.

And went where he sat on a log and led him in and assured him,
And brought water and fill'd a tub for his sweated body and bruis'd feet,
And gave him a room that enter'd from my own, and gave him some coarse
   clean clothes,
And remember perfectly well his revolving eyes and his awkwardness,
And remember putting plasters on the galls of his neck and ankles;
He staid with me a week before he was recuperated and pass'd north,
I had him sit next me at table, my fire-lock lean'd in the corner.

             *   *   *

15

The pure contralto sings in the organ loft,
The carpenter dresses his plank, the tongue of his foreplane whistles its
   wild ascending lisp,
The married and unmarried children ride home to their Thanksgiving
   dinner,
The pilot seizes the king-pin, he heaves down with a strong arm,
The mate stands braced in the whale-boat, lance and harpoon are ready,
The duck-shooter walks by silent and cautious stretches,
The deacons are ordain'd with cross'd hands at the altar,
The spinning-girl retreats and advances to the hum of the big wheel,
The farmer stops by the bars as he walks on a First-day loafe and looks at
   the oats and rye,
The lunatic is carried at last to the asylum a confirm'd case,
(He will never sleep any more as he did in the cot in his mother's bed-
   room;)
The jour printer with gray head and gaunt jaws works at his case,
He turns his quid of tobacco while his eyes blurr with the manuscript;
The malform'd limbs are tied to the surgeon's table,
What is removed drops horribly in a pail;
The quadroon girl is sold at the auction-stand, the drunkard nods by the
   bar-room stove,
The machinist rolls up his sleeves, the policeman travels his beat, the gate-
   keeper marks who pass,
The young fellow drives the express-wagon, (I love him, though I do not
   know him;)
The half-breed straps on his light boots to compete in the race,
The western turkey-shooting draws old and young, some lean on their rifles,
   some sit on logs,
Out from the crowd steps the marksman, takes his position, levels his piece;
The groups of newly-come immigrants cover the wharf or levee,
As the woolly-pates hoe in the sugar-field, the overseer views them from
   his saddle,
The bugle calls in the ball-room, the gentlemen run for their partners, the
   dancers bow to each other,

The youth lies awake in the cedar-roof'd garret and harks to the musical rain,

The Wolverine sets traps on the creek that helps fill the Huron,

The squaw wrapt in her yellow-hemm'd cloth is offering moccasins and bead-bags for sale,

The connoisseur peers along the exhibition-gallery with half-shut eyes bent sideways,

As the deck-hands make fast the steamboat the plank is thrown for the shore-going passengers,

The young sister holds out the skein while the elder sister winds it off in a ball, and stops now and then for the knots,

The one-year wife is recovering and happy having a week ago borne her first child,

The clean-hair'd Yankee girl works with her sewing-machine or in the factory or mill,

The paving-man leans on his two-handed rammer, the reporter's lead flies swiftly over the note-book, the sign-painter is lettering with blue and gold,

The canal boy trots on the tow-path, the book-keeper counts at his desk, the shoemaker waxes his thread,

The conductor beats time for the band and all the performers follow him,

The child is baptized, the convert is making his first professions,

The regatta is spread on the bay, the race is begun, (how the white sails sparkle!)

The drover watching his drove sings out to them that would stray,

The pedler sweats with his pack on his back, (the purchaser higgling about the odd cent;)

The bride unrumples her white dress, the minute-hand of the clock moves slowly,

The opium-eater reclines with rigid head and just-open'd lips,

The prostitute draggles her shawl, her bonnet bobs on her tipsy and pimpled neck,

The crowd laugh at her blackguard oaths, the men jeer and wink to each other,

(Miserable! I do not laugh at your oaths nor jeer you;)

The President holding a cabinet council is surrounded by the great Secretaries,

On the piazza walk three matrons stately and friendly with twined arms,

The crew of the fish-smack pack repeated layers of halibut in the hold,

The Missourian crosses the plains toting his wares and his cattle,

As the fare-collector goes through the train he gives notice by the jingling of loose change,

The floor-men are laying the floor, the tinners are tinning the roof, the masons are calling for mortar,

In single file each shouldering his hod pass onward the laborers;

Seasons pursuing each other the indescribable crowd is gather'd, it is the
fourth of Seventh-month, (what salutes of cannon and small arms!)
Seasons pursuing each other the plougher ploughs, the mower mows, and
the winter-grain falls in the ground;
Off on the lakes the pike-fisher watches and waits by the hole in the frozen
surface,
The stumps stand thick round the clearing, the squatter strikes deep with
his axe,
Flatboatmen make fast towards dusk near the cotton-wood or pecan-trees,
Coon-seekers go through the regions of the Red river or through those
drain'd by the Tennessee, or through those of the Arkansas,
Torches shine in the dark that hangs on the Chattahooche or Altamahaw,
Patriarchs sit at supper with sons and grandsons and great-grandsons around
them,
In walls of adobie, in canvas tents, rest hunters and trappers after their
day's sport,
The city sleeps and the country sleeps,
The living sleep for their time, the dead sleep for their time,
The old husband sleeps by his wife and the young husband sleeps by his
wife;
And these tend inward to me, and I tend outward to them,
And such as it is to be of these more or less I am,
And of these one and all I weave the song of myself.

16

I am of old and young, of the foolish as much as the wise,
Regardless of others, ever regardful of others,
Maternal as well as paternal, a child as well as a man,
Stuff'd with the stuff that is coarse and stuff'd with the stuff that is fine,
One of the Nation of many nations, the smallest the same and the largest
the same,
A Southerner soon as a Northerner, a planter nonchalant and hospitable
down by the Oconee I live,
A Yankee bound my own way ready for trade, my joints the limberest
joints on earth and the sternest joints on earth,
A Kentuckian walking the vale of the Elkhorn in my deer-skin leggings, a
Louisianian or Georgian,
A boatman over lakes or bays or along coasts, a Hoosier, Badger, Buckeye;
At home on Kanadian snow-shoes or up in the bush, or with fishermen off
Newfoundland,
At home in the fleet of ice-boats, sailing with the rest and tacking,
At home on the hills of Vermont or in the woods of Maine, or the Texan
ranch,
Comrade of Californians, comrade of free North-Westerners, (loving their
big proportions,)

Comrade of raftsmen and coalmen, comrade of all who shake hands and
   welcome to drink and meat,
A learner with the simplest, a teacher of the thoughtfullest,
A novice beginning yet experient of myriads of seasons,
Of every hue and caste am I, of every rank and religion,
A farmer, mechanic, artist, gentleman, sailor, quaker,
Prisoner, fancy-man, rowdy, lawyer, physician, priest.

I resist any thing better than my own diversity,
Breathe the air but leave plenty after me,
And am not stuck up, and am in my place.

(The moth and the fish-eggs are in their place,
The bright suns I see and the dark suns I cannot see are in their place,
The palpable is in its place and the impalpable is in its place.)

17

These are really the thoughts of all men in all ages and lands, they are not
   original with me,
If they are not yours as much as mine they are nothing, or next to nothing,
If they are not the riddle and the untying of the riddle they are nothing,
If they are not just as close as they are distant they are nothing.

This is the grass that grows wherever the land is and the water is,
This is the common air that bathes the globe.

18

With music strong I come, with my cornets and my drums,
I play not marches for accepted victors only, I play marches for conquer'd
   and slain persons. . . .

T. V. SMITH
Democracy as fraternity

Perennially there arise in the dreams of men these three goals: liberty,
equality, fraternity. And the brightest of these is fraternity. It would be
difficult indeed to do justice in words to the glamor that human imagination has thrown over the notion of brotherhood. Afar off it has stood like
a divine promise to the deeper longings that men have had about themselves and their destiny. Fraternity is a conception to which humanity's
greatest religious prophets have turned in their ecstasy, and it is a culmination that our finest poets have envisaged in their moments of keenest insight. A lonely Hebrew seer long ago glimpsed through the din of contemporary strife the inspiriting spectacle of a united humanity journeying

From T. V. Smith, *The Democratic Way of Life* (Chicago: University of Chicago
Press, 1926), pp. 15–27, 44–46. Reprinted by permission of the author.

on a way which in his enraptured vision conducted men unto a perfect order. And a recent social prophet has declared, with similar import, that " *Real* defeat will overtake humanity only in so far as men themselves, forgetting that they are comrades in doom and agents of each other's woe or weal, go down the years estranged from the one friend they have — each other." The persistence amid age-old defeat of the longing for a closer tie of man with man suggests that human life cannot reach its highest level except in a world with fewer barriers to friendliness. This challenging ideal will bear inspection both as to depth and breadth.

I

On its intensive side, fraternity reduces in its essence to something closely resembling love. But the word itself means a relation such as that between brothers. Fraternity is thus a family ideal, with all the intimacy and feeling involved in that most closed of social unions. But it is that merely at the beginning. Historically, men have insisted upon a closed family organization, exclusive and intimate, partly at least by way of compensation for the failure of friendship on a larger scale. If the family must stand alone, then of course must it stand foursquare. Plato had noticed the tendency of the family to squander loyalty upon itself; and because his heart was set upon making the fraternal unit as wide as the whole city-state, he felt it necessary to abolish the family as far as he could, since it was proving an enemy of the larger loyalty that he sought. If a man cannot lose himself at the heart of the whole herd, then will he insist upon having exclusive right to one or to a few hearts in which he may shuffle off his coil of individual loneliness. For some deep-lying reason, to be considered later, human life is not good if detached. But man, who is completely cowed if he feels that he is really alone, will brave the whole universe when he knows that he is reinforced unequivocally by a few loving hearts. The brave song of the Mermaid Tavern, as represented by Alfred Noyes, is a fitting hymn for all humanity in challenging even the right of deity to violate friendliness.

> Well, if God saved me alone of the seven,
> Telling me *you* must be damned, or *you*,
> " This," I would say, " this is hell, not heaven!
> Give me the fire and a friend or two! "

But the fact that man will find satisfaction in life with a very few comrades does not mean that his deeper nature does not crave the indefinite enlargement of friendly contacts. Families grew into clans, and clans expanded to tribes, and tribes turned to nations. The human touch tends to grow from more to more. The intrinsic good of intimate kindliness, when objectified, furnishes a goal in terms of which to conceive an ideal community where all would not only have friends, but be friends.

The never dying dream of men for a warless world is testimonial to the unlimited extension that the ideal of brotherhood claims for itself. In whatever conditions men must actually live as regards strife and dissension, they cannot demand of their ideal less than the cessation of wholesale hostility. This indigenous human longing gets its meaning not so much from the negative emphasis on the abolition of war as from the positive content of friendly association that seems to be implied by perpetual peace. Isaiah became the spokesman of all humanity when he foresaw through the vagueness of the years men beating their swords into plowshares, and their spears into pruning hooks. Men indeed want, more deeply than they want success or glory, a social accord which is forbidden them by the specter of war. And when long brooding over the end seems to bring to our hand the means to it, we find ourselves willing to wage a world-wide war with curious gladness because we are led to believe that it is the war that will end war. The faith that men, in spite of differences, can dwell together in amity incarnates a human hope that no disillusion seems able to dim.

Schisms in spiritual bodies lead to two churches rather than to none. The road from the divorce court leads past the office where marriage licenses are issued. And out of the débris of a universal holocaust there rises as on the wings of magic morning the dream of a League of Nations that will spell the end of war, even as out of its dead ashes rose the phoenix to a new life perennially renewed. Out of opposition to this vision rise disarmament conferences and projected associations of nations which, even though they too should wither before the bud turn to fruit, would be followed by other plans clothed out of the habiliments of human hopes, and they in turn by others — on to the end of the unending process. Though it is hard for man, the unsocial social animal, to live with men, nothing is more clear than that he cannot live happily without them.

II

The utter centrality of brotherhood among the natural ends of human hopes and endeavors can be reinforced and somewhat clarified by looking very closely at the stages through which the human being passes on the way from infancy to maturity. Perhaps the most significant thing about every man is that he was at one time a child, and that, furthermore, in becoming a man he did not so much outgrow as just overgrow the child nature. Modern psychology is succeeding at last in helping us to understand more clearly what we have always assumed, that the child is father to the man. The deeper into childhood one probes, the more does friendliness appear both the warp and woof of life. The infant is not really born into the world at all; he is born merely into a family. And there is here a vast difference in the expectations aroused. The harsher physical environment that would bring the helpless infant death in a day is so mediated to him by parental tenderness as to turn what otherwise were an inevitable doom into a heaven of love fairer than the most enchanting phantasy of poets. He awakes to consciousness, his human heritage,

Fretted by sallies of his mother's kisses,
With light upon him from his father's eyes.

And even the inhumanities that man shows man are themselves left also, with the harsher sandals of physical fact, at the threshold of the human nursery. As an infant sees no gruff lineament of nature that can possibly be concealed from him, so also he discovers only the smiling, caressing moods of the Janus-faced human world. His food is warmed and sweetened for him, his clothing is softened, and his random movements are constituted a repertoire on a royal stage where every gesture is enthusiastically encored. In his world, fire is hot but never burns, winter is cold but never freezes, want is pinching but seldom pinches. His facts are tamed down with fancy, and his beliefs are toned up to thrilling story.

Born thus into a mediating, comforting group and sustained by it through helpless years, man would not be the animal he is if, when later confronted by the sterner side of his human world and disillusioned by the gruff demands of his physical environment, he did not turn back in pained surprise upon his early fairy god-mother for confirmation of his rosy expectations. And it is a surprise greater perhaps than ever comes to an adult when the all-sufficient friendliness that has surrounded the infant begins to fail the growing child, when he first discovers that he cannot have everything he wants; it involves the utter reversal of that order of nature which his small group's solicitude had led him to expect. Typical is the perplexity of the four-year old who imperiously demanded why the cupboard was bare, since Mother Hubbard would be kind to the dog. Human life is indeed started on its course overwhelmed with the benedictions of what seems a complete fraternity.

Now this heaven that lies about us in our infancy is of inestimable influence throughout the whole of human life. Whether the first great disillusion leads to rebellion against one's group, or to a developing cynicism, or to an understanding co-operation with one's family in buffeting common hardships, the dream of the blessedness that preceded the awakening does not wholly depart. Dimly remembered and oftentimes utterly unrecognized images from this forgotten Elysium of infancy we project to form our later social utopias. For its reinstatement we unknowingly strive in our quest for romantic love. In conventional religious devotion we flee reality to reconstruct in a timeless, painless clime what we realized in all its mystic fulness ere shades of the prison house began to close upon us. According to the fruits of friendliness that we have known in early years, the nature of our seeking throughout life is largely determined. We cannot be content without at least vaguely striving to reinstate on a genuinely universal scale what in our initial experiences was complete and beatific. Thus does love forever radiate among men its comforting afterglow.

But brotherhood becomes a necessary and natural end of human endeavor not merely because we passed through it and learned to respond to it in infancy and childhood. To put the matter in terms that imply that we started life with a definite personal equipment and then were deeply influenced by our first experiences would be merely to observe the periphery but to fail to see the very heart of the powerful impetus toward fraternity. We start life with no more than a body; we acquire a soul in the stages through which our body grows. Now our first experiences lay the corner-stone of our personality and thus largely determine the kind of full-grown soul we shall have. But our first experiences, as we have seen, are consti-tuted by intimate contacts with a group, and that too with a group that displays in general only kindness. Our very individuality rises thus in the sunlight of brotherhood and breathes the exhilarating air of unreserved friendliness. However much clouds of distrust may later obscure the sun, or gases of discord stagnate our spiritual air, our birthright is sunshine, and pure air is our inheritance. Of these we shall dream even when dark night overtakes us, and we shall refuse to be fully contented except in the glad confidence that the morning cometh again.

The fact that our helplessness in infancy renders it quite necessary that if we are to survive at all we must be surrounded by ministering hands, makes it equally necessary, as already suggested, that we shall later discover the limitations of love. The deepest irony of life lies precisely here: we survive in infancy and childhood only by getting such treatment as later dooms us to disillusion. The inability of our group later to fulfil the ex-pectations raised in us leads to distrust and even at times to alienation. Only the subtle technique of analytic psychology can show us how genuinely blessed is the personality that escapes from the family group into the larger social world without deep scars left by well-intentioned love.

This is, however, but a special case of the general form the irony of living takes when it plants in achievement the seeds of contentment, making thus the goal of every stage of growth mean the doom of further growing. While no one wholly escapes the travail of this second birth, men differ greatly in their adaptive and recuperative ability. Those who suffer least often content themselves with loyalty to the smaller group that has nour-ished them in comforting love, sublimating in one way or another the call of the wider brotherhood which is waiting to be built after the pattern of the smaller one. Those who suffer most may become misanthropic and lose faith in the attempt to universalize fraternity, or they may in impo-tence devote themselves to some ethical or religious abstraction, and thus defeat their ideal potentiality through worship of a dream. Between the wasting of loyalty upon some group smaller than the human whole and the squandering of one's energy upon some abstraction substituted for the whole, enough human benevolence has been lost in our era to have built the heavenly Jerusalem in this green and sunny land. One must out of the best of motives emphasize this leakage; for the shortness of the distance that we have come in progress toward a world-wide community is no less than astonishing in the light of our love for family and friends on the one side and our devotion on the other side to the ideal of human brotherhood. . . .

V

Such a way of life as that here envisaged remains confessedly in large part an ideal, but it is the major part of the end that moved men to institute democratic governments as a means. If men had not seen through the haze of popular legislatures and administrative bureaus the shining ideal of a closer human contact, it is certain that they would not have troubled themselves to set up the democratic machinery. And now that we have at last succeeded in establishing the political means, we must not lose sight of the moral end that inspired us to the effort, the long lasting effort. No generation can afford to forget that where men's hearts are there is humanity's treasure also. There are those who would gladly have us forget that we wanted a universal friendliness as reward for the labor spent in building popular government. It is not that they themselves do not feel the longing for fraternity in some obscure fashion. It is oftentimes they that have suffered the deepest scars in trying to transfer their loyalty from some exclusive to a universal community. Interests that are callously selfish on the periphery are not always so at heart. In a large sense every man wills only his own good, but in ignorance of what his good is he commits himself all too often to ways of living that progressively shut out what, following attainment, he himself would treasure as his greater good. We must not forget the intrinsic meaning of brotherhood and we must work for it in the interest of those who oppose it as well as in our own interest. This conviction itself breeds tolerance and friendliness. Here, then, is the first objective, ethically as well as historically, of the democratic way of life-fraternity.

ERICH FROMM
A behavioral scientist views brotherly love

The most fundamental kind of love, which underlies all types of love, is *brotherly love.* By this I mean the sense of responsibility, care, respect, knowledge of any other human being, the wish to further his life. This is the kind of love the Bible speaks of when it says: love thy neighbor as thyself. Brotherly love is love for all human beings; it is characterized by its very lack of exclusiveness. If I have developed the capacity for love, then I cannot help loving my brothers. In brotherly love there is the experience of union with all men, of human solidarity, of human at-onement. Brotherly love is based on the experience that we all are one. The differences in talents, intelligence, knowledge are negligible in comparison with the iden-

From Erich Fromm, *The Art of Loving,* 1956, pp. 47–48. Reprinted by permission of Harper & Brothers.

tity of the human core common to all men. In order to experience this identity it is necessary to penetrate from the periphery to the core. If I perceive in another person mainly the surface, I perceive mainly the differences, that which separates us. If I penetrate to the core, I perceive our identity, the fact of our brotherhood. This relatedness from center to center — instead of that from periphery to periphery — is " central relatedness." Or as Simone Weil expressed it so beautifully: " The same words [e.g., a man says to his wife, " I love you "] can be commonplace or extraordinary according to the manner in which they are spoken. And this manner depends on the depth of the region in a man's being from which they proceed without the will being able to do anything. And by a marvelous agreement they reach the same region in him who hears them. Thus the hearer can discern, if he has any power of discernment, what is the value of the words." [1]

Brotherly love is love between equals; but, indeed, even as equals we are not always " equal "; inasmuch as we are human, we are all in need of help. Today I, tomorrow you. But this need of help does not mean that the one is helpless, the other powerful. Helplessness is a transitory condition; the ability to stand and walk on one's own feet is the permanent and common one.

Yet, love of the helpless one, love of the poor and the stranger, are the beginning of brotherly love. To love one's flesh and blood is no achievement. The animal loves its young and cares for them. The helpless one loves his master, since his life depends on him; the child loves his parents, since he needs them. Only in the love of those who do not serve a purpose, love begins to unfold. Significantly, in the Old Testament, the central object of man's love is the poor, the stranger, the widow and the orphan, and eventually the national enemy, the Egyptian and the Edomite. By having compassion for the helpless one, man begins to develop love for his brother; and in his love for himself he also loves the one who is in need of help, the frail, insecure human being. Compassion implies the element of knowledge and of identification. " You know the heart of the stranger," says the Old Testament, " for you were strangers in the land of Egypt; . . . *therefore love the stranger!* " [2]

SECTION 3. Freedom

Among the deepest schisms which have developed among the adherents of the democratic way of life have been those which have developed over the *nature* of freedom and the *requisites* for its maintenance. Few would

---

[1] Simone Weil, *Gravity and Grace*, G. P. Putnam's Sons, New York, 1952, p. 117.
[2] The same idea has been expressed by Hermann Cohen in his *Religion der Vernunft aus den Quellen des Judentums*, 2nd edition, J. Kaufmann Verlag, Frankfurt am Main, 1929, p. 168 ff.

deny freedom's urgency or desirability. The heart of the democratic ideology lies in a faith that freedom is not a luxury provided by democratic societies: it is rather a necessity for their very survival. This is the faith upon which the entire American experiment has rested. Perhaps the urgency of this faith can never be more clearly seen than in time of crisis. Within this light it is interesting to hear the Supreme Court of the United States, speaking in the midst of a great world conflict, and concerning itself with the right of school children to refuse to salute the flag if this gesture ran counter to their religious convictions. Tracing the course of the history of repression of the right to differ, the Court spoke as follows:

" Struggles to coerce uniformity of sentiment in support of some end thought essential to their time and country have been waged by many good as well as evil men. Nationalism is a relatively recent phenomenon but at other times and places the ends have been racial or plans for saving souls. As first and moderate methods to attain unity have failed, those bent on its accomplishment must resort to ever-increasing severity. As governmental pressure towards unity becomes greater, so strife becomes more bitter as to whose unity it shall be . . . Ultimate futility of such attempts to compel coherence is the lesson of every effort from the Roman drive to stamp out Christianity as a disturber of its pagan unity, the Inquisition as a means to religious and dynastic unity, the Siberian exiles as a means to Russian unity, down to the fast failing efforts of our present totalitarian enemies. Those who begin coercive elimination of dissent soon find themselves exterminating dissenters. Compulsory unification of opinion achieves only the unanimity of the graveyard.
" It seems trite but necessary to say that the First Amendment to our Constitution was designed to avoid these ends by avoiding these beginnings . . .

We can have intellectual individualism and the rich cultural diversities that we owe to exceptional minds only at the price of occasional eccentricity and abnormal attitudes. When they are so harmless to others or to the State as those we deal with here, the price is not too great. But freedom to differ is not limited to things that do not matter much. That would be the mere shadow of freedom. The test of its substance is the right to differ as to things that touch the heart of the existing order . . ." [1]

It is this faith in maintaining the right to differ as a *social necessity* which is the greatest safeguard of the democratic state and the most significant foundation of democratic education.

Perhaps no finer philosophical defense of the right to differ has been made than that proposed by John Stuart Mill in his classic essay *On Liberty,* published over a century ago. A famous utilitarian philosopher, Mill developed his arguments for liberty in terms of its social utility. In our time it is particularly interesting to note that his essay presages the current concern over the *informal* pressures which can so sharply curtail liberty, and so truncate individuality. To him we are indebted for a clearcut recognition that liberty is not limited solely by the law, since informal pressures can be as great a curtailment of freedom as any legal system devised. Equally important is his treatment of the distinct categories of freedom of thought and freedom of action. Important as Mill's insight into liberty was, his argument essentially reinforced a tendency to view liberty within the context of *absence of restraint*. It is upon this ground that many modern theorists have challenged the nineteenth century concept of liberty. Among the great issues which have been posed in our time,

[1] Mr. Justice Jackson, for the majority in Board of Education v. Barnette, 319 U.S. 624 (1943).

for example, have been: Is a person really free merely because there are no formal restraints placed upon his action? (For example, is a man free to read a newspaper who has never had the chance to learn to read?) What is the role of government in providing the conditions which make for effective freedom? Does it have a responsibility to promote the conditions of positive freedom — learning to read — as well as to refrain from imposing unwarranted restraints, such as censoring the press? Is it consistent with freedom for the individual to choose a system or institution and then surrender his freedom to that system or institution? (For example, does democratic freedom encompass the right to select a political party or religious institution and then surrender one's freedom to choose to those who control that system or institution?) Is the real question of freedom one of *freedom* or *no freedom* — or one of *what freedom* and *for whom?* (For example, is it more important for parents to be free to choose with whom their child shall associate in school, or for all children, regardless of social status, to be free to attend the same school?) The careful contemporary analyses of freedom by Ralph Barton Perry and Robert M. MacIver come to grips with just such problems. The final selection in this section, *The Right to Intellectual Freedom*, by the Philosophy of Education Society, returns once again to the initial question raised by John Stuart Mill a century before: Can a democratic society survive or prosper if it would deny any or all of its citizens the freedom to seek the truth where they can find it, to follow the argument wherever it may lead?

JOHN STUART MILL
A classic statement on liberty

The notion, that the people have no need to limit their power over themselves, might seem axiomatic, when popular government was a thing only dreamed about, or read of as having existed at some distant period of the past. Neither was that notion necessarily disturbed by such temporary aberrations as those of the French Revolution, the worst of which were the work of a usurping few, and which, in any case, belonged, not to the permanent working of popular institutions, but to a sudden and convulsive outbreak against monarchical and aristocratic despotism. In time, however, a democratic republic came to occupy a large portion of the earth's surface, and made itself felt as one of the most powerful members of the community of nations; and elective and responsible government became subject to the observations and criticisms which wait upon a great existing fact. It was not perceived that such phrases as " self-government," and " the power of the people over themselves," do not express the true state of the case. The " people " who exercise the power are not always the same people with those over whom it is exercised; and the " self-government " spoken of is not the government of each by himself, but of each by all the rest.

From John Stuart Mill, *On Liberty*, 1859. Gateway Editions, Inc. Distributed by Henry Regenery Company, pp. 4–7, 21–29, 76–81, 86–93, 98. Reprinted by permission.

The will of the people, moreover, practically means the will of the most numerous or the most active *part* of the people; the majority, or those who succeed in making themselves accepted as the majority; the people, consequently *may* desire to oppress a part of their number; and precautions are as much needed against this as against any other abuse of power. The limitation, therefore, of the power of government over individuals loses none of its importance when the holders of power are regularly accountable to the community, that is, to the strongest party therein. This view of things, recommending itself equally to the intelligence of thinkers and to the inclination of those important classes in European society to whose real or supposed interests democracy is adverse, has had no difficulty in establishing itself; and in political speculations " the tyranny of the majority " is now generally included among the evils against which society requires to be on its guard.

Like other tyrannies, the tyranny of the majority was at first, and is still vulgarly, held in dread, chiefly as operating through the acts of the public authorities. But reflecting persons perceived that when society is itself the tyrant — society collectively over the separate individuals who compose it — its means of tyrannising are not restricted to the acts which it may do by the hands of its political functionaries. Society can and does execute its own mandates: and if it issues wrong mandates instead of right, or any mandates at all in things with which it ought not to meddle, it practises a social tyranny more formidable than many kinds of political oppression, since, though not usually upheld by such extreme penalties, it leaves fewer means of escape, penetrating much more deeply into the details of life, and enslaving the soul itself. Protection, therefore, against the tyranny of the magistrate is not enough: there needs protection also against the tyranny of the prevailing opinion and feeling; against the tendency of society to impose, by other means than civil penalties, its own ideas and practices as rules of conduct on those who dissent from them; to fetter the development, and if possible, prevent the formation, of any individuality not in harmony with its ways, and compels all characters to fashion themselves upon the model of its own. There is a limit to the legitimate interference of collective opinion with individual independence: and to find that limit, and maintain it against encroachment, is as indispensable to a good condition of human affairs, as protection against political despotism.

But though this proposition is not likely to be contested in general terms, the practical question, where to place the limit — how to make the fitting adjustment between individual independence and social control — is a subject on which nearly everything remains to be done. All that makes existence valuable to any one, depends on the enforcement of restraints upon the actions of other people. Some rules of conduct, therefore, must be imposed by law in the first place, and by opinion on many things which are not fit subjects for the operation of law. What these rules should be is the principal question in human affairs; but if we except a few of the most obvious cases, it is one of those which least progress has been made in resolving. . . .

*   *   *

OF THE LIBERTY OF THOUGHT AND DISCUSSION

The time, it is to be hoped, is gone by, when any defence would be necessary of the " liberty of the press " as one of the securities against corrupt or tyrannical government. No argument, we may suppose, can now be needed, against permitting a legislature or an executive, not identified in interest with the people, to prescribe opinions to them, and determine what doctrines or what arguments they shall be allowed to hear. This aspect of the question, besides, has been so often and so triumphantly enforced by preceding writers, that it needs not be specially insisted on in this place. Though the law of England, on the subject of the press, is as servile to this day as it was in the time of the Tudors, there is little danger of its being actually put in force against political discussion, except during some temporary panic, when fear of insurrection drives ministers and judges from their propriety; [1] and, speaking generally, it is not, in constitutional countries, to be apprehended, that the government, whether completely responsible to the people or not, will often attempt to control the expression of opinion, except when in doing so it makes itself the organ of the general intolerance of the public. Let us suppose, therefore, that the government is entirely at one with the people, and never thinks of exerting any power

---

[1] These words had scarcely been written, when, as if to give them an emphatic contradiction, occurred the Government Press Prosecutions of 1858. That ill-judged interference with the liberty of public discussion has not, however, induced me to alter a single word in the text, nor has it at all weakened my conviction that, moments of panic excepted, the era of pains and penalties for political discussion has, in our own country, passed away. For, in the first place, the prosecutions were not persisted in; and, in the second, they were never, properly speaking, political prosecutions. The offense charged was not that of criticizing institutions, or the acts or persons of rulers, but of circulating what was deemed an immoral doctrine, the lawfulness of Tyrannicide.

If the arguments of the present chapter are of any validity, there ought to exist the fullest liberty of professing and discussing, as a matter of ethical conviction, any doctrine, however immoral it may be considered. It would, therefore, be irrelevant and out of place to examine here, whether the doctrine of Tyrannicide deserves that title. I shall content myself with saying that the subject has been at all times one of the open questions of morals; that the act of a private citizen in striking down a criminal, who, by raising himself above the law, has placed himself beyond the reach of legal punishment or control, has been accounted by whole nations, and by some of the best and wisest of men, not a crime, but an act of exalted virtue; and that, right or wrong, it is not of the nature of assassination, but of civil war. As such, I hold that the instigation to it, in a specific case, may be a proper subject of punishment, but only if an overt act has followed, and at least a probable connection can be established between the act and the instigation. Even then, it is not a foreign government, but the very government assailed, which alone, in the exercise of self-defense, can legitimately punish attacks directed against its own existence.

of coercion unless in agreement with what it conceives to be their voice. But I deny the right of the people to exercise such coercion, either by themselves or by their government. The power itself is illegitimate. The best government has no more title to it than the worst. It is as noxious, or more noxious, when exerted in accordance with public opinion, than when in opposition to it. If all mankind minus one were of one opinion, and only one person were of the contrary opinion, mankind would be no more justified in silencing that one person, than he, if he had the power, would be justified in silencing mankind. Were an opinion a personal possession of no value except to the owner; if to be obstructed in the enjoyment of it were simply a private injury, it would make some difference whether the injury was inflicted only on a few persons or on many. But the peculiar evil of silencing the expression of an opinion is, that it is robbing the human race: posterity as well as the existing generation; those who dissent from the opinion, still more than those who hold it. If the opinion is right, they are deprived of the opportunity of exchanging error for truth: if wrong, they lose, what is almost as great a benefit, the clearer perception and livelier impression of truth, produced by its collision with error.

It is necessary to consider separately these two hypotheses, each of which has a distinct branch of the argument corresponding to it. We can never be sure that the opinion we are endeavouring to stifle is a false opinion; and if we were sure, stifling it would be an evil still.

First: the opinion which it is attempted to suppress by authority may possibly be true. Those who desire to suppress it, of course deny its truth; but they are not infallible. They have no authority to decide the question for all mankind, and exclude every other person from the means of judging. To refuse a hearing to an opinion, because they are sure that it is false, is to assume that *their* certainty is the same thing as *absolute* certainty. All silencing of discussion is an assumption of infallibility. Its condemnation may be allowed to rest on this common argument, not the worse for being common.

Unfortunately for the good sense of mankind, the fact of their fallibility is far from carrying the weight in their practical judgment which is always allowed to it in theory; for while every one well knows himself to be fallible, few think it necessary to take any precautions against their own fallibility, or admit the supposition that any opinion, of which they feel very certain, may be one of the examples of the error to which they acknowledge themselves to be liable. Absolute princes, or others who are accustomed to unlimited deference, usually feel this complete confidence in their own opinions on nearly all subjects. People more happily situated, who sometimes hear their opinions disputed, and are not wholly unused to be set right when they are wrong, place the same unbounded reliance only on such of their opinions as are shared by all who surround them, or to whom they habitually defer; for in proportion to a man's want of confidence in his own solitary judgment, does he usually repose, with implicit trust, on the infallibility of " the world " in general. And the world, to each individual, means the part of it with which he comes in contact: his party, his sect, his church, his class of society; the man may be called, by comparison, almost liberal and large-minded to whom it means anything so comprehensive as his own country or his own age. Nor is his faith in this collective authority at all shaken by his being aware that other ages, countries, sects, churches, classes, and parties have thought, and even now think, the exact reverse. He devolves upon his own world the responsibility of being in the right against the dissentient worlds of other people; and it never troubles him that mere accident has decided which of these numerous worlds is the object of his reliance, and that the same causes which make him a Churchman in London, would have made him a Buddhist or a Confucian in Pekin. Yet it is as evident in itself, as any amount of argument can make it, that ages are no more infallible than individuals; every age having held many opinions which subsequent ages have deemed not only false but absurd; and it is as certain that many opinions now general will be rejected by future ages, as it is that many, once general, are rejected by the present.

The objection likely to be made to this argument would probably take some such form as the following. There is no greater assumption of infallibility in forbidding the propagation of error, than in any other thing which is done by public authority on its own judgment and responsibility. Judgment is given to men that they may use it. Because it may be used erroneously, are men to be told that they ought not to use it all? To prohibit what they think pernicious, is not claiming exemption from error, but fulfilling the duty incumbent on them, although fallible, of acting on their conscientious conviction. If we were never to act on our opinions, because those opinions may be wrong, we should leave all our interest uncared for, and all our duties unperformed. An objection which applies to all conduct can be no valid objection to conduct in particular. It is the duty of governments and of individuals, to form the truest opinions they can; to form them carefully, and never impose them upon others unless they are quite sure of being right. But when they are sure (such reasoners may say), it is not conscientiousness but cowardice to shrink from acting on their opinions, and allow doctrines which they honestly think dangerous to the welfare of mankind, either in this life or in another, to be scattered abroad without restraint, because other people, in less enlightened times, have persecuted opinions now believed to be true. Let us take care, it may be said, not to make the same mistake; but governments and nations have made mistakes in other things, which are not denied to be fit subjects for the exercise of authority; they have laid on bad taxes, made unjust wars. Ought we therefore to lay on no taxes, and, under whatever provocation, make no wars? Men, and governments, must act to the best of their ability. There is no such thing as absolute certainty, but there is assurance sufficient for the purposes of human life. We may, and must, assume our opinion to be true for the guidance of our own conduct: and it is assuming no more when we forbid bad men to pervert society by the propagation of opinions which we regard as false and pernicious.

I answer, that it is assuming very much more. There is the greatest difference between presuming an opinion to be true, because, with every opportunity for contesting it, it has not been refuted, and assuming its truth for the purpose of not permitting its refutation. Complete liberty of contradicting and disproving our opinion is the very condition which justifies us in assuming its truth for purposes of action; and on no other terms can a being with human faculties have any rational assurance of being right.

When we consider either the history of opinion, or the ordinary conduct of human life, to what is it to be ascribed that the one and the other are no worse than they are? Not certainly to the inherent force of the human understanding; for, on any matter not self-evident, there are ninety-nine persons totally incapable of judging of it for one who is capable; and the capacity of the hundredth person is only comparative; for the majority of the eminent men of every past generation held many opinions now known to be erroneous, and did or approved numerous things which no one will now justify. Why is it, then, that there is on the whole a preponderance among mankind of rational opinions and rational conduct? If there really is this preponderance — which there must be unless human affairs are, and have always been, in an almost desperate state — it is owing to a quality of the human mind, the source of everything respectable in man either as an intellectual or as a moral being, namely, that his errors are corrigible. He is capable of rectifying his mistakes, by discussion and experience. Not by experience alone. There must be discussion, to show how experience is to be interpreted. Wrong opinions and practices gradually yield to fact and argument; but facts and arguments, to produce any effect on the mind, must be brought before it. Very few facts are able to tell their own story, without comments to bring out their meaning. The whole strength and value, then, of human judgment, depending on the one property, that it can be set right when it is wrong, reliance can be placed on it only when the means of setting it right are kept constantly at hand. In the case of any person whose judgment is really deserving of confidence, how has it become so? Because he has kept his mind open to criticism of his opinions and conduct. Because it has been his practice to listen to all that could be said against him; to profit by as much of it as was just, and expound to himself, and upon occasion to others, the fallacy of what was fallacious. Because he has felt, that the only way in which a human being can make some approach to knowing the whole of a subject, is by hearing what can be said about it by persons of every variety of opinion, and studying all modes in which it can be looked at by every character of mind. No wise man ever acquired his wisdom in any mode but this; nor is it in the nature of human intellect to become wise in any other manner. The steady habit of correcting and completing his own opinion by collating it with those of others, so far from causing doubt and hesitation in carrying it into practice, is the only stable foundation for a just reliance on it: for, being cognisant of all that can, at least obviously, be said against him, and having taken up his position against all gainsayers — knowing that he has sought for objections and difficulties, instead of avoiding them, and has shut out no light which can be thrown upon the subject from any quarter — he has a right to think his judgment better than that of any person, or any multitude, who have not gone through a similar process.

It is not too much to require that what the wisest of mankind, those who are best entitled to trust their own judgment, find necessary to warrant their relying on it, should be submitted to by that miscellaneous collection of a few wise and many foolish individuals, called the public. The most intolerant of churches, the Roman Catholic Church, even at the canonisation of a saint, admits, and listens patiently to, a " devil's advocate." The holiest of men, it appears, cannot be admitted to posthumous honours, until all that the devil could say against him is known and weighed. If even the Newtonian philosophy were not permitted to be questioned, mankind could not feel as complete assurance of its truth as they now do. The beliefs which we have most warrant for have no safeguard to rest on but a standing invitation to the whole world to prove them unfounded. If the challenge is not accepted, or is accepted and the attempt fails, we are far enough from certainty still; but we have done the best that the existing state of human reason admits of; we have neglected nothing that could give the truth a chance of reaching us: if the lists are kept open, we may hope that if there be a better truth, it will be found when the human mind is capable of receiving it; and in the meantime we may rely on having attained such approach to truth as is possible in our own day. This is the amount of certainty attainable by a fallible being, and this the sole way of attaining it.

Strange it is, that men should admit the validity of the arguments for free discussion, but object to their being " pushed to an extreme "; not seeing that unless the reasons are good for an extreme case, they are not good for any case. Strange that they should imagine that they are not assuming infallibility, when they acknowledge that there should be free discussion on all subjects which can possibly be *doubtful*, but think that some particular principle or doctrine should be forbidden to be questioned because it is so *certain*, that is, because *they are certain* that it is certain. To call any proposition certain, while there is any who would deny its certainty if permitted, but who is not permitted, is to assume that we ourselves and those who agree with us, are the judges of certainty, and judges without hearing the other side. . . .

*   *   *

OF INDIVIDUALITY, AS ONE OF THE ELEMENTS OF WELL-BEING

Such being the reasons which make it imperative that human beings should be free to form opinions, and to express their opinions without reserve; and such the baneful consequences to the intellectual, and through that to the moral nature of man, unless this liberty is either conceded, or asserted in spite of prohibition; let us next examine whether the same reasons do not require that men should be free to act upon their opinions — to carry these out in their lives, without hindrance, either physical or moral, from their fellow-men, so long as it is at their own risk and peril. This last proviso is of course indispensable. No one pretends that actions should be as free as opinions. On the contrary, even opinions lose their immunity when the circumstances in which they are expressed are such as to constitute their expression a positive instigation to some mischievous act. An opinion that corn-dealers are starvers of the poor, or that private property is robbery, ought to be unmolested when simply circulated through the press, but may justly incur punishment when delivered orally to an excited mob assembled before the house of a corn-dealer, or when handed about among the same mob in the form of a placard. Acts, of whatever kind, which, without justifiable cause, do harm to others, may be, and in the more important cases absolutely require to be, controlled by the unfavourable sentiments, and, when needful, by active interference of mankind. The liberty of the individual must be thus far limited; he must not make himself a nuisance to other people. But if he refrains from molesting others in what concerns them, and merely acts according to his own inclinations and judgment in things which concern himself, the same reasons which show that opinion should be free, prove also that he should be allowed, without molestation, to carry his opinions into practice at his own cost. That mankind are not infallible; that their truths, for the most part, are only half-truths; that unity of opinion, unless resulting from the fullest and freest comparison of opposite opinions, is not desirable, and diversity not an evil, but a good, until mankind are much more capable than at present of recognising all sides of the truth, are principles applicable to men's modes of action, not less than to their opinions. As it is useful that while mankind are imperfect there should be different opinions, so it is that there should be different experiments of living; that free scope should be given to varieties of character, short of injury to others; and that the worth of different modes of life should be proved practically, when any one thinks fit to try them. It is desirable, in short, that in things which do not primarily concern others, individuality should assert itself. Where, not the person's own character, but the traditions or customs of other people are the rule of conduct, there is wanting one of the principal ingredients of human happiness, and quite the chief ingredient of individual and social progress.

In maintaining this principle, the greatest difficulty to be encountered does not lie in the appreciation of means towards an acknowledged end, but in the indifference of persons in general to the end itself. If it were felt that the free development of individuality is one of the leading essentials of well-being; that it is not only a co-ordinate element with all that is designated by the terms civilisation, instruction, education, culture, but is itself a necessary part and condition of all those things; there would be no danger that liberty should be undervalued, and the adjustment of the boundaries between it and social control would present no extraordinary difficulty. But the evil is, that individual spontaneity is hardly recognised by the common modes of thinking as having any intrinsic worth, or deserving any regard on its own account. The majority, being satisfied with the ways of mankind as they now are (for it is they who make them what they are), cannot comprehend why those ways should not be good enough for everybody; and what is more, spontaneity forms no part of the ideal of the majority of moral and social reformers, but is rather looked on with jealousy, as a troublesome and perhaps rebellious obstruction to the general acceptance of what these reformers, in their own judgment, think would be best for mankind. Few persons, out of Germany, even comprehend the meaning of the doctrine which Wilhelm von Humboldt, so eminent both as a *savant* and as a politician, made the text of a treatise — that " the end of man, or that which is prescribed by the eternal or immutable dictates of reason, and not suggested by vague and transient desires, is the highest and most harmonious development of his powers to a complete and consistent whole "; that, therefore, the object " towards which every human being must ceaselessly direct his efforts, and on which especially those who design to influence their fellow-men must ever keep their eyes, is the individuality of power and development "; that for this there are two requisites, " freedom, and variety of situations "; and that from the union of these arise " individual vigour and manifold diversity," which combine themselves in " originality."

Little, however, as people are customed to a doctrine like that of Von Humboldt, and surprising as it may be to them to find so high a value attached to individuality, the question, one must nevertheless think, can only be one of degree. No one's idea of excellence in conduct is that people should do absolutely nothing but copy one another. No one would assert that people ought not to put into their mode of life, and into the conduct of their concerns, any impress whatever of their own judgment, or of their own individual character. On the other hand, it would be absurd to pretend that people ought to live as if nothing whatever had been known in the world before they came into it; as if experience had as yet done nothing towards showing that one mode of existence, or of conduct, is preferable to another. Nobody denies that people should be so taught and trained in youth as to know and benefit by the ascertained results of human experience. But it is the privilege and proper condition of a human being, arrived at the maturity of his faculties, to use and interpret experience in his own way. It is for him to find out what part of recorded experience is properly applicable to his own circumstances and character. The traditions and customs of other people are to a certain extent, evidence of what their experience has taught *them*; presumptive evidence, and as such, have a claim to his deference: but, in the first place their experience may be too narrow; or they may not have interpreted it rightly. Secondly, their interpretation of experience may be correct, but unsuitable to him. Customs are made for customary circumstances and customary characters; and his circumstances or his character may be uncustomary. Thirdly, though the customs be both good as customs, and suitable to him, yet to conform to custom, merely as custom, does not educate or develop in him any of the qualities which are the distinctive endowment of a human being. The human faculties of perception, judgment, discriminative feeling, mental activity, and even moral preference, are exercised only in making a choice. He who does anything because it is the custom makes no choice. He gains no practice either in discerning or in desiring what is best. The mental and moral, like the muscular powers, are improved only by being used. The faculties are called into no exercise by doing a thing merely because others do it, no more than by believing a thing only because others believe it. If the grounds of an opinion are not conclusive to the person's own reason, his reason cannot be strengthened, but is likely to be weakened, by his adopting it: and if the inducements to an act are not such as are consentaneous to his own feelings and character (where affection, or the rights of others, are not concerned) it is so much done toward rendering his feelings and character inert and torpid, instead of active and energetic.

He who lets the world, or his own portion of it, choose his plan of life for him, has no need of any other faculty than the ape-like one of imitation. He who chooses his plan for himself, employs all his faculties. He must use observation to see, reasoning and judgment to foresee, activity to gather materials for decision, discrimination to decide, and when he has decided, firmness and self-control to hold to his deliberate decision. And these qualities he requires and exercises exactly in proportion as the part of his conduct which he determines according to his own judgment and feelings is a large one. It is possible that he might be guided in some good path, and kept out of harm's way, without any of these things. But what will be his comparative worth as a human being? It really is of importance, not only what men do, but also what manner of men they are that do it. Among the works of man, which human life is rightly employed in perfecting and beautifying, the first in importance surely is man himself. Supposing it were possible to get houses built, corn grown, battles fought, causes tried, and even churches erected and prayers said, by machinery — by automatons in human form — it would be a considerable loss to exchange for these automatons even the men and women who at present inhabit the more civilised parts of the world, and who assuredly are but starved specimens of what nature can and will produce. Human nature is

not a machine to be built after a model, and set to do exactly the work prescribed for it, but a tree, which requires to grow and develop itself on all
sides, according to the tendency of the inward forces which make it a living thing. . . .

It is not by wearing down to uniformity all that is individual in themselves, but by cultivating it, and calling it forth, within the limits imposed
by the rights and interests of others, that human beings become a noble
and beautiful object of contemplation; and as the works partake the character of those who do them, by the same process human life also becomes
rich, diversified, and animating, furnishing more abundant aliment to high
thoughts and elevating feelings, and strengthening the tie which binds
every individual to the race, by making the race infinitely better worth belonging to. In proportion to the development to his individuality, each
person becomes more valuable to himself, and is therefore capable of being more valuable to others. There is a greater fullness of life about his
own existence, and when there is more life in the units there is more in
the mass which is composed of them. As much compression as is necessary
to prevent the stronger specimens of human nature from encroaching on
the rights of others cannot be dispensed with; but for this there is ample
compensation even in the point of view of human development. The
means of development which the individual loses by being prevented from
gratifying his inclinations to the injury of others, are chiefly obtained at
the expense of the development of other people. And even to himself there
is a full equivalent in the better development of the social part of his nature, rendered possible by the restraint put upon the selfish part. To be
held to rigid rules of justice for the sake of others, develops the feelings
and capacities which have the good of others for their object. But to be
restrained in things not affecting their good, by their mere displeasure, develops nothing valuable, except such force of character as may unfold itself
in resisting the restraint. If acquiesced in, it dulls and blunts the whole
nature. To give any fair play to the nature of each, it is essential that different persons should be allowed to lead different lives. In proportion as
this latitude has been exercised in any age, has that age been noteworthy
to posterity. Even despotism does not produce its worst effects, so long as
individuality exists under it; and whatever crushes individuality is despotism, by whatever name it may be called, and whether it professes to
be enforcing the will of God or the injunction of men.
    Having said that the individuality is the same thing with development,
and that it is only the cultivation of individuality which produces, or can
produce, well-developed human beings, I might here close the argument:
for what more or better can be said of any condition of human affairs
than that it brings human beings themselves nearer to the best thing they
can be? or what worse can be said of any obstruction to good than that it
prevents this? Doubtless, however, these considerations will not suffice to

convince those who must need convincing; and it is necessary further to show, that these developed human beings are of some use to the undeveloped — to point out to those who do not desire liberty, and would not avail themselves of it, that they may be in some intelligible manner rewarded for allowing other people to make use of it without hindrance.

In the first place, then, I would suggest that they might possibly learn something from them. It will not be denied by anybody, that originality is a valuable element in human affairs. There is always need of persons not only to discover new truths, and point out when what were once truths are true no longer, but also to commence new practices, and set the example of more enlightened conduct, and better taste and sense in human life. This cannot well be gainsaid by anybody who does not believe that the world has already attained perfection in all its ways and practices. It is true that this benefit is not capable of being rendered by everybody alike: there are but few persons, in comparison with the whole of mankind, whose experiments, if adopted by others, would be likely to be any improvement on established practice. But these few are the salt of the earth, without them, human life would become a stagnant pool. Not only is it they who introduce good things which did not before exist; it is they who keep the life in those which already exist. If there were nothing new to be done, would human intellect cease to be necessary? Would it be reason why those who do the old things should forget why they are done, and do them like cattle, not like human beings? There is only too great a tendency in the best beliefs and practices to degenerate into the mechanical; and unless there were a succession of persons whose ever-recurring originality prevents the grounds of those beliefs and practices from becoming merely traditional, such dead matter would not resist the smallest shock from anything really alive, and there would be no reason why civilization should not die out, as in the Byzantine Empire. Persons of genius, it is true, are, and are always likely to be, a small minority, but in order to have them, it is necessary to preserve the soil in which they grow. Genius can only breathe freely in an *atmosphere* of freedom. Persons of genius are, *ex vi termini*, more individual than any other people — less capable, consequently, of fitting themselves, without hurtful compression, into any of the small number of moulds which society provides in order to save its members the trouble of forming their own character. If from timidity they consent to be forced into one of these moulds, and to let all that part of themselves which cannot expand under the pressure remain unexpanded, society will be little the better for their genius. If they are of a strong character, and break their fetters, they become a mark for the society which has not succeeded in reducing them to commonplace, to point out with solemn warning as " wild," " erratic," and the like; much as if one should complain of the Niagara river for not flowing smoothly between its banks like a Dutch canal.

I insist thus emphatically on the importance of genius, and the necessity of allowing it to unfold itself freely both in thought and in practice, being well aware that no one will deny the position in theory, but knowing also that almost every one, in reality, is totally indifferent to it. People think genius a fine thing if it enables a man to write an exciting poem, or paint a picture. But in its true sense, that of originality in thought and action, though no one says that it is not a thing to be admired, nearly all, at heart, think that they can do very well without it. Unhappily this is too natural to be wondered at. Originality is the one thing which unoriginal minds cannot feel the use of. They cannot see what it is to do for them: how should they? If they could see what it would do for them, it would not be originality. The first service which originality has to render them, is that of opening their eyes: which being once fully done, they would have a chance of being themselves original. Meanwhile, recollecting that nothing was ever yet done which some one was not the first to do, and that all good things which exist are the fruits of originality, let them be modest enough to believe that there is something still left for it to accomplish, and assure themselves that they are more in need of originality, the less they are conscious of the want.

In sober truth, whatever homage may be professed, or even paid, to real or supposed mental superiority, the general tendency of things throughout the world is to render mediocrity the ascendant power among mankind. In ancient history, in the Middle Ages, and in a diminishing degree through the long transition from feudality to the present time, the individual was a power in himself; and if he had either great talents or a high social position, he was a considerable power. At present individuals are lost in the crowd. In politics it is almost a triviality to say that public opinion now rules the world. The only power deserving the name is that of masses and of governments while they make themselves the organ of the tendencies and instincts of masses. This is as true in the moral and social relations of private life as in public transactions. Those whose opinions go by the name of public opinion are not always the same sort of public: in America they are the whole white population; in England, chiefly the middle class. But they are always in a mass, that is to say collective mediocrity. And what is a still greater novelty, the mass do not now take their opinions from dignitaries in Church or State, from ostensible leaders, or from books. Their thinking is done for them by men much like themselves, addressing them or speaking in their name, on the spur of the moment, through the newspapers. I am not complaining of all this. I do not assert that anything better is compatible, as a general rule, with the present low state of the human mind. But that does not hinder the government of mediocrity from being mediocre government. No government by a democracy or a numerous aristocracy, either in its political acts or in the opinions, qualities, and tone of mind which it fosters, ever did or could rise above mediocrity, except in so far as the sovereign Many have let themselves be guided (which in their best times they always have done) by the counsels and influence of a more highly gifted and instructed One or Few. The initiation of all wise or noble things comes and must come from individuals; generally at first from some one individual. The honour and glory of the average man is that he is capable of following that initiative; that he can respond internally to wise and noble things, and be led to them with his eyes open. I am not countenancing the sort of " hero-worship " which applauds the strong man of genius for forcibly seizing on the government of the world and making it do his bidding in spite of itself. All he can claim is, freedom to point out the way. The power of compelling others into it is not only inconsistent with the freedom and development of all the rest, but corrupting to the strong man himself. It does not seem, however, that when the opinions of masses of merely average men are everywhere become or becoming the dominant power, the counterpoise and corrective to that tendency would be the more and more pronounced individuality of those who stand on the higher eminences of thought. It is in these circumstances most especially, that exceptional individuals, instead of being deterred, should be encouraged in acting differently from the mass. In other times there was no advantage in their doing so, unless they acted not only differently but better. In this age, the mere example of non-conformity, the mere refusal to bend the knee to custom, is itself a service. Precisely because the tyranny of opinion is such as to make eccentricity a reproach, it is desirable, in order to break through that tyranny, that people should be eccentric. Eccentricity has always abounded when and where strength of character has abounded; and the amount of eccentricity in a society has generally been proportioned to the amount of genius, mental vigour, and moral courage it contained. That so few now dare to be eccentric marks the chief danger of the time.

I have said that it is important to give the freest scope possible to uncustomary things, in order that it may in time appear which of these are fit to be converted into customs. But independence of action, and disregard of custom, are not solely deserving of encouragement for the chance they afford that better modes of action, and customs more worthy of general adoption, may be struck out; nor is it only persons of decided mental superiority who have a just claim to carry on their lives in their own way. There is no reason that all human existence should be constructed on some one or some small number of patterns. If a person possesses any tolerable amount of common sense and experience, his own mode of laying out his existence is the best, not because it is the best in itself, but because it is his own mode. . . .

The despotism of custom is everywhere the standing hindrance to human advancement, being unceasing antagonism to that disposition to aim at something better than customary, which is called, according to circumstances, the spirit of liberty, or that of progress or improvement. The spirit of improvement is not always a spirit of liberty, for it may aim at forcing improvements on an unwilling people; and the spirit of liberty, in so far as it resists such attempts, may ally itself locally and temporarily with the opponents of improvement; but the only unfailing and permanent source of improvement is liberty, since by it there are as many possible independent centres of improvement as there are individuals. The progressive principle, however, in either shape, whether as the love of liberty or of improvement, is antagonistic to the sway of Custom, involving at least emancipation from that yoke; and the contest between the two constitutes the chief interest of the history of mankind. . . .

ROBERT M. MACIVER
The meaning of liberty

When we contemplate the mass of utterances devoted to the subject of liberty we find it hard to escape the conclusion that of all the arts the most backward is the art of thinking. I am referring not to any profound or highly technical art but to an intrinsically simple one. I do not mean the art of fathoming the secrets of nature or the art of calculation or the art of philosophical speculation. I do not mean an art that depends either on erudition or on the skills of the laboratory. On the contrary it is an art that the metaphysician is as apt to sin against as the common man. It is an art that the leaders of men betray at least as often as do those they lead. It is an art that is not taught in the schools, and rarely in the colleges. Instead, there are special crafts and professions the primary purpose of which is to confound this art altogether. It is an art that established authority always suspects and often represses. In some countries today the practice of it is forbidden under the severest penalties. And yet, in this age wherein the techniques of propagandism are so highly developed, there is perhaps no art that it is more imperative for men to learn.

These are bold statements, but anyone who will take the trouble sincerely to contemplate the history of disputations concerning this word " liberty " and its meaning can be convinced, I believe, of their truth. Whatever liberty is, all men are agreed that its presence or absence is of vital importance to them. Whatever liberty is, they have always been ready to fight for it — or about it. But for all the fighting and all the disputing the same confusions and sophistications flourish today, flourish as persistently and as triumphantly as ever in the past. Here there is no record of progress. While we have conquered great kingdoms of knowledge, while we have been penetrating to the heart of the atom and to inconceivably far-off galaxies, we have attained no consensus concerning the condition of this liberty that touches all of us so nearly. Statesmen and even scientists, men of letters and men of law, perpetuate the same misconceptions about it that we find at

Robert M. MacIver, " The Meaning of Liberty and Its Perversions," from *Freedom: Its Meaning*, Ruth Nanda Anshen, ed., 1940, pp. 278–287. Copyright, Harcourt, Brace and Company, Reprinted by permission.

the very dawn of reflection. And if we have not attained any greater clarity or any greater understanding it is not because we are dealing with something in itself abstruse and baffling — it is rather because our interests, our prejudices, our warm immediate impulses will not let us approach it, examine it, and see it for what it is.

We will devote our attention to one thing only — the meaning of a word. How do we ascertain this meaning? There is no question of validity or invalidity in the mere assertion: " I attach this meaning to this symbol." It may be a kind of antisocial act to use a word in a very different sense from that of its common acceptance, but this is in itself no offense against the integrity of thought. In a specialized context it may be appropriate, or even necessary — since there are always more meanings than available words — to use a common word in a specialized sense. Where then does the offense come in? When can we justly speak of the perversion of meaning?

The word we are concerned with is one of universal use. The philosopher and the scientist have no technical term to substitute for it. It signifies an immediate datum, something that cannot be analyzed into components or reduced to simpler elements. It signifies the state of being free, and this being free is as ultimate as being warm or pleased or angry. One indication of the ultimate character of the concept is that while in the English language we have two words for it (" liberty " and " freedom ") no perceptible nuance of difference has developed in the generic usage of them. How can we define a word of this sort? We cannot use other words that more clearly express its meaning. We can, of course, offer cases and illustrations. We can relate its meaning to other meanings. We can consider the conditions on which the state of being free depends. We can bring out its implications. We can specify particular modes of its manifestation, particular areas in which it is present or absent, as when we speak of religious liberty, economic liberty, political liberty, and so on. We can specify within any given situation who is free and in what respect. We can turn about and define it indirectly, as the absence of its negation, the absence of restraint. But in all this we are merely identifying a meaning, not defining it. It is a meaning we must simply recognize, simply accept. The universality of usage sets it for us. It is understood by the child and by the savage as well as by the civilized man. It is a meaning we cannot do without, and thus we find that when people offer us some alternative and different meaning they nonetheless imply that it is equivalent to the universally accepted meaning. Here, as we shall see, is the root of the worst perversions. On this account much that is written on the subject of liberty is worse than futile. It confuses the issues, obscures that which it pretends to clarify, even sophisticates liberty into its own contradiction. Hence the greatest sinners against reason have been the reasoners, the philosophers, and high priests.

The history of the more pretentious writings on liberty, from the time of Plato to the present day, amply substantiates this charge, but within our

present limits all we can do is to point out the nature of the more persistent and frequent misconceptions.[1]

We begin with those who honestly accept the universal meaning but,
being led to define it by the double negative, as the absence of restraint,
are never able to see it positively again and fall in consequence into immediate error. Their argument runs as follows: liberty is the absence of restraint, therefore all restraint is a curtailment of liberty. They reason in
the void of their negatives. Shall we, to bring them back to common sense,
add yet another negative, and ask them, What then of the restraint of restraint? Is it not obvious that liberty — except on a desert island, where,
alas, it is an unprized commodity — is subject to constant invasion and
must be constantly safeguarded? Is it not obvious that the absence of restraint, whereby men in society enjoy any kind of liberty, is the presence
of superior restraint on the forces that would suppress this liberty?

Here the commonest form of error is that which rests on the simple antithesis of the realm of liberty and the realm of law; one the " free " life of
man in nature or in nonpolitical society and the other the coercive order
of the State. Many writers on liberty have been content with this untenable antithesis. It was the view of Thomas Hobbes that liberty existed
only in the interstices of law. And his contention has been upheld with un-
diminished vigor by many later schools, by the utilitarians such as Ben-
tham and Mill, by the Neo-Darwinians such as Herbert Spencer, by the
robust individualists and nature-worshipers after the manner of Thoreau,
by the philosophical anarchists, and by the economic conservatives who at
the present day echo the sentiments of Herbert Hoover's trumpet blast,
The Challenge to Liberty. Every law, they say, is an encroachment on liberty. Every new law reduces yet further the shrunken area of liberty.

Yet the argument is most patently fallacious. You cannot *think* about it
without discovering its error. True, every law restrains *some* liberty for
some. But in so doing it may well establish some other liberty for some
others — or indeed for all. The law that forbids an employer to dismiss a
worker because he joins a trade union gives the worker a liberty that, as
worker, he lacked before. The law that forbids another to trespass on my
property assures me the liberty to enjoy my property. Every law establishes
an obligation, but the obligation is the reverse side of a right. The obligation may lie on the many and the right rest in the few, as for example under a law imposing a censorship of opinion. Or the right may be established
for the many and the corresponding obligation be imposed on the few, as
when a law compels factory-owners to introduce safety devices. Since liberty does not exist in the void but in the relations between men, all liberties depend on restraints just as all rights depend on obligations. The naïve
Hobbesian stand ignores this simple truth.

[1] The best analysis of the subject within my knowledge is Dorothy Fosdick's book,
What Is Liberty?, New York, 1939.

In a deeper sense too it misapprehends alike the nature of liberty and the nature of law. Laws may be tyrannous, but tyranny is the quality of particular enactments and has nothing to do with the essential character of law. Law is not command, though many jurists have mistakenly defined it so. A legal code is a system regulating human relationships within the frontiers of a State and applying to all who live within it. It is a necessary basis of social order, a guaranty that men will act on certain principles in their intercourse with one another, that, for example, they will fulfill their contracts and will not use violence to gain their ends. Remove this system, and every complex society would be reduced to chaos. Men could not foresee the consequences of their actions, could not undertake any enterprise that looked beyond the moment, could not possess any security of mind or body. The liberties we possess are relative to the social order in which we live and in large measure are created as well as sustained by that order. When our rights perish our liberties perish too. How vain then is the saying that liberty exists only " in the interstices of law "!

When men define liberty as the absence of restraint, the trouble frequently is that they at once think of some kinds of restraint and forget others altogether. They do not realize that in every society all kinds of restraints and liberties — legal, constitutional, economic, social, moral, religious — inevitably coexist in endless combinations for the different groups who live in the same community. There is no simple totality that may be named *the* liberty of the individual or *the* liberty of the people. When Herbert Hoover, in the book already referred to, speaks of " the American system of liberty," he finds it realized in the particular range of economic liberties that depend on equal *legal* rights, with practically no reference to the opportunities and conditions on which the exercise of these rights depends. He opposes economic controls by government, not on the ground that they are misguided but on the ground that they cause " myriad wounds to liberty." He decries " regimented agriculture " as a blow to liberty, without inquiring whether the farmers, wisely or unwisely, want the " regimentation." He decries " regimented currency," without considering that currency is always " regimented " — by someone. The controls he disapproves, wisely or unwisely, he regards as inconsistent with liberty or even as part of " the American system of liberty." He seems scarcely conscious of the fact that if two thousand individuals are in a position to control or direct half the industry of the country, therein also lies an important aspect of the problem of liberty.

Every law restrains some liberty, but before we can condemn it on that account we must put to ourselves two vital questions. First, *whose* liberty? For every law gives some men something that they will to have or to do, while restraining them, and all other men, in the contrary direction. Second, *what* liberty? For there are many kinds of liberty, and they conflict one with another, and some can be attained only by the restriction of others, and the advancement of one man's liberty generally means the setting of a limit to the similar liberty of another man. In the simplest terms, when one man or one group dominates another, they arrogate to themselves precisely the kind of liberty over others that they deny the others over themselves. Certain liberties are incompatible with one another, certain liberties are again incompatible with the possession by others of the like liberty. Therefore the answer to the question, *What* liberty? involves always a comparison of liberties and an assessment of their relative values. Here, incidentally, is where the negative definition of liberty as the absence of restraint proves quite unhelpful. For instance, I regard the liberty of men to think as they please as more important, more valuable, than the liberty of other men to control their thinking. The absence of one kind of restraint means far more to me than the absence of another kind of restraint. So I am driven back to the ultimate, the positive, and yet not further definable meaning of liberty. Then the problem of liberty becomes a far more complex one than it seemed at first, when we were content with the negative definition. For now we have to ask: What combination of liberties and restraints is most serviceable for the existence of what men seek when they place a high value on liberty?

Of such a nature are the more significant and searching questions that emerge when we pass beyond the elementary confusions that beset our thinking on the subject. But our immediate concern is with these confusions, and so we proceed to a second group of them. Here we meet the people who start from the universal meaning of liberty but, finding that the state of being free is realized for themselves under certain conditions, forthwith postulate that liberty itself, liberty for all men, is attained under the same conditions. They confound their personal liberty, or the liberty of some group to which they belong, with universal liberty. There are certain things they want to do, certain goals they want to achieve. If there is no restraint on this doing or achieving, that is liberty enough for all men. If all men are free to worship *their* God, that is religious liberty. If all men are free to express the opinions *they* cherish, that is intellectual liberty. Since their God is the true God and their opinions the right opinions, it must be so. They bid us, for example, distinguish liberty from license, license being the liberty to do the things they disapprove. They believe in economic liberty, meaning thereby, if they are employers, the right to run their business as they please, to hire and fire as they please. They believe in " liberty of contract," and maintain, with the Supreme Court in the case of *Adair* vs. *the United States*, that " the right of the employee to quit the service of the employer, for whatever reason, is the same as the right of the employer, for whatever reason, to dispense with the services of such employee." They think it is no interference with the liberty of opinion to restrain the opinion of radicals, if they themselves are conservative, or the opinion of conservatives, if they themselves are radical. They universalize as liberty for all men what is liberty only for the particular group, persuasion, or class to which they adhere.

This interest-limited conception of liberty explains the defeats that the principle of liberty has suffered in many of the battles won in its name. The demand for liberty is a most powerful incentive when it is directed against a particular oppressor or a particular oppression. But those who win liberty for their own cause often refuse it to others. Sects that resist to the death the intolerance of established faiths may become no less intolerant when they in turn are established. Nations that have won political liberties have often used their new-found strength to dominate other nations. The principle of liberty is most apt to be defeated by its own triumphs.

From the interest-limited conception of liberty it is only one step to the final perversion. We have thus far confined ourselves to such views as profess to mean by liberty that which is its universal meaning. About this universal meaning there can be no doubt. The child knows it who is forced to work when he wants to play. The savage knows it who is prevented from following his tribal customs. The criminal knows it who is put behind prison bars. The property-owner knows it who is not allowed to use his property as he pleases. Everywhere in human society, for better or worse, there are hindrances and prohibitions set by the will of others to that which we want to do, and everywhere the condition of which we are thus deprived is called liberty. The meaning of the term may be extended to include the absence of other obstacles to action than those that depend on the will of men to prevent our acting, though then the word " opportunity " is more appropriate than the word " liberty." Or again it may be extended to include the absence of hindrances in ourselves to the fulfillment of the things our hearts desire. Thus we speak of men as being " slaves to their habits." But this is clearly an analogical variant of the universal meaning, not to be pressed too far, certainly not to be made the ground for a redefinition of a term so necessary, so widely used, so unmistakable in its primary applications. The partisans of every cause have redefined the term " liberty," as something else than that which men everywhere mean by it, as something identifying it with their particular cause, thereby creating the worst confusions. They redefine it, and still they appeal to the emotions generated by the universal meaning. They redefine it, and transfer to this new meaning the values that properly attach to the original meaning. This is a far worse offense than those we have already indicated. This offense is " the lie in the soul."

Yet a long line of philosophers have followed this fashion. In the modern world it was set by Rousseau and it attained its philosophical culmination in Hegel. Today it is exploited most notably, though far from exclusively, by the apologists of antilibertarian forms of government. For the curious thing about these final perversions is that they enable men to justify in the name of liberty the most extreme suppressions of liberty. Our modern sophists draw a distinction between real liberty and apparent liberty. They proclaim that we are free only when we do what we *ought* to do — or rather what they think we ought to do; only when we desire what we *ought* to desire — what they think we ought to desire. They say that liberty is self-realization, the realization of the true self. They say that we find liberty in surrender to the " law " of our being, to the law of God, to the law of the State as the organic whole in which we are fulfilled. They do not say that self-realization is good and liberty is good, and seek for some relation between them. They say the one *is* the other. If they make any distinction at all, it is between a superficial and spurious liberty on the one hand and true liberty on the other. So Bernard Bosanquet, for example, contrasted our " actual " will and our " real " will. With sublime Hegelian arrogance they confer reality on what they think ought to be, and degrade to unreality that which they think ought not to be.

So it is not surprising that they often end by merging liberty in its own contradiction. It is the supreme example of having one's cake and eating it too. Rousseau again led the way when he spoke of men being " forced to be free." He was not content with saying " forced to be good," " forced to be rational." He gloried in what seemed to him only a paradox — instead of a perversion. In this he has had a multitude of followers. They transmuted liberty into self-surrender, self-abnegation, obedience, subjection. Hegel reconciled the opposites by announcing that they were one. The individual who is " forced to be free " might protest, but of course it is not his true self that protests. Hegel knows better. In the same spirit Treitschke explained that Germany would restore the people of Alsace " against their will to their true selves." In the same spirit Gentile explains that the absolute corporate State confers more liberty than the democratic State. In the same spirit Spengler and Spann and Freyer and the whole host of Nazi apologists explain that dominance, mastery, totalitarian authority, assure to those subjected to them the blessing of " true liberty."

These apologists will not face the issue that they value other things more highly than liberty and that they reject liberty for the sake of those other things. That position would at least be honest. Instead, they pervert the universal meaning of liberty in order to deny the most obvious of facts. They would destroy the meaning of liberty because they are afraid to admit its meaning. They call it something else, hoping that thus no one will claim it for what it is.

So after the many centuries in which men have talked and written of liberty we find proclaimed from the high places doctrines more perverse and fallacious than ever were uttered at the beginning of reflective thought. I have tried to show that each of these doctrines rests on a quite elementary error, on the most simple inability — or unwillingness — to apply the art of thinking. Liberty cannot be identified with any cause — except the cause of liberty — for its whole challenge is for the right to choose between causes. The analysis of the meaning of liberty, in its application to social realities, opens up the most fruitful questions. They remain mostly unexplored. We cannot advance to the more meaningful problems because they lie beyond this ever renewed fog of intellectual confusion.

RALPH B. PERRY
Liberty in a democratic state

Misunderstandings commonly arise from the fact that for reasons of linguistic economy a single word is used to carry many meanings. Where, as in the case of " liberty," the word itself is charged with emotional meaning, the effect is to ally parties who really mean different things, or divide parties who really mean the same thing. To clarify such a situation, the first step is to set down the several meanings side by side in order that libertarians may realize precisely what it is that they propose and antilibertarians precisely what it is that they oppose.

There are at least seven meanings of liberty which are relevant to democracy. There is positive versus negative liberty; and there is primitive versus moral liberty. These are all fundamental meanings, prior to government. The introduction of government generates the three additional meanings: legal liberty, or liberty *under* government; civil liberty, or liberty *against* government; and political liberty, or liberty *for* government.

One does not speak of liberty at all unless there is a disposition to perform an act. Given such a disposition, negative liberty implies an external obstacle, as when the child is held in the grasp of an adult, or when some barrier, such as iron bars, is interposed between the prisoner and the place where he would prefer to be. With such an obstacle in mind, negative liberty means merely its absence or removal. In social relations the obstacle commonly takes the form of a threat — what the individual desires to do is penalized, that is, connected by natural causation or human intervention with a strongly repugnant sequel.

Negative liberty is relative to the specific character of a felt interest, and to its intensity. In an age of religious zeal negative liberty will mean liberty from an oppressive Church; when men aspire to the management of their own affairs, they will covet liberty from a tyrannical State; when they are ambitious to rise in the economic scale, negative liberty will mean escape from the limitations imposed by the existing industrial hierarchy. To writers, liberty means relief from censorship; to drinkers, repeal of prohibition; to pacifists, the absence of compulsory military service; to agitators and minorities, unrestricted speech and assembly. Negative liberty plays a small role in the lives of apathetic men; and will take a high place in the code of men whose desires and ambitions are strong, and who feel the impact of the obstacle with a proportional intensity.

Positive liberty, on the other hand, means that the externally unimpeded interest is *capable* of proceeding towards its realization. A man is

Ralph B. Perry, " Liberty in a Democratic State," from *Freedom: Its Meaning*, Ruth Nanda Anshen, ed., 1940, pp. 265–272. Copyright, Harcourt, Brace and Company. Reprinted by permission.

not positively at liberty to walk unless he has sound limbs, or to travel unless he has the fare — even though nothing prevents him, and nobody forbids him. Liberty from prison bars is not positively enjoyed except by an individual who is capable of moving his body; the absence of censorship, persecution, or tyranny implies no positive liberty except to those who possess the resources for artistic creation, for worship, or for self-government.

Liberty, positive and negative, is effective personal choice. No one can be said to be an advocate of full liberty, nor can any State or policy be said to promote it, unless liberty is thus doubly conceived, as both unhampered and implemented.

When liberty is claimed or conceded as a right, there arises a distinction between primitive and moral liberty. Primitive liberty is the claim of any interest to the positive and negative conditions of its realization. This liberty manifests itself on every plane, from the most elemental or selfish appetite to the most spiritual or humane aspiration. It possesses no moral quality in itself, but creates an obligation on the part of other interests. According to democratic theory, every interest is, so far as it goes, an original source of value: to negate it is to do evil, and therefore subtracts something from the sum of goods; to negate it unconsciously, is to be reprehensibly selfish; to negate it willfully, is to be malicious. Its own self-assertion may therefore properly be attended with a consciousness of rectitude; and the disinterested observer will feel a moral sympathy with the victim.

But liberty is not only good in the material sense, as possessing a claim to moral consideration, but may itself possess the form of moral goodness intrinsically. When it does possess this form, whether personal or social, it may be termed " moral liberty."

Moral liberty in the personal sense is liberty internally regulated by reason and conscience. It appears upon that level of integration in which the individual's several appetites have been centered and unified by a reflective will. It is a part of the purpose of the democratic State that individuals should be allowed and encouraged to exercise the prerogatives of personality.

In the second or social sense, liberty is moralized when it assumes the form of a sentiment which moves the individual to approve and to seek the enjoyment of liberty by all. Love of liberty in this sense is tested by the attitude towards another's liberty. The love of one's own liberty creates a needful corrective of oppression, but it is morally defective, because it lacks the intent to provide for the interests of others. Patrick Henry's " Give me liberty or give me death " is thus ambiguous. If he meant that he preferred death to the loss of his own liberty, he did not rise above the level of personal self-interest. But if he meant that he preferred death to the destruction of a social system under which all persons enjoyed their just rights, then his sentiment was " noble," but it would have found a fitter expression in the words, " Give *us* liberty, or give *me* death."

Moral liberty, in the social sense, is also possessed by what may be called " cultural liberty," meaning the " disinterested " activities of science and of art. Truth serves all interests, since all interests embrace judgments concerning their instruments or objects and are effective in proportion as these judgments are true. The use of truth by one interest is compatible with its use by others. In so far as science is successful it results in a fund of truth freely available to all, and its value is therefore social or human, rather than private and selfish. Beauty is a sharable good. The enjoyment of painting, sculpture, poetry, and music does not bring individuals into a relation of rivalry and does not create or exacerbate enmities, but induces a sense of participation and is enhanced thereby.

The liberties on which attention is focused at the present time are those whose meaning is related to government. The first is liberty under government, to which I propose to give the name of legal liberty.

The widely diffused idea that liberty is created by the State is both false and confusing. It is entirely conceivable that an isolated individual possessing suitable faculties and facilities, or an individual living in an unorganized society of individuals whose interests were happily compatible with his own, should possess and enjoy full liberty, negative and positive, primitive and moral. This reservation being made, it is now in order to affirm that no high degree of liberty is normally possible without the protection of the State.

The most serious hindrance to a man's interest is the rival interest of his neighbor, and the remedy lies in the systematic delimitation of interests. There is a greater liberty to be enjoyed through the acceptance of such delimitation than through the claim of limitlessness, because the limited liberties are guaranteed and regularized. In short, while the State neither creates nor justifies liberty, it does create security; and it is upon security that the fuller and more constructive liberties of civilization depend.

The restrictions which government imposes are justified only by the primitive and moral liberties for which they make room — as much room as possible. Any given system of legal liberty may fail to provide the maximum of room, and this failure furnishes the ground for criticism and reform. This priority of primitive and moral liberties is not eagerly accepted by those who under the existing system enjoy the most spacious room, and would therefore prefer to invest their present legal liberties with an ultimate validity.

If it be the duty of government to promote the liberty of every man, this function must be extended to embrace positive and not merely negative liberty. The most ancient, persistent, and oppressive enemies of liberty are not external hindrances, whether physical or human, but poverty and ignorance. It is the chief fault of prosperous and of enlightened men

that they forget this fact. What government does in the way of education, public information, health, housing, increased wages, reduced hours
of labor, or the redistribution of wealth may be as much a service of liberty as is its protection of men against interference, from one another or
from itself. The distinction between "welfare" and liberty breaks down
altogether, since a man's effective liberty is proportional to his resources.

The topic of civil liberty is the most confused, and, next after that of
war, the most prominent of contemporary issues. The phrase has at least
five distinct meanings which are, unhappily, not distinguished. It is sometimes used to mean legal liberty, in the sense already discussed above. It is
sometimes used to mean political liberty, in the sense to be discussed below. It is sometimes used, without definition, to refer to an indeterminate
list of specific liberties: the liberties of speech, press, assembly, and religion, as interpreted in judicial decisions; the so-called "inalienable" rights
of life, liberty, and property or happiness; the rights of petition, habeas
corpus, "due process" of law, trial by jury, and the inviolability of the
home or person; together with other rights embraced under the broad for-
mulas of "common law rights," or "the rights of Englishmen." It is sometimes used, again without definition, to refer to a narrower group of the liberties listed above, namely, those liberties which have to do most directly
with the effective public utterance of opinion. Finally, civil liberty is sometimes taken to mean such liberties as the above, when conceived as limiting the powers of the executive and legislative branches of the government,
or of the government "in power," and as entrusted to some more considered procedure, such as the framing or amendment of the constitution, or
decisions by courts having a constitutional jurisdiction.

The expression "civil liberty" will here be employed in the fifth of
these senses, in the sense, namely, of constitutional liberty. Civil liberty
defines the line between the use and the abuse of the powers of government. It has meaning only in a political philosophy, such as democracy, in
which it is affirmed that government, instead of being an end in itself, possesses obligations beyond itself. It signifies what, to use Jefferson's expression, "the people are entitled to against every government on earth."

The principle of civil liberty implies a tendency of government to defeat its legitimate end and become an abuse rather than a utility. There
are three ways in which government may become the enemy of liberty: by
disloyalty, by excess, and by inefficiency.

By disloyalty of government is here meant any deviation from its public
function due to the private self-interest of the ruler. It signifies the chronic
evil, and the chronic suspicion, associated with the name of tyranny. The
popularity of government does not suffice to save it from tyranny, but may
create new forms of tyranny. Thus popular government lends itself to the
tyranny of the majority or of the masses; and to the tyranny of the demagogue, who conceals his self-interest by flattering the people, and appeals

to their baser instincts against their reflective judgment. The corrective of tyranny in these popular forms does not lie in relating government more closely to the existing will of those who live under it, but in a scrupulous regard for the liberty of minorities or dissenting individuals, and in a system of popular education that shall emancipate the critical faculties and develop a resistance to irrational appeal.

Liberty may be conceived as a just claim not only against disloyal government, or tyranny, but also against excessive government, or paternalism. A popular government is peculiarly liable to this abuse. It tends to be trusted by those who live under it, since it speaks in their name; and it tends to be invoked by them as a utility, since they feel it is their creature.

The issue of liberty versus excessive government derives its present meaning to most Americans from the application to " business." The beginning of sound thinking on this matter is to see that the economic system known as laissez faire capitalism is not an effect of " the silence of the law," but is founded on legal rights. Men who are merely let alone to do as they please do not compete with one another, they plunder one another. " Free competition " depends no more on letting men do as they please, than on preventing them from doing as they please, and forcing them to do as they do not please. The only question regarding government's interference with business is whether it shall interfere more or less, and in old ways or new ways. The only democratic principle applicable to this question is the principle that the restraints imposed by government shall be justified by their positive fruitfulness to the individuals living under government. Judged by this standard, government is always excessive when it is exercised for its own sake.

Civil rights protect men, in the third place, from the inefficiency of government, that is, from the malfunctioning of its mechanisms and agencies. Considering the instruments at its command, government will sometimes most effectively serve liberty by leaving the regulation of private interests to private institutions, such as church, school, or charitable organization, or to the unofficial power of the social conscience. Thus the agencies which will effectively regulate opinion, sentiment, science, and art are coarse instruments, unsuited to so delicate an operation. If a hammer and saw were the only tools of surgery, it would be difficult to remove the diseased portions of the body without injuring the adjoining parts. Similarly, the mechanisms of public enforcement are ill suited to distinguish between art and pornography, or between science and dogma, or between persuasion and propaganda, or between education and indoctrination.

Every instrument may be dulled or broken by overuse. A State which is asked to do too much may do nothing well. Its functions may increase more rapidly than its competence. It is prudent, therefore, to limit the functions of the State out of regard for the human limitations of its rulers.

The inefficiency of government may consist not in the imperfection of its own instruments, but in its failure to profit by other instruments. It is self-evident that the State should derive the utmost public benefit from the motive of private self-interest. There is an area within which public and private interest coincide, and here the motive of private interest may be stronger and more reliable than the disinterestedness of government, and its use more economical. . . .

PHILOSOPHY OF EDUCATION SOCIETY
A statement on intellectual freedom

A vigorous democracy continuously builds upon the faith that in matters of public policy the people can decide what is best for them as a result of open discussion. A democratic people puts its trust in procedures that provide a hearing for contending beliefs and the weighing of differing ideas. Anything which prevents or restricts the process of public inquiry and the free communication of ideas interferes with the process by which the people decide what is good in every aspect of their common life. In this manner, they seek to improve the institutions which serve them.

We have a distinguished tradition which affirms the right to engage in free and open inquiry into problems of public concern. Our Founding Fathers, knowing the free exchange of ideas to be indispensable to the progress of a free people, provided that " Congress shall make no law . . . abridging the freedom of Speech." Throughout our history we have attained, even in perilous times, a vital and abiding faith in the free expression and examination of ideas. Jefferson affirmed clearly this deeply held value. " If there be any among us who would wish to dissolve this Union or to change its republican form, let them stand undisturbed as monuments of the safety with which error of opinion may be tolerated where reason is left free to combat it." This tradition has been the keystone of this country's greatness.

When ideas are not freely exchanged and judged on their merits, decisions and judgments are controlled by the arbitrary authorities of the moment. Then, to hold a belief at variance with the views of those who hold arbitrary power is to risk suppression, perhaps by an official police power. Tyranny, rooted in the effort to control the thoughts of men, may gradually come upon us if in timidity or thoughtlessness we fail to practice our tradition of speaking, hearing, thinking and choosing.

Mature minds cannot be developed where ideas deemed dangerous are kept out of our common life. We must provide, therefore, those conditions which make the full range of alternatives freely available for public inspection. To the degree that the conditions of open inquiry and communication are established we need have no fear but that our citizens will

" The Right to Intellectual Freedom: A Statement by the Philosophy of Education Society," *Educational Theory*, 3:185–186, April, 1953. Reprinted by permission.

choose policies that advance the common good. Failure to accept this responsibility is to deny the very basis of self-government and thereby to surrender to tyranny.

Consequently, the freedom to inquire is a public necessity. Our society will be renewed not by those who know no other way to live but only by those who knowing others, prefer the democratic way. Thus, the rights to inquire, to hear, to speak, are not rights we hold privately, but rights we share in common through our citizenship.

It thus becomes the duty of thoughtful citizens to protest the suppression of freedom of thought, inquiry, and communication wherever it may occur. In each instance, where the rights to hear and study and explore ideas are infringed, there is a present danger to our way of life and to the freedom of each of us. These rights should be exercised, to be sure, in a thoughtful manner, with full regard for the obligations of personal sincerity and integrity and a commitment to the ways of a free society. Yet responsible inquiry and expression are best safeguarded and nourished when intellectual freedom is held so dear that we protect the right of individuals to express even the most unwelcome ideas.

In the light of these considerations we affirm that the indispensable condition for the preservation and enrichment of our democratic heritage is the full and free examination of ideas. A living danger to a free society exists whenever a particular interested group appropriates for itself the right to censure ideas, to determine what others may hear. This course, though pursued in the name of democracy, can lead only to the subversion of our way of life. It is the obligation of a democratic community to provide the maximum opportunity for the full, free and responsible exchange of ideas on matters of public concern.

For the Philosophy of Education Society
By Its Committee on Freedom of Inquiry

George E. Axtelle
H. Gordon Hullfish
Kent Pillsbury
B. Othanel Smith
A. Stafford Clayton, Chairman

SECTION **4. Community and individuality**

" To learn to be human is to develop through the give-and-take of communication an effective sense of being an individually distinctive member of a community; one who understands and appreciates its beliefs, desires, and methods, and who contributes to a further conversion of organic powers into human resources and values." This conception of the intrinsic relationship between *individuality* and *community*, as stated by John Dewey, bridges one of the oldest alleged conflicts in social theory — that of the individual *vs* society. A clear conception of individuality posed in this conflict is revealed in the earlier selection on freedom by John Stuart Mill. Dewey's position transposes, in our century, the focus of attention to a yet more fundamental issue: How can we develop the individual *in* society — the productive individual who realizes his own potentialities and contributes thereby to the enhancement of the common life? In the selections which follow, John Dewey and Mary Follett address themselves to this issue.

The centrality of the issue in our times has been underscored by many social analysts. The postwar decades have been beset with social criticisms which have marked and often decried our tendency toward conformity, toward an ethic of the organization man, toward outer-directedness, toward reverence for the group mind. The telling significance of these criticisms, insofar as they point to social realities or forces which dwarf or stultify human personality, cannot be gainsaid. But the plea against frightened or unwitting conformity, against lack of moral courage, or against the scarcity of creativity and imagination in human life, can in irresponsible minds easily degenerate into a plea in favor of equally unconsidered or asocial eccentricity. Perhaps no greater service to intellectual clarity in this realm could be rendered than to establish those criteria which will enable us to distinguish between worthy and spurious individuality, and to discover and abet those conditions which produce the type of worthy, integrated individuality which remains relevant to the present, not acquiescent but boldly and creatively adaptive, not unexamined but consciously chosen. The task of determining such criteria inevitably faces every classroom teacher.

JOHN DEWEY
The nature of community

That government exists to serve its community, and that this purpose cannot be achieved unless the community itself shares in selecting its governors and determining their policies, are a deposit of fact left, as far as we can see, permanently in the wake of doctrines and forms, however, transitory the latter. They are not the whole of the democratic idea, but they express it in its political phase. Belief in this political aspect is not a mystic faith as if in some overruling providence that cares for children, drunkards and others unable to help themselves. It marks a well-attested conclusion from historic facts. We have every reason to think that whatever changes may take place in existing democratic machinery, they will be of a sort to make the interest of the public a more supreme guide and criterion of governmental activity, and to enable the public to form and manifest its purposes still more authoritatively. In this sense the cure for the ailments of democracy is more democracy. The prime difficulty . . . is that of discovering the means by which a scattered, mobile and manifold public may so recognize itself as to define and express its interest. This discovery is necessarily precedent to any fundamental change in the machinery. We are not concerned therefore to set forth counsels as to advisable improvements

From John Dewey, *Public and Its Problems*, 1927, pp. 146–152. Reprinted by permission of Holt, Rinehart and Winston, Inc.

in the political forms of democracy. Many have been suggested. It is no derogation of their relative worth to say that consideration of these changes is not at present an affair of primary importance. The problem lies deeper; it is in the first instance an intellectual problem: the search for conditions under which the Great Society may become the Great Community. When these conditions are brought into being they will make their own forms. Until they have come about, it is somewhat futile to consider what political machinery will suit them.

In a search for the conditions under which the inchoate public now extant may function democratically, we may proceed from a statement of the nature of the democratic idea in its generic social sense.[1] From the standpoint of the individual, it consists in having a responsible share according to capacity in forming and directing the activities of the groups to which one belongs and in participating according to need in the values which the groups sustain. From the standpoint of the groups, it demands liberation of the potentialities of members of a group in harmony with the interests and goods which are common. Since every individual is a member of many groups, this specification cannot be fulfilled except when different groups interact flexibly and fully in connection with other groups. A member of a robber band may express his powers in a way consonant with belonging to that group and be directed by the interest common to its members. But he does so only at the cost of repression of those of his potentialities which can be realized only through membership in other groups. The robber band cannot interact flexibly with other groups; it can act only through isolating itself. It must prevent the operation of all interests save those which circumscribe it in its separateness. But a good citizen finds his conduct as a member of a political group enriching and enriched by his participation in family life, industry, scientific and artistic associations. There is a free give-and-take: fullness of integrated personality is therefore possible of achievement, since the pulls and responses of different groups reënforce one another and their values accord.

Regarded as an idea, democracy is not an alternative to other principles of associated life. It is the idea of community life itself. It is an ideal in the only intelligible sense of an ideal: namely, the tendency and movement of some thing which exists carried to its final limit, viewed as completed, perfected. Since things do not attain such fulfillment but are in actuality distracted and interfered with, democracy in this sense is not a fact and never will be. But neither in this sense is there or has there ever been anything which is a community in its full measure, a community unalloyed by alien elements. The idea or ideal of a community presents, however, actual phases of associated life as they are freed from restrictive and disturbing elements, and are contemplated as having attained their limit of

---

[1] The most adequate discussion of this ideal with which I am acquainted is T. V. Smith's " The Democratic Way of Life."

development. Wherever there is conjoint activity whose consequences are appreciated as good by all singular persons who take part in it, and where the realization of the good is such as to effect an energetic desire and effort to sustain it in being just because it is a good shared by all, there is in so far a community. The clear consciousness of a communal life, in all its implications, constitutes the idea of democracy.

Only when we start from a community as a fact, grasp the fact in thought so as to clarify and enhance its constituent elements, can we reach an idea of democracy which is not utopian. The conceptions and shibboleths which are traditionally associated with the idea of democracy take on a veridical and directive meaning only when they are construed as marks and traits of an association which realizes the defining characteristics of a community. Fraternity, liberty and equality isolated from communal life are hopeless abstractions. Their separate assertion leads to mushy sentimentalism or else to extravagant and fanatical violence which in the end defeats its own aims. Equality then becomes a creed of mechanical identity which is false to facts and impossible of realization. Effort to attain it is divisive of the vital bonds which hold men together; as far as it puts forth issue, the outcome is a mediocrity in which good is common only in the sense of being average and vulgar. Liberty is then thought of as independence of social ties, and ends in dissolution and anarchy. It is more difficult to sever the idea of brotherhood from that of a community, and hence it is either practically ignored in the movements which identify democracy with Individualism, or else it is a sentimentally appended tag. In its just connection with communal experience, fraternity is another name for the consciously appreciated goods which accrue from an association in which all share, and which give direction to the conduct of each. Liberty is that secure release and fulfillment of personal potentialities which take place only in rich and manifold association with others: the power to be an individualized self making a distinctive contribution and enjoying in its own way the fruits of association. Equality denotes the unhampered share which each individual member of the community has in the consequences of associated action. It is equitable because it is measured only by need and capacity to utilize, not by extraneous factors which deprive one in order that another may take and have. A baby in the family is equal with others, not because of some antecedent and structural quality which is the same as that of others, but in so far as his needs for care and development are attended to without being sacrificed to the superior strength, possessions and matured abilities of others. Equality does not signify that kind of mathematical or physical equivalence in virtue of which any one element may be substituted for another. It denotes effective regard for whatever is distinctive and unique in each, irrespective of physical and psychological inequalities. It is not a natural possession but is a fruit of the community when its action is directed by its character as a community.

Associated or joint activity is a condition of the creation of a community. But association itself is physical and organic, while communal life is moral, that is emotionally, intellectually, consciously sustained. Human beings combine in behavior as directly and unconsciously as do atoms, stellar masses and cells; as directly and unknowingly as they divide and repel. They do so in virtue of their own structure, as man and woman unite, as the baby seeks the breast and the breast is there to supply its need. They do so from external circumstances, pressure from without, as atoms combine or separate in presence of an electric charge, or as sheep huddle together from the cold. Associated activity needs no explanation; things are made that way. But no amount of aggregated collective action of itself constitutes a community. For beings who observe and think, and whose ideas are absorbed by impulses and become sentiments and interests, " we " is as inevitable as " I." But " we " and " our " exist only when the consequences of combined action are perceived and become an object of desire and effort, just as " I " and " mine " appear on the scene only when a distinctive share in mutual action is consciously asserted or claimed. Human associations may be ever so organic in origin and firm in operation, but they develop into societies in a human sense only as their consequences, being known, are esteemed and sought for. Even if " society " were as much an organism as some writers have held, it would not on that account be society. Interactions, transactions, occur *de facto* and the results of interdependence follow. But participation in activities and sharing in results are additive concerns. They demand *communication* as a prerequisite. . . .

MARY P. FOLLETT
The nature of individuality

As the collective idea and the collective will, right and purpose, are born within the all-sufficing social process, so here too the individual finds the wellspring of his life. The visible form in which this interplay of relations appears is society and the individual. A man is a point in the social process rather than a unit in that process, a point where forming forces meet straightway to disentangle themselves and stream forth again. In the language of the day man is at the same time a social factor and a social product.

People often talk of the social mind as if it were an abstract conception, as if only the individual were real, concrete. The two are equally real. Or rather the only reality is the relating of one to the other which creates both. Our sundering is as artificial and late an act as the sundering of con-

From Mary P. Follett, *The New State*, 1920, pp. 60–68. Reprinted by permission of Longmans, Green and Company, Inc.

sciousness into subject and object. The only reality is the interpenetrating of the two into experience. Late intellectualism abstracts for practical purposes the ego from the world, the individual from society.

But there is no way of separating individuals, they coalesce and coalesce, they are " confluent," to use the expression of James, who tells us that the chasm between men is an individualistic fiction, that we are surrounded by fringes, that these overlap and that by means of these I join with others. It is as in Norway when the colors of the sunset and the dawn are mingling, when to-day and to-morrow are at the point of breaking, or of uniting, and one does not know to which one belongs, to the yesterday which is fading or the coming hour — perhaps this is something like the relation of one to another: to the onlookers from another planet our colors might seem to mingle.

The truth about the individual and society has been already implied, but it may be justifiable to develop the idea further because of the paramount importance for all our future development of a clear understanding of the individual. Our nineteenth-century legal theory (individual rights, contract, " a man can do what he likes with his own," etc.) was based on the conception of the separate individual. We can have no sound legal doctrine, and hence no social or political progress, until the fallacy of this idea is fully recognized. The new state must rest on a true conception of the individual. Let us ask ourselves therefore for a further definition of individuality than that already implied.

The individual is the unification of a multiplied variety of reactions. But the individual does not react to society. The interplay constitutes both society on the one hand and individuality on the other: individuality and society are evolving together from this constant and complex action and reaction. Or, more accurately, the relation of the individual to society is not action and reaction, but infinite interactions by which both individual and society are forever a-making: we cannot say if we would be exact that the individual acts upon and is acted upon, because that way of expressing it implies that he is a definite, given, finished entity, and would keep him apart merely as an agent of the acting and being acted on. We cannot put the individual on one side and society on the other, we must understand the complete interrelation of the two. Each has no value, no existence without the other. The individual is created by the social process and is daily nourished by that process. There is no such thing as a self-made man. What we think we possess as individuals is what is stored up from society, is the subsoil of social life. We soak up and soak up and soak up our environment all the time.

Of what then does the individuality of a man consist? Of his relation to the whole, not (1) of his apartness nor (2) of his difference alone.

Of course the mistake which is often made in thinking of the individual is that of confusing the physical with the real individual. The physical individual is seen to be apart and therefore apartness is assumed of the psychic or real individual. We think of Edward Fitzgerald as a recluse, that he got his development by being alone, that he was largely outside the influences of society. But imagine Fitzgerald's life with his books. It undoubtedly did not suit his nature to mix freely with other people in bodily presence, but what a constant and vivid living with others his life really was. How closely he was in vital contact with the thoughts of men.

We must bear in mind that the social spirit itself may impose apartness on a man; the method of uniting with others is not always that of visible, tangible groups. The pioneer spirit is the creative spirit even if it seems to take men apart to fulfil its dictates. On the other hand the solitary man is not necessarily the man who lives alone; he may be one who lives constantly with others in all the complexity of modern city life, but who is so shut-up or so set upon his own ideas that he makes no real union with others.

Individuality is the capacity for union. The measure of individuality is the depth and breadth of true relation. I am an individual not as far as I am apart from, but as far as I am a part of other men. Evil is non-relation. The source of our strength is the central supply. You may as well break a branch off the tree and expect it to live. Non-relation is death.

I have said that individuality consists neither of the separateness of one man from the other, nor of the differences of one man from the other. The second statement is challenged more often than the first. This comes from some confusion of ideas. My individuality is difference springing into view as relating itself with other differences. The act of relating is the creating act. It is vicious intellectualism to say, " Before you relate you must have things to relate, therefore the differences are more elemental: there are (1) differences which (2) unite, therefore uniting is secondary." The only fact, the only truth, is the creative activity which appears as the great complex we call humanity. The activity of creating is all. It is only by *being* this activity that we grasp it. To view it from the outside, to dissect it into its different elements, to lay these elements on the dissecting table as so many different individuals, is to kill the life and feed the fancy with dead images, empty, sterile concepts. But let us set about relating ourselves to our community in fruitful fashion, and we shall see that our individuality is bodying itself forth in stronger and stronger fashion, our difference shaping itself in exact conformity with the need of the work we do.

For we must remember when we say that the essence of individuality is the relating of self to other difference, that difference is not something static, something given, that it also is involved in the world of becoming. This is what experience teaches me — that society needs my difference, not as an absolute, but just so much difference as will relate me. Differences develop within the social process and are united through the social process. Difference which is not capable of relation is eccentricity. Eccentricity, caprice, put me outside, bring anarchy; true spontaneity, originality, belong not to chaos but to system. But spontaneity must be coördinated; irrelevancy produces nothing, is insanity. It is not my uniqueness which makes me of value to the whole but my power of relating. The nut and the screw form a perfect combination not because they are different, but because they exactly fit into each other and together can perform a function which neither could perform alone, or which neither could perform half of alone or any part of alone. It is not that the significance of the nut and screw is increased by their coming together, they have no significance at all unless they do come together. The fact that they have to be different to enter into any fruitful relation with each other is a matter of derivative importance — derived from the work they do.

Another illustration is that of the specialist. It is not a knowledge of his specialty which makes an expert of service to society, but his insight into the relation of his specialty to the whole. Thus it implies not less but more relation, because the entire value of that specialization is that it is part of something. Instead of isolating him and giving him a narrower life, it gives him at once a broader life because it binds him more irrevocably to the whole. But the whole works both ways: the specialist not only contributes to the whole, but all his relations to the whole are embodied in his own particular work.

Thus difference is only a part of the life process. To exaggerate this part led to the excessive and arrogant individualism of the nineteenth century. It behooves us children of the twentieth century to search diligently after the law of unity that we may effectively marshal and range under its dominating sway all the varying diversities of life.

Our definition of individuality must now be " finding my place in the whole ": " my place " gives you the individual, " the whole " gives you society, but by connecting them, by saying " my place in the whole," we get a fruitful synthesis. I have tried hard to get away from any mechanical system and yet it is difficult to find words which do not seem to bind. I am now afraid of this expression — my place in the whole. It has a rigid, unyielding sound, as if I were a cog in a machine. But my place is not a definite portion of space and time. The people who believe in their " place " in this sense can always photograph their " places." But my place is a matter of infinite relation, and of infinitely changing relation, so that it can never be captured. It is neither the anarchy of particularism nor the rigidity of the German machine. To know my place is not to know my niche, not to know whether I am cog no. 3 or cog no. 4; it is to be alive at every instant at every finger tip to every contact and to be conscious of those contacts.

We see now that the individual both seeks the whole and is the whole.

First, the individual, biology tells us, is never complete, completeness spells death; social psychology is beginning to show us that man advances towards completeness not by further aggregations to himself, but by further and further relatings of self to other men. We are always reaching forth for union; most, perhaps all, our desires have this motive. The spirit craves totality, this is the motor of social progress; the process of getting it is not by adding more and more to ourselves, but by offering more and more of ourselves. Not appropriation but contribution is the law of growth. What our special contribution is, it is for us to discover. More and more to release the potentialities of the individual means the more and more progressive organization of society if at the same time we are learning how to coördinate all the variations. The individual in wishing for more wholeness does not ask for a chaotic mass, but for the orderly wholeness which we call unity. The test of our vitality is our power of synthesis, of life synthesis.

But although we say that the individual is never complete, it is also true that the individual is a being who, because his function is relating and his relatings are infinite, is in himself the whole of society. It is not that the whole is divided up into pieces; the individual is the whole at one point. This is the incarnation: it is the whole flowing into me, transfusing, suffusing me. The fulness, bigness of my life is not measured by the amount I do, nor the number of people I meet, but how far the whole is expressed through me. This is the reason why unifying gives me a sense of life and more unifying gives me a sense of more life — there is more of the whole and of me. My worth to society is not how valuable a part I am. I am not unique in the world because I am different from any one else, but because I am a whole seen from a special point of view.[1]

That the relation of each to the whole is dynamic and not static is perhaps the most profound truth which recent years have brought us.[2] We now see that when I give my share I give always far more than my share, such are the infinite complexities, the fulness and fruitfulness of the interrelatings. I contribute to society my mite, and then society contains not just that much more nourishment, but as much more as the loaves and fishes which fed the multitude outnumbered the original seven and two. My contribution meets some particular need not because it can be measured off against that need, but because my contribution by means of all the cross currents of life always has so much more than itself to offer. When I withhold my contribution, therefore, I am withholding far more than my personal share. When I fail some one or some cause, I have not failed just that person, just that cause, but the whole world is thereby crippled. This thought gives an added solemnity to the sense of personal responsibility.

To sum up: individuality is a matter primarily neither of apartness nor of difference, but of each finding his own activity in the whole. In the many times a day that we think of ourselves it is not one time in a thou-

---

[1] This is the principle of the vote in a democracy. This must not, however, be confused with the old Hegelianism.

[2] In art this is what impressionism has meant. In the era before impressionism art was in a static phase, that is, artists were working at fixed relations. The " balance " of modern artists does not suggest fixedness, but relation subject directly to the laws of the whole.

sand that we think of our eccentricities, we are thinking indirectly of those qualities which join us to others: we think of the work we are doing with others and what is expected of us, the people we are going to play with when work is over and the part we are going to take in that play, the committee-meeting we are going to attend and what we are going to do there. Every distinct act of the ego is an affirmation of that amount of separateness which makes for perfect union. Every affirmation of the ego establishes my relation with all the rest of the universe. It is one and the same act which establishes my individuality and gives me my place in society. Thus an individual is one who is being created *by* society, whose daily breath is drawn *from* society, whose life is spent *for* society. When we recognize society as self-unfolding, self-unifying activity, we shall hold ourselves open to its influence, letting the Light stream into us, not from an outside source, but from the whole of which we are a living part. It is eternally due us that that whole should feed and nourish and sustain us at every moment, but it cannot do this unless at every moment we are creating it. This perfect interplay is Life. To speak of the " limitations of the individual " is blasphemy and suicide. The spirit of the whole is incarnate in every part. " For I am persuaded that neither death, nor life, nor angels, nor principalities, nor powers, nor things present, nor things to come, nor height, nor depth, nor any other creature, shall be able to separate " — the individual from society. .

SECTION 5. Experimentalism in the democratic scheme of values

The uncritical adulation of fraternity, liberty, and equality leads to " mushy sentimentalism," as John Dewey puts it in a preceding selection. For these are not static concepts, nor is it a static society within which they function. We are constantly evolving and refining our perceptions of these qualities. If these are indeed not static, how can we be sure that we retain their essential characteristics as they evolve? This is one of the questions to which the following selection by John L. Childs addresses itself.

As a pragmatist, Childs is especially concerned with the place of experimentalism in the democratic scheme of values. This experimentalism embodies the method of intelligence in resolving problems and rests upon the pragmatic principle that the resulting beliefs be judged by the consequences to which they lead. If we exercise this experimental inquiry, so the argument goes, we will have incorporated a self-regulating mechanism for properly reconstructing our social order. In that way we shall be able to modify our conception of what constitutes the essential attributes of democracy without at the same time losing its essence.

Childs deals with experimentalism within a self-imposed limitation of the viewpoints of four individuals — Dewey, Kilpatrick, Counts, and Bode. He begins with a clarification of Dewey's reasons for preferring democracy to other forms of social life and concludes with some common elements in the thinking of Kilpatrick, Counts, and Bode on the matter of experimentalism. The reader should be further aware that the following selection is merely an introduction to the idea of experimentalism; its implications are dealt with more extensively in Chapters 10, 11, and 14.

JOHN L. CHILDS
Strands in the pragmatic theory of education

The kind of values which we have just described persist, however, and they provide the perduring moral standards by which proposals for meeting these changing life conditions are evaluated. Chief among these lasting values, as we have seen, are faith in the potentialities of human beings and regard for their welfare and growth, faith in the principle of equal treatment for all, faith in the desirability of sharing interests and meanings, faith in the possibility of the improvement of man's estate through the process of inquiry, the free exchange of ideas, and the fashioning of more inclusive and significant human ends, and faith in the possibility of the creation of a flexible and stable social and political system in which authority and law rest on the consent of the governed and changes are made by peaceful and cooperative means.

We turn now to the problem of the relation of these values of the democratic way of life to the scientific or experimental method of thought. Obviously, the way in which we view this relationship will have far-reaching educational consequences. Moreover, . . . it is a question about which pragmatists themselves have differed. Some have held that the morality of democracy and the method of experimental inquiry literally merge as one. That the supreme and inclusive aim of education is to teach the child "how to think," and that if he learns to think experimentally, he will necessarily learn how to live democratically. They have even contended that it is immoral to teach the child "what to think," for education then becomes a process of indoctrination for certain chosen ends or values and the immature human being is robbed of his right to choose for himself, to make his own determinations. Thus to manipulate the child for preconceived values is morally wrong, for without the freedom to make his own determinations he is deprived of his chance to become a genuinely self-determining human being. They also believe that the whole program of democratic education suffers whenever we undertake to determine what the young shall think, for education then tends to become a mere scramble by conflicting pressure groups to control and shape the school curriculum so that their special group interests and values will have a privileged position in the molding of the patterns of belief, value, and allegiance of the young. In this period of transition and trouble, these leaders believe that education needs above everything else to maintain its function of untrammeled inquiry, and they hold that we cut the ground from under the process of free inquiry whenever we assume that it is our responsibility not only to teach the child to think and to ground his views on evidence, but also to

From John L. Childs, *American Pragmatism and Education*, 1956, pp. 135–140, 283–286. Reprinted by permission of Holt, Rinehart and Winston, Inc.

nurture him in the values and the attitudes that are foundational in the democratic way of life.

Other eminent pragmatists view the situation somewhat differently. They recognize that the democratic way of life is inherently an *experimental* mode of group living, but they do not believe that the values of democracy can be restricted to the attitudes and the allegiances that are inherent in the experimental mode of thought. As illustrations of values that transcend those of the method of experimental inquiry they point to faith in the worth and dignity of individual human beings, recognition of the principle of equality of treatment, and allegiance to the principle of the resolution of conflicts through peaceful, cooperative means as opposed to violence and reliance on brute force. They also emphasize that according to the pragmatist theory of the genesis and the nature of human personality, these values are not inborn but are acquired through experience and learning and that they are not so embedded in the practices of any society that a child acquires them automatically merely as a by-product of his living and growing up in the community. Hence, they contend, the school has its responsibility for the deliberate cultivation of these values in the beliefs and attitudes of the young. Moreover, they point to a contradiction in the actual educational practice of those who declare that it is wrong to shape the moral outlooks of the immature in this way. Actually, most of those who condemn education for the nurture of democratic values in the young wholeheartedly support the effort to organize the school in the pattern of a democratic community so that the young will have opportunity to experience and learn this mode of human living. These pragmatists also reject the charge that education in these basic democratic values is necessarily a form of immoral manipulation and indoctrination. For them, the practice of indoctrination involves the deliberate effort to cultivate beliefs by the process of withholding or suppressing evidence, and by the use of sloganized, emotional appeals. The virtue of democratic values is that they are of the kind that can stand the most searching sort of scrutiny and therefore do not have to be inculcated by the withholding of evidence and the suppression of knowledge of other life alternatives. But while these democratic values have been confirmed by that which men have experienced in many different life situations, they nevertheless cannot be reduced to the values that are resident in the scientific outlook or practice. Since they are not inborn they must be cultivated in the young, and these pragmatists hold that organized education has its responsibility for undertaking this basic moral task. . . .

As we have seen, Dewey has never rested the case for democracy on the mere fact that we, as Americans, have lived under its institutions, and that its values, as a consequence of this experience, have " become an habitual part of our mental and moral make-up." He is concerned that the values of democracy be grounded not on " causes " which are the result of a particular cultural experience, but rather on "reasons" that have a universal appeal. He asserts that it is stupid to suppose that "all moral principles are so relative to a particular state of society that they have no binding force in any social condition."

In his discussion of the principle of equality he undertakes to define the nature of these more solid social "reasons" for our democratic preference by showing that the principle of equality is grounded in the very facts of community life. His argument may be summarized as follows: Human beings are interdependent. All of us are dependent on the work of others for life necessities. We are therefore inescapably involved in a network of social relations. These social relations define claims we have on others and they also define obligations we owe to others. The duties are as inherent as the claims, and both are as natural as the facts of social life. Hence there is a criterion of right and wrong that is other than a "mere" personal subjective opinion sometimes improperly called "private conscience."

The person upon whom the duty is laid himself makes claims upon others; he expects benefits from others; he holds others to the duties which they owe him, because of his ends and the values which he seeks to obtain. If the claim is, then, of the kind which he himself puts forth, if it serves a good which he prizes for himself, he must, in the degree in which he is fair-minded, acknowledge it to be a common good, and hence binding upon his judgment and action. . . . Wrong consists in faithlessness to that upon which the wrongdoer counts when he is judging and seeking what is good to him.[1]

Now a key phrase in the above quotation is "in the degree in which he is fair-minded" an individual must acknowledge the "common good" as binding upon his judgment and action. Clearly the implication of this phrase is that the obligation to observe the principle of equality is grounded in the personal character of the judger as well as in the social relations in which he is involved. In other words, Dewey's analysis of the factors inherent in the situation in which the concept of equality emerges tends to confirm and not disconfirm the proposition of Morris Cohen that "our conclusion cannot attain an 'ought' if all of our premises are restricted to what 'is.'"

There is much which suggests that this view is in line with Dewey's own thought. He has consistently maintained that all deliberate education is ultimately a moral undertaking. By "moral" he has meant that a choice among alternative patterns of life and thought is inescapable in it. He has written:

All education is an affair of action. . . . Now all truly human action involves preference. It signifies working for one end rather than for another

[1] Dewey and Tufts, *Ethics*, revised edition, (New York: Henry Holt and Company, 1932), pp. 251–252.

in situations where alternatives exist. . . . Nevertheless intelligent choice is still choice. . . . Sincerity demands a maximum of impartiality in seeking and stating the reasons for the aims and the values which are chosen and rejected. But the scheme of education itself cannot be impartial in the sense of not involving a preference for some values over others. The obligation to be impartial is the obligation to state as clearly as possible what is chosen and why it is chosen.[2]

As a matter of fact, Dewey was not undertaking to show that the " preference " for democracy is not a " preference." He was rather seeking to show that it is a significant, and not an arbitrary preference, and that there are solid reasons for preferring the pattern of democracy to all the alternative forms of social life. Nor can it be held that the values of democracy, in the view of Dewey, are restricted to the values inherent in the method of experimental science or to those verified by scientific procedures. Dewey has always believed in philosophy as vision, and vision goes beyond that which has been scientifically demonstrated. He has always conceived of democracy as an experiment and a faith in a way of life — in part, the validation of that experiment and faith depends upon what we do. To be sure, our aspirations must take account of whatever scientific inquiry discloses, but a program of living and of education may be in harmony with the principles and the findings of science, and yet move out into the affirmation of values that have not been scientifically demonstrated. Dewey declares:

In the historic role of philosophy, the scientific factor, the element of correctness, of verifiable applicability, has a place, but it is a negative one. The meanings delivered by confirmed observation, experimentation and calculation, scientific facts and principles, serve as tests of the values which tradition transmits and of those which emotion suggests. Whatever is not compatible with them must be eliminated in any sincere philosophizing. This fact confers upon scientific knowledge an incalculably important office in philosophy. But the criterion is negative; the exclusion of the inconsistent is far from being identical with a positive test which demands that only what has been scientifically verifiable shall provide the entire content of philosophy. It is the difference between an imagination that acknowledges its responsibility to meet the logical demands of ascertained facts, and a complete abdication of all imagination in behalf of a prosy literalism.[3]

In conclusion, we would emphasize that democracy is neither the child of science nor of pragmatism. Basic elements in the democratic morality are older than either of them. As a matter of fact, democracy provided

---

[2] Kilpatrick, Editor, *The Educational Frontier*, pp. 287–288 (New York: The Century Company, 1933).

[3] Dewey, *Philosophy and Civilization*, (New York: Minton, Balch and Company, 1931), p. 10.

the cultural environment in which American pragmatism evolved. In both its methodological and moral aspects the thought of the pragmatists has been deeply influenced by the values inherent in the democratic way of life. What Dewey designates as " causes " are not as separate from " reasons " as his own statement suggests. One of the reasons we prefer democracy is that there is something in the social experience of men in many different cultures that has caused them to affirm the values we identify with the democratic movement. . . .

* * *

THE PRAGMATIC THEORY OF EDUCATION RE-EXAMINED

The analysis . . . of the views of Kilpatrick, Counts, and Bode reveals important similarities and differences in their respective interpretations of the work of the school. From the standpoint of an understanding of the general pragmatic orientation to the educational task, their agreements are, of course, fundamental. But their differences are also significant, for they define and throw light on certain ambiguities and difficulties in the existing formulations of the pragmatic program of education. In this . . . [discussion] . . . we shall examine some of these differences and the factors that underlie them. We shall also explore the position of a group of progressive educators who contend that the discipline of experimental inquiry is not adequate to prepare the young for the making of value judgments, and, therefore, should be supplemented by what they call " the method of practical judgment."

We begin our discussion, however, with a summary of the basic views that Kilpatrick, Counts, and Bode have in common. In this connection we shall also indicate certain tendencies in contemporary education which they all oppose.

Salient features in the pragmatic theory of education. As we have noted, all three of these pragmatic educators are committed to the methods, the perspectives, and the attested findings of experimental science. They all hold that the entire program of the school should be permeated by the intellectual and moral attitudes inherent in the practice of experimental inquiry. They are united in the conviction that the young should be systematically nurtured in those attitudes and procedures which will dispose them in all aspects of their experience to test and " true-up " their ideas by whatever evidence bears on them.

These pragmatic educators also hold that the school should not attempt to implant any belief or doctrine in the young which is contrary to the established findings of science. Nor should any meaning be communicated in such a way that it cannot be reviewed whenever life developments or advances in knowledge make this desirable. Even the principles and the " laws " of science are subject to this continuing test, for ultimate authority rests not with particular findings, nor with the eminence of those who affirm them, but rather with the empirical and cooperative procedures by which meanings are formulated, clarified, and tested.

All three of these educational leaders are in accord with Peirce's dictum that " the scientific spirit requires a man to be at all times ready to dump his whole cartload of beliefs, the moment experience is against them." Throughout their lives, Kilpatrick, Counts, and Bode have worked for a school that would be open intellectually, that is, for a school open to inquiry.

These three leaders are not only committed to the scientific method of thought, they are equally committed to the democratic way of life. Indeed, they believe that each of these human movements requires the other for its own richest development. For them, the essence of democracy is that the good is to be defined in terms of that which satisfies and promotes the interests of human beings, and that human beings are themselves the best judges of what these interests are and of the means by which they are to be realized. Since human beings live not as isolated atoms but as members of a community, it is obvious that they must cooperate in the determination both of their interests and the definite measures by which they are to be met. This, in turn, requires a society open to inquiry, discussion, and group decision, and this democratic principle of government by consent involves the right of all to raise questions about existing arrangements whenever they consider that these arrangements fail to make effectual use of existing resources, or operate so as to advantage some at the expense of others. Thus, the morality of experimental inquiry and the morality of democracy unite in the common demand that intellectual beliefs, social norms, and legal arrangements be judged by the consequences to which they lead. Just as the scientific principle points to the self-correcting community of belief and inquiry, so does the democratic principle point to the self-regulating, self-adjusting, cooperative human society. Both the scientific principle and the democratic principle stress the fundamental role of intelligence in social affairs.

Kilpatrick, Counts, and Bode all share this faith in the capacity of ordinary experience to develop from within its own processes its regulative meanings, beliefs, standards, social norms, laws, and institutions. They also share the conviction that one of the deepest purposes of the school is to develop the person who can responsibly participate in the maintenance of a society thus open to untrammeled inquiry and morally committed to the reconstruction of its ways of living in accordance with the principle of equal opportunity. Each of these educators has given his own characteristic statement of this basic faith. For Bode, a democratic society cannot be secure if certain of its modes of life and thought operate on an empirical basis, while others remain on the traditional, absolutist foundation. As he views it, that which is absolutist is, in the last analysis, authoritarian in nature. He declares: " A democratic program of education must necessarily rest on the perception that democracy is a challenge to all forms of absolutism, that it has its own standards, ideals, and values, and that these must pervade the entire program from end to end." Kilpatrick, with his emphasis on the reality of change and his regard for the child as a person, states: " Our duty is so to prepare the rising generation to think that they can and will think for themselves, even ultimately, if they so decide, to the point of revising or rejecting what we now think." Counts with his interests in the social, economic, and political aspects of our experience affirms that democracy " places its faith in the methods of enlightenment, persuasion, and peace in the adjustment of differences among men, in the formulation of policies great and small, and even in the transformation of the structure and basic institutions of society. It thus proclaims the most revolutionary political doctrine of all history — the doctrine that the process of revolution itself can be institutionalized and conducted without resort to organized violence and civil war."

The faith of these men in the capacity of human experience to develop its own moral foundations and to define and redefine the ends and the means of human existence has brought them into conflict with all those groups in American life — ecclesiastical, nationalistic, militaristic, economic, and racial — who assume that they are the trustees of immutable beliefs and practices, and who therefore seek to abridge the right of the people to inquire into certain departments of life. Many of the current attacks on the new education are inspired by groups who fear a theory and program of education that is committed to the nurture of consistent experimental and democratic attitudes in the young. . . .

SECTION **6. Authority in the democratic scheme of values**

The history of western civilization for the past several centuries has been one of resistance to and emancipation from various forms of authoritarianism. At some times the opposed authorities were represented by monarchs, at other times by ecclesiastics, at still other times by entrenched political figures. The battle cry of many a liberal cause has been freedom *from* such authorities. Only after the battles were fought, and the authorities deposed, did the realization come that freedom does not operate within a vacuum, that is, with the complete absence of some source of authority. Perhaps the comparative unanimity of people in opposing authoritarianism is indicative of the fact that in general they can more readily come to an agreement on what they are fighting

against than they can on what they are fighting *for*. It is easy to oppose authoritarianism; it is difficult to select from valid competing authorities. Yet it is a truism that freedom is not license. In order for a society to maximize its benefits from freedom, it must subscribe to some overriding principles, beliefs, norms, and aspirations. Collectively, these become the authority from which the society derives its rationale for social action.

In the following selection Kenneth D. Benne analyzes the complex nature of authority. He makes a distinction between authoritarianism, which he rejects, and authority, which he accepts as inevitable in any society. He is particularly critical of some liberals who fail to see the interrelationship of freedom and authority. This treatment by Benne is mainly one of analysis and clarification; he does not purport to derive the ultimate authority to which a democratic society should subscribe. In the next chapter of this book Myron Lieberman deals directly with one facet of the problem of authority, i.e., the sources of authority for the classroom teacher.

KENNETH D. BENNE
An analysis of the concept of authority

Without attempting in any way to oversimplify the " causes " of resurgent authoritarianism in the world today, it can perhaps be safely said that a far-flung and confused attempt to deny the principle of authority in human relationships helps to create the social and moral vacuum, the loss of community, which frantic authoritarianism promises to fill. . . . It should be remarked that this is not meant as an argument for a return to the authoritarian family pattern. Its rejection has come not arbitrarily, but from more or less intelligent parents who have seen that the old institutional form of parental authority no longer serves the changed functions of parenthood in democratic, industrial communities. But new functions mean new authority, a new " office " for parents, not the denial of " office " or authority. The function of inducting children into a wider community in part remains to modern parents. To deny their authority is to reject their responsibility for this function. If children are dependent on the responsible exercise of this function, the " freedom " of children from authority is a distinct detriment to both children and parents. To explain further the ill-starred attempt to reject the principle of authority as well as its outmoded specific forms we will turn shortly to the historic liberal tradition which in some large part represents ideologically a large-scale historical effort to do just that. It will be sufficient here to remark that, insofar as the unreconstructed liberal tradition conduces to attempted rejection of authority from social relations, it diverts from the task of necessary reconstruction of authority-relations and even tends in effect to strengthen its opposite — authoritarianism. That is to say, if the issue between democracy and totalitarianism is one of opposing systems of authority, clashing principles of order, then to deny in the name of democracy the principle of authority, i.e., basically to oppose " freedom " to " authority," while exalting " freedom," is to divert the attention of democrats from the real issue and their real task and thus to serve, wittingly or unwittingly, the opponents of democracy.

Before turning to a more extended statement of the contemporary problem of authority in terms of the deficiencies of a persistent liberal tradi-

From Kenneth D. Benne, A Conception of Authority (New York: Bureau of Publications, Teachers College, Columbia University, 1943), pp. 7–28. Reprinted by permission of the author.

tion, what broad parallels to Plant's described rejection of authority of status by parents do we find in the practices of deliberate education and educators? Plant himself has the following to say on this point:

Quite widely through our school systems the teacher is not depending on her position as such. She is a person — one it is true, with a contribution to classroom activities that is different from that made by the children — but yet a person. In many classrooms she has put her desk in the corner so that its impersonal symbol of authority shall not stand between her and the pupils.[1]

Here again many of us would agree that the attempted rejection of the authoritarian pattern of authority by the teacher is admirable. But precisely why? In order to free children from the authority of the teacher or from the authority of the community, which in the " office " of teacher she represents in the group of children? I should say definitely not. The chief reason why I find her attempted rejection of the authoritarian pattern of classroom management admirable is that it better enables her to mediate between a democratic community and the children growing into it. Because, that is, it permits her with less ambiguity and contradiction *to exercise her authority*, an authority based precisely upon her service as vicar of " the pedagogical community," in this case, a democratic one. That teachers and leaders of teachers have at times seen in the rejection of authoritarianism a rejection of authority and not a greater opportunity to exercise pedagogical authority appropriate to our kind of community, the career of the " child-centered school " makes clear.

To focus vaguely upon the " personality " of the teacher as the source of her authority over children as opposed to her community function or " office " as a teacher, as Plant suggests some teachers are attempting to do, is to leave the former criterion without any intelligible basis of definition. It can only thus become some vague intrinsic quality of leadership. Such a basis for teacher authority seems to me, as previously discussed in the case of the parent, to have much more in common with the authoritarian leadership principle than with the democracy it purports to serve.

Of course, educators must be concerned with the teacher's personality, but precisely in order that she may better fulfill her " office." The only intelligible basis on which to define desirable teacher-personality is in terms of the functions she performs in some community. And this leads precisely to a positive statement of the community values which the teacher is authorized by her community function to seek to develop in the children in her charge, i.e., to the responsibilities and limits of her authoritative office.

For the present, I wish to comment briefly upon what seems to me

[1] Plant, *Personality and the Cultural Pattern*, p. 180. Quoted by permission of the Commonwealth Fund, publishers.

another variant of the tendency to self-abdication of the " office " of teacher by teachers — what Otto Rank [2] has called the attempt to conceive education as therapy. This, as I understand Rank, does not refer to the therapeutic help given to individual pupils in promoting their increased socialization in their school and in the wider community. Such help, whatever hazards it faces in a community fraught with serious conflicts and providing very limited opportunity for deeply shared common experiences, presupposes an educational aim based upon (and in some degree consonant with) the aims and purposes of a going community. It presupposes a common ideology into which it is the function of teachers to induct their students, always of psychological necessity with some measure of respect for their individual differences of all sorts (a respect especially emphasized and augmented by moral design in democratic communities). Rather Rank describes by his phrase, " education as therapy," an attempt by some teachers, warned of the " rottenness " of the prevailing ideology and of the fundamental irrelevance to contemporary community demands and purposes of much of what has been traditionally taught, warned alike by the increasing resistance and indifference of normally alert students toward it and by their own profound misgivings, moral and intellectual, to find in the " unique " and " healthy " adjustments of individual students the central aim of educational effort.

The irony of the attempt is, as Rank points out, that such a pedagogic effort runs a real danger of augmenting the neurosis it sets out to prevent. Rank's own words are eloquent on this point:

Striving educationally for individuality apparently tends more to neurosis than would the enforcement of a strong educational ideology permitting rather of a reaction toward constructive individual development. In other words, the suppression of individuality by a strong community ideal may also lead to neurosis, but the educational furtherance of individual development seems to produce still more neuroses, and ever less strong personalities who rather spontaneously develop in resisting the pressure of a collective education. From this it follows that the modern ideal of education cannot simply consist of a replacing of the community type by developing individual personalities. For the formation of individualities can never be the program of education, the very nature and system of which is to form types.[3]

Again, here as before, we see that the effort of teachers, who find the functional basis of the traditional teacher function eroded by changing and confused community relations and demands, to reject the authoritarianism of the traditional teacher-pupil relationship often seems based on the tacit assumption that the opposite of authoritarianism is no authority. Rejecting

[2] Otto Rank, *Modern Education* (tr. by Mabel E. Moxon). See especially Chaps. I, IV, and V.

[3] Otto Rank, *op. cit.*, p. 28. Quoted by permission of Alfred A. Knopf, publishers.

the burden of their authority because of the undeniably grave confusions and complexities which attend any honest contemporary effort to define it, teachers sometimes attempt unwittingly to throw the full burden of what is in some degree *their* central and continuing problem — the problem of locating living and dependable community powers, trends, and processes (i.e., authorities) and of helping students to find working identifications and affiliations with these — upon the presumably less mature and less experienced minds of their students. Again, as noted above, it is admirable for democratic teachers to work for a community in and beyond the schools in which individuality is respected and prized. But the problem involved here is to establish in school and wider community authority relations which stably foster and protect individuality, i.e., to effect a theoretic and practical interpenetration of individuality and authority, not to exempt individual development from the organic security and direction which stable authority relations can alone provide.

I have tried repeatedly, in my previous comments, to suggest that the contemporary tendency toward self-abdication of authority by parents, teachers, and other community " offices," insofar as it exists, is probably in part a response to personal confusion and uncertainty in the presence of the crumbling, under the impact of transformed cultural conditions, of those ideologies which traditionally stabilized and supported their authorities. I have also suggested that the widespread tendency to see the problem presented by this undeniable state of affairs, not as one of building new and dependable authority relations but as one, in effect, of denying the continuing community functions and needs upon which the authority relation is built, can best be understood in the light of the continuing influence of the ideology of historic liberalism.

It is this second suggestion which I wish now to explore. The early revolt of " modern " men against the uncongenial restrictions of ecclesiastical and political institutions was not confined, as their revolt spread, to the repudiation of the authority of specific institutions over the action and belief of men. It is a commonplace that as this reaction against the autocratic state of the eighteenth century grew, the champions of liberty maintained " that the individual must be liberated from the Church which hampered his freedom to believe; from the Mercantilist system which hampered his freedom to trade; from the guilds which hampered his freedom to labor; and from the censorship which hampered his freedom to expression." [4] In the dominant ideology which emerged, as Dewey has put it, this historical accident was erected into a theoretical denial of the principle of authority. Its historically conditioned origin as a revolt from particular uncongenial and hampering authority relations into the positive freedom of authority relations less hampering and more congenial to novelly emerging human functions and purposes was forgotten and con-

[4] J. S. Schapiro, *Condorcet and the Rise of Liberalism*, p. 59.

cealed in the apotheosis of ideally absolute freedom. In Dewey's language, the

attack upon ecclesiastic and political institutions spread to science and art, to standards and ideals of economic and domestic life. For the practical movement of assault, like every other such movement, had to defend itself on intellectual grounds. The best intellectual defense was attack, and so defense grew into systematic justification, and a social philosophy developed that was critical of the very idea of any authoritative control.[5]

Like all inclusive ideologies this outlook, of course, headed up, though not without paradox, in a view of the nature and motivation of Man, i.e., in a human type. In Sterrett's words:

In the eighteenth century forum, freedom from all forms of social and institutional authority was proclaimed. The evils of man were held to be due to society. The individual could only reach perfection by being freed from all restraint and allowed to follow his natural instincts. All relations between individuals were looked upon as artificial, made by compact, and in no way constitutive of them. Hence dissent became the rule and conformity the exception.[6]

For our purposes, the two most important features of the historic liberal ideology are now before us:

1. The attempted denial of the principle of authority;
and
2. The exaltation of individuality, while identifying the individual with elements of variation and uniqueness rather than with common "human" elements that enter fundamentally and centrally into the developing personality.[7]

It is with this dominating ideological equipment that many — parents and educators among them — face today the task of rebuilding stable authority relationships in keeping with the demands of new interdependencies. For it has become a commonplace with modern students of society

[5] J. Dewey, "Authority and Social Changes," in Harvard Tercentenary Publications, *Authority and the Individual*, p. 170. Reprinted by permission of the President and Fellows of Harvard College.
[6] J. M. Sterrett, *The Freedom of Authority*, p. 12. Quoted by permission of The Macmillan Company, publishers.
[7] This represents, of course, only one aspect and one strain of historic liberal thought. Certainly, the broad liberal tradition has produced its own critics and qualifiers of this very emphasis, especially in its twentieth century developments. Nor has the liberal emphasis, "pure" or qualified, ever captured all the minds or all the institutions of the life of any Western nation. Yet, admitting all the qualifications which might properly be made of the above description of historic liberal ideology, it would be wrong to underemphasize the hold which its dominant emphases have upon the minds and consciences of all of us who have grown up in the American liberal climate of opinion.

that with the growth of our industrial society, the web of social-economic interdependence which ties the life and welfare of each of us to that of all others in an everwidening nexus of economic relationships has grown apace. With the consequent growing involvement of the *common, public* interest in the economic decisions of every individual and every group, the demand has grown for *public* planning of a common framework and policy in which the economic decisions of every individual and group are to be made. A growing conviction has arisen that the traditional competitive-individualist patterns of economic control no longer operate and can no longer operate in the public welfare. The unacknowledged partial surrender of these patterns (though not of their passionate defense) by private control groups themselves, the tragic non-employment of our productive resources, human and material, and the recurrence and persistence of economic depression lend strong support to this conviction. The steady growth of political centralism, despite continuous powerful opposition, has been an inescapable concomitant of these developments. This growth of increasingly collective conditions under which all of us must today live out our lives has unavoidably challenged deeply the institutional patterns of our once individualistic society and economy and our related ideological conceptions of individual-social relationships and of social-political control. In thus being forced to reorganize, often fundamentally, our practices and conceptions of proper individual-group relationships, to re-create our operating patterns of economic and political power, the problem of authority becomes centrally and crucially important.[8]

Sterrett may well be right in his contention that the ideas of " evolution," " culture," and the Hegelian contributions to the social thought of the nineteenth century, rightly understood, make the abstract and atomic individualism of our dominant ideology theoretically indefensible. For all of these developments have served to de-emphasize the abstract and isolated individual of eighteenth century liberal thought by emphasizing the inter-involvements of man and his environment. Further, the idea of " culture," in the anthropological sense, and the dominant emphasis of Hegelian thought led to an increased emphasis upon the social environment in thus entering into the warp and woof of human personality. If these ideas are granted, the human individual can no longer be defensibly identified with its elements of variation and uniqueness, as historical liberalism has been wont to do. For the common patterns of belief and conduct of the social group are seen to enter centrally and intrinsically into the constitution of the human person. The customs of the group furnish in some large measure the habits of member men. The group lives and moves in the common patterns of the persons of its members. Its authority over the minds and consciences of men is thus seen to be involved integrally in

---

[8] A vast bibliography might be used to document this development. A succinct and authoritative description can be found in Karl Mannheim's *Man and Society in an Age of Reconstruction*. See especially Introduction, Chaps. I and II; Part I, Chap. IV.

the processes by which persons grow and develop. But Sterrett is probably guilty only of understatement in his further remark concerning the continued prevalence of the individualistic ideology, especially if we include the " common man " as well as the " intellectual " in our purview. " And yet it lingers on in robust form — an encysted, but lively corpse in the cosmic thought of the twentieth century." [9]

It is this very " lively corpse," still confusing the historic battles out of which it was born with a cosmic issue of authority and freedom, that responds in the area of education, for example, to contemporary suggestions of any authoritative teaching with flat opposition, and in the name of " individuality " and " freedom." According to Counts,

The champions of freedom are obviously the product of an age that has broken very fundamentally with the past and is equally uncertain about the future. In many cases they feel themselves victims of narrow orthodoxies which were imposed upon them during childhood and which have severely cramped their lives. At any suggestion that the child should be influenced by his elders they therefore envisage the establishment of a state church, the formulation of a body of sacred doctrine, and the teaching of this doctrine as fixed and final. . . . But this is to create a wholly artificial situation: the choice should not be limited to two extremes.[10]

Nearly every social issue tends to be interpreted, by those of the above persuasion, in terms of a conflict of freedom and authority. In such cases, " authority " is identified tacitly with the " authoritarianism " against which the liberal-democratic movements led their historic revolt. It is not often recognized by those who oppose freedom and " authority " that this identification is, in effect, an acceptance of the view of their anti-liberal opposition. For it is to admit, by implication, that these authoritarian opponents, the authoritarian state based on divine right, the divinely sanctioned authoritarian family, the authoritarian church, etc., have a monopoly of " authority," of all the social " offices " which make for social stability, continuity, and security.

Confirmation of this observation can be found, interestingly enough, in the writings not of liberals but of apologists for various eclipsed " authorities." These not seldom have assumed that to re-establish the validity of the principle of authority is to re-establish one or another of the forms of authority — monarchy, church, or family — which antedate the liberal revolutions. For example, in such suggestive treatments of " authority " as those of Balfour, *Foundations of Belief*, or Sterrett, *The Freedom of Authority*, there seems to operate the tacit assumption that the principle of " authority " is completely missing from the innovations of the " liberal "

[9] Sterrett, *op. cit.*, p. 5. Quoted by permission of The Macmillan Company, publishers.
[10] G. S. Counts, *Dare the Schools Build a New Social Order?*, p. 11. Quoted by permission of The John Day Co., publishers.

community and that the theoretical re-establishment of the necessity of " authority " in human affairs will lend credence to those very authoritative institutions and beliefs which the " liberal heresy " had tried to set aside. It is not unusual for the orthodox thus to deny authority to the community of heretics. It is unusual for the band of heretics to accept and even affirm their denial. And this denial is proving embarrassing precisely when the erstwhile heretics must defend their unacknowledged authoritative beliefs and practices against profound and untraditional challenges, e.g., against the challenges of Fascists and Communists.

When social crises come and the virtues of " authority " — security, order, and discipline — require emphasis in the life of a group, the theoretical denial of the principle cf authority save to authoritarian arrangements tends to force an attempted return by liberals to a reliance upon these arrangements, in which processes of individual creativity and innovation are not centrally valued, respected, and encouraged, not seldom to a revised version one or another of those forms of authoritarianism against which historic liberal forces had led their revolt. Put differently, one who advocates " freedom " but opposes it to " authority " will almost certainly fail to locate and critically maintain and extend the solid and continuing bases of value, method, and practice (the " authorities ") on which he and his group have been operating. The common bases on which " fellow liberals " reared their synthesis are ignored; intentional celebration and propagation of this basis of community may fail to be properly cared for. When the unconscious processes of habituation on which community authority has rested are threatened or undercut, the harassed and insecure deniers of " authority " may react extremely toward " authoritarianism," the only kind of authority recognized by them, as a basis of order, security, and discipline.

Dewey has well described this ideological tendency in men facing the individualistic erosion of the bases of national and international community today:

That all is not well, on the other hand, with the principle of individualistic freedom in the form in which it has been influential up to now, is shown by more than one fact in the present scene of discord and insecurity. Above all is this manifested by the recrudescence of the principle of authority in its most extreme and primitive form — the rise of dictatorships.

As if in substantiation of the old idea that nature abhors a vacuum, it might be contended that economic competitive individualism, free from social control, has created a moral and social vacuum which recourse to dictatorships is filling. In many countries, the demand for collective and organized guidance and support has become so urgent that the very idea of individual freedom has gone into the discard and become an idea, not to be praised, but to be despised. The regime of economic individualistic liberty is attacked by dictatorships from both the right and the left. In coun-

tries in which there are no open and acknowledged dictatorships, the conceptions of liberty and individualism seem to be losing their magic force; and security, discipline, order, and solidarity are, by social transfer, acquiring magic power in their stead.[11]

The difficulty in such violent revolutions is not that they seek to build conscious and deep-rooted community-values in men, values often slighted under the liberal synthesis, but that the value which historic liberalism and individualism has taught us to prize and in some areas at least, to actualize — the potential creativity of each deviate individual and a deep conviction that each individual is in some measure a deviate and hence potentially creative — will be concealed, ignored, or submerged in the reassertion of community power. How can the two values be reconciled?

The same inability to conceive and consciously to practice the interpenetration of freedom and authority operates in the small as well as in the large. It is present in all attempts of thoughtful, responsible men when they see the danger of undirected, inorganic " liberty " threatening to verge upon " license," to invoke a separate sphere of " authority " to take care of the case. The field of social conduct under question is thus divided into two realms, one of authority and one of freedom. This attempt [12] is nowhere better illustrated than in Bertrand Russell's essay on " Freedom or Authority in Education." [13] Mr. Russell recognizes that " freedom in education cannot mean that children should do exactly as they please all day long" since " every child left to itself, will sooner or later swallow pins, drink poison out of medicine bottles, fall out of an upper window, or otherwise bring itself to a bad end." He even feels sure that " most children, if they were left to themselves, would not learn to read or write, and would grow up less adapted than they might be to the circumstances of their lives." Thus " authority " is necessary. " An element of discipline and authority must exist; the question is as to the amount of it, and the way in which it is to be exercised." Or again, " There must be educational institutions, and children must be to some extent under authority. But in view of the fact that no authority can be wholly trusted [he has surveyed the state, the church, the family, and the school and found them all wanting], we must aim at having as little authority as possible, and try to think out ways by which young people's natural desires and impulses can be utilized in education."

Now, I share Mr. Russell's generous belief that children's personalities

11 J. Dewey, Authority and the Individual, p. 182. Quoted by permission of the President and Fellows of Harvard College.
12 It is this attempt, taking the form of the delimitation of separate spheres of individual freedom and state action as in J. S. Mill's and Spencer's outlooks, which Bosanquet criticizes fundamentally in his Philosophical Theory of the State (First Edition, Chap. III, pp. 53–78). In my opinion, though his critique is here valid, Bosanquet's own position is far from acceptable.
13 Century Magazine, CIX (December 1924), 172 ff.

must be respected, his rejection of attempts at willful and coercive imposition on children of creeds and outlooks by parents, priests, or schoolmasters, his belief that the spontaneous interests of learners must be utilized in the education of children, or indeed of anyone else.

But does or can anyone become a stable, secure, and confident person apart from active membership in state, church, family, school, club, vocational association, etc.? Indeed, apart from the habits and attitudes he acquires, under such social auspices, through a common life with others, would he become a personality at all? Memberships in basic human associations do not remain external to the human participant in them — rather they are built into his very nature. Men do not achieve freedom and individuality apart from human associations. They achieve these qualities and working habits only through participation in stable associations which authorize, " patronize," and control processes of individual creation and innovation. The problem is to devise an educational authority (and as Plato made finally clear in his *Republic* this means eventually an organization of all *community* authorities) which provides various and diverse avenues for developing and utilizing various and diverse individual talents and interests in enterprises that are fraught with a common spirit and which issue in common consequences, directly or indirectly. Freedom, if it is to be stabilized and assured for children (or for other human beings), must interpenetrate all the authority relationships under which men must live.

Mr. Russell's " solution," despite his general impulses, is then frankly no solution at all to the problem of freedom and authority in education. His very title, freedom *or* authority, shows the assumption of inherent opposition between the two under which he labors throughout. Whenever Mr. Russell speaks of authority, he uses words like " regimentation," " dominion," " orthodoxy," which he obviously dislikes. The controls of authoritative institutions are conceived as external to men and as remaining external. One can only speculate as to how churchmen, parents, and good citizens — the imposers — came to find their " freedom " in church and state and family. He seems unable, like historical liberalism generally, to disengage " authority " from the authoritarian " authority." The only " solution " to the problem of " freedom " or " authority," in these terms, is thus one of having individual " freedom " as far as possible in the processes of growing life, introducing " authority " (i.e., authoritarianism) only where it must be admitted grudgingly to be necessary in order to avoid catastrophe. Clearly this is only a restatement of the problem plus an expressed mood, albeit a generous and potentially valuable one. Its effect, if seriously acted upon, would be to leave the individual " freedom " it exalts organically undirected, erratic, restless, wayward, and unstable and the " authority " it grudgingly acknowledges organically untinctured by generous respect for and institutional recognition of the uniqueness of individuals and the creative potentialities in these. Friends of " freedom " must look otherwhere for an actual solution of their problem.

If one accepts the principle of authority as integral to the existence and operation of any and every human community, then, as suggested above, the liberal community must have had its own operating bases of authority, even when its frozen philosophy of revolution has tended to prevent their willing acknowledgment and wholehearted affirmation by its membership. It is far beyond the scope and competence of this study to attempt the complex task of revealing these in any detail and of tracing their historical emergence and career.

It will perhaps suffice to suggest how some of the operating bases of authority of the liberal-democratic community have been fundamentally challenged from within and without. Devoted members of that community, faced with fundamental challenge to their way of life by whatever authoritarianism rising within or without the national community, must assess their basic authoritative beliefs and values, must amend them where they are no longer consistent or workable, must seek to promote, conserve, and extend these against the challenge. But it is precisely in such a situation that some liberal-democrats find their traditional opposition to " authority " interfering with their willingness to advocate and propagate any authoritative beliefs, values, or practices, however deeply reassessed and criticized these may have been. Examples could be drawn from many areas of our life today. One example from the field of public education must suffice. I can do no better than to quote a paragraph by Professor J. L. Childs which describes the kind of paralysis which comes to liberal-democrats who deny the principle of authority in a time when their very belief in liberal democracy is being fundamentally challenged.

Does the rejection of authoritarianism imply that authority also has no place in education? Some have so held. Democracy, they contend, involves the right of each person to do his own thinking and to form his own thinking and to form his own conclusions. Ability to think, to evaluate, to judge, are essential characteristics of a developed personality. A program of education, therefore, which is patterned after the democratic conception will not seek to dispose the young to any particular way of life, not even democracy. It will strive, they assert, to present impartially all of the important data and rival theories of social life without consciously attempting to lead the young to favor any one of these as opposed to others. To attempt to cultivate particular outlooks and values in the minds and affections of the young is indoctrination, not education. It is a form of educational manipulation which fails to respect the integrity of the child's experience, and tends to produce the inert, docile conformist, rather than a resolute personality possessed of the capacity of initiative, of independent thought, and of critical judgment.[14]

[14] J. L. Childs, " Education and Authority," *Religious Education*, XXXIII (1938). 149–53. Quoted by permission of the publishers.

Professor Childs rejects the contention which he here describes. In my opinion, he goes to the heart of the difficulty when he declares, " To forego authoritarianism raises but does not in itself answer the question of authority in education." [15] His alternative suggestion seems not dissimilar to that which I have been suggesting throughout this discussion. Educators must redefine the character and limits of their non-authoritarian authority under changed conditions of life. To deny their authority is in effect to surrender responsibility for the community function which, as educators, they exist to serve.

Let us return to the hidden " authorities " of the individualistic community which the turn of recent events has tended to challenge and, in challenging, to reveal in their deep-seated power to at least many of the members of that community. One of the first which any thoughtful contemporary would probably name is the economic system of private enterprise. It was its apparent failure to release the economic possibilities of the new technology, the depth, prevalence, and persistence of economic depression that revealed the ramifications of its " authority " in the liberal-democratic community. Let it be said at once that the revelation of its authority does not necessarily release men from that " authority," though as traditional liberals they may defend it by seeking to deny " authority " to it, by calling it " freedom." This revelation of hidden authorities to the rank and file of men does make possible the study and criticism of the authoritative principles and the consideration of alternatives. The common habits, attitudes, and motivations with respect to economic enterprise, which the authoritative (and, as it has grown, largely authoritarian) system has fostered, live in some measure in all the persons who have depended on it, even in those who have been " dispossessed " by its operation. Operating authorities are never wholly external to the members of the community in which they operate. This accounts for much of their power and persistence, the " willing obedience " which is accorded to them. In any stable community, control through brute coercion is the exception, not the rule.

Dewey has well expressed, though not without critical evaluation, the significance of this " hidden authority," now revealed in the perpetuation of an outmoded ideology, a perpetuation which makes for the continued denial of the principle of authority, the dangers of which for our time I have tried to suggest in several connections previously.

While decrying the principle of authority, and asserting the necessity of limiting the exercise of authority to the minimum needed for maintenance of police order, the new philosophy in fact erected the wants and endeavors of private individuals seeking personal gain to the place of supreme authority in social life. In consequence, the new philosophy, in the very act of

[15] *Ibid.*, p. 153.

asserting that it stood completely and loyally for the principle of individual freedom, was really engaged in justifying the activities of a new form of concentrated power — the economic, which new form, to state the matter moderately, has consistently and persistently denied effective freedom to the economically underpowered and underprivileged. While originating as a social force that effected widespread social change in opposition to, indeed in despite of, the powers that had authority when it began to emerge, economic power has now become, in its turn, an organized social institution that resists all further social change that is not in accord with itself, that does not further and support its own interests as at present existing.[16]

A second " hidden authority " in the liberal synthesis lies in the operation of the deliberate method of organized cooperative intelligence in the guidance of human affairs. Its application in scientific studies illustrates its operation best. Here again there have arisen many, especially among the authoritarians, to challenge its power among men. For this inclusive authority perhaps most successfully shows, among current authorities, hidden and overt, in the spheres of operation where it has found successful application, the organic fusion and interpenetration of freedom, as the potentially creative uniqueness of individual experience, and authority, as the stable, organically directing powers of stability, solidarity, and continuity in human affairs. This fusion of authority and freedom is best seen in the common public processes of limited scientific communities in matters scientific.

In spite of science's dependence for its development upon the free initiative, invention, and enterprise of individual inquirers, the authority of science issues from and is based upon collective activity, co-operatively organized. Even when, temporarily, the ideas put forth in science by individuals sharply diverge from received beliefs, the method used is a public and open method which succeeds only as it tends to produce agreement, unity of belief among all who labored in the same field. Every scientific inquirer, even when he deviates most widely from current ideas, depends upon methods and conclusions that are a common possession and not of private ownership, even though all of the methods and conclusions may at some time have been initially the product of private invention. The contribution the scientific inquirer makes is collectively tested and developed and, in the measure that it is co-operatively confirmed, becomes a part of the common fund of the intellectual commonwealth.[17]

It is not easy to say whether the limitation of this " authority " to operation in relatively limited intellectual areas of culture has been due more to its inapplicability in its " scientific " forms to the management of cer-

[16] Dewey, op. cit., pp. 178–79. Quoted by permission of the President and Fellows of Harvard College.
[17] Ibid., p. 186. Quoted by permission of the President and Fellows of Harvard College.

tain other areas of experience, to the vested opposition of authoritarian powers threatened by its extension, or to the failure of educational agencies consciously to communicate its spirit and morale of operation to wider areas of experience. Certainly, it is beyond the province of this chapter to analyze the reasons for its limitation. Despite these limitations, when we consider the pervasive contribution of scientific findings and method to nearly all functions of modern life our dependence upon it and its authority over us can hardly be denied.

Perhaps my purposes in this brief pointing to two " hidden authorities " which in the past helped to sustain and stabilize and which in some degree still sustain the liberal community have been achieved. These purposes may be summarized as follows:

1. To show that the individualistic community did breed its own " authorities " even as it ignored or sought to explain away their authority. The two named are only examples of these. In no way do I mean to suggest that these particular " authorities " are essential to any future collective existence.
2. To suggest that these " authorities," under challenge, are being revealed to their subjects, as challenge to any way of life drives its proponents back to the revelation of its operating authoritative values and beliefs.
3. To suggest that the operating authorities of the individualistic community, perhaps because of their denial and unconscious operation, are not consistent. Choices must be made among them. The authoritarianism of our private economy cannot be fully or permanently reconciled with the social democracy of scientific pursuits.
4. To suggest that it is in relation to such criticized and selected authoritative beliefs and practices and to the profound problems of human adjustment raised by their conflicts that the functions of bearers of educational authority, the family and the school, for example, must be redefined, recharted, and reasserted.

I can best summarize . . . by attempting to state in brief the inclusive problem of authority for our time and community, as I see it and as I have tried to portray it here. Authority is a necessity of all stable community life. Today, under the impact of growing collective interdependence men are forced to rethink and reconstruct the operating bases of community authority. The widespread attempt under the historic liberal ideology to deny the principle of authority in human relations has helped to blur the recognition of operating bases of authority necessary to stable and responsible individual and group life, thus paradoxically contributing to the restoration of extreme authoritarianism in human affairs. The values of creative individuality which the liberal ideology rightly stressed are basically endangered by the recrudescence of authoritarianism. Liberal-democrats cannot combat authoritarianism with the advocacy or practice of a partly fictitious and abstract "freedom." They must discover (in part rediscover), advocate, and propagate a type of authority organically united with freedom and individuality. Those who accept this challenge must find their redefined functions, their specific authorities, whether as parents, educators, publicists, or statesmen, within the conception and program of such an authority. Only such an authority is a proper foil to a widely resurgent authoritarianism.

SECTION 7. Critiques of democracy

One of the most difficult accomplishments of individuals, as Robert Burns poetically wrote, is "to see ourselves as others see us." Although Burns was writing about individuals, the present day sociologist expresses the same general idea in regard to social groups by employing the concept of ethnocentrism. An ethnocentric person is one who judges another society on the basis of values subscribed to by the members of *his* society. A frequent concomitant of the ethnocentric person is his inability to perceive or understand criticisms of his society on the basis of some *other* value system. The following selections by Alfredo Rocco and Alexis de Tocqueville are critiques of democracy; the one by Rocco is included especially in order to acquaint the reader with a point of view that stems from an anti-democratic value system.

Alfredo Rocco was one of the intellectual leaders of Italian fascism. His academic background consisted of work as both a student and faculty member, mainly in the field of law. He was appointed Minister of Justice in the Italian government in 1925. Mussolini entrusted to him the job of supervising the general reform of Italian legal codes. The most significant of these was the system of syndicates of industry and the professions in which both employers and employees were to reconcile their differences. The state was the final arbiter. This predominant position of the state over the individual constitutes one of the cornerstones of Rocco's philos-

ophy, as well as the philosophy of both Italian and German fascism.

In view of the inclusion of a selection dealing with fascism, the question may be asked as to why this section does not also have a comparable selection representing the communist point of view. For although the editors make no brief for communism, yet we cannot dismiss this position merely because we do not like it. The reason for not including such a selection is that communism at least *professes* to be democratic. True, the communist interpretation of democracy may be significantly different from the interpretation of Western states, but at least communism is *not* avowedly anti-democratic. Note the frequent use of the term " democratic " by communists in describing or identifying nations under communism. Such nations are generally referred to as " peoples' democracies." Fascism, on the other hand, is openly, avowedly and unequivocally opposed to the *principle* of democracy.

The further question may be raised as to why, in a book of readings such as this, with its commitment to a democratic frame of reference, the editors should include a selection which is so boldly anti-democratic. Basically, the answer may be stated in terms of democracy's ability to compete openly in the market-place of ideas. An advocate of democracy should welcome the opportunity to defend it against all types of opposition. It is true that such open consideration of opposing views may put the democrat in the position of advertising the wares of his competitors. But this is much like the situation of the way in which a whetstone is used with a knife. In the hands of the uninitiated a stone may only dull the knife; in skilled hands it may serve as a sharpener. The decision is in the hands of the user. It is in this spirit that the Rocco selection is included.

If one of the criteria of a literary classic is the timelessness of the ideas expressed, de Tocqueville's *Democracy in America* certainly meets this qualification. This young French aristocrat visited the United States in 1831, ostensibly to investigate the penitentiary system here. He travelled extensively through all parts of the new republic studying various levels of government, businesses, occupations, manners, and morals. *Democracy in America* was the first of four volumes on American institutions and their influences. Although it was written primarily for the European reader, it provides Americans probably the most astute view ever presented of " ourselves as others see us."

The major criticism that de Tocqueville makes of American democracy is that the political majority has practically unlimited power. As a consequence of this extreme majority rule there are concomitant failings in public administration, legislative action, public opinion, and the very character of our populace. De Tocqueville's fear of the majority and solicitation for the rights of the minority are reasons for the persistently high esteem in which his writings are held by various segments of American society. We are all members of some minority groups. Interestingly enough, an introduction to the American translation of de Tocqueville's book was written after the Civil War by Senator Morgan of Alabama. In his introduction the Senator took note of de Tocqueville's comment on the " general equality " in the United States. Senator Morgan adds, " He referred, doubtless, to social and political conditions among the people of the white race, who are described as ' We, the people,' in the opening sentence of the Constitution." This interpretation of de Tocqueville is perhaps indicative of the way in which his defense of minorities has been employed to buttress the peculiar beliefs and values of those who express concern about the tyranny of the majority.

Although de Tocqueville does not deal directly with public education, the reader may draw his own inferences about the validity of de Tocqueville's criticisms as they would apply to the control of education. If majority rule may be tyrannical and unwise in a state legislature, may it not be so in a school board? Or, if we have avoided the evil consequences of majority rule in legislatures, are we able to do the same with school boards? For that matter, how valid are the criticisms, both from de Tocqueville and our contemporaries, of conformity in American society? And what can the schools do about it?

In reading the selection from *Democracy in America,* one finds it difficult to resist a genuine feeling of humility about our accomplishments as a democracy. These criticisms were written well over a century ago. Their sting is felt all too sharply even today. Perhaps they can best serve to remind us that democracy is still an experiment — as yet unproved in the hard school of history.

ALFREDO ROCCO
A totalitarian looks at democracy

FASCISM AS ACTION, AS FEELING, AND AS THOUGHT

Much has been said, and is now being said for or against this complex political and social phenomenon which in the brief period of six years has taken complete hold of Italian life and, spreading beyond the borders of the Kingdom, has made itself felt in varying degrees of intensity throughout the world. But people have been much more eager to extol or to deplore than to understand — which is natural enough in a period of tumultuous fervor and of political passion. The time has not yet arrived for a dispassionate judgment. For even I, who noticed the very first manifestations of this great development, saw its significance from the start and participated directly in its first doings, carefully watching all its early uncertain and changing developments, even I do not feel competent to pass definite judgment. Fascism is so large a part of myself that it would be both arbitrary and absurd for me to try to dissociate my personality from it, to submit it to impartial scrutiny in order to evaluate it coldly and accurately. What can be done, however, and it seldom is attempted, is to make inquiry into the phenomenon which shall not merely consider its fragmentary and adventitious aspects, but strive to get at its inner essence. . . .

First of all let us ask ourselves if there is a political doctrine of Fascism; if there is any ideal content in the Fascist state. For in order to link Fascism, both as concept and system, with the history of Italian thought and find therein a place for it, we must first show that it is thought; that it is a doctrine. Many persons are not quite convinced that it is either the one or the other; and I am not referring solely to those men, cultured or uncultured, as the case may be and very numerous everywhere, who can discern in this political innovation nothing except its local and personal aspects, and who know Fascism only as the particular manner of behavior of this or that well-known Fascist, of this or that group of a certain town; who therefore like or dislike the movement on the basis of their likes and dislikes for the individuals who represent it. Nor do I refer to those intelligent and cultivated persons, very intelligent indeed and very cultivated, who because of their direct or indirect allegiance to the parties that have been dispossessed by the advent of Fascism, have a natural cause of resentment against it and are therefore unable to see, in the blindness of hatred, anything good in it. I am referring rather to those — and there are many

From a speech delivered by Alfredo Rocco at Perugia, Italy, on August 30, 1925. Translated by Dino Bigoniari. Reprinted in *International Conciliation Pamphlet* No. 223 published by the Carnegie Endowment for International Peace. Reprinted by permission.

in our ranks too — who know Fascism as action and feeling but not yet as thought, who therefore have an intuition but no comprehension of it.

It is true that Fascism is, above all, action and sentiment and that such it must continue to be. Were it otherwise, it could not keep up that immense driving force, that renovating power which it now possesses and would merely be the solitary meditation of a chosen few. Only because it is feeling and sentiment, only because it is the unconscious reawakening of our profound racial instinct, has it the force to stir the soul of the people, and to set free an irresistible current of national will. Only because it is action, and as such actualizes itself in a vast organization and in a huge movement, has it the conditions for determining the historical course of contemporary Italy.

But Fascism is thought as well and it has a theory, which is an essential part of this historical phenomenon, and which is responsible in a great measure for the successes that have been achieved. To the existence of this ideal content of Fascism, to the truth of this Fascist logic we ascribe the fact that though we commit many errors of detail, we very seldom go astray on fundamentals, whereas all the parties of the opposition, deprived as they are of an informing, animating principle, of a unique directing concept, do very often wage their war faultlessly in minor tactics, better trained as they are in parliamentary and journalistic manoeuvres, but they constantly break down on the important issues. Fascism, moreover, considered as action, is a typically Italian phenomenon and acquires a universal validity because of the existence of this coherent and organic doctrine. The originality of Fascism is due in great part to the autonomy of its theoretical principles. For even when, in its external behavior and in its conclusions, it seems identical with other political creeds, in reality it possesses an inner originality due to the new spirit which animates it and to an entirely different theoretical approach.

COMMON ORIGINS AND COMMON BACKGROUND OF MODERN POLITICAL DOCTRINES; FROM LIBERALISM TO SOCIALISM

Modern political thought remained, until recently, both in Italy and outside of Italy under the absolute control of those doctrines which, proceeding from the Protestant Reformation and developed by the adepts of natural law in the 17th and 18th centuries, were firmly grounded in the institutions and customs of the English, of the American, and of the French Revolutions. Under different and sometimes clashing forms these doctrines have left a determining imprint upon all theories and actions both social and political, of the 19th and 20th centuries down to the rise of Fascism. The common basis of all these doctrines, which stretch from Languet, from Buchanan, and from Althusius down to Karl Marx, to Wilson and to Lenin is a social and state concept which I shall call mechanical or atomistic.

Society according to this concept is merely a sum total of individuals, a plurality which breaks up into its single components. Therefore the ends of a society, so considered, are nothing more than the ends of the individuals which compose it and for whose sake it exists. An atomistic view of this kind is also necessarily anti-historical, inasmuch as it considers society in its spatial attributes and not in its temporal ones; and because it reduces social life to the existence of a single generation. Society becomes thus a sum of determined individuals, viz., the generation living at a given moment. This doctrine which I call atomistic and which appears to be anti-historical, reveals from under a concealing cloak a strongly materialistic nature. For in its endeavors to isolate the present from the past and the future, it rejects the spiritual inheritance of ideas and sentiments which each generation receives from those preceding and hands down to the following generation, thus destroying the unity and the spiritual life itself of human society.

This common basis shows the close logical connection existing between all political doctrines; the substantial solidarity, which unites all the political movements, from Liberalism to Socialism, that until recently have dominated Europe. For these political schools differ from one another in their methods, but all agree as to the ends to be achieved. All of them consider the welfare and happiness of individuals to be the goal of society, itself considered as composed of individuals of the present generation. All of them see in society and in its juridical organization, the state, the mere instrument and means whereby individuals can attain their ends. They differ only in that the methods pursued for the attainment of these ends vary considerably one from the other.

Thus the Liberals insist that the best manner to secure the welfare of the citizens as individuals is to interfere as little as possible with the free development of their activities and that therefore the essential task of the state is merely to coördinate these several liberties in such a way as to guarantee their coexistence. Kant, who was without doubt the most powerful and thorough philosopher of liberalism, said, " man, who is the end, cannot be assumed to have the value of an instrument." And again " justice, of which the state is the specific organ, is the condition whereby the freedom of each is conditioned upon the freedom of others, according to the general law of liberty."

Having thus defined the task of the state, Liberalism confines itself to the demand of certain guarantees which are to keep the state from overstepping its functions as general coördinator of liberties and from sacrificing the freedom of individuals more than is absolutely necessary for the accomplishment of its purpose. All the efforts are therefore directed to see to it that the ruler, mandatory of all and entrusted with the realization, through and by liberty, of the harmonious happiness of everybody, should never be clothed with undue power. Hence the creation of a system of checks and limitations designed to keep the rulers within bounds; and among these, first and foremost, the principle of the division of powers, contrived as a means for weakening the state in its relation to the individual, by making it impossible for the state ever to appear, in its dealings with citizens, in the full plenitude of sovereign powers; also the principle of the participation of citizens in the lawmaking power, as a means for securing, in behalf of the individual, a direct check on this, the strongest branch, and an indirect check on the entire government of the state. This system of checks and limitations, which goes by the name of constitutional government, resulted in a moderate and measured liberalism. The checking power was exercised only by those citizens who were deemed worthy and capable, with the result that a small élite was made to represent legally the entire body politic for whose benefit this régime was instituted.

It was evident, however, that this moderate system, being fundamentally illogical and in contradiction with the very principles from which it proceeded, would soon become the object of serious criticism. For if the object of society and of the state is the welfare of individuals, severally considered, how is it possible to admit that this welfare can be secured by the individuals themselves only through the possibilities of such a liberal régime? The inequalities brought about both by nature and by social organizations are so numerous and so serious, that, for the greater part, individuals abandoned to themselves not only would fail to attain happiness, but would also contribute to the perpetuation of their condition of misery and dejection. The state therefore cannot limit itself to the merely negative function of the defense of liberty. It must become active, in behalf of everybody, for the welfare of the people. It must intervene, when necessary, in order to improve the material, intellectual, and moral conditions of the masses; it must find work for the unemployed, instruct and educate the people, and care for health and hygiene. For if the purpose of society and of the state is the welfare of individuals, and if it is just that these individuals themselves control the attainment of their ends, it becomes difficult to understand why Liberalism should not go the whole distance, why it should see fit to distinguish certain individuals from the rest of the mass, and why the functions of the people should be restricted to the exercise of a mere check. Therefore the state, if it exists for all, must be governed by all, and not by a small minority: if the state is for the people, sovereignty must reside in the people: if all individuals have the right to govern the state, liberty is no longer sufficient; equality must be added: and if sovereignty is vested in the people, the people must wield all sovereignty and not merely a part of it. The power to check and curb the government is not sufficient. The people must be the government. Thus, logically developed, Liberalism leads to Democracy, for Democracy contains the promises of Liberalism but oversteps its limitations in that it makes the action of the state positive, proclaims the equality of all citizens through the dogma of popular sovereignty. Democracy therefore necessarily implies a republican form of government even though at times, for reasons of expediency, it temporarily adjusts itself to a monarchical régime.

Once started on this downward grade of logical deductions it was inevitable that this atomistic theory of state and society should pass on to a more advanced position. Great industrial developments and the existence of a huge mass of working men, as yet badly treated and in a condition of semi-servitude, pushed the labor problem violently to the fore. Social inequalities, possibly endurable in a régime of domestic industry, became intolerable after the industrial revolution. Hence a state of affairs which towards the middle of the last century appeared to be both cruel and threatening. It was therefore natural that the following question should be raised: " If the state is created for the welfare of its citizens, severally considered, how can it tolerate an economic system which divides the population into a small minority of exploiters, the capitalists, on one side, and an immense multitude of exploited, the working people, on the other? " No! The state must again intervene and give rise to a different and less iniquitous economic organization, by abolishing private property, by assuming direct control of all production, and by organizing it in such a way that the products of labor be distributed solely among those who create them, viz., the working classes. Hence we find Socialism, with its new economic organization of society, abolishing private ownership of capital and of the instruments and means of production, socializing the product, suppressing the extra profit of capital, and turning over to the working class the entire output of the productive processes. It is evident that Socialism contains and surpasses Democracy in the same way that Democracy comprises and surpasses Liberalism, being a more advanced development of the same fundamental concept. Socialism in its turn generates the still more extreme doctrine of Bolshevism which demands the violent suppression of the holders of capital, the dictatorship of the proletariat, as means for a fairer economic organization of society and for the rescue of the laboring classes from capitalistic exploitation.

Thus Liberalism, Democracy, and Socialism, appear to be, as they are in reality, not only the offspring of one and the same theory of government, but also logical derivations one of the other. Logically developed Liberalism leads to Democracy; the logical development of Democracy issues into Socialism. It is true that for many years, and with some justification, Socialism was looked upon as antithetical to Liberalism. But the antithesis is purely relative and breaks down as we approach the common origin and foundation of the two doctrines, for we find that the opposition is one of method, not of purpose. The end is the same for both, viz., the welfare of the individual members of society. The difference lies in the fact that Liberalism would be guided to its goal by liberty, whereas Socialism strives to attain it by the collective organization of production. There is therefore no antithesis nor even a divergence as to the nature and scope of the state and the relation of individuals to society. There is only a difference of evaluation of the means for bringing about these ends and establishing these relations, which difference depends entirely on the different

economic conditions which prevailed at the time when the various doctrines were formulated. Liberalism arose and began to thrive in the period
of small industry; Socialism grew with the rise of industrialism and of
world-wide capitalism. The dissension therefore between these two points
of view, or the antithesis, if we wish so to call it, is limited to the economic
field. Socialism is at odds with Liberalism only on the question of the
organization of production and of the division of wealth. In religious,
intellectual, and moral matters it is liberal, as it is liberal and democratic
in its politics. Even the anti-liberalism and anti-democracy of Bolshevism
are in themselves purely contingent. For Bolshevism is opposed to Liberalism only in so far as the former is revolutionary, not in its socialistic aspect.
For if the opposition of the Bolsheviki to liberal and democratic doctrines
were to continue, as now seems more and more probable, the result might
be a complete break between Bolshevism and Socialism notwithstanding
the fact that the ultimate aims of both are identical.

FASCISM AS AN INTEGRAL DOCTRINE OF SOCIALITY ANTITHETICAL TO THE ATOMISM OF LIBERAL, DEMOCRATIC, AND SOCIALISTIC THEORIES

The true antithesis, not to this or that manifestation of the liberal-demo-
cratic-socialistic conception of the state but to the concept itself, is to
be found in the doctrine of Fascism. For while the disagreement between
Liberalism and Democracy, and between Liberalism and Socialism lies
in a difference of method, as we have said, the rift between Socialism,
Democracy, and Liberalism on one side and Fascism on the other is caused
by a difference in concept. As a matter of fact, Fascism never raises the
question of methods, using in its political praxis now liberal ways, now
democratic means and at times even socialistic devices. This indifference
to method often exposes Fascism to the charge of incoherence on the part
of superficial observers, who do not see that what counts with us is the end
and that therefore even when we employ the same means we act with a
radically different spiritual attitude and strive for entirely different results.
The Fascist concept then of the nation, of the scope of the state, and of
the relations obtaining between society and its individual components, rejects entirely the doctrine which I said proceeded from the theories of
natural law developed in the course of the 16th, 17th, and 18th centuries
and which form the basis of the liberal, democratic, and socialistic ideology.

I shall not try here to expound this doctrine but shall limit myself to a
brief résumé of its fundamental concepts.

Man — the political animal — according to the definition of Aristotle,
lives and must live in society. A human being outside the pale of society is
an inconceivable thing — a non-man. Humankind in its entirety lives in
social groups that are still, today, very numerous and diverse, varying in
importance and organization from the tribes of Central Africa to the great
Western Empires. These various societies are fractions of the human spe-

cies, each one of them endowed with a unified organization. And as there is no unique organization of the human species, there is not " one " but there are " several " human societies. Humanity therefore exists solely as a biological concept, not as a social one.

Each society on the other hand exists in the unity of both its biological and its social contents. Socially considered it is a fraction of the human species endowed with unity of organization for the attainment of the peculiar ends of the species.

This definition brings out all the elements of the social phenomenon and not merely those relating to the preservation and perpetuation of the species. For man is not solely matter; and the ends of the human species, far from being the materialistic ones we have in common with other animals, are, rather, and predominantly, the spiritual finalities which are peculiar to man and which every form of society strives to attain as well as its stage of social development allows. Thus the organization of every social group is more or less pervaded by the spiritual influxes of: unity of language, of culture, of religion, of tradition, of customs, and in general of feeling and of volition, which are as essential as the material elements: unity of economic interests, of living conditions, and of territory. The definition given above demonstrates another truth, which has been ignored by the political doctrines that for the last four centuries have been the foundations of political systems, viz., that the social concept has a biological aspect, because social groups are fractions of the human species, each one possessing a peculiar organization, a particular rank in the development of civilization with certain needs and appropriate ends, in short, a life which is really its own. If social groups are then fractions of the human species, they must possess the same fundamental traits of the human species, which means that they must be considered as a succession of generations and not as a collection of individuals.

It is evident therefore that as the human species is not the total of the living human beings of the world, so the various social groups which compose it are not the sum of the several individuals which at a given moment belong to it, but rather the infinite series of the past, present, and future generations constituting it. And as the ends of the human species are not those of the several individuals living at a certain moment, being occasionally in direct opposition to them, so the ends of the various social groups are not necessarily those of the individuals that belong to the groups but may even possibly be in conflict with such ends, as one sees clearly whenever the preservation and the development of the species demand the sacrifice of the individual, to wit, in times of war.

Fascism replaces therefore the old atomistic and mechanical state theory which was at the basis of the liberal and democratic doctrines with an organic and historic concept. When I say organic I do not wish to convey the impression that I consider society as an organism after the manner of the so-called " organic theories of the state "; but rather to indicate that the social groups as fractions of the species receive thereby a life and scope which transcend the scope and life of the individuals identifying themselves with the history and finalities of the uninterrupted series of generations. It is irrelevant in this connection to determine whether social groups, considered as fractions of the species, constitute organisms. The important thing is to ascertain that this organic concept of the state gives to society a continuous life over and beyond the existence of the several individuals.

The relations therefore between state and citizens are completely reversed by the Fascist doctrine. Instead of the liberal-democratic formula, " society for the individual," we have, " individuals for society " with this difference however: that while the liberal doctrines eliminated society, Fascism does not submerge the individual in the social group. It subordinates him, but does not eliminate him; the individual as a part of his generation ever remaining an element of society however transient and insignificant he may be. Moreover the development of individuals in each generation, when coördinated and harmonized, conditions the development and prosperity of the entire social unit.

At this juncture the antithesis between the two theories must appear complete and absolute. Liberalism, Democracy, and Socialism look upon social groups as aggregates of living individuals; for Fascism they are the recapitulating unity of the indefinite series of generations. For Liberalism, society has no purposes other than those of the members living at a given moment. For Fascism, society has historical and immanent ends of preservation, expansion, improvement, quite distinct from those of the individuals which at a given moment compose it; so distinct in fact that they may even be in opposition. Hence the necessity, for which the older doctrines make little allowance, of sacrifice, even up to the total immolation of individuals, in behalf of society; hence the true explanation of war, eternal law of mankind, interpreted by the liberal-democratic doctrines as a degenerate absurdity or as a maddened monstrosity.

For Liberalism, society has no life distinct from the life of the individuals, or as the phrase goes: solvitur in singularitates. For Fascism, the life of society overlaps the existence of individuals and projects itself into the succeeding generations through centuries and millennia. Individuals come into being, grow, and die, followed by others, unceasingly; social unity remains always identical to itself. For Liberalism, the individual is the end and society the means; nor is it conceivable that the individual, considered in the dignity of an ultimate finality, be lowered to mere instrumentality. For Fascism, society is the end, individuals the means, and its whole life consists in using individuals as instruments for its social ends. The state therefore guards and protects the welfare and development of individuals not for their exclusive interest, but because of the identity of the needs of individuals with those of society as a whole. We can thus accept and explain institutions and practices, which like the death penalty, are condemned by Liberalism in the name of the preëminence of individualism.

The fundamental problem of society in the old doctrines is the question of the rights of individuals. It may be the right to freedom as the Liberals would have it; or the right to the government of the commonwealth as the Democrats claim it, or the right to economic justice as the Socialists contend; but in every case it is the right of individuals, or groups of individuals (classes). Fascism on the other hand faces squarely the problem of the right of the state and of the duty of individuals. Individual rights are only recognized in so far as they are implied in the rights of the state. In this preëminence of duty we find the highest ethical value of Fascism.

THE PROBLEMS OF LIBERTY, OF GOVERNMENT, AND OF SOCIAL JUSTICE IN THE POLITICAL DOCTRINE OF FASCISM

This, however, does not mean that the problems raised by the other schools are ignored by Fascism. It means simply that it faces them and solves them differently, as, for example, the problem of liberty.

There is a Liberal theory of freedom, and there is a Fascist concept of liberty. For we, too, maintain the necessity of safeguarding the conditions that make for the free development of the individual; we, too, believe that the oppression of individual personality can find no place in the modern state. We do not, however, accept a bill of rights which tends to make the individual superior to the state and to empower him to act in opposition to society. Our concept of liberty is that the individual must be allowed to develop his personality in behalf of the state, for these ephemeral and infinitesimal elements of the complex and permanent life of society determine by their normal growth the development of the state. But this individual growth must be normal. A huge and disproportionate development of the individual, of classes, would prove as fatal to society as abnormal growths are to living organisms. Freedom therefore is due to the citizen and to classes on condition that they exercise it in the interest of society as a whole and within the limits set by social exigencies, liberty being, like any other individual right, a concession of the state. What I say concerning civil liberties applies to economic freedom as well. Fascism does not look upon the doctrine of economic liberty as an absolute dogma. It does not refer economic problems to individual needs, to individual interest, to individual solutions. On the contrary it considers the economic development, and especially the production of wealth, as an eminently social concern, wealth being for society an essential element of power and prosperity. But Fascism maintains that in the ordinary run of events economic liberty serves the social purposes best; that it is profitable to entrust to individual initiative the task of economic development both as to production and as to distribution; that in the economic world individual ambition is the most effective means for obtaining the best social results with the least effort. Therefore, on the question also of economic liberty the Fascists differ fundamentally from the Liberals; the latter see in liberty a principle, the Fascists accept it as a method. By the Liberals, freedom is recognized in the interest of the citizens; the Fascists grant it in the interest of society. In other terms, Fascists make of the individual an economic instrument for the advancement of society, an instrument which they use so long as it functions and which they subordinate when no longer serviceable. In this guise Fascism solves the eternal problem of economic freedom and of state interference, considering both as mere methods which may or may not be employed in accordance with the social needs of the moment.

What I have said concerning political and economic Liberalism applies also to Democracy. The latter envisages fundamentally the problem of sovereignty; Fascism does also, but in an entirely different manner. Democracy vests sovereignty in the people, that is to say, in the mass of human beings. Fascism discovers sovereignty to be inherent in society when it is juridically organized as a state. Democracy therefore turns over the government of the state to the multitude of living men that they may use it to further their own interests; Fascism insists that the government be entrusted to men capable of rising above their own private interests and of realizing the aspirations of the social collectivity, considered in its unity and in its relation to the past and future. Fascism therefore not only rejects the dogma of popular sovereignty and substitutes for it that of state sovereignty, but it also proclaims that the great mass of citizens is not a suitable advocate of social interests for the reason that the capacity to ignore individual private interests in favor of the higher demands of society and of history is a very rare gift and the privilege of the chosen few. Natural intelligence and cultural preparation are of great service in such tasks. Still more valuable perhaps is the intuitiveness of rare great minds, their traditionalism and their inherited qualities. This must not however be construed to mean that the masses are not to be allowed to exercise any influence on the life of the state. On the contrary, among peoples with a great history and with noble traditions, even the lowest elements of society possess an instinctive discernment of what is necessary for the welfare of the race, which in moments of great historical crises reveals itself to be almost infallible. It is therefore as wise to afford to this instinct the means of declaring itself as it is judicious to entrust the normal control of the commonwealth to a selected élite.

As for Socialism, the Fascist doctrine frankly recognizes that the problem raised by it as to the relations between capital and labor is a very serious one, perhaps the central one of modern life. What Fascism does not countenance is the collectivistic solution proposed by the Socialists. The chief defect of the socialistic method has been clearly demonstrated by the experience of the last few years. It does not take into account human nature, it is therefore outside of reality, in that it will not recognize that the most powerful spring of human activities lies in individual self-interest and that therefore the elimination from the economic field of this interest results in complete paralysis. The suppression of private ownership of capital carries with it the suppression of capital itself, for capital is formed by savings and no one will want to save, but will rather consume all he makes if he knows he cannot keep and hand down to his heirs the results of his labors. The dispersion of capital means the end of production since capital, no matter who owns it, is always an indispensable tool of production. Collective organization of production is followed therefore by the paralysis of production since, by eliminating from the productive mechanism the incentive of individual interest, the product becomes rarer and more costly. Socialism then, as experience has shown, leads to increase in consumption, to the dispersion of capital and therefore to poverty. Of what avail is it, then, to build a social machine which will more justly distribute wealth if this very wealth is destroyed by the construction of this machine? Socialism committed an irreparable error when it made of private property a matter of justice while in truth it is a problem of social utility. The recognition of individual property rights, then, is a part of the Fascist doctrine not because of its individual bearing but because of its social utility.

We must reject, therefore, the socialistic solution but we cannot allow the problem raised by the Socialists to remain unsolved, not only because justice demands a solution but also because the persistence of this problem in liberal and democratic régimes has been a menace to public order and to the authority of the state. Unlimited and unrestrained class self-defense, evinced by strikes and lockouts, by boycotts and sabotage, leads inevitably to anarchy. The Fascist doctrine, enacting justice among the classes in compliance with a fundamental necessity of modern life, does away with class self-defense, which, like individual self-defense in the days of barbarism, is a source of disorder and of civil war.

Having reduced the problem to these terms, only one solution is possible, the realization of justice among the classes by and through the state. Centuries ago the state, as the specific organ of justice, abolished personal self-defense in individual controversies and substituted for it state justice. The time has now come when class self-defense also must be replaced by state justice. To facilitate the change Fascism has created its own syndicalism. The suppression of class self-defense does not mean the suppression of class defense which is an inalienable necessity of modern economic life. Class organization is a fact which cannot be ignored but it must be controlled, disciplined, and subordinated by the state. The syndicate, instead of being, as formerly, an organ of extra-legal defense, must be turned into an organ of legal defense which will become judicial defense as soon as labor conflicts become a matter of judicial settlement. Fascism therefore has transformed the syndicate, that old revolutionary instrument of syndicalistic socialists, into an instrument of legal defense of the classes both within and without the law courts. This solution may encounter obstacles in its development; the obstacles of malevolence, of suspicion of the untried, of erroneous calculation, etc., but it is destined to triumph even though it must advance through progressive stages. . . .

ALEXIS DE TOCQUEVILLE
A Frenchman views democracy in America

UNLIMITED POWER OF THE MAJORITY IN THE UNITED STATES,
AND ITS CONSEQUENCES

The very essence of democratic government consists in the absolute sovereignty of the majority; for there is nothing in democratic States which is capable of resisting it. Most of the American Constitutions have sought to increase this natural strength of the majority by artificial means.[1]

The legislature is, of all political institutions, the one which is most easily swayed by the wishes of the majority. The Americans determined that the members of the legislature should be elected by the people immediately, and for a very brief term, in order to subject them, not only to the general convictions, but even to the daily passions, of their constituents. The members of both houses are taken from the same class in society, and are nominated in the same manner; so that the modifications of the legislative bodies are almost as rapid and quite as irresistible as those of a single assembly. It is to a legislature thus constituted that almost all the authority of the government has been entrusted.

But whilst the law increased the strength of those authorities which of themselves were strong, it enfeebled more and more those which were naturally weak. It deprived the representatives of the executive of all stability and independence, and by subjecting them completely to the caprices of the legislature, it robbed them of the slender influence which the nature of a democratic government might have allowed them to retain. In several States the judicial power was also submitted to the elective discretion of the majority, and in all of them its existence was made to depend on the pleasure of the legislative authority, since the representatives were empowered annually to regulate the stipend of the judges.

Custom, however, has done even more than law. A proceeding which will in the end set all the guarantees of representative government at naught is becoming more and more general in the United States; it frequently happens that the electors, who choose a delegate, point out a certain line of conduct to him, and impose upon him a certain number of positive obligations which he is pledged to fulfil. With the exception of the tumult, this comes to the same thing as if the majority of the populace held its deliberations in the market-place.

From Alexis de Tocqueville, *Democracy in America*, 1835. Volume I, Chapter XV.

[1] We observed, in examining the Federal Constitution, that the efforts of the legislators of the Union had been diametrically opposed to the present tendency. The consequence has been that the Federal Government is more independent in its sphere than that of the States. But the Federal Government scarcely ever interferes in any but external affairs; and the governments of the States are in reality the authorities which direct society in America.

Several other circumstances concur in rendering the power of the majority in America not only preponderant, but irresistible. The moral authority of the majority is partly based upon the notion that there is more intelligence and more wisdom in a great number of men collected together than in a single individual, and that the quantity of legislators is more important than their quality. The theory of equality is in fact applied to the intellect of man: and human pride is thus assailed in its last retreat by a doctrine which the minority hesitate to admit, and in which they very slowly concur. Like all other powers, and perhaps more than all other powers, the authority of the many requires the sanction of time; at first it enforces obedience by constraint, but its laws are not respected until they have long been maintained.

The right of governing society, which the majority supposes itself to derive from its superior intelligence, was introduced into the United States by the first settlers, and this idea, which would be sufficient of itself to create a free nation, has now been amalgamated with the manners of the people and the minor incidents of social intercourse.

The French, under the old monarchy, held it for a maxim (which is still a fundamental principle of the English Constitution) that the King could do no wrong; and if he did do wrong, the blame was imputed to his advisors. This notion was highly favorable to habits of obedience, and it enabled the subject to complain of the law without ceasing to love and honor the lawgiver. The Americans entertain the same opinion with respect to the majority.

The moral power of the majority is founded upon yet another principle, which is, that the interests of the many are to be preferred to those of the few. It will readily be perceived that the respect here professed for the rights of the majority must naturally increase or diminish according to the state of parties. When a nation is divided into several irreconcilable factions, the privilege of the majority is often overlooked, because it is intolerable to comply with its demands.

If there existed in America a class of citizens whom the legislating majority sought to deprive of exclusive privileges which they had possessed for ages, and to bring down from an elevated station to the level of the ranks of the multitude, it is probable that the minority would be less ready to comply with its laws. But as the United States were colonized by men holding equal rank amongst themselves, there is as yet no natural or permanent source of dissension between the interests of its different inhabitants.

There are certain communities in which the persons who constitute the minority can never hope to draw over the majority to their side, because they must then give up the very point which is at issue between them. Thus, an aristocracy can never become a majority whilst it retains its exclusive privileges, and it cannot cede its privileges without ceasing to be an aristocracy.

In the United States political questions cannot be taken up in so general and absolute a manner, and all parties are willing to recognize the rights of the majority, because they all hope to turn those rights to their own advantage at some future time. The majority therefore in that country exercises a prodigious actual authority, and a moral influence which is scarcely less preponderant; no obstacles exist which can impede or so much as retard its progress, or which can induce it to heed the complaints of those whom it crushes upon its path. This state of things is fatal in itself and dangerous for the future.

HOW THE UNLIMITED POWER OF THE MAJORITY INCREASES IN AMERICA THE INSTABILITY OF LEGISLATION AND ADMINISTRATION INHERENT IN DEMOCRACY

I have already spoken of the natural defects of democratic institutions, and they all of them increase at the exact ratio of the power of the majority. To begin with the most evident of them all; the mutability of the laws as an evil inherent in democratic government, because it is natural to democracies to raise men to power in very rapid succession. But this evil is more or less sensible in proportion to the authority and the means of action which the legislature possesses.

In America the authority exercised by the legislative bodies is supreme; nothing prevents them from accomplishing their wishes with celerity, and with irresistible power, whilst they are supplied by new representatives every year. That is to say, the circumstances which contribute most powerfully to democratic instability, and which admit of the free application of caprice to every object in the State, are here in full operation. In conformity with this principle, America is, at the present day, the country in the world where laws last the shortest time. Almost all the American constitutions have been amended within the course of thirty years: there is therefore not a single American State which has not modified the principles of its legislation in that lapse of time. As for the laws themselves, a single glance upon the archives of the different States of the Union suffices to convince one that in America the activity of the legislator never slackens. Not that the American democracy is naturally less stable than any other, but that it is allowed to follow its capricious propensities in the formation of the laws.[2]

The omnipotence of the majority, and the rapid as well as absolute manner in which its decisions are executed in the United States, has not only the effect of rendering the law unstable, but it exercises the same influence upon the execution of the law and the conduct of the public admin-

[2] The legislative acts promulgated by the State of Massachusetts alone, from the year 1780 to the present time, already fill three stout volumes; and it must not be forgotten that the collection to which I allude was published in 1823, when many old laws which had fallen into disuse were omitted. The State of Massachusetts, which is not more populous than a department of France, may be considered as the most stable, the most consistent, and the most sagacious in its undertakings of the whole Union.

istration. As the majority is the only power which it is important to court, all its projects are taken up with the greatest ardor, but no sooner is its attention distracted than all this ardor ceases; whilst in the free States of Europe the administration is at once independent and secure, so that the projects of the legislature are put into execution, although its immediate attention may be directed to other objects.

In America certain ameliorations are undertaken with much more zeal and activity than elsewhere; in Europe the same ends are promoted by much less social effort, more continuously applied.

Some years ago several pious individuals undertook to ameliorate the condition of the prisons. The public was excited by the statements which they put forward, and the regeneration of criminals became a very popular undertaking. New prisons were built, and for the first time the idea of re-forming as well as of punishing the delinquent formed a part of prison discipline. But this happy alteration, in which the public had taken so hearty an interest, and which the exertions of the citizens had irresistibly accelerated, could not be completed in a moment. Whilst the new penitentiaries were being erected (and it was the pleasure of the majority that they should be terminated with all possible celerity), the old prisons existed, which still contained a great number of offenders. These jails became more unwholesome and more corrupt in proportion as the new establishments were beautified and improved, forming a contrast which may readily be understood. The majority was so eagerly employed in founding the new prisons that those which already existed were forgotten; and as the general attention was diverted to a novel object, the care which had hitherto been bestowed upon the others ceased. The salutary regulations of discipline were first relaxed, and afterwards broken; so that in the immediate neighborhood of a prison which bore witness to the mild and enlightened spirit of our time, dungeons might be met with which reminded the visitor of the barbarity of the Middle Ages.

TYRANNY OF THE MAJORITY

I hold it to be an impious and an execrable maxim that, politically speaking, a people has a right to do whatsoever it pleases, and yet I have asserted that all authority originates in the will of the majority. Am I then, in contradiction with myself?

A general law — which bears the name of Justice — has been made and sanctioned, not only by a majority of this or that people, but by a majority of mankind. The rights of every people are consequently confined within the limits of what is just. A nation may be considered in the light of a jury which is empowered to represent society at large, and to apply the great and general law of justice. Ought such a jury, which represents society, to have more power than the society in which the laws its applies originate?

When I refuse to obey an unjust law, I do not contest the right which the majority has of commanding, but I simply appeal from the sovereignty of the people to the sovereignty of mankind. It has been asserted that a people can never entirely outstep the boundaries of justice and of reason in those affairs which are more peculiarly its own, and that consequently full power may fearlessly be given to the majority by which it is represented. But this language is that of a slave.

A majority taken collectively may be regarded as a being whose opinions, and most frequently whose interests, are opposed to those of another being, which is styled a minority. If it be admitted that a man, possessing absolute power, may misuse that power by wronging his adversaries, why should a majority not be liable to the same reproach? Men are not apt to change their characters by agglomeration; nor does their patience in the presence of obstacles increase with the consciousness of their strength.[3] And for these reasons I can never willingly invest any number of my fellow-creatures with that unlimited authority which I should refuse to any one of them.

I do not think that it is possible to combine several principles in the same government, so as at the same time to maintain freedom, and really to oppose them to one another. The form of government which is usually termed mixed has always appeared to me to be a mere chimera. Accurately speaking there is no such thing as a mixed government (with the meaning usually given to that word), because in all communities some one principle of action may be discovered which preponderates over the others. England in the last century, which has been more especially cited as an example of this form of Government, was in point of fact an essentially aristocratic State, although it comprised very powerful elements of democracy; for the laws and customs of the country were such that the aristocracy could not but preponderate in the end, and subject the direction of public affairs to its own will. The error arose from too much attention being paid to the actual struggle which was going on between the nobles and the people, without considering the probable issue of the contest, which was in reality the important point. When a community really has a mixed government, that is to say, when it is equally divided between two adverse principles, it must either pass through a revolution or fall into complete dissolution.

I am therefore of opinion that some one social power must always be made to predominate over the others; but I think that liberty is endangered when this power is checked by no obstacles which may retard its course, and force it to moderate its own vehemence.

Unlimited power is in itself a bad and dangerous thing; human beings are not competent to exercise it with discretion, and God alone can be

[3] No one will assert that a people cannot forcibly wrong another people; but parties may be looked upon as lesser nations within a greater one, and they are aliens to each other: if, therefore, it be admitted that a nation can act tyrannically towards another nation, it cannot be denied that a party may do the same towards another party.

omnipotent, because His wisdom and His justice are always equal to His power. But no power upon earth is so worthy of honor for itself, or of reverential obedience to the rights which it represents, that I would consent to admit its uncontrolled and all-predominant authority. When I see that the right and the means of absolute command are conferred on a people or upon a king, upon an aristocracy or a democracy, a monarchy or a republic, I recognize the germ of tyranny, and I journey onward to a land of more hopeful institutions.

In my opinion the main evil of the present democratic institutions of the United States does not arise, as is often asserted in Europe, from their weakness, but from their overpowering strength; and I am not so much alarmed at the excessive liberty which reigns in that country as at the very inadequate securities which exist against tyranny.

When an individual or a party is wronged in the United States, to whom can he apply for redress? If to public opinion, public opinion constitutes the majority; if to the legislature, it represents the majority, and implicitly obeys its injunctions; if to the executive power, it is appointed by the majority, and remains a passive tool in its hands; the public troops consist of the majority under arms; the jury is the majority invested with the right of hearing judicial cases; and in certain States even the judges are elected by the majority. However iniquitous or absurd the evil of which you complain may be, you must submit to it as well as you can.[4]

[4] A striking instance of the excesses which may be occasioned by the despotism of the majority occurred at Baltimore in the year 1812. At that time the war was very popular in Baltimore. A journal which had taken the other side of the question excited the indignation of the inhabitants by its opposition. The populace assembled, broke the printing-presses, and attacked the houses of the newspaper editors. The militia was called out, but no one obeyed the call; and the only means of saving the poor wretches who were threatened by the frenzy of the mob was to throw them into prison as common malefactors. But even this precaution was ineffectual; the mob collected again during the night, the magistrates again made a vain attempt to call out the militia, the prison was forced, one of the newspaper editors was killed upon the spot, and the others were left for dead; the guilty parties were acquitted by the jury when they were brought to trial.

I said one day to an inhabitant of Pennsylvania, " Be so good as to explain to me how it happens that in a State founded by Quakers, and celebrated for its toleration, freed blacks are not allowed to exercise civil rights. They pay the taxes; is it not fair that they should have a vote? "

" You insult us," replied my informant, " if you imagine that our legislators could have committed so gross an act of injustice and intolerance."

" What! then the blacks possess the right of voting in this country? "

" Without the smallest doubt."

" How comes it, then, that at the polling-booth this morning I did not perceive a single negro in the whole meeting? "

" This is not the fault of the law; the negroes have an undisputed right of voting, but they voluntarily abstain from making their appearance."

" A very pretty piece of modesty on their parts! " rejoined I.

" Why, the truth is, that they are not disinclined to vote, but they are afraid of being maltreated; in this country the law is sometimes unable to maintain its authority

If, on the other hand, a legislative power could be so constituted as to represent the majority without necessarily being the slave of its passions; an executive, so as to retain a certain degree of uncontrolled authority; and a judiciary, so as to remain independent of the two other powers; a government would be formed which would still be democratic without incurring any risk of tyrannical abuse.

I do not say that tyrannical abuses frequently occur in America at the present day, but I maintain that no sure barrier is established against them, and that the causes which mitigate the government are to be found in the circumstances and the manners of the country more than in its laws.

EFFECTS OF THE UNLIMITED POWER OF THE MAJORITY UPON THE ARBITRARY AUTHORITY OF THE AMERICAN PUBLIC OFFICERS

A distinction must be drawn between tyranny and arbitrary power. Tyranny may be exercised by means of the law, and in that case it is not arbitrary; arbitrary power may be exercised for the good of the community at large, in which case it is not tyrannical. Tyranny usually employs arbitrary means, but, if necessary, it can rule without them.

In the United States the unbounded power of the majority, which is favorable to the legal despotism of the legislature, is likewise favorable to the arbitrary authority of the magistrate. The majority has an entire control over the law when it is made and when it is executed; and as it possesses an equal authority over those who are in power and the community at large, it considers public officers as its passive agents, and readily confides the task of serving its designs to their vigilance. The details of their office and the privileges which they are to enjoy are rarely defined beforehand; but the majority treats them as a master does his servants when they are always at work in his sight, and he has the power of directing or reprimanding them at every instant.

In general the American functionaries are far more independent than the French civil officers within the sphere which is prescribed to them. Sometimes, even, they are allowed by the popular authority to exceed those bounds; and as they are protected by the opinion, and backed by the co-operation, of the majority, they venture upon such manifestations of their power as astonish a European. By this means habits are formed in the heart of a free country which may some day prove fatal to its liberties.

POWER EXERCISED BY THE MAJORITY IN AMERICA UPON OPINION

It is in the examination of the display of public opinion in the United States, that we clearly perceive how far the power of the majority sur-

---

without the support of the majority. But in this case the majority entertains very strong prejudices against the blacks, and the magistrates are unable to protect them in the exercise of their legal privileges."

" What! then the majority claims the right not only of making the laws, but of breaking the laws it has made? "

passes all the powers with which we are acquainted in Europe. Intellectual principles exercise an influence which is so invisible and often so inappreciable, that they baffle the toils of oppression. At the present time the most absolute monarchs in Europe are unable to prevent certain notions, which are opposed to their authority, from circulating in secret throughout their dominions, and even in their courts. Such is not the case in America; as long as the majority is still undecided, discussion is carried on; but as soon as its decision is irrevocably pronounced, a submissive silence is observed; and the friends, as well as the opponents, of the measure, unite in assenting to its propriety. The reason of this is perfectly clear: no monarch is so absolute as to combine all the powers of society in his own hands, and to conquer all opposition, with the energy of a majority, which is invested with the right of making and of executing the laws.

The authority of a king is purely physical, and it controls the actions of the subject without subduing his private will; but the majority possesses a power which is physical and moral at the same time; it acts upon the will as well as upon the actions of men, and it represses not only all contest, but all controversy.

I know no country in which there is so little true independence of mind and freedom of discussion as in America. In any constitutional state in Europe every sort of religious and political theory may be advocated and propagated abroad; for there is no country in Europe so subdued by any single authority, as not to contain citizens who are ready to protect the man who raises his voice in the cause of truth, from the consequences of his hardihood. If he is unfortunate enough to live under an absolute government, the people is upon his side; if he inhabits a free country, he may find a shelter behind the authority of the throne, if he require one. The aristocratic part of society supports him in some countries, and the democracy in others. But in a nation where democratic institutions exist, organized like those of the United States, there is but one sole authority, one single element of strength and of success, with nothing beyond it.

In America the majority raises very formidable barriers to the liberty of opinion; within these barriers an author may write whatever he pleases, but he will repent it if he ever step beyond them. Not that he is exposed to the terrors of an auto-da-fé, but he is tormented by the slights and persecutions of daily obloquy. His political career is closed forever, since he has offended the only authority which is able to promote his success. Every sort of compensation, even that of celebrity, is refused to him. Before he published his opinions he imagined that he held them in common with many others; but no sooner has he declared them openly than he is loudly censured by his overbearing opponents, whilst those who think without having the courage to speak, like him, abandon him in silence. He yields at length, oppressed by the daily efforts he has been making, and he subsides into silence, as if he was tormented by remorse for having spoken the truth.

Fetters and headsmen were the coarse instruments which tyranny formerly employed; but the civilization of our age has refined the arts of despotism which seemed, however, to have been sufficiently perfected before. The excesses of monarchical power had devised a variety of physical means of oppression: the democratic republics of the present day have rendered it as entirely an affair of the mind as that will which it is intended to coerce. Under the absolute sway of an individual despot the body was attacked in order to subdue the soul, and the soul escaped the blows which were directed against it and rose superior to the attempt; but such is not the course adopted by tyranny in democratic republics; there the body is left free, and the soul is enslaved. The sovereign can no longer say, " You shall think as I do on pain of death "; but he says, " You are free to think differently from me, and to retain your life, your property, and all that you possess; but if such be your determination, you are henceforth an alien among your people. You may retain your civil rights, but they will be useless to you, for you will never be chosen by your fellow-citizens if you solicit their suffrages, and they will affect to scorn you if you solicit their esteem. You will remain among men, but you will be deprived of the rights of mankind. Your fellow-creatures will shun you like an impure being, and those who are most persuaded of your innocence will abandon you too, lest they should be shunned in their turn. Go in peace! I have given you your life, but it is an existence incomparably worse than death."

Monarchical institutions have thrown an odium upon despotism; let us beware lest democratic republics should restore oppression, and should render it less odious and less degrading in the eyes of the many, by making it still more onerous to the few.

Works have been published in the proudest nations of the Old World expressly intended to censure the vices and deride the follies of the times: Labruyère inhabited the palace of Louis XIV when he composed his chapter upon the Great, and Molière criticised the courtiers in the very pieces which were acted before the Court. But the ruling power in the United States is not to be made game of; the smallest reproach irritates its sensibility, and the slightest joke which has any foundation in truth renders it indignant; from the style of its language to the more solid virtues of its character, everything must be made the subject of encomium. No writer, whatever be his eminence, can escape from this tribute of adulation to his fellow-citizens. The majority lives in the perpetual practice of self-applause, and there are certain truths which the Americans can only learn from strangers or from experience.

If great writers have not at present existed in America, the reason is very simply given in these facts; there can be no literary genius without freedom of opinion, and freedom of opinion does not exist in America. The Inquisition has never been able to prevent a vast number of anti-religious books from circulating in Spain. The empire of the majority succeeds much better in the United States, since it actually removes the wish of publishing them. Unbelievers are to be met with in America, but, to say the truth, there is no public organ of infidelity. Attempts have been made by some governments to protect the morality of nations by prohibiting licentious books. In the United States no one is punished for this sort of works, but no one is induced to write them; not because all the citizens are immaculate in their manners, but because the majority of the community is decent and orderly.

In these cases the advantages derived from the exercise of this power are unquestionable, and I am simply discussing the nature of the power itself. This irresistible authority is a constant fact, and its judicious exercise is an accidental occurrence.

EFFECTS OF THE TYRANNY OF THE MAJORITY UPON THE NATIONAL CHARACTER OF THE AMERICANS

The tendencies which I have just alluded to are as yet very slightly perceptible in political society, but they already begin to exercise an unfavorable influence upon the national character of the Americans. I am inclined to attribute the singular paucity of distinguished political characters to the ever-increasing activity of the despotism of the majority in the United States. When the American Revolution broke out they arose in great numbers, for public opinion then served, not to tyrannize over, but to direct the exertions of individuals. Those celebrated men took a full part in the general agitation of mind common at that period, and they attained a high degree of personal fame, which was reflected back upon the nation, but which was by no means borrowed from it.

In absolute governments the great nobles who are nearest to the throne flatter the passions of the sovereign, and voluntarily truckle to his caprices. But the mass of the nation does not degrade itself by servitude: it often submits from weakness, from habit, or from ignorance, and sometimes from loyalty. Some nations have been known to sacrifice their own desires to those of the sovereign with pleasure and with pride, thus exhibiting a sort of independence in the very act of submission. These peoples are miserable, but they are not degraded. There is a great difference between doing what one does not approve and feigning to approve what one does; the one is the necessary case of a weak person, the other befits the temper of a lackey.

In free countries, where everyone is more or less called upon to give his opinion in the affairs of state; in democratic republics, where public life is incessantly commingled with domestic affairs, where the sovereign authority is accessible on every side, and where its attention can almost always be attracted by vociferation, more persons are to be met with who speculate upon its foibles and live at the cost of its passions than in absolute monarchies. Not because men are naturally worse in these States than elsewhere, but the temptation is stronger, and of easier access at the same time. The result is a far more extensive debasement of the characters of citizens.

Democratic republics extend the practice of currying favor with the many, and they introduce it into a greater number of classes at once: this is one of the most serious reproaches that can be addressed to them. In democratic States organized on the principles of the American republics, this is more especially the case, where the authority of the majority is so absolute and so irresistible that a man must give up his rights as a citizen, and almost abjure his quality as a human being, if he intends to stray from the track which it lays down.

In that immense crowd which throngs the avenues to power in the United States I found very few men who displayed any of that manly candor and that masculine independence of opinion which frequently distinguished the Americans in former times, and which constitutes the leading feature in distinguished characters, wheresoever they may be found. It seems, at first sight, as if all the minds of the Americans were formed upon one model, so accurately do they correspond in their manner of judging. A stranger does, indeed, sometimes meet with Americans who dissent from these rigorous formularies; with men who deplore the defects of the laws, the mutability and the ignorance of democracy; who even go so far as to observe the evil tendencies which impair the national character, and to point out such remedies as it might be possible to apply; but no one is there to hear these things besides yourself, and you, to whom these secret reflections are confided, are a stranger and a bird of passage. They are very ready to communicate truths which are useless to you, but they continue to hold a different language in public.

If ever these lines are read in America, I am well assured of two things: in the first place, that all who peruse them will raise their voices to condemn me; and in the second place, that very many of them will acquit me at the bottom of their conscience.

I have heard of patriotism in the United States, and it is a virtue which may be found among the people, but never among the leaders of the people. This may be explained by analogy; despotism debases the oppressed much more than the oppressor: in absolute monarchies the king has often great virtues, but the courtiers are invariably servile. It is true that the American courtiers do not say " Sire," or " Your Majesty " — a distinction without a difference. They are forever talking of the natural intelligence of the populace they serve; they do not debate the question as to which of the virtues of their master is pre-eminently worthy of admiration, for they assure him that he possesses all the virtues under heaven without having acquired them, or without caring to acquire them; they do not give him their daughters and their wives to be raised at his pleasure to the rank of his concubines, but, by sacrificing their opinions, they prostitute themselves. Moralists and philosophers in America are not obliged to conceal their opinions under the veil of allegory; but, before they venture upon a harsh truth, they say, " We are aware that the people which we are addressing is too superior to all the weaknesses of human nature to lose the command of its temper for an instant; and we should not hold this language if we were not speaking to men whom their virtues and their intelligence render more worthy of freedom than all the rest of the world." It would have been impossible for the sycophants of Louis XIV to flatter more dexterously. For my part, I am persuaded that in all governments, whatever their nature may be, servility will cower to force, and adulation will cling to power. The only means of preventing men from degrading themselves is to invest no one with that unlimited authority which is the surest method of debasing them.

THE GREATEST DANGERS OF THE AMERICAN REPUBLICS PROCEED
FROM THE UNLIMITED POWER OF THE MAJORITY

Governments usually fall a sacrifice to impotence or to tyranny. In the former case their power escapes from them; it is wrested from their grasp in the latter. Many observers, who have witnessed the anarchy of democratic States, have imagined that the government of those States was naturally weak and impotent. The truth is, that when once hostilities are begun between parties, the government loses its control over society. But I do not think that a democratic power is naturally without force or without resources: say, rather, that it is almost always by the abuse of its force and the misemployment of its resources that a democratic government fails. Anarchy is almost always produced by its tyranny or its mistakes, but not by its want of strength.

It is important not to confound stability with force, or the greatness of a thing with its duration. In democratic republics, the power which directs [5] society is not stable; for it often changes hands and assumes a new direction. But whichever way it turns, its force is almost irresistible. The Governments of the American republics appear to me to be as much centralized as those of the absolute monarchies of Europe, and more energetic than they are. I do not, therefore, imagine that they will perish from weakness.[6]

If ever the free institutions of America are destroyed, that event may be attributed to the unlimited authority of the majority, which may at some future time urge the minorities to desperation, and oblige them to have recourse to physical force. Anarchy will then be the result, but it will have been brought about by despotism.

[5] This power may be centered in an assembly, in which case it will be strong without being stable; or it may be centered in an individual, in which case it will be less strong, but more stable.
[6] I presume that it is scarcely necessary to remind the reader here, as well as throughout the remainder of this chapter, that I am speaking, not of the Federal Government, but of the several governments of each State, which the majority controls at its pleasure.

Mr. Hamilton expresses the same opinion in the " Federalist," No. 51. " It is of great importance in a republic not only to guard the society against the oppression of its rulers, but to guard one part of the society against the injustice of the other part. Justice is the end of government. It is the end of civil society. It ever has been, and ever will be, pursued until it be obtained, or until liberty be lost in the pursuit. In a society, under the forms of which the stronger faction can readily unite and oppress the weaker, anarchy may as truly be said to reign as in a state of nature, where the weaker individual is not secured against the violence of the stronger: and as in the latter state even the stronger individuals are prompted by the uncertainty of their condition to submit to a government which may protect the weak as well as themselves, so in the former state will the more powerful factions be gradually induced by a like motive to wish for a government which will protect all parties, the weaker as well as the more powerful. It can be little doubted that, if the State of Rhode Island was separated from the Confederacy and left to itself, the insecurity of right under the popular form of government within such narrow limits would be displayed by such reiterated oppressions of the factious majorities, that some power altogether independent of the people would soon be called for by the voice of the very factions whose misrule had proved the necessity of it."

Jefferson has also thus expressed himself in a letter to Madison: " The executive power in our Government is not the only, perhaps not even the principal, object of my solicitude. The tyranny of the Legislature is really the danger most to be feared, and will continue to be so for many years to come. The tyranny of the executive power will come in its turn, but at a more distant period." I am glad to cite the opinion of Jefferson upon this subject rather than that of another, because I consider him to be the most powerful advocate democracy has ever sent forth.

CHAPTER FIVE BIBLIOGRAPHY

FRIEDRICH, CARL J., editor, *Authority*. Cambridge: Harvard University Press, 1958.

> This volume is the first in a series of annual publications by the American Society for Political and Legal Philosophy. The chapters range from a consideration of authority in general to authority in historical perspective and authority in social-political perspective. The contributors stress our ambivalent attitudes toward authority in the United States.

FRIEDRICH, CARL J., editor, *Community*. New York: Liberal Arts Press, 1959.

> Chapter VIII by George Catlin is an especially good treatment of the meaning of community. He argues that community is to be had at the price of conformity to *homonia* — " and the philosophical problem is whether the price is worth paying." Chapter XVI by John Ladd is a logical analysis of the concept of community and is functionally derived.

KIRK, RUSSELL, *The Conservative Mind: from Burke to Santayana*. Chicago: Henry Regnery Company, 1953.

> Kirk believes we are in an age of " disintegrating liberal and radical philosophies." His book deals with the ideas of those British and American thinkers who have carried on the conservative tradition.

LINDSAY, A. D., *The Modern Democratic State*. London: Oxford University Press, 1943.

> Lindsay stresses the " operative ideals " that underlie modern democratic states. These ideals, derived mainly from Western civilization, were influenced by ideals of the French Revolution, and are changed gradually.

LIPPINCOTT, BENJAMIN E., *Victorian Critics of Democracy*. Minneapolis: University of Minnesota Press, 1938.

> Lippincott has selected those whom he considers to be the outstanding English critics of democracy in the nineteenth century. He assesses their assumptions and the place each held in his time. Their criticisms of democracy are brought forth, and the author evaluates these criticisms. The critics are Carlyle, Ruskin, Arnold, Stephen, Maine, and Lecky.

METZ, HAROLD W. and THOMSON, CHARLES A. H., *Authoritarianism and the Individual*. Washington: The Brookings Institution, 1950.

> A brief consideration is presented of the meaning of freedom and a free society and the proper role of the state. The book as a whole seeks to show the extent and effect of influence of several authoritarian regimes upon various social, economic, personal, and political aspects of life. Feudalism, fascism, National Socialism, and communism are studied.

MUNTYAN, MILOSH, " Community," in Chester W. Harris, editor, *Encyclopedia of Educational Research*, third edition. New York: Macmillan Company, 1960.

> This is a perceptive analysis of the concept of community. Muntyan cites several fallacies and inconsistencies in the typical usage of the term *community* in educational literature. Several research and sociological studies are cited.

PENNOCK, J. ROLAND, *Liberal Democracy: Its Merits and Prospects*. New York: Rinehart and Company, 1950.

> Chapter V, a discussion of equality and fraternity, gives a number of illustrations of the meanings of these concepts by reference to Matthew Arnold, Plato, Herbert Spencer, R. H. Tawney, and others. Discussion and conclusions are written in plain and readable style.

RUSSELL, WILLIAM F., *Liberty vs. Equality*. New York: Macmillan Company, 1936.

> Russell gives a brief sketch of United States history in which he sees liberty and equality in constant conflict. The resolution is to be found in a compromise. Since the compromise is a delicate balance, the conflict reappears with renewed attempts to find a proper balance.

SCHNEIDER, HERBERT W., *Three Dimensions of Public Morality*. Bloomington: Indiana University Press, 1956.

>The three dimensions that Schneider deals with are liberty, equality, and fraternity. He sees the three as aspects of a *single* moral order — a kind of " secular trinity." A straightforward, readable book.

SHEEN, FULTON J., *Liberty, Equality and Fraternity*. New York: Macmillan Company, 1938.

>An outstanding Catholic spokesman here links the ideal of liberty with capitalism, equality with communism, and fraternity with Catholicism.

SOROKIN, PITIRIM A., editor, *Forms and Techniques of Altruistic and Spiritual Growth*. Boston: Beacon Press, 1954.

>Several chapters are devoted to altruistic aspects of religious beliefs — particularly Eastern religions. In Chapter 20 Sorokin describes a study of friendship and enmity patterns among members of a college class of his, in this case students from Harvard and Radcliffe. This book provides many different insights into the concept of fraternity.

STANLEY, WILLIAM O., *Education and Social Integration*. New York: Bureau of Publications, Teachers College, Columbia University, 1953.

>Stanley identifies the democratic tradition as the foundation of social integration. Chapters 8 and 9 contain a discussion of bases of educational authority. A competent methodology of group deliberation is seen as the means for sustaining intellectual and moral authority.

6

The Implications of Democracy for Education

It is periodically popular, in this country and abroad, to criticize American education as being "too democratic." For those who are *not* committed to the democratic way of life, this is a very valid criticism; but for those who *are* committed to the democratic way of life, this reduces itself to a logical fallacy. Democratic education is nothing more than the organized attempt to help individuals capitalize on their unique strengths in ways that are socially useful. It is democracy in practice, and to criticize democratic education is, in the last analysis, to criticize democracy itself. It is easy, indeed, to criticize many of the practices which have been undertaken *in the name of* democracy in education. But there is a difference between criticizing a practice which is mistakenly undertaken in the name of democracy and criticizing education itself for being "too democratic." Anyone who starts out with an initial faith in democracy and recognizes the relationship between education and the way of life of the society which supports it, cannot consistently accept the latter criticism as valid. Although the attacks upon *democratic* education have been numerous, three criticisms — which are, upon analysis, not criticisms of genuine democracy at all — deserve mention.

The first of these criticisms is generally based on a comparison between American education and education in some other land. The critics say: "American education is not as good as education over there. It is too democratic." Comparisons between American education and education in foreign countries can be very useful; they

can help us locate points in our own system which are deserving of special scrutiny. But this comparison never enables us to determine which is *better*. It is only a second comparison made between the practices of each country and the goals we accept which can enable us to determine this. If education in another country, for example, helps individuals to realize their unique strengths better than does American education, then it is in this respect, at least, *more democratic* than our own. The criteria for judgment reside in our democratic frame of reference, not in the practices of the American, or foreign, educational system.

The second of these criticisms stems from a grave misconception of the nature of democracy: the tendency on the part of some persons to view mediocrity as a natural product of democracy. These critics assert: "Democracy in education produces only mediocrity. What we need is excellence!" That American education has sometimes produced mediocrity cannot be gainsaid, but the point is that when it has done so it has been *undemocratic, not democratic*. There is no place in the lexicon of democracy for a concept such as mediocrity; democracy is committed to a respect for the unique — not for the asocial uniqueness of the hermit, but for the constructive uniqueness of the socially dedicated human being. Mediocrity and uniqueness have nothing in common. Mediocrity is a term akin to all those concepts of averaging people out, of categorizing humanity, which have plagued mankind throughout history. Democratic education is never education for mediocrity; it is always education for excellence — but education for the *unique* excellence of each and every individual.

The third of these criticisms stems from an antiquated notion of the nature of democracy; from the tendency on the part of some persons to equate democracy with a concept of laissez-faire control, a concept of nineteenth century liberal economic policy which has, admittedly, sometimes been applied in educational settings. Such critics say: " Democratic education is not education at all — it is leadership of the immature by the immature; it is anarchy! " The discipline of democracy is assuredly the discipline of informed self-control. But it is discipline, not license. It is informed, not random. Democratic education is education designed to help individuals become increasingly effective in their self-direction. Effective self-direction requires not only permissiveness but knowledge. The informed person who has analyzed his values and the alternatives available to him is the only person who is truly self-directive. Producing such persons, and finding increasingly effective ways of producing them, is the business of democratic education. The findings of modern social science can give little comfort to those who would prefer to believe that the way to develop self-direction is to be forever subject to the arbitrary direction of another. Democratic education is education seeking to find the appropriate areas and boundaries of individual choice at each appropriate level of growth or maturity.

Basically then, most criticisms of American education which characterize it as being " too democratic " miss the point entirely. The failures of American education, of which there are certainly many, are not the result of its being characterized by " too much democracy," but by " too little democracy " or, sometimes, by an inadequate conception of democracy. Our challenge is not that of limiting the extent of democracy in education but of tracing out its true educational implications and eliminating those practices which we find to have been spurious or superficial. A social system, such as democracy, which posits its faith in a reciprocal relationship between the individual and society, and which sees the society as achieving its potential only as it serves individuals in achieving theirs, must seek out its own educational paths. It will sometimes make mistakes in doing this, for it is passing through uncharted terrain; but it has along on its quest a self-corrective directional device of great worth — the right to free intellectual inquiry — and this instrument is the greatest safeguard man has yet devised against his own folly.

But what are the central educational corollaries of the democratic way of life as we have defined it? At least the following are clear. No doubt others could be added to the list:

1. *Democracy demands an education that is value-oriented.* The democratic way of life is not a way of life made up of lawn-mowers, washing machines, and television sets. It is a way of life characterized by a set of values which guide men in all their actions. These values are not innate; they are learned. They are not values to be accepted without question; they are subject to inquiry, reflection, and modification. They are not values to be kept apart from daily life; they are values which must be lived. They require commitment. Democratic education is concerned with building such inquiry, such practice, and such commitment.
2. *Democracy demands an education that develops the qualities of self-criticism.* Democracy never rests; it is an impatient way of life. It seeks not the good but the best; it does not accept any of its present social forms as necessarily the final, best means of achieving its ideals. Democratic education is a leader in society's quest for ever better paths into the future.
3. *Democracy demands an education concerned with all aspects of social*

life. Democracy embraces many realms of human activity. It incorporates a faith that the way to improvement in all of these realms is through the application of man's intelligence to them. This does not mean that only the social studies are the democratic part of education; it means rather that knowledge in all fields of study needs to be appraised for its social consequences. Democratic education would apply man's knowledge in man's service.

4. *Democracy demands an education that is characterized by faith in knowledge and free access to knowledge.* Simply, this requirement rests upon the fact that in a democratic society men are self-governing, and effective self-government requires the availability of appropriate knowledge. But there is more to the requirement than this. The very truths of democracy are subject to change. Intelligence is the effective control of change through knowledge. Democratic education is the building of such intelligence.

5. *Democracy demands an education which capitalizes on the unique capacities of individuals and directs them in ways that are socially responsible.* Democracy pins its faith, not on all men being the same, but on the capacity of society to balance off differing individual strengths so that the good life may result for all. Democratic education is characterized not by the equality of identity but by the equality of opportunity for developing uniqueness.

6. *Democracy demands an education which builds toward shared goals through shared activities.* Democracy seeks to capitalize on unique potentialities in socially useful ways. Only as we contribute our individual strengths toward building a common future can the democratic ideal of maximum human growth be achieved. Man's genuine humanity is built not by being apart from his society, but by being part of his society. Democratic education prepares man to participate in such a future by enabling him to participate in such a present.

7. *Democracy demands an education that will change with the advent of new knowledge and new problems.* Democracy is always in the process of becoming, of achieving its potential. The education which will truly undergird democracy must likewise be in a process of becoming, of changing, as man's vision improves. The democratic education of tomorrow will certainly extend far beyond the horizon of man's vision today.

It is only when we have established such beacons as these that we may approach confidently the many problems that confront education and educators in our society. This chapter is designed to help clarify the most pressing of these problems within the context of democratic criteria.

SECTION 1. The extent of education: Who shall be educated?

The various aspects of equality as an attribute of democracy have been explored in the previous chapter. The implications for education of the concept of equality are dealt with in the first group of readings in this chapter. The phrase " equality of educational opportunity " has been used in the United States as a statement of faith by many, a rallying cry by others, and a still sought-after goal by some minority groups. And just as the political idea of equality has various meanings, so also its educational facets are varied and complex. As James B. Conant points out, " In athletics, at least, the coaches are expected to develop only promising material. No one complains if his undersized son with awkward legs does not become a football hero. Some fathers, however, seem to demand the intellectual equivalent of such a miracle."

But the question of who shall be

educated goes beyond the simple matter of the location and cultivation of those with brainpower. Our young are inducted into a society that contains, among other characteristics, that of social class. Concomitants of social class are wealth, employment, residence, and heritage. Since these exist in differing amounts among persons, they act as selective agents in determining who shall advance how far on the educational ladder. These relationships between social class and educational achievement are dealt with by Warner, Havighurst and Loeb in their book, *Who Shall Be Educated?* In this selection they point out some of the more persistent manifestations of our social class system as it affects education. It should be understood that, although some of the factual information may now be out of date, the generalizations about social class are for the most part still considered to be as valid as when they were written.

Conant recognizes the factors of social class that Warner and others refer to, but he takes a very optimistic view of the future and looks forward to the day of a practically classless society. The major agent for bringing about this peaceful revolution is the system of free public education. Both Conant and Warner argue that we should tap the vast reservoir of potentially able students who now have their formal schooling terminated before they have completed the level and kind of education of which they are intellectually capable.

The final selection in this part of the chapter is perhaps the most optimistic and forward-looking of all. It is from the Educational Policies Commission's *Education for ALL American Youth* and is written somewhat in the same vein as Edward Bellamy's *Looking Backward.* In this selection the Commission is writing a hypothetical account of developments in education since World War II — as they hopefully *should* be in the fictitious state of Columbia and its typical communities of Farmville and American City.

W. LLOYD WARNER et al.
The school as a selecting agency

The educational system is a sorting and selecting agency. The educational system may be thought of as an enormous, complicated machine for sorting and ticketing and routing children through life. Young children are fed in at one end to a moving belt which conveys them past all sorts of inspecting stations. One large group is almost immediately brushed off into a bin labeled " nonreaders," " first-grade repeaters," or " opportunity class " where they stay for eight or ten years and are then released through a chute to the outside world to become " hewers of wood and drawers of water." The great body of children move ahead on the main belt, losing a few here and there who are " kept back " for repeated inspection.

At a station labeled " high school " there are several types of inspection and the main belt divides into smaller belts which diverge slightly from each other. From some of the belts the children, now become youths, are

From W. Lloyd Warner, Robert J. Havighurst, and Martin B. Loeb, *Who Shall Be Educated?* 1944, pp. 49–54, 148–150, 162–166. Reprinted by permission of Harper & Brothers.

unceremoniously dumped down chutes into the outside world, while the other belts, labeled " college preparatory," " commercial," " vocational " roll steadily on. The young people are inspected not only for brains and learning ability, but also for skin color, pronunciation, cut of clothes, table manners, parental bank account. Strangely enough they are not inspected for moral integrity, honesty, or other qualities which go under the name of " character."

At the end of the high-school division several of the belts project their human freight into the outside labor market, and the sorting machine is now much smaller, housing a few narrow conveyors labeled " college," " professional school," and " trade school." The inspectors quickly shunt aside the majority of this small band of young men and women into the labor market, leaving a few indeed who reach the next station, labeled " bachelor's degree," which is the end of the machine really, though there is a small extension called " graduate school."

Whatever figure of speech we use, the school system appears to be a sorting device with various selective principles operating. In addition to the principle of intellectual ability, there are such principles of selection as economic status, social class, and social personality. There is little or no selection for moral character.

The Hometown school has already sorted out Tom Brown from Bob Jones. Tom will be promoted regularly and readied for college. Bob will be dropped as soon as possible. It is not yet clear what will happen to Joe Sienkowitz, but it appears that he will finish high school and because of his talent his teachers may help him to get a scholarship for study of music. There are probably two or three other boys in Tom Brown's class, fully as able as Tom, but without any special artistic talent, who will have to stop their education at the end of high school because their way into college is blocked by lack of money. . . .

Educational opportunity is not equally available to all. There are two senses in which we might say that educational opportunity is equally available to all children. We could speak of equal educational opportunity if all children and young people went to schools of their own choosing as long as they or their parents pleased. In that sense we fall far short of providing equal educational opportunity and we shall probably never attain such a goal.

In a more limited sense we might speak of equality of educational opportunity if all children and young people exceeding a given level of intellectual ability were enabled to attend schools and colleges up to some specified level. This is the only practicable kind of equality of educational opportunity. For example, if all boys and girls with I.Q.'s over 100 were able to attend high school up to the age of eighteen, and if all young people with I.Q.'s over 110 were able to attend college for four years, we could say that equality of educational opportunity existed to a considerable degree.

It is possible to investigate the availability of educational opportunity in this sense in various parts of the country. For example, a study of youth in Pennsylvania was conducted about a decade ago by the State Department of Public Instruction and the American Youth Commission. The socio-economic status and educational history were ascertained for a group of 910 pupils with intelligence quotients of 110 or above. It is generally assumed that pupils with intelligence quotients above 110 are good college material. This group of superior pupils was divided into two subgroups on the basis of socio-economic status. Of the upper socio-economic group, 93 per cent graduated from high school and 57 per cent attended college. Of the lower socio-economic group, 72 per cent graduated from high school and 13 per cent attended college. Further study of the data in Table II will show even more clearly that the group with below-average socio-economic status had relatively less educational opportunity than the group with above-average socio-economic status, although both groups were about equal in intellectual ability.

TABLE II

RELATION OF INTELLIGENCE TO EDUCATIONAL OPPORTUNITY

(Record of students with Intelligence Quotients of 110 or above)

Educational advance	Socio-economic status				Total group	
	Above average		Below average			
Dropped school at eighth grade or below	4	0.7%	27	7.9%	31	3.4%
Completed ninth, tenth, or eleventh grade but did not graduate from high school	36	6.2%	69	20.2%	105	11.6%
Graduated from high school but did not attend college	206	36.3%	202	59.0%	408	44.8%
Attended college	322	56.8%	44	12.9%	366	40.2%
Total	568	100.0%	342	100.0%	910	100.0%

A similar conclusion must be drawn from a study made by Helen B. Goetsch on 1,023 able students who graduated from Milwaukee high schools in 1937 and 1938. These students all had I.Q.'s of 117 or above. The income of their parents is directly related to college attendance, as is shown in Table III. The higher the parents' income, the greater is the proportion who went to college.

The same general result is found in the data of the National Health Survey, which was conducted in eighty-three cities in eighteen states dur-

TABLE III

RELATION OF PARENTAL INCOME TO FULL–TIME COLLEGE
ATTENDANCE OF SUPERIOR MILWAUKEE
HIGH SCHOOL GRADUATES

Parental Income	Per Cent In College Full-time
$8,000+	100.0
5,000–7,999	92.0
3,000–4,999	72.9
2,000–2,999	44.4
1,500–1,999	28.9
1,000–1,499	25.5
500– 999	26.8
Under 500	20.4

ing the winter of 1935–36. When boys and girls of ages sixteen to twenty-four are classified by family income, school attendance increases markedly with increase in family income.

It might be argued, in the face of these facts, that children of families in the lower socio-economic levels do not desire as much education as those from the middle and upper levels. Thus, if public grants were available to pay the living expenses of all high-school pupils who wished to go to school and needed financial help, we might still find that more children of the upper economic levels were attending school. But there are three lines of evidence which indicate that children at the lower economic levels do not have all the educational opportunity they or their parents desire. One is the frequency with which " lack of money " is given as a reason for quitting school. Another is the sharp increase in college and high-school enrollment that came with the establishing of the National Youth Administration student-aid program in 1935. A third is the fact that there is a substantial out-of-pocket cost attached to attendance at a " free " high school. Hand has summarized a number of studies on the cash cost of going to a public high school. He finds this to average $125 a year in several cities. Students can go to school and spend little or no money. But they are then barred from many of the school activities, they cannot even take regular laboratory courses, and they must go around in what is to high-school youngsters the supremely embarrassing condition of having no change to rattle in their pockets, no money to contribute to a party, no possibility of being independent in their dealings with their friends. . . .

The hard facts. Education must serve democratic purposes. Education must give all boys and girls their chance. The educational system must select and encourage those with the best abilities wherever they are found.

Education must promote social solidarity through providing equal opportunity, through freeing people from narrow class prejudice and snobbery, and through teaching the kind of morality that democracy requires.

In making education serve democratic purposes, the educator faces many difficult problems. These problems are caused by certain irreducible stubborn facts about human beings and about our society. These are the hard facts:

Children are not born equal. We no longer believe, if we ever did, that all children are created equal biologically. Children are born equal in America only in the sight of God and the law. This means that they have equal spiritual claims to consideration as individual human beings, and that they have equal rights in the law courts. In no other important sense are they born equal. We know that children are born with diverse potentialities. We believe that, even if all children had identical social and physical environments, they would grow up to be different in ability, personality and physique.

We also know that children with talent or unusual ability are born to parents of low as well as high status. Everybody knows that dull, ordinary, and superior children are produced by parents of high social status. Everybody also knows that parents of low social status may produce superior children.

We know that children are not created equal socially. Every individual is born into a set of social positions. A child is born into a social status by sex. From the day of its birth a boy child is treated in a different manner from a girl child. A child is born into a status by his birth order in the family. The first-born will receive different treatment from those who come later. The last child will get a special kind of treatment. A child is born into a status by his family's position in the social structure. The child of the house " on the hill " will have nurses, servants, tutors. He will grow accustomed to having people treat him with deference. He will develop manners and speech that mark him as having grown up " on the hill." The child of the house by the railroad tracks will grow up with entirely different manners and attitudes and expectations in life. A child is born into a status by his nationality or race. If he is Jewish, Italian, Irish, German, Chinese, Hindu, Negro, he will undergo the treatment accorded to people of his group, treatment which varies from one part of the world to another and from one time to another.

These social inequalities quickly become part of the person. They get into his nervous system. They engender habits and attitudes which mark him as a person and over which he has little conscious control. The marks of social status appear in a person almost as soon as the genes which he inherits from his parents' bodies display themselves in observable characteristics, and it becomes impossible to tell how much of the person is due to heredity and how much to environment.

By the time children are five or six years of age, they are such a diverse lot that equality of opportunity for them obviously is not identity of opportunity. To treat them all alike would be like putting little chicks, ducklings, baby swans, puppies, kittens, and bear cubs all in a pond together and waiting to see how they respond to this " equal opportunity." . . .

Organization of the educational program. The educational system should be organized to recognize superior abilities wherever they are found, to reward them, and to train them. This is what we mean by equality of educational opportunity. Equal opportunity does not mean identical opportunity. Children and young people vary in their ability to take advantage of opportunity. Consequently, we must have different kinds of education for different kinds of people.

For younger boys and girls, the common program of elementary education is capable of sufficient differentiation to serve pupils of various abilities. For boys and girls of high-school age, however, a variety of courses is desirable. Equality of educational opportunity means differentiation of educational opportunity. There should be a number of different courses or curricula in secondary schools and colleges designed for people with different abilities and different vocational goals. The high school should offer commercial, homemaking, mechanical arts, agriculture, and college-preparatory courses.

All these differentiated courses should have a substantial common core of " education for the common life." A third to a half of the school day should be spent in this part of the program, with all kinds of students thrown together. In this common core there should be no sectioning of students by vocational aim or social position. But students should be segregated by ability and by vocational aim in the differentiated part of the educational program.

The chief problem which arises in this kind of program is that of placing students in the courses to which they are best adapted. Inevitably, some courses or curricula will have more social prestige than others, and boys and girls, egged on by their parents and by teachers also, will seek admission to the preferred curricula. Nearly all students who desire social recognition now go into a college-preparatory course in high school. In a university the distinctions are not so great among curricula, but still the curricula in agriculture and home economics are often thought of as below the social level of other courses of study.

The kind of change in values which we foresee in American life, away from material success and toward more humane and spiritual values, will make this problem easier of solution. The boy who takes auto mechanics because he likes tools and machines and who promises to become a good husband, father, citizen, and worker in his chosen station in life will not be made to feel guilty because he has not aimed for something " higher." The girl who takes high-school home economics and marries this boy will not be made to feel sorry for herself because she did not become a teacher and marry a lawyer. But this change in social values will come slowly, and the problem of guiding boys and girls into the courses to which they are best suited will continue for a long time to be most difficult.

The best solution of this problem seems to lie in establishing a scientific and honest guidance program. The student's aptitudes, abilities, and expectations in life should be assessed and considered by wise and well-trained counselors who should then give the student and his parents their honest and frank advice. If they should advise a boy to take a commercial course, but in spite of this advice he and his parents should insist on his taking a college-preparatory course, the decision of the boy and his parents should be respected. But standards in the college-preparatory course should be rigorously high, and the boy should be required to meet these standards.

If the boy should succeed in this course, the counselors should give their approval and encouragement. If he should fail, they should advise him once more to follow the course they first suggested. Thus there could be no basis for complaint by the boy or his parents that he was not given equal educational opportunity with others.

In a differentiated educational program of this sort, Tom Brown would probably take a college-preparatory course and go on to college where he would take a course in engineering, or business administration, or law. A friend of Tom's who is also of a middle-class family but has not the proper abilities for a college course would be advised to take a commercial or mechanical course in high school. If he accepted this advice, he would probably graduate from high school in Hometown and go into his father's business, or go to work in a garage or factory, and become a well-adjusted and well-liked citizen. If he and his parents resisted the counselor's advice and insisted on the college-preparatory course, he might fail in this course and then pursue the plan originally advised; or he might barely pass the course, barely get into college, and fail in college after a few months. In this case he would knock about from one job to another until he settled down more or less happily into the kind of job he would have scoffed at a few years earlier. Rarely, this kind of boy would surprise the counselor with some hidden ability and ambition. He would succeed in college and in a vocation requiring abilities that the counselor thought he did not possess.

Tom and his middle-class acquaintances can afford to go to college if they want to. But what about Joe Sienkowitz and a number of other able, ambitious, and talented boys and girls whose parents can barely afford to keep them in high school and cannot hope to send them to college? What does the phrase " equality of educational opportunity " imply in such cases?

Thomas Jefferson faced this same problem in considering an educational program for the state of Virginia a hundred and fifty years ago. Our proposals are essentially the same as Jefferson's when applied to modern conditions. He wrote concerning a proposed law:

This bill proposes to lay off every county into small districts of five or six miles square, called hundreds, and in each of them to establish a school for teaching reading, writing, and arithmetic. The tutor to be supported by the hundred, and every person in it entitled to send their children three years gratis, and as much longer as they please, paying for it. These schools to be under a visitor who is annually to choose the boy of best genius in the school, of those whose parents are too poor to give further education, and to send him forward to one of the grammar schools, of which twenty are proposed to be erected in different parts of the country, for teaching Greek, Latin, geography and the higher branches of numerical arithmetic.

Of the boys thus sent in one year, trial is to be made at the grammar schools one or two years, and the best genius of the whole selected and continued for six years, and the residue dismissed. By this means twenty of the best geniuses will be raked from the rubbish annually, and be instructed at the public expense so far as the grammar schools go. At the end of the six years' instruction, one half are to be discontinued (from among whom the grammar schools will probably be supplied with future masters); and the other half, who are to be chosen for the superiority of their parts and disposition, are to be sent and continued three years in the study of such sciences as they shall choose at William and Mary College. . . .

The general objects of this law are to provide an education adapted to the years, to the capacity, and to the condition of every one, and directed to their freedom and happiness. . . . By that part of our plan which prescribes the selection of youths of genius from among the classes of the poor, we hope to avail the state of these talents, which nature has sown as liberally among the poor as among the rich, but which perish without use if not sought for and cultivated. But of the views of this law none is more important, none more legitimate, than that for rendering the people the safe, as they are the ultimate, guardians of their own liberty. . . .

In every government on earth is some trace of human weakness, some germ of corruption and degeneracy, which cunning will discover and wickedness insensibly open, cultivate, and improve. Every government degenerates when trusted to the rulers of the people alone. The people themselves therefore are its only safe depositories. And to render even them safe, their minds must be improved to a certain degree.

To make educational opportunity effectively equal there must be a broad scholarship program that reaches down into the high school and extends through college and graduate school. Scholarships must be available at the age of fourteen and fifteen when youth begin to drop out of school for financial reasons. The number of scholarships must be large enough to care for some 5 per cent of the boys and girls of high-school age. Such a program will be costly enough to call for support from the federal government.

While careful study and some experience would be necessary in order to determine the number of scholarships that should be provided, a rough estimate can be easily reached. Scholarships for 5 per cent of the youth of high-school age and 2 or 3 per cent of the youth of college age would go far toward meeting the needs of poor but able students.

The cost of such a scholarship program would be large, but not prohibitive. It would cost approximately as much as was spent by the National Youth Administration about 1938 when its load was greatest.

In order to make a broad scholarship program fair to all, we should have to develop selective methods that are both sound and democratic. With our present ability to diagnose intelligence and other capacities and with the knowledge that our better schools possess of the character and family background of their students, it is possible to do a reasonably good job of selecting boys and girls for scholarship aid at the age of fourteen or fifteen. Of course we could not place major reliance on verbal tests of intelligence, since they favor middle-class children. But there are tests of intelligence and other abilities which do not penalize lower-class youth.

A proposal of this sort is bound to attract the charge that it is undemocratic. Some people resist the thought of selecting a small group to receive special help toward social mobility, no matter how democratic the selective procedure may be. Such people prefer to indulge in the fantasy that the really able and deserving young people can all get an education and get ahead in the world if they will only work hard enough. But the hard fact is that we do not have equal educational opportunity and that many able boys and girls are now denied opportunity through no fault of their own. A scholarship program of the sort that we have described would give Joe Sienkowitz and several other talented and industrious Hometown boys and girls a chance which they otherwise would not get. Such a program would contribute to social solidarity through increasing the amount of social mobility without increasing it too much. . . .

JAMES B. CONANT
The school as a class-leveling agency

There are probably some who feel that I am indulging in nostalgic fancy when I hope for the evolution of a less stratified and more fluid society. You may say that the modern world of large cities, vast industries, and scientific methods of communication has made the America of a hundred years ago as irrelevant as the Middle Ages. You may argue that a way of life which was possible in the 1840's is impossible in the 1940's; that in the near future we shall all of us have to move in a quite contrary direction. You may contend that soon we shall have to take sides in a bitter class struggle and choose between an American brand of Fascism and an American brand of Socialism.

From James B. Conant, " Education for a Classless Society," *Atlantic Monthly*, 165: 593–602, May, 1940. Reprinted by permission of the author.

I know that many believe this to be inevitable. I venture to disagree. And here is the reason for my rash dissent. In my opinion, our newly erected system of public education has potentialities of which we little dream. In this century we have erected a new type of social instrument. Our secondary-school system is a vast engine which we are only beginning to understand. We are learning only slowly how to operate it for the public good. But I have hope that it will aid us in recapturing social flexibility, in regaining that great gift to each succeeding generation — opportunity, a gift that once was the promise of the frontier.

Let me explain. Today some six million boys and girls attend our secondary schools, ten times the number enrolled a half century ago. Today nearly three quarters of those of high-school age are enrolled as pupils; fifty years ago schooling at this level was a privilege of less than ten per cent of those who might attend. Opportunity can be evaluated only in terms of personal capacity. What is opportunity for one young man is a blind alley for another. In rapidly expanding pioneer communities, openings for capabilities of all sorts automatically appeared. Only doctors, lawyers, and ministers needed an extensive education. Opportunities were ready at hand for all other types of talent. In our highly industrialized, relatively static society, the situation is otherwise. The personal problem of each boy or girl is much more difficult. Abilities must be assessed, talents must be developed, ambitions guided. This is the task for our public schools. All the future citizens pass through these institutions. They must be educated as members of a political democracy, but, more important still, they must be equipped to step on to the first rung of whatever ladder of opportunity seems most appropriate. And an appropriate ladder must be found for each one of a diverse group of students. This may seem an overwhelming burden to put upon our educational system. But is it not possible that our public schools, particularly our high schools, can be reconstructed for this specific purpose?

Jefferson thought of universal schooling of younger children chiefly in terms of educating potential voters. His selective process for higher studies was conceived in terms of intellectual pursuits of preparation for the learned professions such as law and medicine. To continue the tradition he started, we must expand both of his ideas today. The roads which lead to those careers which depend on aptitude for "book learning" still run through the universities. We must fight to keep them open. State-supported universities have blazed the way. But the task is far from done. In many localities the opportunities for the children of the really poor are lamentable indeed. Outside of metropolitan areas and college towns, the privileges of a professional training are hard to win. An expanded scholarship policy in our privately endowed universities is imperative. Wisely administered student aid will go far to right the balance. Perhaps this device merits more attention even by institutions supported by the state.

The changes required to provide adequately for the intellectually gifted are relatively slight. The real problems of reconstruction of our schools and colleges do not lie in this area. The real difficulties are with the careers of a different sort. Our schools must be concerned with educating for a useful life a great variety of boys and girls. They must be concerned not only with the able scholar, but with the artist and the craftsman. They must nourish those whose eye or ear or manual dexterity is their greatest asset. They must educate others whose gifts lie in an ability to understand and lead their fellow men. The school curricula must include programs for developing the capacities of many who possess intuitive judgment on practical affairs but have little or no aptitude for learning through the printed page.

It has been a natural consequence of our history that many false values now permeate the entire educational system. " Book learning " is placed too high in the scale of social ratings by some; too low by others who profess to scoff at " brains." That type of ability which can handle easily the old-fashioned subjects of the curriculum is often glorified by being equated with " intelligence " by educational snobs. On the other hand, the same ability often suffers from lack of stimulation when there is failure to maintain high standards. As a result, we have a great deal of make-believe in our schools and colleges — too many feeble attempts at tasks which are proper only for a restricted type of individual; too many failures to explore talents which fall outside orthodox academic bounds. Jefferson in the simpler society of his day naturally thought of only a few avenues of opportunity open through education. Today we must recognize the existence of many and strive for the social equality of all.

Parents who expect miracles worked upon their children must be reminded of the limitations imposed by nature. In athletics, at least, the coaches are expected to develop only promising material. No one complains if his undersized son with awkward legs does not become a football hero. Some fathers, however, seem to demand the intellectual equivalent of such a miracle. We expect our college health departments to direct each student into that form of sport which is suited to his physique and power. We need a parallel form of educational guidance in both schools and colleges to assist the development of the skills of brain and hands.

But again I venture to be optimistic. I see signs everywhere of enormous strides forward in such matters. Our educational pattern is becoming daily more diversified; a recognition of the need for a radically different type of education is growing. We look forward to the opening of many channels which lead to a variety of attractive goals; we can envisage the building up of more than one " élite."

Of course, in any realistic discussion of these problems we cannot neglect the social and economic factors. As long as the shadow of unemployment is upon the land, some method of providing food and clothing for the children of many families must be found. For even free schools offer little real opportunity to famished youngsters; public education is only theoretically available to those in rags. Providing food and clothing for those to whom assistance is essential is clearly necessary for a satisfactory functioning of the entire educational system. Many a talented youth is lost by dropping out of the competition, for financial reasons, during the high-school years. In short, we must explore every method of developing the individual capacity of each future citizen for useful labor based on individual initiative.

Political and economic changes must go hand in hand with educational innovations — the revision of methods of perpetuating control of many large industries, the overthrow of nepotism and patronage wherever possible, the stimulation of small enterprises, the spreading of private ownership. All this and more is needed if a free classless society is to become once again an ideal which affects our lives.

Freedom of the mind, social mobility through education, universal schooling — these, let me repeat, are the three fundamentals of the Jeffersonian tradition. They have represented the aspirations and desires of a free people embarked on a new experiment, the perpetuation of a casteless nation. Popular enthusiasm for enlightenment, for overturning dogmas, for intellectual exploration, has temporarily waned. I have given my reasons for hoping that the black reaction of these years is only a passing phase. The ideal of a free republic without classes has likewise suffered an eclipse. To many of the present college generation the phrase "equality of opportunity" seems a mockery, a trite collection of idle words. In this I see the major challenge to our educational system, a challenge which can be met only by a radical reconstruction. If the nation wants to bend its efforts to have as free and classless a society *as possible*, then for those of us concerned with schools and colleges our course is clearly plotted.

So it seems to me. If we as educators accept the American ideal, then this acceptance must be the major premise for all our thinking. Without neglecting the older roads designed for those of academic brilliance, we must construct many new approaches to adult life, and we must do so very soon. Extreme differentiation of school programs seems essential — differentiation of instruction, but not necessarily a division into separate schools. From this it follows that rapid improvement in our testing methods must be forthcoming; a much more conscientious and discriminating form of educational guidance must be developed soon if we are not to fail. In short, a horde of heterogeneous students has descended on our secondary schools; on our ability to handle all types intelligently depends in large measure the future of this country.

Is it too late — too late for our schools to revitalize the idea of a classless nation? Can we complete the necessary major readjustments in our educational system in time to prevent the extinction of the Jeffersonian tradition? I believe we can, if we make haste. I predict at least another century of vigor for the American ideal. I envisage a further trial on this continent for many generations of our unique type of social order. I look forward to a future American society in which social mobility is sufficient to keep the nation in essence casteless — a society in which the ideals of both personal liberty and social justice can be maintained — a society which through a system of public education resists the distorting pressures of urbanized, industrial life. I have faith in the continuation of a republic composed of citizens each prepared to shoulder the responsibility for his own destiny. And if at each step in the educational journey opportunity truly beckons, will not each student rejoice in the struggle to develop his own capacities? Will he not be proud of the continuing American tradition and find in contemplation of our national history ample courage to face those risks and hazards that come to all who would be free?

EDUCATIONAL POLICIES COMMISSION
A glimpse of what might be

Compulsory school attendance until the eighteenth birthday. Shortly after the end of World War II, the state legislature changed the laws relating to required school attendance. Under the new law, attendance is required until completion of the twelfth grade or until the eighteenth birthday, whichever is the earlier.[1]

This change was deemed desirable chiefly because the majority of the secondary schools of the state, like those of Farmville and American City, were moving rapidly to serve the educational needs of *all* youth. It was therefore held that the state was justified in requiring its young people to use the services provided.

The change in the employment situation was also a factor. With the approach of the end of the war, the employment of sixteen- and seventeen-year-old boys and girls fell off. Most of the youth who lost their jobs had only a single skill and were ill-fitted to compete in the labor market with returning veterans and older, more experienced workers. Thereafter, there were fewer jobs to be found for untrained, inexperienced youth in their middle teens, and these were chiefly of the " blind-alley " type. It was thought better by far, for both youth and society, to have young people in attendance at schools in which they could secure occupational training, work experience, and a well-rounded general education than to have them enter the labor market without training, experience, or adequate educational background.

Public secondary education beyond the high school. The decision to extend free public secondary education upward so as to include general and

From Educational Policies Commission, National Education Association, *Education for ALL American Youth: A Further Look*, 1952, pp. 325–329, 335–337. Reprinted by permission.

[1] A student in Grade XI or XII, with his parents' consent may be absent from school in order to be employed on a job which is under school supervision and which is considered a part of the student's educational program.

vocational education in the thirteenth and fourteenth grades was reached after careful study of the conditions likely to develop in the years immediately to come. It seemed probable that many, perhaps most young people would find it difficult to secure employment consistent with their abilities without more general education, vocational training, and supervised work experience than could be supplied in the high schools alone. It was clear, moreover, that some public institution was needed to prepare young men and women to enter a large number of military, technical, commercial, and semiprofessional occupations, requiring education beyond the twelfth grade. And it was agreed that the needs of society for educated citizens would alone justify the continuation of a sound program of civic and general education for another two years. These and other considerations have already been discussed in the chapters on the schools of Farmville and American City.

The development of junior colleges, public and private, during the score of years preceding World War II gave evidence of public demand for institutions of this type. In the state of Columbia, the growth had been uneven. The law permitted school districts to levy taxes to support junior colleges, and it did not prohibit tuition. The results were a small number of well-developed public junior colleges in some of the wealthier and more populous areas and a larger number of high schools which offered a few postgraduate courses and often assumed the name of " junior college." The large junior colleges charged fees while the small institutions charged both fees and tuition. The situation was one which proponents of free pub-

GROWTH OF JUNIOR COLLEGES IN THE UNITED STATES *

Year	Publicly Controlled		Privately Controlled		Total	
	No.	Enrol.	No.	Enrol.	No.	Enrol.
1919–20	10	2,940	42	5,162	52	8,102
1929–30	129	36,501	148	19,115	277	55,616
1935–36	187	70,557	228	31,896	415	102,453
1937–38	209	82,041	244	39,469	453	121,510
1939–40	217	107,553	239	42,301	456	149,854
1941–42	231	100,783	230	40,489	461	141,272
1943–44	210	56,439	203	28,177	413	84,616
1945–46	235	109,640	225	46,816	460	156,456
1947–48	242	178,196	230	61,977	472	240,173
1949–50	290	170,899	221	58,312	511	229,211
1951–52	289	191,798	224	47,714	513	239,512
1953–54	292	241,626	211	43,027	503	284,653
1955–56	299	298,559	226	49,724	525	348,283
1957–58	309	331,671	248	54,840	557	386,510
1959–60	334	393,553	259	60,064	593	453,617

Source: U. S. Office of Education
* Editor's note: Original table included data only through 1947–48. Data for period 1949–60 are also from U. S. Office of Education.

lic education believed to be wrong. They urged state action that would make higher secondary education available for all.

New legislation, therefore, authorized both vocational and non-vocational instruction for two years beyond the conventional high school as an integral part of the system of secondary education. It abolished fees and tuitions for such instruction and placed financial support upon the same basis as that of elementary and high schools. The new laws carried a mandate to the state department of education to establish a system of post-high-school institutions in order to serve the educational needs of all the young people of the state.

Two types of advanced secondary schools. Two types of institutional service, well illustrated by the Farmville Secondary School and the American City Community College, have been developed. In Farmville and many other small communities, two years of instruction, intended primarily for the young people who expect to live in these communities or others like them, have been added to the regular secondary schools. These schools of the Farmville type offer advanced training in the major local occupational fields, together with civic, cultural, and physical education appropriate to older youth. They do not give training in occupations not well represented locally, nor do they undertake to offer courses comparable to those of the junior colleges or four-year colleges and universities. Indeed, as we shall see, schools of this type are required to remain within the limits just mentioned as a condition for receiving state financial aid.

In American City and ten other cities, new institutions of advanced secondary education have been developed, of which the American City Community College is an example. These institutions provide vocational education in many fields, each institution including the chief occupations of a large region as well as of the city itself. Together they cover practically all the occupations of the state which do not require education beyond the fourteenth grade. They also offer courses comparable to those of the first two years of four-year colleges and universities. In common with secondary schools of the Farmville type, they supply continuing civic, cultural, and physical education to all their students and are responsible for local programs of education for adults and out-of-school youth.

The name " community college " is used throughout the state for this second type of institution. The term " junior college " already had a variety of meanings because of the diversity of practices in institutions bearing that title. Therefore, it was deemed advisable to use a name free from associations with past practices.

Not all community colleges have the same organization. The state laws about community colleges refer to the thirteenth and fourteenth grades of public education, but they do not prescribe how these two advanced secondary grades shall be related to the rest of the school system. In some communities, as in American City, the two upper grades constitute an advanced secondary school which is housed and staffed separately from the senior high schools. In other cities, such as Three Rivers, the thirteenth and fourteenth grades have been joined with the eleventh and twelfth to form a four-year community college, while Grades VII to X, inclusive, constitute the lower secondary school, known locally as the " intermediate school."

Whatever the particular form of organization may be, the program of Grades XIII and XIV is looked upon as an integral part of the eight-year structure of secondary education. . . .

Thirteenth and fourteenth grades in other secondary schools. A great deal of public education beyond twelfth grade takes place quite apart from the community colleges, however. Any school district which does not have a community college may now offer instruction at the thirteenth and fourteenth grade levels in its secondary school or schools if it meets the minimum standards set by the state department of education and if its vocational education is limited to the chief occupational fields represented in the local community. The Farmville Secondary School is a good example of a secondary school embracing the eight years from Grade VII through Grade XIV and offering advanced courses in agriculture, homemaking, retail trade, business education, and mechanics. Although Farmville pioneered in this field, one now finds comparable arrangements in most of the secondary schools which are not within commuting distance of community colleges. A secondary school receives state aid for its thirteenth and fourteenth years on the same basis as a community college. The law makes it clear, however, that the two upper years in such a school do not constitute a community college.

This suggests the question of the relationships of community colleges to the secondary schools in districts which do not have community colleges. Each such secondary school, it is believed, should be closely and permanently related to a community college, preferably the one most conveniently located with respect to transportation. For one thing, competition for out-of-town students among the community colleges is considered highly undesirable. A more important reason is that a close relationship greatly facilitates the operation of a continuous guidance program, bridging the transition from high school to community college. The Columbia State Department of Education, with the advice of the commission on secondary education, has mapped out a tributary area for each community college and has adopted the regulation that a high-school graduate will normally attend the community college in whose area his high school is located. Exceptions are made, of course, in the cases of students interested in vocations not represented in the curriculum of their local community college. We have already had occasion to observe many contacts and examples of cooperation in the case of the American City Community College and the

Farmville Secondary School which lies in the tributary area of American City.

Education for out-of-school youth and adults. All these provisions, however, were not enough. The members of the state planning groups were quick to see that, even in the best of school systems, all the educational needs of youth could not possibly be met within twelve or fourteen years of school attendance. Some aspects of education must wait upon experience and maturity. When a youth joins the armed forces; when he takes his first full-time job; when he loses that job and has to find another; when he marries and establishes a home; when he becomes a voter; when he joins a labor union, a farmers' organization, or a businessman's association; when he finds that he has four hours of leisure time a day at his disposal — then he is likely to become keenly aware of educational needs which only a few months before had seemed remote.

Legal provisions were therefore made for the support of a comprehensive program of free public adult education which would be open to all youth not in full-time attendance at school. The law authorized but did not require districts to admit adults and out-of-school youth to regular classes in community colleges and in the thirteenth and fourteenth grades of secondary schools. It also authorized districts to organize and maintain part-time and evening classes in any subject and to receive financial aid from the state for classes in subjects approved by the state board of education. The board's approvals, we may add, have been broad enough to encompass practically the whole range of interests of adults and older youth — vocational, avocational, civic, cultural, family life, homemaking, and health. A satisfactory formula was developed for translating units of attendance in part-time classes into units of school population as a basis for distributing state financial aid.

In anticipation of the possible establishment of work camps for youth in public parks and forests and on public conservation and construction projects, the law provides that state aid may be applied to the support of educational programs in such camps. It further authorizes the state legislature to appropriate funds to pay for the difference between the total costs of such programs and the state funds supplied under the regular plan of state aid. Since work camps are usually remote from the larger school districts, the state department of education is authorized to operate and control educational programs in camps, but it may contract with local school systems to carry all or part of this responsibility. . . .

SECTION **2. The educational system: One track or many?**

One of the great demands which democracy places upon its formal educational system is that it provide schooling which recognizes the claims of community and fraternity, on the one hand, and individuality and freedom on the other. The truly unique and praiseworthy characteristic of our American school system is that it has, albeit often in a faltering manner, attempted to meet this demand. Upon our willingness to stand by this unique venture in humane education, and upon our willingness to seek out and remedy its present imperfections, may well rest the future of our democracy as a comprehensive way of life. But the very difficulty of the problem, coupled with our all-too-human characteristic of stereotyped thinking and our tendency to *classify* people rather than *respect* their uniqueness, has stood as an ever-present danger to the very system we have constructed.

In education this tendency to stereotype human beings has taken three distinct forms — each of which has challenged democratic education. The first of these has been the attempt to stereotype individuals *by race or social status,* a type of thinking which has led to segregation in the public schools. In some sections of the country this has been done by the erection of double school systems; in other sections of the country it has too often been done by such devious devices as gerrymandering of school districts and attendance areas or by the " selective guidance " of students. The decision of the United States Supreme Court in *Brown vs. Board of Education,* included first among the selections below, has spoken to the undemocratic nature of this practice. The second of these forms of stereotyped thinking about students has been shown in the attempt to segregate individuals *by vocational goal,* a type of thinking which has led to the separation of individuals through *rigid curricula* based on ultimate vocational goals. For example, many schools require students to pursue either commercial, industrial, general, homemaking, or academic curricula. These curricular programs often effectively separate students from interaction with other youngsters pursuing quite different goals. This system of stereotyping or segregation, so common in other countries characterized by rigid class or caste systems, has often led educators to overlook the need for those common, unifying experiences so vital to building our sense of community and brotherhood. The third of these forms of stereotyped thinking about students has shown itself periodically in the attempt to segregate students *by intelligence quotient,* an attempt which has led to the organization of quite separate tracks for the intellectual elite and the non-intellectual mass. The claim that educational systems which separate individuals into such tracks are democratic in that they recognize individual differences is taken to task severely by John Dewey in the selection on individuality and education which follows, and which was written as a rejoinder to just such a proposal.

But the challenge to American education still remains. Is it truly possible to construct and operate an educational system which will both build a sense of community and brotherhood and yet provide for the unique qualities, strengths, and interests of individuals? In the final selection in this section, a noted educator answers this question in the affirmative. James B. Conant, scientist, diplomat, and former President of Harvard University, deals with the essential characteristics of American secondary education and relates these to the demands of American society and the world in which we live.

U. S. SUPREME COURT
The decision on desegregation

Mr. Chief Justice Warren delivered the opinion of the Court.

These cases come to us from the States of Kansas, South Carolina, Virginia, and Delaware. They are premised on different facts and different local conditions, but a common legal question justifies their consideration together in this consolidated opinion.

In each of the cases, minors of the Negro race, through their legal representatives, seek the aid of the courts in obtaining admission to the public schools of their community on a nonsegregated basis. In each instance, they had been denied admission to schools attended by white children under laws requiring or permitting segregation according to race. This segregation was alleged to deprive the plaintiffs of the equal protection of the laws under the Fourteenth Amendment. In each of the cases other than the Delaware case, a three-judge federal district court denied relief to the plaintiffs on the so-called " separate but equal " doctrine announced by this Court in *Plessy* v. *Ferguson*, 163 U.S. 537. Under that doctrine, equality of treatment is accorded when the races are provided substantially equal facilities, even though these facilities be separate. In the Delaware case, the Supreme Court of Delaware adhered to that doctrine, but ordered that the plaintiffs be admitted to the white schools because of their superiority to the Negro schools.

The plaintiffs contend that segregated public schools are not " equal " and cannot be made " equal," and that hence they are deprived of the equal protection of the laws. Because of the obvious importance of the question presented, the Court took jurisdiction. Argument was heard in the 1952 Term, and reargument was heard this Term on certain questions propounded by the Court.

Reargument was largely devoted to the circumstances surrounding the adoption of the Fourteenth Amendment in 1868. It covered exhaustively consideration of the Amendment in Congress, ratification by the states, then existing practices in racial segregation, and the views of proponents and opponents of the Amendment. This discussion and our own investigation convince us that, although these sources cast some light, it is not enough to resolve the problem with which we are faced. At best, they are inconclusive. The most avid proponents of the post-War Amendments undoubtedly intended them to remove all legal distinctions among " all persons born or naturalized in the United States." Their opponents, just as certainly, were antagonistic to both the letter and the spirit of the Amendments and wished them to have the most limited effect. What others in

Brown v. Board of Education, 347 U.S. 483. May 17, 1954.

Congress and the state legislatures had in mind cannot be determined with any degree of certainty.

An additional reason for the inconclusive nature of the Amendment's history, with respect to segregated schools, is the status of public education at that time. In the South, the movement toward free common schools, supported by general taxation, had not yet taken hold. Education of white children was largely in the hands of private groups. Education of Negroes was almost nonexistent, and practically all of the race were illiterate. In fact, any education of Negroes was forbidden by law in some states. Today, in contrast, many Negroes have achieved outstanding success in the arts and sciences as well as in the business and professional world. It is true that public school education at the time of the Amendment had advanced further in the North, but the effect of the Amendment on Northern States was generally ignored in the congressional debates. Even in the North, the conditions of public education did not approximate those existing today. The curriculum was usually rudimentary; ungraded schools were common in rural areas; the school term was but three months a year in many states; and compulsory school attendance was virtually unknown. As a consequence, it is not surprising that there should be so little in the history of the Fourteenth Amendment relating to its intended effect on public education.

In the first cases in this Court construing the Fourteenth Amendment, decided shortly after its adoption, the Court interpreted it as proscribing all state-imposed discriminations against the Negro race. The doctrine of " separate but equal " did not make its appearance in this Court until 1896 in the case of *Plessy* v. *Ferguson, supra*, involving not education but transportation. American courts have since labored with the doctrine for over half a century. In this Court, there have been six cases involving the " separate but equal " doctrine in the field of public education. In *Cumming* v. *County Board of Education*, 175 U. S. 528, and *Gong Lum* v. *Rice* 275 U. S. 78, the validity of the doctrine itself was not challenged. In more recent cases, all on the graduate school level, inequality was found in that specific benefits enjoyed by white students were denied to Negro students of the same educational qualifications. *Missouri ex rel. Gaines* v. *Canada*, 305 U. S. 337; *Sipuel* v. *Oklahoma*, 332 U. S. 631; *Sweatt* v. *Painter*, 339 U. S. 629; *McLaurin* v. *Oklahoma State Regents*, 339 U. S. 637. In none of these cases was it necessary to re-examine the doctrine to grant relief to the Negro plaintiff. And in *Sweatt* v. *Painter, supra*, the Court expressly reserved decision on the question whether *Plessy* v. *Ferguson* should be held inapplicable to public education.

In the instant cases, that question is directly presented. Here, unlike *Sweatt* v. *Painter*, there are findings below that the Negro and white schools involved have been equalized, or are being equalized, with respect to buildings, curricula, qualifications and salaries of teachers, and other " tangible " factors. Our decision, therefore, cannot turn on merely a comparison of these tangible factors in the Negro and white schools involved in each of the cases. We must look instead to the effect of segregation itself on public education.

In approaching this problem, we cannot turn the clock back to 1868 when the Amendment was adopted, or even to 1896 when *Plessy* v. *Ferguson* was written. We must consider public education in the light of its full development and its present place in American life throughout the Nation. Only in this way can it be determined if segregation in public schools deprives these plaintiffs of the equal protection of the laws.

Today, education is perhaps the most important function of state and local governments. Compulsory school attendance laws and the great expenditures for education both demonstrate our recognition of the importance of education to our democratic society. It is required in the performance of our most basic public responsibilities, even service in the armed forces. It is the very foundation of good citizenship. Today it is a principal instrument in awakening the child to cultural values, in preparing him for later professional training, and in helping him to adjust normally to his environment. In these days, it is doubtful that any child may reasonably be expected to succeed in life if he is denied the opportunity of an education. Such an opportunity, where the state has undertaken to provide it, is a right which must be made available to all on equal terms.

We come then to the question presented: Does segregation of children in public schools solely on the basis of race, even though the physical facilities and other " tangible " factors may be equal, deprive the children of the minority group of equal educational opportunities? We believe that it does.

In *Sweatt* v. *Painter, supra,* in finding that a segregated law school for Negroes could not provide them equal educational opportunities, this Court relied in large part on " those qualities which are incapable of objective measurement but which make for greatness in a law school." In *McLaurin* v. *Oklahoma State Regents, supra,* the Court, in requiring that a Negro admitted to a white graduate school be treated like all other students, again resorted to intangible considerations: ". . . his ability to study, to engage in discussions and exchange views with other students, and, in general, to learn his profession." Such considerations apply with added force to children in grade and high schools. To separate them from others of similar age and qualifications solely because of their race generates a feeling of inferiority as to their status in the community that may affect their hearts and minds in a way unlikely ever to be undone. The effect of this separation on their educational opportunities was well stated by a finding in the Kansas case by a court which nevertheless felt compelled to rule against the Negro plaintiffs:

Segregation of white and colored children in public schools has a detrimental effect upon the colored children. The impact is greater when it has the sanction of the law; for the policy of separating the races is usually interpreted as denoting the inferiority of the negro group. A sense of inferiority affects the motivation of a child to learn. Segregation with the sanction of law, therefore, has a tendency to [retard] the educational and mental development of negro children and to deprive them of some of the benefits they would receive in a racial[ly] integrated school system.

Whatever may have been the extent of psychological knowledge at the time of *Plessy* v. *Ferguson*, this finding is amply supported by modern authority. Any language in *Plessy* v. *Ferguson* contrary to this finding is rejected.

We conclude that in the field of public education the doctrine of " separate but equal " has no place. Separate educational facilities are inherently unequal. Therefore, we hold that the plaintiffs and others similarly situated for whom the actions have been brought are, by reason of the segregation complained of, deprived of the equal protection of the laws guaranteed by the Fourteenth Amendment. This disposition makes unnecessary any discussion whether such segregation also violates the Due Process Clause of the Fourteenth Amendment.

Because these are class actions, because of the wide applicability of this decision, and because of the great variety of local conditions, the formulation of decrees in these cases presents problems of considerable complexity. On reargument, the consideration of appropriate relief was necessarily subordinated to the primary question — the constitutionality of segregation in public education. We have now announced that such segregation is a denial of the equal protection of the laws. In order that we may have the full assistance of the parties in formulating decrees, the cases will be restored to the docket, and the parties are requested to present further argument on Questions 4 and 5 previously propounded by the Court for the reargument this Term. The Attorney General of the United States is again invited to participate. The Attorneys General of the states requiring or permitting segregation in public education will also be permitted to appear as *amici curiae* upon request to do so by September 15, 1954, and submission of briefs by October 1, 1954.

It is so ordered.

JOHN DEWEY
Individuality, mediocrity, and conformity in education

Individualism is about the most ambiguous word in the entire list of labels in ordinary use. It means anything from egoistically centered conduct to distinction and uniqueness. It is possible to say that excessive individualism is

John Dewey, " Mediocrity and Individuality," *New Republic*, 33:35–37, December 6, 1922; " Individuality, Equality and Superiority," *New Republic*, 33:61–63, December 13, 1922. Both articles reprinted by permission of the *New Republic*.

an outstanding curse of American civilization, and that absence of individualism is our marked deficiency. When the former remark is made, economic and legal conditions are in mind; when the latter, intellectual life is in question. Individuality is a surer word; it carries with it a connotation of uniqueness of quality, or at least of distinctiveness. It suggests a freedom which is not legal, comparative and external but which is intrinsic and constructive. Our forebears who permitted the growth of legal and economic arrangements at least supposed, however mistakenly, that the institutions they favored would develop personal and moral individuality. It was reserved for our own day to combine under the name of individualism, laudation of selfish energy in industrial accomplishment with insistence upon uniformity and conformity in mind.

Now that we have reached the point of reverence for mediocrity, for submergence of individuality in mass ideals and creeds, it is perhaps not surprising that after boasting for a long time that we had no classes we now boast that we have discovered a scientific way of dividing our population into definite classes. Just as Aristotle rationalized slavery by showing how natural it was for those superior by nature to constitute the ends for others who were only tools, so we, while marvelling perhaps at the callousness of the Greek philosopher, rationalize the inequities of our social order by appealing to innate and unalterable psychological strata in the population. Thus Mr. George B. Cutten in his inaugural address as president of Colgate University recently informed us that it is now " discovered " that " only fifteen percent of the people have sufficient intelligence to get through college." From this " discovery " he draws the conclusion that as we have never had a real democracy, so " the low level of the intelligence of the people will not permit of our having one." He not only makes the undeniable statement that we are ruled by an aristocracy in industry, commerce, professions and government, but he terms this aristocracy an *intellectual* aristocracy! The adjective seems incredible. But President Cutten thinks there is the same scientific warrant for assuming that conspicuous success under present conditions is a sign of innate intellectual superiority as for saying that twenty-five percent of the population are mentally subnormal and that only fifteen percent are capable of higher education.

Mr. Cutten begins his presidential career with a startling view of the social stratification which is to be the ultimate outcome of an educational classification based on intellectual classifications by means of mental testing. We are to arrive at a caste system like that of India, " but on a just and rational basis." For " when the tests for vocational guidance are completed and developed, each boy and girl in school will be assigned to the vocation for which he is fitted." There will be no difficulty about filling the ranks of unskilled labor and mechanical operators, for Mr. Cutten implicitly believes the yarn that the army tests have shown that the " average mentality " of the population is slightly over thirteen years. Considering only the energy and unspoiled curiosity of the average thirteen year old in comparison with the dulled observation and blunter vigor of the average adult one might hope that this statement were true. It would be most encouraging. But it is more to the point to remark that, as Mr. Lippmann has so clearly shown in these pages, the statement interpreted as Mr. Cutten means it is like saying that perhaps sixty-five percent of the population rank below the lowest fifty percent; it takes absolutely what is only a comparative statement, thereby rendering it literally senseless. What makes this performance more than a mere individual mistake is that it affords striking evidence of the habit of ignoring specific individualities, of thinking in terms of fixed classes, intellectual and social.

There is no need to re-traverse the ground so admirably covered by Mr. Lippmann. But why has it been so generally assumed among our cultivated leaders that a purely classificatory formula gives information about individual intelligence in its individuality? To say that Johnnie Jones who was born in 1913 has in 1922 a mental age of eight or of ten years only means that he belongs, on the basis of his performance of certain exercises, to a class of persons at least over a million in number, who were born in 1912 or 1914 respectively. Why then is it so frequently supposed that the individual mentality of John Jones has been definitely determined? To say that one belongs in a class which is a million or so large, with respect to which one is accelerated or retarded by a year in comparison with another class of a million, does not, after all, throw much light on the intrinsic capacities of a given individual.

The assumption seems to indicate one thing. We are irretrievably accustomed to thinking in standardized averages. Our economic and political environment leads us to think in terms of classes, aggregates and submerged membership in them. In spite of all our talk about individuality and individualism we have no habit of thinking in terms of distinctive, much less uniquely individualized, qualities. The inference to be drawn from the popular reception of mental testings concerns the acquired habits of intellectual spokesmen, rather than the inherent intellectuality of the populace. This fact is indeed significant for the prospects of democracy. But the reason it is ominous for democracy is radically different from that often assigned. For it reflects not upon the innate mentality of the mass but upon the acquired intelligence of men in high positions. It shows how their education, that given by their surroundings as well as by their schools, has fixed in them the disposition to judge by classification instead of by discrimination, and by classifications which represent the average of massed numbers, mediocrities instead of individualities.

We may be thought to ignore the interest which many testers have shown in pupils of superior abilities. For some of the testers tell us that one of the chief beneficial consequences of testing is that it enables us to pick out the superior tenth, to rescue the saving remnant from the ruck in which they are now submerged. But the seeming exception proves the rule. The idea of classification still fatally pursues and dominates. " Superior " is still a classificatory word. The size of the class is reduced, say from a million to a hundred thousand. But what kind of superiority marks a particular individual is still unrevealed to us.

The practical educational use to which testers propose that the results of testing should be put strengthens the proposition that even cultivated minds are dominated by the concept of quantitative classes — so much so that the quality of individuality escapes them. For many of them are now telling us that the chief use of the results of the tests is to secure a more accurate ranking or grading of pupils. Instead of mixing up together a lot of pupils of different abilities we can divide them into a superior, a middle and an inferior section, so that each can go its own gait without being kept back or unduly forced by others. An individual is not conceived as an individual with his own distinctive perplexities, methods and rates of operation. The classificatory submergence of individuals in averaged aggregates is perpetuated: it is standardized and rendered more efficient. It may turn out that the net result will be to postpone the day of a reform of education which will get us away from inferior, mean and superior mediocrities so as to deal with individualized mind and character. The movement is on a par with the movements to make instruction more efficient while retaining the notion of teaching which emphasizes the receptively docile mind instead of an inquiring and pioneering purpose.

These remarks are in no sense a hostile criticism of the scientific procedure of mental testing. They are an attempt to suggest its proper goal and to indicate the stage which has now been reached in moving toward that goal. The goal is a method of discrimination, of analysis of human beings, of diagnosis of persons, which is intrinsic and absolute, not comparative and common. Before this goal can be reached it is necessary that certain average statistical norms should be determined. But their function is scientific, not practical either for schooling or for the conduct of democracy. They are of value in working out a system of tests to be used ultimately in analysis of an individual. You cannot be sure, for example, that you have a good test for mechanical ingenuity in a particular person until you have seen how large numbers react to different exercises. The pity is that a scheme for testing tests which are ultimately to be used in diagnosing individuality has been treated as if it already provided means of testing individuals.

Life insurance is impossible, for example, without extensive statistical investigations, establishing quantitative mean norms. Individuals are graded as to their degree of insurable risk on the basis of these norms. But no one supposes that the result determines the fate of any particular person. If to be accepted as a good risk were a guarantee of long life, clearly no one after being accepted would insure himself. And similarly to a sensible person rejection is not a fatalistic sign of sure death. It is a warning to have a thorough individual examination made, and to undertake individualized remedial measures on the basis of this individual diagnosis. An I.Q.

as at present determined is at most an indication of certain risks and prob-
abilities. Its practical value lies in the stimulus it gives to more intimate
and intensive inquiry into individualized abilities and disabilities.

As a matter of fact, President Cutten's educational outlook in the concrete is much more intelligent and humane than is indicated by his credulous use of the army tests. He saves himself by losing his logic. He says
that education is conservative as compared with theology and philosophy;
he declares that if we are teaching the wrong subjects, the better the teaching the more disastrous the results; his conviction that we are largely teaching the wrong subjects is perhaps indicated by his statement that our curricula have not changed much in the last millennium. He points out that
the whole system is strong on its receptive side and weak on the creative
side; and that the consequence is the comparative scarcity of creative artists
and thinkers among us. Students who merely pass in college and who are
conspicuous for breaches of discipline become later in life leaders and
executives.

Is it possible to admit these facts and not also admit that as a practical
measure we should devote ourselves to changes in education which are
within our control rather than worry about innate differences which are
not within our control? If there prevailed from the elementary school up
the kind of inquiring and creative education which President Cutten desires for the college, perhaps democracy, in spite of native inequalities and
inferiorities, would not be in such a parlous condition. Until we have tried
the educational experiment, we simply do not know and shall not know
what individual capacities and limits really are. For it is not just the quantity of our education which is confessedly at fault; it is its quality, its spirit,
method and aim.

A change from a receptive education to a creative one, to one which as
President Cutten well says would result in " ability to meet a unique situation," obviously implies studying and treating individuals in their distinctive and unique qualities. It involves getting away from that class and
averaged education to which the current interpretation of the results of
mental testing the more rigidly commits us. One appeals with unusual
pleasure from President Cutten dealing with a subject matter of a science
in which he is a somewhat credulous non-expert to the field of education
in which he is a wise expert. From an ad hominem point of view, the difference of attitude in the two fields indicates how much what is termed intelligence is an acquired matter, due to opportunity and experience. No
matter how much innate qualities may set limits, they are not active forces.
Experience, that is to say education, is still the mother of wisdom. And
we shall never have any light upon what are the limits to intelligence set
by innate qualities till we have immensely modified our scheme of getting
and giving experience, of education. Barring complete imbecility, it is safe
to say that the most limited member of the populace has potentialities

which do not now reveal themselves and which will not reveal themselves till we convert education by and for mediocrity into an education by and for individuality.

* * *

An article entitled Mediocrity and Individuality pointed out that the current reception of the results of mental testing proves the extent to which we are given to judging and treating individuals not as individuals but as creatures of a class, a quantitative class which covers up truly individualized traits. Our mechanical, industrialized civilization is concerned with averages, with percents. The mental habit which reflects this social scene subordinates education and social arrangements to stratifications based on averaged gross inferiorities and superiorities. We accept standards of judging individuals which are based on the qualities of mind and character which win under existing social conditions conspicuous success. The " inferior " is the one who isn't calculated to " get on " in a society such as now exists. " Equals " are those who belong to a class formed by like chances of attaining recognition, position and wealth in present society.

This intellectual acceptance of standards for valuing individuals of a society which every candid mind admits to be lopsided and disordered gives occasion for a reexamination of the fundamental ideas of superiority and equality. What do these words mean? Professors have one measure of superior ability; captains of industry another. One class esteems aptitude for learning academic subjects; the other class appraises in terms of power in execution. Suppose that investigators and artists were so socially dominant that they were effectively articulate. Should we not then employ quite other standards of measurement? At present superior races are superior on the basis of their own conspicuous achievements. Inferior races are inferior because their successes lie in different directions, though possibly more artistic and civilized than our own.

Superiority and inferiority are meaningless words taken by themselves. They refer to some specific outcome. No one should use the words until he has asked himself and is ready to tell others: Superior and inferior in *what?* Is a student inferior for purposes of reciting lessons, of fitting into a school administration, of influencing companions, of " student activities " or what? Is an adult superior in money-making, in music, in chicanery and intrigue, in being a wise parent or good neighbor, as a homemaker, a chauffeur or a librarian, a congenial companion, a confidence man, an investigator of higher mathematics, an expert accountant, a tractable worker or a revolutionist, in writing acceptable movie scenarios or in research in the laboratory?

There are as many modes of superiority and inferiority as there are consequences to be attained and works to be accomplished. And until society becomes static new modes of activity are continually developing, each of which permits and exacts its own specific inferiorities and superiorities.

There is doubtless some degree of correlation between traits which promote superiority in more than one direction. But the idea of abstract, universal superiority and inferiority is an absurdity. The current loose use of these conceptions suggests overcompensation on the part of those who assume that they belong to a superior class. It appears like an attempt to escape from the limitations and incapacities which we all know, subconsciously at least, that we possess.

When classifications are rigid, the quantitative, the more or less, phase of superiority is inevitably conspicuous. Castes are ranks or grades of superiority; within each caste the hierarchical order of higher and lower is repeated. The endeavor to discover abstract degrees of mental superiority which fit for "leadership" in the abstract is evidence of the hold upon us still exercised by feudal arrangements. Our new feudalism of the industrial life which ranks from the great financier through the captain of industry down to the unskilled laborer, revives and reenforces the feudal disposition to ignore individual capacity displayed in free or individualized pursuits. Sometimes in theory we conceive of every form of useful activity as on a level with every other as long as it really marks the performance of needed service. In these moments we also recognize in idea at least that there are an infinite number of forms of significant action. But these ideas are usually restricted to religiously accented moments. When it comes to "practical" matters, the very person who in his religious moods asserts the uniqueness of individuality and of opportunity for service falls back upon a restricted number of conventionally formulated and esteemed occupations and is content to grade persons in a quantitative comparative scale.

It was once supposed, at least by some, that the purpose of education, along with equipping students with some indispensable tools, was to discover and release individualized capacities so that they might make their own way with whatever of social change is involved in their operation. But now we welcome a procedure which under the title of science sinks the individual in a numerical class; judges him with reference to capacity to fit into a limited number of vocations ranked according to present business standards; assigns him to a predestined niche and thereby does whatever education can do to perpetuate the present order. The motto concerning genuinely individual distinctions is that of the tank corps. "Treat 'em rough" — except as they give promise of success in this or that established social classification. Otherwise, the person might grow up to be a conscientious objector or a social innovator, or be inclined to demand social recognition for activity in free scientific inquiry or in art or some other luxurious and ornamental calling.

The irony of the situation is that this course is usually taken in the name of aristocracy, even of intellectual aristocracy, and as part of an attack upon the tendencies of democracy to ignore individuality. It may be that the word democracy has become so intimately associated with a particular political order, that of general suffrage and elective officials, which does not work very satisfactorily, that it is impossible to recover its basic moral and ideal meaning. But the meaning remains whatever name is given it. It denotes faith in individuality, in uniquely distinctive qualities in each normal human being; faith in corresponding unique modes of activity that create new ends, with willing acceptance of the modifications of the established order entailed by the release of individualized capacities.

Democracy in this sense denotes, one may say, aristocracy carried to its limit. It is a claim that every human being as an individual may be the best for some particular purpose and hence be the most fitted to rule, to lead, in that specific respect. The habit of fixed and numerically limited classifications is the enemy alike of true aristocracy and true democracy. It is because our professed aristocrats surrender so gladly to the habit of quantitative or comparative classifications that it is easy to detect snobbery of greater or less refinement beneath their professed desire for a régime of distinction. For only the individual is ultimately distinctive; the rest is a matter of common qualities differing merely in degree. Even in the crudest pioneer democracy there was something more distinctive, more aristocratic, than in that smoothed-off communal worship of qualities belonging to certain classes which is characteristic of present day critics of democracy.

The most ardent of the early advocates of equality never fell into the stupidity of alleging that all persons are qualitatively alike. Rousseau was one of the first to insist upon natural differences, psychological and physical. It was his profound conviction of the intensity and scope of these differences which made him so insistent upon political, legal and, within certain limits, economic equality. Otherwise some form of native superior energy would result in the enslavement of the masses, adding artificial enfeeblement to their natural deficiencies, while corrupting those of superior ability by giving them an artificial mastery of others and a cruel, contemptuous disregard for their welfare.

In our own earlier history, John Adams is perhaps the chief proponent of the unavoidable necessity of recognizing the aristocratic principle in politics because of inequality of natural endowments. But Adams was a realist. He did not assume that superiority of gifts meant intellectual superiority or that aristocracy in practice means the rule of the mentally and morally superior. He saw that the native superiorities which were bound in any political system to find outlet and to warp institutions to their ends are indefinitely many kinds — power, power to command and influence the action of others, being their only common divisor. In his own realistic words: "Any aristocrat is any man who can command two votes, one besides his own." And this superior influence may be due, he points out, to virtue, talent or intrigue and debauchery; to loquacity or taciturnity, to frankness or reserve, to good fellowship or fraud, violence and treachery, to deism or atheism. Powerful is as powerful does. Adams never fell into that mealy-mouthed sentimentalism of contemporary defenders of aristocracy who assume that native superiorities are all in the direction of talent and virtue, and inferiorities all in the opposite direction.

Thomas Jefferson is associated with the democratic school. But he writes to John Adams: " I agree with you that there is natural aristocracy among men . . . The natural aristocracy of virtue and talents is the most precious gift of nature . . . That government is best which provides the most effectively for selection of these natural aristocrats into the offices of government." And he proceeds to state that the differences between Adams and himself concern the means which are best calculated to secure this result. Adams thought that some express and definite institution was necessary; Jefferson thought that such explicit recognition would encourage the " tinsel " aristocracy of wealth and birth at the expense of natural aristocracy; for the wealthy will manage to protect themselves anyway and need no artificial protection against the feebleness of the poor. Both agreed that equality is moral, a matter of justice socially secured, not of physical or psychological endowment.

No intelligent defender of democratic equality has ever believed anything else. Today he is not as sure as men were a century ago that any legal and political system can of itself prevent the untoward working of native differences of power. He sees very clearly that a regime of economic anarchy like the present overstimulates many of the least desirable forms of superior native power, and that the result overrides the legal and political bulwarks of moral equality. In consequence he sees that moral equality cannot be conceived on the basis of legal, political and economic arrangements. For all of these are bound to be classificatory; to be concerned with uniformities and statistical averages. Moral equality means incommensurability, the inapplicability of common and quantitative standards. It means intrinsic qualities which require unique opportunities and differential manifestation; superiority in finding a specific work to do, not in power for attaining ends common to a class of competitors, which is bound to result in putting a premium on mastery of others. Our best, almost our only, models of this kind of activity are found in art and science. There are indeed minor poets and painters and musicians. But the real standard of art is not comparative, but qualitative. Art is not greater and less, it is good or bad, sincere or spurious. Not many intellectual workers are called to be Aristotles or Newtons or Pasteurs or Einsteins. But every honest piece of inquiry is distinctive, individualized; it has its own incommensurable quality and performs its own unique service.

Upon reflection, however, it is apparent that there is something academic in confining the models of moral equality to art and intellectual pursuits. Direct personal relationships, the affections and services of human companionship are its most widespread and available manifestations. The snobbery of the snobbish, who call themselves aristocrats, is nowhere as evident as in their neglect of the superior gifts and attainments of the humble of the earth in these respects. No contact of this human sort is replaceable; with reference to it all are equal because all are incommensurable, infinite. Democracy will not be democracy until education makes it its chief concern to release distinctive aptitudes in art, thought and companionship. At present the intellectual obstacle in the way is the habit of classification and quantitative comparisons. Our pseudo-aristocrats with their flourishing of abstract and uniform superiority and inferiority are now the main defendants of a concept of classes which means only the mass divided into smaller portions. The democrat with his faith in moral equality is the representative of aristocracy made universal. His equality is that of distinction made universal.

JAMES B. CONANT
Characteristics of American education

The school board members and the school administrators to whom this report is directed are familiar with the basic assumptions underlying the present pattern of American education. They realize that the task of the American high school is a task which arises out of the historical developments of our schools, colleges, and universities and, in particular, reflects certain basic changes in the structure of our society which have occurred during this century. Some readers of this report, however, who have had little or no opportunity to study American public schools may not be aware of the processes by which our school and college arrangements have come to diverge so markedly from those in other free nations. Therefore, as an introduction to a study of one segment of the educational pattern — the tax-supported high school — a brief summary of the characteristics of American public education may be in order.

To a foreign observer several aspects of the American educational scene seem so strange as to be almost incomprehensible. First of all, our colleges and universities are baffling. There are so many institutions with so great a variety of requirements for admission and with so many different types of program that a foreign visitor has difficulty in identifying those portions of a university which are concerned with what he regards as the true university function. In European universities there is no equivalent of our undergraduate liberal arts college, no provision for general education. European universities are essentially a collection of faculties concerned with the education of future members of the learned professions. The general or liberal education of the doctor, lawyer, theologian, engineer, scientist, or professional scholar is provided by special secondary schools, admission to which is determined by a highly selective procedure at age ten or eleven. Not more than 20 per cent of an age group are selected from the ele-

From James B. Conant, *The American High School Today* (McGraw-Hill Book Company, 1959), pp. 1–8, 11–13, 95–96. Reprinted by permission of the author.

mentary school and enrolled in the preuniversity schools. Therefore there is a waste of talent under the European system. No one has estimated how much potential talent goes undeveloped in Germany, France, Italy, and Switzerland because of the early selection of the preuniversity students — a selection often influenced by the class system of European lands. The other 80 to 85 per cent stop their formal education at age fourteen and go to work. Of course, the selection of those who are to be enrolled in the pre-university school is on the basis of academic ability, but family tradition plays a big role and many boys and girls from the farm and working class never even think of trying to enter a preuniversity school.

In the European preuniversity schools an eight- or nine-year rigorous course in languages, mathematics, science, history, and literature prepares the student to pass a state examination for a certificate which admits him to a university. The failures during the long course are many, and a con-siderable number fall by the wayside, but those who succeed finish with a mastery of two foreign languages, a knowledge of mathematics through calculus and of physics and chemistry at the level of our sophomore col-lege courses. Those who are not enrolled in the preuniversity schools, ex-cept for a small fraction who enter an intermediate school, complete their full-time education at age fourteen.

One often sees a comparison made between the proportion of the youth of college age who are studying in an American college or university and the proportion of German, or Swiss, or French youth who are attending a university. It is true that something like a third of our young people are " going to college," and only about a fifteenth or twentieth of the boys and girls in a European country are university students. But the vast majority of the Americans are *not* university students in the European sense of the term — that is, students preparing for a profession. Actually, the percentage of young men who are preparing to be doctors, lawyers, engineers, sci-entists, scholars, and teachers of academic subjects is about the same in this country as in Europe — a surprisingly small percentage, by the way — some-thing like 6 per cent of an age group.

To understand American colleges and universities, one must be aware of their history. The existence of a few American four-year colleges during colonial days and the persistence of these institutions during the early years of the American republic have had a determining influence on higher edu-cation in this country. Of perhaps equal significance has been the move-ment to establish agricultural and mechanical arts colleges which started just about a century ago. The passage of the Morrill Act during the Civil War provided federal support for a new type of college in each state, the " land-grant colleges," as they were soon called. As these institutions de-veloped, collegiate instruction in such practical fields as animal husbandry came to have the same academic standing as that of education for the pro-fessions. A proliferation of professional and semiprofessional areas of in-struction, running from architecture to wild life conservation, started in the closing decades of the last century and has continued in this century until today a catalogue of many an institution (privately controlled or publicly supported) bears little resemblance to a corresponding pamphlet issued by a European university.

The widening of the fields of instruction in the nineteenth century was part of a drastic educational reform that was taking place on both sides of the Atlantic. The main objective of this reform was the recognition of the physical and biological sciences as reputable subjects to be studied in a university. On this continent, because of the special history of the American people, the movement took on many special characteristics. The definition of what was a " university subject " widened and widened as the decades passed.

As the fields of study of applied science and practical subjects broadened at the university level, instruction at the secondary level also changed. A hundred years ago one assumed a lawyer would have studied Greek and Latin; it was argued that a classical education was essential for him as a professional man. Fifty years later, it was hard to make a convincing case that the preprofessional education of an electrical engineer or an agriculturist should include instruction in reading Latin. And at no time in the educational history of this country has mastery of a modern foreign language come to be recognized as the hallmark of a well-educated man or woman.

The transformation of the European university tradition on this continent is a theme about which much has been written. But the impact of this mutation on the high school seems at times to have been overlooked. Having spent considerable time talking to university professors and schoolteachers in several European countries, I have been impressed by the basic differences in the total pattern of tax-supported education on the two sides of the Atlantic. And, having tried to explain American public education to German audiences, I am aware of some of the peculiarities of our system — peculiar from a European standpoint. Yet I have found that by pointing out certain differences between American and European history one can lead a German, for example, to a better understanding of our schools (and also of some of our political institutions, but that is another story).

When Thomas Jefferson wrote of equality, he was certainly thinking of political equality. It is clear that the contrast between a new society without hereditary titles and an old society with an aristocracy was what he had in mind. The absence of conqueror and conquered, of a feudal system in our history, when pointed out to a European, provides a clue to understanding something of our present situation. So too does a realization of the importance of the pioneer movement westward in the nineteenth century. Frontiers — in the American sense of the term — have had no influence on the development of European nations, but the American frontier has in fact shaped our institutions. To a large extent, it was responsible for widening the concept of equality. For the American of the nineteenth century equality became, above all, equality of opportunity — an equal start in a competitive struggle. This aspect of equality acted like a magnet on inhabitants of other lands and attracted those immigrants whose settling on this continent so enriched our culture and invigorated our stock. And this wave of immigration placed on our tax-supported schools many educational tasks of a special nature. This fact is recognized by European educators who have studied our educational history, and more than one of them has spoken to me of the success of our public schools in bringing together the children of so many diverse peoples.

Equality thus came to mean for many new Americans not only political equality but also equality of opportunity. It came to mean too, especially west of the Alleghenies, equality of status of all honest labor. The land-grant colleges were both a symbol of equality of status and a means to the realization of the idea. One academic manifestation of this doctrine is our unwillingness to state frankly that a bachelor's degree has long since lost any meaning as a mark of scholastic attainment or the completion of a course of formal academic training. Whether one has a degree in engineering, agriculture, home economics, commerce, physical education, or in the arts and sciences, he is entitled to be called a " college graduate."

It is important to remember that the contrast between American and European education at the college and university level is nothing new. Except in terms of numbers, the differences were almost as great at the beginning of the century as they are now. Although only 4 per cent of the American youth were then attending a college or university compared to over 35 per cent today, the situation was as surprising to a European then as now. He then saw, as he still sees, a multitude of colleges and universities having no uniform standards for admission or for graduation, even in professional fields, and offering a wide range of practical subjects in which a student could major.

In the half-century that has elapsed, there have been no drastic changes in the basic pattern of education in either Europe or the United States. But in two respects the American pattern has diverged even more from that to be found in other countries; certain unique characteristics have been emphasized, so to speak. The percentage of youth attending a college or university has jumped from 4 to 35, and, at the same time, the percentage enrolled in grades eleven to twelve of the high school has about doubled. In 1910, only 35 per cent of the seventeen-year-olds were in school; today, the corresponding figure is over 70 per cent. These changes could easily have been predicted in 1900 by a student of American education. He would already have seen how enormous was the power of the twin ideals of equality of opportunity and equality of status; it was evident that the American people had come to believe that more education provided the means by which these ideals were to be realized. But two other factors also played a role. First, there was the urge for institutional expansion — the drive for larger faculties and student bodies in the colleges and universities; fifty years ago expansion was more than welcomed. Second, there was a radical change in the picture regarding the employment of youth. When this century began, approximately half of the boys and girls fifteen years of age were *not* attending school; many were at work. Thirty years later the percentage of this group attending school had reached 85. This alteration was not a consequence of state laws raising the school-leaving age; the laws were rather a consequence of profound economic and social changes. To explore adequately the background of this shift in the American scene would require many pages; suffice it to remind the reader that in the second decade of this century the campaign against child labor was being pushed vigorously at the state and national levels. Today, as a result of laws affecting employment, as well as the attitude of management and labor, it is difficult for boys even at the age of seventeen to obtain many types of jobs. In European countries three quarters or more of the youth go to work at fourteen or fifteen years of age.

As a consequence of the changes in universities and colleges in the nineteenth century and the alteration of the employment situation since World War I, the American public high school has become an institution which has no counterpart in any other country. With few exceptions, for the most part in large eastern cities, the public high school is expected to provide education for *all* the youth living in a town, city, or district. Such a high school has become known as a " comprehensive " high school in contrast to the " specialized " high schools which provide vocational education or which admit on a selective basis and offer only an academic curriculum. The local factors which have determined, and still determine, some of the features of a comprehensive high school are discussed later in this report, as are the pros and cons of the selective academic high school and the specialized vocational school.

Thousands of comprehensive high schools of considerable size exist throughout the United States. Though generalization about American public education is highly dangerous (and I shall avoid it as far as possible in this report), I believe it accurate to state that a high school accommodating all the youth of a community is typical of American public education. I think it safe to say that the comprehensive high school is characteristic of our society and further that it has come into being because of our economic history and our devotion to the ideals of equality of opportunity and equality of status. . . .

* * *

A UNIQUE FEATURE: THE COMPREHENSIVE HIGH SCHOOL

As everyone directly concerned with American secondary education is well aware, there are a number of different types of high schools in the United States. In the first place, in many school systems the arrangement is what is known as a " 6–3–3 " system, in which a junior high school of three years plays an intermediary role between the elementary school and the senior high school of three years. In the older pattern, a senior high school course of four years follows eight years of an elementary school. I shall not attempt to pass judgment on the relative advantages of the 6–3–3 and 8–4 schemes or on certain variants of these two patterns which are also found in the United States. It would appear that in some communities, for historical and geographic reasons, the existence of two or more junior high schools sending students to the senior high school with a three-year course has advantages. Even in those systems in which there is a junior high school, it is customary to regard grades nine through twelve as a unit, from the point of view of scheduling the students' work and arranging programs. Indeed, one finds that it is common practice in a three-year senior high school to consider the tenth grade as the sophomore class, although this group of boys and girls have only just entered the high school in question.

Leaving aside the differences between the three-year and the four-year senior high schools, we can conveniently divide all the high schools in the United States into two general categories. In the one category are the specialized high schools found in certain large cities and, in the other, the comprehensive high schools, which are found in communities of all sizes. The specialized high school offers a program adapted to a special group of students and usually requires evidence of certain aptitudes on the part of candidates for admission. For example, there is a specialized high school in New York City called The Bronx High School of Science. The Central High School in Philadelphia, which is usually spoken of as an " academic " or " college-preparatory " school, and the six-year Boston Latin School are other examples of specialized high schools which have entrance requirements and whose programs are of a strictly academic nature. Finally, one should mention among the specialized high schools the vocational high schools which are located in many cities along the Atlantic Coast and in a few of the large midwestern cities. These schools are also to be found in smaller communities in a few states in which federal funds provided under the Smith-Hughes Act of 1917 and such supplemental acts as the George-Barden Act of 1946 have been used by state authorities to develop separate vocational schools.

Limitations on the comprehensiveness of a high school. I have already defined the comprehensive high school as a high school whose programs correspond to the educational needs of *all* the youth of the community. In those cities in which there are specialized high schools, particularly vocational schools, it may well happen that some of the boys and girls who reside in the district served by a comprehensive high school attend the specialized school, and to this degree the breadth of the program in the comprehensive high school is limited. Likewise, in those states in which separate vocational schools have been developed and supported, the comprehensive high school will not have among its programs the vocational offerings supported by federal funds. One can therefore speak of the " degree of comprehensiveness " of a high school.

As will be pointed out more than once in the course of this report, there are high schools whose comprehensiveness is limited not by the existence of a specialized high school, but by lack of interest in the community in certain types of programs which develop special skills immediately useful upon graduation. High schools whose comprehensiveness is thus limited by the nature of the community are to be found particularly in suburban areas and in high-income residential sections of large cities. In these schools one finds that the vast majority of boys and girls desire to enter a four-year college or university, largely because of the collegiate ambitions of parents. In such schools, one will find that courses in stenography, auto mechanics, mechanical drawing, or the building trades are either not offered or are elected by very few students. . . .

*   *   *

A CONCLUDING WORD

More than once in the course of this report, I have pointed to the diversities among our tax-supported schools. I have reported not only on the diversity of solutions of pedagogic problems but also on the diversity of the communities served by the high schools I have visited. I cannot emphasize too strongly the differences I have found between small industrial cities, suburban areas, and the districts I have visited in certain large cities. I hope this last section of the report has conveyed to the reader some idea of the way the problems faced by school administrators often depend on the attitudes of the families in the city or town in question. If I have made myself clear, it will be evident that there is no such thing as a typical American high school. Furthermore, it is impossible to draw a blueprint of an ideal high school. A school that would be highly satisfactory in a small industrial city would be unsatisfactory in many suburban areas, and vice versa. Within a large city great diversity will be found from district to district; it would be most unwise to attempt to say what is the correct curriculum or organization of all the high schools under the management of the city school board.

As I have already stated, I am convinced American secondary education can be made satisfactory without any radical changes in the basic pattern. This can only be done, however, if the citizens in many localities display sufficient interest in their schools and are willing to support them. The improvements must come school by school and be made with due regard for the nature of the community. Therefore, I conclude by addressing this final word to citizens who are concerned with public education: avoid generalizations, recognize the necessity of diversity, get the facts about your local situation, elect a good school board, and support the efforts of the board to improve the schools.

SECTION **3. The curriculum: What shall be taught?**

The curriculum for American schools was not handed down from Mount Sinai nor concocted by infallible human beings. Like other social instruments, it has evolved out of the experiences of the past. In common with other social instruments, it is characterized by haphazardness, internal inconsistencies, and cultural lags. Among the major decisions facing professionally minded educators is that of determining just what curricular content should be retained, what should be added, and what should be deleted. Two fundamental factors account for the complexity of this task. The first arises out of the fact that the sheer amount of our extant knowledge is increasing at a tremendous pace, and thus the selection process becomes more critical. The second arises out of the fact that we have honest differences of opinion as to what the ends of education should be, and thus there are differences on what the curriculum, as a means to these ends, should contain.

The first of these factors, although a truism, has implications that are not so obvious. Because the storehouse of potential content that could be incorporated into the curriculum is so vast, only an infinitesimal amount — probably less than one per cent — can ever become part of the curriculum of any one school system. As a consequence, no teacher of any course can possibly " cover the subject " during one school year — or even twelve school years. One of the persistent delusions under which some teachers still operate is that they can or should accomplish this impossible task.

As for the second factor involving differences of opinion about the ends

of education, all of the following selections deal directly or indirectly with this relationship between educational philosophy and the curriculum. All recognize this inescapable relationship between ends and means. Of the following three selections, the one by Phillip Phenix takes perhaps the broadest view of the curriculum, stressing its importance in meeting both individual and societal needs. Smith, Stanley, and Shores consider four possible criteria for determining the curriculum: current social practice, universal social institutions, current social trends, and significant social problems. The first three of these are found inadequate. Their statement of the case for a curriculum based upon the study of social problems is contained in the second reading selection. Stephen M. Corey concludes this section with his tongue-in-cheek article, " The Poor Scholar's Soliloquy." As with all good satire, this brief tale of woe contains just enough truth to make even the most complacent educator wince a bit.

Decisions about curricular content are not something that some nebulous " other person " makes for the teacher. Probably in no other country of the world is the classroom teacher given as much freedom to determine the curriculum as in the United States. Within the broad outlines of system-wide courses of study or curriculum guides, the teacher has a very wide latitude of choice as to specific content, method, and materials of instruction. This freedom of choice imposes a corresponding responsibility on the teacher to make decisions in regard to curricular content that are in keeping with an educational theory appropriate to a democratic society.

PHILLIP PHENIX
The nature of curriculum

Having now considered the school and its teachers, we turn next to the curriculum, or course of study. The term curriculum is simply a name for the organized pattern of the school's educational program. A complete description of the curriculum has at least three components: (1) *what* is studied — the "content" or "subject matter" of instruction — (2) *how* the study and teaching are done — the "method" of instruction — and (3) *when* the various subjects are presented — the order of instruction.

The first of these components — the content — includes the whole range of matters in which the student is expected to gain some competence. There are the obvious academic subjects which are customarily associated with the idea of curriculum, such as language and literature, mathematics, the several natural sciences, history and the social sciences, and the fine arts. All of these are primarily intellectual in character. The curriculum may also include practical studies which develop skill in the manual arts and crafts either for personal enjoyment or more often for vocational purposes. Other studies combine the practical and intellectual, in preparation for service in the learned professions, such as law, medicine, or the ministry. Still another group of studies, neither primarily intellectual nor practical, may best be described as personal in orientation. In this category would fall provisions for physical and mental health education, for development of mature human relationships, and for growth of desirable attitudes and values.

In the following pages we shall be chiefly concerned with the philosophy of curriculum as content or subject matter, with brief reference also to the order and units of instruction. The question of method has been taken up in the preceding chapter. It should be stated, however, that this separation between content and method is artificial and to a certain extent misleading. The possibility of separation presupposes a certain view of the relation between truth and personality. If truth is regarded as having an existence independent of persons, and if it is thought to be more or less faithfully embodied in books and other cultural artifacts, then subject matter is a definite body of material to be acquired, and the question of how it is made available has no relation to the content.

The opposite view is that truth has meaning only as known by persons, and that the way of knowing enters into the very nature of the truth. Hence the content of what a person learns is determined by the complete nature of the experiences in which the learning takes place. Since the methods of teaching are an integral part of these experiences, content and

From Phillip Phenix, *Philosophy of Education*, 1958, pp. 57–75. Reprinted by permission of Holt, Rinehart and Winston, Inc.

method cannot be separated. The strength of this position is particularly evident in those studies referred to above as " personal." Here the method of teaching (e.g., in matters of human relationships) is of the very essence of what is taught. In the more traditional academic subjects the independence of the subject matter can be more easily defended. The practical subjects lie in between the personal and academic. This suggests that the possibility of separating content from method may be a function of the subject studied, being most feasible in the purely intellectual disciplines and least so in such personal matters as emotional and moral instruction.

CURRICULUM AS A PROBLEM

It is obvious that the school must have a curriculum, for without a course of instruction it would not be an educational institution. Is it equally obvious what the curriculum should be? Does the curriculum present a problem? Under certain cultural and social conditions there is no problem in deciding what to teach. If there is a limited body of knowledge and a definite set of skills which constitute the basic cultural capital of a society, these are the necessary and appropriate subjects of study. When the student has mastered them, he is an educated person; he has completed the course. Again, in a society where to each person certain fixed and circumscribed functions are assigned, the course of study is easily prescribed. Nor is there any appreciable problem in deciding what shall be taught when the time and resources for schooling are extremely meager. In such cases instruction must clearly center about those elementary competences required for social intercourse and making a living.

Curriculum is a problem only in advanced, relatively free societies where considerable opportunities for schooling are available. It is a problem because a choice must be made among a great variety of different possibilities. In modern civilization the cultural inheritance is no longer a circumscribed, standard, and relatively stable body of content. It has become enormous in size and profoundly complex. It continually undergoes revision and receives accessions at an accelerating rate. It is not possible now, as it once was, for even an exceptionally able person to obtain a reasonable mastery of all the major fields of learning. For each individual a choice must be made from the virtually unlimited store of materials to be learned. Assuming that society is organized so that choice is possible, and assuming that schooling is provided, the problem of curriculum is to make the wisest decision about which few things among the many valuable subjects should be studied.

Essentially curriculum is a problem of economy. Unfortunately, the capacity of the human being to learn is limited. No person can learn everything that now waits to be known. If one spent a whole lifetime in study it would not suffice to produce universal competence; life is too short, and forgetting takes its toll. Many people are not endowed with more than modest learning capacities. Furthermore, there are many things to be done with life besides acquiring new knowledge; most people spend most of their time in these other pursuits. All of these limiting factors increase the disproportion between the vast cultural capital available and the limited learning capacity of the individual person. The problem of curriculum is to economize scarce learning potential by making the most judicious and appropriate selection of study content. Human intelligence is too rare and precious a thing to squander on a haphazard program of instruction.

CURRICULUM AND VALUES

The choice of what shall be taught requires a principle of selection. There must be a measure of which subjects are more important than others, indicating which ones can be sacrificed — since not everything can be mastered — and which ones are absolutely essential. Criteria are needed to decide the optimum proportion of available school time to be devoted to the various studies selected. Such standards presuppose a scale of values. The central problem in all education is that of values. The educator must choose the direction in which he believes the student's growth may best proceed. He can make no decision whatever without a conviction that in that instance one way is preferable to all other possible paths. Now beliefs about what is best or preferable imply a scale of values. Hence all educational activity drives one to the question of underlying values.

The curriculum is a schedule of proposed instruction embodying the preferred direction of student development. It rests upon and manifests a certain system of values. These values constitute the aims, objectives, or purposes of education, and the curriculum is the means by which the aims are achieved, the objectives realized and the purposes fulfilled.

Oftentimes the educator is not aware of the values which are implicit in his chosen curriculum. This may result in inconsistency and indecisiveness because the foundation for choice is not clear and explicit. One important function of educational philosophy is to promote reflection on curricular offerings in order to reveal what educational values or purposes are presupposed by them. Furthermore, certain aims may be affirmed and sincerely espoused and yet be quite at odds with the objectives implied in the curriculum. For example, the teacher may honestly desire to promote a scientific outlook and yet by the choice of study materials in fact encourage passive acceptance of authoritative pronouncements. Philosophic analysis of the curriculum may help to overcome such incongruities, bringing convictions about the purposes of education into closer accord with the aims embodied in the curriculum, through a revision of stated goals, of the course of study, or of both.

In the following paragraphs some of the classes of component values which enter into the determination of the curriculum, together with illustrations of the corresponding subjects of instruction, will be discussed. Every person and every society gives a characteristic weight to the several types of general objectives, and the relative importance assigned to each of them determines the curriculum selected. This process of assigning relative degrees of importance to general educational goals in turn rests upon the application of a still more ultimate system of values, such as that contained in a personal " philosophy of life," in a religious faith, or in the ideology of a community. . . . Our purpose in what follows is . . . to indicate some of the kinds of general but less than ultimate factors which must be considered in deciding the content of the course of study.

BASIC HUMAN NATURE

The first requirement of any education is that it answer the basic need to be human. In constructing the curriculum the starting point is to make provision for developing those capacities which are fundamental to man as man. Just as reflection on the curriculum raises the central question of values in education, so also does it require a consideration of this other root issue — the nature of man. If there are certain features which are humanly essential — i.e., without which one would not truly be a person — the recognition and development of these should clearly be the primary objective of the curriculum. . . . A brief . . . selection of fundamentals will have to suffice for illustration here. Following are six suggested constituents of a curriculum for essential humanity.

Elementary physical skills. The young child must learn to perform the usual physical functions of eating, walking and running, manipulating, and observing. He must develop muscular coordination and habits of sense perception which will preserve him from danger and enlarge his powers of enjoyment and control of the environment. Most of these abilities are acquired automatically as the child matures, and it is generally necessary only to provide a safe yet appropriately challenging environment, together with older persons to demonstrate what is to be learned.

Basic social skills. A person is inescapably social. His satisfaction and effectiveness in living depend upon developing productive relationships to other people. The child must early learn that there are persons besides himself with feelings and demands like his own, and that he must govern his conduct to take account of them. Hence the necessity for opportunities for planned social activity, with lessons in sharing and experience of the resulting satisfactions, instruction in manners and courtesies which make social existence more pleasant, as well as teaching of the sterner disciplines of making one's way properly in a world where injustice and deceit often prevail.

Use of symbols. Man's most notable possession is his intelligence. This power of mentality is manifest most clearly in the use of symbols, especially in the form of language. Intelligence is based upon the ability to utilize ideas or concepts, which embody the sense of meaning, and symbols to express and communicate these meanings. The ability to use language to speak, to read, and to write is therefore necessary to the achievement of essential humanity. Mathematics is another form of symbolic activity, in some ways even more powerful and more perfectly an expression of human reason than language. "The three R's" (the symbolic disciplines) have traditionally and rightly been regarded as basic to the curriculum because they help man realize his essential rationality.

Constructive activity. Human reason finds expression not only in language and mathematics, but also in various constructive activities. Man is not only a thinker and speaker, but also a maker. He fashions objects of beauty and use. He employs tools to do what his unaided hands cannot accomplish. He invents and builds. He puts his creative imagination to work in conceiving and embodying ideas in a variety of material forms. It is to supply these basic human needs that programs of arts and crafts are included in the curriculum.

Play. It is perhaps not widely enough appreciated that play is also a fundamental human function. In play a person participates in a world fashioned by the free imagination, orderly yet unconstrained by the ordinary rules of social existence, and serious yet not directed to the long-term purposes of vocational life. Learning to play is a vital part of the educational process. School recreational activity is not merely recess from the real business of learning. It is itself an essential factor in the development of freedom, imagination, and perspective.

Moral responsibility. A final constituent of basic human nature is the ability to make wise and responsible choices. It is of the essence of manhood to be able to decide between alternative courses of action. The curriculum, therefore, should provide ample opportunities for the student to exercise intelligence in choosing and opportunities to assume responsibility for his decisions. This moral instruction is generally not provided in specific segments of the curriculum, as the other five elements to a considerable extent are, but may be an ingredient in every type of activity. Its efficacy depends upon preserving the right balance, at every stage of maturity, between freedom and authority, so that the student has enough guidance to give him some foundation for choice yet enough liberty to make the alternatives genuine and the responsibility his own.

DEMANDS OF THE ACTUAL SOCIETY

The course of study clearly ought to be designed to serve the basic human needs. These are the fundamental values, but they are by no means the only ones which enter into curriculum decision. Human development goes beyond growth in basic human competences, and it is in relation to these further elaborations that other claims are advanced and other values affirmed. The present section and the four to follow describe the general nature of five such types of claims.

Language, geography, and history. First, there are the educational demands created by the special character of the actual society. For example, the language usually taught first and most intensively is the one which is in actual use in the society where the school is situated. Instruction in arithmetic employs the customary number system and usual designations of weight, length, volume, and monetary value. In the teaching of geography, attention is directed primarily to the features of the student's own state and country which he may need to know in order to be an intelligent citizen. For the same reason, in the study of history major emphasis is placed on those events which were most relevant to the making of the civilization in which the student shares.

Manners and customs. The actual society also determines the nature of the manners and customs which are taught. Such matters as clothing styles, eating habits, common courtesies, patterns of relation between the sexes, and types of recreation engaged in are of great interest to the young and are of major significance in achieving a sense of belonging in his society. The curriculum necessarily includes instruction in these concerns, usually informally and implicitly, but sometimes in regular courses of study.

Occupations. The claims of the existing social order are advanced with particular insistence in relation to education for the occupations. Society needs workers to fill its jobs. The structure of the society is reflected in part in the kinds and relative numbers of available positions, and thus pressures tend to be exerted on the school to emphasize particular types of vocational preparation. For example, a highly industrialized society can exist only as it is provided with a constant supply of scientific and technical personnel. This demand forces the schools to offer a full complement of courses in mathematics, the basic sciences, and the various technical disciplines. Again, a predominantly religious society requires a ready supply of priests and teachers, and the educational system must accordingly give major attention to instruction in the beliefs and practices of the faith. Political conditions make it expedient for many nations to advance or defend their interests by force of arms and hence to include military training in the instruction of the young, whether in the civil schools or in the military establishment itself. In each of the above examples the emphasis given to the respective studies in the curriculum depends to a large extent upon how insistent the social demand is and how critical the respective competences appear to be for the health and security of the society.

Common values. Perhaps the most fundamental demand made by the actual society is that the young be given a clear awareness of the common values upon which the society rests. An English child is nurtured in the traditions of his people. A child in the Soviet Union is taught how to be a loyal Communist. In the United States the curriculum conveys a sense of what America stands for, including such values as freedom, equality, individual dignity, enterprise, cooperation, and the special meanings given to these in American culture. One of the ways of teaching the main common values of a people is to provide courses which trace the development of the civilized heritage from its sources. Thus, an American student can learn the values of his culture through the study of the great men and movements in Western civilization from its ancient roots in Greece, Palestine, and Rome down to the present day.

IDEAL SOCIAL NEEDS

A curriculum designed in response to the demands of the actual society subserves conformity and adjustment to what now is. The school fits the child for the existing society. No challenge is provided for the improvement of the social order, and the individual is regulated by society rather than society being dedicated to the service of the individual. Against these tendencies reformers and individualists champion other types of values which need to be considered in determining the curriculum.

In a changing and forward-looking social order there is concern not only for adjustment to existing conditions, but also for the creation of a better society. Since the school may be an important means of effecting the desired improvements, the curriculum may be expected to include elements of response to the claims of the social ideal. The course of study will then be designed to prepare the student for participation in the society that ought to be rather than for conformity to the world as it is.

There is, of course, the question as to how far the educator's ideal should depart from what now exists. If the student were prepared for life in a perfect world, he would probably be unable to participate effectively in any actual society. Education for social perfection thus appears to be irrelevant. Perhaps the rule is that the social ideal embodied in the curriculum should be an advance over what now is, but should not be so radical a departure that all connection with the imperfect conditions of actual life is lost. By this principle the social order for which the student is prepared should be reasonably possible to attain, and not a visionary utopia.

Transcending the particular culture. As pointed out above, the study of one's native language, history, and geography reflects the claims of the actual society. Mastering other languages and learning about other cultures may also prove of use in adjusting to existing conditions, as in travel or international trade. But such broadening of horizons may better be justified as a general practice by appeal to the claims of the ideal, in which purely national and ethnic loyalties will be transcended and other people and their ways will be understood and appreciated in and for themselves rather than for any practical use they may now serve.

Social cohesion. An example of appeal to the ideal is the case of a heterogeneous nation made up of peoples with many different dialects seeking through education to unify the society by teaching everyone a common language. Again, a study of the main ideas and practices of the major religious groups in a plural culture is a means of furthering mutual understanding and acceptance. More generally, the entire curriculum of public schools, as contrasted with private ones, is designed to advance the ideal of inclusive social cohesion rather than of solidarity within special groups of the society.

The ideal of social unity also underlies the consideration of controversial issues in the schools. Differences of economic, political, moral, and religious belief and practice often seriously interfere with the harmony and efficiency of society. The informed discussion of such problems in schools, under expert guidance and by students who are sufficiently mature, may contribute to the ideals of greater mutual understanding, respect for differences, and the use of constructive means for resolving conflicts.

When the accepted mark of success in a given society is power over other people, the school in response to the ideal of a cooperative commonwealth may give less weight to preparation for the competitive struggle, and more to mutual assistance, than sole concern for social adjustment would dictate. Again, where military necessity requires that the young be taught how to kill, the educator may feel a duty to supplement that demand by studies which will prepare the pupil to heal, construct, and conciliate, even though the occasion for such peaceful pursuits is not yet within sight.

Occupational balance. Consideration of the ideal society prevents the school from responding too directly to appeals for narrow vocational preparation. While the efficiency of the social mechanism may in the short run depend upon the preparation of highly trained specialists, the long-term goal of society may better be served by broadly educated citizens. If this is so, the curriculum will not only reflect the immediate demands but will also take due account of the needs of the better society that may yet come. Furthermore, when the distribution of occupations in the actual society lacks proper balance, the educational institutions by encouraging students to prepare themselves for those callings which ideally need larger representation can contribute to a more satisfactory condition.

The question of weighing ideal social needs against the demands of the actual society in the determination of curriculum is another form of the issue . . . concerning the relation of the school to the rest of society. If the school is regarded as servant and tool of the community, its curriculum will reflect the claims of the actual society. If, on the other hand, the school is considered at least in some degree as leader and molder of the community, then its curriculum will be fashioned in the light of practicable but as yet unrealized social ideals.

DEMANDS OF THE ACTUAL INDIVIDUAL

Since individual persons always develop within a social context and societies are made up of individuals, it is not possible entirely to separate personal and social values. There are, however, legitimate differences of emphasis which in practice make it useful to distinguish the one from the other. In particular, decisions about curriculum must take account of personal as well as of group demands. The unique qualities and capabilities of each person are values to be weighed along with those which measure the well-being of the community as a whole.

Individuation. One of the characteristic features of living things is the tendency toward individuation. Every organism is a unique integration of specialized parts. The more complex the organism, the greater is the variety of possible organized wholes. In the human being, with his amazing brain and nerve structure, and with the resulting capacity to learn from experience rather than to behave largely according to instinctive patterns, individuation reaches its highest level. Most things are best described by indicating the classes of objects to which they belong. Their nature is defined by what they have in common with other members of their kind. Though this sort of description is possible with human beings, perhaps such classification obscures the most important aspect of the person, namely, his uniqueness; the special significance of human life may rather lie in individuality.

Obviously a curriculum dedicated to the development of individuals differs considerably from one designed to produce certain classes of persons prepared to exercise specified functions within the society. The primary fact is that a curriculum which seriously takes account of individual differences cannot be a standardized course of study but must be specially constructed for each person. The same sequence of instruction cannot be used for all. Each student engages in those studies which are most consonant with his interests and abilities.

Such individual curricula are, of course, expensive. A high ratio of teachers to students must be maintained to insure the requisite individual attention. Ideally, a tutorial rather than a class system of instruction is called for, though group activities, planned with individual needs in mind, may well be part of the study program. When economic considerations make class instruction necessary, the needs of the individual may still be taken into account by grouping students of similar interests and capacities and by making allowance in the work of the class for personal choice and maximum flexibility. In fact, the whole system of grouping students into grades is a method of doing maximum justice to individual needs within the limits set by economic considerations.

Exceptional students. Concern for the individual underlies the provision of special curricula for exceptional students. The great majority of pupils can be given a reasonably standard course of instruction designed for persons of average ability. This curriculum is not, however, suitable for the relatively small proportion of exceptional persons who have unusual talent or who are markedly deficient in ability. The very able ones are not sufficiently stimulated by the average curriculum, and the slow learners are discouraged and confused by it. To care for these unusual individuals special courses of study may be designed, based upon the particular capabilities of the students. These programs may or may not call for the separation of the exceptional students into special classes or tutorial sessions, depending upon the extent of the individual's needs for social interaction with persons of different abilities and upon the possibilities for variation of assignment within a heterogeneous group.

Testing. Curriculum planning in the light of the actual individual's demands calls for a well-developed system of counseling and testing. By a variety of psychological tests the student's interests and abilities can be assessed, and in the counseling process he may be directed into the program of study which best fits him. The fundamental assumption on which the entire guidance and psychological service program of the school is based is the value of adjusting the educational program as far as possible to the unique characteristics of the individual.

IDEAL INDIVIDUAL NEEDS

There is another dimension of individuality beyond that of the actual person, just as there are social needs which transcend the demands of the existing community. This is the dimension of ideal individual needs. The educator is concerned with what the person now is, but only as this bears upon what he may become. The existing individual has capabilities which may or may not be worthy of development. The demands which the person makes and the needs which he feels may or may not be worthy of affirmative response. The present characteristics of the student do not provide a complete guide to what he ought to become. Granted that what the person now desires and can do should be considered in organizing his course of study, these factors do not in themselves answer the question of what direction development should take. It may well be that some present interests should be left unsatisfied and new ones encouraged, that certain abilities should be ignored and other ones cultivated.

The ideal person. Accordingly, the curriculum maker needs some conception of the ideal individual to guide his selection of teaching materials. He must have an idea of what the good man, the complete person, the mature individual is like. Value systems differ, and no single definitive and universally accepted set of ideals can be stated. For some the ideal would be the kingly man, combining knowledge, practicality, strength, and justice. For others the goal would be the saint, with his humility, holiness, compassion, and reverence. Still another objective would be the sage, endowed with intellectual power, penetrating insight, and breadth of perspective.

The claims of the ideal individual as they are usually reflected in the curriculum can be summarized under four headings.

Intellectual. First, there are the requirements of intellectual excellence. The pupil at the beginning is ignorant and perhaps quite uninterested in acquiring knowledge. Nevertheless, truth has a claim on him, and the course of study should help to stimulate the spirit of inquiry and the love of knowledge. The standard academic fields — mathematics and the natural sciences, psychology and the social sciences, history, philosophy, and literature — are the customary means of intellectual discipline. It is not ultimately a question of whether or not the student is interested in such knowledge. He ought to know, he would be a better person through knowing; therefore, the curriculum should be designed to generate intellectual interests and then to satisfy them.

Moral. A second set of claims is ethical in nature. The ideal individual is not only intelligent; he is also morally good. Moral standards differ, of course, but every curriculum must include some instruction about right conduct. Whether these moral concepts are based upon custom, upon revelation, or upon rational or empirical inquiry is at this point irrelevant. In whatever way derived and sanctioned, ideas of right and wrong are an important element in the curriculum. Whether or not the student wishes to do right, the moral code makes its claim, and the course of instruction ought to create the desire for and achievement of goodness.

Esthetic. Third, there are esthetic claims. The individual ideally should have well-developed tastes for what is beautiful. The esthetic sensibilities of the immature are not trustworthy guides to the development of higher appreciations. There are ideals of balance, harmony, and fitness which serve as values to be grown toward and not as enjoyments in possession. The curriculum should therefore make provision both through courses in the arts and perhaps even more through incidental and informal means for habituating the student to things of beauty.

Religious. A fourth component in the ideal for the individual is the religious claim. This is difficult to define and takes many different forms, but essentially has to do with the person's basic outlook on the meaning of life and with his ultimate loyalties and commitments. Religious faith is not a simple extension of immediate interest. It comes from instruction in an ideal which has taken root in those of spiritual maturity. By means of specific courses in religion and more informally through the perspective of teachers in other subjects the religious ideal may be given its place in the curriculum. . . .

CLAIMS OF THE CULTURAL TRADITION

In the preceding five sections the types of values entering into determination of curriculum have had specific reference to societies or to individuals, in both cases either actual or ideal. There is, finally, a kind of value which really belongs to all five of the above categories and yet deserves special reference. This sixth type of value is based on the claims of the cultural tradition. Some things are learned by some people not because they meet any actual or ideal demand of persons singly or in association but simply to preserve and extend the cultural heritage. There is a great and growing body of knowledge much of which cannot be shown to contribute directly to human well-being but which is treasured for its own sake.

This work of conserving and augmenting the cultural capital is primarily the task of the scholarly community. The scholar is one who devotes himself to caring for and improving the received store of knowledge regardless of whether or not it has any demonstrated individual or social use. There are ancient civilizations which he seeks to keep alive, long unused languages which he explores, and curious skills which he cultivates. These things the scholar does because he believes that there is intrinsic worth in the hard-won creations of the race, which should not be allowed to fall into oblivion for lack of clear present or future relevance.

In the light of these claims, certain courses of study are designed for the express purpose of perpetuating the scholarly tradition. Often such studies can also be justified on grounds of social and personal needs, but it seems worth while to draw special attention to the trans-personal dimension in the ideal of pure scholarship and to set this off as a specific kind of value in the determination of curriculum.

THE DETERMINATION OF CONTENT

In the above sections six types of value have been suggested as relevant to decisions concerning the course of instruction. Generally all of these kinds enter in some degree into the construction of any actual curriculum. Every maker of the school's program to some extent adjusts the course to the needs of society and of the individual and never wholly neglects the lure of the ideal nor the integrity of the tradition. The application of these values differs, however, from one case to another, and their respective weights vary widely. In one situation the immediate demands of society are most insistent, in another interest in perfecting the individual predominates, in still a third the preservation of the heritage seems most crucial. Where the balance falls depends upon prevailing conditions, personal, social, and cultural, and upon the pattern of ultimate values which at the deepest level govern the educator's decisions.

In determining curriculum content the educator must translate the value types into specific study units which will serve to realize them. A rough numerical weight must then be assigned to each value, and from this the school time and teaching resources must be proportionately allocated to the various units. Curriculum is, of course, primarily a matter of quality, but there must finally also be a quantitative rating of the various qualities, since a decision has to be reached on how the limited available study time shall be distributed among them.

THE PROBLEM OF TIMING

Decisions about when each subject is to be taught also enter into the construction of the curriculum. The course of study is not determined solely by reference to content, that is, to the distribution of subject matter, but also involves the distribution of study units in time. There are three types of factors which govern the decision about timing. These are respectively developmental, logical, and personal-social factors.

Developmental. The human being grows in accordance with an orderly plan. Beginning with a single fertilized cell at the time of conception, a definite process of development ensues. Following the pattern determined by the original germ-cell genes, a step by step progression of cell multiplication, differentiation, and organization occurs, resulting eventually, if all goes well, in the mature individual. Environment decisively influences this development, but always in accordance with the given hereditary potentials and the laws of organic growth. The person cannot learn to perform any activity for which the requisite physical organs, nervous structures, and emotional patterns have not yet matured. For example, it is futile to try to teach a two year old how to write poetry, drive a car, or decide political issues. The developmental sequence imposes a certain order upon the learning process. What can be taught at any given time is subject to the limitation that the organism must be in readiness for the learning to occur.

Hence, the curriculum must be organized in such a way that the order of studies does not conflict with the order of development. To give instruction in any subject prior to the time when it can possibly be learned is to invite failure, frustrate the student, and waste precious learning time. To teach a subject much later than the time when it can first be learned may unnecessarily retard personal growth. Yet knowledge of development stages is not a sufficient basis for curriculum determination, since at any point much more could in principle be taught than there is in fact time to learn. Hence, further principles of selection are required.

One important developmental principle is that the growth of intellectual powers increases the ability to think in abstractions. Instruction must begin on the level of the concrete, with specific situations and objects of immediate sense perception. As the person matures, generalizations and abstract processes of reasoning can be introduced in greater measure. The temptation of the adult is to impose his own relatively abstract ways of thought on the child for whom only the particular has any vivid meaning.

Another illustrative principle of development is that proper maturation involves a movement from emotional dependence, to growing independence, into eventual fruitful interdependence. The school program should, therefore, provide ample emotional support in the early years, recognize the need for enlarged autonomy as the child develops, and finally give opportunity for truly responsible social participation in the years of maturity. The stages of emotional growth are particularly important also in providing the clue to motivation. The student may be intellectually capable of mastering certain materials but emotionally apathetic to them. If intellectual capacities can be linked with emotional drive, the most efficient learning occurs. Curriculum timing should take account of the interplay of these factors in development.

Logical. In addition to the patterns of organic development, there are logical structures within the subject matter of the curriculum which may further affect the sequence of studies. Knowledge is to some extent, and especially in certain of its branches, cumulative in nature. Each item depends upon the establishment of a connected series of previous ones and cannot be understood until these prior elements have been assimilated. Algebra as usually taught presupposes familiarity with arithmetic, and success in analytic geometry similarly depends upon a prior mastery of algebra and the elements of geometry. To understand American government there must be some basic knowledge of American history, and the latter in turn requires some insight into the European roots of American civilization. Again, one cannot usefully study the principles or the philosophy of education in the absence of a prior acquaintance with the elementary facts of educational practice.

In general, the logical order and the developmental sequence are compatible. Both proceed from the simpler to the more complex, from concrete particulars to abstract generalizations. However, a distinction may usefully be made between the psychological and the formal logical sequence for the teaching of a given body of organized knowledge. The strict logic of the subject sometimes dictates its formulation in a pattern which presupposes considerable familiarity with its facts and principles. For example, formal logical exposition of a system in mathematics might begin with definitions and axioms, the reasons for which would not be clear to the novice. In such a case the teacher might better adopt a psychological presentation, that is, one which would start where the student is and build the system inductively with ample use of illustrative instances, diagrams, and applications. In decisions about timing in the curriculum it is this *psychological* rather than the *formal* logical order which should be primary. Only after the subject has become familiar can the student be introduced to the strictly formal structure.

Personal-social. A third complex of factors in curriculum timing are the demands and expectations of the individual and society. A student who has unusual interests or talents in a certain type of endeavor may well be advised to apply himself to it early. Abilities which society requires of everyone must be taught from the beginning. Thus, in an urban society of highly literate people whose life is largely governed by written symbols, the child must be taught to read early. In an agrarian civilization the priority would probably be given to learning the manual skills necessary for successful farming; reading could be deferred indefinitely.

The several types of values — personal and social — entering into decisions about content are also relevant to timing. Within the limits set by developmental and logical factors, the temporal priority will generally be given to those subjects which are most valued and the subjects considered less important will be postponed.

THE ORGANIZATION OF INSTRUCTION

Even after the problems of general curriculum content and timing have been settled, there still remains the task of organizing the materials of instruction. Assuming, for example, that the student is to be taught to read, beginning at age six, how does one select from the virtually unlimited stock of reading materials those which will be most effectively learned? Given the political system of the nation as the subject of instruction, how does the educator decide in what form to teach it? What criteria of choice will insure the maximum economy of learning resources and the greatest teaching efficiency? Three main ways of organizing instruction will now be described.

Systems of ideas. One time-honored way of organizing what is to be learned is around systems of concepts. This is the traditional " academic " approach. Knowledge is divided into definite subjects or departments, each of which has its characterstic ideas. Arithmetic is a distinct and separate kind of study, with its own set of meanings and methods; language is another well-defined subject; and art is a third. From the multitude of ideas contained in each field the teacher chooses those which best typify the whole subject. These central or key ideas, once well understood, provide a basic grasp of the entire field of study and enable the student with relative ease to acquire further detailed knowledge of the subject.

As the student becomes more advanced in knowledge the subjects often become more specialized in nature and the idea-systems more limited and intensive. On the other hand, it becomes increasingly important to establish connections between the special departments of study, and for this purpose " bridge " subjects like biochemistry or art history are created. In addition to these, as the student matures intellectually, he may be taught to consider all of his knowledge philosophically, critically examining assumptions, noting the structure and interrelations of ideas, and even creating tentative syntheses including hierarchies of organizing concepts with all grades of generality. . . .

Things. A second approach to organization is through actual things rather than through systems of ideas. The fields-of-knowledge approach is essentially abstract. It introduces the student to the end-products of scholarship, reflection, and research. Many people do not respond readily to such an approach. They live in the world of concrete things rather than of logic and abstraction. Hence they learn better if their study is organized around real objects, and if ideas are employed for the purpose of understanding these things. For example, if a study were organized around " American Indians," it would be useful to introduce ideas from such fields as geography, history, religion, and anthropology to understand the subject well. A study of " trees " could utilize concepts from such fields as biology, physics, chemistry, economics and history. In each case the abstractions would not be studied systematically or for their own sakes but would be selected for their relevance to the concrete object being considered.

The approach through things has the great advantage of vividness. Human experience is founded upon perception of the concrete, from which abstractions are drawn. Things are in this sense closer to reality than idea-systems. Concrete things also provide immediately and naturally for the interconnections of ideas. Concepts are most clearly linked together not in chains of systems, but in their common relevance to actual things. On the other hand, the concepts employed in the description of concrete things have been developed through the efforts of systematic thinkers, and the student should not be without understanding for these abstract modes of thought. Hence the curriculum should generally include both types of organization, the proportion of each depending largely upon the maturity and abstractive power of the student.

Problems. The first type of organization discussed above was idea-centered. The second type was thing-centered. The third is centered on the student and his problems. This approach is based on the theory that effective thinking occurs only when the person is faced with a problematic situation — a real difficulty to be overcome, an obscurity to be clarified, or a confusion to be resolved. The problem then becomes the focus of study, and ideas and things are investigated only as they provide assistance in reaching a solution. A student may see no point in studying arithmetic for its own sake, and he may have no interest whatsoever in learning about trees, for their sake, but if he has an opportunity to earn some spending money by working in an orchard, he may eagerly learn whatever is necessary about trees and arithmetic in order to do the job and calculate his earnings. The basis for study is then an activity or project motivated by a need felt as such by the student.

Problem-organization shares with thing-organization the virtues of vividness and concreteness, and it has the further merit of obvious personal relevance. Its use raises the question as to whether " natural " problems, arising out of the student's immediate perplexities, are to be the basis for inquiry, or whether the function of the teacher may not create other " artificial " problems for the student which in the long run will lead him to more valuable learnings than the largely fortuitous natural problems would provide. Furthermore, things and systems of ideas in themselves present challenges to the student's intelligence. For many students the motive of intellectual curiosity and the desire for clarity and completeness of comprehension are sufficient stimulus for learning. When that is the case, the idea-centered or thing-centered approach suffices, and there is no need to organize the curriculum around the student's immediate problems. In any event, a broad conception of " problem " extending beyond purely material or practical interests, seems necessary.

Problems are particularly useful in taking account of individual needs. By the same token they may require more ample teaching resources than would be required if the course of study were organized around concept systems or things.

Finally, the basic assumption of the problem approach needs to be critically examined. Do students think only when they face difficulties? May not learning also occur as students participate in any sort of experience, of satisfaction as well as frustration, of illumination as well as perplexity, of assurance as well as uncertainty?

Uses of the three approaches. There are special advantages and defects in all these major types of curriculum organization. Normally it would be wise in constructing any course of study to make use of all three as they seem respectively appropriate to age level, personality characteristics, and types of knowledge to be acquired.

For example, the program of young children may properly emphasize things, with less concern for problems and still less for systems of ideas, while for adolescents problems are the most appropriate approach in many cases, and for advanced graduate students the systematic method is most fitting. Some persons learn best through things, others are of more practical bent and need the challenge of problems, while still other personalities are gifted with abstractive power and are better served by a systematic approach. Finally, the three types of organization will clearly receive different weight depending upon whether the knowledge sought is primarily descriptive, prescriptive for practice, or theoretical.

B. OTHANEL SMITH et al.
Criteria for selecting curricular content

THE CURRICULUM PREMISED UPON SIGNIFICANT SOCIAL PROBLEMS

The fourth and last curriculum theory predicated on social reality takes the position indicated by the criticism of the previous theories. It defines the curriculum in terms of the significant and persistent social problems of the society in which the school is located. The way in which a group conceives its problems, however, is always relative to its interests and goals. Since the aspirations and purposes of a people are both revealed and shaped by their intellectual and moral commitments, the definition of the significant and persistent problems of any society always entails a determination of the ideological basis of its culture. The resolution of social problems, moreover, is an affair of knowledge and fact. But judgments respecting social policy inevitably involve standards of the good and of the just which, in their turn, are grounded in the ethical and intellectual commitments of a people. Hence both the definition and the study of social problems are intimately related to these commitments.

The adherents of the social-problems theory, in common with many other social realists, locate this basic commitment in the American demo-

From B. Othanel Smith, William O. Stanley, and J. Harlan Shores, *Fundamentals of Curriculum Development*, revised edition, 1957, pp. 627–631. Reprinted by permission of the World Book Company.

cratic tradition. The term *tradition* must be employed with considerable caution in this instance. The American democratic faith is traditional in the sense that it has historically represented the supreme social and political allegiance of the American people. It is not traditional in the sense of being traditionalistic; its tenets have never been regarded as immutable, nor have they been validated primarily by an appeal to antiquity. On the contrary, the democratic doctrine, on its own terms, is a growing and developing faith, resting its case on human reason and experience. Accordingly, the adherents of the social-problems school of curriculum determination have usually recognized that, in an age of social transformation, the democratic tradition, if it is to retain its vitality and strength, must be redefined and reconstructed in terms of the problems and conditions of the time. In short, while the democratic tradition is accepted as the ultimate standard that gives point and direction to the selection and study of social problems, that tradition is regarded as problematic in some degree — and, hence, as an object of critical study and revision. This position logically demands the acceptance of the thesis that a growing and changing faith can, at the very time that it is undergoing reconstruction, serve as the touchstone of intellectual and moral judgment.

The major principle espoused by the social-problems school of curriculum construction is, then, that the curriculum should be organized around the problems encountered by a democratic society, compelled by profound scientific and technological changes to adapt its thinking and its institutions to the requirements of a highly interdependent and industrialized world order. This means, of course, that the school must become a laboratory engaged in the analysis and study of the issues and problems involved in social reconstruction through democratic, as opposed to authoritarian and violent, methods. This conception of the curriculum represents the view that a paramount purpose of the school is to develop in the young the understanding and the attitudes required to facilitate social reconstruction along democratic lines and by democratic means.

Difficulty of studying social problems in the school. An educational conception of this type places a heavy burden upon the schools. Yet it is a burden that cannot be avoided save at the price either of arbitrary imposition or of confusion and disorder in education. For, as the previous analysis has revealed, the school in a transitional era is caught between the partially disintegrated conceptions of the old order, not yet wholly dead, and the emerging conceptions of the new society, not yet fully determined or established. Under these conditions the school must seek order and clarity in education in a method of dealing with the confusions and conflicts of the time.

The task of the school can be simplified. The issues and problems encountered in the course of democratic social reconstruction are, in detail, multitudinous and complex. They come to a focus, however, in two great questions, which, from a democratic point of view, define a major task. First, upon what principles and by what means can the consensus required to hold society together be restored, along essentially democratic lines, under the conditions imposed by an interdependent and industrialized world order? And, second, in what ways and by what methods can the institutional structures of society be reconstructed so that they are both compatible with the democratic faith as defined by the emerging consensus and capable of smooth and efficient operation under the conditions set by modern technology? At bottom the criteria of democratic compatibility and efficient operation, measured by democratic goals, are intimately related. Institutions are merely the means by which a society realizes its ideal ends. Hence, any institutional structure which, under a given set of conditions, is incapable of effectively actualizing democratic goals for the vast majority of the population cannot, in that situation, be regarded as efficient.

In the solution of the two basic problems — restoring consensus and reconstructing institutions — almost every phase or aspect of organized social life is potentially involved in one way or another. Three such aspects, however — world organization, economic structure, and class and race relationships — appear particularly crucial. The disruptive influences of war, of prolonged economic dislocation and depression, and of race and class dissension are so great that it is probably not too much to say that the ultimate destiny of the democratic way of life depends primarly upon its ability to restore, by peaceful and democratic means, consensus and order in these vital areas of social life. The successful achievement of this triple task entails technical issues of a high order — not the least important of which is the discovery of more adequate means of individual participation in the control and direction of group activity on a large scale.

Skill in group deliberation and action. It would be difficult to exaggerate the significance of this problem. Group activity is becoming increasingly important in modern life — so much so that many students of society have declared with Woodrow Wilson that the fundamental relationships of men are now with groups rather than with individuals as such. Moreover, it is clear — documented by a trend that has persisted for more than fifty years — that the conditions of modern life will require more, not less, group control and action. Under such circumstances democracy can be destroyed by a theory that equates democracy with purely individual choice and action. It can also be destroyed, no less effectively, by a theory that defines democracy in terms of individual participation in group decision and action, in the absence of adequate machinery and techniques through which individuals may actually participate in group deliberation and choice. Yet it could hardly be maintained that existing techniques are fully satisfactory, even in the case of small and intimate groups. Where major decisions must be made, as frequently happens in a modern society, by large groups scattered over a considerable territory, the machinery and techniques now available are grossly inadequate. On the technical side, therefore, the discovery of vastly improved techniques of group deliberation and decision is probably the most significant problem of democratic reconstruction (unless it is the problem of insuring that the people have full access to real facts on any issues that concern them — a problem that is, at bottom, simply a phase of the larger problem of group control and action).

Despite the great importance of these technical problems, the major difficulties, as the previous discussion has indicated, are not technical. They are moral and intellectual, growing directly out of conflicting conceptions of the ends of social policy.

The significance of this analysis for public education is relatively clear. A school designed to grapple with the problems of democracy in the present crisis must undertake to develop three qualities in its pupils: first, a democratic personality and character; second, a clear understanding of the major issues involved in the restoration of intellectual and moral consensus and in the reconstruction of the institutional structure of society, particularly with respect to the three areas noted above; third, a considerable facility and skill in the use of democratic techniques of group deliberation and action.

Accordingly, the social-problems criterion must be construed in these terms. It does not imply a narrow study of particular social issues considered in isolation from the social context and from one another. Rather, it calls for a curriculum that would provide the student with the necessary bases for intelligent thought and action, in a period of social transformation, by providing him with the experiences and the materials required to develop a broad and penetrating comprehension of the present social situation, with its trends, its problems, and its potentialities. Nor does the social-problems criterion imply a curriculum limited to intellectual understanding alone. On the contrary, its meaning must be interpreted in such a way as to include also within its purview the experiences and materials required to build democratic personalities skilled in techniques of group deliberation and action.

STEPHEN M. COREY
A " failure " assesses the curriculum

No I'm not very good in school. This is my second year in the seventh grade and I'm bigger and taller than the other kids. They like me all right, though, even if I don't say much in the schoolroom, because outside I can

Stephen M. Corey, " The Poor Scholar's Soliloquy," *Childhood Education*, 20:219–220, January, 1944. Reprinted by permission.

tell them how to do a lot of things. They tag me around and that sort of makes up for what goes on in school.

I don't know why the teachers don't like me. They never have very much. Seems like they don't think you know anything unless they can name the book it comes out of. I've got a lot of books in my own room at home — books like *Popular Science, Mechanical Encyclopedia,* and the Sears' and Ward's catalogues, but I don't very often just sit down and read them through like they make us do in school. I use my books when I want to find something out, like whenever Mom buys anything secondhand I look it up in Sears' or Ward's first and tell her if she's getting stung or not. I can use the index in a hurry to find the things I want.

In school, though, we've got to learn whatever is in the book and I just can't memorize the stuff. Last year I stayed after school every night for two weeks trying to learn the names of the Presidents. Of course I knew some of them like Washington and Jefferson and Lincoln, but there must have been thirty altogether and I never did get them straight.

I'm not too sorry though because the kids who learned the Presidents had to turn right around and learn all the Vice Presidents. I am taking the seventh grade over but our teacher this year isn't so interested in the names of the Presidents. She has us trying to learn the names of all the great American inventors.

I guess I just can't remember names in history. Anyway, this year I've been trying to learn about trucks because my uncle owns three and he says I can drive one when I'm sixteen. I already know the horsepower and number of forward and backward speeds of twenty-six American trucks, some of them Diesels, and I can spot each make a long way off. It's funny how that Diesel works. I started to tell my teacher about it last Wednesday in science class when the pump we were using to make a vacuum in a bell jar got hot, but she said she didn't see what a Diesel engine had to do with our experiment on air pressure so I just kept still. The kids seemed interested though. I took four of them around to my uncle's garage after school and we saw the mechanic, Gus, tearing a big truck Diesel down. Boy, does he know his stuff!

I'm not very good in geography either. They call it economic geography this year. We've been studying the imports and exports of Chile all week but I couldn't tell you what they are. Maybe the reason is I had to miss school yesterday because my uncle took me and his big trailer truck down state about two hundred miles and we brought almost ten tons of stock to the Chicago market.

He had told me where we were going and I had to figure out the highways to take and also the mileage. He didn't do anything but drive and turn where I told him to. Was that fun! I sat with a map in my lap and told him to turn south or southeast or some other direction. We made seven stops and drove over five hundred miles round trip. I'm figuring now what his oil cost and also the wear and tear on the truck — he calls it depreciation — so we'll know how much we made.

I even write out all the bills and send letters to the farmers about what their pigs and beef cattle brought at the stockyards. I only made three mistakes in 17 letters last time, my aunt said — all commas. She's been through high school and reads them over. I wish I could write school themes that way. The last one I had to write was on, " What a Daffodil Thinks of Spring," and I just couldn't get going.

I don't do very well in school in arithmetic either. Seems I just can't keep my mind on the problems. We had one the other day like this:

If a 57 foot telephone pole falls across a cement highway so that $17\frac{3}{6}$ feet extend from one side and $14\frac{9}{17}$ feet from the other, how wide is the highway?

That seemed to me like an awfully silly way to get the width of a highway. I didn't even try to answer it because it didn't say whether the pole had fallen straight across or not.

Even in shop I don't get very good grades. All of us kids made a broom holder and a bookend this term and mine were sloppy. I just couldn't get interested. Mom doesn't use a broom anymore with her new vacuum cleaner and all our books are in a bookcase with glass doors in the parlor. Anyway, I wanted to make an end gate for my uncle's trailer but the shop teacher said that meant using metal and wood both and I'd have to learn how to work with wood first. I didn't see why but I kept still and made a tie rack at school and the tail gate after school at my uncle's garage. He said I saved him $10.

Civics is hard for me, too. I've been staying after school trying to learn the " Articles of Confederation " for almost a week because the teacher said we couldn't be good citizens unless we did. I really tried, because I want to be a good citizen. I did hate to stay after school, though, because a bunch of boys from the south end of town have been cleaning up the old lot across from Taylor's Machine Shop to make a playground out of it for the little kids from the Methodist home. I made the jungle gym from old pipe and the guys made me Grand Mogul to keep the playground going. We raised enough money collecting scrap this month to build a wire fence clear around the lot.

Dad says I can quit school when I'm fifteen and I'm sort of anxious to because there are a lot of things I want to learn how to do and as my uncle says, I'm not getting any younger.

SECTION **4. The classroom situation: Methods and discipline**

Closely related to the problem of *what* should be taught is that of *how* to teach. In all areas of the curriculum, method and content interact; in some areas they are inextricable. Although this is not a textbook on methods of teaching, this brief section on methods and discipline is included to recognize the interrelationship of the what and the how of teaching.

Perhaps the most effective way of dealing with methods of teaching would be to describe hypothetical teaching situations in each subject matter area. Since this is impractical, a next most effective substitute would be to identify a general method that has applicability to all learning situations. And this is precisely what Earl S. Johnson does in his sprightly selection that follows. He is concerned with a method of inquiry that is applicable to " all *problems* in the area of human affairs — and which are not necessarily *social* problems. They are all, however, problems of cause-and-effect."

As you read the selection by Johnson, note especially the tacit relationships between method, content, and aims of education. In the hands of a skillful teacher the process of problem-solving becomes as significant as (and sometimes more significant than) the subject dealt with. It is this process which has the carry-over and transfer value to other problematic situations. Furthermore, the very decision to use a problem-solving rather than a rote, mechanistic, or authoritarian method more suitably reflects the aims of education in a democratic society. In an authoritarian society an open-ended problem-solving approach would be either unnecessary, undesirable, or intolerable — especially in the area of social problems.

This selection is concluded with two readings dealing with discipline. Probably no other aspect of teaching poses as much immediate concern to the beginning teacher (and sometimes even to the experienced one) as the matter of maintaining discipline in the classroom. Unfortunately, no standard set of admonitions can be given to all teachers because differences in personality make-up among teachers result in each disciplinary situation's being uniquely different for each teacher. A uniform handbook of gimmicks for teachers will not do. It is for this reason that Herbert J. Klausmeier deals with underlying reasons for disciplinary behavior and suggests constructive, positive approaches to forestall such behavior. William C. Morse follows with an analysis of the " get tough " versus the mental health approach to discipline. Morse particularly recognizes the relationship between discipline and the establishment of desirable value orientations in pupils. Here again we see how such a theoretical matter as the aims of education in a democratic society exerts a profound influence on such a practical matter as classroom management.

EARL S. JOHNSON
The method of inquiry

The method of inquiry is tentative. The method of inquiry has none of the lock step, certainty, or the cocksureness of the Herbartian or Morrison methods. It has a tentativeness which does not permit the teacher to know the exact order of steps to be taken respecting a given problem of inquiry. This is just the state of mind in which the scientist, bent on scientific research, finds himself. The absence of certainty as to the order of steps is,

From Earl S. Johnson, *Theory and Practice of the Social Studies*, 1956, pp. 207–214. Reprinted by permission of The Macmillan Company.

however, more than compensated for by the thrill which accompanies inquiry which takes its cue from whatever lies at hand.

An ideal order of the steps in inquiry. The method of inquiry is a *method*; hence it does not operate at haphazard. Each phase or step seems almost to suggest if not dictate the next step. This is true, wherever you start. I shall now show the ideal order of its steps or phases. I shall leave the area of study unnamed and I shall not give a name to the problem on which it is used. I wish to make it clear, however, that the method of inquiry is applicable to all *problems* in the area of human affairs — and which are not necessarily *social* problems. They are all, however, problems of cause-and-effect. . . .

1. The identification or creation of a problem situation of some kind: " Who killed Cock Robin? " — or its social studies equivalent. Note that it is a problem situation, not a discrete problem. The *Gestalt* or form is not clear; there is a field of things which appear to belong together but the lines of relationship are obscure. The *Gestalt* has no clear center.

There is an " idea " in it, but do not worry if it cannot be stated at once. That is just why it is a problem situation rather than a problem. If the idea is readily apparent then you have nothing about which to invite a search. It is " too easy " and the task is over before it is begun. Even if the idea which is central to the problem situation were stated that would not, of itself, guarantee that its meaning is known. Only to " say it " is not to find it.

You try to excite the class: the response is variable. You are manipulating stimuli. All sorts of exploratory activities might be employed: a movie, a short talk, suggestions from the class, etc. These are to serve the purpose of putting the class in *a tension* to bring it to *attention*. This is an ever-so-slight frustration, not more than that. Or call it the creation of a block or a doubt. You want to get the class in a " slight jam " — from which you wish to help to rescue it. If there is nothing to overcome, if there is no tension to release, then there is no beginning. If no beginning, no middle; and if no middle, no end.

In short, in this phase — which may reappear in the course of the enterprise because the path of inquiry, like true love, seldom runs smoothly — you try to create such a state of concern and interest that every other object except the one at hand is banished from the minds of all. That takes some doing.

You and the class have but one objective at this time: to get a clue which will give insight into how the problem may be stated in explicit terms. The more the class shares in the planning of it, the greater interest you start with. If your students press you to teach about it, you may be sure that they have some views and opinions on it — whatever the " it " turns out to be. These will range from cocksure to cloudy ones.

But what is your aim or objective? Only this: to get a sharper picture of what makes something " tick," how something works, etc. You state your objectives only in a very general way: one or more hunches, clues or call them hypotheses if you wish, so that the act of inquiry may begin and go forward. You are simply " going hunting " — what explicit game will be bagged no one knows. Scouting for game is the first objective; the more specific objectives will follow when the game shows up — rabbits, quail, or maybe larger " animals."

2. Throughout this phase you are doing your best to suggest clues without giving the plot away. You know the answer but you are not going to take your students by the hand and lead them to it. You want a *hunt* — not a sure-fire *find*. Your attempt to stimulate interest takes the form of raising and planting questions. I say " raising questions " rather than " asking questions." The difference is this: to ask a question suggests a direct answer response; to raise a question connotes that some time must elapse before it is " lowered "; it is for consideration, not for immediate answer.

Many kinds of assignments, many enterprises or projects may enter here; if questions are asked facts will be needed, and facts suggest further questions. The problem situation is beginning to clear up — a problem is emerging. The questions tease it out of hiding. They might be such as these: to whom is this a problem? To whom not and why in both cases? What facts seem to suggest this? How did the problem arise? How widely is it felt? What specific interest or stake do various groups have in it? What facts are known about it? What would happen if it were solved? Would new problems be created in the very solving of this one? What resources — machinery, finance, leadership — are needed to solve it? Are the causal factors simple or complex? How readily can they be seen by ordinary people? How deeply is the community affected by the problem? Who will be hurt if it is solved?

3. These questions help to narrow the field of your students' perceptions, and help to sharpen the *Gestalt* by putting things into place. They have their origin in wild, vague, or random hunches but they are the raw materials for specific hypotheses. They give you the search leads. Research is quite as appropriate because there is always a trace of common-sense wisdom at work which needs to be reworked or researched. Assume that two or more promising hypotheses (*née* hunches) come to light. That's right, come to light. They spring to the mind by the provocation which questions create. (Teaching is always more provoking than " telling.") These hypotheses suggest a division of labor which will be filled out in terms of the different interests and ideas that have been aroused and manifested. Some students will work alone — don't force people to co-operate; we want some lone wolves, the good kind! Committees may be formed: research committees who will dig and delve. Such activities as these may be tried out to see what they produce: interviews, " resource people " brought into class, bibliographies assembled, a map may be appropriate — it is better hand-made than " bought " — all learning has a kinesthetic aspect — biology is part of

thinking; a movie, a filmstrip may throw some light on the problem, a field trip, etc. At appropriate times, difficult if not impossible to plan with calendar precision, the findings will be pooled — discussion may ensue, even ought to.

4. In this net of experience, the " right " hypothesis is caught.

5. This " right " hypothesis has earned its place through competition. It is now put to work. It leads to the appropriate data. These data are the ground for a judgment or conclusion. Once the data confirm it, it is put to test in similar situations. This may require some changes in it and subsequent changes in a judgment or conclusion. But this depends on the size of the universe which is being examined as well as its complexity. Once these revisions have been made the inquiry is satisfied.

The teacher's role in inquiry. This continuum of learning experiences applies to both you and your students. For them it should have a fresh and exciting character. For you it may be pretty routine, even " old stuff," because of your greater knowledge. You may, nevertheless, find a great reward in a new experience in *communication* rather than in the discovery of new truth. This suggests what your role is, as distinct from your students'. You have an idea (or more than one) in the back of your head. It is as clear and precise as you can state it to yourself. This is the bull's-eye of the enterprise, which may be a whole unit or a part of one. (For your students it is much less clear, even unknown.) If the matter at hand has to do with the provisions of the Constitution you have, in your head, the *idea* that learning them by heart will be well-nigh worthless *unless* they are seen as *means to insure justice* or whatever else you wish to emphasize. This *idea of justice* is your central and crystal-clear idea. You will, eventually, seek to make it as central and crystal-clear to your students. Suppose that the enterprise has to do with the importance of *distance in space* as a factor related to the ability of the people, in a country with such great land expanse as ours, to act in concert on some public issue. Many other factors are, of course, involved but at this time you want to drive home the significance of " distance in space." That is *your* central idea. And so it goes. But, not until you are sure of *your* central idea, or sense one that the students seem to be trying to work out, can you know which stimuli to manipulate. Your selection and manipulation of them is guided by an idea.

Although, ideally, everything I have said involves the fullest participation of your students, the responsibility which you have inherited as *leader* cannot be minimized. This involves you in suggesting, correcting, demonstrating, asking questions, giving encouragement, praising, and the many things which no teacher can completely delegate to students. Nothing can escape *you.* You are all eyes and ears. You are the teacher and it is your business to *teach.* . . .

While I would not for a minute suggest that you arrogate to yourself the role of authoritarian, you have every right to think of yourself as an *author-*

ity in both method and substance. This requires the balance of a sense of humility and genuine pride — in what proportions I cannot tell you.

The conception of your role which I have in mind was given by H. G. Wells.

I want simply this world better taught . . . I will not suppose that there is any greater knowledge of things than men actually possess today, but instead of its being confusedly stored in many minds and books and many languages, it has all been sorted and set out plainly so that it can easily be used. . . .

When I ask you to suppose a world instructed and educated in the place of this old traditional world of unguided passion . . . a world taught by men instead of a world neglected by hirelings, I do not ask you to imagine any miraculous change in human nature. I ask you only to suppose that each mind has the utmost enlightenment of which it is capable instead of its being darkened and overcast. Everyone is to have the best chance of being his best self. Everyone is to be living in the light of the acutest self-examination and the clearest mutual self-criticism.[1]

A classification of aims. Although a later chapter will deal with aims, it is appropriate now to identify those which are basic to every unit of study: reliable knowledge, skill in inquiry, and attitudes. These will, we hope, defeat ignorance, muddle-headedness, and apathy. New methods of perceiving will be learned, new facts acquired and these, in turn, will engender new attitudes and patterns of conduct. Thus knowledge, policy, and action will be related. Doubts, dissatisfactions, and states of unrest will take the form of ideas and these will be tested. The *activities* in which you and your students co-operatively engage will mediate the whole enterprise. In it all, the fallacy that the mind is first sharpened and then used will be exposed for what it is. The mind will be sharpened by its *use*. Learning will be interpreted as problem solving. Interest will be the shaft which gives unity and continuity to the whole experience. Thus the course of productive thinking will run.[2]

The rhythm of romance, precision, and romance. There is a cyclical rhythm to its course. This is the rhythm of romance-precision-romance. In giving structure to the teaching-learning act, this cycle performs a useful function which is, of course, the purpose of structure. These phases of the teaching-learning act are not sharply and distinctly separable because they

---

[1] *The Undying Fire* (New York: The Macmillan Co., Copyright 1919), pp. 182 and 184.

[2] An account of the dynamics and logic of productive thinking is to be found in Max Wertheimer, *Productive Thinking* (New York: Harper & Brothers, 1945). See especially " Introduction," pp. 1–13, in which Tables I, Ia, and II set forth the course of thinking under the rules of deductive and inductive logic, and the association theory, respectively. Read " Conclusion," pp. 189–215, in which these theories are examined and compared with the logic of the method of inquiry which I have used.

are *phases* rather than fixed steps. Whitehead calls them " distinctions of emphasis," each one of which is present throughout the act. There is only " alternation of dominance " among them.[3]

Manifestations of romance. The hallmark of romance, wherever it enters into inquiry, is imagination. Inquiry begins with it, for the thing sought must be sought first by imagining *how it may be sought.* Without curiosity there can be no quest: the thrill of the quest is the romance of it. Rote learning is dead, unimaginative, provokes no curiosity — hence is unromantic. Romance is the art phase of the work of the scientist. Work does not dull romance, only make-work dulls it. Assignments that have only the purpose of setting tasks that are unrelated to anything but a teacher's notion that through them the student will be made to learn are also death to romance. If you would encourage your students to learn you must appeal first to their imagination and from that, romantically invite them into reasoning and thinking.

Romance is the affective phase of learning without which it will be idle to expect much on its effective side. It inheres in the very nature of the experimental outlook and attitude. It inheres also in the thrill which attends discovery. It is part of the ferment with which all genuine inquiry begins, and which exists throughout its course. If affection for the object of study can be fixed there will be something to deal with through sympathetic imagination.

Interest is another name for romance. This is the dynamic which sustains the student when the discomfort of thought, the " painful suspension " of inquiry seems more than he can bear. It renders difficulties less difficult. It keeps him from losing heart.

It may, sometimes, impede or forestall inquiry by jumping over it. Human interest in consequences is sometimes so romantic as to seek to escape the discipline of reason. Pascal once said that most of the evils of life arise from man's being unable to " sit still in a room." That is hard; he wants to be up and doing.

The demands of the romantic mood in learning dictate that you begin not with abstractions but with concretions. The abstractions they may illustrate will then come easier. This means that you begin where the student is: with his own involvements which, if not romantic, are at least emotional. There is also some danger in overdoing reference to the purely contemporary. It is often too commonplace and the task of rendering it uncommon is not easy. Knowledge sometimes requires that it be *suffered*; romance can relieve some of the suffering, but not all of it, for discipline cannot be denied its claim.

But there is some discipline and precision in the romantic phase. No part of an education can do without discipline, rigor, and precision. But

---

[3] See Whitehead, *The Aims of Education,* Chapter 3, " The Rhythmic Claims of Freedom and Discipline."

do not forget that the adult world is not like the world of youth. The former is more complicated and will repel inquiry about it if it is thrust on the student in its demanding and complex form.

Romance will persist throughout if learning can be made a game. The essence of a game is continuous novelty. The sheer joy of playing it overcomes the ardor of playing it. Without this spirit knowledge is inert. Without romance, knowledge may even be held in contempt.

The cadence changes. But the cadence changes and the act of inquiry becomes more demanding. If romance has dominated the beginning it has put the student in the mood for doing more precise things. The phase of precision calls for patience, waiting, and ultimate rather than immediate rewards. It demands an investment which does not pay off at once. It changes the emphasis to concentration, to the use of skills, to studying, figuring out, making connections, and arriving at conclusions.

Precision is misunderstood. Not infrequently this is the only stage, not by necessity but by virtue of a teacher's believing that you have to " make 'em work." This is the view which Mr. Dooley reported in his aphorism that " it doesn't matter what you teach the child so long as he doesn't like it." But teaching does not find its genuine directives in seeking to please the student. It finds them in making learning as rewarding and hence as pleasurable as possible. The limit of precision is reached when imagination is stifled; when rules are followed in rote fashion, when the student is commanded to do this or that. Precision does not inhere in teacher authority. It inheres in the attractiveness of the enterprise.

Skill demands repetition but this need not be rote. It can be made to combine romance and precision by the will to solve a problem. Order is not enough. The requirements of precision are more complex than that. Precision permits order with a touch of novelty in it. Without it, precision degenerates into punishment. It is brute facts with which your students must work. Only by a mixture of novelty and romance can their nature be tamed.

Romance and precision co-operate. Hypothesis-making is both romantic and precise. Here the rhythm is one of up and down and of shuttling between. Facts come hard. The printed page is often uninviting; it is too impersonal. But hard work may be no less hard but less onerous, and the printed page may be worth interpretation if the pitch of interest can be kept high. Thus romance serves precision. The truth and the hardness of a fact or a proposition may be the more rewarding if they can be presented with an appeal not only to reason but also to sentiment.

If the object with which you are dealing is abstract show its nature in concrete examples. If it be unfamiliar show, by analogy, that it is like something the student already knows. Students cannot imagine anything with which they have had no acquaintance. The approach to the unknown is through the known. This makes it no less precise — only knowable. If the matter be difficult and almost beyond their reach, couple it with their interest. Theirs will be the gain. It is not the precise truth of an idea that leads to its acceptance as much as its truth-appeal; it must be as congenial truth as you can make it.

The transition from romance to precision. The big problem comes in the transition from romance to precision. At this time the breadth of treatment narrows and you seek what is exact, more than what is picturesque. This is the state of " the grammar of science." This is the phase when activity is more than play. It is the activity of analysis under rules of the game. The rules are dominant; the game spirit is recessive. Still there can be what Whitehead calls " the adventure of thought." But hard work need not be irksome, however much it demands precision. It need not turn into drudgery. Right and wrong ways must be distinguished.

Romance again dominates. Then follows the phase when romance is again dominant. Whitehead calls this the phase of generalization. Its romance inheres in the fact that doubt is now turned to belief. The roadblock is down; action can go on. The judgment which has been made can now be tested — even played with to see how well it works in like situations. This is the fun of proof. The garden which was weeded in the middle stage of precision now yields its crop. This is the stage of consummation.

Romance becomes orderly. Romance is not unorderly now, as it was in the beginning. It is orderly and in that fact lies a sense of accomplishment. Order has been *created:* this is the productive, the creative, the working act. Synthesis brings its own reward. The student may now show what he has learned. He is now effective and finds even an affective thrill in being that. He is now in command of principles; his conduct may thus be principled in both intellectual and moral ways. He can now direct his thinking. He can now generalize; he is relieved from the pressure of mere events; facts are now clothed with meaning. He may sense the meaning of Emerson's belief that " generalization is always a new flux of divinity into the mind: hence the thrill that attends it."

HERBERT J. KLAUSMEIER
Mental hygiene and classroom discipline

How Robert Merriman, now a junior-high-school principal, promoted mental health and encouraged self-discipline as an experienced teacher is reported as follows:

My teaching responsibilities are three freshman classes of General Science, two classes of Senior Forum, and one General Review class for seniors who have had academic difficulties. The total number of students per week

From Herbert J. Klausmeier, *Teaching in the Secondary School*, 1958, pp. 378–397. Reprinted by permission of Harper & Brothers.

is about one hundred and eighty. We have an hour-and-four-minute class period, five periods a day, and all students take five subjects per day with no free periods.

Let us first consider the freshman General Science group. This group consists of about eighty per cent rural students and students coming from parochial schools. The class is required for these students and is elective for those who have come up through our city school system. Obviously, there is a wide variety of abilities, characteristics, interests, and backgrounds represented in this group. . . .

The first day in class I distribute books, make assignments, and spend about fifteen minutes explaining what I expect so far as class procedure is concerned. The main discussion is about mutual respect, one student for another and my respect for each of them. This acts only as an introduction to the subject but I stress this phase each day as we continue through the year. Only a short time passes before the student realizes the idea of respect and responsibility, and " discipline problems " do not exist.

Though we teach a basic background of subject matter, my primary job is to know each student as well as possible as soon as possible. I check cumulative records and make whatever notations I feel important in my class book. Then I spend several weeks trying to learn the characteristics of each student. Usually by the end of the first four weeks I know the special interests of each student. I know how he will respond in class and the type of question he can handle best. I become familiar with the student's home environment and learn who his friends are. By this time I have had an opportunity to meet most of my students informally and have had a chance to talk farming with an interested farm youngster, hunting and trapping with another, shows with some, or sewing, or any of a number of different activities in which they are interested. I want to be interested in their activities and want them to know I am because soon I share their interest and confidence. The net result: the class is not a formal " sweat session " but is rather informal and becomes fun.

After becoming acquainted more or less personally with each student it is an easy matter to " bend " subject matter toward the interest and ability of the student, and the student responds confidently because he feels that this information applies to him. Soon the " slow " student feels success and achievement and he is willing to go ahead and try the next assignment. The " fast " student likewise feels he can master the current subject and there are individual projects and assignments for him in addition.

Assignments are made in a block form covering a total unit of work. I also propose dates for completion but include with this schedule the statement that these are only probable dates, that discussions, slides, or the students' projects may delay this schedule. My main emphasis is that I do not care how fast we go but I do care how well they do and I want to include all the phases of the subject in which they are interested. So far this approach has worked very well. One of the contributing factors lies in our schedule. During the hour-and-four-minute period there is ample time for study and discussion, demonstration, or activity. Quite often the first part of the hour, about thirty minutes, is used for study and the last part for activities, demonstrations, etc. My thought here is that each student has had a chance to stretch between classes and it is easier to study the first part of the hour. As soon as interest lags, students become uneasy, or tired of reading and individual study, I get them into discussions, moving around in lab work, etc. This program in class is not " iron-clad " but is changed in accordance with the day. Some days the group is uneasy and not inclined to study. When I sense this I move them into some active participation. Other days it seems they want to continue studying throughout the period so we do just that. With the students in class for study instead of in study hall, the individual help theory becomes practice.

Differences in abilities and interests are provided for in several ways. Probably the most important adjustment to ability and interest is to avoid a set scale of accomplishment that all students must attain. For some students a grade of 75 would be a high mark and their test scores would average about 65 per cent. But the final grade would probably be a " C " or even higher. If someone wanted to know how a student with an average of 65 got a " C " I would show him that class participation, interest, effort, extra credit activities, along with tests and daily work, are all incorporated in the final mark.

My " discipline " is handled on a mutual respect basis. I have yet to " bawl out " a student in class, nor do I send him to the office as I feel he has not violated anything in the office. Instead when he leaves class I ask if he would please stop in after school as I feel we had better arrive at an understanding before both of us get into trouble with each other. In eight years of experience no one has failed to appear for that after-school meeting, and no one has left without a satisfactory explanation and readjustment for both of us so that we can each do a better job. I try to make my " discipline " a matter of mutual agreement instead of my telling the student what I think of him and letting it go at that.

Seating arrangements in all classes are primarily determined by the students. There are two exceptions. First, if the student has a physical defect, I try to seat him where it will suit him best. The other exception occurs only if the student feels he is headed for trouble if he continues to sit where he is and requests to have his seat changed. In this instance someone else has to be moved as we have no spare seats.

Generally speaking, an individual or a group of individuals lives up to a reputation that they feel they have or that others have for them. By instilling in the student or the group a feeling of security, mutual respect, and a display of compatibility, I soon have a sound, harmonious learning situation. By earning respect instead of demanding respect and by steering the students instead of commanding them, a good learning situation is readily achieved.

In spite of a heavy teaching load, Mr. Merriman was able to adhere to the following principles:

1. Students are understood as individuals.
2. An orderly work situation is maintained.
3. The classroom climate focuses on self-discipline and group control.
4. Correction and sometimes punishment are necessary.
5. Some students and classes require special treatment.

Mr. Merriman taught in a moderate-sized community where education is generally valued highly, the curriculum is flexible enough to meet the needs of all the students well, and the number of antisocial groups and maladjusted students is relatively small. In communities where these conditions do not prevail, some of the principles he followed might need to be modified. But everyone, regardless of where he teaches, must recognize that discipline is closely related to the overall learning situation. No teacher can have a poor learning situation and at the same time maintain good discipline and promote the mental health of the students.

The above implies that the goals of classroom discipline are twofold: to help each student grow out of dependence on adults for direction and control to self-direction and self-discipline, and to set up an orderly work situation so that learning will proceed smoothly for all students. Promoting mental health requires that these two goals be achieved, and the other principles stated above are also conducive to mental health, as will be shown in the subsequent discussion.

STUDENTS ARE UNDERSTOOD AS INDIVIDUALS

Knowing a student as an individual involves, among other things, becoming acquainted with him and identifying his interests, aptitudes, and achievements. There are many ways in which a teacher may become acquainted with a student — visiting his home, making a seating chart the first day of school so he can associate names with faces, and allowing each student to talk about his interests soon after the school term starts. Also useful are the cumulative record, tests, and informal evaluation procedures. . . . It is especially important to discover how to meet the developmental needs of adolescents if the teacher wants to promote mental health and to minimize disruptive conduct and shy, withdrawing behavior.

Classroom disturbances are often related to the adolescent's need to control his emotional expression, to make satisfactory adjustments to his agemates, and to establish new and satisfying relationships with adults.

Disciplinary procedures designed to help students make good adjustments to their agemates utilize the need for attention and approval. Opportunity is provided for students to discuss problems and lessons with one another, to work together and to make rules of conduct for working together, and to evaluate progress in living up to individual and group standards. In this classroom situation the teacher serves as the leader to insure that the need for attention and approval is satisfied in socially approved ways; thus this need becomes a positive motive for providing a better learning situation. The teacher who helps adolescents gain attention and approval by doing their work well is capitalizing on this need. Not to permit the adolescent to satisfy this need while directing his activities toward useful ends is to invite a variety of behaviors not conducive to a good learning situation. The antisocial behavior manifest in an extreme form in gangs of delinquents may have originated in the classroom. These gangs enable adolescents to satisfy their need for the attention and approval of their agemates; the means of doing so are destructive rather than constructive, and hence are injurious to society and the adolescents.

Young people's need for attention and approval from their teacher is perhaps not so strong as it is from their agemates; however, many show this need. The adolescent's feelings toward adults are often ambivalent; that is, he wants to be completely independent of adult control but at the same time he feels very insecure unless he knows that his parent or teacher approves of him. High-school students are in various stages as far as this need is concerned; some need a great deal of approval from their teacher, whereas others are relatively mature. Constructive disciplinary procedures take into account the differences in development, give the students increasing freedom of decision when they are ready for it, and use their need for adult approval to help them in making choices. The teacher who makes all the rules and strives for uniform obedience is not helping his students increase their self-control.

Controlling emotional expression often presents problems for students. Adolescents frequently find themselves in situations in which disruptive emotions are involved. As preventive measures, teachers need to be familiar with the kind of situations which arouse such emotions, to recognize symptoms of emotional stress, and to avoid crises in their classrooms. The teacher who would help young people mature emotionally organizes constructive activities in which they learn about emotions, learn how to analyze situations objectively, recognize socially approved methods for relieving emotional tensions, develop skill in meeting problem situations, and learn how to discard immature patterns of emotional response. In many classrooms these kinds of learnings are largely incidental. Nevertheless, every teacher may well give attention to the student who is highly immature or infantile emotionally because he will be a constant source of irritation for the group until he becomes more mature.

AN ORDERLY WORK SITUATION IS MAINTAINED

All human beings try to find meaning in their activities. An individual does this as he can perceive order in an assignment, in work, in his relationships with others. Disorderly, meaningless situations are not conducive to mental health. Disrespect for constituted authority and the resulting disorder are not good for the adolescent, for the teacher, or for society. Therefore, the teacher should manifest enthusiastic, confident leadership.

This and some of the other characteristics of an orderly work situation are considered in this section.

Manifest confident leadership. In his first meeting with a class, the teacher has the responsibility of establishing his position as the figure of authority in the classroom. Everyone — parents, students, and those who hire him — expect him to maintain order, using means appropriate to the age and characteristics of the students and the size of the class. The means of securing order vary widely. The means used by the woman teacher with a soft voice differ from those used by a large man with a commanding voice. Moreover, the same teacher may vary the methods used from class to class. The following account by an experienced teacher describes one of the many ways to establish student respect for the teacher as the leader.

It is the first meeting with a tenth-grade woodwork class, which is elective and has 24 students. So that everyone has a definite understanding of what is expected of each student and each student has a good idea of what to expect of me, I discuss the general procedures to be followed by the class. These include definite things to do at the beginning of the period, at the end of the period, and during emergencies.

In the first part of the period, I list the special materials needed and discuss the care of equipment in the shop. During the last part of the period, I discuss briefly the objectives of the course and the outcomes expected, with the students raising questions at any point in the discussion.

I find that the large majority of the students are interested in doing what is expected of them when they know what to do. The very small minority that does not want to conform usually follows instructions in order to get the approval of the large majority. Also, if a student violates safety rules or disobeys instructions, he is not allowed to continue on a project or use a machine until he and I have had opportunity for a conference.

In this teacher's classes, the work situation is good from the start; and when the students are ready to accept responsibility, it is given to them.

It is wise to be firm in early meetings with students rather than easy-going. The degree of firmness needed varies widely with the situation, as the following reports from experienced teachers suggest.

My first teaching experience, years ago, was in a Vermont high school. I started confidently, full of hope and enthusiasm. I was going to be the kind of teacher I always liked as a student — a teacher who was kind, courteous, and humorous. In this school, corporal punishment was widely practiced. Pupils were hit by teachers over the knuckles or finger tips with a ruler. Some were sent to the principal for paddlings. I had contempt for all of this.

I started with kind, humorous treatment of the students. Early in the school term, before I got far with the humorous part, I found myself in front of an auditorium study hall, with a ninth-grade boy on the floor and my foot on his chest, listening to the boy's protestations of what his father and big brother were going to do to me. Youngsters like this mistook kindness and humor for weakness but they regarded firm severity as an indication of strength. They came to school because state law compelled them to. Fortunately, this latter group was in the minority.

We shall not debate the wisdom of this teacher's means of establishing his role as the authority. There is a tendency in some schools, however, for students to see how far they can go with a new teacher. Generally, firmness during the first contacts does not frustrate the students who come to school to learn, and it pays with those who are testing the teacher. But students in many schools accept the teacher as authority without question, as shown in the following:

My classes are in United States History, eleventh-grade, with classes of thirty to thirty-six students. The majority of these students assume much responsibility for mature conduct. The problem of discipline, with very few exceptions, does not occur. The students and I have a feeling of mutual acceptance; courteous behavior is neither difficult to develop nor hard to maintain.

These students, as individuals, have every right to expect and receive treatment that I also desire to have afforded to me. When they come to me with reasons for failure to finish an assignment on time, I accept their reasons without questioning. Few take advantage of this, and instances are far between when students fail to have assignments in on time. In cases of disputed questions or wording in tests, I listen to their criticisms, and many times find it highly valuable and constructive. I believe that this acceptance of their ideas and views lends stature to the class and encourages growth in self-discipline.

This teacher, who is in a large senior high school, not only displays a desirable attitude toward his students but has established a school-wide reputation among the students as a good teacher. His students like his classes, do well in them, and learn self-discipline and control.

Establish zest for learning. Everyone who has observed small children closely marvels at their exploratory behavior. Preschool children ask questions concerning all phases of their environment: What is the moon? What makes lightning? Where do babies come from? Where is the airplane going? Why does the baby cry? Most mothers spend a considerable amount of time trying to discover where curiosity has led young children in their outdoor play. The nursery school and kindergarten build fences around playgrounds to keep this curiosity within supervisory limits. With few exceptions, young children are curious, exploratory, and eager to learn.

For many children, this zest is blunted during elementary and secondary school by restrictions imposed in the home, the neighborhood, and the school. In the first grade the urge for activity that leads to new discovery is thwarted by the need to conform to a confining situation — the classroom. Answers the child wants now to solve an important problem are deferred because a problem an adult wants solved takes precedence. Subjects in the high school are frequently taught as if every student needed the same dosage of an identical prescription. Eventually, the student no longer finds a challenge in the classroom learning situation; his previous eager search for solutions becomes passive tolerance or even open resistance.

The need for relating classroom experiences to out-of-school life and for helping the student see practical applications has been mentioned earlier several times. However, this need in no way denies that students should be helped to feel the thrill of discovery for its own sake. Typing for five minutes without error, playing something on the piano for the first time, giving a five-minute talk to one's classmates, building a desk, discovering how to solve a problem using a letter for an unknown quantity — all of these may be thrilling explorations. To what extent secondary-school classrooms may be workshops in which students may feel the thrill of making important discoveries is not known. In some classes this situation does prevail.

In classrooms where students are frustrated by having identical assignments, conforming to overly restrictive rules of conduct, or having to use monotonous work methods, many discipline problems arise. A teaching method that encourages passivity tends to destroy the zest for learning. Adapting learning experiences to student needs, using a variety of instructional materials, and encouraging students to find new solutions give zest to learning, promote mental health, and avoid discipline problems.

Set reasonable levels of achievement. Some teachers set requirements that are beyond reasonable limits. The student who is capable of doing slightly above average in geometry is encouraged to strive for perfection — to make a perfect score on timed tests. He is led to believe that he can and should do this, and he feels guilty when he fails to do so. Feelings of guilt which stem from failing to meet the ideals are common among better-than-average students. Teachers and parents who attempt to push adolescents beyond their ability by holding that perfection is the only goal create emotional hazards for normal development.

Perfectionism is often manifest in directions to students: " Do not be satisfied until your work is perfect "; " Work to get to the top "; " Solve the ten problems correctly in five minutes "; " Everyone should make one hundred percent on this test." Generally, these demands are unrealistic because of the nature of the distribution of abilities among students.

If requirements are set too low — the opposite extreme — students become complacent; they have no need to work for higher achievement or to improve their work or study methods. When students are not challenged sufficiently, they become satisfied with doing just enough to get by or with being near the top with minimum effort.

To help a class set reasonable levels of achievement, the teacher must understand each student's abilities in relation to the work at hand, help him set realistic goals, and aid him in making progress toward the goals.

Every teacher should realize that students are relatively unequal in abilities, and that when equal time is used to develop understandings and skills, differences in achievement become more rather than less evident. Each student needs to have standards that are in line with his ability. When he is frustrated because he cannot reach a teacher-set standard, he may cheat, lie, become unruly, or give up. When the standard is too low, he becomes complacent; and time he should use for improving his performance is spent idling, harassing the teacher and classmates, or engaging in other unproductive activities which tend to disrupt the classroom.

Closely related to the setting of standards is the use of tests. Tests may facilitate learning when the students know that they are being used to discover the extent to which correct responses have been established, to measure 'progress, and to overcome difficulties. Usually a teacher-led discussion after the test has been scored serves these purposes. Knowledge of his scores in relation to those of his classmates is also useful when interpreted properly. The student should realize that he may have done poorly because he did not study or is using a method of work which interferes with his progress. The student who has worked hard and done poorly in relation to his classmates but well in relation to his abilities should of course not be ridiculed or made to feel insecure. As long as curricula cannot be sufficiently broad to fit the varying abilities of school-age youth, students who do their best should not experience failure repeatedly, be " flunked out " of high school, or be encouraged to cheat or use other devious methods for passing tests.

Any test may be used to arouse fear, jealousy, and antagonism among students. It is easy to construct a difficult test and set such a high standard for passing that few students reach it. Students will surely become fearful of tests and antagonistic to them if the teacher writes unfavorable notes to parents, criticizes the class as a whole, or criticizes individual students in front of the class for having done poorly. Taking away privileges and assigning extra work have the same effect.

Students frequently fear tests because they cannot do as well as their parents hope, because they want to excel a sibling or a classmate, or because they want to win recognition based on competitive test scores. Some adults fear all test situations largely because of the way these were handled in school. Testing can be made constructive in the following ways: Make sure that the purposes of the tests for both student and teacher are clearly understood; give tests frequently so that each one does not become so important; give tests only as scheduled; use tests as a method by which students can measure their progress; help students recognize the factors that produce differential test scores; and finally, use the test results as a means of understanding students better and of organizing more effective learning experiences.

These elements of creating an orderly work situation — manifesting confident leadership, establishing a zest for learning, and setting reasonable levels of achievement — are related to understanding students as individuals and also to managing interpersonal group relations.

THE CLASSROOM CLIMATE FOCUSES ON SELF-DISCIPLINE AND GROUP CONTROL

The feelings of students and the expression of those feelings toward one another, toward learning and work procedures, and toward the teacher; and the feelings of the teacher toward the students and the classroom situation — all these forces operating simultaneously are responsible for the social climate of the classroom. Because the social climate vitally affects conduct and work, it should focus on self-discipline and group control. Social climates may be grouped in four categories: (1) anarchic, (2) repressed, (3) competitive, and (4) cooperative.

Anarchic climates. An anarchic climate is one in which there is great confusion and disorder, in which standards for conduct and work have not been established. This climate frequently appears when a teacher overestimates the maturity of the class and puts the students too suddenly completely on their own. It may also appear when the teacher has a poor sense of educational values or does not know how to guide adolescents. In any event, because there are no accepted group standards of control and no feeling of unity among the members, the conduct of the group is erratic, undisciplined, and disruptive.

The teacher whose sense of educational values is poor allows students to loaf instead of working, to ridicule one another, to express prejudices openly and maliciously, and to settle differences with fists. Such behavior, when condoned by a teacher, leads to great confusion in the class, to disunity, and a poor learning situation.

The teacher who overestimates the maturity of adolescents and suddenly makes them wholly responsible for deciding about work and controlling their conduct fails to recognize that progressing from dependence to independence is a gradual process that needs careful direction. . . . [L]aissez-faire leadership does not give students security or establish a feeling of unity and accord among them. This type of leadership led to low work output, much aimless activity, aggressive conduct, and frequent withdrawal from activities.

Repressed climates. A repressed climate is characterized by the absence of student initiative and participation in planning work or setting goals. The students do not talk or work together, or move about. They sit quietly and work individually in accordance with a leader's direction and rules. This climate results when the teacher remains aloof from his students and confines discussion to that between himself and a student. Repressed climates range from apathetic to covertly rebellious.

An apathetic repressed group is one in which the members are thoroughly dominated by their leader. They have lost initiative and no longer want responsibility for discovering problems or trying to solve them. This climate is exemplified outside the classroom in a caste system — a social organization in which individuals have accepted an inferior status and do nothing about improving it. Also typical is the home where the father rules with an iron hand and subjugates other members so thoroughly that they become apathetic. Some prisons and schools for delinquents are operated in this fashion. This climate is possible in the classroom only when the home and community are also active in repression. Children who have learned at home that it is better to submit than to resist may be perfectly willing to yield to a repressive teacher.

A covertly rebellious group is one in which the leader must constantly suppress surface aggression against him. The members of the group are united in feeling resentment against him and, outside the situation he controls, devise methods for resistance. When there is a unified feeling against the leader, the members use various methods for frustrating him — they refuse to work to full capacity or to carry out his suggestions promptly, and they discover ways for irritating him. In the classroom, loud blowing of the nose, faked crying, loud coughing and clearing of the throat, " accidental " dropping of books, and similar devices are indicative of a repressed rebellious attitude.

Continued repression leads to widespread maladjustment because of denial of the satisfaction of the needs for activity, attention, and approval. Any repressed group, whether in the home, the school, or the community, fails to achieve its potential production because initiative is lost or it is directed against the leader. As suggested early in the . . . [discussion] . . . , a teacher may wish to establish a repressed climate in his early meetings with a class in order to provide a good working situation. This climate should give way as quickly as possible to an atmosphere in which the focus is on the development of self-discipline and group control.

Competitive climates. A competitive climate is one in which group members direct their energy to becoming superior to others. Because our society is to a great extent competitive, many adolescents have learned to respond to competition as motivation. However, it is imperative to recognize that our society is also to some extent cooperative, and that, as a civilized society, we are committed not to sacrifice children or less effective adults for the sake of achieving and maintaining superiority. It is false to assume that because our society is somewhat competitive, adolescents should experience failure based on competitive standards in school. On the contrary, it is a well-established fact that children need to be successful in school if they are to meet competitive situations outside school with a fair degree of emotional stability. Delinquents, criminals, and psychotics frequently have histories of many school failures, but few successes.

Competitive climates may be classified as friendly, hostile, and punitive.

Friendly competitive. Competition in which rules have been established and are followed may be friendly and conducive to higher morale among group members. This, however, depends largely on the rules and on the goals being aimed at. The group leader is responsible for both these factors. In high-school wrestling, for example, definite rules are established and equality in competition is provided for by having only wrestlers of fairly equal weights compete. The rules eliminate danger of serious physical injury, and a referee decides when violations have occurred. So also with basketball, state regulations hold that competing schools must have relatively equal enrollment. Frequently, competitive athletics provides that the losers take on other losers. When the goal is to be at the top and the desire to win becomes stronger than the willingness to abide by the rules, the friendly feeling is lost.

Competition in the classroom may be friendly and stimulate work activity. The following factors make for friendly competition: Students who are relatively equal are competing; they understand and follow the rules; the goal is higher achievement or a better method of working rather than a material or symbolic reward; the goal is not so desirable that the students evade rules or take unfair advantage of one another to reach it; losing does not result in continuing inferiority feelings or eliminate the desire for further participation.

Hostile competitive. When members of a group compete with one another for material rewards such as tickets to a movie, for symbolic rewards such as marks, or for favors and approval from the leader, hostility may develop. In reward-directed competition, where all the members participate actively but relatively few obtain the reward, intense rivalry is inevitable. The work output of the whole group will decrease unless rewards are made progressively more desirable. That of the losers inevitably drops once they realize that they can never win the rewards.

Hostility manifests itself in various ways, among them the following: (1) Friendly relationships tend to break down. It becomes increasingly difficult for Mary to be considerate and interested in Esther's problems, for Esther is doing her utmost to be made class valedictorian, an honor that Mary also wants. (2) Aggressiveness increases. Jim, who wants to lead the violins in the orchestra, verbally attacks his competitor, Bill, and encourages Sally to date Bill so that he will be late for practice or miss it entirely. Bill may take more direct action and hide Jim's music. (3) Withdrawal conduct increases. Frequently the extremely hostile individual hides his feelings in a shell of isolation; he is not satisfied unless he wins, so he withdraws from normal social relationships, devoting his time and energy to beating others. Because he feels that others are out to beat him, he distrusts their motives and thus creates an unsurmountable barrier to normal interpersonal relationships.

Punitive competitive. In some competitive situations the losers are punished. This is extremely vicious when the individuals in a competitive situation are relatively unequal and when the losers are made scapegoats for the near winners. In punitive competition the leader frequently imposes the punishment; sometimes he arranges for the winners to punish the losers. Under such conditions, hostility is comparatively unrestrained, and open aggression is encouraged.

To some extent, the teacher who fails students who have done their best in a required class creates a punitive-competitive climate. When students are marked according to a predetermined system — for example, the top 10 percent A's, the next 23 percent B's, the next 34 percent C's, the next 23 percent D's, and the lowest 10 percent F's — those who do their best and still receive F's are being punished, for they must repeat the class, substitute some other one, or not be graduated. Equally important, each student who hoped for a mark higher than the one he got may feel that he is being punished for not having done well enough. This may be true of the student who wants an A but gets a B, especially if he needs the A to win a scholarship or some other award that he particularly desires.

Members of classroom groups may punish other members. The French teacher organizes his thirty students into five teams for a vocabulary contest, with the first-place team getting an A, the second-place team a B, and so on; the team in last place receives an F and is given extra work or is deprived of some privilege. In organizing the groups, the teacher picks out the five top students and tells them to choose, in rotation, five other members for their teams. Then the teacher says a French word; each student writes the English equivalent. At the end of the contest, team scores are computed on the basis of the total number all members had correct. In such a situation the better students on the losing teams will undoubtedly penalize the poorer ones for making them lose. The punishment will take the form of not choosing these students in the future, finding fault with them, snubbing them outside class, or making them feel humiliated or inadequate.

These examples show that the way achievement is handled may produce a punitive competitive climate. The teacher as the leader of the class may also consciously or inadvertently create this climate because of the way he handles conduct, as when he encourages students to ostracize other students who have had little or no opportunity to learn the particular code of conduct he wants observed. Here again rewards for measuring up to codes of conduct are put on a competitive basis for students whose ability to achieve them is unequal. The teacher praises a particular kind of conduct, bestows favors on the students who conform, and either punishes or urges their classmates to punish those who do not conform. This is especially vicious when students are punished for conditions they cannot control.

Cooperative climates. There is a basic difference in the motives underlying competition and cooperation. The motive for competitive action is twofold: winning, and personal gain. The motive for cooperative action is also twofold: to improve oneself and make a significant contribution to the group. The extent of personal achievement in the two may not vary significantly, but personal feelings do. In well-managed competitive groups, friendliness may be present; in poorly managed groups hostility and overt aggression are present. When members of a group are motivated to improve themselves for the group's advancement, there is no room for hostility or aggression; on the contrary, the group members are encouraged to help one another.

To establish a cooperative spirit among students who have already been strongly conditioned by competition is rather difficult because the winners are often unwilling to give up personal objectives for the group's advantage, and, having been accustomed to receiving rewards, they do not accept group goals as incentives for effort. The " What's in it for me? " attitude may be as difficult to overcome as any form of prejudice. Furthermore, students accustomed to occupying a middle or low place on the competitive ladder may not work toward a group goal because they feel inadequate in their relationships with one another.

Students usually work together better . . . when the groups are small; the members have similar interests and backgrounds; they are friendly toward one another when the groups are first formed; the goal they are working for is clearly understood; the leader's responsibility in the group is clearly established; and each member knows his responsibilities. The teacher who is planning to divide his class into groups, each group to contribute to a whole-class goal, should carefully consider all these factors. If his students are relatively immature or already strongly conditioned for competition, he may need to specify the members of each group so that students who are friendly and interested in similar work activities will be in the same group. Moreover, it is often wise to appoint the leader for each group and clearly outline the leaders' responsibilities to the class, to outline the work to be done by each group, and to help each group subdivide its responsibilities among its members. Though the ultimate goal is to have students assume responsibility for self-discipline and group control, the teacher must be careful to decrease his control gradually.

To summarize this discussion of social climates, the cooperative climate is best for encouraging self-discipline and group control. The friendly competitive climate is also useful in this respect. Anarchic climates produce no good results. A repressed climate is sometimes necessary at first to set up a good working situation. The best test of whether students are becoming self-disciplined and responsive to reasonable group control is to arrange cooperative projects, with the teacher's control gradually lessening. If the students are well disciplined and responsive to group standards, they will proceed with committee assignments and various group projects with relatively little need for teacher control of their conduct. The teacher will serve mainly as a resource person, helping the students to obtain information, develop better work methods and study habits, and evaluate the outcome of their efforts.

WILLIAM C. MORSE
Needed: New theory and practice in discipline

Much more is written about cultural disorganization than is done to master its effects. The same could be said of the current situation relative to discipline and that particular facet of cultural breakdown we are to discuss. Endless articles describe the need for discipline for today's youth, but few writers generate methods to deal effectively with the problem. In spite of words and attempts to develop programs, delinquency continues to increase. Apprehension and downright fright dictate that something must be done immediately.

Who is to inherit the major responsibility for action? Society already is quietly in the process of bequeathing this task to the schools, and one can hear many interesting rationalizations as to why this is the logical step. After all, the school is the one agency which enrolls all children. The school has trained personnel. The school has special services. And the school has over the years assumed increasing responsibility for pupil adjustment. Schools are the social agent for forming the new generation. Of course it follows that the schools should take the major responsibility in discipline.

Regardless of the truth or falsehood of what is implied by such assertions, the schools had best get ready for the additional responsibility. This making ready will not be a simple process, and the following considerations are offered as orientation to the school's role in discipline. After a brief examination of certain background factors, consideration will be given to the need for new direction in both theory and practice. The classroom teacher and the specialists must find a new team relationship. The techniques of discipline now in vogue must be examined.

BACKGROUND FACTORS SET THE STAGE

There are certain background factors which must be recognized before schools can formulate guidelines for their future action. These background factors put realistic limits on what the school should or can do. The following heterogeneous listing is a rapid overview of important items. Each item actually deserves far more extensive treatment than is possible here.

1. Many of the current difficulties evidenced in discipline and delinquency control are part of the over-all cultural condition. Schools cannot be expected to provide an antidote for total cultural defects.[1] Simplified solutions and exaggerated expectations are doomed to failure with attendant recrimination against the school.

William C. Morse, "School Discipline in the Next Decade," *Michigan Journal of Secondary Education*, 1:3–10, Winter, 1960. Reprinted by permission.

[1] A. K. Cohen, *Delinquent Boys* (Glencoe, Illinois: The Free Press, 1955).

2. The school's role has changed from *enhancing* values already implanted in the child elsewhere to one of *inculcating* the values in the first place. One more frequently finds parents who have consciously or unconsciously given up the attempt to train their children and have delegated this huge responsibility to the school.

The actual building of a value system in a pupil is a complex and difficult task, not too well understood by even the most wise of our professionals.[2]

The traditional laws of learning do not provide cues, and usual teaching techniques will not be adequate. One does not teach character like spelling. The process of fostering identifications will require a different order of pupil-teacher relationship. If it is to be accomplished, time will have to be provided in already crowded schedules. For some pupils, it will mean smaller groups working with fewer teachers over longer periods. A great deal of experimentation with the human and physical resources of the school will be necessary before an effective new format is evolved. If the schools assume the responsibility for inculcating discipline, they are also tacitly agreeing to flexibility far beyond that practiced at present.

The schools are ill-equipped to meet the burden of socialization of all the children, implied by the task of discipline. Teachers today have high standards which imply internalized acceptance of values rather than mere surface compliance. Our goal is maturity rather than outward conformity. Already there are many children who require more help than the school can give. Special school services are swamped.

3. *Schools must work closely with other community agencies,* but there are not enough referral agencies for children with severe problems. Schools continue to struggle with many children who should be receiving intensive treatment. When the school continues to act as a holding company for these pupils, it does them no good. The community is thus encouraged to escape its responsibility to provide help. Schools will need courage to exclude from the regular classroom some of the most serious discipline problems and unmanageable delinquents.

4. The outcropping of serious discipline problems is no longer confined to one age (such as adolescence) or one area (the unfavored schools in blighted areas). It is omnipresent, and its seriousness vexes the career teacher as well as the neophyte. The type of problem differs from school to school, but all schools are involved. Prevention efforts will have to move to younger ages.

5. The Sputnik hangover in education has increased the discipline problem. Uniform pressure on pupils for academic involvement has further jeopardized the status of those who lack the capacity to accept such values. From the practice of " lifting " pupils whether or not they were ready for the tasks of the next class, we have overreacted by failing more students

[2] E. H. Erikson, " Identity and the Life Cycle," *Psychological Issues,* I, No. 1 (1959).

when arbitrary standards are not met. Pupil hostility has increased. Unwittingly, the schools themselves, by not recognizing these individual differences, have made discipline harder to maintain.

NEW DIRECTIONS ARE NEEDED

The starting point: a new theoretical framework. For the schools merely to do more of what now is being done will not provide a solution to the problem of discipline. Even if we could afford to double our efforts there still would be a problem. As we seek new guidelines, our point of beginning will be a new psychology, a theoretical synthesis which is generic to the school as an institution and keyed to the realities of the school setting. The school is neither a treatment facility nor a detention home. When it tries to assume the posture of either the orientation becomes confused.

Stated in caricature, which embodies more truth than proponents would like, we have been invited to choose between a " get tough " theory and a so-called mental health approach. The first would suggest that character building is the consequence of hard knocks, the harder the better. Harsh discipline, physical or otherwise, is expected to stamp out the will to misbehave. The watchword is " beware of mollycoddling youth." Historically we passed through this stage a generation ago but it is back as a reaction against presumed permissiveness. There is a resurgence of physical punishment and its companion, ridicule, both administered by the teacher authority.[3]

Urged by desperation, we have allowed physical punishment to become respectable again. The school must control the children. Before we become too psychologically self-righteous, let us ask what other procedures we have to offer as replacements. Most teachers who use stringent methods would be happy to find more hygienic methods which would work.

Opposed to this " get tough " approach is the mental hygiene attitude, a position with extensive and erudite antecedents. The mental health movement brought in needed emphasis on child study, awareness of unconscious motivations, attention to children's needs, and the importance of accepting the child as he is. But the other school problems involved in control of impulses were not attended to with the same diligence.

The mental hygiene movement has always been scented with the aroma of therapy; no one questions the effectiveness of therapy for its specific purpose, but when transplanted these concepts can lead to confusion. The distinction between what is teaching and what is therapy becomes hazy and in some instances teachers are admonished to forget the distinctions altogether. The indirect consequence is a devaluation of the function and role of teaching as a discipline. We live in the age of therapy, where pres-

---

[3] Reports have been presented in the press with dismaying frequency in the last few years.

tige is attached to specialized relationships and the teacher is often regarded as only a handmaiden in the work of adjustment. And yet, the teacher is the first line of defense in meeting the discipline crises, and the child spends much more time in the classroom than in individual therapy.

Certainly the time is ripe for a new theoretical synthesis. The discipline theory must have as its core the goal of hygienic management of children. The procedures for hygienic handling will follow diagnosis of the dynamics of the individual pupil rather than any list for rules for discipline. For example, the pupil with only a trace of feeling or empathic potential will not be treated in the same manner as a child acting out his school failure frustration, or as another bound by a dominating fear of peer rejection. Control and discipline procedures depend on the defect and not on a theoretical predisposition to one best way.

This presupposes a more sophisticated psychology for educators, a psychology emerging from an analysis of school situations and valued for its worth in providing solutions to everyday learning and discipline problems. Psychologists will continue, as they have in the past, to export borrowed theory until educators demand theory which is really generic to schools. Unless this demand is made teachers will still be translators trying to make concepts fit, whether or not they actually apply. In short, we cannot be satisfied with a warmed-over clinical, counseling, or animal psychology, entrancing though this may be to the specialist. Neither can we settle for a simple " tough " or " soft " position. It is obvious that much work remains to be done in the realm of theory before there is an adequate psychology of school discipline.

The realignment of the school specialist team to follow the development of a new theory. The school must be seen as a milieu,[4] an operating culture with curriculum, adult, and peer instigated forces. Particularly in the case of the specialist team members, there must be coherent action. This team includes the classroom teacher, the special remedial teacher, the visiting teacher, the psychologist, the curriculum skills expert, and the administrator. These separate disciplines will begin to share knowledge and skills until they develop considerable overlap in functions.

We have learned, for example, that the " power " factor usually residing in the person of authority is essential in creating and maintaining effective discipline. This control function cannot be separated from the acceptance function of the therapeutically oriented personnel. If one agent becomes the listening ear and the other the restraining hand, we have split two functions which the pupil must see as a unified core. The administrator must operate along with the other specialists, and learn how to use authority, delegate authority, and infuse the total setting — particularly the classroom — with adequate authority needed for control. This will certainly

[4] Fritz Redl, " The Concept of a Therapeutic Milieu," *American Journal of Orthopsychiatry,* XXIX, No. 4 (1959), pp. 721–737.

be a change of involvement for some administrators, bogged down with details for years. Those with special mental health training will have to aid the classroom teacher and all other personnel as they learn how to talk effectively with pupils. Only the extra special skills will be retained as the sole possession of the specialist.

The psychologically trained specialists, particularly, have to examine their communications to other school personnel, their language (including jargon), and sometimes even a precious attitude about their sacred relationship with the child. They will have to move their practice from the protected office more toward the school in action and even to the midst of trouble. No longer separated by time and distance from the impact of misbehavior, they will find they have training which can solve many problems. Since this has already been done by some psychologists and visiting teachers,[5] it is clear that a new pattern can be developed.

Finally, as all of these specialists focus on serving and training the classroom teacher, these experts will need to learn more about groups. They will need methods for diagnosing group problems and procedures for ameliorating difficulties. Group counseling, now the exception, may become the rule. Fortunately, many of the special practitioners in schools already are leading the way in this metamorphosis. One of the specific responsibilities of these specialists is to help with decisions about children who are too disturbed to be kept in regular classrooms. The school needs both courage and technical assistance in setting cutoff points.

The expert in curriculum technique has a crucial role to play in many discipline problems. When the regular curriculum is unsuited, the teacher needs help in revising the learning content. If basic skills are not acquired, special remedial work is in order. It is well known that many children with behavior problems and many delinquents have fallen hopelessly behind in reading and other skills. Frequently the remedial specialists are not seen as first line help in meeting discipline difficulties, but they may very well be just that.

New skills for the classroom teacher. We have purposely left the most important educational worker until last. The more one works with classroom teachers, the more it becomes clear that their problem is no longer that of acquiring proper attitudes or the so-called mental hygiene ideology. The teachers' problem is technique. They are concerned about the emotional life of their charges. Many have a good grasp of dynamic psychology. They are strongly motivated to help children. They want to do the right thing. Very few need lectures on why they should love children. The problem is, what can the classroom teacher do to make effective inroads on current discipline problems? With this ability will come a new respect for the classroom teacher.

[5] J. Vosk, "The Clinical Psychologist in a Difficult School," *American Journal of Orthopsychiatry*, XXIX, No. 1 (1959), pp. 157–165.

We should not attempt to make them into therapists, or pseudothera-pists. The popular nondirective counseling methods are designed for an-other purpose and will not answer the teacher's needs. Moralizing or puni-tiveness are not useful devices. In truth, for years we have been at a loss for methodology suited to the teacher's role in classroom discipline. There is, however, a new development by Redl which teachers can learn and use. It is called " life space interviewing." [6] To do this interviewing requires training and insight, to be sure, as would any significant skill. It is particu-larly suited to the " on the line " worker's task.

Training programs have demonstrated that teachers are ready learners and effective practitioners of such interviewing methods. Since this method is designed for hygienic management of behavior, with it the teacher can manage many discipline problems right in the classroom. Adding skill in interviewing of this type to more diagnostic awareness, the teacher at last has twin processes designed for him. Specialist time must be devoted to on-the-spot teacher training in this regard.

If this skill is coupled with consultation with the specialists and the right to exclude from and readmit to his classroom, the teacher will be ready to play his full part in discipline and delinquency control. Referrals will continue, but referrals will be only those in which the teacher cannot be of enough support to the child in the regular classroom.

Finally, the need for special classes. The trained teacher, the adjunct psychological service, and the remedial provisions still may not be enough to keep a disturbed or delinquent within acceptable bounds for a regular classroom. We must remember, as things now stand, that *even with indi-vidual therapy the child spends the vast majority of his time in the regular classroom*, and many will not be able to survive.

When the resources which can be brought to bear in the classroom have failed to bring control, special classes must be provided for the re-calcitrant, the delinquent, and the nonlearner. This type of special edu-cation still lags behind the others. Discipline is a special case of emotional learning. We have special classes for visual, intellectual, and motor handi-caps, but we act as if this emotional area should still be handled in the regular classroom. Courageous educators are starting this work and barriers have been overcome. The reluctance to face emotional problems can be met. Small classes, specially trained teachers, and a tailored program for each group are anticipated. Each class will have its own unique constella-tion of clientele and school content. We now know that this, too, can be done.

Some very delinquent, neurotic, or psychotic pupils will not be able to accommodate themselves even to this. When the school has done all it can, the child must be excluded from school and referred to other com-

[6] Fritz Redl, " Strategy and Techniques of the Life Space Interview," *American Journal of Orthopsychiatry*, XXIX, No. 1, (1959), pp. 1–19.

munity services for intensive treatment. By separating pupils who cannot be successfully treated in the public school setting, we will be doing them a service, and the teachers will be able to give the majority of pupils the needed supportive discipline, and the marginal pupils special attention in areas of control.

CONCLUSION

The school is faced with increasing responsibility in discipline for today's youth. A brief survey of the conditions producing the problems makes it clear that no simple panacea will work. We will move ahead only with a theory related to school situations. The specialists-teacher team will require some realignment. The classroom teacher must be taught new skills. Special classes will be needed. Even with all these services, there will be pupils who cannot be accommodated and need institutional treatment. Keeping untreatable pupils in the regular school because there is no other place has enabled the community to evade its responsibility for adequate community services.

SECTION 5. The control of teaching: Who decides what?

The role of the expert in a democratic society is probably nowhere more demanding of clear delineation than in the field of public education. Many arguments have been advanced for maintaining the supremacy of lay authority and control over professional authority in this particular field. Three such arguments stand out. First, it is apparent that in a humane society, rooted in family life, there is a deep and legitimate concern on the part of the parents for their children and their welfare. It is children and their future that we are dealing with in education, and parents feel, rightly or wrongly, that they are the best judges of what that future should be. Second, education is a *social* function — concerned with the maintenance and development of the society. It is thus argued that only society itself, through its political structures, can appropriately control education, that no single segment of the public can be entrusted with the relevant decisions. Third, it is argued that there is little genuine expert knowledge in education — that the main problems we must solve are ethical problems — problems of judging right and wrong and in these, it is claimed, " one man's opinion is as good as another's." Or sometimes it is argued that our insufficient knowledge in the human sciences has provided us too unsure a foundation to merit placing the kind of confidence in a professional teacher that we would, say, in a professional physician. The prevailing public sentiment in favor of lay authority and control over all important educational matters is stated by a contemporary lay critic of education in the following words:

" . . . I submit the only way we can find the teachers we want is first to know exactly what we want the courses we offer to be and to do, and then try to find the men and women willing to do the job we want done. It is important to understand that we won't get what we want from people *unwilling* to do the job our way. At any rate, we certainly cannot allow our educators to tell us what the job should be, any more than we'd let the sheriff tell us what laws he had suddenly decided to enact and enforce. We should by all means listen to our schoolmen's advice, and get as much advice as possible, but in the matter of what is taught, and how and why, as in the matter of teacher qualifications, as in all other public school matters, the basic policy decisions must be ours." [1]

That *legal* control of education in America currently reflects this point of view is not debatable. The real question we must ask ourselves, however, is this: Does the present legal system of controls vest power in those persons who possess the knowledge which will best assure the making of wise educational decisions?

The two selections which follow present two responsible elaborations of conflicting points of view. The first selection, taken from a yearbook of the American Association of School Administrators, accepts the present legal position and attempts to place those possessing expert knowledge of education — the professional teacher and administrator — in a position where they possess purely advisory functions in all determination of policy but administrative functions in the implementation of policy. It accepts the common assumption that legal control, employed appropriately through boards of education, rests upon sound bases of intellectual and moral authority derived from the democratic ethos. The second selection, representing the position of a current critic of educational practice who is himself a member of the teaching profession, takes strong exception to the existing position. Within this selection, Myron Lieberman makes a clear distinction between the concepts of educational *control* and educational *authority* and attempts to point directions in which we must move if *control* and *authority* are to become com-

patible with one another. His judgments as to the areas which are appropriate for professional determination differ sharply from those accepted by the authors of the American Association of School Administrators' yearbook. The juxtaposition of these two points of view raises some of the most significant educational problems confronting America today: Can we make a clear distinction between *ends* and *means* in education, giving authority over *ends* to lay persons and authority over *means* to professional persons? Is the role of the expert in a democratic society limited to an *advisory* function, real determination appropriately resting in the hands of non-experts chosen as representatives of the people? Are there certain areas which are appropriately the domain of the public, others which are appropriately the domain of the expert in a democracy? Obviously the role of the professional teacher is going to vary widely depending upon which of these two interpretations of the requirements of a contemporary democratic society is accepted.

Even while these broad issues of policy are being resolved, the classroom teacher who is conscientiously fulfilling his mandate to educate must face the immediate practical problems which they in turn raise: Should he teach in areas which are " closed " in the community conscience? Should he accept the dictates of the public as to what should or should not be taught? How can he help parents and the community recognize and respect the professional knowledge of teachers and their obligations as members of a profession? How does he determine what he has a right and an obligation to teach? What he does not? How can he determine that his teaching really rests upon sound moral and intellectual authority and does not merely reflect a set of unexamined personal preferences and biases? Integrity in a philosophy of education requires that any teacher come to grips with just such problems.

[1] John Keats, *Schools Without Scholars* (Boston: 1958), p. 153. Quoted by permission of Houghton Mifflin Company.

ASSOCIATION OF SCHOOL ADMINISTRATORS
Why we have school boards

Nothing is more uniquely American than local control of public education through boards of education composed of lay citizens. Visitors from foreign countries find this feature of our educational system completely baffling to them. They ask: "How can you safely entrust to laymen the professional, technical tasks of organizing and operating a school system? Do you not find constant interference with the experience and professional skill of educators?"

They say: "Your system makes it almost impossible to have uniform educational standards. Each board can tell its employees what to teach!"

They conclude: "You waste most of the talents and energies of your top administrators in negotiations with these amateur boards. The superintendent has to convince them that what he and his colleagues want to do is what should be done. Why go through all that lost motion?"

In 1934 the eminent Charles H. Judd, at that time dean of the School of Education of the University of Chicago, developed the thesis that school boards were an obstruction to the advance of public education and that in time they would be completely abolished. He wrote:

The fact is well known that boards of education frequently disregard the technical advice of their expert appointees, thus substituting lay opinion for professional judgment. . . . New members of boards of education frequently enter upon their duties inspired by a zeal for reform born of the profoundest ignorance and conceit. . . . Boards of education are survivals, inherited from an age when professionalization of schools was less advanced than at present.[1]

He suggested that the appointment of the superintendent be left to the state department of education or to officials of local government. Although seriously proposed by an educator of national prominence and influence, no support arose for the abolition of school boards. The question, "Are school boards necessary?" if posed today, would receive an unqualified Yes in reply from the American people.

School board members represent the people who own and support the schools. They form a grass roots organization which is closer to the people than any other form of government. They voice the wishes and aspirations of the parents and the children. They spend the local taxpayers' money

From American Association of School Administrators, *School Board-Superintendent Relationships.* Thirty-Fourth Yearbook, 1956, pp. 26–28, 35–36, 41–43, 153–159. Reprinted by permission of the American Association of School Administrators.

[1] Judd, Charles H. "School Boards as an Obstruction to Good Administration." *Nation's Schools* 13:13–15; February 1934.

and are responsible to their neighbors for the action. They are trustees of a great public responsibility.

School boards are necessary. The school board is typical of the form of government of many institutions in the United States — churches, hospitals, schools, libraries, welfare and character-building agencies as well as business and commercial organizations. It is American tradition to form a governing board when the affairs of the organization get too complicated for the membership to operate.

The American school board has strived to keep the public schools an immediate possession of the people rather than of general government or of professional educators or of private corporations. It has also served as a prime protection against the domination of schools by an *ism* or any centralized pattern for remolding society. Our schools began as local institutions; school boards keep them that way.

School boards constitute a check on the proprietary interests developed by professionals and thus carry out our basic American concept of checks and balances. School boards afford a means for bringing to bear multiple minds and varying points of view in formulating school policy. They make possible, but do not guarantee, the direct exercise of the people's will in regard to public education. . . .

Developing the educational program. The board is constantly having to say Yes or No to many conflicting pressures. The answers depend on the board's understanding of the total school program. Does the board define public education broadly or within narrow limits? Where does public schooling end and where does welfare — or charity, or penology, or public recreation, or community advertising, or religion, or higher education, or industry, or individual initiative — take over? What are the relationships of the public schools to these other forces? What is the purpose of the school system? What is its program? Each board has the duty and the right, within legal mandates, to decide these questions.

The classroom is the heart of the school system and should be the primary interest of the board and the professional staff. People are more interested in what the children are taught than in any other phase of the school program. A member with long tenure on his board of education remarked recently that he had heard more about " curriculum " and especially the " Three R's " in the last five years than he had in the other 10 years he had been on the board. He reflected the experience of many others.

Board members and the superintendent should concern themselves with the philosophy and purposes underlying the curriculum, methods of teaching being used in the classroom, and results obtained. The interest shown by the parents should be recognized by board and superintendent by inviting patrons to serve as members of curriculum committees, to visit the schools, and to contribute to the policies of the school.

The schools can also use this community interest by working with community organizations on projects that will improve the community as well as the schools. Community recreation, sanitation, safety, housing, and the like are fields in which the schools can make a real contribution, through educational means, to the over-all welfare of the community. This type of cooperative program strengthens both the community and school. . . .

How the school board works. School boards are agencies of the state and operate all their services under state law — the constitution, the statutes, the attorney general's rulings, and court decisions. The state educational agency, operating under law, issues administrative regulations on such items as certification, state aid, reports, transportation, and other matters inherent in the operation of a public school. Some functions are mandatory upon the board to perform, others are permissive. In addition there are implied or discretionary powers; these the local board should recognize and exercise courageously when new occasions demand new solutions.[2]

Members come on the board with little knowledge of school law and procedures. It should be the duty of the superintendent to advise with the board so that costly or embarrassing mistakes are not made. Legal counsel may be secured as needed. Not merely knowledge of the law but integrity is also necessary. Unfortunately, there have been instances of acquiring money from the state through inaccurate reports. Ignorance of the law, of course, excuses no board member or superintendent of schools.

Legislating through policy. The state vests the members of the board of education with the legal right and responsibility for establishing and operating the public schools. Wise policies undergird and support a well-organized school. How to make policy often confuses board members. They wonder what a policy is, how to make it, and where to start. A policy of a school board is simply a statement of a rule or principle which the board agrees should be followed in deciding *types* of cases or problems that may confront the board.

Policies grow out of the legal provisions for education, the board's previous experiences, and study of other boards' policies. Policies are not formulated at one or a few meetings devoted exclusively to policy making; they accumulate over the years. A proposed new policy or a change in an old one is frequently initiated in the form of a recommendation by the superintendent.[3]

Wise policies, well made, should be stated by the board and amplified in written rules and regulations. Rules should stipulate and clarify the duties and relationship of all personnel, budgetary procedures, school plant

[2] Messick, John D. *The Discretionary Powers of School Boards.* Durham, N. C.: Duke University Press, 1949. 147 p.

[3] Texas Association of School Boards and Texas Association of School Administrators; Texas Committee of Ten. *Handbook for Texas School Board Members.* Bulletin 546. Austin: Texas Education Agency, 1953, pp. 1–2.

operation, personnel policies, and regulatory conduct of the entire system. Too many rules and regulations, however, can cripple or slow down efficient operation. A minimum number of good rules administered by the superintendent with fairness and judgment is the ideal balance.

Confusion in drawing a line between what is policy and what constitutes rules and regulations may grow out of a lack of clear understanding of the relationship between the school board and its chief administrative officer. The school board is the final authority in setting policy. A board is functioning within its recognized sphere of activity when it approves the rules and regulations that are consistent with its policies. But it can quickly find itself in a position of meddling and interfering if it attempts to deal with administrative details. Execution of policy through the procedures of school administration is the job of the school superintendent.[4]

Wise policy making includes long-term planning. It includes statements of a school philosophy and objectives. It provides a picture of the present and a blueprint for the future.

Some boards and superintendents let practices develop by precedent — one decision at a time; one based upon the other. As a result no definite policy for future action is laid down. When confronted by even the simplest problems the superintendent has to say, " I will have to take this up with the board before making a decision." This evidence of poor planning and lack of policy can sap the public's confidence in the school leadership.

Where school boards have taken a long look in school planning and where well-thought-out policies have been interpreted into rules and regulations, the way is clear for the superintendent to make administrative decisions and to act efficiently. . . .

* * *

TAILORING THE PROGRAM TO THE COMMUNITY

Participants in a workshop session for new school board members in a Midwestern state were amazed to discover that they had any responsibility for the development of the curriculum. Further discussion revealed that most of these new members believed that the limit of their trusteeship was to provide the financial support for the schools and for new buildings. One of the most important things they learned was that they are responsible for the kernel of education as well as the shell.

The power to modify the school program from one community to another is demanded by the very nature of school administration. The board must do many things for which the law makes no specific provision, in order to serve the community effectively.

Beyond the area of legislative mandate to boards of education, which

[4] American Association of School Administrators and National School Boards Association. *Written Policies for School Boards.* Washington, D. C.: American Association of School Administrators, a department of the National Education Association, 1955. 24 pp.

says what the schools *must* do, and the area of legislative consent, which says what the schools *may* do, there is a third area — of *implied* power, that type of duty or power which may be reasonably inferred from the general powers given to school boards to operate schools.

It is in this area that school boards and superintendents operate in tailoring the school program for a specific community. Unless the superintendent of schools is really on his toes, the school board may be completely ignorant of many of the responsibilities and opportunities which it has in this tailoring process.

Boards sometimes forget that the courses taught and the services provided by the schools are subject to the decision of *each successive* board of education. Nothing should be taught just because nobody remembered to take it out of the curriculum; no needed subject or service should be missing just because a public outcry has not demanded it.

The function of the board goes beyond keeping its fingers on the pulse of community sentiment. The board cannot wait for the community to come knocking at its door. If a situation has reached the point of general dissatisfaction with the leadership of the superintendent and the board of education, the school officials have failed their responsibilities to the community.

The board must lead. After studying school problems as they are analyzed and presented by the superintendent and his professional staff, and after getting as much advice as possible from community groups, the board must determine those policies which seem to be best for the community. It should identify the community needs which the schools might help to meet, and explore the ways through which the school program may be adapted for the purpose.

What is a community? Most of us think of a community as a self-contained unit for living, which embraces all the economic, social, political, and educational needs of those who live within its bounds. Many of today's school districts coincided with the boundaries of such communities when they were formed, several decades ago.

Today, the residents of many historically constituted " communities " are going outside for most of the goods and services they require. In many school districts the old boundaries must be enlarged in order to enclose a genuine community. In others it must be accepted that the school district is still a community only in the sense of being a social and residence unit, and that many economic interests extend farther.

Some school districts are so large that they include many communities — whose interests should be recognized separately. There are also overlying areas of interests which sometimes are called " communities." Thus, within the limits of a single school system we speak of the industrial community, the business community, the suburban community, and in some cases, several rural communities. School board members and superintendents must be sensitive to the interests of each in constructing a comprehensive school program.

What is the school program? All the opportunities that the schools give for learning new facts and processes, and all that the schools provide in meeting the needs of individual pupils of every age, constitute the school program. All school services are included.

In a given community the program may serve various age levels, from nursery school through adulthood. It may serve various vocational interests and provide for varied cultural interests. It may provide a laboratory for training the future leaders and followers of the community in the fundamentals of good citizenship. It may provide recreational centers, during both the school year and the summer, with facilities for athletics, dramatics, music, art, handcrafts, and similar leisure-time activities for adults and young people.

The past decade has brought about a tremendous growth in guidance and counseling services. Psychological and psychiatric services have been introduced, and health services have been greatly expanded. Examinations, inoculations, safety education, and sanitation instruction have become important phases of the school program. Pupils ride to school in buses provided by the school district.

Classroom instruction is central to the school program. The actual content of what is taught in the classroom evolves from year to year to meet new conditions. How *does* Johnny learn to read? Teaching methods, teaching materials, and subjects taught must be considered in thinking of the scope and effectiveness of the school program.

The type of school organization is part of the program. Shall schools follow a traditional pattern of eight elementary grades and a four-year high school, or shall the secondary school begin earlier? Shall there be separate classes for the handicapped, or ability grouping in regular classes, or separate high schools for girls, or vocational high schools separate from comprehensive high schools? Questions of this kind must be answered in building the program.

The community and the program. Many elements in the program should be related to local problems and local needs. Health problems of different communities, for example, may not be the same. Orange juice may be needed to supply vitamin deficiencies in the reservation schools in Arizona. In a metropolitan area, a free milk program may be needed to bolster nutritional deficiencies. School recreational facilities in Florida will be different from those in Minnesota. Summer activities in large cities differ from those in rural areas where children of school age have definite jobs to do at home. The demands upon an adult education program in Scranton, with its industrial emphasis, might be expected to differ markedly from the program required in a residential suburb such as Evanston. But whatever the program of the school, the problem of relating it to the community is present.

Communities differ greatly in what they expect the schools to do for them and also in what they are able to pay for in their school program. They differ, too, in what they know about the school program now offered.

This community background should be studied in the process of meeting community needs. Because his professional training should prepare him to make such an analysis, and because he is less deeply rooted in local ways than the board members, the superintendent can render special service here.

With so many people asking the schools to provide more services, it is easier today than it was 50 years ago to integrate the school with the community. But school boards and superintendents in many school systems are overlooking the opportunity to study the community directly in developing the school program. They are more likely to survey practices elsewhere when evaluating the present program or considering a new service. They get information from other districts of the same size, or the same type of organization, or the same type of population. State and local school annual reports and studies by educational associations often provide facts. Such information may be useful in showing the way that the educational winds are blowing. But it offers no direct guidance for the local board to follow.

Suppose that the community's major industry is the making of copper wire. The board and superintendent might find out what could go into the school curriculum that will help the community understand the product and the processes to which so many of its citizens devote their working careers. There may be special skills which the factory needs. Should the schools offer elective courses in their vocational department for workers who wish to equip themselves for employment in the factory? Could the board and the factory work out a cooperative plan for on-the-job training? How far should the board go in such plans? Is what is good for the wire works always good for the community?

Another district might depend upon the winter tourist trade for its chief source of income. Should the school board provide a particularly attractive program of adult education for its part-time residents? Does the school board do its best for the community's young people when it gives much emphasis to such interests as food service and entertainment skills? For what age pupil should such community specializations begin — or should it affect every age level?

Whatever the answers may be, the board and the superintendent fail in their responsibility if they fail to raise and answer questions such as these.

The board makes choices. In moving toward the community's ideal school program, the members of the board of education must pick a precarious path, with two sets of extremes to waylay them.

There is the choice between the old and the new. Few citizens other than school board members have any notion of the things that the board is asked to add to the course of study. The labor unions want a fairer and longer treatment of the meaning of the labor movement in American history. The chamber of commerce and the board of trade want a fairer and longer treatment of the meaning of free enterprise in American history.

The local athletic association proposes cooperation in a plan to teach every pupil to swim. The automobile association offers cooperation in establishing a required course in driver education. And the school faculty have ideas of their own, gained from their teaching and the findings of educational research, as to needed improvements.

Sooner or later, some new things are added, and some of the old must be sloughed aside. But community pressures cling to the traditional elements. The old labels are precious. Such useful combinations as the " social studies " and " core " and " general education " become color words and may need constant reinterpretation. But innovations can be introduced into the teaching of history, geography, civics, English, and arithmetic if the old names are used. In time, however, change is accepted. Parsing, Greek, and cube root give ground, and speech training, world history, and consumer education work their way into the curriculum.

The other pair of extremes that the board faces is the choice between the general and the particular. This itself is a double problem: (a) the individual's vocational career versus his life as a member of society as a whole, and (b) the community's needs versus those of state and nation.

The first choice is between vocational training and learning to live a good life as a human being in whatever vocation. A particular individual may be gifted in mathematics and destined for a career in engineering or abstract science, but for much of his school career he studies many things of general rather than specific interest and value to him. This is equally true of the future housewife, secretary, or machinist. The atomic scientists who were grief-stricken at their ignorance of the society their work might destroy give a classic example of over-individualized education. The physician who knows that he should treat the whole man, but actually knows little about humanity, is another. The school authorities must always be aware of this dilemma in making choices about the school program. What are the needed general learnings? How far should the school go in meeting the individual needs of pupils who have thousands of vocational choices before them?

The second kind of choice between the particular and the general balances the community's needs against those of state and nation. What do the children of a community high in the mountains of Idaho need to study that is different from what is needed in a school near Florida's seacoast, or in the outskirts of Detroit? What should be taught that the community needs to have its citizens know? Over against the community's particular need is the general need of the state and the nation. Many of these children will live as adults in other cities and in other states. Wherever they live, they will one day be citizens of a state and of the United States; they need a common core of learning that will fit them into our national life. And as American citizens they must understand and direct their nation's course in world affairs. *If they stay in the locality where they go to school,* there are special local knowledges that will prove useful. How far shall the board go? Provincialism is to be avoided, and yet an exact knowledge of some one local community's traditions, growth, and current problems may enrich the individual life. The decision may be to do a great deal of special local education or almost none — but a conscious decision is called for on the part of the board.

Boards of education are more likely to travel on the side of tradition and on the side of the general program of education that is typical of all parts of the United States than to go too far toward innovations and local adaptations. But the path of the pioneers in American education has been marked by board-superintendent teams who fitted the work of the schools to new needs or local needs which they saw and tried to meet. . . .

MYRON LIEBERMAN
Authority and control in education

The classroom teacher is always in a position in which choices must be made. The teacher wants to know: " If I have my students study these materials (perhaps a unit on the races of mankind), what will the consequences be? " Presumably studying these materials would have different outcomes than studying other materials. This means that after the teacher decides what the consequences of studying the different materials are likely to be, he still has another decision to make. Should the students study a unit which will lead them to the conclusion that the races of mankind have a common biological origin, and are considered as members of one family by the world's great religions? Or should they study materials that lead to different conclusions on this subject? Or should they ignore the subject altogether? The teacher must judge the probable consequences of different lines of action and also which consequences he ought to bring about. Teachers are not free to bring about any results they wish. They are in the classroom to accomplish certain results and not others.

Moral and intellectual authority. The distinction between moral and intellectual authority is based upon the distinction between the kinds of decisions teachers must make. *Intellectual authority* is invoked in deciding what are the facts, what actually happened, or what will happen if certain things are done or not done. *Moral authority* is invoked in deciding whether a certain course of action is right or wrong. Intellectual authority is used to decide what will happen if a certain action is taken. Moral authority is used to decide whether it is right or wrong to take such action.

The necessity for a source of authority. It is impossible to avoid reliance upon some source of moral and intellectual authority. This is sometimes overlooked by teachers who assume that avoidance of all authority is the

From Myron Lieberman, *Education as a Profession,* 1956, pp. 49–50, 71–73, 84, 87–88, 90–91, 97–100, 122–123. Reprinted by permission of Prentice-Hall, Inc.

mark of an independent thinker. The notion that it is wise or even possible to avoid completely reliance upon any authority, stems from the mistaken idea that authority is necessarily *dictatorial* authority or that reliance upon authority is a characteristic of weak-minded individuals who need someone to tell them what to do. A rejection of *undesirable* authority, however, does not call for a rejection of *all* authority.

Geography teachers have not visited every place they discuss in class. If geography teachers were to teach about only the places they have visited personally, geography would be a very narrow subject. The geography teachers must rely upon some authority in assuming the existence of places and conditions unknown to them through first hand experience. Science teachers cannot personally test every scientific law they teach. They too must rely upon authority in assuming the validity of the laws of science they teach to students. Demonstrations in the classroom may make it easier for the students to understand the laws of physics or chemistry, but no science teacher would say a law was valid solely on the basis of a classroom experiment.

Likewise, when it comes to deciding what ought to be done, reliance upon authority is inescapable. The authority may be parents, the school board, the superintendent, a religious leader, or some other source. The teacher may even regard himself as the ultimate moral authority in education. In this case, however, the teacher would be saying that whatever I do is right *because I think it is right*. Few teachers would be willing to say this. Most teachers do what they think is right, but they usually think their action right because it is or would be sanctioned by a " higher " source of authority. . . .

The democratic ideals as the source of the educator's moral authority. We have analyzed briefly the major positions concerning the educator's source of moral authority. All the positions involve logical and practical difficulties which cannot be ignored. Still, teachers cannot wait until a perfect theory is formulated. They must teach now, hence they must choose an ultimate source of moral authority now. Which alternative, regardless of its difficulties, should they accept?

The position that seems to hold the most promise is that the democratic ideals of the national community should be the ultimate source of moral authority for education. This position in itself is not new. Many educators accept it at a verbal level. The point is that they usually balk at the implications of this view by also stating that the teacher must always follow the wishes of the local community or administrative superiors. This view never comes to grips with the problem of the teacher's duty when local pressures or administrative orders conflict with the teacher's independent judgment. If we accept the notion that the teacher's ultimate responsibility is to the national community, we must honestly face up to the fact that teachers will have to do many things which are unpopular at the local level.

Conflict over the meaning of democracy. Probably the major criticism of the view that teachers should rely upon the democratic ideals of the national community as their source of moral authority is based upon the widespread disagreement over the meaning of democracy. What are the democratic ideals according to which teachers should guide their actions?

These ideals have been stated in different ways by different persons. Each way of stating them is subject to qualification. For present purposes, however, the following statement of them is probably adequate to bring out the main issues.

1. The personal worth and dignity of every individual must be respected.

2. Every person should be free to speak, to read, to write, to think, and to worship according to his own conscience; freedom should be curtailed, if at all, only to the extent necessary to protect freedom for others.

3. Government should rest upon the informed, responsible, and freely given consent of the governed.

4. Differences between individuals, groups, and peoples are not necessarily undesirable; many of these differences are invaluable resources which should be respected and encouraged as an invaluable means of progress and of enriching the lives of everyone.

5. Individuals should have equal opportunity to develop themselves and to contribute to the development of others.

One obvious criticism that can be made at this point is that people who accept these ideals often disagree on what they mean in practice. For example, persons who support racial segregation assert their belief in the worth and dignity of every individual just as do the people who oppose racial segregation. How can both groups be relying upon the same source of moral authority when they draw such contradictory conclusions from it? Whose version of the democratic ideals should teachers accept, and why?

It will help us to answer these questions if we note that no specific political, economic, educational, or other social arrangement has been included in the statement of the democratic ideology. For example, the ideals listed did not include the free enterprise system, although many persons assert that the free enterprise system is an essential ingredient of the democratic way of life. Other persons, who also affirm their faith in these ideals, assert that public ownership and control of basic industries is necessary to effectuate them. Both the advocate of free enterprise and the advocate of public ownership insist that their economic proposals should be regarded as part of the meaning of democracy. Whose interpretation should the teacher accept?

The answer is neither interpretation, because *no* economic system can be regarded as an *essential* part of the democratic creed. For the sake of argument, let us concede that the free enterprise system contributes more than any other economic system to promote the ideals of democracy. The possibility (not the probability) *always* exists that at some future time a different economic system might make a greater contribution to those ideals. The American people do not adhere to the free enterprise system regardless of its effects. They adhere to it because they believe it contributes more effectively than any other economic system to certain objectives. They do not evaluate such things as the dignity of individuals, freedom of conscience, and freedom of speech by whether they contribute to a particular economic system. Instead, they evaluate economic systems (and political, educational, and other social systems as well) by how adequately such systems contribute to the dignity of man, freedom of conscience, and freedom of speech. This may help to explain why no particular social institution or social arrangement can be regarded as a part of the democratic creed, and why it has been asserted that the democratic creed should be regarded as the teacher's ultimate source of moral authority. . . .

The teacher's source of intellectual authority. What source of intellectual authority should teachers rely upon? What source of intellectual authority, if any, should they attempt to get their students to accept? Because reliance upon some source of intellectual authority is inevitable, and because the choice of intellectual authority has an important bearing upon action, these are fundamental questions for any teacher in the public schools.

The answer to the first question would seem to be science. Reliance upon any religious source of intellectual authority would run afoul of the same objections encountered in reliance upon a religious source of moral authority. Reliance upon parents, the local community, or even the national community as a source of intellectual authority has practically no justification. Whether or not a course of action is right may come to depend upon whether or not parents or the community are willing to accept it. But the truth of a statement does not depend upon acceptance of it as true by parents or the community. The world was no flatter for everyone's having thought it flat.

Teachers generally ignore the problem of what source of intellectual authority students should be taught to accept. This neglect is not always intentional. Probably it is due more often to the teacher's failure to appreciate the significance of this problem, than it is to any intentional evasion on his part. In either case, evasion is educationally unsound, because it leaves students without the intellectual tools needed to solve the questions of fact which confront them. . . .

* * *

PROFESSIONAL AUTONOMY

Expert authority. In order to analyze professional autonomy intelligently, we need first to clarify further the concept of authority. " Authority " has several meanings. Sometimes a person is referred to as " an authority " on a certain subject. When we try to settle a dispute by appealing to authority, we are saying in effect: " Here is what the person who knows the most about the matter has to say about it." We shall use the term " expert authority " to refer to this meaning of authority, and the term " experts " to refer to persons who possess such authority. Obviously, every member of a genuine profession is an expert.

At the present time, widespread confusion and uncertainty prevail throughout our society concerning the role of experts. Sometimes lay groups insist upon making and executing decisions which should be left to expert decision and execution. This frequently happens over the vigorous and completely justified protest of the experts concerned. Such incidents have involved every profession at one time or another, but they occur more often with respect to teachers than with any other group claiming professional, and hence expert, status. Resistance to such indiscriminate decision-making by lay groups is often labelled " undemocratic " by people who identify democracy with the absence of expertness. As a result, issues which should be decided by experts are frequently settled by lay individuals who are not qualified to make a judgment on the issues.

If we are to preserve our democratic institutions in an age characterized by highly specialized knowledge and by expert authority concerning matters of survival for entire societies as well as for individuals, it is essential that our people achieve a better understanding of the functions, rights, privileges, and responsibilities of expert groups generally. Otherwise, there is little hope that we will ever cease shuttling from the one extreme of attempting to decide every question by counting noses, to the equally irrational extreme of leaving all fundamental questions of policy and purpose up to " experts." Democracy requires a third alternative; one which recognizes the indispensability of expert judgment. We must not mistakenly identify democracy with the absence of expertness. We must also guard against experts or leaders who try to gain power by promises to solve all problems for us. . . .

The scope of professional autonomy in education. Since there is much disagreement over the functions of education, whatever teachers do will appear to many persons to exceed the scope of their professional autonomy. Nevertheless, it is still possible to analyze certain aspects of professional autonomy in a meaningful way. No matter what the functions of an occupation are, the practitioners will have certain powers if they are a professional group. For instance, the practitioners of a profession, regardless of its function, will control entry into the profession. Hence, we can meaningfully discuss the extent to which educators control entry into education while recognizing that we have not settled the problem of function. Among those who agree that teaching is or ought to be a profession, there might be disagreement over the criteria used in evaluating professional qualifications. There should be no disagreement on the point that teachers themselves ought to formulate and apply the criteria, whatever they are. On particular occasions, we could not always agree whether teachers had abused their professional autonomy without prior agreement on the functions of education, but we should agree that teachers lack an essential element of professional status if they lack the power to expel or suspend teachers for such causes as the teachers themselves deem sufficient.

. . . [D]isagreement over the functions of education [is] paralleled by disagreement over the nature of the teacher's expert authority. However, despite all these disagreements, there are certain things which we can definitely say should be decided by educators if they are a professional group. Among them are the following:

The subjects to be taught and the materials (such as textbooks) to be used in teaching them; the criteria to be used in deciding who should be admitted, retained, and graduated at all levels; the forms to be used in reporting pupil progress; school boundary lines and the criteria for permitting students to attend schools outside the boundary lines; the qualifications for entrance into teacher training; the length and content of the teacher training program; the standards for entry into and expulsion from education; the standards of professional conduct and the power to judge if and when practitioners have violated these standards; and who should lead the profession and speak for it on matters of broad professional concern.

We shall not attempt to explain in detail why these are all matters for professional rather than lay decision. The professional character of some of them should be obvious, especially since they are matters for professional decision in all the professions. The professional character of others seems equally clear, although the activities involved are peculiar to education. We shall consider both types of professional decisions, that is, those which are peculiar to education, such as selecting teaching materials, and those which are common to all the professions, such as setting the standards for entry into the profession. . . .

Textbooks and teaching materials. The choice of textbooks and teaching materials is clearly a professional matter. This is apparent from a brief consideration of the factors that should be taken into account in selecting textbooks. An incomplete list would include the following: The reading level of the text, its choice of topics and the space devoted to each topic, the value of its teaching aids, the amount of overlap with other materials in courses in the same subjects at higher and lower grade levels, the style and format of the book, and the way a particular book compares with others in the field. Making an adequate judgment about these things presupposes a great deal of knowledge about the abilities, interests, and previous educational experiences of the students who will be using the textbooks. It presupposes further a knowledge of the school program and the availability of other materials besides textbooks.

These things are not matters of common knowledge. A sound judgment concerning them requires professional training and experience. Textbooks are as much the tools of the teacher as scalpels are the tools of the doctor. Telling a teacher what textbook to use is equivalent to telling a doctor what instrument or what drug to use.

It should not be inferred that every individual teacher should always be completely free to choose whatever textbook he wishes. In a local or state school system, it may be more feasible for reasons of economy to adopt one or a few textbooks than to permit each individual teacher to choose the textbook he prefers. In such cases the fact that an individual teacher has to use a textbook which he personally would not have selected does not necessarily constitute a violation of his professional autonomy. For instance, in a large city school system, it may be necessary to adopt one English textbook. If the textbook is adopted by a group selected by the English teachers themselves, there is no violation of professional autonomy even for the English teacher who disagrees with the selection that is made. Professional autonomy would be violated if the selection were made by the school board or superintendent or even by English teachers not chosen by the teachers who would have to use the textbook selected. Decisions or rules made by the professional group itself are not a violation of the professional autonomy of the individual practitioner who happens to disagree with them.

Violations of professional autonomy over the selection of textbooks occur at many different levels. They occur at the state level when the selection is made by a state school agency dominated by laymen. They occur at county or local levels when school boards select or ban textbooks. They occur within a school when a principal dictates the choice. It is just as much an invasion of professional autonomy for an administrator to dictate the choice of textbooks or teaching materials as it is for a lay agency to do so.

There is no handy way to measure the extent of lay interference with professional autonomy with respect to the selection of textbooks and teaching materials, but it may be worthwhile in this connection to consider briefly the status of professional autonomy with respect to textbook selection at the state level. In 1950, the adoption of textbooks at the state level was in the hands of the state board of education in sixteen states. At that time, however, only two of these sixteen boards were required by law to have a majority of educators on the board. Even in these two states (Arizona and Indiana) the educators on the state boards were not chosen by educators. In many other states, the approval of textbooks was under the jurisdiction of other agencies not controlled by the profession.

The situation may not be quite so bad in practice as these facts suggest. It is very probable that the state boards usually give some weight to the recommendations of educators even though they are legally free to disregard completely such recommendations and have on occasion done so. The fact that the educational advisers or representatives on these boards have not been selected by the teachers affected means that we do not know to what extent the educators on the state boards of education really represent professional opinion. In general, having members of a professional group serve as advisers to a lay board which has the power to make what should be professional decisions is not a satisfactory arrangement, even when the professional representatives are chosen by the professional group. This arrangement has not worked out satisfactorily in other professions and there is no reason to expect any better results in education.

Subjects and courses of study. Agreement that textbooks and teaching materials should be a matter for professional decision is probably more widespread than agreement that educators should decide what subjects shall be taught. Yet the same basic considerations apply in both cases. Indeed, it is illogical to say that the subject taught should be a matter for lay decision and the textbooks and teaching materials a matter for professional decision. In the last analysis, the power to decide what materials shall be used *is* the power to decide what subjects shall be taught.

As in the case of textbooks, violations of professional autonomy with reference to what subjects shall be taught occur at several different levels. Again, we shall consider the problem only at the state level. In 1949, the responsibility for adopting courses of study was vested in the state board of education in thirty-one states. Not one board was controlled by educators. Many were completely devoid of professional representation. It is very probable that this situation has not changed materially since 1949.

One reason why lay control over the subjects taught is even more pronounced than lay control over the materials used in teaching the subjects, is that few educators regard the determination of the subjects to be taught as basically a professional matter. This may be due to a mistaken application of the idea that the public should determine the ends of education and teachers the means. The mistake lies in not realizing that the subject taught should be regarded as a means and not an end. The public, local, state, or national, does not really regard the teaching of courses labelled " English " as an *end*. The end it has in mind is people who can communicate clearly and effectively. The decision as to whether this end requires *courses* in English, and if so how long and at what grade levels, should be strictly a professional matter. . . .

Professional autonomy is a practical goal. Absolutely nothing in this entire discussion can or should be taken to mean that educators should adopt an arrogant, know-it-all, " public be damned " attitude. The mark of a profession is dedication to public service. There is no need to choose between a spineless abdication of professional autonomy and an arrogant dictatorial attitude toward the public. The proper attitude for educators to take is the same as that in any other profession. When the decision should be made by an agency outside the profession, educators should feel free to offer professional suggestions and criticisms. When the decision is a professional one, educators in turn ought to welcome and encourage suggestions and criticisms from sources outside the profession. But educators ought not to relinquish control over such decisions any more than the public ought to relinquish control over decisions which are essentially non-professional in nature.

Undoubtedly one reaction to the suggestion that educators insist that their professional autonomy be respected will be that the suggestion is an impractical one. It will be said that the advice " may be all right in theory but it won't work in practice " or that " people just won't stand for it." Others will predict that educators who insist upon lay respect for professional autonomy will be unemployed in short order.

At the present time the public expects to decide many things which should be decided by educators. Getting the public to respect and value professional autonomy in education is not going to be an easy task. There is, however, no basic reason why this task cannot be accomplished. The present attitude of the public, which takes lay interference with the educator's professional autonomy for granted, is a logical reaction to the uncritical notions of democracy and professionalism which prevail among educators. A much different attitude on the part of laymen can be expected only if and when educators themselves understand the need for professional autonomy and are alert to every opportunity to strengthen it. The transition will take time. There will be many temporary setbacks here and there. However, the dangers of insisting upon professional autonomy are great only insofar as it is assumed that it must be solitary individuals here and there who will make the effort. Implementation of professional autonomy need not be an invitation to educational martyrdom. . . . It should be recognized that there is a world of difference between doing everything possible to uphold the principles of professional autonomy (while recognizing that compromises are sometimes unavoidable), and being unaware of the principles of professional autonomy in the first place. . . .

CHAPTER SIX BIBLIOGRAPHY

BAYLES, ERNEST E., *Democratic Educational Theory*. New York: Harper and Brothers, 1960.

> In Chapter Eleven, " Democracy and Keeping School," the problems of curriculum, the classroom situation and control of teaching are dealt with in a straightforward manner. Examples are given which are based on a concise definition of democracy as elaborated in the preceding chapter.

BRACKENBURY, ROBERT L., *Getting Down to Cases*. New York: G. P. Putnam's Sons, 1959.

> This is a case book which presents various practical problem situations, gives solutions by several hypothetical people, and then analyzes each solution. In Chapter Two, " Art and the Role of the Specialist," the superintendent and board discuss their roles and the teacher's role in deciding what is the responsibility of each for what and how to teach.

BRIGGS, THOMAS H., *Secondary Education*. New York: Macmillan and Company, 1933.

>Although this book is dated, it raises the question of whether the secondary school should be selective, a topic still discussed at times today. The author's educational philosophy is evident in the answers offered in Chapters 10, 11, and 14. His attitude on the special functions of the secondary school furnishes insights into the philosophical positions developed by readings in the present chapter.

NATIONAL SOCIETY FOR THE STUDY OF EDUCATION, *Curriculum-making: Past and Present*, Part I. Chicago: The Society, 1927.

>Of particular interest here are Sections III and IV. Each chapter is a presentation of a program of curriculum-making in a particular public school or private laboratory school. Examples are from Denver, St. Louis, Winnetka, and the laboratory schools connected with the Universities of Chicago, Columbia and Iowa.

NATIONAL SOCIETY FOR THE STUDY OF EDUCATION, *The Foundations of Curriculum-making*, Part II. Chicago: The Society, 1927.

>In Chapter XII, Harold Rugg has presented a series of representative quotations of Dewey's thinking about curriculum. Some of these are " The Logically Organized Curriculum vs. the Child Growth Curriculum," " On the Role of Studies and Subject Matter," and " On the Role of Manual Occupations in the School." The book also contains the views of such men as William C. Bagley, George S. Counts, Ernest Horn, and William H. Kilpatrick, on curriculum-making.

NORBERG, KENNETH D., *American Democracy and Secondary Education*. New York: Bureau of Publications, Teachers College, Columbia University, 1943.

>Chapters II, III, and IV critically review the progressive, subject-centered, and Hutchins views of the curriculum. Chapter V concerns a functional curriculum for a democratic, industrial society. This brief book is a thoughtful review of important curriculum positions with the author's proposals for fundamental improvements.

7

Cultural Foundations of Education

It is impossible to divorce the educative process from the society in which it occurs. Consider the following excerpt from an account dealing with the education of a shepherd boy in the rugged Khyber Hills of West Pakistan:

". . . Sheep and their care are vital to the needs of this boy, his family and nation. From the wool his mother and sisters will make clothes to protect the family against the January winds which sweep the barren hills. The family's meager ration of meat will come from the sheep. The hide, surplus wool and meat will provide cash for the family's needs and, if exported, much needed foreign exchange for the nation's treasury. This lad's indigenous education is directed at the basic needs of underdeveloped nations — food, human protection and purchasing power.

There is hope, too, in the manner in which this shepherd boy acquired his skill in tending sheep. The learning sprang from experience. From early childhood he was aware of the importance of sheep to his family's welfare. As a little boy he scrambled over the rocks after his father as he shepherded the flock. He watched at lambing, shearing and slaughtering time. Almost without being aware of it, he learned his skill by practicing it. There was nothing remote or theoretical about the way he learned. It was practical, to the point, effective." [1]

[1] Cole S. Brembeck, " Education for National Development," (mimeo, undated), p. 1.

Contrast the above description with a typical scene of education in a middle-class suburban American community with its modernistic single story school building; the plethora of books, equipment and teaching aids; the neatly cleaned clothes adorning neatly scrubbed young children. It does not take much astuteness to see that in any society there is a relationship between its patterns of education and its patterns of social life. A necessary step, therefore, for any student of American education is to examine the multi-faceted pattern of American society. One of the purposes of this chapter is to provide the reader with a glimpse of some of these facets.

A second purpose of this chapter is far more significant — and correspondingly difficult to achieve. For out of the examination of the nature of our society the professionally competent teacher is to extract relevant meanings and make appropriate judgments. To assist in this task the teacher has access to the findings, methodology, and tools of the trade held by two groups of scholars — the behavioral scientists and the philosophers. It has become commonplace to make a rather simple and short-circuited distinction between these two disciplines. The behavioral scientists (including those who engage in the study of the individual in society as well as society itself) are said to be concerned with what *is;* whereas the philosophers (especially the students of ethics) are said to be concerned with what *ought* to be. As Dewey and Humber point out in the first reading selection of this chapter, the statements of the scientist about human or natural affairs are of the order of " If such-and-such is done, then such-and-such will, within certain limits of probability, result." He has assumed the image of the man in the white coat, adept in the manipulation of switches and knobs, precise in stating his findings, and reluctant or downright averse to making any value judgment about the consequences of his actions.

Putting aside for the moment the question of the validity of such an image, one may justifiably conclude that the natural and social scientists have provided us with an ever-increasing storehouse of verified knowledge about our physical world, our personality structure, and our inter-group relationships. Since our schools operate within this total environment, we may assume that such knowledge about the whole will give us some valuable clues for understanding one of its parts. And even that knowledge about society which may not appear immediately to have any " practical " value may take on immensely significant proportions in the future in much the same way that the apparently " useless " knowledge about the internal structure of the atom later assumed such frightful importance.

But what now about the validity of the image itself? Some would seriously question whether the scientist is really as divorced from value judgments as he assumes. Whether the scientist likes it or not, so the argument goes, he is concerned with values for the following reasons: (1) The very selection of topics to investigate and the rejection of others presupposes some valuation of what is more and what is less important for a society to know about. (2) The persistent rejection of an area of investigation may attenuate or even close off our knowledge about such an area; and what we don't know may hurt us. (3) The very method of scientific investigation rests upon certain *a priori* assumptions of an epistemological nature; in other words the scientist tends

to accept knowledge that is verifiable by one or more of our sense organs and reject as spurious that knowledge which is arrived at through non-scientific means such as dreams, visions, hunches, or intuition.

The philosopher, on the other hand, is assumed to deal with value judgments as a normal part of his stock in trade. It makes no difference to him, for example, if a Gallup Poll were to show ninety per cent of the American people in favor of euthanasia (mercy-killing). He still is concerned with the goodness or badness, the rightness or wrongness, of the act. He would argue that people *ought* to behave morally once they have established a reference or ethical standard by which to act. Note that such value judgments of the philosopher are not the result of mere whims or personal prejudices. They are the logical end-product of a systematic and objective method of dealing with ethical issues.

But even this commonly accepted image of the philosopher is open to modification. Some would divide his role into two sub-categories, of which the first would be the one described above. In the second category he would be as objective and scientific in his study *about* the elements of philosophy as his natural science colleague would be, for example, in his study of nuclear energy. In this role the philosopher would deal with the various aspects, ideas, concepts, and systems of thought associated with philosophy in a detached, impartial, and analytical manner. His purpose would be to understand and explain, not to exhort. He would be less concerned with proscribing certain immoral acts than he would be with describing and identifying an ethical system that related to such an act.

Where does all this leave the prospective teacher? In effect he takes on attributes of *both* the scientist and the philosopher — with all four of their roles. First — in order to understand the school, he must know something about the society in which it operates. Secondly, since he cannot possibly study *all* aspects of society, the decisions that he makes about assigning priority to various aspects will be dependent upon his judgments of value. Thirdly, as a classroom teacher he cannot avoid making decisions about the rightness or wrongness of specific behaviors by his pupils, certain social conditions in the community, or current events of social significance; nor will he be able long to conceal his own preferences for what ought to be done or ought not to be done. Finally, and perhaps most difficult of all, he will attempt to deal with the factors involved in making ethical decisions in an objective, analytical, and fair-minded way; he will see his role not as one who *preaches* the truth but as one who, along with his students, *seeks* the truth.

All of this adds up to a truly staggering responsibility for the teacher. The less intrepid are likely to say that they cannot possibly perform all such roles. But this is of no avail. The very nature of the profession demands tacit or express recognition of them. As has been repeatedly stressed in this volume, the teacher is a member of a profession that demands numerous and persistent normative decisions by its members. This fact alone warrants the high esteem in which many actually hold the profession; subconsciously it may also account for the lip-service rendered the profession by others.

The first two readings for this chapter elaborate on various parts of the relationship between science and philosophy. The final selection, by Max Lerner, is of a different order. It deals with one part of the cultural milieu in which the American schools are found, that is, the popular and the fine arts. Lerner takes a view somewhat different from many of the current criticisms of TV, movies, and " low brow " art. He particularly stresses the relationship between various art forms and the culture out of which they emerge.

RICHARD DEWEY and W. J. HUMBER
Social scientists and the good society

For several decades talk of " the good society " or " the good life " has been shunned by almost all social scientists. Perhaps one could say without fear of successful refutation that the more respected the social scientist, the more apt he is to avoid any evaluative discussion of society or culture. Such evaluations are all right, they say, for theologians, reformers, and " do-gooders," but not for anyone who professes to call himself *scientist*. The terms " good," " bad," " ought," and " should " have been, and are, taboo. The scientist's job, we are told, is to describe, define, categorize, and seek regularities in the natural order in its physical, biological, and social aspects. His is the province of the means to the ends or goals — never man's goals or ends as such. His statements about the world or universe are always to be of the order of " If such-and-such is done, then such-and-such will, within certain limits of probability, result." That " such-and-such " *should* be done, should (sic) never come from the lips or pen of a scientist

From Richard Dewey and W. J. Humber, *The Development of Human Behavior*, © 1951, pp. 711–729. Reprinted by permission of The Macmillan Company.

as a scientist. Thus the scientist can point out that if certain conditions are permitted to continue, then widespread mental and physical illness, or widespread criminality will result — but he must *never*, under the prevailing viewpoint, say, in his role as a scientist, that such conditions *should* be eliminated. This general attitude effectively removes the consideration of ethics from the province of science. In this view, ". . . all ethical statements [are] necessarily ethnocentric — relative to some culture." [1] This is the view held currently by most social scientists.

If such a division between science and ethics is to be, then there is no objective meaning in the terms "good society," or "sick society." The regimes of Hitler, Caligula, Nero, and Stalin are equally as "good" or "bad" as are the cultures found in present day Scandinavia, England, Switzerland, Canada, New Zealand, or the United States. The scientist's judgment of these cultures is placed upon the same basis as the layman's judgment of a woman's hat — one likes it or not, depending upon his taste habits. Nothing is good or bad, better or worse — just different. The most that one can say is that different proportions of the society support given social orders. The slave system, whether of ancient Egypt, Greece, Rome, or of nineteenth-century America, is in no way a bad, or less-good, social system. Ethics can never, according to this view, be subjected to the gaze of science except for purposes of description. Wars are fought, and legislators quarrel, we are told, over purely ethnocentric, cultural values. Buchenwald, Belsen, and other extermination camps of the Nazis are not, the social scientist says, good or bad except as the Nazis or the anti-Nazis so define them.

Why does this attitude prevail among the social scientists? This rejection of the ethical viewpoint among the social scientists has, of course, its explanation. It would seem that this explanation is in two parts. First is the newness of the social sciences. In terms of man's history, the attitude that social behavior of man is subject to the same sort of study as other aspects of the natural world is of relatively recent origin. In certain individuals this view is very old, but as a culture pattern it is very young. Psychology as a separate field of study is among the youngest of established disciplines, and the word "sociology" was not known until August Comte coined it in 1839, a scant century ago. It was long after its coinage that the word developed a field of study as a referent, and it was even later that objectivity became a component of sociological study. It is just this late arrival of scientific methodology that accounts in part for the rejection of evaluation of social phenomena by the sociologists of today. Although it is true to some extent among all students of society and social behavior, it is especially true among sociologists that they can look back a few short years to the time when their field was dominated by persons whose attitudes

[1] George A. Lundberg, "Some Comments on Jessie Bernard's 'The Power of Science,'" *American Sociological Review*, XIV (December, 1949), p. 796.

toward social behavior were essentially subjective in nature. They were, first of all, reformers who " knew " about the world and were bent upon getting others to conform to their way of thinking. Their viewpoints were strongly ethnocentric, prejudiced, and frequently very unrealistic. Their " social problems " approach to the study of society and social behavior was provincially oriented and devoid of objectivity. In their understandable desire to disavow any kinship to these early " sociologists," the sociologists of today are found among the most vigorous supporters of the separation of social science and ethics. Anyone among them who mentions " good society " is likely to be pigeonholed with the utopian, the unscientific, the " do-gooder," and the subjectively oriented reformer.

A second factor which gave support to the social scientists' attitude toward ethics is their worship of the physical and biological sciences. In their desire to keep subjective evaluations out of their findings, the social scientists sought to emulate the other scientists. This is commendable, but on that score they have far outstripped their fellow investigators of the world's phenomena. Actually, in their reluctance to label a social environment as " good " or " bad," the social scientists set themselves apart from the physical and biological scientists. The latter do not hesitate to speak of good and bad environments for animals, plants, insects, and so on. Nor do they lose status by so doing. With regard to foods, fertilizers, soils, medicines, and many other such items, the biological and physical scientists use the terms good and bad, or their equivalents, with what must appear to the social scientist as prodigal abandon.

RELATIVITY OF VALUES — DUAL MEANINGS

Social values, it will be recalled, are objects, material or nonmaterial, which have gained social significance. They are the things which are esteemed or disesteemed by man. Thus honesty, political systems, houses, churches, schools, religion, formal education, divorce, marriage, punctuality, ambition, and so forth, are all social values. The term " relativity of values " means that these things which men hold to be valuable are not meaningful or valuable in and of themselves, but only as they are related to something else. In other words, they are to be judged as good or bad, desirable or undesirable, not by themselves in isolation, but by referring them to some other factor. So far we can find nothing to quarrel about in the concept " relativity of values," but the discussion cannot stop here. If values are not absolute, but are relative, in regard to what are they relative? What is the " something else " which serves as the criterion for the judgment of the value as a good or a bad one?

In the sense in which the term " relativity of values " is commonly used, the referent is determined by the cultural or personal-social experiences of the individual or group. What is good or bad is that which a given culture or individual says is good or bad, nothing else. War, family-decimating feuds, killing of war prisoners for experimental purposes, monopoly of land by the few, dictatorship, and patricide are good if the culture or the individual says so. Everybody and anybody, regardless of his training or competence, determines the good and the bad. Everybody, that is, except the social scientist. The only reason why some values are dominant over others, according to this scheme, is that some people have the power to enforce their values, by direct force or by education and propaganda, whereas others do not. No one, neither the ones in power nor the ones who want to be in power, can go to the social scientist with any hope of finding out from him which is the better system of values. The best that one can hope to hear from the social scientist who holds to this version of the relativity of values is a " Well, if you do this, then such-and-such probably will happen." The demagogue and the democrat, the sadistic megalomaniac or the good Samaritan all receive the same impersonal treatment and good advice. The scientist under these circumstances cannot question the applicant's ends; he can but suggest means for him to attain such ends.

This conception of the relativity of values has no fixed or constant base. The relationship between value and criterion is a free-floating one, with no independent variables. Within this framework there is no room, of course, for the terms " good " or " bad." It is this orientation of many social scientists which provides some theologians with the ammunition they seek in their running battle with secular education. The barbs they throw hurt because the person so oriented has no defense against them. This sort of relativism can say nothing in response to the assertions of the church about the good society, neither in support nor in refutation. Whatever the social scientist says under this system must be said as a layman, and as such he is no match for the professional subjectivists. In his zest to avoid subjective judgments he has turned the ethics of the world over to the persons least qualified for interpretation of right and wrong; least qualified, that is, if objective judgments have merit. In reality, however, when the social scientist acts on social issues " as a layman " his behavior is sufficiently different from that of the complete layman that the fruits of his scientific studies show clearly through his layman's disguise. The fact that the social scientists, regardless of the culture within which they live, tend to support many common ethical values, suggests strongly that they do not behave in keeping with the baseless, free-floating relativism we have described here, but do see an independent variable which serves as the referent of the social values. It is to a discussion of such an interpretation of relativism that we now turn.

Values are relative, yes, but not to each other as mutually dependent variables. *Values are relative to the nature of man as this nature is revealed in social action.* The criterion by which the works of man or other aspects of nature are judged to be good or bad is man's nature, and this relationship gives an entirely different perspective to the picture of social values. It removes the discussion of social values from the void of complete relativism and places them upon the only real data the social scientist can know, *viz.,* human interaction. The social nature of man is knowable only through observation of his social behavior, and the foregoing chapters of this book and the many other books in the field attest to the fruits of such observation. Lest the reader fear that a narrow interpretation of the good society is about to be presented, let him be assured that by tying down values to the stable base of man's nature, we preserve almost intact the traditional position of the social scientist, viz., that there is no single way of meeting man's felt needs. The tremendously flexible, modifiable nature of man's basic needs, both biogenic and sociogenic, provides bases for judging social behavior to be good or bad which are broad enough to allay any fears of a narrowly conceived " good society."

It is untrue that we have lured the social scientist from any scientific ideal by suggesting that he is in a position to talk of the good society because of his study and training. Suppose that one were to approach an entomologist and ask for information about the corn-borer. In response to his question of " What can I do about them? " the entomologist does not do as many social scientists say he should, and reply, " Well, that depends upon whether or not you want to enhance the life chances of the corn-borer, or enhance the life chances of the corn." With no fear of violating his status as scientist, the entomologist will tell what is " good " for the corn, and what is " bad " for it. If we ask a botanist or animal scientist what is a good environment for a certain flower, or shrub, or cow, he does not hedge his reply by saying, " That depends upon whether you want the plant (or cow) to live or to die." We assume that a good environment for anything is one which permits it to live and mature according to its natural needs, whether the object be an orange tree, a field of corn, a dog, or a person. Conversely, we assume that a bad environment is one which stunts or destroys the nature of any growing thing, be it man, beast, or plant. Actually, as we shall try to demonstrate, most social scientists believe this too, despite their protestations to the contrary.

If it were true that the social scientist believed that his status as scientist had nothing to do with ends or goals except to view them as data for study, it is logical to assume that his own goals would not be affected by his scientific study. It is logical to assume that the goals which he sought prior to the time when he began to study human nature would not be affected by his inquiries and observations of man's interactions. If the division between means and ends existed in his own thinking as he says it should, then his new intellectual orientation would in no way influence his conceptions of what the good life really is. His increased knowledge of the nature of man would be kept apart from his emotional preferences. In short, his subjective ideas about the way life should be lived would not be influenced by his objective knowledge about the nature of man.

Such a division of intellectual and emotional attitudes does not exist, because many of the emotional attitudes are based upon intellectual conceptions, or misconceptions, as the case may be. In as much as this is true, the knowledge about man which comes as a result of objective study cannot help having an influence upon one's ethical conceptions. The student of criminology has a picture of the good society which differs widely from that of the average man who sits on a jury. The social psychologist, psychologist, and psychiatrist see the ideal school situation from a perspective that differs from that of the teacher of mathematics who has had training only in his chosen field. The sociologist and anthropologist do not share the ethical judgments of many laymen in so far as race relations and interethnic relations are concerned. One could continue for a long time indicating the way in which ethical orientations differ from individual to individual because of differences in objective knowledge about man's nature. Why, if the social scientist's objective knowledge about man is accepted by him as sufficient basis for shifting his ethical judgments, is it not a sufficient basis for others? If he believes that such-and-such social behavior is good or bad in terms of what he knows about man's needs and nature, why is he loath to speak of it as good or bad, *as a social scientist?* Only continued adherence to the fiction of the separation of knowledge and ethics prevents him from speaking out with ethical judgments.

NONSCIENTIFIC ASSUMPTIONS

There are three assumptions which the social scientist must make if he is to judge social behavior on an objective basis. The first is that it is good that man be able to satisfy his basic physiological, psychological, and social needs. The second is that objective criteria are better or more desirable than purely subjective bases for judgment. The third assumption is that the " good " in society has a quantitative character as well as a qualitative one, that a given society, or culture, is better than another to the extent that a greater proportion of the populace shares in the goods of life. It is freely granted that there is no way of scientifically verifying these assumptions. However, this should not be disquieting to the scientist, because only the most naïve social scientist believes that he makes no nonscientific assumptions in his scientific endeavors. Once one has made these assumptions, and most scientists do make them implicitly, there is no need to depart from his role of scientist in order to say that this or that society, or culture, is a better or worse society, or culture.

Objective criteria for the " good society." A given society is good in the degree to which it permits man to grow and act in accordance with his nature. It is bad to the extent that it thwarts man's attempts to live fully according to his nature. In the first part of this book considerable time and space were taken up by a detailed account of man's nature, and it is with reference to these factors that we judge a society, or the way of life which it permits, to be desirable or undesirable, good or bad. Were man's nature different, then the nature of good or bad society would be different. To the degree that man's fundamental nature remains constant, the criteria for a good way of life likewise remain constant.

One of the most profound students of social action tells us that ethics ". . . presupposes the knowledge of the world in all its aspects." [2] *With full realization that we are far from knowing the world " in all its aspects," we use the remaining pages of this book to speculate about the good society and the good life, guiding ourselves with the knowledge with which we have been provided by man's efforts to date.* The adequacy of our ethical speculations, we readily grant, is determined by the adequacy of our objective knowledge. Whatever the resulting ethical orientation, it is more consistent than the more commonly used subjective judgments.

The good society recognizes man's biogenic needs and capacities for what they are, and accepts them as some of the given factors in the situation. It permits of a way of life that is not burdensome in the amount of physical effort required to gain a livelihood. Physical labor which makes men old before their time, and from which there is no respite except through sleep, sheer exhaustion, or death is not part of the good life. Physical comfort is measured not only in terms of optimum amounts of heat, moisture, and food, but also by adequate rest and leisure time. The labor-saving devices which have come to man's aid through the centuries have done much to permit the attaining of the good life. However, as we shall emphasize later, freedom from all work is not man's goal, nor would it conduce to satisfactory living.

In addition to providing for sheer physical comfort, the good society makes provisions for the satisfaction of those physiological motivations which we call psychological. The impulses or drives which we have discussed under the headings of random activity and sex must be recognized. Most societies make adequate provision for the former, but the latter aspects of man's psychological equipment are rarely accepted as a legitimate feature of man's human nature. The cultures which have been dominated by what has come to be called a " puritanical " attitude toward sex do not qualify as settings for the good life. Sex must be accepted as a fundamental, inevitable impulse to activity which has important implications for one's social adjustment. It must be accepted as a motive which can be instrumental in social and personal adjustment or maladjustment. Any society which denies its existence or misconceives of its nature is undesirable. The culture in which the assumption is made that the sex impulse will somehow " take care of itself," that the individual needs no guidance in learning of its nature, is no less undesirable than the ones of puritanical bent. In the good society the sex impulse is studied, understood, and accepted as part of man's nature.

Were we to stop at this point in the development of the good society,

[2] E. Jordan, *The Good Life* (Chicago: University of Chicago Press, 1949), p. 13. The reader for whom the relationship between science and ethics is an interesting problem is urged to study this volume. This is a book to study, not to read, but one cannot say that he has examined the nature of ethics and its relationship to knowledge and social action unless he is familiar with the viewpoint provided in Jordan's book.

much would be left to be desired. Man does not live merely for the satisfaction of his biogenic needs. It is this fact which distinguishes him most
sharply from the other members of the animal kingdom. The beasts of the
field find contentment in life if their needs for food, water, a certain
amount of physical exercise, and sex expression are met. The motivations
which we call sociogenic are found in animals other than Homo sapiens
only in token amounts at best. The good life for man involves the satisfaction of his desires for a variety of stimulating experiences, for social approval and recognition, for affection and companionship, and for security
or predictability. The good, or adequate, society cannot neglect any one of
these. An excess of one does not compensate for a deficiency of another.

Man's capacity for boredom exceeds by far that of any other living thing,
and the accumulation of culture is to be accounted for in significant part
by the motivation which we variously identify as the desire for new experience, for a variety of experiences, or as curiosity. The good society is so
made up that it permits the population to find satisfaction of this basic
drive to action. Other things being constant, the more opportunities there
are for new and different experiences in a given society, the better that society will be. The dull, monotonous, uneventful way of life which is characteristic of the areas of this country in which most of the lynchings take
place is not a good life. The importance of lynchings, barn-burnings, religious meetings often with heightened emotional content, weddings, and
even funerals in remote rural areas suggests the need for greater variety in
the offerings of life in these areas. The festive appearance of funerals in the
colonial period of this country may appear odd to a modern urbanite, but
when one thinks of the isolation and routine aspects of life at that time,
the huge banquets with their " a good time was had by everybody " atmosphere are not difficult to explain, if we keep in mind this need of man
for variety of experiences. To be sure, such occasions fulfilled other functions than the breaking of monotony. In present-day America, one should
not underestimate the value of movies and radio in breaking the monotony
of the day-by-day living. Neurosis is apt to be found among persons who
are bored with a life that is not sufficiently stimulating to keep them from
excessive self-contemplation.

One of man's most urgent sociogenic needs is the desire for recognition.
Cognizance of this must be made in any society which makes a pretense
of being good. To deny a person ways in which he can gain social approval
will result in his seeking social recognition at any cost. From the hell-raiser
in the schoolroom to the vengeful murderer, we see the need for recognition operating. The good society will provide a variety of ways in which a
person can gain this basic satisfaction, and will not ridicule the ways in
which one secures this recognition if it is not harmful socially. Skill at playing bridge, owning the finest collection of medium-sized glazed elephants,
being first to cross a number of new bridges, or any other claim to fame is
justified and is no less commendable than some of the more popular ways

of gaining recognition. The more ways there are for persons to seek and gain social approval, the less need there will be to find this satisfaction in neurotic fantasies or in the more serious forms of mental illness.

The greater freedom given the members of a family, a community, or a nation to seek recognition, the more widespread is likely to be the satisfaction of this need. Social statuses rigidly assigned by authoritarian leaders reduce the possibility of the populace's gaining social approval or recognition because of the differential preparation and abilities of individuals. A society which demands that all of its members be members of athletic teams and honors only the outstanding athlete is bound to have dissatisfaction on this score prevalent. Obviously everyone cannot be a leader in a given pursuit, and the differences in physique, intelligence, interest, and training all determine that some shall fail and others succeed in any one line of endeavor. The good society recognizes these personal differences and provides opportunities in accordance with the differential abilities.

Much has been said by child psychologists and psychiatrists about the need for affection. The good society emphasizes this need and makes adequate provision for it. There is little that need be said here on this point because of the widespread agreement of specialists in personality development of its importance. The customs, institutions, and organizations that make for the satisfaction of this need are component parts of the good society. The need for affection or companionship is met not only by the family group, but by other primary groups which are associated with school, church, groups of employees, and other associations and organizations. In the good society there is no need for a " lonely hearts " club.

The concept " security " is no newcomer to the literature of the social sciences. If any one trend could be said to characterize the last two decades in western Europe and the United States, it probably is the effort of individuals, groups, and nations to attain a greater degree of security of the basic physiological needs of life. America is well beyond the swashbuckling stage of her development, and recent surveys indicate that the high school graduate of today is more willing to settle for a " safe " income than to gamble for big stakes. As we have emphasized earlier in the book, security is in no small measure made up of predictability. Man wants to be able to predict that he will have certain goods of life as long as he lives. However, if we are to use the desire for security as a basis for judging the good society, it must not be restricted to the desire for predictability of just food, housing, and an optimum temperature. Security does not have a specific referent as do the desires for recognition, response, and new experience. The threat of loss of any one of these is a threat to one's security. Too, predictability carried to the extreme can spell boredom.

THE GOOD LIFE IS A BALANCED ONE

The balance of need fulfillment must occur not only between the biogenic and sociogenic needs, but also among the needs of each of these two categories. Here we encounter the question of the priority of needs, of whether or not there is a hierarchy of human needs. If we push the question to the extreme, there can be little doubt that the majority of mankind would elect to fulfill first the vegetative needs for food, water, and the required amount of heat in the case of extreme deprivation of all needs. The . . . effect . . . of near-starvation . . . emphasizes this point, and the reports of American soldiers in prison camps where the food allotment was insufficient further illustrate the priority given to the hunger impulse when that need is grossly neglected. However, we all know of numerous instances when people are motivated to deny a basic need of the biogenic level in order to secure the satisfaction of certain sociogenic ones. The person who diets to a near malnutrition level in order to get into a size twelve dress is common in our culture. The unmarried woman who denies herself any overt expression of the sex impulse in order to maintain an acceptable status in society is another instance of the seeming reversal of the priority of motives.

In any event, the good society does not require that one or more of the basic needs be fulfilled at the expense of the others. On the other hand, the society which emphasizes one to the exclusion of the others sets the stage for widespread dissatisfaction. A few examples of social situations in which provision is made for one, but not all, of the needs will demonstrate the inadequacy of such situations.

Perhaps no better illustration of a one-sided system is available than the system of slavery. Here the needs for security and predictability of basic biogenic needs are pretty well met. Because of the economic value to the owner, the physical well-being of the slave is carefully watched. His future is as predictable as anyone's can be, and he does not have to worry about his food, shelter, or clothing. An oft-told anecdote illustrates the failure of such security to meet the needs of man. In the pre-Civil War period when the underground railway was in full swing, there arrived in a northern city a fugitive from the slavery system of the South. In response to the inquiries of a northern citizen, the Negro reported that his master had treated him kindly, had given him sufficient and good food, and had not overworked him. To the further inquiry, " Why, then, did you run away? " the ex-slave is supposed to have replied, " The job is still open if you want it." To state the obvious, the lot of the slave denies him satisfaction of his sociogenic needs for recognition and variety of experiences. The sociopsychological weakness of the Communist appeal lies in this realm. It can hope to reach only those who are deprived of the most elementary needs of life, or those who believe that they will be the ruling clique in a supposedly cliqueless or classless society. The exceptions to this rule are those intellectually oriented persons who believe that the good society is based upon homogeneity of social values and a security of life needs at the vegetative level. They overlook the fact that once the basic biogenic needs are met, the quest for fulfillment of sociogenic needs will demand a heterogeneity of social values and a freedom of social action that cannot be permitted in an authoritarian system. It is interesting to note the extreme use of medals and citations as measures of social control in a dictatorship which demands conformity that is not in keeping with man's basic needs.

The influence upon the personality of parents' overemphasis upon security is well known and documented. The overprotection of the child is one of the best preparations for social maladjustment in adulthood that can be invented. The fears engendered by this protection serve to perpetuate the protective relationship between the individual and others.

On the other hand, a social system in which the need for variety of experience is unduly emphasized is not an ideal situation either. Perhaps the situations surrounding the recent war effort set the stage for satisfaction of this need in the extreme. Here predictability of the future was at a minimum, at least in so far as most individuals were concerned. The constant change and movement, the repeated encounter with novel situations, and the lack of security characterized this period. No society, however, can hope to be based upon such constant flux. The frontier town, particularly the " boom " town near oil, gold, or silver mines, is another example where thrills (i.e., new, unpredictable situations) are a " dime a dozen." Institutions do not exist, and immediate expediency is the " order " of the day. All except the most adventurous, and those whose life chances seem to be enhanced by the constant changing situations, view the conditions of the frontier as undesirable. The history of any frontier, pioneering community reveals the gradual provision for greater security and order in the ways of the community's social life. Frontier life is not a way of life that meets the needs of man in a balanced fashion.

It grows clear that the most desirable way of life involves some sort of compromise among the various human needs. No one of them can be given full and complete satisfaction without payment of high social and personal cost. The good life is a life guided by mature personalities who have learned that there can be too much of a good thing. Satiety does not spell satisfaction. This fact brings us to the question of the relative value of a life based upon a crass hedonism, upon doing only that which one wishes to do, and a life which includes a significant amount of obligation in social behavior. There is much more than just humor in the inquiry of the child in the extremely " progressive " school in which he asks, " Teacher, do we *have* to do what we want to do today? " Not only is it essential to the functioning of the social structure that people fulfill obligations and carry tasks beyond the point where the pleasure principle carries them, it is also essential to the living of the full life from the viewpoint of the individual. . . . [O]ne aspect of pleasure is the removing of the unpleasant or of escaping the unpleasant. There is no need to resort to a masochistic explanation of motives to see the truth of this. No one has fully enjoyed food who has not been really hungry, rest unless he has been weary, nor companions who has not been lonely. The ones who appreciate and enjoy a bit of social approval or recognition are those who have not been surfeited of it. Accordingly, the good society is one which imposes work upon its citizens beyond the dilettante stage. The average person's conception of heaven is a most unrealistic one if the inhabitants of such a place are to have the attributes of human beings. As usually conceived, it would be a place of boredom and one from which the majority would soon be tempted to escape to the nether regions — that is, if the latter region is as usually described by those who disapprove of it. With no intention of denying the positive aspects of pleasure, we insist upon the importance of recognizing the negative aspects of it.

Institutions and the good life. Many of the arguments which attend almost all discussions of the merits and demerits of such institutions as formal educational, religious, economic, and political systems are traceable to the lack of agreement about what the good society or good life is. Until consensus of what is good about life and society is attained, the debates on the activities of the schools, churches, business associations, and states will remain subjective and fruitless. None of these is good or bad in its own right, but only as it is related to the larger society and to the nature of human nature. Time does not permit the elaboration of the relationship between any one institution and the good society, but a few statements will serve to indicate the trend of thinking which our position sponsors.

Education and the good life. Much valuable time is wasted disputing about whether our educational systems should equip the populace to secure for itself the material things of life or the nonmaterial. The good life demands both so there can be no " either/or " educational program. The terms " a full life " or " a rich experience " perhaps convey more meaning than a statement of the good life in terms of fulfillment of basic biogenic and sociogenic needs. In any event, *in our culture* the content of liberal education, including the arts, humanities, and sciences is essential to the good life. The satisfactions of basic needs that can be secured through the mastery of an art, through comprehensive reading or study of literature, both fictional and nonfictional, cannot, of course, be measured in terms of dollars or credits or degrees. Nor is research of profound proportions necessary to demonstrate the value of a large store of knowledge about the universe in which we live. Merely to contrast the eagerness with which Dr. H., whom we briefly describe below, fills his leisure time, with the frantic boredom of the grossly ignorant individual during his periods of enforced idleness is to demonstrate the value of a liberal education.

Dr. H. lives in a small city in New York State. He is a respected physician in that community and has a medical practice which takes up much of his time, but to mention merely his status of physician is to tell little about him. He taught modern languages in a university to finance his medical education, and some of the older residents of an area of the city peopled by immigrants from Europe may remember him as he stumbled through the district, studying his surgery text on his way to class. There was no other time to study surgery. Earlier as an undergraduate, Dr. H. had played his violin for dances, and worked summers as a union carpenter.

In his adult years his skills of early years were not lost. In addition to building much of his furniture, he turned attention to making violins. Although some did not prove to be of a quality he would like, most of them were excellent and several of the world's finest violinists are owners of his violins. He still plays the violin, mostly now for his own pleasure. In his observatory, which he built himself, he has taught astronomy to interested young people in the community. He also has taught trigonometry, French, and German to members of the community, all for the love of teaching and of knowledge. He is an amateur botanist and geologist with more than a small amount of knowledge in each field. A cabin in the Adirondacks which he built, with the assistance of good friends, afforded him and his family recreation. He is an omnivorous reader and seeker after knowledge of all sorts, often driving miles to neighboring metropolitan centers to attend lectures, concerts, or to prowl around a museum of one sort or another.

It is incredible that Dr. H. could ever experience boredom. His world is too full of things that remain unfinished, of things to do that are very satisfying to him, to leave room for boredom. Surely his is the good life. He and his wife now plan to retire to a smaller house which is largely of his own building, to enjoy the leisure that his long practice has earned for him. The interests of a lifetime are still with him, and now there will be more time in which to pursue them. We are not suggesting that Dr. H. is the average citizen of tomorrow. We include this briefest of sketches of his personality in order to indicate some of the aspects of a " good life." Not everyone can possess the fortunate combination of unusual energy, innate ability, early motivation, and fortunate environment which are essential to such a way of life. However, man falls so far short of using the things which are potentially at his command that this way of life can be approached, if not actually attained, by many people. The more closely it is approximated, the closer we will come to the " good society." This need not require extensive formal education, but man being what he is, it probably would mean just that in the majority of cases. Such education would necessarily recognize individual differences in learning ability and interest.

No fuzzier field of debate can be found than the current arguments about the respective merits of " content " or knowledge, and " method " (really, techniques of pedagogy). Not until the educators, and their detractors, realize that the answer to the query " knowledge for what? " is " knowledge for the good life," and have some clear concept of the nature of the good society and good life, will the discussions about educational institutions be anything but fuzzy.

Religion and the good society. No discussion of the good society can afford to omit some reference to the question of religion, surely one of the most debated, and debatable, questions of the day or any day. The question really has two aspects which are in some degree independent of each other.

Some of the confusion in current thinking about religion and church traces to the failure to distinguish clearly between these two parts of the problem. One aspect of the problem concerns the validity of the dogma set forth by the exponents of the various supernatural religions. For the most part they are subjective in nature, and the problem of how to substantiate or refute them is probably not of finite dimensions.

Another aspect of the problem centers around the social and personal consequences of belief, or disbelief, in these religious viewpoints. This problem cannot be solved by proving or disproving the assertions of the churchmen. The question is whether or not the good society needs something called religion, regardless of the validity of its dogmas. We do not have in hand the answer to this second part of the religion-life problem. However, there are a few tentative evaluative statements about religion and the church which can be made in our discussion of the good society.

Many of the older interpretations of mental and physical illness are now called superstitions and have yielded to objective interpretations that are acceptable to almost all modern churchmen, clergy and laymen alike. It seems likely that some of the pre-scientific interpretations of social behavior will likewise yield to objective interpretations. This does not mean, however, that there will not still exist large areas of experience for which no objective interpretations are known, and for which some philosophical orientation is necessary. Just what that orientation will be cannot be known now, but it seems certain that there will continue to be a place for the organization of the church in the good society. The dependence of the clergy and many members upon the organization of the church for the fulfillment of their needs will, in all probability, assure the continued existence of the church. It is equally certain that some of its viewpoints and functions will change.

It is unlikely in the good society that there will be but one church, and certainly not a state church. Ideally, the collective values of the church would be consistent with those of the state, but in any event, the former would be free to evaluate the functions of the state. In the good society the churches will examine their doctrines and activities in the light of their relationships to mental health and community welfare. No organization can be called " good " if its attitudes and activities engender social animosities, limit social mobility, conduce to the development of inadequate personalities, or in any way frustrate man in his quest for the good life. Religious views must be reconcilable with objective knowledge in the good society. The various churches, appealing to the variety of human natures in the community, will support the general welfare by inspiring group activity and community ideals that will serve as a cohesive force and media of social control in the society of which they are functional parts.

Economic systems and the good society. The most significant change in the world's economic system has been the shift from a rural-agricultural one to a system which is both rural-agricultural and urban-industrial, with the latter becoming dominant. The implications which this shift has for the good way of life are not yet fully understood. Our remarks on this point are speculative and suggestive, not definitive and sure. One of the accompaniments of the urban-industrial-commercial economic system is the increased specialization of labor, with each worker contributing a smaller and smaller part to the completed whole, whether that whole be a material object or some form of service. This specialization brings with it the fact that the opportunity for a worker to satisfy more than sheer economic needs by his activity is definitely lessened. In the former, nonspecialized, nonfactory type of production and service efforts, the need for variety of experience and recognition were often met through the economic activity. In making a whole chair, the former craftsman was more closely identified with the finished object than is the modern furniture factory worker who merely sands the wood after someone else has cut it and before someone else assembles it and it is passed on to another who paints or varnishes it. Making the whole chair is a less montonous task, if a less efficient one from the viewpoint of time and cost.

The craftsman who creates the whole finished product has greater opportunity to secure social approval and variety of experiences than has the man who uses a power wrench to tighten bolts on an automobile. The pride of craftsmanship is nearly lost in the larger mass-production industries. The " plums " are reserved for the designer and a few other specialists and part of the construction process left for the majority of other specialists is work in its strictest sense.

The stripping of a job of its satisfying, noneconomic aspects poses one of the major problems for modern society. Can the good society have as one of its components a mass-production system wherein the workers' tasks are so specialized and minute that they receive no recognition for [their] part in the finished product, and find the job highly monotonous? Lest one jump to the conclusion that such an economic system is inadequate or bad, he must be cautioned that an institution or organization which may be found wanting when viewed in isolation may prove to be quite adequate when judged in terms of the whole cultural context. Perhaps, for instance, the assembly-line worker may be able to compensate adequately for the social shortcomings of the job by wise use of his increased leisure time which is afforded by the factory system. Perhaps the negative identification of line worker with management and ownership which results from the large size and necessarily impersonal relationships which characterize our large factories and commercial houses, can be compensated for by carefully designed educational programs and personnel departments. These things remain to be demonstrated. The absence of adequate research of these problems involved in our economic system is in part attributable to the absence of any clear-cut concept of the good society. Until research is so oriented, the debates about the capitalistic, socialistic, and communistic economic systems will continue at the nonobjective, emotional level.

MANY KINDS OF GOOD SOCIETIES ARE POSSIBLE

As we have emphasized throughout this book, man's capacity for adaptation of his environment is greater than that of any other living thing. His basic needs can be met in almost innumerable different ways. As long as the societal pattern of institutions and organizations, and acceptable variations from the normal patterns, are of such a nature that man's biogenic and sociogenic needs can be satisfied within their framework, it matters not what the content of them is. There is no one diet, no single form of recreation, nor occupational set-up that is best. Within the limits set by the nature of human nature, social values *are* relative.

Within the larger framework, internal consistency is a measure of adequacy. All types of institutions or organizations do not fit together equally well. The type of economic system determines in part the type of school, family, or church system best suited for that culture. All good societies have the same basic framework, but the content of that framework may, and inevitably will, vary widely from group to group, and from culture to culture.

The things which all good societies have in common tend to be at the level of mores, whereas the variations from culture to culture are more apt to be at the folkways level. This gives all good societies a common morality, but permits wide variety in the expedient way of doing things. The terms morality and immorality gain new and specific meaning in a society which looks to the nature of man as the basis for its rules of moral behavior.

SUMMARY

There is a general reluctance among social scientists, perhaps among the better social scientists, to evaluate any society or any culture. The current opinion of many social scientists is that their job includes the task of discovering means to attain certain ends, but they disavow any ability or right to evaluate the ends. For them Nazi Germany and the way of life in this country are equally good or bad. The most that they will say is that they are different, that the evaluations all have a cultural basis and therefore are not objective bases.

Among the social scientists, particularly the sociologists, the memory of the many subjectively oriented reformers who call themselves social scientists is still vivid. These reformers " knew " the answers to the world's ills and were intent upon getting the rest of the world to think and act as they did. In their legitimate desire to dissociate themselves from these reformers, the social scientists of today may have swung too far in the opposite direction.

A second factor in this zeal of social scientists to avoid any evaluation of man's behavior or society lies in the worship of the physical and biological sciences. In their commendable attempts to be as objective as other scientists, the social scientists have outstripped the other scientists. The biological scientists, for instance, do not hesitate to speak of environments for plants or animals as good or bad.

The term "relativity of values" has two meanings. One suggests that social values are evaluated only in terms of themselves, the one value being good or bad in terms of another value or other values. Viewed this way, the scientist cannot, of course, call any social value good or bad. However, if we view social values in terms of the nature of man, if we judge a society or culture to be good or bad to the degree that it meets, or fails to meet, the basic needs of mankind, then the social scientist *can* evaluate social values and still not relinquish his claim to the status of scientist. In fact, the intellectual attitudes which come from one's scientific study of human nature effect changes in the evaluation of the social scientist. The uniformity of the changes which occur among social scientists' attitudes toward social values strongly suggests that the separation of objective knowledge about man and evaluations of man's social behavior as good or bad is fiction. Were it true that there is no objective basis for judging man's behavior, then the increase in objective knowledge by the social scientists would not have any influence upon their social attitudes. If the social scientist makes the three nonscientific assumptions (1) that it is good for man to live and develop according to his nature, (2) that objective criteria are better than subjective criteria, and (3) that there are degrees of goodness and badness in societies, he is then free to judge cultures and societies *as a scientist.*

The good society is one in which the basic biogenic and sociogenic needs of man are fulfilled. Even though in extreme instances of deprivation, such biogenic impulses as hunger and thirst usually assume priority over others, in the good society all of the needs must be satisfied in a balanced fashion. Provision for one in excess will not satisfy the others. Because of man's extremely modifiable nature, there are many combinations of culture patterns which are equally good or bad. It is perhaps this fact that gave rise to the belief that *any* society is a good society, that there is no basis of objective judgment of man's behavior or his works. However, man's nature sets limits to the variation which societies can exhibit and still qualify as "good societies."

CHARLES FRANKEL
Decision-making and aspirations by modern man

Why is it said that the sickness of modern society goes back to the fact that it was born sick, and that all the signposts we have been using to measure our progress have in fact been measures of the progress of this disease? Why is it felt that something very fundamental has gone wrong?

The answer is that something very fundamental *has* gone wrong. But what has gone wrong is not the result of a faulty philosophy of history. A social philosophy and a philosophy of history provide men with guidelines, a set of leading principles, that enable them to formulate their problems. There have been weaknesses and equivocations in modern liberal theory which have led men to emphasize certain factors, to select certain strategies, and to disregard other issues; and in this sense, the philosophy of liberalism, along with a great many other philosophies, and along with the absence of any philosophy, is " responsible " for our present doubts and anxieties. But at bottom these doubts and anxieties are not the result of a faulty philosophy any more than a tornado is the result of our ignorance about its causes. The collapse of some liberal hopes, the obvious threat to others, is the consequence of fundamental social dislocations that have overtaken us.

War, the business cycle, and the disorganized international scene have had an obvious influence. But there have been other tidal movements in our institutions which are hardly less important, and which stand behind the present feeling that the liberal ideas and ideals with which we grew up are on the way out. These institutional developments have given us the feeling that history is something that goes on behind our backs, that there is a power someplace we can't get at, and that the individual cannot affect the conditions of this life. They have created a kind of social experience which makes the philosophies of history we have been studying seem credible.

First of all, there is the role that technology plays in our lives. In no other age have men lived with so dizzying a sense of change, or seen their basic material and social environment being made over, and made over again, so steadily. Technology, plainly, is the fundamental dynamic element in modern society. It affects everything from the size, shape, look, and smell of our cities and suburbs to the mobility of populations, the character of social classes, the stability of the family, the standards of workmanship that prevail, and the direction and level of moral and æsthetic sensibilities. The decision as to when, where, and how to introduce a technological change is a *social* decision, affecting an extraordinary variety of values. And yet these decisions are made in something very close to a social vacuum. Technological innovations are regularly introduced for the sake of technological convenience, and without established mechanisms for appraising or controlling or even cushioning their consequences.

A current example is the impact of television. It has affected education and home life, changed the patterns of congressional behavior and political discussion, and fundamentally altered, for better or worse, the operating conditions and purposes of traditional political institutions like legislative investigations and political conventions. But the decisions on how to use television, and how not to use it, have been made almost entirely by men whose area of responsibility is very narrow, and who have to think about only a very few, selected values. The engineers, we say with pride, are the true revolutionaries. We forget to add that if they came dressed as social planners many of us would regard them as tyrants. The engineers and industrialists who make decisions concerning technological changes have enormous power to affect the quality and conditions of our lives even though they do not know they have this power and have no interest in exercising it. This does not change the fact that their decisions are often decisions about basic social policy, and that the traditional liberal mechanisms of public consultation and consent, on which the authority for such basic decisions has been supposed to rest, have next to no influence here. From the point of view of most of us these decisions just seem to happen; and it is one reason why so many ordinary men and women have come to feel that they are being manipulated by invisible persons whom they do not know and cannot control.

The problem cannot be met by reminding engineers of their social responsibilities, or by calling conferences to discuss the human use of human inventions. The problem is institutional. Contemporary industrial society is an elaborately interconnected affair; large-scale organization plays an inevitable role in that society. This means that decisions made in certain central places have consequences that flow out farther and wider than the decisions made by most absolute despots in the past.

> Gone are the days when madness was confined
> By seas or hills from spreading through Mankind:
> When, though a Nero fooled upon a string,
> Wisdom still reigned unruffled in Peking. . . .

And yet, despite the extraordinary range of these decisions, those who make them are frequently anonymous even to themselves. The Madison Avenue account executive does not think of himself as an educator; the industrialist who believes that men who are out of work should be willing to travel two thousand miles to find a job does not think of himself as advocating an unsettled home life. They do not know they are making the kind of broad social decision they are making; they neither intend, nor can they foresee, most of the consequences of what they are doing; they are likely to feel as much caught in the drift of events as the rest of us. As individuals they may have, of course, a sense of power and a feeling that they are making the wheels go round. But they are not likely to know, and no one asks them to care, how many wheels they are turning, or the direction in which they are carrying us along.

There are other institutional changes as well which have tended to throw liberal hopes in the shadow. Technological developments have eaten out the social texture of modern society. To begin with, the simple physical mobility of an industrial population makes social ties impermanent and thin. When a man's place of residence depends mainly on his job, and when jobs are changed frequently, community pressures are weakened, and community affections diluted. But even more important, the kind of social relation into which men tend to enter in an industrial society has changed fundamentally. Once individuals joined only one or two groups which took care of a wide variety of things; they now join many groups, each of which has only a single purpose. A man joins a trade association or a union to take care of his working life, a bridge club or a bowling team to take care of his recreation, and a Better Citizenship Society to take care of his unharnessed moral impulses. In each of these groups he deals with different people; and in each of them only a part of himself is involved, and the general social significance of what he is doing tends to be hidden from view. This has depleted the reservoir of community feelings and common interests on which liberal societies have counted for the resolution of disagreements.

An example of what this means is offered by the local church. Even fifty years ago, the local church in many places was still the focus of a community. Men met at the church to get the news, to enjoy themselves, to deal with common disasters, to receive or to dispense charity, to be confirmed and married and to bury their dead. When they came together to pray, it was as a community which had been meeting regularly to deal with common problems. Now, however, the local church is one more specialized association with a special business. Men get their news elsewhere, they get their entertainment elsewhere, and when they realize they have a common problem they usually form a special association — a Youth Board, for example, or a Civic Association — to deal with that problem. As a result, church membership has become more formal and occasional, and prayer more abstract. The problems of our churches do not come mainly from the inducements of a rival " materialistic " philosophy. They come from the basic institutional changes that have taken place in industrial society.

Another example is the family. In preindustrial societies, the family is usually in only one of its aspects an arrangement for mating and bringing up children. It is an economic arrangement, and, even more, it is the basic form of social insurance. A marriage represents the union not of two people, but of two clans. It gives a man additional protection against his enemies, extends his influence in the community, cushions him against sudden disasters like disease or bad crops, and guarantees that he will be cared for in his old age. And it is, consequently, a relatively permanent arrangement. But in an industrial society the variety of functions which were once served by the single institution of the family have been parceled out to separate agencies. Men find their social security by investing in stocks and bonds, by joining unions, or by turning to the State. The family has been reduced in function; and with this reduction in function has gone a reduction in its size, power, and permanence.

Before we become nostalgic about all this, it is well to remember that these changes in the associations that govern men's lives have meant considerably more personal freedom for most men, and have released them from what were often stifling pressures. And a type of specialized social group has been created which is undoubtedly more efficient in achieving specific purposes. But these changes do mean that the sort of powerful, independent social group which once stood between the individual and the abstraction known as " society at large " has been progressively devitalized. The most powerful groups to which individuals now belong are mass organizations like trade unions or political parties, where power is highly bureaucratized. The individual can no longer have the sense — except vicariously — that he is taking an active part in the making of public decisions that affect him. His access to centers of social power becomes increasingly difficult; he comes to experience social authority as something remote and abstract; he feels isolated and depersonalized. Allowing for exaggeration, the experience, and the world view, of the ordinary member of contemporary industrial society is the reverse of the experience of the member of preindustrial society. The major cataclysms that affected preindustrial man came from a physical world which he tended to think of in personal terms; the major cataclysms that affect industrial man come from a human world which he tends to think of in impersonal terms. Once the physical world was thought to be largely uncontrollable, something to be propitiated or cajoled or paid off. We take that attitude now toward our social fortunes. The destruction of the vigorous, multipurpose private associations that once stood as centers of power between the State and the individual has created that feeling of helplessness before the ebb and flow of massive social events which is expressed in contemporary philosophies of history.

Such changes in our institutions are the sort of thing which threatens to engulf the liberal image of a society made up of men who set their own standards, run their own lives, and co-operate as equals in dealing with common problems. The overhanging problem for contemporary liberals — a problem which challenges their courage and intelligence and, most of all, their imaginations — is this drift of decision-making authority into key positions that are anonymous, the development of an institutional structure that denies the individual genuine options, and the increasing inadequacy of our inherited mechanisms of public discussion and consent to control this situation. It is a problem to which none of the old models apply. We are not governed by what used to be called an " oligarchy." At the moment, and for the foreseeable future, most of us in the United States at any rate (with the large exception of the salaried middle class) cannot claim we are being economically exploited. And certainly there is no single design behind the policy decisions that are made. Those who occupy key positions — in industry, communications, organized labor, the military, or politics — are not a unified group, they have limited objectives, and they mutually check and restrain one another. But if it is not oligarchy, it is not what has been envisaged by modern liberal democracy either.

The problem, then, is that of restoring responsibility to the decision-making process. Responsibility is the analogue in politics and society of objectivity in intellectual affairs. And like objectivity, it is the product of definite social arrangements. A decision is responsible when the man or group that makes it has to answer for it to those who are directly or indirectly affected by it. To introduce this kind of responsibility, those who are affected by social decisions have to be in a position to ask the relevant questions; they have to know whom to ask; they have to have enough power to force their questions to be taken seriously; and, in the end, they have to have some power of free choice. They have to be in a position to take their business elsewhere if they do not like the answer they get. To create such a structure of responsibility in a mass society is the overarching problem, I think, to which a contemporary liberal program must be addressed. For what we have now approaches the organization of irresponsibility.

There is no single strategy for dealing with all the problems for which this phrase stands. On the simplest level, they call for changes in existing legislative processes so as to make party responsibility for political decisions clearer and more definite. On a deeper level, they require experimentation, wherever possible, with methods of administrative decentralization and devolution. In a secular society, symbols, rituals, and abstract statements of ideals can go only so far. The etiquette and the public spirit that are necessary to make institutions of free discussion and consent work must come out of the habitual personal experience of men and women with these institutions. And they can only have this experience if they have the chance to participate meaningfully in the work of social groups that have some independent power and are doing something important.

But most of all, the creation of a structure of responsibility requires the extension of the activities of both the State and voluntary mass associations into fields where they are not now active. The pattern of competition is the basic pattern which liberal societies have traditionally employed to make the decision-making process responsible. The problem now is to find ways of extending the area in which individuals have real choices by restoring genuine *social* competition. The major social decisions that are now made — decisions affecting a broad spectrum of values — are made by specialized agencies whose business it is to be concerned with only one or two of those values. Quite different decisions might be made by agencies whose context of activity and reason for existence are different. It would be interesting to explore the possibilities, for example, of bringing other agencies than those that are now active — and not only government agencies, but private agencies ranging from our great philanthropic foundations to our labor unions — into fields such as public communications and community planning. This might broaden the choices available to the individual at the same time as it brought more responsibility on all sides. Alternatives would be brought into the open that are now overlooked; and when social decisions were made they might be recognized as the kind of thing they are — genuine options involving a wide range of values. The essential point is to introduce a competition of powers into the decision-making process that does not now exist. And what is required to do this is a new attitude toward the proper role of the State and of our large voluntary associations, a willingness to use them to introduce new standards and broader choices.

The great problem, in short, is to reconstruct the liberal tradition to make it applicable to an age of technical specialization, bureaucratized power, and mass movements. To do so will require a revision and amplification of the liberal tradition at two of its weakest points. There has been a tendency, on one side of liberalism, to neglect the importance for the freedom and power of individuals of secondary associations in between the individual and the State, and to overlook the possibility of any kind of collective action for the achievement of broad social purposes that is not State action. The other side of the omnicompetent State is the isolated individual. Liberal opposition to the State, and liberal dependence upon the State, are frequently two sides of the same coin. There has also been a tendency, on another side of liberalism, to take a primarily legalistic and political view of power, and to forget that property, managerial authority, and inequalities in social class or status, give men dominion over other men which needs to be controlled, not only by formal legal safeguards, but by the deliberate redistribution of social power. Free speech, for example, is not the business of the courts alone, but is also affected by the structure of the communications industry. Although liberalism in the twentieth century has gone far toward correcting both these weaknesses, it has not yet quite got over them. It has developed neither a systematic program for eliminating the growing vacuum between the individual and centralized authority, nor does it have a full-fledged theory of social power at its disposal.

But however difficult these problems with which liberalism is confronted may be, it is clear that they are institutional, not psychological — political, not moral. They cannot be dealt with by reaffirming our faith in absolute moral principles, or by reducing our faith in human potentialities, or by admitting that rationality is a will-o'-the-wisp, or by waiting for spiritual transfiguration. The revival of liberal hopes depends upon their being attached to specific programs and definite objectives; it does not depend on initially disparaging the technical powers and the secular intelligence which must be our main instruments in dealing with our problems. " So much does the soul require an object at which to aim," wrote Montaigne, " that when it does not have one, it will turn its violence upon itself, and create false and fantastic problems, in which it does not even believe, rather than not have something to work upon."

It would be absurd to say (though it is done every day in four-color advertisements) that the hopes which the liberal outlook on history expressed have not been disappointed. But before we decide that it was these hopes that misled us, it would be well to look at the nature and quality of the disappointments we have suffered. For there is something quite distinctive about them. It suggests how very new and special these disappointments are, and what the context is in which they have arisen. And it suggests, too, that our disappointments, while real, need not be final.

There is an obvious fact about recent history which it is easy to forget. We have had wars which have involved whole populations as have no wars in the past, depressions which have left a third of the working population unemployed, and political tyrannies whose power to penetrate into the daily lives of individuals puts all past tyrannies in the shade; we live now with weapons that threaten the sheer physical survival of the race, weapons we have invented but are not quite sure we know how not to use. And yet on certain simple standards of progress, progress in the last hundred and fifty years has been unprecedented. Basic conditions of human life have changed for the better, and almost beyond recognition. The average length of life has been steadily extended; illiteracy has been progressively eliminated; leisure time has grown; work, while much of it is routine, mechanical, and dispiriting, is at least less back-breaking; a certain degree of uniformity and equity has been introduced into our legal systems; special privilege, while great, is now recognized as special privilege. These may be limited indices of human progress, but only the most improbable callousness could altogether neglect them. In these respects, men's lives have changed more radically in the last hundred and fifty years than in all history before that time.

This progress throws our present disappointments into perspective. For the simple fact is that men's happiness depends upon their expectations — and the expectations of modern men have grown tremendously. This is the setting in which our present sense that we are going to the dogs must be understood. If there is now a widespread sense of guilt and failure, it is in part because humanitarian feelings have increased, and because the moral sympathies of many ordinary men and women now have an immeasurably greater scope than the sympathies of any but the most exceptional leaders of mankind in the past. If there is a sense that we in this century have a peculiar talent for sin, it is because the collective disasters we have suffered are almost all of them clearly man-made — a token of human power which represents a quite new state of affairs in human experience. If the existence of poverty oppresses us, it is because we do not think it is inevitable. If intellectual inquisitions shock our sensibilities, and seem like inexplicable eruptions of irrationality, it is because our moral expectations have been profoundly altered by the prestige which institutions of free inquiry now enjoy. And if we are worried about the chances of the human race for survival, this is painful, but it is a little like the gout. Most men in the past, most men in Asia and Africa today, have had to worry about their own short-run personal survival.

Indeed, the very bitterness with which we contemplate the difference between our expectations and our actual performance has arisen within this context. There is bound to be some difference between the professions and the actual practice of any society; in most societies this difference has been very large. But this gap between theory and practice has been what most men in the past have expected. It is precisely what their absolutistic moral codes explained and justified. The steady development of an experimental attitude toward morals and society in the modern era has meant, in contrast, that men expect human ideals and human practices to be closer together. It means that they demand that myths and symbols stand for some reality. And it has subjected both our ideals and our institutions to a more constant test, and has made it harder to maintain a gap between theory and practice without insupportable tensions.

In short, there is a sense in which the philosophies of history we have studied are right. Our present complaints have arisen within the context of a secular society, a pervasive science and technology, and a liberal outlook on human history. But those who blame this outlook for our problems are taking the very context in which we define these problems and converting it into their cause. It is like saying that the invention of arithmetic is the cause of Junior's troubles at school.

For the revolution of modernity has not been only a material revolution or an intellectual revolution. It has been a moral revolution of extraordinary scope, a radical alteration in what the human imagination is prepared to envisage and demand. And it has changed the basic dimensions in which we measure happiness and unhappiness, success and failure. It has given us the sense that we make our own history; it has led us to impose new and more exacting demands on ourselves and our leaders; it has set loose the restless vision of a world in which men might be liberated from age-old burdens, and come to set their own standards and govern their own lives.

To be " modern " is not a monopoly of modern man. There have been modern men in most eras, and there have been other modern eras. At least once before, during the Greek Enlightenment, the Western mind envisaged a world in which the critical spirit would be preferred over the pious spirit, and in which doubt, not dogma, would be regarded as the leaven of a high civilization. Such modernity has been only one strain in the present era, and not always a dominant one. But it has lasted longer, gone deeper, and spread farther than has the modern spirit in any other time. No other age has gone so far in the belief that the spirit of modernity might be widely shared, and that all men might participate in the goods and responsibilities of a modern civilization. The modern spirit in Athens was a brief and glimmering thing, arising in a society based on slavery. The modern spirit in fifteenth-century Italy was an aristocratic phenomenon, limited to an elite. But our own revolution of modernity has led to the unprecedented vision of a society in which the opportunity for personal achievement and social power would be generally diffused among men, and not limited to a selected group.

And as its crowning symbol, it developed a radically new outlook on human destiny, which saw the meaning of history in terms of the progress of the human mind, and held that human history could be made to follow the direction that men chose to give it. Prometheus was the first modern. The revolution of modernity proposed to put men squarely on Prometheus' side. It is a unique venture in human affairs, and we can only relieve the strains and tensions it has created by taking it seriously. Our disappointments are real. But they are real because our powers are great and our expectations legitimately high. . . .

MAX LERNER
Artist and audience in a democratic culture

Periodically, when the arts in America are in the doldrums, the blame is put on one of the new media. But it is idle to talk of any art as the enemy of the others. The theater lives in the golden shadow of Hollywood, and the novel seems at times tributary to it: but that does not make Hollywood their enemy. Nor is photography an enemy to painting, nor jazz to " serious " music, any more than night baseball is an enemy to the concert hall or the mystery to the novel. Even TV, whose shadow seems to have fallen on movies, radio, and book publishing, can scarcely be regarded as the Adversary. For to think of the arts as rivals is to think of them as flowing from a fixed fund of energy, so that a popular devotion to one of them means anemia for the others. It is true that some of the newer and lustier popular arts display an imperialistic bent in crowding their neighbors, but in its youth each of the elite arts was also arrogant in its imperialism. Actually the movies and jazz, radio and TV, the paperbacks and the spectacle arts, have reinforced one another because their vitality is contagious rather than sterilizing.

I am not talking here of the question of what medium commands a larger segment of the Big Audience. Given limited leisure, it is plausible that a revolutionary increase in the TV audience should have a drastic effect on movie attendance. But such audience rivalry is different from the rivalry in the intellectual and æsthetic standards of the media. Quite possibly American radio may be able to reach better levels of achievement by limiting itself to good music, news commentary, political discussion, and suspense shows, than it reached when it spread itself thin into areas where TV can do better. The movies may discover that TV cannot be surpassed in the histrionic display of sex and violence, or in the presentation of a documentary sense of the immediate moment: by concentrating on emotion and characterization it may perform for TV the kind of generative function that the theater over several generations performed for the movies. There is a big enough audience in America to furnish for each popular art some perceptive portion of the population that will sustain it economically, especially since another popular art may use it as a feeder for ideas and talent.

In thus dismissing the necessity of a Big Audience I do not accept the view that any art which has one is thereby cheapened. This would be to hold that the chief enemy of the arts is their popularization. One may believe that the spreading of an art wide among a mass audience necessarily brings with it a dilution of its standards: " the wider you spread it, the thinner it spreads." But to hold this view mechanically means, for example, to forget the creative achievements of an art like the movies. It implies a curious antipopulism — a fear that the wide support of an art must taint its quality or destroy its fine bloom. This is the Great Fear that one finds in American literary and art criticism; and one can match it only by the Great Contempt that one finds in turn on the part of the Big Audience — a contempt for the elite arts it cannot understand and whose aestheticism it distrusts. The contempt and the fear together split a society into a Big Audience and a Little Audience, driving a wedge between the creative people and those who are needed to nourish their creativeness.

The fear of the " horde " in art undercuts one of the cultural assumptions of a democracy — that the human personality is a bundle of potentials irrelevant to income or social or even educational rating, and that the richness of popular culture will depend on how well those potentials are fulfilled. The Elizabethan theater in Shakespeare's time, the great church music of the Middle Ages, the acting of Chaplin and Garbo in Hollywood in our own time: all have been people's arts. To be sure, the need for reaching a Big Audience has often been used to excuse the trivial and unexacting. But there is proof enough that, if greatly conceived, the popular arts can derive strength from a massive popular base and can reach the many by reducing themselves to simplest elements — that is, to their broadest humanity.

If we take American painting as an instance, we find an art that has never appealed to a wide audience. It has suffered from the twin plagues of the Expensive and the Esoteric. Having made their fortunes, the American captains of industry ransacked European galleries for their best works and brought them home at big prices. Since the dead masters were the object of their pecuniary piety, they stored them in museums; and Americans came to think of painting as something in a museum or a rich man's house, removed from their lives — and so they ignored it. The painter, in turn, cut off from his audience except for an inner circle of means and sensibility, came to despise those whom he could not reach.

This isolation of artist and audience from each other has been attributed to the machine, which revolutionized the market for art products as for other commodities. Where the product is one of unique workmanship and is not reproducible, as in painting and sculpture, the arts have remained much as they were during the Age of Handicraft. Even in painting the revolutionary techniques of reproduction have made possible a " museum without walls." In the case of the printed and spoken word and of images and movement, the press and film and electronics have made them infinitely reproducible and infinitely accessible. The machine has made possible the widespread appreciation of music, the cheap distribution of literary classics, the enactment of dramatic performances in thousands of movie centers and millions of homes.

The problem of distribution in the arts has been effectively broken. What remains is the question of the conditions of creativeness. I have suggested that in America this problem focuses not on the fact of popularization but on the isolation of the artist. The pushing, successful people among the Americans regard him as an outsider. They do not make a hero of him, as they do of the technical or moneyed genius or the man of power, or even the successful performer in a Big-Audience medium. At best they regard him as a luxury a culture can perhaps afford. Where once the American artist had to wage the Emersonian fight for self-reliance and for freedom from a sense of provincialism, his main fight now is for acceptance in a culture that values the pecuniary. This has led him periodically to flight abroad, especially to France and Italy, where he could thrive in a social climate of acceptance. Sometimes it has led to surrender to the idols of the market, sometimes to a flight into himself. The European apprenticeship has been of value to American artists, but the surrender has been uniformly destructive, and the flight into himself has usually led to obscurity rather than depth. But the American artist has been maturing, and some have achieved the power of synthesis — of exploring their own being without cutting themselves off from the currents of their place and time.

Since the pressures to conform are strong, the artist still works in a difficult environment in America. When he fights against them he runs the danger of joining a coterie which spins out a narrowly private universe with an incommunicable language. He finds it hard to assimilate the rapid pace of cultural change and the vast human deposits of his own culture. He may retreat to the realism of describing one " slice of life " he knows, but he makes no connections between it and the universal values he has failed to grasp. The poet or painter may single out a few crucial items of experience as symbols for the whole, but he soon finds that to handle symbolism as well takes even greater grasp than to handle naturalism. He may concentrate on a locale or region which seems manageable, only to find that the problems of creativeness are not diminished by shrinking the map. Failing there, he almost always turns to the popular arts. Sometimes the

Pilgrim's Progress of a writer or artist in America is a progression through all these phases.

The fatal magnetic force is that of the Big Prizes. Given the Big Audience, the prizes are big enough to engender cupidity and enforce timidity. There is no scorn in America more withering than the scorn felt for " the highbrow." The charge against him is not only that he cuts himself off from the people but also from " reality " — which is identified with making money. The easiest way to get at the Big Prizes is by pandering to the culture traits in all classes that will mean a sure-fire sale. The Midas touch which turns everything in American life to gold does not spare the energies that might otherwise go into difficult reaches of the intelligence and imagination.

If the artist decides to take the pecuniary culture in his stride, aiming at a good living without chasing the Big Prizes, he will still come up against another obstacle — the increasing bureaucratization of the arts. He will need an agent and a lawyer to take care of his contracts; or he may go on concert and lecture tours, barnstorming across the country, largely repeating himself but making money enough to let him do the work he loves the rest of the year. If he is a playwright, he must deal with Broadway producers, theater owners, stage-hand unions. If he is a musician he must pay for an initial recital and " paper the house " with free tickets. As a painter he must be *persona grata* to galleries, museums, rich customers. As an actor or radio performer, he must deal with the networks and sponsors, and with their agents and his own. If he is an architect he must tangle with building codes and city officials and the construction unions. As a novelist he must reckon with serial rights, book-club and cheap reprint rights, movie rights. For the novelist, playwright, and actor there is the guild of reviewers to reckon with, who have it in their power to damn an author or performer who has proved a literary or political heretic, slaying him either with abuse or silence. For the short-story writer there is either the poverty of a host of " little magazines " or the Big Circulation magazines that pay well but may exact in return a large measure of conventionality in art and a conformity in politics.

Even the star system, which seems at the opposite pole from bureaucracy in the arts, works in much the same way. The movie star, the boxing champion or baseball hero, the TV comic of national fame — all represent a huge investment in which many financial groups may have a stake. Highly personalized though their lives may seem, they are actually depersonalized since they must move within narrow patterns set by the bureaucracy their public image serves. It is usual for the writer, composer, or designer in the popular arts to remain anonymous while the performer is played up. It is not the creator but the executor whom the public gets to know as symbol — not the novelist or script writer or composer, but the starred actors and perhaps the director or producer; not the radio or TV writer but the gagster or crooner or the M.C. of the variety shows. The folk

heroes of popular culture, as is true of all folklore, are not the creators but°
the protagonists — of radio serial or comic strip, baseball field or movie
studio. There is thus an anonymity in the popular arts that does not exist
in the elite arts — the anonymity of the creator but not of the hero. This
lack of interchange between the creator and his audience may account for
much of the isolation of the artist of which I have spoken. It is a tossup
whether the anonymity of the creator or the stardom of the performer is
more destructive to personality.

Despite these obstacles, the American artist has one advantage the European artist lacks — the sense of cultural hope and dynamism in a people
reaching out for new ways of expressing itself. The American feels he has
a future, while the European feels caught. Out of this sense of being
caught may come a quality, at once mellow and doomed, which will not
be found in the American writer, who has new media always opening for
him. Thus the American artist has typically a more meteoric rise and a
more abrupt collapse than the European. This has proved true of young
novelists who start as sensitive recorders of what they remember, catching
the characteristic tone of their generation and pinning it down as you
might mount a butterfly. But the high expressive moment of the generation passes, and if the young novelist or playwright has no other resources
than gaiety and vitality and the gift of transcription, he stops in his tracks
as a writer and goes to pieces in his life.

If the career of the artist in America has its dangers, which I have described, it also has its strength. Popular culture has performed a great
ground-clearing function by breaking the monopoly over taste that the elite
arts held so long in the Western World. But to clear the ground is only
a first step toward constructing a new structure of sensibility. There remains the question of by whom and for whom it will be built.

This is not a new problem in America. The split between the " vernacular " and the " cultivated," which I have discussed earlier, started with the
long-barreled rifles of the frontier and the economical lines of the farmer's
tools. The issues of battle have never been sharply defined: it is not always
the mass-produced as against the unique product, nor the popular as against
coterie art, nor the " modern " and " functional " as against the academic.
Nor can one agree that when the vernacular has won out against the cultivated, as has repeatedly happened in American history, it has always been
to the advantage of the product. Yet if it is possible to speak of an artistic
culture predominantly phrased in the vernacular — that is to say, a popular
culture — America must be counted its most fateful experimental instance.
What some of the younger art historians and critics call a " democratic
æsthetic " will either be shaped in America or nowhere.

One question about it is whether it must rest on indigenous art forms
alone. If this is taken to mean exclusively home-grown forms and techniques it would be absurd, since it would force each culture to cut itself off

from the world and retraverse every step other cultures have taken. Throughout American history there has run a demand for a nativist art, whether in architecture or literature, music or aviation design. In part this has been a recoil from an earlier cultural provincialism, but it has maintained its self-assertiveness and been sustained long after the declaration of cultural independence. At their best the nativists have seen that an indigenous art may and must borrow widely: what makes it indigenous is how it uses the materials it finds at home and abroad, and how it weaves them into a pattern expressing the common experience.

An indigenous art in this sense need not be troubled by the question of the classes, from which its material derives or by which its product is accepted. Just as Joyce could appropriate scatological language and make out of it a complex art product intelligible only to the few, so the American language has shown that it can adapt the restricted phrases of the educated classes and integrate them — often with a saving grace of irony — into its own mood and pattern. American ballet has taken traditional dance form derived from the aristocratic societies of St. Petersburg and Vienna and fused it — as in Agnes De Mille's *Fall River Legend* — with the folk material of America, giving it a tongue-in-cheek hyperbole that stamps it as American popular culture. Because these forms have been mixed with the sweat of American experience the lowly do not distrust them as highbrow, nor does the elite despise them as vulgar, but all classes can relax and accept the accents of the universal in the indigenous. These art forms are in turn accepted abroad because they bear the smell of the soil from which they came, yet break through the walls of cultural separation.

Within this frame of the universal the accents of the American vernacular often crop up in very diverse arts. Thus, there are a stridency and exaggeration running through folklore and speech as they do through the comic gag, the radio and TV program, and the spectacle sports — as if the tone of the frontier swaggerers were able to be maintained because the richness of the unbroken wilderness still persisted among the towers of the city. Thus also there is, throughout the popular arts, a blending of the rustic and urban such as will be found in few other cultures. This is illustrated by the blues songs and jazz, whose themes and overtones belong to a preindustrial people but whose beat carries the tensions of the big cities.

To a curious degree the American popular culture, unlike the " Socialist realism " of Marxian cultures, stays clear of the descriptively naturalistic. On the surface it uses the method of realism, but it achieves its characteristic effects in the abstractions from reality. It is a kind of cartoon or gargoyle art, in which everything is bigger than life. This is true of a rich vein of the comic tradition in Hollywood from the Keystone Cops and Charlie Chaplin through W. C. Fields, Harry Langdon, and the Marx Brothers, and of the radio comic tradition which Jimmy Durante expresses. It is also part of the American theater, from the early traveling minstrel shows through the masks of O'Neill's characters and the poetic expressionism of

Tennessee Williams. The same abstraction from life will be found at once in movie musicals and spectacles, in jazz and in the skyscrapers (the " jazz of architecture "), as it will also be found in painting. The younger expressionist painters and sculptors who have never won popular acceptance have a quality similar to that of " cool jazz."

This makes hash of much of the " battle of the brows " in the controversies over American taste. I have mentioned in an earlier chapter the amusing discussion by Russell Lynes, in the manner of Thackeray's *Book of Snobs*, on the highbrow, lowbrow, and middlebrow in America. The truth is that tastes of Americans, like their classes, are hopelessly intermingled. Legend has it that Justice Holmes, a Yankee Brahmin, slapped his knee while sitting at a burlesque show and muttered to his neighbor, " Thank God for our low tastes." The American who likes Jackson Pollock is likely also to delight over the travail of Li'l Abner; the enthusiast for Frank Lloyd Wright may devour cheap mystery stories and roar over the obsessive adventures of Groucho Marx. The fluidity of the class system, the sweep of common experience, and the spread of the big media have done havoc to the hierarchy of the brows, and American society never remains stable long enough for the brows to rigidify in their angle of elevation. Moreover, one can discern in contemporary American literary circles (as Riesman suggests) a separation between the Old Highbrow and the New Highbrow. The Old Highbrow has an attitude of either reserve or hostility toward popular culture, either because as an aristocrat he regards it as vulgar or because as a radical he sees it as a corrupt product of capitalist incentives. The New Highbrow, recoiling both from the genteel tradition and from Marxism, has come to embrace popular culture, finding in it — shoddiness and all — something of the mystique the eighteenth-century intellectual found in the Noble Savage.

There are signs, however, of a new criticism which will separate the true vernacular from the spurious mob language and combine the best of the vernacular with the best from the elite arts. Such a critic will face the fact that the big media will tend to gravitate toward whatever is flat, stale, and profitable, that the press lords will debase their product and the radio sponsors will narrow the imaginative world of the radio to the compass of their own shriveled intellectual universe. But he will not retreat in despair, but will see the growth of popular culture in perspective, just as he looks back at the history of the elite arts and sees in perspective that they too had the vigor to outgrow their excesses.

Where the Old Highbrow regards every Big Audience as a bad one and the New Highbrow sees the Big Audience as a great one, the critic I speak of will understand that the great audience is only a potential in the Big Audience, and that the potential will not be fulfilled except in an intellectual climate that affirms its possibilities even while it criticizes the actual product. He will not despise the movies and TV because mainly the young are drawn to them, but neither will he count that fact in itself an index of vitality. He will recognize that every form of popular culture has varied levels of audience appeal, and that a mature art will shape its product — as Chaplin did in the movies — to reach each audience on its own terms, yet hold them all in suspension by universals which give each a new dimension. He will respect the subtleties and richness of the American language, and the capacity of the common speech to express the common experience of Americans. He will not scorn the escapist in the arts, since imagination must create a sheath within which to feel secure before it can release its quickening energies. But he will refuse to the popular arts — as to any art — the easy, jerry-built solutions to old human dilemmas, exacting from them the emotional honesty with which a mature man cannot dispense.

This is the final test of a democratic æsthetic, whose parallel will be found in the politics and economics of a democracy. No one expects a general leveling of either income or power, but a democracy does require that the whole personality of every man be valued by giving him access to the common political and economic opportunity. Similarly, a democratic æsthetic will not level intellectual and taste standards; but it will reject the principle of a frozen elite of the arts. It will open a hospitable door to any experience which can be phrased in a universal language of art from which no one need be shut out. It will value the indigenous material not because it is " native " or " American " but because — coming out of the common experience — it can be couched in this common language of emotion, so that the reader or listener is at once source and receiver of the creative process. In this sense a democratic æsthetic, like a democratic ethic, gives dignity to every personality.

The foreigner's picture of American popular culture, whether in Europe, Asia, or Latin America, is often wide of the mark. The Communist campaign against " degenerate " American jazz or the " corrupt " press or " degrading " movies or " Coca-Cola imperialism " sometimes impresses many who are otherwise sympathetic to America and its democratic experience. But Americans are needlessly worried about this obviously ephemeral phase. Foreign cultures have accepted and absorbed American movies — and in some cases gone on to produce better ones of their own; they have picked up the more colorful phrases of the American language from soldiers, travelers, and books; they have been deeply influenced by American jazz, by American design in the items of daily use, by American novelists and playwrights. Whatever proves to be universally valid in American culture will make its way in other cultures.

The idea that movies or jazz or literature is a " weapon " in the international struggle has been overstressed in American anxieties about them. It is foolish to use this as an argument for censorship or for changing the direction of the arts themselves. Movies cannot be prettified merely because they will give Communists abroad a handle for attacking America, nor can the historic fact that jazz originated in the brothels of Storyville be muted because it is used against America. In the domain of artistic integrity, cold wars intrude a dimension of irrelevance. The popular arts will serve American interests best when they express with depth and universality the surging impulses of the common American experience. . . .

CHAPTER SEVEN BIBLIOGRAPHY

BRAMELD, THEODORE, *Cultural Foundations of Education*. New York: Harper & Brothers, 1957.

> This is " an interdisciplinary exploration " into the relationship of anthropology and education. Brameld proposes a framework for professional training in education which is capped with a unifying theory that is both temporal and spatial, descriptive and normative. He proposes goals for school and society; he is critical of cultural relativism.

COWELL, F. R., *Culture in Private and Public Life*. New York: Frederick A. Praeger, 1959.

> Cowell gives a brief exposition of the forces of change in our society which are weakening the reliance on tradition and which leave us with more and more unanswered questions. The book explores a great many facets of culture, leading toward a better definition of that term.

DEWEY, JOHN, *The Public and Its Problems*. New York: Henry Holt and Company, 1927.

> Dewey defines the concepts of the public and democracy and their functions. Conditions which prevent the fulfillment of these functions in real life are analyzed.

FROMM, ERICH, *The Sane Society*. New York: Rinehart and Company, 1955.

> It is the belief of Fromm that while science has not yet defined human nature with any completeness, it will approach this. Such scientific knowledge is a guide to a conception of what a good society should be. Meanwhile, societies like our own have developed some patterns which are not compatible with human nature and give rise to socially developed defects in the people who have adapted to that society. While people suffer in consequence, they often do not realize the source of their suffering since it is culturally ingrained. Fromm contends that our mass communication and entertainment media are necessary as an escape; that many people would become ill if thrown back upon their own resources.

GRISWOLD, A. WHITNEY, *Liberal Education and the Democratic Ideal*. New Haven: Yale University Press, 1959.

> In Chapter 14 the author expresses a deep concern for the loss of respect of individuals for themselves and their powers of decision. The size, number, and power of organizations necessary to our age are seen as encroaching upon and diminishing the individuality necessary to man and culture.

NATIONAL SOCIETY FOR THE STUDY OF EDUCATION, *Social Forces Influencing American Education*. Chicago: The Society, 1961.

A variety of social influences are analyzed from the viewpoint of several social science disciplines. This is a good reference for reviewing those social influences affecting education.

OPLER, MARVIN K., *Culture, Psychiatry and Human Values.* Springfield: Charles C. Thomas — Publisher, 1956.

The author describes how culture shapes the psychological manner of expression and also determines what may be expressed. Pages 173–179 are especially good in depicting the influence of culture upon personality.

RUGG, HAROLD and WITHERS, WILLIAM, *Social Foundations of Education.* New York: Prentice-Hall, Inc., 1955.

Chapter 2 is a good review, both for the effect of culture in molding a human being, and for the teacher's role as a guide in this process.

SAIYIDAIN, K. G., *Education and the Art of Living.* New York: Bureau of Publications, Teachers College, Columbia University, 1959.

This distinguished Indian educator looks upon the American culture, selecting some significant problems for discussion in two lectures which he was invited to give. He focuses attention upon those problems of communication and attitudes in our society which impede our really knowing and appreciating others.

8

Education for Transmitting Discovered Truth

We live in a very real world confronted by very real problems. No competent educational philosopher, no competent teacher, denies this. But the state of the world in which we live can at best only pose the educational problem; it does not provide answers to that problem. As Arthur Bestor, one of the severest critics of our contemporary American education, has stated in one of the selections which follow, "Education must, of course, provide the intellectual tools to enable young men and young women to live in this complex and changing world. It has always aimed to do so, and it always must. The question is not *whether,* but *how*." The educational conservatives believe they have the answer to this question.

Today the very term conservative is most frequently used in a depreciatory sense. Most persons would seek to cast the halo of liberalism over themselves and over the programs they espouse. At heart, however, conservatism is an orientation toward life which would attempt to preserve the best that man has attained in the past for his present service. It is an orientation which looks to the *past,* to man's accumulated experience, and attempts at all costs to hold fast to that which has been proven. All contemporary theories of education, of course, look to the accumulated experience of mankind for clues to the solution of educational problems. The conservative generally finds his appropriate patterns there. All contemporary theories of education also look to the *present*. The conservative generally holds that the patterns of the past can, with slight modi-

fication, meet the problems of the present. Some educational theories look to the *future*. The educational conservative is confident of the future, for to him the tried and proven trails of the past will be our surest highways through the uncharted terrain of our tomorrows.

The real challenge to conservative education comes in times of change and crisis. As long as everything is progressing smoothly, as long as a good life appears to be certain and widespread, traditional patterns of education are little questioned or disturbed. But when, as in our century, the very moral and intellectual bases upon which our society rests have been challenged, when changes engulf us at a rapid rate, when our society shows signs of disorganization or confusion, the existing educational program is inevitably called into question. New educational panaceas are proposed and tried. Educational devices which were once thought adequate are often re-evaluated and scrapped. Social change is said to carry educational change as its regular corollary. It is against this assertion that education should vary as a function of changes in culture that educational conservatives have mustered their forces.

The conservative challenge to educational innovations has struck at the heart of the issue. It has not denied the changing world in which persons live out their lives. It has rather asked the question of what it is that people really need to lead worthy, full lives, and it has come up with a conservative answer. In the words of William C. Bagley, one of its early spokesmen,

" Paradoxical as it may seem, it is the conservative functions of education that are most significant in a period of profound change . . . The very time to emphasize in the schools the values that are relatively certain and stable is when the social environment is full of uncertainty and when standards are crumbling." [1] The fundamental issue in the social theory of education may be summarized as follows: In a changing and uncertain society, does the educational system best serve its function by holding to those values which have endured from the past and are being challenged by the tides of change, or does it best serve its function by clarifying the issues of the present and seeking out new beacons for the future? The remaining chapters of Part Three face this issue.

Educational conservatism faces two related questions and comes up with a spectrum of answers. The questions concern the *content* and *method* of education. In dealing with these conservatism sets its own definition of discipline. It makes its own claim to liberality, in the name of liberal education. Its answers to the question of content run the gamut from the traditional academic subjects of the school curriculum in the 1920's to the classical trivium and quadrivium of the twelfth century. Most fundamentally, however, its advocates divide into those who would ground their position in the organized fields of knowledge and their social utility and those who would ground their position in the " immutable nature of man *as man*" and the eternal and universal verities which it is and has been his destiny to discover and cherish.

" Tradition," writes Clifton Fadiman, " is the mechanism by which all past men teach all future men. . . . The primary job of the school is the efficient transmission and continual re-

appraisal of what we call tradition." For centuries the schools have been engaged in this process of transmission of the cultural heritage or tradition. In Western educational systems it has generally been assumed that the most effective method of passing on this tradition was through the organized fields of knowledge, often referred to as the *disciplines*. These fields of knowledge or disciplines have regularly been translated into the *subjects* of the public schools. These subjects are generally assumed to be the ideal vehicle for the " efficient " transmission of the heritage. If one accepts the conservative's definition of education, and his assumption that this is the way to organize the curriculum, a few questions still remain. Which of the organized fields of knowledge are most worthy of being transmitted? What within these fields of knowledge shall be selected for inclusion at each level of instruction? What methods of instruction will best assure this transmission? But more fundamental than these questions remains the persistent challenge: Is this all that education really is?

The first of the selections included below represents a social-evolutionist interpretation of the essential elements to be transmitted to the young. It is the position of the Essentialist Committee for the Advancement of American Education. Reflecting the viewpoints of such notable educators of the 1930's as Henry Morrison and William C. Bagley, it addresses itself both to the question of *content* of education and to the question of the *climate and methods* of education. In terms of content it appeals for inclusion of those accepted values which the evolution of man has stamped with the seal of permanence, and of that knowledge which has been considered as essential to progressive cultures everywhere. In terms of climate and methods it appeals for renewed emphasis on the role of the mature in guiding and directing the immature and for less concern with the immediate needs, in-

---

[1] William C. Bagley, *Education and Emergent Man,* New York: Thomas Nelson and Sons, 1934, pp. 154–155.

terests, and personal experiences of youngsters as a basis for laying out the educational program.

Contemporary traditionalism is not as clearly rooted in a social philosophy as was the traditionalism of the 1930's. If its philosophic roots are to be found anywhere, they are to be found in rationalism, in a faith that an intellectual discipline in traditional areas of human knowledge can best cope with the problems of the world. The program of the present day traditionalist is likewise directed to the question of the *content* and the *climate and method* of education. With Bagley he will decry any atmosphere characterized primarily by concern with the immediate interests, needs, or problems of daily living of students. Going beyond the position of Bagley, he will attempt to delimit the content of education quite exclusively to those subjects which are essential tools for further learning. These are generally seen as the traditional academic subjects of the school — foreign languages, English, history, mathematics, and science. Within such subjects a degree of mastery and control must be attained, a standard of excellence must be achieved. The Council for Basic Education, established to advance this point of view, makes this position clear in its original statement of purpose: "The Council for Basic Education . . . insists that only by the maintenance of high academic standards can the ideal of democratic education be realized — the ideal of offering to all the children of all the people of the United States not merely an opportunity to attend school, but the privilege of receiving there the soundest education that is afforded anyplace in the world." It is within this framework that the selections by Clifton Fadiman and Arthur Bestor should be examined.

The assessment of these positions is not an easy task. No one would deny the importance of sound education to a democratic society. Few would deny that it is important not only to educate people in school but, more important, to prepare them to continue to educate themselves. Many respondents to the positions here advocated have pointed out that Bestor's figures, being percentage figures, are misrepresentations of the actual pattern of American education today. It is undoubtedly true that the smaller *percentage* of persons taking foreign language, advanced science, and mathematics is largely a result of the increased drawing power of the school, the fact that the school now attracts and retains a multitude of youngsters from a variety of backgrounds, youngsters who formerly failed to continue into high school and thus received no formal secondary education. A more fundamental question remains, however: Are we really convinced that the human mind, genuine intellectual power, or moral purpose are really best developed for all within the context of the traditional arts and sciences? We must consider whether learning to repair a television set and going on to intellectualize and generalize this experience may not lead to as strong an intellectual power, and as unquenchable a thirst for knowledge as that acquired through traditional subjects; whether puzzling over the inequities of *Apartheid* policies in South Africa, or social segregation at the school dance may not produce a moral insight as deep, a democratic commitment as great, and a character as soundly human as that of the most careful academic scholar.

The humanist doctrine in education — the belief that education is essentially a function of our common human nature and our heritage of truth, eternal and determinable — has been clearly enunciated by Robert M. Hutchins:

"One purpose of education is to draw out the elements of our common human nature. These elements are the same in any time or place. The notion of educating a man to live in any particular time or place, to adjust him to any particular environment, is therefore foreign to a true conception of education.

" Education implies teaching. Teaching implies knowledge. Knowledge is truth. The truth is everywhere the same. Hence education should be everywhere the same. I do not overlook the possibilities of differences in organization, in administration, in local habits and customs. These are details. I suggest that the heart of any course of study designed for the whole people will be, if education is rightly understood, the same at any time, in any place, under any political, social, or economic conditions." [2]

On these foundations Hutchins has built a philosophy of education which purports to deal not only with the current world situation but with any subsequent situation, unforeseen or unforeseeable.

A critic of contemporary American education, and a critic with an alternative program to propose, Hutchins has faced up resolutely to both the question of *content* and the question of *climate and method* in education. In *The Higher Learning in America,* an early critique of American education which drew heavily upon medieval models, he advocated " a course of study, consisting of the greatest books of the western world and the arts of reading, writing, thinking and speaking, together with mathematics, the best exemplar of the processes of human reason." Such a course of study, described as *liberal education,* is ably defended in the selection from

[2] Robert M. Hutchins, *The Higher Learning in America* (New Haven: Yale University Press, 1936), p. 66.

Hutchins which follows. The method which he sees for education is the method of the dialectic — the intellectual pursuit of an argument wherever it might lead, a method characterized by faith in verbal analysis and mastery of the arts of communication. Such a method can stand by itself. Any attempt of the school to duplicate or replicate the everyday experience which the student receives in the process of living is to be decried. " Today as yesterday we may leave experience to other institutions and influences and emphasize in education the contribution that it is supremely fitted to make, the intellectual training of the young." It is with the importance of this conception of the content and method of education that Hutchins concerns himself in the final selection in this chapter.

The intellectualist conception of education, advocated by Hutchins, raises a number of questions which touch the very heart of any educational theory. Are we to accept his verdict that education is concerned exclusively with the intellectual powers of man? Are we to accept his assumption that vocational life is demanding and not a means for the development and expression of essential human characteristics? Should education concern itself only with what is common in man at the expense of what is unique in each person? Can the great issues of our time, and the significant problems in the individual's life, be best resolved by consideration of the intellectual discoveries of the past? Is truth unchanged and unchangeable, or is it in a process of continual reconstruction and refinement? These are questions with which every teacher must, indeed, ultimately come to terms.

WILLIAM C. BAGLEY
A party platform for conservatives

EDUCATIONAL THEORIES THAT ARE ESSENTIALLY ENFEEBLING

6. Throughout the long history of education — and organized education is practically as old as civilization — two opposing theories have been in evidence. Although over-simplification is always dangerous, one with this caution may contrast these two theories of education by certain conflicting concepts summed up in pairing such opposites as " individual *vs.* society," " freedom *vs.* discipline," " interest *vs.* effort," " play *vs.* work," — or to use more recently current expressions, " immediate needs *vs.* remote goals," " personal experience *vs.* race experience," " psychological organization *vs.* logical organization," " pupil-initiative *vs.* teacher-initiative." The fundamental dualism suggested by these terms has persisted over the centuries. It came out sharply in Greek education during the Age of the Sophists. It was reflected in the educational changes brought about by the Italian Renaissance. It appeared in the 17th Century in a definite school of educational theory the adherents of which even at that time styled themselves the " Progressives." It was explicit in the successive educational reforms proposed by Rousseau, Pestalozzi, Froebel, and Herbart. In American education it was reflected in the theories advocated and practiced by Bronson Alcott, in the work of Horace Mann, and later in the work of E. A. Sheldon and Francis W. Parker; while the present outstanding leader, John Dewey, first came into prominence during the last decade of the 19th Century in an effort to resolve the dualism through an integration expressed in the title of his classic essay, now called " Interest and Effort in Education."

7. Under the necessity which confronted American education of rationalizing the loosening of standards and the relaxation of rigor if mass-education were to be expanded upward, the theories which emphasized interest, freedom, immediate needs, personal experience, psychological organization, and pupil-initiative, and which in so doing tended to discredit and even condemn their opposite — effort, discipline, remote goals, race-experience, logical sequence, and teacher-initiative — naturally made a powerful appeal. Over more than a generation these theories have increasingly influenced the lower schools. They find specific expression today in a variety of definite movements so numerous that only the more outstanding can here be listed.

(*a*) *The complete abandonment in many school systems of rigorous standards of scholastic achievement as a condition of promotion from grade to grade, and the passing of all pupils " on schedule."* This policy, which

From William C. Bagley, " An Essentialist's Platform for the Advancement of American Education," *Educational Administration and Supervision*, 24:244–256, April, 1938. Reprinted by permission.

found a strong initial support thirty years ago in the studies of " retardation and elimination " has of late been given even a wider appeal by the teachings of mental hygiene regarding the possible effects of failure in disintegrating personality. The problem is extremely complicated as a later reference to it will show, but the movement has already resulted in at least one very important change. Instead of having " overage " pupils piling up in the intermediate grades, we now have " overgraded " pupils handicapped in the work of the junior and senior high schools by their lack of thorough training in the fundamentals already referred to.

(b) *The disparagement of system and sequence in learning and a dogmatic denial of any value in, even of any possibility of learning through, the logical, chronological, and causal relationships of learning materials.* This has led to an enthronement of the doctrine of incidental learning. Only as one becomes acquainted with facts and principles through applying them to vital problems that appeal to one as worth solving at the moment (so the theory holds) can one truly learn such facts and principles. And on the side of skills — such as the fundamental arts of language, measurement, and computation — mastery as far as possible should await an occasion when one of them is needed. As someone has said in effect, " These things are only tools, and when a workman needs a tool he goes to the shop and gets it." And yet this theory that " mind will not learn what is alien to its fundamental vital purposes," Thorndike has pronounced on the basis of extended experimentation, " to be attractive and plausible but definitely false." The disparagement of systematic and sequential learning has also been criticized in no uncertain terms by John Dewey.

(c) *The wide vogue of the so-called " activity movement."* This is an outgrowth of the so-called " project-method " which in its turn was an effort to find, or to encourage the learner to find, problems or vital purposes in the solution of which desirable learnings could be effected. The activity movement and resulting " activity programs " and " activity curricula," like the project-method, have an important place — a central function in the primary school, and a very useful supplementary function on all educational levels. The tendency to make them a substitute for systematic and sequential learning and to go even further and regard activity as a sufficient end in itself irrespective of whether or not anything is learned through the activity is another matter. It is, however, an intriguing proposal. As one enthusiastic activist said, " Let us not use activities as pegs on which to hang subject-matter." If the schools only provide an abundance of " rich experiences " for the learner, it seems, other things will miraculously take care of themselves. This is not at all absurd if one accepts the premises; it is a thoroughly consistent result of the theory of incidental learning carried to its logical conclusion.

(d) *The discrediting of the exact and exacting studies.* The most significant barrier to opening the high schools to the masses was at the outset the practically universal requirement of Latin, algebra, and geometry in the secondary program. Perhaps inherently and certainly as commonly taught, the difficulties in mastering these subjects were quite beyond a large proportion of pupils. At the same time the practical value of the subjects was difficult to defend. Their central place in the curriculum, however, was believed to be justified in a high degree by the mental discipline that their mastery involved. Anything that would tend to discredit this justification was seized upon by those responsible for the upward expansion of mass-education. Most fortunately for their purposes there appeared just at the turn of the century the report of the first careful psychological experiments testing the validity of the theory of mental discipline. These really classic experiments of Thorndike and Woodworth were followed by a long series of similar investigations that aimed to determine in how far learnings acquired in one subject were, or could be, applied in other situations. The results in general indicated that such a " transfer " was far from inevitable and in some cases either quite negative or so slight as to bring the whole theory into question.

The proponents of the universal high school and of other educational movements that were impeded by the requirement of subjects inherently difficult to the average mind were not slow to capitalize these experimental findings. As is natural under conditions of this sort, the evidence was generalized to a far greater extent than the experiments warranted, and with far-reaching results in school practice. Although the absolute number enrolled in Latin classes has increased, only a small proportion of pupils graduating from the high schools during the past ten years have even been exposed to Latin. Increasing proportions, too, are quite innocent of any training in elementary mathematics beyond the increasingly ineffective modicum of arithmetic acquired in the elementary schools. But the important fact is that there has been a growing practice of discouraging even competent learners from undertaking the studies that are exact though exacting; hence the upward expansion of mass-education, while sincerely a democratic movement, is not guarding itself against the potentially most fatal pitfall of democracy. It has deliberately adopted the easy policy of leveling-down rather than facing resolutely the difficult task of leveling-up — and upon the possibility of leveling-up the future of democracy indisputably depends. As John Dewey has contended, the older curriculum of classics and mathematics does have a unique value to those competent to its mastery — a value for which the so-called reform movements have not as yet, in his judgment, provided a substitute.

(e) *An increasingly heavy emphasis upon the " social studies."* While the exact and exacting studies were in effect being discredited the primrose path of least resistance was opened ever wider in the field known as the social studies. The argument here is plausible and appealing. " Education for citizenship " is a ringing slogan with limitless potentialities, especially in an age when high-sounding shibboleths, easily formulated, can masquerade as fundamental premises and postulates wrought through the agony of hard thinking.

Obviously no fundamental premise in educational thinking could fail to recognize the importance of a firm foundation in the history of human institutions, or of an acquaintance with present and pressing social problems especially in the light of their genesis, or of an acquaintance with such principles of economics, sociology, and political science as have been well established.

But just as obviously the social sciences, so called, are not in the same class with the natural sciences. Their generalizations permit trustworthy predictions only in a few cases and then only in a slight degree. When the human element enters, uncertainty enters — else the world could have anticipated and adjusted itself to Hitler and Mussolini and Stalin and the military oligarchy of Japan and would not be standing dazed and impotent as it stands today. And while to expect an educational pabulum of social studies in the lower schools essentially to overcome this inherent limitation of the social sciences is an alluring prospect, it is to expect nothing less than a miracle. It is, indeed, just as sensible as would be a brave and desperate effort to incite immature minds to square the circle.

(*f*) *Using the lower schools to establish a new social order.* The proposal definitely and deliberately to indoctrinate immature learners in the interest of a specific social order and one that involves wide departure from that which prevails in our country is to be questioned, if for no other reasons, upon the grounds set forth in the preceding paragraphs. With the growing ineffectiveness of the lower schools in failing to lay adequate foundations in fundamental and established learnings of unquestioned permanence and value, such efforts would necessarily be superficial in the last degree. It would be an extreme case of building what may be characterized for the sake of argument as a perfectly splendid edifice on shifting sands — in this case, quicksands would be the more appropriate metaphor. And here we might well study certain peoples that have actually achieved a social order which is pointed to by our idealists as exemplifying in many ways the realization of their dreams. Reference is made, of course, to such countries as Sweden, Denmark, Norway, and New Zealand. An oustanding fact of fundamental significance is that these countries have *not* achieved these laudable results by emasculating their educational systems. Their peoples indeed would stand aghast at the very suggestion.

(*g*) *The " curriculum-revision " movement and its vagaries.* The various reform proposals just discussed have culminated in the general movement known as curriculum-revision which has dominated the lower schools for nearly twenty years. A primary emphasis has been the alleged need of building the programs of instruction around the local community. As long ago as 1933 more than 30,000 different curricula were on file in the curriculum-laboratory of Teachers College, Columbia University. Most of these had been prepared during the preceding decade by committees of teachers in local school systems throughout the country. Sometimes the committees were personally directed by a " curriculum-expert "; in practically all cases a rapidly developing theory evolved by these specialists guided the work. In so far as we can learn, this theory has never explicitly recognized that the state or the nation has a stake in the content of school instruction. The need of common elements in the basic culture of all people, especially in a democracy, has in effect been denied. Furthermore, with the American people the most mobile in the world, with stability of residence over the period of school attendance the exception and not the rule in many sections of the country, and with a significantly higher average of school failure among pupils whose parents move from place to place than among those who remain in the same community, the curriculum theorists have been totally insensitive to the need of a certain measure of uniformity in school requirements and in the grade-placement of crucial topics. In addition to all this, the clear tendency of the curriculum-revision movement has been to minimize basic learnings, to magnify the superficial, to belittle sequence and system, and otherwise to aggravate the weakness and ineffectiveness of the lower schools.

THE PROBLEM AND THE PLATFORM

8. It is particularly unfortunate that American education should be unnecessarily weak at a time when the situation both at home and abroad is critical in the last degree.

The American people are facing an economic problem which both in nature and in magnitude is without an even remotely similar precedent in all history. In the richest country in the world, two thirds of the world's unemployment is now concentrated. In the midst of potential abundance, the cogs in the wheels of production, distribution, exchange, and consumption have lamentably failed to mesh.

It is the indicated and imminent task of the present dominant generation to solve this problem under whatever expert guidance at the hands of the economist and the social engineer it may find and accept. The student of education must coöperate with all other citizens in this task. It is his own specific duty, however, to consider the problems in his field that are bound to arise in the changes that seem now to be inevitable, regardless of the form which the solution of the present desperate economic situation may take — this with one exception, for if in desperation the American people discard democracy and yield to a dictator the sincere student of education will have no function and consequently no duty. The yes-man and the rubber-stamp will take his place. He will be a luxury without a purpose; and the dictators have standardized a simple but effective technique for liquidating luxuries of this sort.

9. We shall assume, however, that "it can't happen here" and that, whatever may be the new economic and social order, the political order

based upon representative government and the Bill of Rights will persist. Hence a primary function of American education will be to safeguard and strengthen these ideals of American democracy, with especial emphasis upon freedom of speech, freedom of the press, freedom of assembly, and freedom of religion. It is clear enough now that whenever any one of these is permitted to collapse, the whole democratic structure will topple like a house of cards. These, then, are among the first essentials in the platform of the Essentialist.

10. Democracy is now distinctly on trial. It is under criticism and suspicion. Every weakness will be watched for and welcomed by its enemies. Inevitably the future will bring competition if not clashes and conflicts with the now militantly anti-democratic peoples. Democratic societies cannot survive either competition or conflict with totalitarian states unless there is a democratic discipline that will give strength and solidarity to the democratic purpose and ideal. If the theory of democracy finds no place for discipline, then, the theory will have before long only historical significance. French education, much closer to the danger, has recognized this imperative need. Still unswerving in fidelity to the ideals of democracy, and still giving its first emphasis to clarity of thought and independence in individual thinking as the time-honored objective of French education, it recognizes no less the fundamental importance of social solidarity in the defense of democracy.

American educational theory long since dropped the term " discipline " from its vocabulary. Today its most vocal and influential spokesmen enthrone the right even of the immature learner to choose what he shall learn. They condemn as " authoritarian " all learning tasks that are imposed by the teacher. They deny any value in the systematic and sequential mastery of the lessons that the race has learned at so great a cost. They condone and rationalize the refusal of the learner to attack a task that does not interest him. In effect they open wide the lines of least resistance and least effort. Obedience they stigmatize as a sign of weakness. All this they advocate in the magic names of " democracy " and " freedom."

Now, obviously, the freedom of the immature to choose what they shall learn is of negligible consequence compared with their later freedom from the want, fear, fraud, superstition, and error which may fetter the ignorant as cruelly as the chains of the slave-driver — and the price of this freedom is systematic and sustained effort often devoted to the mastery of materials the significance of which must at the time be taken on faith.

11. This problem is far more than merely personal or individual in its reference. A democratic society has a vital, collective stake in the informed intelligence of every individual citizen. That a literate electorate is absolutely indispensable not only to its welfare but to its very survival is clearly demonstrated by the sorry fate that so speedily overtook every unschooled and illiterate democracy founded as a result of the War that was to " Make the world safe for democracy."

And literacy in this sense means, of course, far more than the mere ability to translate printed letters into spoken words; it means the development and expansion of ideas; it means the basis for intelligent understanding and for the collective thought and judgment which are the essence of democratic institutions. These needs are so fundamental to an effective democracy that it would be folly to leave them to the whim or caprice of either learner or teacher.

Among the essentials of the Essentialist, then, is a recognition of the right of the immature learner to guidance and direction when these are needed either for his individual welfare or for the welfare and progress of the democratic group. The responsibility of the mature for the instruction and control of the immature is the biological meaning of the extended period of human immaturity and necessary dependence. It took the human race untold ages to recognize this responsibility. It is literally true that until this recognition dawned man remained a savage. Primitive societies, as numerous students have observed (and their testimony seems to be unanimous), pamper and indulge their young. Freedom of children from control, guidance, and discipline is with them a rule so nearly universal that its only brief but significant exception during the nearly universal savage ceremonies marking the adolescent onset of maturity is regarded as the first faint beginning of consciously directed human education.

It would be futile to deny that control and discipline may be stupid and brutal and used for unworthy ends. It would be futile to deny the need for the development of self-discipline and for the relaxation of external discipline with the growth of volitional maturity. But all this does not alter the fundamental truth that freedom must go hand in hand with responsibility, and that responsible freedom is always a conquest, never a gift.

12. An effective democracy demands a community of culture. Educationally this means that each generation be placed in possession of a common core of ideas, meanings, understandings, and ideals representing the most precious elements of the human heritage.

There can be little question as to the essentials. It is by no means a mere accident that the arts of recording, computing, and measuring have been among the first concerns of organized education. They are basic social arts. Every civilized society has been founded upon these arts, and when these arts have been lost, civilization has invariably and inevitably collapsed. Egypt, Asia Minor, and Mesopotamia are strewn with the ruins of civilizations that forgot how to read and write. Contemporary civilization, for the first time in history, has attempted to insure its continuance by making these arts in so far as possible the prerogative of all.

Nor is it at all accidental that a knowledge of the world that lies beyond one's immediate experience has been among the recognized essentials of universal education, and that at least a speaking acquaintance with man's past and especially with the story of one's own country was early provided for in the program of the universal school. Widening the space horizon

and extending the time perspective are essential if the citizen is to be protected from the fallacies of the local and the immediate.

Investigation, invention, and creative art have added to the heritage, and
the list of recognized essentials has been extended and will be farther extended. Health instruction and the inculcation of health practices are now
basic phases of the work of the lower schools. The elements of natural science have their place. Neither the fine arts nor the industrial arts are
neglected.

We repeat that there can be little question as to the essentials of universal education. As Charles A. Beard has so well said: " While education
constantly touches the practical affairs of the hour and day, and responds
to political and economic exigencies, it has its own treasures heavy with the
thought and sacrifice of the centuries. It possesses a heritage of knowledge
and heroic examples — accepted values stamped with the seal of permanence."

13. A specific program of studies including these essentials should be
the heart of a democratic system of education. In a country like ours with
its highly mobile population there should be an agreement as to the order
and grade-placement of subjects and especially of crucial topics. There is
no valid reason for the extreme localism that has come to characterize
American education. There is no valid reason for the failure of the American elementary school to lay as firm a foundation in the fundamentals of
education as do the elementary schools of other democracies. It is especially
regrettable that contemporary educational theory should in effect condone
and rationalize scamped work by ridiculing such traits as thoroughness, ac-
curacy, persistence, and the ideal of good workmanship for its own sake.
One may be very sure that democracy schooled to the easy way will have
short shrift in competition or conflict with any social order dominated by
objectives which, however reprehensible, are clear-cut and appealing, and
are consequently embraced even by disfranchised masses.

14. Generally speaking, the recognized essentials should be taught as
such through a systematic program of studies and activities for the carrying
out of which the teachers should be responsible. Informal learning through
experiences initiated by the learners is important, and abundant opportunities should be provided for such experiences throughout the range of organized education. Beyond the primary grades, however, where as we have
said it may well predominate, informal learning should be regarded as supplementary rather than central.

15. Failure in school is unpleasant and the repetition of a grade is costly
and often not very effective. On the other hand, the lack of a stimulus that
will keep the learner to his task is a serious injustice both to him and to
the democratic group which, we repeat, has a fundamental stake in his effective education. Too severe a stigma has undoubtedly been placed upon
school failure by implying that it is symptomatic of permanent weakness.
By no means is this always the case. No less a genius than Pasteur did so

poorly in his first year at the Higher Normal School of Paris that he had to go home for further preparation. One of the outstanding scientists of the present century had a hard time in meeting the requirements of the secondary school, failing, it is said, in the most elementary work of the field in which he later became world-famous. The list could be extended almost indefinitely.

Obviously not all learners can progress at the same rate. Some will go very, very slowly. Others will have trouble in getting started but will progress rapidly when they overcome the initial handicaps. Let us not stigmatize failure as we have done in the past. On the other hand, if education abandons rigorous standards and consequently provides no effective stimulus to the effort that learning requires, many persons will pass through twelve years of schooling only to find themselves in a world in which ignorance and lack of fundamental training are increasingly heavy handicaps. This in an all too literal sense is to throw the baby out with the bath.

16. The transition from a predominantly rural to a predominantly urban life has laid increasing burdens upon American education. For four decades or more we have been told that the school must provide opportunities for types of education that the normal bringing-up of children once provided on the farm and in the home. Manual training and the household arts were among the first responses to this demand. The parallel development of physical training with its later ramifications into various forms of health education are traceable in part to the same causes. Playgrounds, gymnasiums, and swimming pools are material expressions of the effort to meet these recognized needs. School and college athletics are lusty by-products representing in a very real sense the importance of finding a substitute for the vigorous physical work that once devolved of necessity upon the great majority of young people.

With the profound changes in the conditions of life already in progress, and with their clearly predictable extension and intensification in the immediate future, analogous substitutes must be sought for other educative experiences which the simpler conditions of life naturally and normally provided. Bread-winning employment is now postponed for vast numbers of young people. Willy-nilly they must remain dependent upon society, whether in attendance at school or college, or in such highly important educational enterprises as the Civilian Conservation Corps, or in " made work " of one variety or another.

The analogy of our civilization with the older civilizations based upon slavery is in no sense far-fetched. It has, indeed, a profound significance. Our slaves, it is true, are mechanical and not human. They are power-driven and increasingly they are being automatically controlled. They can do much more economically than human slaves the heavy work and the routine work. In some tasks they can perceive distinctions far too fine to be detected by the human senses, and they can respond far more quickly and far more accurately and dependably than can human nerves and muscles. Fortunately they can neither feel nor suffer, and so the grossest evils of the old slave civilizations are avoided. The fact remains, however, that the perils to those who are the supposed beneficiaries of a slave civilization are in no significant degree changed, whether the slaves be men or robots. Every slave civilization has within it the seeds of degeneration, decay, and ultimate extinction. Struggle and competition, selection and rejection, have often been cruel, but in both biological and social evolution they have been primary factors of progress. In societies that have lifted themselves above the plane of the brute and the savage, a most powerful steadying and civilizing force has been the ideal of personal economic responsibility for one's own survival and for one's old age and the care of one's dependents.

Generally speaking, then, " social security," like responsible freedom, has been a conquest, not a gift. Making it a gift involves some definite dangers. In our own country, few families have long survived the social security that comes through inherited wealth. " Three generations from shirt-sleeves to shirt-sleeves " has usually told the story. But this rule has had its exceptions. Here, as in some other countries, social security has, with occasional families, remained secure over a much longer time — but under the condition that each generation has been rigorously disciplined to its responsibilities and made clearly aware of the pitfalls that await the spendthrift and the idler. These exceptions, and especially those among them that have exemplified the development in each generation of a vigorous and highly sensitized social conscience, warrant the hope that an economy of abundance with social security for all may be so organized that our machine-slave civilization can escape that fate of the slave civilizations that have gone before. Herein lies an educational problem of the first magnitude which our educational theorists seem not even dimly to have sensed — so busy have they been in condemning out of hand the economic system which has made possible an economy of abundance based upon a machine-slave civilization.

A clear and primary duty of organized education at the present time is to recognize the fundamental character of the changes that are already taking place, and to search diligently for means of counteracting their dangers. Let us repeat that an educational theory meet to these needs must be strong, virile, and positive, not feeble, effeminate, and vague. The theories that have increasingly dominated American education during the past generation are at basis distinctly of the latter type. The Essentialists have recognized and still recognize the contributions of real value that these theories have made to educational practice. They believe, however, that these positive elements can be preserved in an educational theory which finds its basis in the necessary dependence of the immature upon the mature for guidance, instruction, and discipline. This dependence is inherent in human nature. " What has been ordained among the prehistoric protozoa," said Huxley, " cannot be altered by act of Parliament " — nor, we may add, by the wishful thinking of educational theorists, however sincere their motives. "Authoritarianism" is an ugly word. But when those who detest it carry their laudable rebellion against certain of its implications so far as to reject the authority of plain facts, their arguments, while well adapted perhaps to the generation of heat, become lamentably lacking in light.

CLIFTON FADIMAN
The case for basic education

The present educational controversy, like all crucial controversies, has its roots in philosophy. One's attitude toward the proposals advanced in this book depends on one's conception of man. It depends on one's view of his nature, his powers, and his reason for existence.

If, consciously or unconsciously, one takes the position that his nature is essentially animal; that his powers lie largely in the area of social and biological adaptation; and that his reason for existence is either unknowable or (should he advance one) a form of self-delusion — then the case for basic education, and consequently for education itself, falls to the ground. By the same token the case for physical, social, and vocational training becomes irrefutable.

On the other hand, if one takes the position that man's nature is both animal *and* rational; that his powers lie not only in the area of adaptation but also in that of creation; and that his reason for existence is somehow bound up with the fullest possible evolution of his mental and spiritual capacities — then the case for basic education, and consequently for education itself, is established; and further discussion becomes a matter, however interesting and important, of detail.

A crisis period is not necessarily marked by disaster or violence or even revolutionary change. It is marked by the absence of any general, tacit adherence to an agreed-upon system of values. It is in such a crisis period that we live. Of the two positions briefly outlined above, a minority adheres to the first. Another minority adheres to the second. But most of us waver between the two or have never reflected on either. Our present educational system quite properly mirrors this uncertainty of the majority. It mirrors our own mental chaos. There is nothing else it *can* do, for ours is a democratic society, and all our institutions are representative.

Now neither of the positions is logically demonstrable, though some have tried to bend them to logic, as well as to propaganda. They are faiths. The scholars whose essays comprise this book deal explicitly with questions of curriculum. Implicitly, however, they are proclaiming the faith by

From *The Case for Basic Education*, edited by James D. Koerner, pp. 3–14. Copyright, ©, 1959, by The Council for Basic Education. Reprinted by permission of Little, Brown & Co.

which they live. Furthermore they are proclaiming that this is the faith by which Western civilization lives.

Because all faiths are attackable, everything they say can be attacked. Indeed everything they say may be wrong. But the attack can only be sustained by the proclamation of an opposing faith. And if they are wrong, they are wrong only in the sense that no faith can be " proved " right.

Thus the *Metaphysics* of Aristotle opens with the well-known statement: " All men by nature desire to know." This is not a statement of fact in the sense that " All men are born with lungs " is a statement of fact. It is not statistically checkable. It is not a self-evident truth. Cursory observation of many men seems to give it the lie. Depending on whether we prefer the language of logic or the language of emotion we may call it either an assumption or a declaration of faith. If the assumption is denied, or the declaration countered by an opposing declaration, this book, as well as education itself, becomes an irrelevancy. But in that case the cultural fruits of civilization also become an irrelevancy, because they would appear to flow, not from some blind process of unending adaptation, but from Aristotle's proposition. Any doubt cast on that proposition also casts doubt on the permanent value of culture.

It may be that the proposition *is* untenable. Perhaps all men do not by nature desire to know. We can then fall back on a second line of defense. We can say that at least men have acted *as if* they did so desire. Aristotle's dictum may be an illusion. But it looks like a creative illusion.

He has another dictum. He tells us that man is a social animal. Put the two statements together. Were man not a social animal but an anarchic animal, his desire to know would have both its origin and its terminus located in himself. But, as he is a social and not an anarchic animal, he socializes and finally systematizes his desire to know. This socialization and systematization are what we mean by education. The main, though not the only, instrument of education is an odd invention, only three thousand years old, called the school. The primary job of the school is the efficient transmission and continual reappraisal of what we call tradition. Tradition is the mechanism by which all past men teach all future men.

Now arises the question: If all men by nature desire to know, and if that desire is best gratified by education and the transmission of tradition, what should be the character of that education and the content of that tradition? At once a vast, teeming chaos faces us: apparently men desire to know and transmit all kinds of matters, from how to tie a four-in-hand to the attributes of the Godhead.

Obviously this chaos cannot be taught. Hence in the past men have imposed upon it form, order, and hierarchy. They have selected certain areas of knowledge as the ones that, to the exclusion of others, both *can* and *should* be taught.

The structure of this hierarchy is not a matter of accident. Nor is it a matter of preference. The teacher may not teach only what happens to interest him. Nor may the student choose to be taught only what happens to interest him. The criteria of choice are many and far from immutable. But there is an essential one. Basic education concerns itself with those matters which, once learned, enable the student to learn all the other matters, whether trivial or complex, that cannot properly be the subjects of elementary and secondary schooling. In other words, both logic and experience suggest that certain subjects have generative power and others do not have generative power. When we have learned to tie a four-in-hand, the subject is exhausted. It is self-terminating. Our knowledge is of no value for the acquisition of further knowledge. But once we have learned to read we can decipher instructions for the tieing of a four-in-hand. Once we have learned to listen and observe, we can learn from someone else how to tie a four-in-hand.

It has, up to our time, been the general experience of men that certain subjects and not others possess this generative power. Among these subjects are those that deal with language, whether or not one's own; forms, figures and numbers; the laws of nature; the past; and the shape and behavior of our common home, the earth. Apparently these master or generative subjects endow one with the ability to learn the minor or self-terminating subjects. They also endow one, of course, with the ability to learn the higher, more complex developments of the master subjects themselves.

To the question, "Just what are these master subjects?" the contributors to this book supply a specific answer. It happens to be a traditional answer. That is, these are, more or less, with modifications in each epoch, the subjects that Western civilization has up to very recent times considered basic. That they are traditional is not an argument in their favor. The contributors believe that they are sanctioned not only by use and wont but by their intrinsic value.

The word *intrinsic* is troublesome. Is it possible that, as the environment changes, the number and names of the basic subjects must also change? At a certain time, our own for example, is it possible that driver-education is more basic than history? Many of us think so, or act as if we thought so. Again I would suggest that if we do think so, or act as if we thought so, it is not because we wish to lower the accident rate (though that is what we say) but because we unconsciously conceive of man primarily as an adaptive animal and not as a rational soul. For if he is primarily the first, then at the present moment in our human career driver-education *is* basic; but if he is primarily the second it is, though desirable, not basic.

I think the authors of this book would concede that with environmental changes the relative importance of the basic subjects will also change. It is obvious that a post-Newtonian world must accord more attention to the mathematical and physical sciences than did the pre-Newtonian world. But *some* science has at all times been taught. Similarly in a hundred years the American high school student may be universally offered Russian rather than French or German. But this does not affect the principle that *some* systematic instruction in *some* leading foreign language will remain a basic necessity.

In other words, however their forms may be modified, a core of basic or generative subjects exists. This core is not lightly to be abandoned, for once it is abandoned we have lost the primary tools which enable us to make any kind of machine we wish. Other subjects may seem transiently attractive or of obvious utility. It is pleasant to square-dance, for instance, and it is useful to know how to cook. Yet we cannot afford to be seduced by such " subjects." Hard though it may be, we must jettison them in favor of the basic subject matters. And there is no time for an eclectic mixture: only a few years are available in which to educe, to educate the rational soul. We cannot afford bypaths. We cannot afford pleasure. All education, Aristotle tells us, is accompanied by pain. Basic education is inescapably so accompanied, as well as by that magnificent pleasure that comes of stretching, rather than tickling, the mind.

I have briefly outlined the standard case for basic education insofar as it rests on an unchanging philosophic faith or view of human nature. But there is a more urgent, though less fundamental, argument still to be advanced. In sum it is this: while basic education is *always* a necessity, it is peculiarly so in our own time.

Perhaps I can best make this clear by a personal reference which I hope the reader will forgive.

I am a very lucky man, for I believe that my generation was just about the last one to receive an undiluted basic education. As this is written, I am fifty-four years old. Thus I received my secondary school education from 1916 to 1920. Though I was not well educated by European standards, I was very well educated by present-day American ones. For this I am grateful to my country, my city, and my teachers. Of personal credit I can claim little.

My high school was part of the New York City system. It had no amenities. Its playground was asphalt and about the size of two large drawing rooms. It looked like a barracks. It made no provision for dramatics or square dancing. It didn't even have a psychiatrist — perhaps because we didn't need one. The students were all from what is known as the " underprivileged " — or what we used to call poor — class. Today this class is depended on to provide the largest quota of juvenile delinquents. During my four years in high school there was one scandalous case in which a student stole a pair of rubbers.

Academically my school was neither very good nor very bad. The same was true of me. As the area of elective subjects was strictly limited, I received approximately the same education my fellows did. (Unfortunately Latin was not compulsory: I had to learn it — badly — by myself later on.) Here is what — in addition to the standard minors of drawing, music, art and gym — I was taught some forty years ago:

Four years of English, including rigorous drill in composition, formal grammar and public speaking.

Four years of German.

Three years of French.

Three or four years (I am not sure which) of history, including classical, European and American, plus a no-nonsense factual course in civics, which was dull but at least didn't pretend to be a " social science."

One year of physics.

One year of biology.

Three years of mathematics, through trigonometry.

That, or its near equivalent, was the standard high school curriculum in New York forty years ago. That was all I learned, all any of us learned, all all of us learned. All these subjects can be, and often are, better taught today — when they are taught at all on this scale. However, I was taught French and German well enough so that in later years I made part of my living as a translator. I was taught rhetoric and composition well enough to make it possible for me to become a practicing journalist. I was taught public speaking well enough to enable me to replace my lower-class accent with at least a passable one; and I learned also the rudiments of enunciation, placing, pitch, and proper breathing so that in after years I found it not too difficult to get odd jobs as a public lecturer and radio-and-television handyman.

I adduce these practical arguments only to explode them. They may seem important to the life-adjuster. They are not important to me. One can make a living without French. One can even make a living without a knowledge of spelling. And it is perfectly possible to rise to high estate without any control whatsoever over the English language.

What *is* important about this old-fashioned basic education (itself merely a continuation and sophistication of the basic education then taught in the primary schools) is not that it prepared me for life or showed me how to get along with my fellow men. Its importance to me and, I believe, to most of my fellow students, irrespective of their later careers, is twofold:

(1) It furnished me with a foundation on which later on, within the limits of my abilities, I could erect any intellectual structure I fancied. It gave me the wherewithal for the self-education that should be every man's concern to the hour of his death.

(2) It precluded my ever becoming Lost.

In drawing the distinction between generative and self-terminating subjects we have already discussed (1).

I want now to explain (2) because the explanation should help to make clear why in our time basic education is needed not only in principle but as a kind of emergency measure.

Again I hope the reader will forgive the intrusion of the autobiographical note.

Considered as a well-rounded American I am an extremely inferior product. I am a poor mechanic. I play no games beyond a little poorish tennis and I haven't played that for five years. I swim, type, dance and drive raggedly, though, with respect to the last, I hope non-dangerously. I have had to learn about sex and marriage without benefit of classroom instruction. I would like to be well-rounded and I admire those who are. But it is too late. I take no pleasure in my inferiorities but I accept the fact that I must live with them.

I feel inferior. Well and good. It seems to hurt nobody. But, though I feel inferior, I do not feel Lost. I have not felt lost since being graduated from high school. I do not expect ever to feel lost. This is not because I am wise, for I am not. It is not because I am learned, for I am not. It is not because I have mastered the art of getting along with my peers, for I do not know the first thing about it. I am often terrified by the world I live in, often horrified, usually unequal to its challenges. But I am not lost in it.

I know how I came to be an American citizen in 1959; what large general movements of history produced me; what my capacities and limitations are; what truly interests me; and how valuable or valueless these interests are. My tastes are fallible but not so fallible that I am easily seduced by the vulgar and transitory — though often enough I am unequal to a proper appreciation of the noble and the permanent. In a word, like tens of millions of others in this regard, I feel at home in the world. I am at times scared but I can truthfully say that I am not bewildered.

I do not owe this to any superiority of nature. I owe it, I sincerely believe, to the conventional basic education I received beginning about a half century ago. It taught me how to read, write, speak, calculate, and listen. It taught me the elements of reasoning and it put me on to the necessary business of drawing abstract conclusions from particular instances. It taught me how to locate myself in time and space and to survey the present in the light of an imperfect but ever-functioning knowledge of the past. It provided me with great models by which to judge my own lesser performances. And it gave me the ability to investigate for myself anything that interested me, provided my mind was equal to it.

I admit this is not much. But it is something, and that a vital something. And that something — here we touch the heart of our discussion — is becoming ever rarer among the products of our present educational system.

The average high school graduate today is just as intelligent as my fellow students were. He is just as educable. But he is Lost, in greater or less degree.

By that I mean he feels little relation to the whole world in time and space, and only the most formal relation to his own country. He may "succeed," he may become a good, law-abiding citizen, he may produce other good, law-abiding citizens, and on the whole he may live a pleasant — that is, not painful — life. Yet during most of that life, and particularly after his fortieth year or so, he will feel vaguely disconnected, rootless, pur-

poseless. Like the very plague he will shun any searching questions as to
his own worth, his own identity. He will die after having lived a fractional
life.

Is this what he really wants? Perhaps it is. It all comes round again to
what was said at the opening of these remarks. Again it depends on one's
particular vision of man. If we see our youngster as an animal whose main
function is biological and social adaptation on virtually a day-to-day basis,
then his fractional life is not fractional at all. It is total. But in that case
our school curriculum should reflect our viewpoint. It should include the
rudiments of reading so that our high school graduate may decipher highway markers, lavatory signs, and perhaps the headlines of some undemand-
ing newspaper. It should include a large number of electives, changing every year, that may be of use to him in job hunting. And primarily it should
include as much play and sport as possible, for these are the proper activities of animals, and our boy is an animal.

Yet the doubt persists. *Is* this really what he wants? And once again the
answer depends on our faith. For example, the " Rockefeller Report " on
Education (published in 1958 and called *The Pursuit of Excellence*) did
not issue, except indirectly, from surveys, analyses, polls or statistical abstracts. It issued from faith. The following sentences do not comprise a
scientific conclusion. They are an expression of faith, like the Lord's
Prayer:

" What most people, young or old, want is not merely security or comfort or luxury — although they are glad enough to have these. They want
meaning in their lives. If their era and their culture and their leaders do
not or cannot offer them great meanings, great objectives, great convictions, then they will settle for shallow and trivial meanings."

There is no compulsion to believe this. If we do not believe it, and unqualifiedly, there is no case for basic education. Which means that, except
for the superior intellect, there is no case for traditional education at all. In
that event we should at once start to overhaul our school system in the
light of a conception of man that sees him as a continually adjusting,
pleasure-seeking, pain-avoiding animal.

But if we do believe it, and unqualifiedly, then the proposals contained
in this book might at least be considered as guidelines, subject to discussion and modification.

The root of our trouble does not lie in an unbalanced curriculum, or in
an inadequate emphasis on any one subject, or in poor teaching methods,
or in insufficient facilities, or in underpaid instructors. It lies in the circumstance that somehow the average high school graduate does not know
who he is, where he is, or how he got there. It lies in the fact that naturally enough he " will settle for shallow and trivial meanings." If nothing
in his early education has convinced him that Newton, Shakespeare and
Lincoln are both more interesting and more admirable than Frank Sinatra,
Jerry Lewis and Pat Boone, he will find answers to his questions in Sinatra,

Lewis and Boone, and not in Newton, Shakespeare and Lincoln. If he has learned little or no history, geography, science, mathematics, foreign languages, or English he will, naturally enough, learn (for even if all men do not desire to know, in Aristotle's sense, surely they desire to know *something*) golf, quail-shooting, barbecuing, and some specialized technique of buying and selling.

In accordance with his luck and his temperament, he may become happily lost, or unhappily lost. But lost he will become. Lost he will remain. Lost he will die.

And if we allow these lost ones to multiply indefinitely, they will see to it that our country is lost also.

ARTHUR BESTOR
Intellectual discipline via formal subject matter

When Lemuel Gulliver, surgeon and ship's captain, made his celebrated voyage to Laputa in 1707, he was permitted to inspect the Grand Academy of Lagado. There, in the School of Languages, he found the professors (typically enough) in a committee meeting, discussing measures for the improvement of communication skills. Although some scholars have been known to possess an exaggerated notion of the importance of the things they have mastered, these particular professors of language were completely free of that contemptible vice. Instead of selfishly advancing the interests of their own subject, they were actually working on " a scheme for entirely abolishing all words whatsoever." The well-being of society was uppermost in their minds. They were saddened by the knowledge that " every word we speak is in some degree a diminution of our lungs by corrosion; and consequently contributes to the shortening of our lives." As semanticists, moreover, they were well aware that "words are only names for *Things*." Acting upon this hint, they inaugurated a progressive program, which revolutionized not only the curriculum but also the intellectual and social life of the community as a whole. " It would be more convenient," they announced, " for all men to carry about them, such *Things* as were necessary to express the particular business they are to discourse on." Gulliver witnessed two of the sages, carrying packs like pedlars, " who when they met in the streets would lay down their loads, open their sacks, and hold conversation for an hour together; then put up their implements, help each other to resume their burthens, and take their leave."

There was nothing wrong with the motives of this scheme. It was thoroughly altruistic. Nay more, it was an act of self-abnegation on the part of the professors of language who devised it. A strong social consciousness prompted it. Behind it lay also a desire for international understanding,

Arthur Bestor, " The Education Really Needed for a Changing World," *Harvard Educational Review*, 27:1–8, Winter, 1957. Reprinted by permission.

since what was offered was " an universal language to be understood in all civilized nations." The proposal had a plausible theoretical foundation, moreover, for it rested on the proposition that words and things are related, a proposition that no one could well deny. There was only one difficulty with the plan: It was absurd.

It was absurd, of course, because its projectors, though purporting to *improve* the intellectual tools of mankind, were actually casting aside the most significant gains that mankind had already achieved through the intellectual processes of generalization and abstraction, and were offering a bumbling, literal-minded substitute, wretchedly inadequate to the needs of a complex society. In the midst of a changing world they were changing education, but they were changing it in precisely the wrong direction.

We live in an even more complex and even more rapidly changing society than that of the eighteenth century. Education must, of course, provide the intellectual tools to enable young men and young women to live in this complex and changing world. It has always aimed to do so, and it always must. The question is not *whether*, but *how*. To deal with novel conditions we need something more substantial than mere novelties. Several searching questions must be answered: What are the powers of mind and the resources of character that men must develop if they are to ride the wild horses of change? If the future is bound to be different from the present, what can we learn today that will serve us in good stead in an altered tomorrow?

Perhaps one can best attack this problem by creeping up, as it were, from the rear, and asking first of all a diametrically opposite question: What kind of education would we provide if this were a completely *static* world?

Let us imagine a spell to have been cast over our present world, arresting all change and freezing all institutions in their existing form. John Keats pictured such a world in his " Ode on a Grecian Urn," with its

> happy melodist, unwearièd,
> For ever piping songs for ever new.

Life under such circumstances would be strangely frustrating and yet, I suppose, strangely idyllic — like undergraduate years prolonged to decades. Keats suggested the paradoxes of the situation:

> Bold Lover, never, never canst thou kiss,
> Though winning near the goal — yet, do not grieve;
> She cannot fade, though thou hast not thy bliss,
> For ever wilt thou love, and she be fair.

The merits and demerits of such a world I shall not attempt to examine. My present purpose is simply to inquire into the qualifications needed for a successful existence in a static society like this. To be specific, what kind of education would we prescribe for the youth and the maiden preparing to live in a world immune to change, where they themselves would be forever unacquainted with crisis, unconcerned with progress, unshadowed by possible disaster or decay?

The answer should not be difficult to find. First of all, we would doubtless concentrate our effort upon vocational training, confident that nothing could possibly render obsolete the skills we would thereby impart. In the second place, we would prescribe a concentrated study of contemporary issues, confident that no novel and unexpected problems were ever going to arise. In the third place, we would labor to bring about complete personal adjustment between the individual student and his immediate companions and immediate environment, for we could be certain that he would never have to make any more difficult or more understanding or more tolerant kind of personal adjustment.

On the negative side, we would hardly bother to offer instruction in such complex subjects as the physical sciences. It would suffice, in a static society, to know how to push the right buttons, squirt oil in the proper holes, replace the fuses, and, in general, operate the gadgets already devised. To comprehend abstract principles would be pointless, because, by hypothesis, no new applications of basic theory would ever be made.

We would not ask our students to master the fine points of language, their own or others', because no special need would exist for clear and accurate analysis and communication of ideas. A little purring and squealing and growling, eked out by occasional phrases of pidgin English, would doubtless suffice for everyday discourse.

History would certainly form no part of the curriculum, because history is a discipline concerned, above all, with change — a concept for which these Arcadian young people would have no manner of use.

All philosophical pursuits, all cultivation of theoretical and abstract thinking could be safely abandoned. Such intellectual efforts are, in the last analysis, quests for elements of stability or regularity or certainty beneath the surface flux of the changing world as *we*, but not as the inhabitants of a changeless society, are obliged to know it.

In summary, vocational training, " life-adjustment " education, the study of contemporary problems, a concern with immediate everyday experience — these elements, in combination, would constitute an ideal scheme of education *for a static world*.

Let us now suppose the spell to be broken, and our imagined community swept back once more into the stream of living, changing reality. What will happen to the young men and women upon whom we have bestowed our admirably static education, now that mutability is again a feature of their lives?

First of all, their vocational training will gradually fail them. The skills they have acquired will one by one grow obsolete, and they will have learned no general principles to give them a head start in learning new techniques. As citizens, moreover, they will become increasingly incompe-

tent and unreliable, once the contemporary problems they have studied
are replaced by new problems they know nothing about. Every item of
change, every novel event, every unfamiliar situation is bound to come as
a terrific shock each time to these young men and women. Their education
will not have provided the historical perspective that might have enabled
them to brace themselves for the unexpected. As their static world is
pounded to pieces, they will quickly discover how lacking they are in the
developed intellectual power — the philosophic insight and the command
of theory — that are necessary to rebuild it.

In summary, again, vocational training, " life-adjustment " education, the
study of contemporary problems, a concern with immediate everyday experience — these elements, in combination, constitute a hopelessly *inadequate* scheme of education for a *changing* world.

If our schools and colleges are to educate for a changing world, it is not
enough for them to change. They must change in the right direction. That
is to say, changes in education must be of the same character as the changes
in intellectual life as a whole. Otherwise education becomes not a preparation for, but a retreat from, the actual world.

The question of direction is all important. In what direction, then, have
American public schools been moving during the last twenty or thirty
years? Are the fundamental studies receiving greater emphasis, or less, in
the programs of all students? Are trivial activities and short-sighted vocational programs being eliminated from the curriculum, or are they increasing in number and diversionary effect? Are standards of academic achievement rising for every pupil, or are intellectual requirements being relaxed
so that even the least able can effortlessly pass?

Some of these questions are answered for the high school by the official
statistics of the United States Office of Education. " Enrollments in both
mathematics and foreign languages in the last 4 years of high school," it
recently reported, ". . . were smaller percentages of the total pupil bodies
in 1949 than in 1934." Moreover, " percentage enrollments in algebra, geometry, physics, and Latin have shown progressive decreases in all investigations since 1915." The Office of Education appears to be not alarmed
but encouraged by this trend. " For the most part," said its complacent
comment, " the changes are in the direction of more functional education.
They represent efforts to meet the life needs of increasingly diverse bodies
of pupils."

This comment is even more disconcerting than the statistics themselves.
It reveals with startling clarity the anti-intellectual assumptions that underlie the thinking of substantial groups of educational theorists and administrators today. Only a total obliviousness to the real needs of contemporary society can explain the equanimity — even the satisfaction — with
which many up-and-coming professional educationists contemplate each
decrease in the percentage of high-school students who are enrolled in
mathematics, physics, and foreign languages. Frequently this attitude mas-

querades as mere opposition to a " classical " curriculum. The implication that the shift now under way is from Latin and Greek to science and mathematics — from " bookish " subjects to laboratory ones — is simply not true. In 1900 some 84 per cent of all high-school students were enrolled in one of the natural sciences; this had declined from 85 to 54 per cent by 1949. In mathematics the decline was from 86 to 55 per cent in the same period. Latin gathered in slightly more than 50 per cent of all high-school students in 1900. Today all foreign-language classes put together (classical and modern alike) enroll less than 22 per cent of all students.

The fault is not primarily that of the students. The blame must rest upon educational authorities who have refused to stand up and say, with clarity and emphasis, that fundamental knowledge is still fundamental. In increasing numbers today, students are wandering off the high-road of learning into the dead-end streets of job training and life-adjustment education. In part this is the consequence of the counselling that students receive, guidance being too largely in the hands of those who are preoccupied with emotional and personal problems and too little in the hands of those who know from personal experience the satisfactions of intellectual endeavor. In part the shift away from the fundamental disciplines is an indication of the alarming fact that courses in them are no longer being offered, thanks to a quarter of a century of systematic disparagement of their value.

The actual dropping of courses from the curriculum is more marked in certain fields than in others. Foreign languages would appear to have suffered most grievously. The situation in one state with a well-supported school system has been carefully surveyed by Prof. Boyd Carter of the University of Nebraska and his colleagues in modern languages and literatures. In 1918–19 nearly 57 per cent of high-school students in 110 towns of over 1000 population in Nebraska were studying foreign languages. Today (1954–55) the figure stands at less than 9 per cent. What lies behind this precipitous decline? The answer is not diminished need for these studies, but drastically diminished educational opportunity. In 1918–19 some 308 high schools were teaching foreign languages. By 1933–34 (at the depth of the depression) the number had increased to 448. Today only 68 schools in the state are offering any instruction at all in foreign languages.

In the sciences and mathematics the decline in percentage enrollments is apparently attributable less to the curtailment of offerings than to " a lack of sufficient concern for science education in the schools," such as the Office of Education noted in 1950. The publication containing this statement did point out what appeared to be an appalling denial of educational opportunity when it reported that a statistically appropriate sample showed only 49.4 per cent of American high schools offering chemistry and only 47.8 per cent physics. The study neglected to indicate what percentage of all students attended these deficient schools, and the figures were accordingly widely publicized as given. In 1956 the Office of Education published a subsequent study, covering the situation in 1954, and on this occasion it partially rectified its earlier omission. The new study did show only 57 per cent of all schools offering chemistry and only 52 per cent offering physics; and it recorded the fact that no less than 23 per cent offered neither physics nor chemistry. It pointed out, however, that only 5.8 per cent of all pupils were enrolled in schools of the last-mentioned class. In mathematics the same study showed that only 78 per cent of all schools offered plane geometry (normally a tenth-grade subject), but it pointed out that a mere 6.8 per cent of all tenth-graders were in schools without the subject. Similarly, it reported: " About one-third of the high schools offered no trigonometry, solid geometry or intermediate algebra. This third enrolled about one-tenth of all pupils in the 12th grade — the grade where such courses are normally offered." There is still a serious denial of educational opportunity, but one may rejoice that its magnitude is no greater.

Unfortunately, however, one cannot gainsay the evidence of percentage declines in enrollment in science and mathematics as well as foreign languages. In its new revisionist mood, the Office of Education has recently reworked its figures so as to show enrollments in science and mathematics as percentages of enrollment in the particular grade in which the subject is normally offered, instead of as percentages of enrollment in the last four years of high school. This is a much more realistic base, which the Office of Education might well have adopted decades ago. The new look may be examined in the case of physics. In 1954–55 only 4.6 per cent of the students in the last four years of high school were studying physics. On the other hand, the students taking physics were 23.5 per cent of the total number of pupils in the twelfth grade. Shifting to the new base increases the percentage by a factor of 5.1. Unfortunately the Office of Education neglects to apply a comparable adjustment to the figures for earlier years. In 1890 and 1900, 22.8 per cent and 19.0 per cent, respectively, of all high-school pupils were studying physics. If the base were changed to all twelfth-graders, the adjusted figure would be close to 100 per cent. It would appear that virtually every twelfth-grader at the beginning of the century was studying physics. The decline to less than a quarter today is even more dramatic when presented on the new base than when presented on the old.

Any educational philosophy that accepts this tendency as tolerable and healthy is not a progressive but a regressive theory. The real intellectual world is moving in precisely the opposite direction. Science and mathematics are becoming more, not less, important in contemporary life. Foreign languages are more, not less, likely to be needed by American citizens in the second half of the twentieth century than in the first. A school that pays proportionately less attention to these intellectual disciplines than in earlier days, or offers instruction less thorough and systematic in them, is not preparing young men and women to live successfully in the actual world. Such a school is building for its pupils a high-walled playground within which the realities of modern intellectual life are forbidden to intrude.

Certain intellectual disciplines are fundamental in education because they are fundamental in mature contemporary life. It is not tradition — as sometimes falsely alleged — but a realistic appraisal of the modern world, which points out the studies that are fundamental. Science is clearly one of mankind's central concerns today, even more than in the nineteenth century. Mathematics underlies not only science but also the increasing host of other modern activities that make use of quantitative data and require statistical and mathematical controls. History is a discipline peculiarly relevant to a rapidly changing world, for the nature of change is one of its paramount concerns. Command of his own language and of the literature written therein is one of the indisputable marks of the educated man. And among nations that must, to use Franklin's phrase, either hang together, or most assuredly hang separately, knowledge of one another's languages has become an essential element of effective citizenship.

Liberal education is designed to produce self-reliance. It teaches a man, not the answers to particular problems, but the way to use his general intelligence to find the answers to all kinds of problems, especially those without precedent. To deny that liberal education in the basic disciplines is a preparation for life, to say that it is an aristocratic concept of education and inappropriate to democracy, is to misunderstand and hence to betray both education and democracy.

Schools exist to equip young men and women with the intellectual tools required to cope with modern life. There was a time when such tools were needed by relatively few. In the past, only a small number of professions called for systematic knowledge and well-developed intellectual skill of the sort that schools are capable of imparting. In the past, one class was responsible for governing, and they alone were required to possess the knowledge of languages and of history without which wise and prudent government is impossible.

In modern democratic societies all this is changed. Every man and woman belongs to the governing class. Virtually every occupation has become, if I may use the term, intellectualized. Science and technology enter into almost every human activity. Precision instruments and accurate calculations have replaced rules of thumb. Practical knowledge of every sort is laid up in books. Today, as a consequence, scientific and historical knowledge, a command of mathematics, an ability to write accurately and well, and, above all, the power to read widely with thorough understanding have become practical necessities for every man and woman who hopes to live in freedom and to work with effect.

There are practical skills to be learned, of course. Men and women have their jobs to perform. They have always had. Universal education did not come into being because suddenly the entire population went to work. Universal education became necessary because every task began to include an *intellectual* component. The mere know-how of a given job is always best learned in the process of doing it. This is as true now as it has ever been. Schooling is necessary when, and only when, there are things that must be learned systematically *before* the practical work can be commenced. The school does not — it cannot — offer training *on* the job. Its function is to provide training *for* the job, in other words, training in the intellectual processes that now underlie all jobs. So long as the life and the work of ordinary men and women included no intellectual component, schooling could be looked upon as a needless luxury for most of them. Because every kind of work has now come to include an intellectual component, universal education has become a necessity. The purpose of the school has not changed. Intellectual training is still its purpose and its justification. The change that has occurred is the increased need of society for precisely this kind of training. The school now takes in virtually the whole population because today virtually the whole population has practical need for the intellectual training that the school is peculiarly fitted to provide.

If the nation is to survive and remain strong, we must have an educational system that is thoroughly up-to-date. The way to bring our public schools up to date is not to experiment with substitutes for intellectual training, but to find ways of teaching the fundamentals more thoroughly than ever before, and to an ever-increasing proportion of all the students in our schools. Our object, after all, is to produce educated men and women, not to reward our youngsters with a diploma for merely growing up.

To educate young men and women for the contemporary world as it really is, we must emphasize the sciences in their theoretical rather than merely their applied aspects. We must lay increased stress upon formal mathematics. We must restore history as history, not being content with short-sighted and superficial discussion of current problems. We must make the great classics of literature and thought an integral part once more of the heritage of our children. We must begin instruction in foreign languages early in the elementary-school years. We must do these things because modern life increasingly demands increasing competence in the use of all these intellectual tools, and it demands it of all citizens.

No direction contrary to this can possibly be the proper direction for a modern school. No direction contrary to this can possibly be the proper direction of a democratic school.

ROBERT MAYNARD HUTCHINS
Education and the eternal verities

The obvious failures of the doctrines of adaptation, immediate needs, social reform, and of the doctrine that we need no doctrine at all may suggest to us that we require a better definition of education. Let us concede that every society must have some system that attempts to adapt the young to their social and political environment. If the society is bad, in the sense, for example, in which the Nazi state was bad, the system will aim at the same bad ends. To the extent that it makes men bad in order that they may be tractable subjects of a bad state, the system may help to achieve the social ideals of the society. It may be what the society wants; it may even be what the society needs, if it is to perpetuate its form and accomplish its aims. In pragmatic terms, in terms of success in the society, it may be a " good " system.

But it seems to me clearer to say that, though it may be a system of training, or instruction, or adaptation, or meeting immediate needs, it is not a system of education. It seems clearer to say that the purpose of education is to improve men. Any system that tries to make them bad is not education, but something else. If, for example, democracy is the best form of society, a system that adapts the young to it will be an educational system. If despotism is a bad form of society, a system that adapts the young to it will not be an educational system, and the better it succeeds in adapting them the less educational it will be.

Every man has a function as a man. The function of a citizen or a subject may vary from society to society, and the system of training, or adaptation, or instruction, or meeting immediate needs may vary with it. But the function of a man as man is the same in every age and in every society, since it results from his nature as a man. The aim of an educational system is the same in every age and in every society where such a system can exist: it is to improve man as man.

If we are going to talk about improving men and societies, we have to believe that there is some difference between good and bad. This difference must not be, as the positivists think it is, merely conventional. We cannot tell this difference by any examination of the effectiveness of a given program as the pragmatists propose; the time required to estimate these effects is usually too long and the complexity of society is always too great for us to say that the consequences of a given program are altogether clear. We cannot discover the difference between good and bad by going to the laboratory, for men and societies are not laboratory animals. If we believe that there is no truth, there is no knowledge, and there are no

From Robert M. Hutchins, *The Conflict in Education in a Democratic Society*, 1953, pp. 67–84, 88–90. Reprinted by permission of Harper & Brothers.

values except those which are validated by laboratory experiment, we cannot talk about the improvement of men and societies, for we can have no standard of judging anything that takes place among men or in societies.

Society is to be improved, not by forcing a program of social reform down its throat, through the schools or otherwise, but by the improvement of the individuals who compose it. As Plato said, " Governments reflect human nature. States are not made out of stone or wood, but out of the characters of their citizens: these turn the scale and draw everything after them." The individual is the heart of society.

To talk about making men better we must have some idea of what men are, because if we have none, we can have no idea of what is good or bad for them. If men are brutes like other animals, then there is no reason why they should not be treated like brutes by anybody who can gain power over them. And there is no reason why they should not be trained as brutes are trained. A sound philosophy in general suggests that men are rational, moral, and spiritual beings and that the improvement of men means the fullest development of their rational, moral, and spiritual powers. All men have these powers, and all men should develop them to the fullest extent.

Man is by nature free, and he is by nature social. To use his freedom rightly he needs discipline. To live in society he needs the moral virtues. Good moral and intellectual habits are required for the fullest development of the nature of man.

To develop fully as a social, political animal man needs participation in his own government. A benevolent despotism will not do. You cannot expect the slave to show the virtues of the free man unless you first set him free. Only democracy, in which all men rule and are ruled in turn for the good life of the whole community, can be an absolutely good form of government.

The community rests on the social nature of men. It requires communication among its members. They do not have to agree with one another; but they must be able to understand one another. And their philosophy in general must supply them with a common purpose and a common concept of man and society adequate to hold the community together. Civilization is the deliberate pursuit of a common ideal. The good society is not just a society we happen to like or to be used to. It is a community of good men.

Education deals with the development of the intellectual powers of men. Their moral and spiritual powers are the sphere of the family and the church. All three agencies must work in harmony; for, though a man has three aspects, he is still one man. But the schools cannot take over the role of the family and the church without promoting the atrophy of those institutions and failing in the task that is proper to the schools.

We cannot talk about the intellectual powers of men, though we can talk about training them, or amusing them, or adapting them, and meeting their immediate needs, unless our philosophy in general tells us that there is knowledge and that there is a difference between true and false. We must believe, too, that there are other means of obtaining knowledge than scientific experimentation. If knowledge can be sought only in the laboratory, many fields in which we thought we had knowledge will offer us nothing but opinion or superstition, and we shall be forced to conclude that we cannot know anything about the most important aspects of man and society. If we are to set about developing the intellectual powers of men through having them acquire knowledge of the most important subjects, we have to begin with the proposition that experimentation and empirical data will be of only limited use to us, contrary to the convictions of many American social scientists, and that philosophy, history, literature, and art give us knowledge, and significant knowledge, on the most significant issues.

If the object of education is the improvement of men, then any system of education that is without values is a contradiction in terms. A system that seeks bad values is bad. A system that denies the existence of values denies the possibility of education. Relativism, scientism, skepticism, and anti-intellectualism, the four horsemen of the philosophical apocalypse, have produced that chaos in education which will end in the disintegration of the West.

The prime object of education is to know what is good for man. It is to know the goods in their order. There is a hierarchy of values. The task of education is to help us understand it, establish it, and live by it. This Aristotle had in mind when he said: " It is not the possessions but the desires of men that must be equalized, and this is impossible unless they have a sufficient education according to the nature of things."

Such an education is far removed from the triviality of that produced by the doctrines of adaptation, of immediate needs, of social reform, or of the doctrine of no doctrine at all. Such an education will not adapt the young to a bad environment, but it will encourage them to make it good. It will not overlook immediate needs, but it will place these needs in their proper relationship to more distant, less tangible, and more important goods. It will be the only effective means of reforming society.

This is the education appropriate to free men. It is liberal education. If all men are to be free, all men must have this education. It makes no difference how they are to earn their living or what their special interests or aptitudes may be. They can learn to make a living, and they can develop their special interests and aptitudes, after they have laid the foundation of free and responsible manhood through liberal education. It will not do to say that they are incapable of such education. This claim is made by those who are too indolent or unconvinced to make the effort to give such education to the masses.

Nor will it do to say that there is not enough time to give everybody a liberal education before he becomes a specialist. In America, at least, the waste and frivolity of the educational system are so great that it would be possible through getting rid of them to give every citizen a liberal education and make him a qualified specialist, too, in less time than is now consumed in turning out uneducated specialists.

A liberal education aims to develop the powers of understanding and judgment. It is impossible that too many people can be educated in this sense, because there cannot be too many people with understanding and judgment. We hear a great deal today about the dangers that will come upon us through the frustration of educated people who have got educated in the expectation that education will get them a better job, and who then fail to get it. But surely this depends on the representations that are made to the young about what education is. If we allow them to believe that education will get them better jobs and encourage them to get educated with this end in view, they are entitled to a sense of frustration if, when they have got the education, they do not get the jobs. But, if we say that they should be educated in order to be men, and that everybody, whether he is a ditch-digger or a bank president, should have this education because he is a man, then the ditch-digger may still feel frustrated, but not because of his education.

Nor is it possible for a person to have too much liberal education, because it is impossible to have too much understanding and judgment. But it is possible to undertake too much in the name of liberal education in youth. The object of liberal education in youth is not to teach the young all they will ever need to know. It is to give them the habits, ideas, and techniques that they need to continue to educate themselves. Thus the object of formal institutional liberal education in youth is to prepare the young to educate themselves throughout their lives.

I would remind you of the impossibility of learning to understand and judge many of the most important things in youth. The judgment and understanding of practical affairs can amount to little in the absence of experience with practical affairs. Subjects that cannot be understood without experience should not be taught to those who are without experience. Or, if these subjects are taught to those who are without experience, it should be clear that these subjects can be taught only by way of introduction and that their value to the student depends on his continuing to study them as he acquires experience. The tragedy in America is that economics, ethics, politics, history, and literature are studied in youth, and seldom studied again. Therefore the graduates of American universities seldom understand them.

This pedagogical principle, that subjects requiring experience can be learned only by the experienced, leads to the conclusion that the most important branch of education is the education of adults. We sometimes seem to think of education as something like the mumps, measles, whooping-cough, or chicken-pox. If a person has had education in childhood, he need not, in fact he cannot, have it again. But the pedagogical principle that the most important things can be learned only in mature life is supported by a sound philosophy in general. Men are rational animals. They achieve their terrestrial felicity by the use of reason. And this means that they have to use it for their entire lives. To say that they should learn only in childhood would mean that they were human only in childhood.

And it would mean that they were unfit to be citizens of a republic.[1] A republic, a true res publica, can maintain justice, peace, freedom, and order only by the exercise of intelligence. When we speak of the consent of the governed, we mean, since men are not angels who seek the truth intuitively and do not have to learn it, that every act of assent on the part of the governed is a product of learning. A republic is really a common educational life in process. So Montesquieu said that, whereas the principle of a monarchy was honor, and the principle of a tyranny was fear, the principle of a republic was education.

Hence the ideal republic is the republic of learning. It is the utopia by which all actual political republics are measured. The goal toward which we started with the Athenians twenty-five centuries ago is an unlimited republic of learning and a world-wide political republic mutually supporting each other.

All men are capable of learning. Learning does not stop as long as a man lives, unless his learning power atrophies because he does not use it. Political freedom cannot endure unless it is accompanied by provision for the unlimited acquisition of knowledge. Truth is not long retained in human affairs without continual learning and relearning. Peace is unlikely unless there are continuous, unlimited opportunities for learning and unless men continuously avail themselves of them. The world of law and justice for which we yearn, the world-wide political republic, cannot be realized without the world-wide republic of learning. The civilization we seek will be achieved when all men are citizens of the world republic of law and justice and of the republic of learning all their lives long.

LIBERAL EDUCATION

As Aristotle remarked, politics is the architectonic science. This is one way of saying that the political philosophy accepted by a state will determine the kind of education it has. It is also a way of saying that the practical political situation in which a state finds itself has an overwhelming effect on its educational system. Plato arrived at his curriculum by asking what made a good man and a good soldier. A discipline was included only if it met both requirements. If, as it is sometimes argued, it is the destiny of the West to go to war with the East, then the educational system of the West will have to be designed with this end in view. Education is a secondary subject.

One difficulty is that we cannot answer any educational question of importance by appealing to the test of experience. The countries of the West appear determined to become industrial, scientific, and democratic. There

---

[1] I owe this discussion to the suggestions of Scott Buchanan.

have never been countries that were industrial, democratic, and scientific before. Entirely apart, therefore, from the usual difficulty of proving anything from history, and entirely apart from the difficulty of showing that any social experiment has succeeded or failed, which results from the inordinate number of variables that is always present, the experience of earlier societies would be of little use to us in solving the present problems of education. Even if we knew what their experience showed, it would be almost irrelevant now.

And yet there has always been an education that has been regarded as the best for the best. It has been regarded as the education for those who were to rule the state and for those who had leisure. Unless experimental science has made all the difference, it would seem that some light might be obtained by asking whether and to what degree the education that has always been regarded as the best for the best is still good for them or for anybody else.

How much difference can experimental science make? If it is true that the truth can be discovered only in the laboratory, then we can know very little indeed about education; for we cannot know even whether the statement is true that truth can be discovered only in the laboratory. The truth of that statement cannot be and has not been proved in the laboratory. The questions that science can answer are questions of fact about the physical world. They deal with the material conditions of existence. What is called social science cannot tell us what kind of society we ought to aim at. It is doubtful whether it can even tell us what the consequences of a given social policy will be. The reason, again, is the enormous number of variables that enter into any social situation. I do not deprecate the efforts of social scientists to understand society. I would merely indicate the limits of their disciplines. The great successes of physical science should not blind us to its limitations, either. We can learn from science and technology how to build a bridge. We may, perhaps, learn from social science what some of the social, political, and economic consequences of building the bridge will be. But whether those consequences are good or bad is not a question in either physical or social science.

And so it is of all the most important questions of human existence. What is a good life? What is a good society? What is the nature and destiny of man? These questions and others like them are not susceptible of scientific investigation. On some aspects of them science can shed some light, and such light should be welcomed. But these questions do not yield to scientific inquiry. Nor do they become nonsense, as the logical positivists would have us believe, because they are not scientific.

Here we see again that education is a secondary subject, depending in this case upon philosophy. If there is no knowledge except scientific knowledge, if one object of education is to communicate knowledge, then the object cannot be achieved except through education in science. Unfortunately, the question whether there is knowledge other than scientific knowledge is one that science can never answer. It is a philosophical question.

If the rise of experimental science does not change the educational situation beyond adding new and most important branches of knowledge, does the rise of industry and democracy change it? It certainly does change it in very significant respects. But does it change it in the respect in which we are now interested, in respect to content? Let us look at the education that has been regarded as the best for the best and ask ourselves whether this is still the education that states the ideal, to what extent it is the best today, and to what extent it may be usefully offered to those who were not regarded as the best when this education was developed.

In the West this education has gone by the name of liberal education. It has consisted of the liberal arts, the arts of reading, writing, listening, speaking, and figuring, and of the intellectual and artistic tradition that we inherit. It was designed for those who were to rule the commonwealth, and for those who had leisure. It has always been thought that those who could profit by it were a small fraction of the population. It has never been denied, as far as I know, that it was the best education for the best. The question I wish to raise is first, whether it actually was the best education, and second whether it is so today, and for whom.

For reasons I have already given, I cannot prove that this education was the best. I cannot prove it in any scientific way. It is dangerous to try to prove it by the quality of the men it produced. Who knows that it produced the men? So it is dangerous for a university president to boast about his distinguished alumni. If he is entitled to credit for them, he must also take the responsibility for those who go to the penitentiary. I can appeal to the common opinion of mankind; but mankind could have been wrong. I think it enough to show that this education was characteristically human and that it was characteristically western. When I say that it was characteristically human, I am saying once more that education is a dependent subject; for what I mean is, of course, that liberal education conformed to an idea of man that I regard as sound. This is the conception of man as a rational animal, an animal who seeks and attains his highest felicity through the exercise and perfection of his reason. It is impossible to avoid being a liberal artist; for a man cannot choose whether he will be human or not. He can make the choice only between being a good liberal artist or a poor one.

Liberal education was characteristically western, because it assumed that everything was to be discussed. Liberal education aimed at the continuation of the dialogue that was the heart of western civilization. Western civilization is the civilization of the dialogue. It is the civilization of the Logos. Liberal education made the student a participant in the Great Conversation that began with the dawn of history and continues at the present day. Great as other civilizations have been in other respects, no other civilization has been as great as this one in this respect.

Such an education can be called a good education, relative to the conditions under which it developed and flourished. But can it be called nothing more than that? Must we say that industrialism and democracy mean that some other education should now supplant it? We know that this education has already been supplanted in the United States.

By the end of the nineteenth century liberal education in the United States was largely in the hands of the teachers of Greek and Latin. A liberal education was a classical education. The teachers of the classics devoted themselves for the most part to instruction in the languages. It was possible to spend years in the study of the Greek and Latin writers without discovering that they had any ideas. The teachers of Greek and Latin were not interested in ideas. They were drillmasters. The languages in which they gave instruction were required for graduation from all respectable colleges, from all preparatory schools, and even from some public high schools.

In the first twenty-five years of this century the flood overwhelmed the high schools and colleges of the United States. Neither the students nor their parents were prepared to believe that what the classical drillmasters were doing was of any importance. And it must be admitted that the students and their parents were largely right. The classical drillmasters did not reform. They did not insist upon the importance of the classical heritage to modern western man. They were, as I have said, not much interested in that. Instead they insisted that their courses continue to be required. By 1925 the flood swept them away. It was characteristic that in the final battle at Yale, at which I was present, the issue was not about liberal education, or about the importance of the classical heritage, but only about whether one year of Latin should be required for the degree of Bachelor of Arts.

The Twentieth Century was right about the classical drillmasters. It was wrong about liberal education. And it was certainly wrong about what it substituted for liberal education. It substituted for it an infinite, incoherent proliferation of courses largely vocational in aim.

Liberal education consists of training in the liberal arts and of understanding the leading ideas that have animated mankind. It aims to help the human being learn to think for himself, to develop his highest human powers. As I have said, it has never been denied that this education was the best for the best. It must still be the best for the best unless modern times, industry, science, and democracy have made it irrelevant. The social, political, and economic changes that have occurred have not required that liberal education be abandoned. How could they? It is still necessary to try to be human; in fact it is more necessary, as well as more difficult, than ever.

Liberal education was the education of rulers. It was the education of those who had leisure. Democracy and industry, far from making liberal education irrelevant, make it indispensable and possible for all the people. Democracy makes every man a ruler, for the heart of democracy is universal suffrage. If liberal education is the education that rulers ought to have, and this I say has never been denied, then every ruler, that is every citizen, should have a liberal education. If industry is to give everybody leisure, and if leisure, as history suggests, tends to be degrading and danger- ous unless it is intelligently used, then everybody should have the educa- tion that fits him to use his leisure intelligently, that is, liberal education. If leisure makes liberal education possible, and if industry is to give every- body leisure, then industry makes liberal education possible for every- body. . . .

When I urge liberal education for all, I am not suggesting that all the people must become great philosophers, historians, scientists, or artists. I am saying that they should know how to read, write, and figure and that they should understand the great philosophers, historians, scientists, and artists. This does not seem to me an unattainable goal. If it is, unless some better kind of liberal education can be invented than the one that I have described, we shall be forced to abandon universal suffrage; for I do not believe that men can solve the problems raised by their own aggregation unless they can learn to think for themselves about the fundamental issues of human life and organized society. If anybody knows a better way of helping them learn to think for themselves about these issues, I hope he will present it. It seems to me that we must agree at least on this: the alternatives are democracy, with liberal education for all, and aristocracy, with liberal education for the few. If we choose the latter alternative, as Plato did, we may ignore, as Plato did, the education of the masses. All the educational system has to do with them is to find some innocuous way in which they can put in their time until we are ready to have them go to work.

Since education in the West is built very largely on the doctrine of indi- vidual differences, so that the study of the individual child and his indi- vidual interests is supposed to be the principal preoccupation of his teachers from his earliest days, and premature and excessive specialization is a common characteristic of both the American college and the British public school, it will be argued that a program of liberal education for all ignores the most important thing about men, and that is that they are different. I do not ignore it; I deny it. I do not deny the fact of individual differences; I deny that it is the most important fact about men or the one on which an educational system should be erected.

Men are different. They are also the same. And at least in the present state of civilization the respects in which they are the same are more im- portant than those in which they are different. Politics, the architectonic science, teaches us that we are remorselessly headed toward the unification of the world. The only question is whether that unification will be achieved by conquest or consent. The most pressing task of men every- where is to see to it that this consummation is achieved by consent. And this can be done only by the unremitting effort to move toward world community and world organization. The liberal arts are the arts of communication. The great productions of the human mind are the common heritage of all mankind. They supply the framework through which we understand one another and without which all factual data and area studies and exchanges of persons among countries are trivial and futile. They are the voices in the Great Conversation that constitutes the civilization of the dialogue.

Now, if ever, we need an education that is designed to bring out our common humanity rather than to indulge our individuality. Our individual differences mean that our individual development must vary. If we all struggle to make the most of our individual human powers, the results will be different, because our powers differ. But the difference is one of degree, and not of kind. In a modern, industrial, scientific democracy every man has the responsibility of a ruler and every man has the leisure to make the most of himself. What the modern, industrial, scientific democracy requires is wisdom. The aim of liberal education is wisdom. Every man has the duty and every man must have the chance to become as wise as he can. . . .

CHAPTER EIGHT BIBLIOGRAPHY

ADLER, MORTIMER J. and MAYER, MILTON, *The Revolution in Education*. Chicago: University of Chicago Press, 1958.

> Chapter 19 deals with the split between democratic idealists who are traditionalists and those who are modernists. Conceptions of knowing, methods, content, and the place of science are argued well from both sides. Other philosophical positions and issues are also treated in this book.

BARZUN, JACQUES, *The House of Intellect*. New York: Harper and Brothers, 1959.

> In the process of criticizing schools for their lack of concern for imparting knowledge, Barzun caustically criticizes, with examples, several things — attitudes, language, and activities which go on in the name of education.

MARITAIN, JACQUES, *Education at the Crossroads*. New Haven: Yale University Press, 1943.

> Maritain argues for a harmony of knowledge which may enable mankind to achieve wisdom. Motivation, knowledge, learning, and curriculum are here treated from a conservative point of view.

MARTEN, WILLIAM OLIVER, *The Order and Integration of Knowledge*. Ann Arbor: The University of Michigan Press, 1957.

> The introductory chapter contains a philosophical discussion of the nature of knowledge and the problems associated with organizing it. It helps to clarify the concept of " discovered truth."

9

Education for Meeting Individual Needs

" Nature provides for the child's growth in her own fashion, and this should never be thwarted. Do not make him sit still when he wants to run about, nor run when he wants to be quiet. If we did not spoil our children's wills by our blunders, their desires would be free from caprice. Let them run, jump, and shout to their heart's content. All their own activities are instincts of the body for its growth in strength; but you should regard with suspicion those wishes which they cannot carry out for themselves, those which others must carry out for them. Then you must distinguish carefully between natural and artificial needs, between the needs of budding caprice and the needs which spring from the overflowing life just described . . .

" Present interest, that is the motive power, the only motive power that takes us far and safely. Sometimes Emile receives notes of invitation from his father or mother, his relations or friends; he is invited to dinner, a walk, a boating expedition, to see some public entertainment. These notes are short, clear, plain, and well written. Some one must read them to him, and he cannot always find anybody when wanted; no more consideration is shown to him than he himself showed to you yesterday. Time passes, the chance is lost. The note is read to him at last, but it is too late. Oh! if only he had known how to read! He receives other notes, so short, so interesting, he would like to read them. Sometimes he gets help, sometimes none. He does his best, and at last he makes out half the note; it is something about going to-morrow to drink cream — Where? With whom? He cannot tell — how hard he tries to make out the rest! I do not think Emile will need a ' bureau.' Shall I proceed to the teaching of writing? No, I am ashamed to toy with these trifles in a treatise on education.

" I will just add a few words which contain a principle of great importance. It is this — What we are in no hurry to get is usually obtained with speed and certainty. I am pretty sure Emile will learn to read and write before he is ten, just because I care very little whether he can do so before he is fifteen; but I would rather he never learnt to read at all, than that this art should be acquired at the price of all that makes reading useful. What is the use of reading to him if he always hates it? " [1]

Jean Jacques Rousseau, who penned the previous words in his *Emile,* not only rebelled against the formalism of the eighteenth century, but also proposed a system of education based upon naturalism. Under formalism children were treated as miniature adults. Education was a " pouring in " process from teacher to pupil. The teacher was the authority who knew the answers, who knew what children should learn, and who was satisfied if children repeated the answers which he had given them, whether children understood them or not. In his opposition to this type of schooling, Rousseau argued that edu-

[1] Jean J. Rousseau, *Emile,* edited by Ernest Rhys (New York: E. P. Dutton and Company, 1911), pp. 50, 81–82.

cation should follow nature — an idea which is central to the philosophical school of naturalism. Although the acquisition of knowledge was not rejected, it generally took a secondary position, as it was acquired incidentally in the natural process of growing up. Knowledge was obtained through experience. Thus, it was considered to be meaningful, not as an end in itself, but as a tool for the solution of problems. The spontaneous self-activity of the child received the major share of attention. Some educators felt the goals of education could be found within the child himself. If we ascertained the interests and needs of the child, we would find a real blue-print for curriculum and methodology. The evaluation of the success or failure would be evident as the observer could readily see whether the child had reached his own potentialities. The naturalists believed that education should be pleasant, as this was conducive to learning. They also felt that any punishment which was imposed should be the normal consequence of the misdeed. Instead of imposing artificial punishment, the child was to be permitted to make errors; he was to learn from the unpleasant results of such endeavors that misdeeds did not bring pleasure. Few would dare to suggest that the child be permitted to run out in the street and into the pathway of a speeding wagon, since the resulting consequences were too disastrous. They suggested adult interference to prevent such a painful learning experience; yet they did feel that children would learn from errors, provided the price they paid for them would not be too expensive. Much was said about maturation. All precocity seemed to be bad. A child should never be pushed; in fact, often there was real value in developing the art of delay. Finally, there was also recognition that the body as well as the mind needed development if the natural method were to be followed. Thus, the emphasis upon the education of the whole child, which included the emotions and feel-ings, received a central position in this theory.

Rousseau's extreme position has not received much support in modern educational literature, yet it has been verbalized and practiced by some teachers. Certainly it has been criticized and lampooned by many writers. In fact, it has been attacked with tremendous vigor. Some critics have tried to leave the impression that American schools for the past quarter century have been committed to such a laissez-faire principle. The attacks upon progressive education have often distorted both the principles and practices of such education, and have exaggerated the amount of education based upon these premises. There are very few educational writers who advocate the extreme position of the " lunatic fringe," who would establish the immediate interests and whims of children as the objectives of education, and who would develop a curriculum based entirely on the desires of children, neglecting planning, preparation, or guidance by the teacher. These same critics have depicted schools as anarchy " in extremis," with pupils exercising license instead of freedom, where teachers become slaves to infants who rule the educational institution without either knowledge or understanding of their own actual interests and needs. Despite the fact that many of the critics distorted facts and that little has been written advocating an extreme naturalistic and individualistic position, there were some outspoken advocates of extreme liberalism in education. There were some vocal proponents of an education based upon the interests and needs of children. It is important for the teacher to be aware of this school of thought and to find out what actually was said.

As in Rousseau's time, the educators favoring a child-centered education generally revolted against the formalism of the educational program which often was adult-centered and dealt with future probable responsibilities rather than with the present problems and needs of children. Some of these individuals did work out a rationale for an educational program consistent with their basic premises. A. S. Neill, an English educator and headmaster of a private school, was one of the extreme members of this group. Although the first selection taken from Neill was written in 1944 and does include some references to that period, it portrays the author's opposition to a type of prevailing formal education. Neill also presents clearly defined objectives and practices. Lest we think that he was merely another Rousseau who could offer advice for others, while he placed his own children in an orphanage, let it be said that Neill practiced what he preached. An excellent description of this is presented in Neill's recent book *Summerhill.* Thus, the question is not, " Can it be done? " but rather, " Is this the way it should be done? "

The second reading is from *Child Life and the Curriculum* by Junius L. Meriam, who was professor at the University of Missouri and superintendent of the University Schools. The University of Missouri Elementary School received much attention from educators while Meriam was its director. It attempted to put into practice many of his ideas and certainly differed from the traditional school. This was one of the early progressive schools of the twentieth century. Meriam not only attacks traditional education, but makes a case for a school which will " help boys and girls do better in all those wholesome activities in which they normally engage." " The curriculum must be made to suit the boy and girl, not the boy and girl shaped to the Procrustean curriculum." Although addressing himself primarily to the elementary level of education, Meriam also proposes his basic principles for secondary education.

Boyd Bode, quoted previously in this book, identifies some of the weaknesses in the needs theory in his article in *Progressive Education.* This article, presented in its entirety, points out the difficulties in defining needs, the problems of choosing which need to follow when several are in conflict, and the fact that not all needs are inherent in the individual. He opposed Rousseauism and instinct psychology, which he felt was basic to much of the enthusiasm in the advocates of children's interests and needs. This selection may help the reader to identify some of the weaknesses of those who had a starry-eyed devotion to childhood.

A. S. NEILL
School subjects as the natural enemy of the child

THE TEACHER AND THE SCHOOL SUBJECT

I have already suggested that the school subject is one of the means used by the State to prevent the child from being educated. It is a safety valve. The only dangerous subject is History, and the textbooks are so written that they are almost dangerproof. Fortunately the State cannot eliminate the teacher's adding his own version to that of the approved book unless it is a State of the totalitarian type with a terror behind its commands.

The other subjects are only useless and sidetracking. This is especially true of the secondary school in which boys learn the Theory of Quadratics

From A. S. Neill, *The Problem Teacher,* 1944, pp. 40–53. Reprinted by permission of the author and A. P. Watt & Son, London.

before they go out to deliver newspapers or beef. They learn French which they are compelled by life to forget when they leave school, compelled because they can never go to France, and having learned mostly the grammar, can never read a French book with ease or pleasure. The little Chemistry and Physics they acquire cannot possibly be kept up after school is left, for no clerk, no shopkeeper, no tradesman has the apparatus or facility for going on with the subject. We rightly thunder against dead end occupations for youth, but it seems to me that our education system is an excellent training for such occupations, for nearly every subject is a dead end one.

The elementary school is less dangerous than the secondary school. Its ambition is less: it is more or less content with the Three R's, that is, the tools necessary for further education. The teacher is not a specialist in one subject, and is able to avoid the narrowness that the subject specialist is almost bound to acquire. True the elementary school has its own dead ends of the long division, multiplication of vulgar and decimal fractions variety, yet in the main the elementary teacher does good work and too often gets the minimum of appreciation for it. He has the chance, if he can take it, to give children up to fourteen a liberal education, in spite of the Education Code. I think of some of the rural schools I knew in Scotland long ago. The village teacher often did give his pupils a good education for that time. This was largely due to the fact that, having four to six classes to attend to, he had to leave the children to themselves for long periods, but it was also due to the ability of the teacher to teach in an interesting way.

I can never take the evergreen controversy about the school-leaving age seriously. I see no point in keeping children at school as schools are today. If a boy leaves a secondary school at seventeen instead of fifteen he will only have a larger smattering of dead end subject to dump before he begins his life work. Under a sensible and just civilisation a boy would probably be allowed to remain at school till he was nineteen, but the school would be adapted to his psychological needs, and the subjects would be very minor affairs in it.

Both elementary and secondary schools fail to be educative because they only provide for the intellect and the memory. Education should be creative all the time, but every schoolmaster knows that his work is almost without creation. Only when creation is recognized as the only dynamic factor in education will our schools be real places of education. So long as learning poetry is preferred to writing verse: so long as vulgar fractions on a blackboard are of more moment than fractions used creatively in making something in wood or metal, our schools are failing to educate.

Most teachers have a more or less vague feeling that their work is pouring water down a drain. In a way the unconscious teacher who thinks that his little subject is a big subject is the lucky one. The really tragic teacher is he who feels keenly that he is giving his best to an unworthy cause, fighting a battle under a flag that he does not honour. Other professions are envious of the teacher's short hours and long holidays. The teacher needs them more than the children do: his work is psychically much more exhausting than that of a lawyer or doctor, not only because he has to regress to the level of the child all the time, but also because he has a job that never finishes, a job in which he never can see the end. The barrister after a trial can say with a sigh of relief: Something attempted, something done: the doctor can say it after the recovery . . . or the funeral. The teacher can never say it. His is a voice crying in the wilderness, and he never knows how much the young ears have taken in. He is in very much the same position as the man who screws a certain nut on a car that travels along the belt: he never sees the completed car. The simile suggests that about the only thing a teacher has to do is to screw on one nut and leave the car to be completed by experience. Our schools are as much mass production factories as the Ford or Morris works.

I don't want to carry the comparison too far. Ford knows what kind of a car he wants, but no teacher knows or should know what kind of a man or woman he should produce from his factory. It is right that the teacher should never see the end of his work. If, however, he had some confidence in the beginning of his work, if he felt that he was on the right lines, he would do more valuable work and would enjoy it more. That is why I manage to have a staff in Summerhill. The teachers know that they are coming to a salary that is wretched compared with what they could earn in a State school, yet they prefer to do this because they know that they can work optimistically in their own way, content in the belief that freedom will turn out a Rolls Royce that has not been made by mass production. (This, of course, is just swank on my part, for Summerhill has produced one or two T Fords as well as some Rolls Royces.)

It is the inability to see the end of his work that makes it so incumbent on a teacher to be politically minded, that is to look beyond and ahead. His subject may be his bread and butter, but he should look for his cake outside the school. If he doesn't he will stagnate and become what so many are, a mechanical drudge with his eye on the clock.

The problem teacher is bounded by his subject. That is why teachers should be moved from one subject to another. The Maths man should be put on to the History class for a year, the German teacher on to Painting. Jack of all trades, master of none? Why not? A specialist in any line of trade or profession sees only the trees and seldom the wood. I shouldn't go so far as to advocate that the man who is an expert on a screw-cutting lathe should be put to emery-clothing chunks of steel, although psychologically it might do him a world of good. I am not suggesting that the Latin master should take on the school porter's job either. If that were the only way to save him from the perils of specialisation I should plump for it.

No specialist can retain an open mind for very long. To the shoemaker there is nothing like leather. The most honest surgeon in the world has somewhere in his unconscious the suspicion that pain in the tummy may have something to do with a diseased appendix. The osteopath will be pretty sure that the same pain has something to do with the spine, and the dietician will be sure that a balanced diet will cure it. If I heard of a psychologist who was curing young thieves by making them eat baked beans I should smile in a very superior fashion, because, as a specialist, I am convinced that my way is the only one. I find the same limitations in famous scientists: they reject a new work without deigning to examine it thoroughly.

What happens is that the specialist gets his subject and his ego mixed up inextricably. Those teachers who have attended staff meetings at the beginning of a term, when the timetable is being made out, will understand what I mean when they think of the savagery with which each expert will fight for his or her subject. . . . " But I've only got the Betas twice a week! I must have them at least four times." It is an excellent spirit: it shows that as a body the teaching profession is sound and enthusiastic. Would that all its enthusiasm could be used in a better cause! The specialist gets hold of the erroneous notion that the subject is more important than the child. New pupils come to me with long Reports from their previous school.

Mathematics — fair.

English — some advancement on last term's work.

Drawing — very good, but is apt to be careless in detail.

General Behaviour — inclined to show off too much in class, but improving.

If I issued Reports at the end of term, I should feel inclined to make them after this fashion: —

Mathematics — lousy, but that doesn't matter.

English — his vocabulary has improved since last term, but he should be warned against using it in Aunt Mary's presence.

History — haven't the least idea and have no wish to discover.

General Behaviour — his parents will find out how that is before he has been an hour in the house.

Now I am being skittish, yet I cannot see what attitude one can take up other than a humorous one. The whole subject racket is a joke, only the specialists cannot see it, and the children dare not see it. When Smith Minor is fifty how much will it matter to him or any one else what opinion his English teacher gave of him when he was twelve? Negatively it may matter a lot, for the millions of school reports that have been issued have helped to lower the self-confidence of millions of children: have given unnecessary fears to millions of children. This is known to all of you who carried home the damning Report to a father you knew would be irate.

But it isn't the Report that is the culprit: the evil lies in the teachers' attitude to the subject. If Reports are to be retained I propose that they should be written by the children themselves, about themselves with an appendix about each teacher. Such a Report might run something like this:

" I hate Maths and the Maths Mistress is a beast. I like English because Mr. Brown lets us write gangster stories or anything we like. My history is pretty bloody, but Miss Green is so dreadfully dull with her tiresome talk about Roman Civilisation. Handwork is O.K. in a way, but we aren't allowed to make what we want to. Who wants to make a pen tray? I want to make guns and aeroplanes. I loathe drawing since Miss X came because she keeps breathing down the back of my neck all the time. Worse still she eats garlic."

What an excellent thing it would be for schools if the children were allowed to write Reports of their own! How spring-cleaning! How disastrous to century-old cobwebs. How exhilarating to subject specialists! How humanising such Reports would be! Alas, most of the Reports would be lies: even if they could be published in a School Magazine anonymously, each critical child would fear that anonymity would fail to protect from staff vengeance. This subject leads on to the next chapter, The Teacher and Psychology.

THE TEACHER AND PSYCHOLOGY

In the medical profession the students are taught much more about disease than about health. I do not know how it is now, but in past years the medical course did not include the subject of diet. The big London hospitals still feed their convalescent patients on white bread. The interest in and the knowledge of diet came from outside the profession, and long before science had discovered Vitamin C, lay practitioners were feeding their patients on lettuce and lemons and oranges. It is seldom that one comes across a medical practitioner who attempts to go to the root of a disease. If I have a skin disease the average doctor will treat the skin without enquiring what is wrong with my living conditions that an outbreak of pimples should take place. He has been taught to treat symptoms, and that is why so many patients have fled to the lay Nature Cure man, for he, at least, puts the symptom in a second place and tries to build up the general health. He has successes because his method is fundamental.

The training of the teacher has similar limitations to those of the medical training. We might compare it to the training that makes a doctor a specialist in — say — Ear, Nose, and Throat. We should be reluctant to call in such a specialist to an appendix case.

The hospitals give a man training in diagnosis and general treatment and he goes out to treat bodies that medical science knows very little about. So the universities and training colleges equip a young teacher to go out and deal with human personalities that he knows little about. Because I take a B.A. in Classics at Oxford I am automatically supposed to be able to teach Latin and Greek. If I spend two years at a training college I am qualified to guide and control a group of children, even although my training has taught me nothing whatever about the nature of a child.

The teacher's chief concern should be the psychology of the child, and all school subjects should be relegated to an inferior place. The issue is evaded by the adoption of the easiest method — that of discipline. Keep the class in order so that you can hand your stuff over the footlights. Obviously if an actor wants to put his stuff across the footlights he has to make it such that his audience will discipline themselves in order to hear it. The method of the theatre should be the only one applicable to the school: the well grac'd actor would command interest, while the actor whose prattle was merely tedious would find himself declaiming to empty benches.

Discipline is the substitute for knowledge of children. True enough it is necessary so long as school is an institution that for the most part militates against child nature: so long as children are compelled to sit at desks and to learn what they have no wish to learn, school discipline will be found necessary. But although today the child is made for the school, there is reason to believe that tomorrow the school will be made for the child. The new era will come much more quickly if the teachers assist in the birth of it, and that they cannot do if they are ignorant of child nature and if they accept the old discipline as a gospel.

Today the chief law in school is: Thou shalt obey. But the chief law in life is: Thou shalt refuse to obey. The only obedience of value is the obedience a man has to his inner self. All external obediences are a curse to his growth. In its psychological component this is the conflict between Fascism and Democracy. Grant that democracy is largely a sham, that the workers in this democratic country are slaves to their capitalist masters. Grant that, but deep down in their hearts the people of Britain desire freedom from obedience, freedom to get rid of the indignity of being yes-men. The men of the International Brigade were democrats who obeyed their own leaders because their leaders had the same cause as they had. That obedience is necessary. The obedience of the school is stamped with the other kind of motive: it is the Heil, Hitler variety, the army variety. Theirs not to reason why.

Obedience should be dynamic: its purpose should be the wish of the one who obeys and at the same time the wish of the one who commands. I think of the orchestral conductor and the band. Obedience should be reciprocal: if the child obeys the teacher the teacher ought to obey the child. To the old-fashioned teacher this may sound nonsense, but I have had this reciprocity in my school for many years, and it has been a complete success. Our school laws are made by the community by majority vote, and I have to obey them just as dutifully as the child of five has. I can order a child out of my room when I don't want his presence, and he can order me out of his room for a similar reason. We both obey.

That this system could not be readily applied to a disciplined and desk school is evident. For one thing it requires not only a study of child nature:

it requires an infinite faith in children, and perhaps of more moment, an infinite faith in one's own attitude to the child. It implies a *Weltanschauung* that relegates knowledge to its proper place, that believes that what a child knows is much less important than what a child is. In other words it makes human behaviour the chief factor in education.

Yet I wonder if teachers were trained for ten years in child psychology would they be prepared to drop their pedestal position? Many, of course, would, as many do already. Teaching is not a science: it is a special kind of art, and it may be that only the artist can teach properly. I do not mean by teaching the presentation of a lesson: I mean the art of living with children and understanding them, and being one of them. Belonging to the gang, as that great teacher Homer Lane put it. A gramophone can present a good lesson just as a soulless teacher can. But a soulless gramophonic teacher can never really get into vital contact with the child.

That is the question — to get in vital touch with the child. To see the school and to see life from the child's point of view. The old idea that a child has to be guided is as false and stupid as Solomon's law about the stick.

What is a child? A child is a being that is largely unconscious. Its life is in great measure spent in phantasy and its play is an expression of this life. Childhood is playhood. The child is naturally active and noisy and unaware (as the state of the furniture in my school testifies). It is primarily concerned with doing, not with thinking — phantasy thinking, yes: reality thinking, no. That comes later.

Now in the classroom the phantasy side of the child has no outlook except the dangerous one of day-dreaming instead of attending to the lesson. The active side is inhibited by the necessity of sitting still, under an ignorant teacher in sitting with arms folded. The noisy side is completely suppressed until playtime. The creative side in a desk school has the minimum of opportunity for expression.

Head work is the rule of the school. This is against the holy law of child nature. Head work belongs to a later stage, much later than we think perhaps. We apply rules to children that we would never think of applying to adults. We have no desire to convert into thinkers Charlie Chaplin or Greta Garbo. Many golfing teachers admire the prowess of Henry Cotton, but not one would try to improve his game by advising him to get up the history of the Hundred Years' War. The boy at the bottom of the class may be the future golf champion of England, but we treat him as if it were taken for granted that he is to be a professor.

Think what is behind the child we see sitting at a desk. We know what his arithmetic is like, but we don't know what is behind the insincere mask that conventional discipline compels him to wear all day long. Let me guess a few of the things behind his mask. He is concerned about his origin and the lies told to him about it. He is concerned about his sex, wondering if he will die or go to hell if he touches his genitals. He is concerned with all sorts of home problems, his fear of father when father raises his voice, his jealousy of his brothers and sisters. Perhaps he has a guilty conscience because he stole something, or because he told a big lie. Maybe he thinks anxiously about death. In all likelihood he is filled with fears, trembling to walk in the dark. Then there is religion. Who is God or is there a God? Further fears because of the dangerous thought. These among a thousand other troubles and doubts.

And his teacher sees only the mask, his teacher is only interested in his work, not realising that all the hidden hopes and fears can easily destroy the ability to concentrate on work. The frequent nervous break-downs in school children are due to education's complete disregard for the deep traits of character. Many a new parent says to me: " The last school over-worked my boy." In Norway, where I am now, the overworking is worse than it is in England, for here apparently you can't become a scavenger without passing an examination. If Norwegian children are not more neu-rotic than English children it must be because their wonderful open air life of ski-ing and skating counteracts the stupidity of their national edu-cation.

The class teacher may reply: It isn't my job to deal with the inner life of the child. I am paid for teaching the little devil arithmetic. Yes, but whose job is it then? Suppose Tommy has phobias: suppose he has inordi-nate death fears or wishes: suppose he is miserably unhappy. If the teacher cannot help him who can? Not his parents, not the clergyman, not the local doctor. If he steals, your punishment will make him worse, for he is seeking love and you will give him hate. If you punish him for bullying he will retain his bullying attitude longer than he would have done because he is reinforced by the added knowledge that you are also a bully.

It is the teacher's job to be the soul doctor to the child, to every child in the classroom. This of course cannot be carried out if the teacher at-tempts to serve God and Mammon, to be the soul doctor and the sergeant-major at one and the same time. In my own work I have this difficulty. New children identify me for a long time with their former teachers, and if these teachers have been strict disciplinarians, I find that it takes me weeks and often months to get into touch with the child. Only when they feel that I am not an authority do they come to me with their soul trou-bles. When children come young enough, at three to seven, they never show this hate and fear of authority, but then when they come so young they seldom need much in the way of soul-doctoring.

Teachers have often said to me: " It's all very well for you. You have been at the job for years, but although I want to help kids sometimes, I simply don't know how to begin. I don't know enough about psychology."

But neither do I. I may know more than many teachers because I have concentrated on the subject for years, but if a child has night terrors I have to begin at the beginning and slowly try to find out, by what the child says, what the possible cause is. Sometimes I succeed: sometimes I fail. In the latter case the trouble often disappears mysteriously without the root having been discovered. The cure is in all likelihood due to the comfort the child finds in getting an adult to side with it and comfort it.

I really do not think a training in psychology is so necessary as a sympathetic attitude. It must be non-moral. You would have to receive with as much emotion the news that a child had murdered its grandmother, as the news that the child had got a new teddy bear. It would depend on your attitude to your own grandmother anyway.

A moral attitude judges and condemns. In a teacher such an attitude is fatal. Even if the teacher hides it with a smile or a look of indifference the child feels it, for he has so uncanny a gift of seeing behind the adult mask.

Most teachers know or should know the story of how Homer Lane cured a rebel by encouraging him to break plates and saucers. I visited Norman MacMunn's school in Tiptree Hall round about 1920. Later when I saw Lane I told him this story: —

" MacMunn tried your method and it failed. His boys began to break up the classroom and Norman thought he would do what you did with your destructive lad, so he joined in and helped them to complete the destruction. Then there was hell, for the boys all began to cry."

" That was because he only acted consciously," was Lane's verdict. " The boys felt that he was swindling them and of course they wept."

There is a warning in the story. One can only help the child if one is sincere in doing it. Otherwise the child will classify the teacher with the bishops and other moral danger.

The art of teaching is the art of leaving children alone. It is a most difficult art to acquire if one is not born a believer in freedom. The natural instinct of an adult is to mix in and show the child the way. This is bad enough when the way is only the way to draw a straight line, but it is tragically wrong when the way is the way to live. It takes infinite patience not to mix in. I watched with fearful doubt a boy from the age of seven to eighteen, watched him making mistakes, watched him waste his time (apparently). He is now doing a difficult job well.

But the poor class teacher cannot wait. The mill goes on grinding and he must feed it with raw fodder. As the years go on he comes to expect more chaff than golden grains. With the best will in the world how can any teacher get into contact with the souls of forty, fifty, perhaps sixty children? I can take a child to my little Private Lesson room, but where can an L.C.C. teacher take a boy or girl in his barrack school? I am free to tell a child that there is no harm in masturbation, but if a State teacher did so he might well lose his job. I can run a school without religion, and tell the children a story of their going to heaven and finding God a benevolent old gentleman who keeps bees, but the State teacher is never free to reject religion or to make it human.

So I am forced to return to the sad truth that until the schools are humanized the teachers cannot be human or even honest. The chains cannot fall from the ankles of the children until the slave teachers are freed from their own bondage. Perhaps when our capitalist civilisation has disappeared for ever . . . but I often doubt if Socialism will retain our prison schools, because the abolition of profit does not necessarily imply the miraculous transformation of mankind from moralism to humanity. . . .

J. L. MERIAM
Present needs as the basis of the curriculum

Children and the present. If the boy or girl were consulted as to school work he would suggest little of the past or the future for study. He lives in the immediate present. He knows little of the past; he forecasts little of the future. He applies himself assiduously to his occupation for the time. He wastes no time in regrets for what might have been; he is too much engrossed with present profit to himself to question as to later results. He is naïvely wrapped up in his own present environment, an environment very rich for him now, richer and more extensive as his experience increases.

But why consult the boy or girl in school about what shall be taught him? Has not racial experience developed what the present generation should acquire, and have not men of varied experiences studied into the future sufficiently to determine what is good for the young? An affirmative answer seems, at first, very plausible; but such an answer is set aside by the favorite thesis in this whole discussion: *the great purpose of the elementary school is to help boys and girls do better in all those wholesome activities in which they normally engage.*

The nature of the boy and girl must be consulted if the curriculum is wisely selected and organized. The curriculum must be made to suit the boy and girl, not the boy and girl shaped to the Procrustean curriculum.

Motives in the present. In this connection a word on children's motives is important. . . . Much emphasis has been given in recent years to the importance of using children's instincts, their interests, their feeling of need, in short, their motives. In their own real life children's motives are strong and they are many. There is a strong motive at every normal turn. Here motive is merely the clear recognition of a situation and the importance of acting so as to adjust oneself better to that situation. Any subject matter must be used by the pupil exactly as a hoe or spade is used by the farmer: it is an instrument by which he does what is wished. It is impossible, then, if we are conscientiously consistent, to arrange first our " instruments " — the set lesson units — and then create situations for the purpose of building up motives. Motives are thus made subordinate to instruments.

Children are naïve if allowed to be. They are natural, not artificial. They

From J. L. Meriam, *Child Life and the Curriculum*, 1921, pp. 147–154, 163–168, 203–204. Reprinted by permission of the author.

normally meet real needs, they experience genuine motives. Situations artificially constructed by adults for the purpose of giving pupils "motives" for attending to previously prescribed tasks are not in harmony with the real nature of children. This artificiality is understood by the child sooner than teachers or parents realize. The teacher's difficulty is then very considerably increased.

Motives may be operative in the immediate present or guide action with reference to a later time. The traditional curriculum is almost universally recognized as a plan of preparation for later use. Motives that lead to a study of arithmetic, for example, are to be found in the recognition of a later need for such subject matter. We may *seem* to appeal to present motives when we construct an artificial situation calling for certain knowledge of arithmetic. But if the situation is artificially constructed by the teacher and is not found in the normal experience of the pupil, the need is not a *real* need. Motive is consequently artificial and has a reference only to later possible needs. The child's motive must be found in his recognition of a real need in the present.

Activity in the present. Boys and girls of elementary school age are intensely active. The period of infancy, including more than the school age, is the period of growth, and this growth is dependent upon activity. In spite of the too common attempt of the adult to repress the child, his activity will out. Repression must yield to expression. Without this strong tendency to activity the development of the child would be hopeless. It is the active pupil, even if mischievous, that promises most. Advocates of the culture-epoch theory support this position and call attention to the interest of children in imitating the activities of primitive men — children enjoy tomahawking and scalping excursions. But one need only observe, on streets where children play, how they enjoy "dressing up" and acting, not in representing primitive peoples or racial experience, but merely in being *more active.* Feathers, paint, dagger, and helmet serve as an "extension of personality" and incite to increased activity. In the same way adults' clothing, false faces, paper hats, and the like incite children to a parade and other forms of active expressions. A dull monotony is the impression which the usual school makes upon the pupils; monotonous and dull largely because of the lack of childlike activity inherent in the regular work of the school. Free play at recess, boisterous as it may be, cannot compensate for the repression practically necessitated by the traditional curriculum.

Many writers and practical school men tacitly assume that the traditional school subjects must be taught. The problem then becomes one of method of infusing into the work such activities as will meet children's needs and serve as motives in inducing them to "take hold." This procedure is inadequate.

Child nature insists upon present interests — for the child. Appreciation of the past and insight into the future vary with the character and the amount of experience. The elementary school pupil has had but little experience. His interests are thus largely limited to the present. Children have motives in the normal course of their lives — many motives, and rich motives, but practically all these motives relate to present needs. Children are intensely active, not in searching out the past nor prospecting as to the future, but in adjusting themselves to their own increasingly complicated and increasingly interesting environment. The curriculum . . . [should be] . . . planned to meet child nature by providing activities and studies of activities that constitute the real environment of children of elementary school age.

PRESENT NEEDS IN THE HOME AND COMMUNITY

Relation of school and home. Boys and girls need help in their activities at their homes and in their communities. So also, the homes and communities in which children live need the assistance of the schools in directing these young people. This need is scarcely questioned, but the immediacy of this need is quite generally overlooked. The stress of the traditional school upon preparing pupils for the exigencies of later life is only an expression of the custom of thinking by the people. The adult looks forward in the interests of children and communities later, and quite overlooks present conditions. Present needs are slighted.

A great deal is being said and written on the importance of bringing the home and the school more closely together. " What can be done . . . to bring the school into closer relation with the home and neighborhood life — instead of having the school a place where the child comes solely to learn certain lessons? What can be done to break down the barriers which have unfortunately come to separate the school life from the everyday life of the child? " [1] Dewey here presents one side of this closer union; that is, the bringing of school life nearer to out-of-school life. But the more usual theory and the more evident practice are on the other side; that is, the bringing into the school such of real life as may be adapted to educational work. The school is made central. One rather conspicuous organization contributing to this policy is the mothers' club. This organization is clearly independent of the school but coöperates with teachers and officials. The real intent in these mothers' clubs is unquestionably good. However, there is a serious weakness in evidence, largely due to a misunderstanding as to the real relation between school and home, and the possibilities of service on the part of such clubs. The International Congress on Home Education has expressed much that is in keeping with the work of the mothers' club. Instead of looking upon the school as in need of their help, these parental organizations should point out to the school its opportunities to help the home and community. The school is in danger of atrophying by living within itself rather than by serving the interests of home and community.

The most practical purpose of the elementary school is to *help boys*

[1] Dewey, J., *School and Society* (first edition), page 116.

and girls do better in all those wholesome activities in which they normally engage, quite aside from the school. We must not, of course, expect too much of the school in improving the home life of children. Teachers rightly complain of the difficulty of doing much in the development of good habits in children when school influence is limited to such a small amount of time compared with home influence. But this disproportion of time only increases the opportunity and responsibility of devising an educational plan that extends much further than school yard and school hours. Teachers and school officials must not shirk this responsibility. Opportunity carries with it responsibility.

Moreover, care must be taken not to judge too favorably the homes of the masses of children by the homes of teachers, college students, or the more cultured of public school pupils. These are the select few and probably come from homes superior to those of the masses of little people who make comparatively little headway in school. There are no suitable data at hand for judging the specific needs of homes. But think of what is included in the usual list of virtues called for: Honesty means being honest in scores upon scores of daily relationships with others of the family; coöperation means helping in all the multiplicity of home activities; generosity means the giving attitude in thousands of cases. So with all the virtues belonging to home life. Virtues are practiced in concrete instances only. In each of these, children need helpful direction.

Play and work at home. Students of social problems find in the decadence of the home the great cause of social evils especially among young people. Industrial evolution leading to the factory system has broken the unity of the home. It is bad enough when two thirds of the men and nearly one fifth of the women in America work away from the home. It is yet worse when, under such circumstances, common interests and sympathetic coöperation are scattered to the winds. All this may be unavoidable under prevailing social and economic conditions. The school cannot ameliorate these conditions at once — it can do directly but little to collect the fathers and mothers and give them work within their own home. The opportunity of the school is to give boys and girls an interest in a variety of commonplace activities of mutual helpfulness in the home — to counteract, so far as possible, the baneful influence of our modern industrial life.

In a very simple way, what a need to study in school things already experienced in the home and in other places of daily life! Children have their associations with other children. Mothers are called upon to suggest games for them to play, and then to show them how to play. Ere long these same good, busy mothers are again under obligation to settle some small dispute between the players. How usually at children's parties is there a real difficulty in providing a genuinely suitable entertainment! There is thus need *now* in our homes that children learn how to make provision for such social hours. Parents, mothers especially, would appreciate such assistance from the schools. Children are probably best reared in those homes where some duties, more particularly in some form of handwork, are required. What an advantage to parents and children *now* if the schools enabled the children to make many things useful and ornamental — holders, doilies, mats, etc.! The practical value of such things is equaled or even exceeded by the aesthetic influence of such articles when they are worked out with artistic design. Home means the more to those children who participate the more in the real life of the home. ". . . The more immediate purposes of instruction must be found among the leading things necessary for proper daily living, — that is, we must look directly to the life about us to find what subject matter the school should offer, and how this should be treated. Its curriculum will be good to the extent that it contains problems . . . that are socially vital and yet within the pupils' appreciation. . . ." [2] Here is a theory commonly accepted. But not until subject matter is actually outlined in terms of home life can the school contribute positive help to children in their home life. . . .

The problem as personal. It is of importance that the situation be sufficiently well understood that a real problem may be appreciated, and that this problem be deeply felt as a personal one. The teacher's arbitrary assignment of the next ten pages in history, or nine problems in arithmetic, or certain descriptions in geography, cannot be felt by the pupil as a real problem and a personal problem. A laboring man, a clerk, any subordinate who merely executes directions of a superior is not solving real problems. He is efficient only as a machine is efficient. Genuinely real problems cannot be assigned to one by some one else. Real problems develop in one's normal experience. They are the result of conflicting conditions. The arbitrarily assigned problem is virtually only a contentless exercise — a sort of mechanical drill. An efficient clerk in a grocery store must observe sufficiently well to know why his employer's trade is decreasing; it may be because of lack of cleanliness in the store. He senses the problem as personal because he himself can effect a change. Such is the case in other industrial or business occupations. In school work such a problem grows out of common interest in the activities that affect the pupils. A class is studying the grocery store as a local industry directly affecting them all. How does the merchant serve his patrons with vegetables? This question becomes a personal problem. Efficiency calls for an attitude of sensing problems and regarding them as personal.

Initiative essential. Initiative in working at the problem is essential for effectiveness. Those who must be constantly told to work or study accomplish little. Assigned lessons in school are virtually directions to go to work. Very little effective studying is done by the students under such circumstances.

[2] McMurry, F. M., *Interim Report, Committee on School Inquiry, City of New York,* 1911–1912, pages 6–7.

It is not at all natural that this initiative display itself upon the traditional curriculum. Work there is not upon normal but only upon artificial problems. Initiative is aroused when one meets, under normal circumstances, a situation which is felt as a personal problem. School work is not the most effective, in the present or as preparation for later work, when it is in response to assigned tasks — lessons — as many each day as the pupil has subjects for study. Pupils soon learn to work upon their own initiative when a large problem covering several days or even weeks is before them. There is no definite amount of work that must be accomplished each day, but a large piece of work is to be done to the best of one's ability. This opportunity presents a strong appeal to initiative in young people, who need more of this opportunity. Too little of this type of work is offered in the traditional curriculum. A curriculum that deals more specifically with the activities of everyday life presents in a large way this opportunity. Initiative is very potent in efficiency. The spirit of initiative carries over into later life.

Method of study. How to study [3] is one of the new problems in educational discussion. Methods of teaching have been much discussed for some time. Processes of learning have been given considerable attention. But study is different from learning.[4] Discussions on methods of study are limited too much to the formal school lessons. Study is too narrowly considered; it belongs to the real life of children far more than in school lessons. School problems ought not to be essentially different from out-of-school problems. A boy of twelve is given a camera by his father. The boy has seen the photographer at work using a tripod. He wishes a tripod for his camera. The price of a manufactured tripod is not at his command, but a bench and tools are within his reach. He observes another tripod; he notes certain essentials, e.g., stability and adjustability. But in the commercial product are fixtures which he cannot duplicate. He must invent a more homely device. This *method of attack* is an essential in efficiency. One must analyze conditions and then construct measures under the guidance of the personal problem before him. In the usual school work there is little call for such study. There is usually learning rather than study. So-called " problems " are artificial, designed for training, rather than growing naturally out of the meeting of real needs. School work may have the *form* of a real out-of-school problem. For example: " A hare is 80 leaps before a hound. The hare takes four leaps while the hound takes three. But two of the hound's leaps are equal to three of the hare's. How many leaps must the hound take to catch the hare? " [5] Such a problem might represent a real situation, but even if it did, no boy or girl would be at all interested in the conclusion that the hound must jump 480 times before he pounced upon

---

[3] McMurry, F. M., *How to Study*; Earhart, Lida, *Systematic Study in the Elementary Schools.*

[4] In German schools the term " lernen " has applied to the work of young pupils; " studieren," to the work of older pupils.

[5] As remembered from an old text in arithmetic.

this exceptional and foolish little animal. The problem is clearly presented as an exercise in fractions. It is a real puzzle to most pupils. Real problems, true to life, normally arising as a common interest or experience, invite the pupil to analyze conditions and invent means to satisfy needs. Such a method of attack is common to all problems in experience, and is carried over from earlier into later life.

Persistence. Persistence is a requisite in efficiency. This statement needs no support by way of discussion. It may be pointed out, however, that in the traditional school work, the artificial problems are too limited to provide the opportunity for the sort of persistence which is really valuable. " Lessons " are comparatively short. Real life problems vary in length and difficulty. If problems arise by reason of real needs felt by the pupils as personal, persistence is natural. In the curriculum herein proposed sixth-grade pupils spend about eight weeks of two and one half hours each day on the one problem, how manufacturing is carried on. This is an industry that affects all and in a variety of aspects is felt by pupils as a personal problem. This spirit of persistency in working out a real problem is carried over from an earlier to a later experience.

Tentative attitude. The tentative attitude toward results is a characteristic of the efficient man. In real life no problems are finally settled. " Circumstances alter cases." Changes are taking place. Market prices depend upon supply and demand. In the traditional curriculum pupils usually get the notion that the several " problems " on which they are working are solved; conclusions are reached and set aside as final. The hound must take 480 leaps. The artificial problem of the school leads too much to the " rest-on-your-oars " attitude. It prompts to idleness until the next assignment. The tentative attitude — the open-mindedness toward all results — is the attitude that spurs one on to the discovery of new conditions and the sensing of new problems. This is the spirit that is fostered by the curriculum which deals directly with the social and industrial activities in real life. This open-mindedness is carried over to later experiences.

OPPORTUNITY FOR A CURRICULUM OF PRESENT ACTIVITIES

" It has been held that interests in the school must in the nature of the case be at first largely artificial. The child is supposed to be preparing for adult life, but he is not surrounded by the conditions of adult life and has not within himself the natural impulses of adults. It is assumed therefore that interests in adult activities must be artificially stimulated. It may be questioned in the first place whether the child cannot in a large measure better be prepared for adult life by living most completely the life of a child and developing in a natural way the interests of childhood, later youth and manhood, as the conditions and instinctive tendencies change." [6]

Dewey states Rousseau's central idea in these words: " The child is best

[6] Kirkpatrick, E. A., *The Individual in the Making*, page 32.

prepared for life as an adult by experiencing in childhood what has meaning to him as a child, and further, the child has a right to enjoy his childhood. Because he is a growing animal who must develop so as to live successfully in the grown-up world, nothing should be done to interfere with growth, and everything should be done to further the full and free development of his body and his mind." [7]

. . . Emphasis has been given [here] to the importance of attending to immediate needs. On the contrary, the custom of preparing for later occasions is due largely to the adult viewpoint. Quite naturally the adult asks: How shall the boy prepare for the duties he must meet at my stage of life? The boy, whose vision is limited according to his experience, acts as though the question were: How can I get the very most out of what I am now doing? The traditional curriculum is accepted as the answer to the adult's question. The curriculum presented in this volume is proposed as an answer to the boy's question. By reason of early withdrawal from school most boys and girls never reach just the adult stage designed in the Three-R curriculum. Further, as the boy and the girl are concerned, by nature, primarily with their present, the essentially preparatory curriculum does not, it cannot, appeal to their motives and provoke in them the generous responses as a curriculum that concerns itself primarily with their present environment. Again, the traditional curriculum, in its emphasis upon preparation, misses a great opportunity to serve both individual and community when both need such service. Finally, preparation for efficiency later is more effectively made when children of the elementary school age are given the opportunity to exercise those traits that contribute so much to efficiency in all phases of life. This opportunity is conspicuously larger in a curriculum of present activities than in the curriculum of traditional forms. . . .

THE CONCRETE NOT A REJECTION OF THE THREE R'S

In closing this . . . [discussion], . . . the reader may be cautioned against a possible misinterpretation. A curriculum in terms of the concrete and the practical would not mean a rejection of arithmetical, geographical, or linguistic subject matter in school work. A pupil's understanding of quantity, of language, and of geography would probably be more extensive and more effective by reason of the stronger motive under which this work was done. These are his tools in studying real life. This . . . [discussion] . . . calls for a change in viewpoint. The school should be concerned primarily with specific activities in social and industrial life.

Traditional Three-R subject matter is not to be ruthlessly cut out of the curriculum merely because it is traditional. It must be placed on a par with subject matter taken directly from real life, *in so far* as it functions in the equipment of boys and girls for community life. However, as has been

[7] Dewey, J., *Schools of Tomorrow*, pages 17–18.

pointed out, the subject matter taken directly from life activities contributes more, and that more directly, to preparation for participation in real life than do the traditional subjects. That which contributes less must yield to that which contributes more in the equipment of children for their work and play activities. The relative values of these two types of subject matter must be determined by their service in real life, and this in turn determines the relative position in the curriculum.

The traditional, formal Three R's are strictly subordinate. From the point of view of method, instruction in these formal subjects is incidental to instruction in the concrete and practical affairs of everyday life. . . .

BOYD H. BODE
A critique of the concept of pupil needs

Any discussion among " progressive " educators is likely to bring in an early reference to the " needs " of pupils. In former years the phrase " felt needs " had considerable currency. The qualifying adjective had the great merit of providing an indication of what was meant by needs. A felt need was identical with desire; it was generated by the nature of the pupil and it pointed to an appropriate course of action. Consequently, an inquiry into needs was supposed to have a quality of objectivity comparable to that of studies dealing with the stratification of rocks or with spots on the sun. A felt need was a desire; although there seems to have been some hesitation about classifying all desires as needs. The hankering of an old soak for another drink, for example, or the yearning of a small boy to punch his playmate's nose, might not qualify as a real need in the mind of a pious educator. Labelling a desire as a need gives it a preferred status; the implication of the term " need " is that we are dealing with a legitimate claim and that something should be done about it.

If, then, we take the concept of felt needs as our point of departure, we at once encounter a problem. How are we to distinguish between desires which are to be recognized as " needs " and those which are not? Even if the desires which we encounter are innocent in themselves, their number and variety are such that we cannot give recognition to all of them. There are no discoverable limits to human desires. As William James says, " Not that I would not, if I could, be both handsome and fat and well dressed, and a great athlete, and make a million a year, be a wit, a *bon-vivant*, and a lady-killer, as well as a philosopher; a philanthropist, statesman, warrior, and African explorer, as well as a ' tone-poet ' and saint. But the thing is simply impossible. The millionaire's work would run counter to the saint's; the *bon-vivant* and the philanthropist would trip each other up; the philos-

Boyd H. Bode, " The Concept of Needs in Education," *Progressive Education*, 15:7–9, January, 1938. Reprinted by permission.

opher and the lady-killer could not well keep house in the same tenement of clay." [1]

In principle there is no difference in this respect between adults and younger people. When desires conflict, as they constantly do, a decision, to be intelligent, must be based, not on the quality or urgency of the desires, but on a long-range program. It is the program, the more remote aim or purpose, that decides which desires are relevant and which are interlopers. Even so elementary a craving as hunger, for example, must be dealt with in this way. Perhaps the person concerned has what he considers to be an unesthetic tendency towards overweight; perhaps he deems it his duty to tighten his belt and help conserve the national food supply; perhaps he believes that eternal salvation can be won only through complete subjugation of the body; or again he may have a primitive conviction that the world owes him a living and act accordingly. It all depends. The fact that he is hungry does not in itself give a clue to his needs. The need is determined in each case by the end to be achieved, by the underlying philosophy. It is related that a man once said to the celebrated Dr. Samuel Johnson: " But doctor, a man has to live! " To which the crusty old doctor replied: " Sir, I do not see the necessity."

We may assume then that some kind of guidance and selection is indispensable. It is different, of course, if we start with Rousseau's assumption that the patterns for development are inherent in our nature because man is created in the image of God. In that case it is reasonable to suppose that desires are the expression of this inherent pattern or divine image and therefore not subject to regulations of any kind. We can understand, too, how a believer in the instinct theory might reach such a conclusion, since the instinct theory merely changes Rousseau's terminology without changing anything else. In either case we have the idea of an inherent pattern from which education is to take its clues. We can then base education on the nurture of needs or desires as they happen to arise, with the comforting assurance that such procedure has the endorsement both of the Almighty and of science. This is logical, even if it does not make sense.

We usually assume that these older views have long since been abandoned. But perhaps this assumption is not wholly warranted. It is true that we place more emphasis on guidance and that we are less inclined than formerly to take the " feltness " of a desire as evidence of a need. A need, it seems, may be a real need, even if it is not recognized as such by the person concerned. Thus a man may be deemed to be greatly in need of a noble woman who loves him and has faith in him, even though the man himself be wholly unable to diagnose his case in any such fashion. In other words, we grant that needs are not the result of purely inner determination, but we seem to persist in the belief that we can ascertain, in an objective way,

[1] James, W., *Psychology*, Vol. I, p. 311.

what the nature of the individual calls for, if we interpret this nature in the light of surrounding circumstances. This is not a surrender of the old point of view, but a refinement of it.

Antecedently the presumption is all against the notion that adolescent needs, for example, can be ascertained by a detailed study of the individual in relation to his social environment. If there is no fixed pattern either in the individual or in the social environment, it is altogether unlikely that such a pattern will be found if we take the two together. Yet, as was said before, the only way to discover a need is in terms of a " pattern " or scheme of values. Let us suppose, for illustration, that a youngster is found to be maladjusted with respect to parental relationships. What light does this shed on his " needs "? This depends altogether on our theory of what these relationships ought to be. According to one view, he may be sadly lacking in the virtue of obedience to parental authority. According to another view, he may be in urgent need of a clearer insight into the limitations of this authority, so that he may persist in his course without being oppressed by a sense of guilt. Either of these views will provide a basis for the determination of needs, but neither one can be regarded as inherent in the nature of the individual or in the cosmic structure of things. Studies of adolescence may be immensely valuable as portrayals of the difficulties that beset modern youth. But it is misleading to call them studies of needs, because the needs still remain to be determined after the investigation is completed. The claim that needs are discoverable in this way would have to be rated, not as a scientific truth but as academic bootlegging. To expect " needs " to emerge from such studies is like expecting an architectural design to result from a study of the structural materials that are to be used for a building.

All this is but a roundabout way of saying that needs refer to ends or aims. In specific situations where the end in view may be taken for granted, it is entirely appropriate to speak of needs, since the end or purpose furnishes a point of reference for judging the needs. But to undertake to build an educational program by starting with needs is quite another matter. Unless we assume that there is a predestined end for human living and that we are in on the know as to what this end is, there is no justification whatsoever for talking so blithely about needs. An authoritarian scheme of education could make excellent use of a doctrine of needs, for it would be in a position to know at every point what it was talking about. In a democratic system of education the center of the plot must always be the continuous rebuilding of the scheme of values, the underlying philosophy or social outlook, by the pupil, as a basis for determining his needs. At most the social and material environment can only furnish an opportunity to choose between alternative conceptions of needs — and even this opportunity is largely dependent on co-operation by the school in supplying the conditions for making an intelligent choice.

The point at issue is far more than the verbal question of how the term "need" is to be employed. It concerns the question of what education should be primarily concerned to achieve. The failure to emancipate ourselves completely from Rousseauism and the instinct psychology is responsible for most, if not all, the weaknesses of the progressive movement in education. The attitude of superstitious reverence for childhood is still with us. The insistence that we must stick like a leech at all times to the "needs" of childhood has bred a spirit of anti-intellectualism, which is reflected in the reliance on improvising instead of long-range organization, in the overemphasis of the here and now, in the indiscriminate tirades against "subjects," in the absurdities of pupil planning, and in the lack of continuity in the educational program. It has frequently resulted in an unhealthy attitude towards children, an attitude which suggests that there is no such thing as a normal child, and that we must be everlastingly exploring his insides, like a Calvinist taking himself apart day after day to discover evidences of sin.

It is a commonplace that the infant's only chance to grow into a human being is through social relationships. This is only another way of saying that growth is not directed from within but by the "patterns" embodied in the social order. If we believe in progress, in a democratic sense, we must believe that these patterns require continuous revision. As they actually exist in our complex modern world, they not only present conflicting types, but the basic patterns are severally incoherent and internally contradictory. In business, for example, we accept both the profit motive and the ideal of social service; in government we hold to both rugged individualism and the ideal of social security; in the field of esthetics we find that standards are both absolute and relative. Yet these are the patterns which must serve as instrumentalities for "growth." In a properly organized educational system this confusion in our cultural heritage will be the constant point of reference, instead of being merely appended, like the tail to the kite, as an additional item after we have set up the program in terms of "needs," the concept of needs thus making a red herring drawn across the trail. What we need is a moratorium on needs, so that we can get down to serious business and bring to fruition the splendid promise that is contained in the philosophy of progressive education.

CHAPTER NINE BIBLIOGRAPHY

ARMENTROUT, W. D., "Individuality and Commonality," *Educational Theory.* 1:186–87, 1951.

> The central ideas which the author deals with are the proper balance between the needs of individuals and the needs of a society, and the development of individuals adequately educated to keep such a balance.

DURKHEIM, EMILE, *Education and Sociology,* translated by Sherwood D. Fox. Glencoe: The Free Press, 1956.

In his description of the social nature of education, Durkheim illustrates his contention that there is no real antagonism between the society and the individual, that individual and social needs have a harmony and mutually supportive relationship.

KAHL, JOSEPH A., "Aspirations of 'Common Man' Boys," *Harvard Educational Review.* 23:186–203, Summer, 1953.

This interesting study gives a good indication of some reasons why boys of ability often do not continue their formal schooling. Family attitude is evidently a primary factor.

NEILL, A. S., *Summerhill: A Radical Approach to Child Rearing.* New York: Hart Publishing Company, 1960.

Radical is the word for this book. Neill describes the beliefs and practices underlying the program at Summerhill school in England. Some would say it was total chaos and license. Neill argues that it provides a balance in child-parent relationships; it is freedom without license.

RUGG, HAROLD and SHUMAKER, ANN, *The Child-Centered School.* New York: World Book Company, 1928.

The authors present a soundly liberal approach to education. In Chapter 5 child interest, creative self-expression, and personality and social adjustment are analyzed as a basis for learning experiences for children.

SIMPSON, RICHARD L. and SIMPSON, IDA HARPER, "The School, the Peer Group, and Adolescent Development," *Journal of Educational Sociology.* 32:37–41, September, 1958.

The discrepancy between the school instructional program and the social needs of adolescents is emphasized. The school can influence the direction of development for which the peer group takes primary responsibility.

TAIT, WILLIAM D., "Psychology, Education and Sociology," *School and Society.* 21:36–37, January 10, 1925.

Tait argues that democracy ought not to provide uniform and leveling conditions, but promote the best in each person, with culmination in an intellectual aristocracy.

IO

Education for Coping with Contemporary Society

Although many critics have found fault with the traditional school, not all have agreed upon an underlying educational philosophy for a more functional education. As we noticed in the last chapter, some have felt that the interests and needs of children should furnish the direction for educational planning and practice. Critics of this position have been convinced that this might be a starting point but would give no direction and would eventually lead only to anarchy. If the individuality of each child were to be supreme, then a laissez-faire operation would ensue. When children's interests and needs come in conflict, no criteria for their resolution is available, unless one adopts the principle that might makes right. Although the educators who accepted this position realized that children rather than subject matter were the prime center of attention, the individualism of Rousseau left much to be desired.

A number of educational philosophers are convinced that education should center in the problems of contemporary society. "Education is life," becomes the battle-cry. Schooling has to be functional or practical. It has to deal with the present problems facing children in society. But several questions arise. Which problems should be chosen? Should the problems be of immediate concern to children? Should problems on a national or international scale take precedence? Are there *persistent* social problems which keep recurring from generation to generation which should have pri-

ority in the curriculum? Even though the answers to these questions have varied from one educator to another, a strong case has been made that certain crucial problems in contemporary society could be isolated and a school program could be built around these. Many advocates of this position believe that the most important function is helping children learn to live in a democratic society. No better way to do this, they believe, could be found than by developing a school which actually practices democracy. By actually practicing democracy, and living democratically, children would be equipped to take their place in society upon graduation. Then education would *be* life rather than *preparation for* life. These educators have argued that the world is dynamic and ever-changing. With everything in flux and no one possessing a crystal-ball, it is impossible to predict adequately what the society of the future will be like. Hence, it is likewise impossible to be dogmatic concerning the future. If the student learns how to solve the problems of the present, he will acquire a technique which will equip him to solve problems he will face later in life regardless of changing conditions. The rapidly changing technology, the dislocations caused by the Depression of the 1930's, the impact of two world wars within the short span of thirty years, the advances in transportation and automation, the developments of the space age, and the remarkable advances in science have shattered our faith in normalcy and stability. Change seems to be the only constant. Thus, to these educators, the security proposed by emphasizing the essentials of the social heritage and the eternal verities seems to be a delusion and incongruous with life in the twentieth century.

John L. Childs, a pragmatist and contemporary of John Dewey, is one such educator who has analyzed the situation and believes that the school can find direction within a changing society. To him, an education geared to the problems of a changing world need not follow one fad after another. In fact, he feels that the school dare not be neutral on moral issues. To him, "Education is a value-conditioned activity." This means adult guidance is necessary. The school must have a purpose, and the emphasis must be upon the fact that education is a moral enterprise. Even though problems change, education can continue to adjust to these changes. In such instability moorings must be found in a commitment to democracy. Thus, if education is to help children cope with the problems of contemporary society, the total program of the school must not only take these changes into account, but must also practice democracy in all the aspects of its diversified program. The topics chosen in a class for discussion, the regulations, the way students and teachers are treated and treat one another, the assembly programs, and the celebration of national holidays will all indicate whether or not democracy is being practiced, and if practiced, learned. The school, then, becomes a huge laboratory of life. Not only will the child be able to solve the problems facing him and live effectively with

his classmates, but he will also be cognizant of the significant events occurring throughout the nation and the world. He will also be able to live with his parents and neighbors and to assist in the solution of domestic and international problems. As he graduates from school, he will not face years of adjustment to novel problems, but will be ready to meet the vicissitudes of life. He will know the techniques of locating and defining a problem, of proposing and testing hypotheses, and of making an effective choice of the best solution. The selection by Childs elaborates upon such an educational system.

John Dewey, leading educator and philosopher for the first half of the twentieth century, continually addressed himself to the problems of the day. He succinctly states his position regarding his educational beliefs in his article "My Pedagogic Creed," part of which has been reproduced in this chapter. Although Dewey preceded Childs and his article was written 53 years before the one quoted from Childs, the basic theme is the same. The pithy manner in which Dewey has stated his beliefs should not only challenge the reader but also help him in comparing the various positions regarding the purposes of education presented in this section of the book. The reader should consider carefully the implications of this position for school organization, curriculum, methodology, and evaluation. He should, finally, ask himself whether this philosophy does express the prime function of the school. Is it in harmony with democracy as a way of life? Can it be implemented?

JOHN L. CHILDS
Education in a changing society

Education and choice among life alternatives. The moral nature of education stems from the fact that schools are organized and maintained by adults, not by the children who attend them. Adults engage in deliberate education because they are concerned to direct the processes by which their children mature and learn to become participating members of their society. A manifestation of preference for certain patterns of living as opposed to others is therefore inherent in every program of deliberate education. Schools always exhibit in their purposes and their programs of study that which the adults of a society have come to prize in their experience and most deeply desire to nurture in their own children. Hence the curriculum of a school is an index to the values of the particular human group that founds the school. It is because some conception of what is humanly significant and desirable is implicit in all nurture of the young that we may say without exaggeration that each program of deliberate education is, by nature, a moral undertaking.

Our thought about education will be confused at its very root if we do not perceive that a school can never be a morally indifferent institution. Each school operates within a definite historical-social situation. This situation is marked by genuine life alternatives. Amid these plural and competing patterns of living, the school seeks to emphasize and to foster certain types of growth, and to hinder and to avert other types of growth. Were one invariant line of development alone open to the young, there would be no need for adult guidance. Thus, both lay and professional educational leaders misconceive the essential meaning of a school whenever they pretend to be neutral or indifferent to what happens to the children under their jurisdiction. In the last analysis, the success or failure of a school is measured in *moral* terms, that is, by what it does with and for the human beings entrusted to its care. All of the other functions of a school are ancillary to this primary responsibility of directing the growth of the immature members of its society.

Obviously, there can be important differences in judgment about what kinds of human behavior are so fundamental and desirable that they should be cultivated in the school. In view of our present limited knowledge of the process of human maturation and learning, there can also be legitimate differences about the best means of nurturing cherished attitudes, techniques, interests, tastes, outlooks and patterns of conduct in the young. But the fact that we still have much to learn about both the ends and the means of education provides no sound ground for the notion that

From *Education and Morals* by John L. Childs, pp. 6–8, 14–20, 27–38. Copyright, 1950, Appleton-Century-Crofts, Inc. Reprinted by permission.

we can educate, and at the same time avoid responsibility for making judgments about the kind of person, or persons, we want the immature to become. This elemental moral responsibility is inherent in each program of deliberate education, for the cultural selections and rejections inescapably involved in the construction and direction of an educational program necessarily have consequences in the lives of those who are nurtured in it.

This tendency to pattern the intellectual and emotional dispositions of the young is present in every type of educational program — democratic as well as authoritarian, secular as well as religious, scientific as well as humanist, liberal as well as vocational, individualist as well as collectivist. In sum, the making of choices that have to do with the destinies of human beings cannot be eliminated from that directing of experience and learning which is the distinctive function of the school. It is choice among significant life alternatives that is the essence of the *moral* act, and choice among values necessarily pervades those human actions by which the program of a school is organized and communicated. . . .

Ends and means in education. It is also important for educators to recognize that a scientifically grounded pedagogy is no substitute for clear ideas about the values and purposes of education. The scientific study of both the nature of the child and the process of human maturation and learning is making indispensable contributions to the work of education. No teacher worthy of the name can afford to ignore these tested findings. But knowledge of these scientific findings does not in and of itself define our educational objectives. For example, knowledge of the fact of individual differences, and of the uniqueness of each child, does not relieve us of responsibility for making judgments about the way in which that inherited uniqueness is to find its appropriate expression within the context of our changing modes of life and thought.

Studies in human learning show that learning is an active, dynamic affair, and the leaders of progressive education have rendered an important service by developing an activity curriculum to provide more adequately for these dynamic aspects of the learning process. But " pupil initiative " and " wholehearted purposeful projects " are in no sense a substitute for adult guidance; they should rather be viewed as improved means of making that guidance more effectual. The more knowledge that we can get about the process by which the powers of the child ripen, the better we shall be able to plan the program of the school, but knowledge of " the human maturation sequence " does not justify a " hands-off " policy in education. As a matter of fact, such findings as we have about child development show that " the human maturation sequence " is by no means exclusively an affair of the biological organism; it is deeply influenced by environmental factors, and after the first years, the rôle of a culturally conditioned experience becomes primary in determining the further lines of personal growth. Confronted with plural and conflicting cultural patterns, educators cannot escape responsibility for choosing main lines of human development.

Those educators who have combined the psychological principles of child growth with the moral principles of democracy and have developed the conception that the supreme aim of education should be the nurture of an individual who can take responsibility for his own continued growth have made an ethical contribution of lasting worth. But acceptance of the objective of developing a person who can eventually take over his own education does not at all imply that the school should arrange its affairs so that each child, unhindered by adult guidance, will be left " free to develop in his own way." To attempt to do this is to negate the very purpose of deliberate education. We establish schools because we recognize that the child does not know the principles and the means of his own development, and because we also realize that the kind of scientific and humane conduct we call " mature " and which is presupposed in the principle of responsible " self-education " is not an original endowment. It is a genuine ethical insight that distinguishes intellectual and emotional maturity from mere slavish conformity to custom, but we err whenever we assume that what is prized as " maturity " is the product of an unguided, spontaneous unfolding of an inborn pattern of human personality.

Although method is fundamental in the nurture of the young, method, in and of itself, cannot determine the objectives of our educational program. To define these educational objectives we must have a definite conception of the kind of person we are seeking to develop. If that conception is to be more than a formal abstraction, it must take account of the actual life conditions and relationships of the society in which the child is to live, along with those more general principles of human conduct which men of many different societies have come to honor because these principles have been confirmed by all that they have experienced.

Education is grounded in respect for the achievements of human beings. If man did not have regard for that which he has learned and created, he would not organize schools to communicate his culture to his young. But in a democratic society, education is also grounded in respect for each human personality. It seeks the growth, not the enslavement, of the immature members of its society. Fortunately, these two basic values are not in conflict; on the contrary, they mutually support one another. We can manifest respect for the child and contribute to his progressive liberation through the procedures of deliberate education only as we have respect for the knowledge and values that man has derived from that which he has suffered and undergone. No educational theory or method is to be trusted which opposes respect for the child to respect for human experience and knowledge.

In fine, education is a value-conditioned activity. The school seeks to cultivate selected values in the young by means of both the subject-matters and the methods that it employs in its program. In education, as in other human arts, our practice becomes intelligent as it grows, both in its awareness of the ends that it is seeking to attain and in its mastery of the means which it must use to attain these ends. The fact that these ends or outcomes involve the lives of the immature deepens — it does not diminish — our responsibility to know what we are trying to accomplish when we undertake to educate.

The moral nature of deliberate education. As we have emphasized in all the foregoing, deliberate education is never morally neutral. A definite expression of preference for certain human ends, or values, is inherent in all efforts to guide the experience of the young. No human group would ever bother to found and maintain a system of schools were it not concerned to make of its children something other than they would become if left to themselves and their surroundings. Moreover, in order to develop the preferred and chosen patterns of behavior, it is necessary to hinder other and incompatible kinds of growth. A school is ineffective as an educational agency whenever the emphases in certain aspects or departments of its work are denied or negated in other parts of its program. In education, as in other realms of human activity, the actual practices of a school are more potent than its verbal professions. Maximum results are achieved when both the declared aims and the actual deeds of a school are unified, and its children are reared in an environment that supports in its daily practices that which it affirms in its theory.

As we have already stated, the term *moral*, as used in this discussion, does not pertain to a restricted phase of the work of the school. The moral interest pervades the entire educational program. It is involved whenever a significant choice has to be made between a better and a worse in the nurture of the young. The moral factor appears whenever the school, or the individual teacher or supervisor, is *for* certain things and *against* other things. The moral element is preëminently involved in all of those selections and rejections that are inescapable in the construction of the purposes and the curriculum of the school. It appears, for example, in the affairs of the playground — in the kind of sports that are favored and opposed, and in the code of sportsmanship by which the young are taught to govern their behavior in the actual play of the various games. It appears in the social life of the school — in all of the behaviors that are approved or disapproved as the young are taught the manners — the conventional or minor morals — of their society. It appears in the school's definition of the delinquent and in its mode of dealing with him. It appears in the way children are taught to treat those of different racial, religious, occupational, economic or national backgrounds. It appears in the department of science; in the methods the young are expected to adopt in conducting their experiments, in their reports of what actually happened during the course of their experiments, as well as in the regard of the teachers of science for accuracy, for precision, and for conclusions that are based on objective data rather than on wishful thinking. It appears in the department of social studies: in the problems that are chosen to be discussed, in the manner in which they are discussed, in the historical documents and events that are emphasized, as well as in the leaders that are chosen to illustrate the important and the worthy and the unimportant and the unworthy in the affairs of man. It appears in the department of literature: in the novels, the poems, the dramas that are chosen for study, in what is considered good and what is considered bad in the various forms and styles of human conduct and expression. It appears in the organization and the government of the school: in the part that superintendent, supervisors, teachers, pupils are expected to play in the making and the maintenance of the regulations of the school. It appears in the methods of grading, promoting, and distributing honors among the children of the school. It appears in the celebration of national holidays: in the particular events that are celebrated as well as in the historical and contemporary personalities who are chosen to exemplify the qualities of citizenship and worthy community service. It appears in the programs for the general assemblies of the schools: in the various leaders from the community who are brought in to speak to the children. It appears in the way teachers are treated: the amount of freedom and initiative they enjoy, in the extent to which teachers are permitted to take part in the life of their community, and the degree to which the young believe that they are studying under leaders who are more than docile, routine drillmasters in assigned subjects. It appears in the way the community organizes to conduct its schools: in the provision it makes in its schoolgrounds, buildings, and equipment, in the kind of people it chooses to serve on the school board, and in the relation of the members of the board to the administrative and teaching staff. In sum, the moral factor enters whenever and wherever significant decisions have to be made about either the organization, the administration, or the instructional program of the school. All of these decisions, whether they relate to curriculum or to extra-curriculum affairs, exert an influence on the attitudes and the behaviors of the young.

Thus judgments about life values inescapably pervade and undergird the whole process of providing and guiding experience. More than many teachers recognize, a scheme of values — a structure of things considered significant, worthful and right — operates in their endless responses to the daily behavings of their pupils. Many of these educational values concern the very fundamentals of human existence. They have to do with such elemental things as the rights, the responsibilities, the beliefs, the tastes, the appreciations, the faiths and the allegiances of human beings. As we introduce the young to the various aspects of human experience — familial, economic, scientific, technological, political, religious, artistic — we inevitably encourage attitudes and habits of response in and to these affairs. In order to encourage, we must also discourage; in order to foster, we must also hinder; in order to emphasize the significant, we must identify the non-significant; and, finally, in order to select and focus attention on certain subject-matters of life, we have to reject and ignore other subject-matters. Were our values different, our selections and our rejections would also be different. The process of selecting and rejecting, of fostering and hindering, of distinguishing the lovely from the unlovely, and of discriminating the important from the unimportant, is unending in education. It is this process of choice and emphasis that defines what is meant by the term *moral* as it is used in this book.

As thus interpreted, the concept of the *moral* refers not primarily to the particular ethical quality of the life interests, outlooks, and practices involved in any given educational program, but rather to the more elemental fact that *choices* among genuine life-alternatives are inescapably involved in the construction and the actual conduct of each and every educational program. These choices necessarily have consequences in the lives of the young, and through them in the life of their society. Viewed from this perspective, education undoubtedly ranks as one of the outstanding moral undertakings of the human race. . . .

The democratic conception and the aims of education. The development of democracy has also eliminated certain historic types of educational purpose and program. In any society that is really governed by the democratic principle of the worth and dignity of each human personality exploitive systems of education are necessarily precluded. The democratic community negates its own moral foundations whenever it regards the child as a mere potential " bayonet " for its armed forces, as a mere future " hand " in its system of factory production, or as a mere instrument of any kind to be fashioned for the perpetuation of an established institution, or the interests of a special class. A society that is grounded in the conception that governments are instituted among men to promote " life, liberty and the pursuit of happiness," and which holds " that whenever any form of government becomes destructive of these ends, it is the right of the people to alter or to abolish it " cannot consistently support an educational practice that is designed to fashion human beings into the mere instruments of the state. The supreme moral trait of the democratic community is that it has no good other than the good of individual human beings.

Moreover, in a democratic society authority and leadership in education, as in government, are not supposed to be lodged in the hands of any ruling group — hereditary, military, ecclesiastic, or economic. It is the very essence of democratic theory that authority and ultimate control in all public affairs should be transferred from all such limited groups to the people as a whole. In accordance with this principle we have sought to organize a system of public schools in the United States in which the responsibility for the determination of the educational program would rest with the local communities, and with the various state authorities, not with the Federal government — that is, with the parents and their own chosen representatives on local school boards, not primarily with national or church officials.

It has been our conviction that a school system thus responsive to the interests and the preferences of parents would tend to make the needs and the welfare of the child its primary concern. We have also assumed that schools which are controlled by the very groups whose children are enrolled in them could not easily be manipulated to serve the special interests of privileged classes. On the whole, events have justified this faith; the American school has been disposed to make the growth, not the exploitation, of the child its controlling objective.

But even in a democratic society the needs of the immature do not define themselves, nor do they remain constant in a world in which change is real. As we have already emphasized, in order to define desirable patterns of growth for the individual child, we must take account of the kind of life that we expect and desire him to lead. This pattern of life is not an isolated and private thing. It involves, to be sure, the individual child with his distinctive native endowment, but it equally involves the community with its public modes of life and thought. The deeper the regard of the educator for the worth and dignity of the child, the deeper his interest in the community should become. Any program of education tends to become abstract, formal, and therefore a mechanical routine whenever its purposes and materials are considered to be the property of a self-sufficient school, for this means that dynamic continuity between the work of the school and the life that goes on outside the school has been disrupted. A school best provides for the growth of the child when it maintains living interaction with the community of which he is a part.

Names and realities in human conduct. A theory of morals is of course implicit in the foregoing view of the relation of the program of the school to the ongoing affairs of its society. This moral theory holds, in the first place, that human rights and human responsibilities do not constitute a separate and fixed system, but that they are conditioned by the concrete ways in which a human group makes its living and carries on its whole schedule of interrelated life activities. This theory assumes, in the second place, that as knowledge grows and new means of control and modes of living develop, traditional patterns of human rights and duties may also have to be modified. In other words, this social conception of education is the correlative of a moral theory which holds that morals are related to human interests and evolving conditions of life, and hence are not absolute and transcendental, but empirical, institutional, and historical in nature.

It is easy to deceive ourselves and to conceal this empirical and social character of morals. All that is necessary to make morals appear to be unconditioned and immutable is to concentrate attention on moral terms or names, and to ignore the actual human relationships and behaviors that are denoted by these moral terms. Thus an educator may affirm that even revolutionary social changes are of no concern to him, for he knows that in each and every society a child should be taught to be unselfish, to be honest, to be chaste, to be loyal, and to make his behavior conform to all of the fundamentals of the moral code. There is, to be sure, a measure of truth in this educational affirmation, for in the course of its experience the human race has gained many ethical insights. But this emphasis on continuity and permanence in the moral life of man becomes harmful whenever it is taken to mean that new knowledge and powers of human control, and altered conditions of life, do not make necessary fresh appraisals of the behaviors that are to be considered authentic expressions of these traditional moral principles.

For example, changes in modes of production have in no way eliminated the importance of the distinction between the " selfish " and the " unselfish " in human conduct, but these economic changes are calling for a fundamental review of the rights of both the owner and the worker. Considerations of public welfare in our interdependent world are now demanding that the right of the owner to do as he pleases with that which he owns, and the right of the worker to leave his job when and as he desires, be altered. Now these are not superficial moral changes; they involve fundamentals in human relationships and behaviors in the economic sphere. The meaning of the concepts of " selfishness " and " unselfishness " must be revised to correspond to these new realities in our interdependent ways of making a living. So also in the realm of family relationships. The development of effectual contraceptive measures has aroused deep controversies about what should now be considered " moral " in this aspect of human behavior. The evidence indicates that a new standard is developing in this ancient sphere of the " moral," and already important church groups are strongly supporting on ethical grounds the principle of planned parenthood. Nor does the concept of " loyalty " in the realm of political affairs automatically define itself. World-wide totalitarian political movements have resulted in novel political affiliations and practices which have raised the most difficult kind of questions about the meaning of citizenship and the criteria by which " loyalty " is to be measured in contemporary political, educational and similar public undertakings.

In brief, unless education is to serve outmoded and reactionary ends, it must accept responsibility for defining the kind of behaviors which now should be associated with such traditional and basic moral categories as " honesty," " unselfishness," " chastity," " loyalty," " equality," " responsibility," and " freedom." The present has its deep continuities with the past, but it also has its significant discontinuities. The discontinuities, moreover, are as real as the continuities. Education, during this period of social transition and strain, will not promote democratic interests, if it seeks to make " moral absolutes " out of historic rights and forms of human conduct. To serve democratic purposes, education must play its part in the important task of moral discovery. It can do this only as it is willing to continue to examine and test its educational values by whatever we gain of new knowledge and also by that structure of human relationships and activities which is ever developing in the society outside the school. An unexamined morality is not fit to fashion the educational program of a democracy in this period of social transition. Apart from intelligent study of the changing affairs of its society, the school has no adequate means of determining the worth of its moral foundations. Recognition of the reality of change must be one of the fundamental principles in the philosophy of education of our period.

Basic meanings in the social interpretation of education. Measured by all the crucial scientific criteria, human beings constitute a common *biological* family. All members of this human family share a basic organic inheritance. But *culturally* they are members of many different human societies. These societies, located in various parts of the world, are the products of a long development. They have their common features, but they also have their distinctive traits. Each of these societies, taken as a whole, is unique. The things which differentiate one human group from other territorial and cultural groups are no less real than those elements in its ways of life and thought that it shares with other human societies. It was this perception which led the Commission on the Social Studies of the American Historical Association to declare that:

Education always has a geographical and cultural location; it is therefore specific, local, and dynamic, not general, universal, and unchanging; it is a function of a particular society at a particular time and place in history; it is rooted in some actual culture and expresses the philosophy and the recognized needs of that culture. . . .

Although the basic biological equipment of man seems to be comparatively invariant and may therefore be expected to give certain common elements to education everywhere and at all times, human civilization has characteristics of neighborhood, region, nation, and more extended cultural areas, which lend unique qualities to every working educational program, however persistent and pervasive may be the universal elements entering into it.[1]

It is significant that the eminent members of this Commission of the American Historical Association decided to emphasize in their concluding Report that deliberate education should be viewed not primarily as a function of humanity in general, but rather as a function of particular human societies, each with its own individualized past, its own language and literary heritage, its specialized skills and modes of making a living, its distinctive structure of customs, laws, and institutions, as well as with its own unique beliefs, sentiments, moral outlooks, and conceptions of human excellence and of human destiny. For the historian, accustomed to think in

---

[1] American Historical Association, *Conclusions and Recommendations*, The Report of the Commission on Social Studies (New York, Charles Scribner's Sons, 1934), pp. 31–32.

the categories of time and place, societies are many, not one; dynamic, not static; individualized and evolving, not fixed specimens of an immutable human pattern. Individual human beings, in their actual psychological natures, are creatures of these historical cultural groups. They think, evaluate, and respond out of an intellectual and moral consciousness that is saturated and hallowed by the history and the achievements of their people. It is not surprising then that when these culturally conditioned groups of human beings undertook the deliberate nurture of their young, they should have created systems of schools which in their subject-matters and their purposes reflected the societies into which they had been born, and which had shaped the very forms of their own being.

But this argument from history is not decisive. The fact that education down to the present has been an undertaking which has varied with factors of time and place, does not in and of itself warrant the conclusion that education in our shrinking and closely integrated world should continue to be that sort of an enterprise. It is wholly fair to ask those who adopt the social interpretation of education to justify their position in terms not of historical origins, but rather in terms of present human values. Certainly a discussion of education and morals should be willing to meet this demand, for the deepest concern of morals is with what *should be*, not simply with the description of what *has been*, or *now is*. We shall therefore conclude this discussion of society and education by enumerating some of the considerations that make it desirable for us to continue to view education as a human undertaking in which factors of time and place are centrally important.

In the first place, this social theory of education is in harmony with the imperatives of educational practice. In spite of present cultural changes, no advocate of universalism in education has been bold enough to contend that the children of the United States should be nurtured in the Chinese language, or that the children of China should be nurtured in the English language, or that the children of these two countries should be educated in a new world-language. In other words, in the case of such basic interests as language and literature, it is generally recognized that stubborn historical factors make it both necessary and desirable that the program of the school be rooted in the cultural heritages of actual human groups. Even following the total military defeat of Japan and Germany, no one has recommended that the children of these two countries be educated in the language of one of the victorious Powers.

The situation is no less compelling when we come to the subject of history. Men in different parts of the world have had their own and distinctive experiences, and these diversified pasts are not dead; they constitute the very substance of the cultures in which men now live and through which they develop their objects of allegiance and devotion. History, moreover, is the past of the present, and to be significant must be explored from the perspective of some actual present. These perspectives are as many as are present human societies. Hence proposals for "objectivity" in the teaching of history have never assumed that the children of the world should be taught a colorless, universalized human history. These proposals for more impartial historical textbooks have recognized the necessity and the desirability of plural accounts of what human beings, organized in different societies, have done and undergone. The demand for objectivity in the preparation of school history books has therefore been the demand that these various cultural and national accounts strive to be more accurate and fair in their report of other cultures and other national groups, particularly in their interpretations of past transactions and conflicts with these groups. It has been accepted that it would mean impoverishment, not enrichment, were all of these individualized human records to be merged in one common, authoritative history of universal man.

The same considerations obviously hold for vocational education, for education in citizenship, for worthy home membership, and for the creative use of leisure time. Without taking into account the operating institutions and practices of its own society, the school would have no adequate means for the construction of its educational program in these vital dimensions of human experience.

Since the school, in one way or another, must make this reference to the affairs of its society, the adherents of the social interpretation of education hold that this evaluation of the life of a people should be made deliberately with public responsibility for whatever cultural selections and rejections are actually involved in the construction of its program. The ends of objectivity will be better served in education when choices among life-alternatives are recognized and avowed, not concealed or denied.

This social view of education, in the second place, can help us overcome the tendency to *formalism* in the work of deliberate education. The constant temptation of the school is to permit its materials and schedules of activities, once they have been selected, classified, graded, and organized into a curriculum, to become an autonomous program of self-perpetuating interests and subjects. The school begins to die both emotionally and intellectually whenever it thus becomes imprisoned in an inherited curriculum and begins to turn its back on the society that it was organized to serve. To make the communication of meaning a living thing, the teacher must grasp the connection of his "subject" or sphere of human interest and knowledge with that which his people have suffered and enjoyed and with that which they now do and undergo. Education, moreover, is an affair of the young just as literally as it is an affair of the heritage of the group. These young are living as well as learning. They live by participating in the affairs of their family, neighborhood, community, and country. A primary aim of education should be to make this participation more meaningful by placing it in a wider historical and geographical and cultural context, and by helping the young to acquire the knowledge, the skills and the techniques which make this participation more effectual. Growth in meaning and growth in capacity for participation in the life of a human group are not effectually cultivated in a school which makes its own world a rival and a substitute for the world outside the school. An increasing number of educators perceive that both " subjects " and " children " become abstractions whenever they are dealt with as entities independent of the life of the community. They recognize that educators can become wise about the nurture of the immature members of their society only as they continue to grow in their understanding of that world *from* which the young come to school, *in* which they continue to live during the period they study as pupils in the school, and *to* which they must go to work out their own careers when their years at school have been completed.

The social conception of education, in the third place, can help save us from the evil of utopianism in education. By utopianism is meant any projection of social and educational ends which fails to take responsible account of actual cultural conditions, and hence evades responsibility for developing the concrete means by which its ideal ends are to be achieved. Whenever we view moral ideals as absolute and unconditioned things, we are apt to get involved in this kind of romanticism. Our country, for example, is committed by both religious and political ideology to the principle of the dignity and worth of " all men." To the extent that we believe in democracy we are necessarily opposed to all patterns of discrimination and enforced segregation based on factors of religion, race, color, sex, class, or national origin. But notwithstanding our official democratic affirmations, the plain fact is that the ideal of equality in the economic, political and cultural affairs of our country is at present most inadequately realized. Our historic system of property ownership often operates in present-day industrial society so as to favor a privileged few at the expense of the many; our political system in its actual operation in many states now denies Negroes elemental civil rights; and existing American attitudes and practices tend to subject the members of minority religious groups to a variety of discriminations. Education in and for democracy must share in the struggle to get rid of these inequalities. But educators can assist in this important task of democratic, social reconstruction only as they recognize that these discriminations are stubbornly grounded in the past experience of the American people. That experience still lives in characteristic mental habits. The pioneer and agrarian experience of the American people, for example, has disposed many of both farm and city to a firm faith in the system of economic individualism, even though their own interests would now be better served in a regime of coöperative planning. We misconstrue the nature of the present economic problem if we do not appreciate the strength of this faith in individualism, and discern the ways in which it is often manipulated by minority groups that have a vested economic interest in the maintenance of the *status quo.* Experience also demonstrates that racial attitudes and the group mores that underlie our segregated school system have deep roots in the past. It is apparent that education can serve as an agency for social progress only as it takes full account of these group attitudes and the factors in our cultural history which have produced them.

But to take account of existing attitudes and prejudices does not mean that we must weakly surrender to them; it rather means that our proposals for reconstruction should be so formulated that they will strengthen, not weaken, the forces that are striving to dissolve this legacy of discrimination. Democratic advance is undoubtedly a function of human courage as well as of intelligence, but no amount of courage will bring us nearer the goal of equality unless that courage is informed by the kind of understanding which comes from historical and social analysis.

Education frequently fails to enjoy the cooperation of many thoughtful people of genuine democratic interest because of its tendency to make vague moral slogans a substitute for analysis of the conditions with which it has to deal. Actually we know our moral ends only as we know something of the means by which these ends are to be attained. Because the social interpretation of education tends to focus attention on conditions and means it gives promise of developing a morality in education that will be free from the weakness of sentimental utopianism.

Finally, the social interpretation of education can help us discern the defects of traditionalism in education. By traditionalism is meant not sincere regard for the human past, but rather the social and educational view which assumes that we already have a completed system of truth concerning the essentials of human nature, moral values, and the patterns of human civilization, and which also assumes that this completed system contains the answers to whatever problems of human belief, human conduct, and social policy may beset us. On this basis, education becomes merely a process by which the young are indoctrinated with the truths of this closed, authoritarian system. Only those educators who are so immersed in a system of intellectual and moral abstractions that they are immune to the instructions of ordinary human experience, can thus convince themselves that change, and novelty, and moral uncertainty are not real factors in the experience of human beings.

In our period of profound social transformation and transition it is no contribution to the resolution of the problems of mankind to minimize the drastic nature of the adjustments which men must now make if they are to continue to survive. . . . [W]e shall explore in some detail the nature of these adjustments and the importance of nurturing the young in a morality that is more consonant with the life imperatives and life possibilities of the new age we are now entering. Every resource in our intellectual and moral heritage will be needed to help us make satisfactory adjustments to these emerging modes of life, but we shall also do well to accept the fact that we are confronted with novel life conditions which call for real moral pioneering if we are to make our new powers of control over the physical environment serve the ends of a good life. Both the nature of our problems and the means for resolving them will be more adequately understood if old and young seek to educate and re-educate themselves in terms of the actual social situations in which they are now involved. A fundamental merit of the social interpretation of education is that it invites educators to view their task as a significant part of the total task of building a civilization that is in harmony with the deep moving forces in the modern world.

JOHN DEWEY
A statement of pedagogic faith

ARTICLE I — WHAT EDUCATION IS

I Believe that

— all education proceeds by the participation of the individual in the social consciousness of the race. This process begins unconsciously almost at birth, and is continually shaping the individual's powers, saturating his consciousness, forming his habits, training his ideas, and arousing his feelings and emotions. Through this unconscious education the individual gradually comes to share in the intellectual and moral resources which humanity has succeeded in getting together. He becomes an inheritor of the funded capital of civilization. The most formal and technical education in the world cannot safely depart from this general process. It can only organize it or differentiate it in some particular direction.

— the only true education comes through the stimulation of the child's powers by the demands of the social situations in which he finds himself. Through these demands he is stimulated to act as a member of a unity, to emerge from his original narrowness of action and feeling, and to conceive of himself from the standpoint of the welfare of the group to which he belongs. Through the responses which others make to his own activities he comes to know what these mean in social terms. The value which they have is reflected back into them. For instance, through the response which is made to the child's instinctive babblings the child comes to know what those babblings mean; they are transformed into articulate language, and thus the child is introduced into the consolidated wealth of ideas and emotions which are now summed up in language.

— this educational process has two sides — one psychological and one sociological — and that neither can be subordinated to the other, or neglected, without evil results following. Of these two sides, the psychological is the basis. The child's own instincts and powers furnish the material and give the starting-point for all education. Save as the efforts of the educator connect with some activity which the child is carrying on of his own ini-

John Dewey, "My Pedagogic Creed" (originally published 1897), in *Education Today*, pp. 3–17. Copyright 1940 by John Dewey. Reprinted by permission of G. P. Putnam's Sons.

tiative independent of the educator, education becomes reduced to a pressure from without. It may, indeed, give certain external results, but cannot truly be called educative. Without insight into the psychological structure and activities of the individual, the educative process will, therefore, be haphazard and arbitrary. If it chances to coincide with the child's activity it will get a leverage; if it does not, it will result in friction, or disintegration, or arrest of the child nature.

— knowledge of social conditions, of the present state of civilization, is necessary in order properly to interpret the child's powers. The child has his own instincts and tendencies, but we do not know what these mean until we can translate them into their social equivalents. We must be able to carry them back into a social past and see them as the inheritance of previous race activities. We must also be able to project them into the future to see what their outcome and end will be. In the illustration just used, it is the ability to see in the child's babblings the promise and potency of a future social intercourse and conversation which enables one to deal in the proper way with that instinct.

— the psychological and social sides are organically related, and that education cannot be regarded as a compromise between the two, or a superimposition of one upon the other. We are told that the psychological definition of education is barren and formal — that it gives us only the idea of a development of all the mental powers without giving us any idea of the use to which these powers are put. On the other hand, it is urged that the social definition of education, as getting adjusted to civilization, makes of it a forced and external process, and results in subordinating the freedom of the individual to a preconceived social and political status.

— each of these objections is true when urged against one side isolated from the other. In order to know what a power really is we must know what its end, use, or function is, and this we cannot know save as we conceive of the individual as active in social relationships. But, on the other hand, the only possible adjustment which we can give to the child under existing conditions is that which arises through putting him in complete possession of all his powers. With the advent of democracy and modern industrial conditions, it is impossible to foretell definitely just what civilization will be twenty years from now. Hence it is impossible to prepare the child for any precise set of conditions. To prepare him for the future life means to give him command of himself; it means so to train him that he will have the full and ready use of all his capacities; that his eye and ear and hand may be tools ready to command, that his judgment may be capable of grasping the conditions under which it has to work, and the executive forces be trained to act economically and efficiently. It is impossible to reach this sort of adjustment save as constant regard is had to the individual's own powers, tastes, and interests — that is, as education is continually converted into psychological terms.

In sum, I believe that the individual who is to be educated is a social individual, and that society is an organic union of individuals. If we eliminate the social factor from the child we are left only with an abstraction; if we eliminate the individual factor from society, we are left only with an inert and lifeless mass. Education, therefore, must begin with a psychological insight into the child's capacities, interests, and habits. It must be controlled at every point by reference to these same considerations. These powers, interests, and habits must be continually interpreted — we must know what they mean. They must be translated into terms of their social equivalents — into terms of what they are capable of in the way of social service.

ARTICLE II — WHAT THE SCHOOL IS

I Believe that

— the school is primarily a social institution. Education being a social process, the school is simply that form of community life in which all those agencies are concentrated that will be most effective in bringing the child to share in the inherited resources of the race, and to use his own powers for social ends.

— education, therefore, is a process of living and not a preparation for future living.

— the school must represent present life — life as real and vital to the child as that which he carries on in the home, in the neighborhood, or on the playground.

— that education which does not occur through forms of life, forms that are worth living for their own sake, is always a poor substitute for the genuine reality, and tends to cramp and to deaden.

— the school, as an institution, should simplify existing social life; should reduce it, as it were, to an embryonic form. Existing life is so complex that the child cannot be brought into contact with it without either confusion or distraction; he is either overwhelmed by the multiplicity of activities which are going on, so that he loses his own power of orderly reaction, or he is so stimulated by these various activities that his powers are prematurely called into play and he becomes either unduly specialized or else disintegrated.

— as such simplified social life, the school life should grow gradually out of the home life; that it should take up and continue the activities with which the child is already familiar in the home.

— it should exhibit these activities to the child, and reproduce them in such ways that the child will gradually learn the meaning of them, and be capable of playing his own part in relation to them.

— this is a psychological necessity, because it is the only way of securing continuity in the child's growth, the only way of giving a background of past experience to the new ideas given in school.

— it is also a social necessity because the home is the form of social life in which the child has been nurtured and in connection with which he has had his moral training. It is the business of the school to deepen and extend his sense of the values bound up in his home life.

— much of present education fails because it neglects this fundamental principle of the school as a form of community life. It conceives the school as a place where certain information is to be given, where certain lessons are to be learned, or where certain habits are to be formed. The value of these is conceived as lying largely in the remote future; the child must do these things for the sake of something else he is to do; they are mere preparations. As a result they do not become a part of the life experience of the child and so are not truly educative.

— the moral education centers upon this conception of the school as a mode of social life, that the best and deepest moral training is precisely that which one gets through having to enter into proper relations with others in a unity of work and thought. The present educational systems, so far as they destroy or neglect this unity, render it difficult or impossible to get any genuine, regular moral training.

— the child should be stimulated and controlled in his work through the life of the community.

— under existing conditions far too much of the stimulus and control proceeds from the teacher, because of neglect of the idea of the school as a form of social life.

— the teacher's place and work in the school is to be interpreted from this same basis. The teacher is not in the school to impose certain ideas or to form certain habits in the child, but is there as a member of the community to select the influences which shall affect the child and to assist him in properly responding to these influences.

— the discipline of the school should proceed from the life of the school as a whole and not directly from the teacher.

— the teacher's business is simply to determine, on the basis of larger experience and riper wisdom, how the discipline of life shall come to the child.

— all questions of the grading of the child and his promotion should be determined by reference to the same standard. Examinations are of use in which he can be of the most service and where he can receive the most help.

ARTICLE III — THE SUBJECT-MATTER OF EDUCATION

I Believe that

— the social life of the child is the basis of concentration, or correlation, in all his training or growth. The social life gives the unconscious unity and the background of all his efforts and of all his attainments.

— the subject-matter of the school curriculum should mark a gradual differentiation out of the primitive unconscious unity of social life.

— we violate the child's nature and render difficult the best ethical results by introducing the child too abruptly to a number of special studies, of reading, writing, geography, etc., out of relation to this social life.

— the true center of correlation on the school subjects is not science, nor literature, nor history, nor geography, but the child's own social activities.

— education cannot be unified in the study of science, or so-called nature study, because apart from human activity, nature itself is not a unity; nature in itself is a number of diverse objects in space and time, and to attempt to make it the center of work by itself is to introduce a principle of radiation rather than one of concentration.

— literature is the reflex expression and interpretation of social experience; that hence it must follow upon and not precede such experience. It, therefore, cannot be made the basis, although it may be made the summary of unification.

— once more that history is of educative value in so far as it presents phases of social life and growth. It must be controlled by reference to social life. When taken simply as history it is thrown into the distant past and becomes dead and inert. Taken as the record of man's social life and progress it becomes full of meaning. I believe, however, that it cannot be so taken excepting as the child is also introduced directly into social life.

— the primary basis of education is in the child's powers at work along the same general constructive lines as those which have brought civilization into being.

— the only way to make the child conscious of his social heritage is to enable him to perform those fundamental types of activity which make civilization what it is.

— the so-called expressive or constructive activities are the center of correlation.

— this gives the standard for the place of cooking, sewing, manual training, etc., in the school.

— they are not special studies which are to be introduced over and above a lot of others in the way of relaxation or relief, or as additional accomplishments. I believe rather that they represent, as types, fundamental forms of social activity; and that it is possible and desirable that the child's introduction into the more formal subjects of the curriculum be through the medium of these activities.

— the study of science is educational in so far as it brings out the materials and processes which make social life what it is.

— one of the greatest difficulties in the present teaching of science is that the material is presented in purely objective form, or is treated as a new peculiar kind of experience which the child can add to that which he has already had. In reality, science is of value because it gives the ability to interpret and control the experience already had. It should be introduced, not as so much new subject-matter, but as showing the factors already involved in previous experience and as furnishing tools by which that experience can be more easily and effectively regulated.

— at present we lose much of the value of literature and language studies because of our elimination of the social element. Language is almost always treated in the books of pedagogy simply as the expression of thought. It is true that language is a logical instrument, but it is fundamentally and primarily a social instrument. Language is the device for communication; it is the tool through which one individual comes to share the ideas and feelings of others. When treated simply as a way of getting individual information, or as a means of showing off what one has learned, it loses its social motive and end.

— there is, therefore, no succession of studies in the ideal school curriculum. If education is life, all life has, from the outset, a scientific aspect, an aspect of art and culture, and an aspect of communication. It cannot, therefore, be true that the proper studies for one grade are mere reading and writing, and that at a later grade, reading, or literature, or science, may be introduced. The progress is not in the succession of studies, but in the development of new attitudes towards, and new interests in, experience.

— education must be conceived as a continuing reconstruction of experience; that the process and the goal of education are one and the same thing.

— to set up any end outside of education, as furnishing its goal and standard, is to deprive the educational process of much of its meaning, and tends to make us rely upon false and external stimuli in dealing with the child.

ARTICLE IV — THE NATURE OF METHOD

I Believe that

— the question of method is ultimately reducible to the question of the order of development of the child's powers and interests. The law for presenting and treating material is the law implicit within the child's own nature. Because this is so I believe the following statements are of supreme importance as determining the spirit in which education is carried on:

— the active side precedes the passive in the development of the child-nature; that expression comes before conscious impression; that the muscular development precedes the sensory; that movements come before conscious sensations; I believe that consciousness is essentially motor or impulsive; that conscious states tend to project themselves in action.

— the neglect of this principle is the cause of a large part of the waste of time and strength in school work. The child is thrown into a passive, receptive, or absorbing attitude. The conditions are such that he is not permitted to follow the law of his nature; the result is friction and waste.

— ideas (intellectual and rational processes) also result from action and devolve for the sake of the better control of action. What we term reason is primarily the law of orderly or effective action. To attempt to develop the reasoning powers, the powers of judgment, without reference to the selection and arrangement of means in action, is the fundamental fallacy in our present methods of dealing with this matter. As a result we present the child with arbitrary symbols. Symbols are a necessity in mental development, but they have their place as tools for economizing effort; presented by themselves they are a mass of meaningless and arbitrary ideas imposed from without.

— the image is the great instrument of instruction. What a child gets out of any subject presented to him is simply the images which he himself forms with regard to it.

— if nine-tenths of the energy at present directed towards making the child learn certain things were spent in seeing to it that the child was forming proper images, the work of instruction would be indefinitely facilitated.

— much of the time and attention now given to the preparation and presentation of lessons might be more wisely and profitably expended in training the child's power of imagery and in seeing to it that he was continually forming definite, vivid, and growing images of the various subjects with which he comes in contact in his experience.

— interests are the signs and symptoms of growing power. I believe that they represent dawning capacities. Accordingly the constant and careful observation of interests is of the utmost importance for the educator.

— these interests are to be observed as showing the state of development which the child has reached.

— they prophesy the stage upon which he is about to enter.

— only through the continual and sympathetic observation of childhood's interests can the adult enter into the child's life and see what it is ready for, and upon what material it could work most readily and fruitfully.

— these interests are neither to be humored nor repressed. To repress interest is to substitute the adult for the child, and so to weaken intellectual curiosity and alertness, to suppress initiative, and to deaden interest. To humor the interests is to substitute the transient for the permanent. The interest is always the sign of some power below; the important thing is to discover this power. To humor the interest is to fail to penetrate below the surface, and its sure result is to substitute caprice and whim for genuine interest.

— the emotions are the reflex of actions.

— to endeavor to stimulate or arouse the emotions apart from their corresponding activities is to introduce an unhealthy and morbid state of mind.

— if we can only secure right habits of action and thought, with reference to the good, the true, and the beautiful, the emotions will for the most part take care of themselves.

— next to deadness and dullness, formalism and routine, our education is threatened with no greater evil than sentimentalism.

— this sentimentalism is the necessary result of the attempt to divorce feeling from action.

ARTICLE V — THE SCHOOL AND SOCIAL PROGRESS

I Believe that

— education is the fundamental method of social progress and reform.

— all reforms which rest simply upon the enactment of law, or the threatening of certain penalties, or upon changes in mechanical or outward arrangements, are transitory and futile.

— education is a regulation of the process of coming to share in the social consciousness; and that the adjustment of individual activity on the basis of this social consciousness is the only sure method of social reconstruction.

— this conception has due regard for both the individualistic and socialistic ideals. It is duly individual because it recognizes the formation of a certain character as the only genuine basis of right living. It is socialistic because it recognizes that this right character is not to be formed by merely individual precept, example, or exhortation, but rather by the influence of a certain form of institutional or community life upon the individual, and that the social organism through the school, as its organ, may determine ethical results.

— in the ideal school we have the reconcilation of the individualistic and the institutional ideals.

— the community's duty to education is, therefore, its paramount moral duty. By law and punishment, by social agitation and discussion, society can regulate and form itself in a more or less haphazard and chance way. But through education society can formulate its own purposes, can organize its own means and resources, and thus shape itself with definiteness and economy in the direction in which it wishes to move.

— when society once recognizes the possibilities in this direction, and the obligations which these possibilities impose, it is impossible to conceive of the resources of time, attention, and money which will be put at the disposal of the educator.

— it is the business of every one interested in education to insist upon the school as the primary and most effective instrument of social progress and reform in order that society may be awakened to realize what the school stands for, and aroused to the necessity of endowing the educator with sufficient equipment properly to perform his task.

— education thus conceived marks the most perfect and intimate union of science and art conceivable in human experience.

— the art of thus giving shape to human powers and adapting them to social service is the supreme art; one calling into its service the best of artists; that no insight, sympathy, tact, executive power, is too great for such service.

— with the growth of psychological service, giving added insight into individual structure and laws of growth; and with growth of social science, adding to our knowledge of the right organization of individuals, all scientific resources can be utilized for the purposes of education.

— when science and art thus join hands the most commanding motive for human action will be reached, the most genuine springs of human conduct aroused, and the best service that human nature is capable of guaranteed.

— the teacher is engaged, not simply in the training of individuals, but in the formation of the proper social life.

— every teacher should realize the dignity of his calling; that he is a social servant set apart for the maintenance of proper social order and the securing of the right social growth.

— in this way the teacher always is the prophet of the true God and the usherer in of the true kingdom of God.

CHAPTER TEN BIBLIOGRAPHY

DEWEY, JOHN, *Democracy and Education.* New York: Macmillan Company, 1916.

> Dewey's view that the present situation furnishes the motive and purpose for the study of the past is here presented concisely and clearly.

HODGKIN, R. A., *Education and Change.* London: Oxford University Press, 1957.

> " The Good Citizen," Chapter VII, considers the active, social, and creative personalities as goals of education. A brief insight into how society and its schools may work for these goals follows.

LANGFORD, HOWARD D., *Education and the Social Conflict.* New York: Macmillan Company, 1936.

> Langford advocates democratic action by an oppressed majority to secure basic economic rights in the crisis of the Great Depression. This is a critical and radical view, advocating much more democracy in the economic sphere.

LASKI, HAROLD J., *Liberty in the Modern State.* New York: Viking Press, 1949.

> Laski shows why the fight for freedom continues anew periodically. Man wants power. Once it is obtained — whether economic, political, or social — there will appear some who want to share in it. Their liberty is restricted. His argument is for reason and tolerance so that the recurring changes will be less disruptive.

MOORE, ERNEST C., *What Is Education?* Boston: Ginn and Company, 1915.

> Education is world building. The school presents the environment in which the student will use his mind in socially profitable ways. In Chapter 4 the author emphasizes that education must deal with life issues. Language should not be a substitute for experience.

MURSELL, JAMES L., *Education for American Democracy*. New York: W. W. Norton and Company, 1943.

> In Chapter 9, Mursell critically reviews curriculum developments based on ideas of formal discipline, arbitrary sequences, and realistic service. The major part of the chapter is taken up with his exposition of " The Making of the Democratic Curriculum." He holds to a plan which is continuous and dynamic, and which involves the entire profession of education.

POWELL, JOHN W., *Learning Comes of Age*. New York: Association Press, 1956.

> Chapter 3 is an excellent presentation of the concerns of adults for further education and of the author's view that the aim of keeping alive one's intelligence is what is really sought.

II

Education for Social Reconstruction

"We really don't differ so much about goals or ends as we do about the means for achieving these goals." This has become a commonplace statement made by one or both disputants involved in a discussion or debate about economics, politics, international relations — or education. Not so with the social reconstructionist, however. His major difference with most other educators *is* with ends rather than means. He sees as the primary purpose of the schools the reconstruction of the social order. The schools become agencies for inducing, not following, social change.

Social reconstructionism is the most radical of all educational philosophies. It is radical because it would call for both the most thoroughgoing changes in our educational institutions as well as sweeping changes in economic, political, and other institutions. In this respect it usually goes a step or more beyond progressivism. The aspects of progressivism that relate to the learning process and the nature of the learner — his needs, interests, and motivations — are for the most part acceptable to the adherent of social reconstructionism. Pragmatism, experimentalism, and a problem-solving method in coping with contemporary problems — these are all regarded as desirable, but they do not go far enough. The schools should incorporate these as desirable *procedures* for accomplishing specified *goals*. Such goals in turn involve the conscious modification of some facets of our society.

Because of the close relationship between reconstructionism as an *educational* philosophy and as a *social* philosophy, it may be inferred that the extent to which reconstructionism is accepted by the people is a reflection of their political preference. The period of the 1930's in the United States, for example, was one during which radical political proposals were freely suggested, openly discussed, and frequently enacted into law. The temper of the times was much more amenable to drastic social changes than was the case in either the previous decade or succeeding two decades. It is not surprising, therefore, that some of the most vigorous statements on behalf of social reconstructionism appeared during the 1930's. A group of " frontier thinkers " emerged, led principally by Harold U. Rugg, George S. Counts, and John Dewey. But just as there was a period of reaction to some of the more radical political philosophies of the 1930's, so also there was a lessening of influence of the educators who subscribed to social reconstructionism. This decline in influence was not too perceptible because of the fact that even in a presumably " favorable climate " the philosophy associated with reconstructionism never really made significant inroads in the American school. The early 1950's, which were characterized by a conservatism in politics and an uneasiness in academic circles, saw a further reduction in the impact of social reconstructionism. As for the contemporary cult of conformity among segments of the American public, perhaps it is sufficient to point out that there is an inverse relationship between social reconstructionism and social conformity.

All in all, the direct influence of reconstructionism on American education has been rather negligible. Its impact on education has been roughly comparable to the impact of third parties in American politics. At no time has it become accepted by the majority; frequently its banners are borne by only a small minority. But it has been an articulate, persistent, and vigorous minority. Some of the educational practices originally stressed by reconstructionists have come to be more generally accepted in the schools today. Examples of these are the fused or unified approach to social studies teaching, which was given its greatest impetus by Harold Rugg, and the need for considering contemporary social problems in the schools, which has been a persistent theme of George Counts. Of course, other educators besides reconstructionists also espoused some of these same causes.

As with all significant social or educational movements, reconstructionism has different shades of meaning and different emphases for its various proponents. Dewey, for example, uses the word *reconstruction* when he speaks of the " reconstruction of experience " as a necessary part of the learning process, and he tends to use the word *construction* when he speaks of the need for schools to prepare persons " to take part in the great work of construction and organization that will have to be done." Dewey's position as a social reconstructionist is relatively mild and conservative compared with others'. He does not see the school as a prime initiator of social change. The role that he would like to see educators pursue is one in which ". . . they may select the newer scientific, technological, and cultural forces that are producing changes in the old order; may estimate the direction in which they are moving and their outcome if they are given freer play, and see what can be done to make the schools their ally." [1] Note

[1] John Dewey, " Education and Social Change," *The Social Frontier*, May, 1937.

that Dewey sees the school as an " ally " of these forces; it is not in the vanguard. The schools should be attuned to these forces and supplement their efforts at social change.

Another emphasis associated with reconstructionism is the stress on a world outlook and the recognition of the close interrelationship between the nations of the world. No one nation is considered an island unto itself. Two corollaries of this emphasis follow: Drastic social, economic and political changes within a given nation are likely to have world-wide repercussions; Nazi Germany is an example. Secondly, since educational changes in any one nation may be cancelled out by competing trends in the society at large, it is necessary for social reconstructionists to concern themselves with social institutions within other nations. The selection by Harold Rugg in this chapter illustrates the concern of the social reconstructionist with education in other nations. The " frontier thinking " is especially evidenced in this selection when we consider that it was written during a period of strong isolationism in the United States. We are just beginning to do, in our study of international affairs, some of the things Rugg advocated in the 1930's.

The most far-reaching and radical form of social reconstructionism is one which purports to have the schools act as the major agency for revising society in accordance with some grand plan or " blue-print " for the future. Probably the most articulate spokesman for this point of view is Theodore Brameld. The selection from his book, *Toward a Reconstructed Philosophy of Education*, constitutes the other reading for this chapter. In espousing his reconstructionism, Brameld stresses the argument that we live in a " crisis-culture," that we as a people should and can determine our long-range goals, and that the schools ought to direct their efforts toward achieving these goals — even to the extent of demonstrating " defensible partiality " toward certain economic, social, and political ends. But he hastens to point out that this is not synonymous with indoctrination.

A further word of explanation about the Brameld selection is needed. What is reproduced here is a rather specific curricular design. In fact it is rather rare for an educational philosopher to be as specific in designating topics, organizational pattern, and procedures as Brameld is. But it should be remembered that this is all based upon a previous exposition of the basic ingredients of reconstructionism as Brameld views them. He especially points out the relationship between *educational* philosophy and philosophy in general. A key ingredient of his educational philosophy is the idea of " social consensus," which is essentially a process by which the people agree upon broad social goals. It is analogous to the idea of the " general will " that Rousseau writes of in his *Social Contract*. Social consensus is an expression of the overwhelmingly agreed upon wishes of the people; these wishes are structured into social goals; the task of the schools is to prepare both the young and the adult population to understand, work for, and re-define these goals.

This introduction to the readings on reconstructionism would not be complete without some mention of a major criticism that has been directed toward this philosophy. The substance of this criticism goes something like this: Reconstructionism depends upon and necessitates more *collective* action with a corresponding decrease in *individual* action and initiative. Collectivism tends to increase the functions and power of government. As governmental functions increase, individual liberties decrease. Even if we were to reconstruct society so as to achieve some of the material goals (and it is not always granted that this would follow) the resulting loss of personal freedom would be too high a price to pay." Since the end product of reconstructionism is unacceptable, we should not use such an invalid philosophy as a guide for our school curriculum.

Probably no other educational philosophy has features that are as sharply identifiable as does reconstructionism. This is an advantage both to those who want to analyze it and to those who want to criticize it. It is hoped that the following pages will provide some basis for your own evaluation of this philosophy.

HAROLD RUGG
Reconstructionism and a world outlook

Industrial civilization is on trial. Its leaders are asking frankly: Can an interdependent civilization that ramifies around the earth manage itself? The current chaos throws out boldly the opportunity and obligation of educators. " Education for a changing society " implies that we shall introduce youth to the understanding of our rapidly changing civilization. But much more is needed than that. The world is on fire, and the youth of the world must be equipped to combat the conflagration. Nothing less than thoroughgoing social reconstruction is demanded, and there is no institution known to the mind of man that can compass that problem except education.

In every changing culture of the world today, two insistent problems

Harold Rugg, " Social Reconstruction Through Education," *Progressive Education*, 10:11–18, January, 1933. Reprinted by permission.

should engage the attention of educators: (1) What are the concepts and problems of our changing civilization which should constitute both the needed social program of action and the outline of the educational program? (2) What are the elements of a creative philosophy which shall be appropriate for the new social order?

II

Before the school can be used as an agent for social regeneration, it must undergo thorough reconstruction. In the past century, a system of primary education has been set up in every industrial country. More than ninety-five per cent of the people have been taught to read, write, and reckon. The tabular contrast of the amount of illiteracy in the agricultural and the industrial countries is a striking revelation of the success of this first attempt to make the peoples of the earth literate. Certainly, we must feel that this is a striking achievement.

But literacy must not be confused with education. There is grave doubt, indeed, whether it should have been taken as the first objective of education. In every country which has done so, there has been produced a top-heavy, white-collar class, a false hierarchy of social classes; and the literate masses of people have been made easy subjects for propaganda. In England, France, Germany, Japan, America, and in the regions on which they have imposed their scheme of intellectual education, has already emerged a huge white-collar class, overcrowding the paper occupations, imbued with contempt for nonintellectual work, discontented, looking down on their elders. I have just been an eyewitness of the condition in one *hsien* in China. In that county, there are one hundred and eighteen college graduates residing in tiny isolated farming villages, unable to find work which they will accept, living on their families; instead of leading China out of her difficulties, they are breeders of unrest and mischief.

This is indicative of the dangerous social effects of a lopsided academic education. For thus far, we of the West, have produced but a partial education, an education which consists merely in the study of words and abstractions. Furthermore, it is an education obsessed with the halo of the past, blind to the insistent problems of the present, and impotent to project alternative solutions.

This phenomenon of hyperintellectual education imposed upon peoples needing a handicraft-citizenship one is world-wide. We Americans have contributed to it in the Philippines, Porto Rico, and Hawaii, and in thousands of our own rural villages. The British, French, Germans, Dutch, Belgians, Italians have done it in India, in Malaya, in Africa, in Australia, in the islands of the seven seas.

Is it not clear that the leaders of the entire earth must join together in thoroughgoing educational reconstruction? Whatever their race or nationality, two great needs confront them: first, the construction of a realistic program of education directly from the problems and needs of the people; second, the development of a creative philosophy indigenous to our new civilization and constructed directly from the materials of each national culture. The educational leaders of this generation confront the first supreme test of modern civilization. They must answer such basic questions as these: Can a compact minority of the peoples of the earth be educated in the scientific attitude and habit of mind? Can they be informed concerning the chief characteristics and problems of our new civilization? Can they be practiced in tolerance? Can they be made critical of the propaganda of dominant economic groups? Can they be taught to see the superficialities of quack remedies for fundamental social ills?

Certainly these things cannot be done by fiat; they can be achieved only through a fundamental reconstruction in education. Only by uniting the educational workers of the world in a dynamic social program of action appropriate to world needs can the current impasse be managed.

III

How is the problem to be attacked? The first step is the building of a new program of work, a new content for the curriculum, directly out of the problems, issues, and characteristics of our changing society. The great central concepts which epitomize the characteristics of our society shall constitute the very skeleton of that program.

To do so will demand courage and concentrated study of modern problems. We must become students of economic, social, and political life, as well as students of artistic self-expression and of growing childhood. No longer can the educationist remain aloof from the frontiers of social and artistic life, for it is the problems on the frontier that constitute the nucleus of the educational program.

This first step is of such importance that I venture to consider it somewhat more fully. I shall state merely the basic concepts that should constitute the guiding skeleton of our new educational program.

First and foremost, the fragile interdependence of this world-mechanism of trade and culture that we have created. Youth in every land must grow up with the sense of responsibility for helping to carry on that mechanism, for preventing the cutting of any single nerve of the new economic-political organism.

Second, the accelerating change with which the cultures of the world are being transformed. The generation shortly to be given the responsibility of self-government must be practiced in the attitude of expectancy of change — change in industry and farming, change in transportation, communication and trade; and therefore change in standards and norms of life, in standards of morality, in family life. And correspondingly, of the need for change in political, economic and social government.

Third, the powerful role of the great economic concepts of private property, the desire for economic gain, and the doctrine of individual success through competition. Youth will learn that all group problems are colored by these prevailing concepts. They will be brought to see how the concept of *laissez-faire* in the marriage of politics and economics has produced enormous inequalities in wealth and social income, the export of large amounts of capital from Europe and America, the disastrous imperialistic exploitation of agrarian and non-militarized peoples, and thus to mad international rivalries and world war. They will understand that underneath most of the activities of individuals, and the political maneuverings of nations and groups, is the desire for economic gain; that throughout the history of the race the desire for trade has been the central thread of continuity; and that the political history of the past few centuries has been largely the story of the conflict between struggling economic classes.

Fourth, experiments in political democracy. Must we not build systematically the attitude among the young people of the world that the trend toward representative democracy has produced nothing more than important *experiments* in government? The need for understanding is twofold: first, that the trend for two hundred years has been from autocracy toward democracy, from government by One Man to government by Many Men. Second, that every form of government on earth today must be regarded frankly as an experiment, tentative, and to be changed as new social and economic conditions develop. The trend has revealed scores of experiments, a great variety of forms and methods of collective living. The danger is that the young nationals of each of the sixty countries will grow up with the conviction that the form peculiar to his country is of proved superiority, rather than that it is one of many experiments and could very likely be greatly improved by the substitution of many foreign practices.

Fifth, it is equally important for youth to understand that effective democracy, whatever the form, postulates the adequate education of the people in understanding, and a dynamic interest in collective affairs. They should grasp the established fact that, as people have herded into cities, they have increasingly lost both interest in collective problems and ability to understand them. Nothing short of heroic efforts of mass education can successfully combat the new conditions of urban democracy.

Sixth, the utter lack of economic government in the modern world. Our new materials of instruction shall illustrate fearlessly and dramatically the inevitable consequence of the lack of planning and of central control over the production and distribution of physical things; namely, recurring cycles of unemployment of increasing intensity, and an unfair division of social wealth and income. Thus through the schools of the world, we shall disseminate a new conception of government — one that will embrace all of the collective activities of men; that will postulate the need for scientific control and operation of economic activities in the interest of all of the people; and one that will successfully adjust the psychological relations among men. Political government in a new connotation, then, including economic government and social government.

Seventh, the dangers inherent in growing economic nationalism. We shall illustrate clearly the manner in which gross differences in standards of living and in machine and military power have produced a destructive nationalism. One conspicuous example will be found in the mad erection of tariff barriers around nations that are almost completely interdependent. We shall introduce into our schools such a dramatic description of modes of living around the world that youth will respect the difficult endeavors of peoples of varying standards of economic life to exchange goods equitably.

Eighth, central world economic government. The recognition of these conditions will expedite the acceptance of the trend toward increasing centralized world control, allocation and exchange of basic commodities — especially foods, fuels, fibers, fertilizers, and metals. We shall illustrate the inevitable destructive effect of economic rivalries and the over-production of all basic commodities and consequent unemployment of millions of workers under a nationalistic competitive system. Thus our youth of the world, while developing a warm loyalty for their native homeland, will hold to an equally strong loyalty for the brotherland of all men on the earth.

Ninth, dangerous overpopulation and crowding into cities. We shall teach the startling multiplication of the peoples of the earth since 1800 and their huddling together in steel-and-concrete cities; the great unnatural trends toward machine production, the raising of standards of living, the discovery and spread of scientific knowledge of sanitation, hygiene, and control of disease, and of universal education will be comprehended in close relationship. Correspondingly, the physical as well as social dangers inherent in this trend will be grasped by youth. Thus can direct education in the control and distribution of population develop.

Tenth, the roles of the promoter, the political, and the creative mind in our acquisitive society shall be made clear. The dangerous stratification of a society which minimizes or ignores the contribution of the creative mind of every frontier of thought and feeling, and puts into a position of power the exploiter and the aggrandizer, be he financial promoter or practical politician.

Eleventh, examples of the psychology of individual and group behavior shall pervade the dramatic content of our new program. Young people will study human conduct in action. They shall see the role of such deeplying fears as those of economic insecurity and social disapproval. They will learn that he who controls the formation of attitudes, opinions, and beliefs by social groups and by the non-personal agencies of communication is in a fair way to control the mind of the nation.

Twelfth, running through the entire program, from kindergarten to college and through all the adult agencies of education, shall be the attempt to build two great coordinate and controlling attitudes and methods of thought. The one is the attitude of experimental inquiry, the scientific attitude which is to control man and men in all the individual and group problem-solving situations of life. The other is the attitude of appreciative awareness, with which men shall adjust to all the personalized, expressive, non-problem-solving situations. These attitudes are coordinate in importance and no curriculum is complete that ignores either.

IV

This, then, illustrates the first step in educational reconstruction — the construction of a new program of studies directly out of the content of our changing cultures. Phrased in another way, this step amounts to preparing and introducing into the schools of the world a courageous and intelligent description of our new society.

I have concentrated my attention on those parts of the curriculum known conventionally as the social sciences. Indeed, I am convinced that two great central themes will dominate the new curriculum — one broad strand of human and social science, and another of creative self-expression and aesthetic appreciation.

V

Thus we have illustrated the need of reconstruction for social action. But there must be equally far-reaching reconstruction in philosophy, and this leads us to our second great task — the development of a new and indigenous theory of life and education. This program of action must have an orienting and directing basis. To determine the content of our curriculum, we must know what manner of man we would produce. And it is at this point that I have found less hard thinking than upon the content of the new curriculum. There is much concern in America, in England, in Germany, in China with the questions: "What shall we teach?" but altogether too little concern with: "What kind of American? What kind of Chinese? What kind of world citizen shall we produce?"

That we need urgently a new theory of individual and group conduct is shown by the drastic changes in our culture in the past generation. The new industrial revolution, which has developed since 1890, has not only changed our external modes of living; it has also swept away the objects of allegiance in our inner culture. One by one the loyalties to which our fathers clung have disappeared, and less personalized ones have emerged to take their places. For the loyalty to the personal ruler, we are asked to substitute allegiance to abstract concepts — democracy . . . my country . . . liberty, equality, fraternity. For our religious loyalties, we are offered reason, personal initiative, and independence. In place of the authority of old age and governmental prestige, we are asked to set up the experimental attitude. Thus, as Waldo Frank first reminded us, the old objects of allegiance around which our fundamental institutions grew up — the family, the community, the church, the nation — are breaking down. A new culture is being produced in this first half of the twentieth century. New mores, new norms of conduct, are being precipitated by social trends. How shall we measure them? Which shall we deliberately build into our basic educational theory?

In China, and less drastically in the West, the old family system is breaking down; the one-generation family is taking the place of the three- and four-generation clan. As this happens, the older loyalties to parents, to elders, to the family group disappear. What shall the Chinese educators teach their children and youth? Are there not fine outcomes from the old family culture which should be kept, which could be kept by nationwide systematic preservation in the schools?

Similarly, we confront grave difficulties in determining the role of national and international loyalties. We know full well that selfish nationalism is dangerous, and history teaches clearly that present social trends are moving us all swiftly toward the need for world unity. But in laying our platform for internationalism, shall we ignore or negate national enthusiasm for our native fatherlands?

Thus we confront the problem of determining what the objects of allegiance of our new culture shall be. The question: " What kind of man shall we aim to produce? " becomes, " What attitudes and points of view, shall we definitely set ourselves to create? " What attitudes toward self, neighbor, family, nation? What attitudes toward our social relations, toward productive labor, the social classes? It is these psychological materials that constitute the very heart of our educational theory. Unless these are clearly thought through and clearly phrased, the educational program will drift aimlessly in no planned course, and social reconstruction will be impossible.

Our search for a new theory of life and education appropriate to the new and changing culture reveals the inadequacy of the pragmatic theories which are subscribed to by educators generally in the West. Indeed, careful study shows us that the pragmatism of Peirce and Dewey is not a philosophy; it is essentially a method of thought. It is a conspicuously fine phrasing of the experimental method of inquiry. It is an exposition of " how we think " when solving problems. It is an intellectual test, not a theory of life, and hence of education.

We need a philosophy, the loyalties of which shall be so inclusive as to guide men in all the situations of life. Our theory must embrace two attitudes, two outlooks on life. The first is the experimental attitude, the scientific outlook that has enabled men increasingly to master nature. It is education in this attitude that will enable men to devise economic government and to master social relations.

The second attitude is that of appreciative awareness. It is the all-embracing attitude of receptivity. These two attitudes are fundamentally different, and the techniques of mind that spring from them are equally different. Yet they are not different in the sense that they oppose each other; they are different in the sense that they complement each other. An educational system built upon either one or the other alone will be incomplete.

I should like to comment briefly here on one important factor or method in the development of the attitude of appreciative awareness. We have discussed one of the two fundamental ways in which social reconstruction shall take place; namely, the building of a new content for the educational program out of the culture of the people. But there is another and equally important one — the building of a new conception of labor and the method of its application in the school.

The new conception that I have in mind embraces two clear connotations — first, labor that is socially useful; second, labor that is creative. The old education denied labor of these types a place in its program. It recognized only intellectual activity, and assumed a hierarchy of social organization in which its product would have no contact with "labor." Under such an educational regime, and in cooperation with the growing mechanization of productive activities, the concept of labor came to emphasize manual skill and repetition. With the decline of the craftsman, the concept of creative labor steadily passed away.

Furthermore, other factors cooperate to urge upon us the reconsideration of our concept of labor and its place in education. These are the world-wide emergence of an unwieldy white-collar class, the aspiration of youth to enter the "paper" occupations, the increasing dislike, even contempt for hand labor, and the belittling of social and manual intelligence in the modern educational programs.

This two-fold concept of socially useful and creative labor is, in the hand of the educator, an effective instrument for social reconstruction. For, while it centers attention on the development of individual personality as the basis of a fine social life, it also recognizes definitely the role of the social group. The current nation-wide experiments of the Russians are bringing out clearly the intrinsic educational value of socially useful work. Correspondingly, the experiments of the child-centered schools in America and Europe have established the creative act as an indispensable factor in the complete education of the individual. And the astute studies of practical philosophers, such as Aaron Gordon, establish creative labor as an indispensable factor in the building of a sound national personality. Thus the new concept of labor, socially useful and creative, if incorporated in our educational theory, will have both individual and social implications.

In the past fifteen years of the new education, no event has been of more significance than that of the creative artist crossing the threshold of the classroom. As he has done so in increasing numbers, he has established beyond the possibility of doubt the fact that maximum appreciation and maximum personality eventuate only from participation in the creative act. Surround the young people with fine creative products, practice them in discriminating judgment, develop the thrill of rich aesthetic experience — all these steps we shall also employ. But for the finest production of persons — and that is our supreme goal, if we would produce a fine social order — we must employ the creative act.

I cannot escape the conclusion, therefore, that bodily education and especially creative handcraft, must come to have a place in the new education coordinate with that of literary education. Leaders and followers alike, the talented few as well as the mediocre mass, must be equipped with a respect for handcraft, as well as mindcraft, and practiced in appreciation of form with every medium of expression.

The production of craftsmen, then, is to be the supreme aim of the new education; not, in industrial countries, as the means of producing food, shelter, and clothing, but as the means of producing sound personalities. Especially is this demanded of us by the swiftly increasing mechanization of all the productive activities, and by the rapid decline of hours of labor and the consequent social danger of an idle and uncultured mass.

For the craftsman, working lovingly at his total product, not only molds his whole personality into it; his molding of it produces in him a new personality. Whatever the medium of expression, this is the process and the result. They work their wonders alike in the Japanese farmer tenderly nursing his garden plot, the Moro metal worker hammering a silver ring out of a Spanish peso, the New England cabinet-maker rubbing his wood surface, or Brancusi shaping his marble. In the process, product and laborer change together — if the labor is creative, that is, if it is an original, honest expression of the worker, of his moods, of his comprehension of and feeling for life. Thus the new educational program shall consist of a stream of activities, each of which, so far as possible, involves socially useful and creative labor.

THEODORE BRAMELD
A proposed curriculum based on reconstructionism

We shall now present designs for a structure of curriculum principles to be erected upon the foundations of reconstructionist philosophic beliefs. Because concrete application of theory has just begun, the designs we shall present are largely conjectural. They are meant only to suggest possible alternatives; obviously no one fixed or universal curriculum could be, or should be, proposed. Nevertheless, it is clear that certain experimental patterns of practice must have early and widespread adoption if public education is to meet its urgent obligation to implement the guiding beliefs of this philosophy. The over-all plan to be presented is, like the concept of learning as social-self-realization, essentially a normative one; that is to say, it provides a goal toward which to move and a standard by which to measure alternative curriculums.

This . . . [discussion] . . . will outline flexible designs for curriculums on the three traditional levels of secondary education, elementary educa-

From Theodore Brameld, *Toward a Reconstructed Philosophy of Education,* 1956. pp. 211–213, 218–228. Reprinted by permission of The Dryden Press.

tion, and higher (including adult) education.[1] Many of the concepts that were presented abstractly . . . [elsewhere] . . . are given concrete illustration here.

SECONDARY EDUCATION: THE CENTER

Why secondary education? Although the curriculums on all three levels are of inestimable importance to the task which reconstructionism has set for itself, and although all three support one another, the center of the program is " secondary education " — the period of about four years covering the last two years of the conventional senior high school course and the two years of junior college. Here our special principles of learning — based always upon foundational beliefs about reality, knowledge, and value — bear most directly upon the organization and content of all studies. In the schooling of the student's more mature years — from seventeen to twenty — earlier schooling is brought to fruition and tested; and subsequent programs of the universities and of adult education . . . retroact to the benefit of the secondary program. The success of secondary schooling depends largely, therefore, upon the effectiveness of both the earlier and later programs, and its own effectiveness strongly influences them.

In defining the period to be called " secondary education," the important point is that the ceiling age for compulsory education, which has risen steadily for generations, should be placed at about twenty years. In this discussion it is assumed that beyond the age of twenty the total number of students who pursue formal education as their major occupation will decrease rapidly with each year of age. In the years between seventeen and twenty — the crucial period in which most young men and women are crystallizing their plans for mature responsibilities — they should still have access to schooling. Therefore the reconstructionist considers this period to be of key importance.

We are visualizing secondary education, moreover, on a world-wide scale. It is true that at present the capacity of nations to provide compulsory education of any kind, much less education up to the age of twenty, varies widely. It is true, also, that countries cannot construct good systems of public education at the same rate everywhere on earth. Nevertheless, this objective is not impracticable if a world order sanctioned by the majority of all peoples is not impracticable. Reconstructionists would argue

---

[1] The indebtedness of the author to various curriculum experts will be obvious. For a summary of American plans, see National Society for the Study of Education, *Twenty-sixth Yearbook*, Part II, " Foundations of Curriculum Making," and Harold Rugg, *Foundations for American Education,* Chap. 20. See also Franklin J. Keller, *The Double-Purpose High School*; Laurence S. Flaum, *The Activity High School*; Marion Nesbitt, *A Public School for Tomorrow*; and especially B. Othanel Smith, W. O. Stanley, and J. Harlan Shores, *Fundamentals of Curriculum Development,* which also contains a rich bibliography. But the " design " proposed in this chapter and the next is based upon assumptions different, both in degree and kind, from any of those above.

that the rate of improvement can be accelerated so rapidly, once authority is provided, as to make all previous educational progress seem pathetically slow.

In believing, further, that secondary schooling should be governed largely by patterns of general education and common learnings, rather than by the older pattern of college preparation and vocational training, we are in agreement with a recent trend among thoughtful educators. We do not mean by this that education in the late teens should not provide for specialization or certain kinds of concentrated study; but specialization and concentration should always be subordinate to and controlled by the main purpose of the curriculum — a goal-centered general education.

It is important to develop a design covering the entire span of this period of four years of secondary education. We shall begin by considering practices that will be followed more or less universally throughout the four-year period, and shall then outline the program for each of the four years in turn. Let us reiterate, meanwhile, that our design is chiefly hypothetical and open to whatever modification is necessary when it is tested in practice. . . .

YEAR ONE OF THE SECONDARY SCHOOL

The first year has two chief objectives:

1. to provide the student with motivation and orientation and to build in him a sense of the importance of the entire secondary program; and

2. to examine the need for goals in the sphere of economic-political reconstruction and to determine their character.

Neither objective can, of course, be attained in a single year; these objectives, perhaps even more than those of the three remaining years, are constantly given further consideration as the student moves forward.

Nevertheless, the necessity of beginning with political-economic objectives should be made clear. However excellent his earlier schooling has been, the young person approaching adulthood may still need to perceive *why* it is important that secondary education be devoted to the governing task of goal-seeking. It is equally important for him to perceive that the crucial ontological realities of that task center in economic-political experience; hence, it is essential for him to understand that these realities must be discerned, analyzed, and refashioned constructively as early as possible in his secondary schooling if other areas are to receive proper consideration.

MOTIVATION AND ORIENTATION

Beginning with the student. Movement toward the first objective can begin through cooperative examination of contemporary culture and of the empirical relations of individuals — in this case, students — to it. We tap John's well springs of interest by detecting his uncertainties, tensions, instabilities, and confusions as they are related to those of his family and to Centerville, where he lives. We then relate these difficulties to whatever certainties, stabilities, and clarities constitute, by contrast, the positive aims of John, his family, and Centerville.

Establishing motivation in this way requires that the school foster a spirit of mutual respect and insist upon honesty of expression. Teachers speak of their uncertainties as well as their certainties, and the class seeks to enlist the interest of parents and other townspeople in its problems. Students make a concerted effort to estimate in a preliminary way how secure or insecure the local community is; how much agreement or disagreement there is about its own problems, practices, and plans. Meanwhile the reconstructionist teacher, governed though he is by his utopian values and therefore critical of many such existing practices and future plans, will not impose his convictions upon any one. He directs this initiating period of study chiefly by making sure that students penetrate deeply enough to discover the actual, rather than the merely ideological, picture of the community. He lets the picture speak for itself.

Moving outward. The student's understanding increases as the status of Centerville is seen to be dependent upon the status of other Centervilles and of the state, region, nation, and world. The aim is to widen the analysis, both geographically and historically; to see, for example, how the prosperity or poverty of Centerville depends upon the state of the economy of the entire nation and indeed the world, and how this dependence emerges directly from the forces of contraction and expansion in recent history. There is, accordingly, a need to study the past in order to foster concern for both present and future — indeed, history is indispensable throughout the four years.

From consideration of the best evidence obtainable both through firsthand observation and through books, students begin to feel the impact of the crisis-culture on themselves and their community. They recognize the achievements of capitalism, of liberal democracy, of the arts, and in human relations, and they assess them as dispassionately as possible. But they weigh these achievements against such stubborn realities as depression, insecurity, and war — in short, they begin to discover group conflicts, group allegiances, and group conditioners, and therefore begin to sense the power of the unrational that underlies those realities. The whole tone of the study, indeed, is indicated by our earlier interpretation of the reconstructionist ontology; the examples cited there are illustrative of the approach to cultural reality that is needed here.

Beginning the quest for the normative. As more and more motivation is established, students are ready to consider the question of what *would be* better by comparison with what now *is*. Technically speaking, ontological investigation soon gives rise to axiological study. With John, his family, and his community still in the forefront of attention, the final process in this introductory period is the attainment of a crude, preliminary consensus about common values.

The temptation to jump quickly from the concrete and graphic level on which study has thus far proceeded to a high and nebulous level of generalization is to be strictly avoided. But once the insecurities that students discover in their own environment are grasped, it should not be difficult to move to defining the simple and specific meanings of such a value as security. It should be possible to analyze its meaning to John and his family first in its immediate economic sense of adequate income, and then to go on to define security in its more complex psychological senses — as it is understood by psychologists, for example, when they speak of the need of children for parental security or of adults for a sense of belongingness and recognition.

These discussions should also begin to develop the student's awareness of the palpable inconsistencies in the value patterns of modern culture — inconsistencies that reflect a basic cultural disequilibrium. The cultural conflicts . . . should be articulated in terms which are in keeping with the experience of students; for example, it will be recognized by students that acceptance of the belief that " honesty is the best policy " is very often associated in the same person with the belief that, in a competitive society, sharp dealing is necessary to economic success and therefore desirable. Because the search for values is a thoroughly inductive process, any imposition by the teacher of his own value system is unnecessary and undesirable. The value of social-self-realization, or some verbal equivalent, although it is more than likely to emerge as a generalized ideal from our methods of learning, need not necessarily be understood in exactly the same way by any two groups. It is a value too rich, too complex, too dynamic to be subjected to rigid definition.

In this connection students should become aware of one question that is particularly important to the entire curriculum: Is it, or is it not, reasonable to expect that people in sharply different environments (assuming that sufficient schooling is available) could be expected to reach a consensus about their values that will provide a common basis for the world-wide reconstruction of culture? Or, to put the issue in another way: If they could have access to dependable evidence and could communicate freely, would a majority of the people in such widely separated and different regions as our deep South, the far West, New England, China, India, Finland, and Liberia be likely to agree upon a definition of such a single goal as security? Would they be able to agree, also, that " security " means not only adequate food, shelter, and clothing — although these are basic — but group protectiveness and other satisfactions as well? And so with the other goals we named earlier as essential to our reconstructed civilization: Can it be expected that these, too, will be agreed upon by a majority (two thirds, shall we say?) of people of all races, nationalities, and classes?

These questions are not merely of intriguing interest. The answers will determine the practicability of achieving national and international goals for our age of reconstruction, and therefore of the means to be used in winning those goals. The reconstructionist teacher believes . . . that such a consensus *can* be won as his kind of education reaches more and people. The extent to which students will agree with him will vary, of course, according to their own socio-economic position (upper-class and upper-status students are less likely to agree than others), upon the thoroughness of their study, upon their experience with people belonging to different races and classes and to other groups in their own community. Given, however, widespread and conscientious participation, plus general meetings that pool the partial consensuses of smaller groups, there is a reasonably good expectation of achieving positive agreements among people in general and students in particular.

A backward and forward look at the curriculum. Two interrelated outcomes of the motivation and orientation period of Year One are sought. First, it is desirable that students regard any consensus achieved about our crisis-culture, with all its dangers and failures, as complementary to any consensus they have reached about the need for normative standards and the nature of such standards. Secondly, it is desirable that students now possess a broad perspective upon the large areas of life that are to be studied during the remaining three years of the secondary program. These areas, although there may be some variation in terminology or order, are fundamental to any four-year program governed by goal-seeking interests as we have defined them. The remainder of Year One is devoted to the first of these areas.

THE ECONOMIC-POLITICAL AREA

The length of time to be allowed for the economic-political area must depend, obviously, upon the amount of time consumed in motivation and orientation. It is probable that at least a third of the year will have been taken up, leaving approximately eight months for the second main task. There is no need to determine the division of time in advance; this will be determined by the rapidity with which initial motivation is established. It is well not to wait too long, however, before plunging directly into the economic-political field, for this study in itself provides further motivation.

How, then, shall we study the first area? A number of principles may be taken as guides to selection and organization of the issues to be considered. Like those to be outlined as guides in the succeeding areas, these principles do not exhaust, but rather suggest, the scope and character of study.

Beginning again where we are. Although the long-range aim is to reach beyond the local community to encompass regional, national, and world reconstruction, the point of departure and the point of return is again the immediate situation of John, his family, and Centerville. This motivation is made easier by the fact that the study of economic-political issues began in the introductory period of Year One. But in the second part of the year study is more intensive and systematic. It includes a critical survey of the community — the average income, kinds of employment, patterns of savings and expenditures, labor and employer organizations, taxes, structure and operation of local government, leading political groups, public services, and as many other pertinent factors as possible.

Accordingly, the kind of understanding gained at this stage depends in a measure upon the nature of the region in which the school is located. In a farming district there will naturally be more concern with agricultural productivity than in an industrial center. A coal-mining town is sharply different economically from a seaport; each requires study of local factors that do not exist in the other.

An interlocking economy. Investigation of the community quickly reaches far beyond Centerville, however. The degree to which absentee ownership prevails (ownership of businesses, farms and other income-producing enterprises by bank mortgage holders or corporations whose directing offices are located elsewhere) is one factor of great importance. In considering the local wage scale it is necessary to investigate such factors as the regional labor supply, the strength of the unions to which local workers belong, and the market elsewhere for products manufactured locally. All these are keys to the way in which Centerville's economy is linked into a complex, world-wide network.

Historic causes and trends. This reaching-out process also extends into time. A study of history is needed, more than at the outset of the year, in order to determine how Centerville reached its present stage of economic development; how the earlier relative self-sufficiency of such communities has been supplanted by dependence upon a tightly interwoven economic system; how political institutions have tended toward more and more interdependence both among themselves and with economic institutions.

History, in addition to illuminating factors in economic development, is indispensable to the anticipation of future trends. With the help of history, students are able to observe the trend away from small, free business enterprise toward corporate monopoly. They can see the record of the shift of population from the countryside to urban industrial districts. They can observe how technology continues to increase productivity and to intensify the consequent problem of increasing the rate of consumption. They find that the new and frightful weapons of the twentieth century utilize technology for mass destruction even more readily than for mass construction.

Such study is a concrete application of the ontological principle of " history as future." Time as duration, as we noted earlier, extends from the past through the present and into the future. Although the study of trends does not make possible the prediction of the inevitable, it does make it possible to become aware of the course that history is running — a course which we can redirect according to the goals that we agree upon, thus actually creating our future.

It is also desirable to view history in the perspective of " expansion and contraction of freedom " — to observe how some economic practices encourage the one, some the other. The same examination can be made of political practices. The aim is always to see how history is moving in our own time and how men must act to ensure greater expansion of freedom in the future.

Economic-political fusion. As already suggested, the economic and political strands of culture are treated inseparably. The chief, though not the sole, purpose of political arrangements is to guarantee the effective operation of sanctioned industrial, agricultural, commercial, and other economic processes. When students discover this fact in the course of interpreting past and present institutions, they are grasping the basic fact that there is a fusion of the economic and the political in our culture. They are learning that legislative representatives may be, and often are, primarily the representatives of organized economic groups, and that in order to analyze their frequently ideological language we must discover in whose interests they are speaking.

It is possible, of course, to examine political structures and operations separately from the economic sphere, and there are times when this should be done both descriptively and normatively. From the normative point of view it is necessary to study such proposals as those for the reorganization of the federal government, the abolition of state boundaries in favor of regional ones, the establishment of unicameral legislatures, the organization of enforceable world government, and the establishment of a world citizenship that is on a par with national citizenship. But all such proposals, as well as analyses of historic or contemporary political practices, are best considered in relation to economic factors as often as possible.

Consideration of proposed programs. The critique of economic-political practices, always on a realistic level, is constantly integrated with consideration of leading proposals for changes in those practices — the one emphasis stimulates the other. It is necessary to give thorough and dispassionate consideration to all important alternative programs among which the people of America and other countries are asked to choose — programs whose sponsorship ranges from the extreme right to the extreme left. Accordingly, students become familiar with the fascist ideas of a Franco in Spain; with the conservative proposals of the Republican Party; with the forward-looking proposals of the liberal wing of the Democratic Party; with the Labour Party of England; with the programs of the Socialist, Communist, Liberal, and other minor parties in America and their major positions in certain other countries.

Although economic issues are central to the programs of these political parties, it is also important to study economic programs as such, apart from political considerations. Students should study the free-enterprise school, the programs of organized labor, the consumer-cooperative movement, the pump-priming theories of liberal economists, the famous Beveridge Plan, the principles of the Tennessee Valley Authority, the meaning of " planned economy," and other basic theories and programs.

Finally, and by no means of least importance, there is the need to study major proposals for establishing a world order. The present United Nations organization, " Union Now," World Federalist, and other plans should be analyzed. Involved in these proposals are such crucial issues as the abrogation of national sovereignty and the need for international policing.

Evaluation of programs. The principles that unite the study of economic-political practices with the study of economic-political proposals are, of course, axiological. It is of the utmost importance that students do not merely review competing programs one by one; they should also evaluate each one carefully to determine the degree to which it offers maximum satisfaction of maximum wants to the maximum number of human beings. Although a beginning in the enunciation of guiding values has already been made in the motivation-orientation period, more effort to agree upon these values is both desirable and practical as students move deeper into the economic-political area, for they are now able to test their criteria against specific situations.

Let us illustrate by means of such a value as security in the American culture. The first question to be considered is the extent to which any program — whether put forward by the Republican Party, the Democrats, or a labor party — can guarantee full employment and a standard of living that will provide all necessities of life. To answer the question requires further historic reference: For example, has any American political party succeeded in producing, or even approaching, such security?

Contemporary reference to other cultures is also required: Are countries in which a labor party is now in power raising standards of living for the masses of citizens? Understanding of revolutionary changes in technology is required: Are programs based upon earlier, more competitive and individualistic arrangements likely to be adequate in view of the world-wide increase in the number of noncompetitive and collective arrangements? Above all, there is required consideration of what design for production, distribution, and consumption (and what correlative political design) is most likely to provide the fullest measure of security for the individual on a world-wide scale.[2]

Methods of learning. Consideration of methods of learning by which all of the above principles can be put into practice brings us back to the plan of the school as a whole.

The range of this first study area is clearly too great to be encompassed equally well by all students. One of the most important tasks of the faculty, therefore, is to help students locate points of concentration in accordance with particular interests; to do this, they repeatedly relate the larger design of national and world purposes to the goals of the student himself. This kind of concentration is encouraged through work in the small groups of the first daily period. Here students practice together such techniques as

---

[2] For a rich example of the relations of economic and political issues and proposals, see Robert A. Dahl and Charles E. Lindblom, *Politics, Economics and Welfare.*

role-playing and observation and utilize resource persons from the faculty or community. Always, the aim is to learn not only about the economic-political problems of the specific group but also about the group's individual members and its character as an emerging " group mind."

As an illustration, recall the extensive consideration given to proposed economic-political programs. Five or six students, because their families are " co-op " members, may find themselves intrigued by the consumer cooperative movement; several others may be interested in the Farmers' Union; still others, by proposals of the Committee of Economic Development; and so on. Therefore those with common interests join together for joint exploration of a specific program. Each group collects and analyzes pamphlets and other documentary material, reaches into the history of sponsoring organizations, interviews officers, attends local meetings if possible, and critically evaluates its own findings, conclusions, and disagreements. Eventually all groups present their findings, agreements, and disagreements for study by the general assembly in the third period of the day.

This assembly serves as a center for integration and comparison. Therefore the group process is often used in much the same fashion as in the smaller groups. Each of the small groups communicates often with all other groups; these in turn raise questions and criticize, frequently requesting particular groups to look still further into programs that have been investigated. At regular intervals throughout the eight months or so devoted to the economic-political area the general assembly attempts to reach a consensus about institutional goals that squares most satisfactorily with its axiological goals. A kind of flexible design is therefore in process of development from month to month; earlier versions are altered as later elements are added. As the year draws toward its conclusion, the whole design is re-examined, re-evaluated, and remodeled.

Meanwhile, students are at work in the second and fourth periods on more specialized skills and contents that are related, whenever possible, to the year's study. We have suggested that intensive practice in writing and speaking is geared to the work of discussion groups and general assemblies. Other methods and materials capable of integration include foreign languages, mathematics, commercial studies, and history. For example, although study of Spanish, Russian, French, or any foreign language is not compulsory, students who desire to do so may elect one or more of these in order to become acquainted as soon as possible with the problems and institutions of other countries through direct contact with their literature and, where possible, their people. The knowledge gained through language studies, moreover, can often be related to group and assembly study of world reconstruction — a central objective always. Mathematics and commercial training give practice in a wide range of economic processes, such as tax and interest computation. As is sometimes done in progressive education, a whole unit in arithmetic could be planned around a consumer cooperative or even around running a school store on cooperative principles. Intensive study of American or European history develops, as far as practicable, in direct relation to the need for background already stressed. If this is done a student whose interest in history is especially strong may satisfy that interest systematically, meanwhile being motivated also by his desire to contribute to the work of the entire class.

In addition, students who engage in vocational training are made more conscious of the relation of their specialization to the wider economic and political pattern. One of the chief weaknesses of vocational education — its narrowness — is thus avoided. A young man who wishes to be an automobile mechanic can devote as much as a half day through a full year to this training, which he would receive in the second and fourth periods. But because he is also a part of the first-period groups and general assembly, he can hardly help but sense the relations of his chosen occupation to the wider pattern. He comes to see that the chances of his achieving self-realization through that occupation depend upon the strength of the whole economy, upon labor organization, and upon the kind of government in power. In turn, he contributes to the learning of others through the technological knowledge that he acquires; for example, he may show other students that the rate of deterioration of machinery under given conditions is a factor of considerable economic significance.

These typical methods of learning are not confined, let us remember, to the classroom or shop. Study groups utilize the community whenever possible by bringing resource materials (plants, soils, products) and people (labor leaders, businessmen, politicians) into the school as consultants. They also go directly and purposefully into the community — into stores, farms, union halls, granges, produce markets, newspaper offices, legislatures, and courts. Of still greater value is their utilization of midwinter recesses, and often midsummer recesses as well, for trips to more distant cities or farm regions or for working (under careful school supervision) in factories, offices, or shops. Work experience is an essential aspect of the entire program; therefore, whenever work experience is clearly related to the plan of the year, certain periods of the week may be set aside regularly for this kind of activity.

Finally, learning in the economic-political area is geared to study of the remaining areas. This is accomplished not only by fostering constant awareness that scientific developments, let us say, have profound bearings upon economic organization; more dramatically, representative committees of students from Years Two, Three, and Four often join with students of Year One for mutual consultation in a particular discussion group or a general assembly. Reciprocally, first-year students join with those of succeeding years. Likewise, teachers of art or science may work with teachers of social studies or human relations at many specific points. The principle is one of learning not only horizontally within the first-year class but vertically through all four classes. In this way, recognition and anticipation of the total design develop steadily from the beginning. . . .

CHAPTER ELEVEN BIBLIOGRAPHY

BECKER, HOWARD, *Man in Reciprocity*. New York: Frederick A. Praeger, 1956.

> The concluding chapter is a summary of what sociology tries to accomplish, the way it looks at society, and the kinds of conclusions it reaches. The cost of social change in individual suffering and disorganization is stressed.

BIDDLE, WILLIAM W., *Growth Toward Freedom*. New York: Harper and Brothers, 1957.

> Chapter One is a plea for the greatly expanded use of higher institutions of education in the development of communities everywhere — a plea for the practical application of educational resources to help humanity in helping itself.

BRAMELD, THEODORE, " The Meeting of Educational and Anthropological Theory," in Spindler, George D., editor, *Education and Anthropology*. Stanford: Stanford University Press, 1955.

> Brameld discusses how anthropological theory may help educational theory in evolving practical reconstructionist goals.

COLLIER, K. G., *The Social Purposes of Education*. London: Routledge and Kegan Paul, 1959.

> The author looks at British society and its problems and then prescribes an education for meeting the society's needs. The book is based on the idea of challenge (knowing the major problem situations in society) and response (the creation of a spirit and attitude for the reshaping of these) which will carry society to higher levels of achievement. This response intimately involves the work of the schools.

COUNTS, GEORGE S., *Dare the Schools Build A New Social Order?* New York: John Day Company, 1932.

> Two great evils in our culture are (1) lack of real democracy since basic material security is still unstably controlled by the few, and (2) lack of vigorous, profound faith in the ideals and possibilities growing out of America's past. Counts argues that the culture imposes a way of life upon its people, generally in an unthinking manner. The schools ought to be used to deliberately impress upon youth a vision of what can and ought to be, so that our society will create people endowed with the vision and the will to improve the society.

SMITH, B. O., STANLEY, W. O. and SHORES, J. H., *Fundamentals of Curriculum Development*. New York: World Book Company, 1950.

> In our changing society the authors see the need for the school to take a major hand in re-educating youngsters who are often, in part, becoming imbued with values which are out of step with the changed and changing values of the larger society.

12

The Teaching Profession

Is teaching a profession? Clearly this question cannot be answered until one has determined what distinguishes between those occupations which merit the designation of *profession* and those which do not. This distinction is a difficult one to make, partly because of the historical development of occupations. With the increasing complexity of society and with the expansion of the knowledge available to carry out social functions, occupations which were at one point in history quite mechanical and routine have subsequently become highly complex and intellectual in nature. If the requirement of a high degree of skill in making decisions based upon theoretical knowledge is *one* of the defining characteristics of the profession, it is easy to see that occupations which once had been classified as trades on the basis of this criterion might at some subsequent point in time become professions. This has, in fact, been the history of the development of professions. The development of architecture as a profession illustrates this process very well.

But why should the members of any occupation, and why should teachers in particular, strive to be known as *professional?* There are cheap and tawdry answers to this question, of course. The designation " professional person " carries with it an aura of prestige and class. Persons who are regarded as " professional people " tend to occupy the higher social rungs in our social system and power structure. But there are other reasons why the claim to professionalism might be pursued, reasons which are not so tawdry or self-centered. One example might suffice to illustrate these sounder reasons. Professional groups in a society are accorded considerable freedom with the expectation that they will themselves regularly maintain the discipline necessary to assure that essential social functions are carried out scrupulously. This has certain advantages in an occupation such as teaching. Because of its confidence in the professional group and the ability of that group to maintain standards of service, the public relies on the judgment of members of the profession in the areas of their expert knowledge. This means that members of recognized professions can work in their areas of expert knowledge without undue infringement by those who are uninformed in it. Professions can further advise the public, with the expectation that their advice will be respected, on those matters of public policy with which the profession is concerned. In a society such as ours, where no one person can be an expert in all things, those who make policy decision have to rely upon the expert knowledge of professional people.

Under these circumstances it is clear that professional status tends to attract those individuals who prize the intellectual freedom to make decisions based upon systematic knowledge. Such persons are especially needed in the teaching field. This is one of the more legitimate reasons why members of the teaching group wish to achieve assured professional status. You can undoubtedly think of other equally significant reasons.

SECTION 1. Education as a profession

The task of developing a comprehensive definition of *profession* is a difficult one. In 1915, while addressing the social workers, Dr. Abraham Flexner made just such an attempt at a definition. This definition has been concisely summarized by Esther Brown:

"According to Dr. Abraham Flexner's frequently quoted criteria of true professions: (1) they involve essentially intellectual operations accompanied by large individual responsibility; (2) they are learned in nature, and their members are constantly resorting to the laboratory and seminar for a fresh supply of facts; (3) they are not merely academic and theoretical, however, but are definitely practical in their aims; (4) they possess a technique capable of communication through a highly specialized educational discipline; (5) they are self-organized, with activities, duties, and responsibilities which completely engage their participants and develop group consciousness; and finally (6) they are likely to be more responsive to public interest than are unorganized and isolated individuals and they tend to become increasingly concerned with the achievement of social ends." *

But even while offering this definition, Dr. Flexner recognizes in the following words that the defining characteristics he proposed might not remain constant:

"The nature of a profession has undergone a readily traceable development, and the number of professions has not remained stationary. Occupations that were once non-professional have evolved into full professional status. These changes will continue to

* Esther Brown, *Social Work as a Profession*. Russell Sage Foundation, 1942, pp. 20–21.

go on. The definition that we may formulate to-day will therefore need recasting from time to time . . ."

Many educators feel that the time is due for a Flexner-type of report specifically on education. Its absence is taken by some to be a cause of the lack of professionalism in teaching; others feel that its failure to appear results from the fact that teaching is not a profession.

The reading selection which follows, by Myron Lieberman, represents a recasting of the criteria of professionalization which Dr. Flexner foresaw in terms of the modern scene. You may wish to measure teaching, as you have experienced it and as you have studied it, against Lieberman's criteria. You may further wish to compare your own assessment of the current professional status of teaching against Lieberman's scholarly study of the profession as this is developed in his volume *Education as a Profession,* from which this selection is taken. The second selection which follows, by T. M. Stinnett, attempts to assess what education must do if it is to acquire genuine professional status. Dr. Stinnett, Executive Secretary of the National Commission on Teacher Education and Professional Standards, reflects the point of view that professional status can never be *conferred* on the teaching group; it must *earn* this status. Such status can only be acquired, he believes, as the group improves its standards of performance through recruitment, careful selection of those entering teaching, improved education of the prospective and practicing teacher, and increased attention to the problems involved in the retention and disciplining of members. The commission of which he is executive secretary has addressed itself particularly to the second and third of these tasks.

MYRON LIEBERMAN
The criteria of a profession

NATURE AND SIGNIFICANCE OF THE PROFESSIONS

1. *A unique, definite, and essential social service.* A profession must have a unique social service to perform. For all practical purposes, only doctors perform surgery or prescribe drugs for sick persons. The practice of law is limited exclusively to lawyers.

The requirement that the social service performed by the occupational group be unique is closely related to the requirement that the scope of its service be clear and definite. Where the occupational group itself or the public is not sure of the function of the group, or is substantially divided on this matter, it is impossible to agree on issues of professional training, ethics, compensation, and so on. Professionalization is inevitably delayed where there is substantial disagreement and uncertainty over the function of an occupational group.

The notion that the service performed be an essential one goes back to the origin of the professions. The professions arose because people believed that certain services were so important that they should be made available to everyone who needed them, regardless of whether the recipient of the services was able to pay for them or not. At one time the clergy was the most important occupation in society, because everyone accepted the doctrine of salvation. It was obviously unfair to permit a person's opportunity to achieve salvation to depend upon whether or not he could afford the services of the clergy. For this reason, the clergy was organized, theoretically at least, in such a way that its services were available to everyone. If education has made any progress toward becoming a profession in the past one hundred years, such progress is undoubtedly due in part to the growing conviction that educational services are so important to the welfare of children and of society that they must be made available to all children, rather than be limited only to those children whose parents could afford to pay for them.

2. *An emphasis upon intellectual techniques in performing its service.* A profession depends to a very high degree upon intellectual rather than physical techniques in carrying on its work. Professional work emphasizes such intellectual techniques as defining problems, searching for relevant data, and formulating possible solutions. Proficiency in physical techniques may or may not be required. In legal work, the use of physical techniques is at a minimum. In certain kinds of surgery, however, the doctor's problem is not so much an intellectual one as it is the exercise of skill and dexterity in conducting the operation. (Before the discovery of anesthetics,

From Myron Lieberman, *Education as a Profession*, 1956, pp. 2–6. Reprinted by permission of Prentice-Hall, Inc.

the proof of a good surgeon was that he could amputate a limb in a few seconds.) In most professions, mastery of physical techniques is required as well as mastery of intellectual techniques. Strictly speaking, all professions require physical operations in varying degrees. The point is that the physical activities of professional workers are guided by a high level of intellectual activity. In any case, it is not the absence of physical or manual operations, but the requirement of complex intellectual operations, that characterizes the professions.[1] Several authorities on the professions have even gone so far as to practically identify the professions with intellectual occupations.[2]

3. *A long period of specialized training.* Entry into the professions usually requires a long period of preparation. No one would care to employ a physician who did not have an extensive education, including a number of years beyond the bachelor's degree.

Part of the extensive period of training must be specialized. Just how long is a much debated question in all the professions. In fact, one of the most common criticisms of education for the professions today is that such education is too specialized. Too many professional workers are said to be uneducated outside their field of specialization. Whether or not this criticism is justified, it remains true that an occupation must require a substantial period of specialized training in order to rank as a profession.

The fact that professional *work* is primarily intellectual suggests that professional *training* will likewise be primarily intellectual in character. Some nonprofessional occupations require long periods of specialized training, but most of the training is not intellectual. It must be recognized, however, that the distinction between intellectual training and other kinds of training is a matter of degree and not a hard and fast distinction. Much of the training for medicine and dentistry puts more stress upon physical skill and dexterity than upon intellectual operations. Just as no occupation is either wholly intellectual or wholly nonintellectual, it follows that no occupation requires training which is either all one or all the other. To repeat, professional training is *primarily*, not *wholly*, intellectual.

4. *A broad range of autonomy for both the individual practitioners and for the occupational group as a whole.* Individuals and groups have auton-

[1] Unless we accept Tawney's view that " A Profession may be defined, most simply as a trade which is organized, incompletely, no doubt, but genuinely, for the performance of function." R. H. Tawney, *The Acquisitive Society* (New York: Harcourt, Brace and Company, 1920), p. 92. This definition would enable *any* legitimate occupation, regardless of its intellectual requirements, to be regarded as a profession if it were efficiently organized to perform its function.

[2] A. M. Carr-Saunders and P. A. Wilson, *The Professions* (Oxford: The Clarendon Press, 1933), pp. 284–85; Also: Alfred North Whitehead, *Adventures of Ideas* (New York: The Macmillan Company, 1933), p. 72; Abraham Flexner, " Is Social Work a Profession? " *School and Society*, Vol. I, (June 26, 1915), p. 902 (from a paper presented at the 42nd Annual Meeting of the National Conference of Charities and Corrections, in Baltimore, Maryland, May 17, 1915).

omy to the extent that they are free to exercise their own best judgment. In occupations of a routine and mechanical nature, decision-making by the worker is at a minimum. A worker on an assembly line may have an extremely important task in the sense that the entire assembly line may break down if he does not perform his duties efficiently, but his duties may require him to make only a few simple decisions over and over again in the entire course of his work. This factor is regarded as one of the advantages of the assembly line system, since it reduces the possibility of error and the labor required can easily be trained and replaced.

Professional work presents a radically different picture. The professional worker is confronted by a wide variety of problems which require the application of a high degree of intelligence and specialized training. Lack of autonomy, in the form of supervision by personnel lacking the specialized training, usually does great harm and is strongly resented. Professional work is not amenable to the kind of close supervision often present in factories and offices. Professions necessarily require a broad range of autonomy, that is, freedom to exercise independent skill and judgment.

In addition to the autonomy of the individual practitioners, the practitioners of a profession enjoy a broad measure of autonomy as a group. Thus in most states lawyers have the sole power to decide such things as the qualifications for admission to the bar, the grounds for suspension or exclusion from practice, the distinctions between ethical and unethical conduct, and many other important matters concerning the occupation itself. The contrast with other occupations is obvious. If an individual wishes to open a retail store, he is not ordinarily required to conform to regulations laid down by the people who operate retail stores. In brief, professional groups have a great deal of freedom to regulate their occupation, whereas nonprofessional occupations generally lack such freedom. They are regulated and supervised by lay agencies rather than by their own membership.

5. *An acceptance by the practitioners of broad personal responsibility for judgments made and acts performed within the scope of professional autonomy.* A large measure of autonomy implies a correspondingly large measure of responsibility. As Flexner puts it, " This quality of responsibility follows from the fact that professions are intellectual in character, for in all intellectual operations, the thinker takes upon himself a risk." [3] This statement must be qualified by the fact that the kind of decision being made is also important in producing a sense of responsibility. Even if it required more intellectual ability to diagnose and treat automotive ailments than human ailments, the responsibilities of doctors would probably be considered greater than those of automobile mechanics, because the decisions made by doctors have much more direct effects upon human welfare.

6. *An emphasis upon the service to be rendered, rather than the eco-*

[3] *School and Society, op. cit.,* pp. 902–3.

nomic gain to the practitioners, as the basis for the organization and per-formance of the social service delegated to the occupational group. An emphasis upon the service rendered rather than the rewards to the prac-titioners is generally acknowledged to be an important characteristic of the professions. However, this criterion does not refer to the *motives* of the average professional worker. The motives of people in the professions are probably no higher than the motives of workers in any other major occu-pation. The point is that professions are so organized and controlled that professional workers cannot avoid certain obligations, regardless of their personal feelings.

7. *A comprehensive self-governing organization of practitioners.* Groups as large as the professions must have some kind of orderly procedure to set the standards for entry into and exclusion from the profession, to promote high standards of practice, and to raise the social and economic status of the group. Professional organizations provide the machinery necessary to carry out these related functions.

In the absence of an organization which can enforce professional stand-ards among the practitioners, each practitioner would soon be a law unto himself. Educational institutions would tend to disregard the standards of training for the professions if there were no permanent machinery to en-force such standards. The practitioners must organize to see that these things do not happen. It would be a mistake, however, to assume that the task of the professional organization is primarily to punish unethical mem-bers or to advance the selfish interests of the membership. Historically, the efforts to raise the levels of compensation for professionals have been the immediate reason for most of the lay criticism directed at professional organizations. [There are] . . . difficult problems involved in maintaining a reasonable balance between the interest of the professional group in securing an adequate level of compensation, and the public's interest in having essential services available at a reasonable cost.

There are many situations in which it is necessary for the public or gov-ernmental agencies to get the thinking of a profession on a particular issue. This means that the practitioners must choose persons to represent them in various capacities. Otherwise, it would be very difficult, if not impossi-ble, to know when a particular professional person was giving his private preferences or really expressing the weight of collective professional opin-ion on an issue. For this reason, the organization of practitioners must be as comprehensive as possible. Otherwise, there is the danger that the think-ing of an active minority will be accepted instead of the thinking of an inactive majority. It should not be thought, however, that professional workers belong to only one professional organization. Where there is a good deal of specialization within a profession, it is a common practice for the professional workers to belong to both comprehensive organizations which include all the practitioners in a given area and organizations of specialists. For example, doctors belong to both the American Medical

Association, which is a comprehensive organization of doctors regardless of specialization, and to organizations composed entirely of specialists in one particular field; such as the American College of Surgeons.

8. *A code of ethics which has been clarified and interpreted at ambiguous and doubtful points by concrete cases.* One of the reasons for the formation of professional organizations is that some definite machinery is needed to enforce high standards of professional conduct. For the more advanced professions, these standards are embodied in codes of ethics which are interpreted and enforced by the professional group. Just as the constitution of the United States required a number of cases to clarify its meaning at various points and continues to require clarification and interpretation, the codes of ethics in the advanced professions have been and are being continually clarified and interpreted by concrete cases. . . .

T. M. STINNETT
Is teaching a profession?

The prospective teacher early encounters the phrase, " the teaching profession," in such courses as " Introduction to Education," " History of Education," or " Orientation of Teaching," and in the literature of education. Encountering the word, " profession," he thinks immediately of medicine, law, the ministry, architecture, or engineering. Less often and with greater hesitancy will he put teaching in this category. In the minds of many people, including many teachers, teaching cannot yet be considered a full-fledged profession. This viewpoint will be described below.

WHAT IS A PROFESSION?

How does a given occupational group acquire recognition as a profession? Obviously the general public must give this recognition. It is not enough just to have recognition within the occupation itself. Professional status is measured largely by the status of the individuals comprising the occupational group. A fairly common practice is to ascribe professional status to a group chiefly on the basis of earning power or income. Remuneration commensurate with the quality and importance of the service rendered to society is, of course, one of the factors in the making of a profession, but this is not an exclusive factor. An examination of the professions will reveal several factors which go together to earn professional recognition in the minds of people.

Professional occupations may be contrasted with trades or skilled jobs, such as carpentry, bricklaying, plastering, and tool making. The skilled trades usually are mastered by work through an apprenticeship under the guidance of a master craftsman. Workers in the trades are almost always

From T. M. Stinnett, *The Teacher and Professional Organizations*, third edition, 1956, pp. 3–7. Reprinted by permission of the National Education Association.

unionized and follow the procedure of collective bargaining in the determination of wages and working conditions. Both work output and pay scales are generally standardized; that is, each worker is expected to turn out the same amount and quality of work and to receive the same pay.

By contrast, preparation for a profession now is attained through completion of a college or university curriculum especially designed for that purpose, quite frequently in conjunction with laboratory or internship experience. Professional education originally was centered in apprenticeship but now is carried on in colleges and universities. The quality and amount of work performed by professional workers will vary according to the individual. In the so-called private professions, such as law, medicine, dentistry, rewards vary with the ability and accomplishments of the professional worker. Collective bargaining and standardization of work output are obviously not practicable in such professions, although standard fees or scales of pay for a given service are sometimes charged or advocated.

By what other means shall we identify a profession? The most commonly used method is to list the distinguishing characteristics of a profession.

Characteristics of a profession. The NEA Division of Field Service has suggested eight criteria as follows: A profession
1. Involves activities essentially intellectual
2. Commands a body of specialized knowledge
3. Requires extended professional preparation
4. Demands continuous inservice growth
5. Affords a life career and permanent membership
6. Sets up its own standards
7. Exalts service above personal gain
8. Has a strong, closely knit professional organization.[1]

Characteristics suggested for appraising another profession, social workers, are as follows:
1. Does the profession have a well-defined function, the nature and scope of which can be identified?
2. Does the profession have a philosophy, code of ethics, and other means of self-regulation which assure that its practice transcends the bounds of political, sectarian, and economic self-interest?
3. Does the profession have a unified pattern of organizations that can speak for it with one voice?
4. Does the compensation received by the professional practitioners indicate that the public is willing to pay them as skilled and responsible professional workers?
5. Is the practice of the profession limited, or tending to be limited, to persons with approved general and professional preparation?

[1] National Education Association, Division of Field Service. "The Yardstick of a Profession." *Institutes on Professional and Public Relations,* 1938–1947. Washington, D. C.: the Association, 1948. p. 8.

6. Is there, in fact, a recognized systematic body of knowledge, skills, and attitudes which can be identified and transmitted as a regimen of professional preparation?

7. Is the regimen of professional education recognized as a quality appropriate for inclusion in the graduate and professional offerings of a university? [2]

Carr-Saunders has described the role of the professional organization as three-fold: (1) to guarantee professional competence, (2) to guarantee professional conduct of their members, and (3) to raise the status of the profession. He writes:

> As soon as a profession emerges, the practitioners are moved by the recognition of common interests to form a professional association. . . . What then are the motives common to the members of every profession which lead to the formation of professional association? . . . Of these, the first is that, as a profession emerges, the better equipped among the practitioners realize that they possess a certain craft . . . but the public does not accord them an exclusive right to that description. Not only may the poorly-equipped call themselves by these titles and obtain public recognition, but also may those without any equipment whatever. The better equipped desire that they should somehow be distinguishable, and to that end they form associations, membership of which is confined to those possessing certain minimum qualifications. . . . [Later these associations] come to desire that all practitioners should possess at least the minimum qualifications. . . . With a few unimportant exceptions, professional associations can now be said to be exclusive only in the sense that they exclude the unqualified. . . . [A second motive of the responsible members:] a profession in fact desires to see a proper standard of professional conduct set up and maintained. Just as the qualified are not readily distinguished from the unqualified, so the scrupulous are not so readily distinguished from the unscrupulous. Thus professional associations define and enforce rules of professional conduct. The members, in other words, mutually guarantee not only their competence but also their honor. . . . There is a third motive — to raise the status of the profession. [3]

Criteria of professions as suggested by Flexner are: [4]

[2] Hollis, Ernest V., and Taylor, Alice L. *Social Work Education in the United States.* Report of a study made for the National Council on Social Work Education. New York: Columbia University Press, 1951. p. 109–110.

[3] Carr-Saunders, A. M. "The Professions in Modern Society." As abstracted in *Readings in the Social Aspects of Education* (compiled by B. Othanel Smith, et al). Danville, Illinois: Interstate Printers and Publishers, Inc., 1951. p. 547–552.

[4] Flexner, Abraham. "What are the Earmarks of a Profession?" As quoted in *Readings in the Social Aspects of Education* (compiled by B. Othanel Smith, et al). Danville, Illinois: Interstate Printers and Publishers, Inc., 1951. p. 553–556.

1. They involve essentially intellectual operations with large individual responsibility.
2. They derive their raw material from science and learning.
3. They work up this material to a practical and definite end.
4. They possess an educationally communicable technique.
5. They tend to self-organization.
6. They are becoming increasingly altruistic in motivation.

Definition of a profession. Another way of identifying a profession is to define it. One dictionary offers the following:

The occupation, if not commercial, mechanical, agricultural, or the like, to which one devotes oneself; a calling in which one professes to have acquired some special knowledge used by way either of instructing, guiding, or advising others, or of serving them in some act; as the professions of arms, of teaching.[5]

Another dictionary defines a profession as:

An occupation that properly involves a literal education or its equivalent, and mental rather than manual labor; especially one of the three so-called learned professions. Hence, any calling or occupation involving special mental and other attainments or specific discipline, as editing, acting, engineering, authorship, etc.[6]

THE TEACHING PROFESSION

This book takes the view that teaching is a profession. But the evidence is mixed and the answer to the question " Is teaching a profession? " can hardly be categorical. In most respects teaching does exhibit the characteristics of a profession. In some, it does not. Again, in some teaching areas and in some places teaching exhibits all the earmarks of a profession. In others, there are conditions which still mark it as semiprofessional or even as a trade. Let us examine the conditions which tend to mitigate against teaching being recognized as a profession comparable to the other major professions in American life.

First, there is the matter of preparation. Requirements for preparation for teaching still vary widely among the states. In a few states elementary-school teachers can still secure licenses to teach in rural districts upon completion of a few or no college hours of preparation (one state still certificates such teachers by examination). In others, the requirements range from a minimum of one to four years of college preparation, and in four states the requirement for high-school teachers is five years. In some places preparation for teaching is still pretty largely a matter of apprenticeship; that is, the securing of a teaching job after meager acadamic preparation

[5] *Webster's New Collegiate Dictionary.* Second edition, 1951. p. 674.
[6] *Funk and Wagnall's New Standard Dictionary of the English Language.* 1938 edition. p. 1978.

and then learning the job on the job. Although the concept of professional preparation for teaching has been applied in the United States since about 1839, when the first state normal school was established, in several states people with little or no professional preparation can still be employed in the schools. The persisting idea that teaching simply requires that one complete a certain amount of general college education has tended to retard the progress of teaching toward professional status.

A second factor is that of public respect. People generally do not yet regard the professional competence of teachers as being on the same level as that of physicians, lawyers, or dentists. Teaching will not become a full-fledged profession until the average parent will consult his child's teacher with the same confidence that he would seek professional advice from the members of other professions. This lack of public acceptance of teaching as a profession is illustrated by the fact that, when qualified teachers are not available to fill all teaching positions, substandard or entirely unqualified teachers are licensed on emergency certificates. This method of staffing the classroom is based upon the assumption that, while specific preparation for teaching may be desirable, it is not always necessary.

Other factors which tend to prevent teaching from achieving the status of a profession are the prevalence of relatively low scales of remuneration for teachers, the acceptance by some employers of the holder of any kind of a teaching certificate as being equal to teachers with standard certificates, the considering of teaching as an appropriate stopgap occupation for young people until marriage or the securing of a more desirable job.

The areas in which teaching does exhibit the characteristics of a profession are: (1) Preparation is tending rapidly to be based exclusively upon completion of specific curriculums in higher education designed to prepare for teaching. (2) A comprehensive body of knowledge about teaching has been derived through research and experimentation, and this body of knowledge is being increased rapidly. (3) Minimum entrance requirements are rapidly approaching the degree level. (Thirty-one states in 1955 specified this minimum. The number of such states requiring the degree has more than doubled since 1946.) (4) Continuous professional growth of practitioners is rapidly becoming a common practice. The chief clientele of college and university summer sessions are teachers, striving to complete five, six, and seven years of college preparation. (5) The trend toward development of strong unified professional organizations is rapid and pronounced. (In 1955, about 92 per cent of all public school teachers were members of their state education associations and nearly 60 per cent belonged to the NEA.) (6) Remuneration of teachers is beginning to compare favorably with that in some of the other professions. (In 1955 the average salary of all teachers was about $4,000, but in at least two states the average was $5,000 or better.)

In summary, it may be said that at the present time teaching has many characteristics of a profession and a few characteristics of a skilled trade.

There yet remains much to be done to bring the occupation up to the level which will mark it as a true profession in every sense. . . .

SECTION 2. Professional organizations in teaching

One of the defining characteristics of a profession listed by Lieberman in the selection contained in the first section of this chapter was that to be a profession an occupation must be characterized by a *comprehensive self-governing organization of practitioners.* Although not truly comprehensive in the sense of including all members of the educational profession, a number of national teacher organizations have developed during the last century. The two most conspicuous and inclusive of these have been the *National Education Association* and the *American Federation of Teachers.* Each of these organizations has pledged its support to furthering the cause of education and to improving the welfare of the teaching group. These two organizations differ, however, on the most effective method of achieving these purposes. The National Education Association has represented the belief that this improvement can come best if teachers organize themselves into a distinct " professional " association which avoids " organic affiliation with any lay organization which has as its primary purpose the promotion of interests outside the field of education." The American Federation of Teachers represents, on the contrary, the conviction that the cause of education, and the cause of the teaching profession, can best be advanced if teachers affiliate themselves with the labor movement — a movement which they see as facing many problems similar to those faced by teachers, as being necessarily devoted to the cause of public education, and as being in a strategic position to assist the teaching profession in bringing about needed changes.

The National Education Association, an organization of persons in various fields and positions in education, is dedicated by its charter " To elevate the character and advance the interests of the profession of teaching and to promote the cause of education in the United States." This organization was formed in 1857 as the National Teachers Association and has since grown to the point where membership in its affiliated state and territorial associations now numbers over six hundred thousand. The national organization, divided into local and state units, and having as affiliates professional organizations in the various fields of teaching and administration, is by far the largest teacher organization in the western world. The selection by T. M. Stinnett which follows reflects the general spirit of this organization and the part that it attempts to play in enhancing professionalization and in helping the beginning teacher. The Platform of the N.E.A., which follows the selection by Stinnett, reflects the comprehensive scope of its concerns.

The American Federation of Teachers is of more recent origin. It was founded as a national organization in Chicago in 1916, at which time a number of existing local teachers' unions combined into a national federation. Although its membership has never been as large as that of the National Education Association, it has included among its members many of the outstanding leaders of American education. John Dewey was a charter member of the organization; George S. Counts has served as its president. Although one of the member unions of the A.F.L.-C.I.O., the American Federation of Teachers is unique among members of that organization in that (1) its constitution includes a no-strike provision and (2) the parent organization has granted school teachers the right to cross picket lines in the course of their professional duties. Persons in administrative, as contrasted with teaching, positions can join the union only by special permission or invitation of the union local. Dedicated to the proposition "Democracy in education; education for democracy," the union has been concerned with both teacher welfare and the broader relationships between the school and the social order. The Commission on Educational Reconstruction of the American Federation of Teachers, from whose work the final selection which follows is taken, numbers among its members such respected philosophers of education as John L. Childs, George S. Counts, Robert Ulich, and George Axtelle. This selection reflects clearly both the social orientation and the theory of social change held by this organization.

T. M. STINNETT
The National Education Association

THE EDUCATION STUDENT AND PROFESSIONAL ORGANIZATIONS

Theodore Roosevelt once said, "Every man owes some of his time to the upbuilding of the profession to which he belongs." The idea that the teacher's responsibility ends with the teaching in the classroom was discarded long ago. It is now recognized that all members of the teaching profession have at least a fourfold responsibility in their service to society: (a) continuous personal and professional growth toward maximum competency and thus toward maximum service to children; (b) cooperative work with immediate colleagues toward well-rounded educational services throughout the school system; (c) participation in community activities to the end that the teacher may carry his share as a member of the community, as an interpreter of the schools to the community, and as a participant in cooperative action and adult education; (d) participation in the work of the organized teaching profession so that the standards of the profession may be raised, the quality of the service of its members increased, and the welfare of all members may be enhanced.

Kinney has defined six roles of the qualified teacher: (1) a director of learning; (2) a counselor and guidance worker; (3) a mediator of the culture; (4) a member of the school community; (5) a liaison between school and community; and (6) a member of the profession.[1] On the last point, he says, "Many of the important responsibilities are fulfilled by the teacher, not as an individual in the classroom, but as a member of the

From T. M. Stinnett, *The Teacher and Professional Organizations*, third edition, 1956. Reprinted by permission of the National Education Association. pp. 51–52, 63–65, 103–107, 125–130.

[1] Kinney, Lucien B. (Analyst) *Measures of Teacher Competences.* (Report of Special Group D, The Miami Beach Conference.) Washington, D. C.: National Commission on Teacher Education and Professional Standards, National Education Association, 1953. (Planographed) p. 12.

organized profession. In general these include two general functions: securing support in building the educational program needed for our times; and improving the welfare and quality of membership of those in the profession, to attract and hold those who should enter."

Members of the profession believe that procedures to secure maximum efficiency, whether in the classroom, the school system, the community, or the profession as a whole, must be based upon the ideals of democracy. The creative power of individuals and groups working together toward common objectives is an instrument of great strength.

Professionalism involves a feeling of respect and pride in belonging to a professional group, an active desire to give effective service, a willingness to share both in the privileges and responsibilities, and the facing of reality regarding the needs and problems of the profession.

The obligation to one's professional organization extends beyond the obligation of membership and financial support. It requires active, enthusiastic participation in the affairs of the organization, sharing in the decisions on policies, and helping in the continuous refinement of its program. Democratic education implies democratic determination of its direction and scope. A united profession means not only universal membership, it means universal sharing in the responsibilities of the professional organization. Actual membership in a professional organization should begin while the prospective teacher is preparing for the profession. Such participation should be as much a part of preservice preparation as student teaching. . . .

THE BEGINNING TEACHER AND PROFESSIONAL ORGANIZATIONS

The beginning teacher will immediately be immersed in a cluster of new and baffling problems. These will largely center around problems of adjustment and orientation to his first job, to a totally new environment and to new co-workers. His first concern will be that of getting his specific teaching job in hand.

In such a situation, it is natural to give only casual attention to or ignore peripheral factors such as the affiliation with and the beginning of active participation in the professional organization. But this is one phase of the beginning teacher's orientation to his new life that is all-important. It should not be postponed. In the first place, the local teachers' organization should provide valuable help to the new teacher in making the necessary adjustment. The majority of its membership are experienced teachers. They will know intimately the community and its problems. They will know the children the new teacher is to work with. They will be familiar with the administrative policies of the school system. Thus, they will be able to help the beginning teacher to get started well in his new assignment. It is, therefore, imperative to get started in the professional organization at once.

For most beginning teachers getting started in the professional organization should not be too difficult. They will have had preliminary preparation for the step. In their preservice period of preparation, they will have gained a reading knowledge of the functions and work procedures of local, state, and national teachers' organizations. They will have gained a vicarious knowledge of salary schedules; group insurance; credit unions; tenure; academic freedom; inservice growth; professional ethics; curriculum development; administrative problems; and relations of teachers with administrators, school boards, and the public. Through experiences, provided during their college days, they will have had some participation in teachers' professional organizations and will have gained an understanding of the relationship of the organization to all these phases of the teacher's job.

Such knowledge and experience will enable the beginning teacher to make the transition from student to teacher. They will enable him to gain a comprehension of the opportunities and responsibilities within the profession. The beginning teacher will recognize the force for good which comes from cooperative planning and action — the essence of the unified teaching profession; he will realize the value of membership in learned societies and of having a part in the work of local, state, and national professional organizations.

What professional organization should you join? This is a question that eventually confronts every teacher. It will be of concern to the education student. The emphases in this book are upon the professional associations of the teaching profession. There are, of course, other organizations which seek to serve the organized interests of teachers, but the author has attempted to describe only teachers' professional organizations.

From this viewpoint, the teacher should hold membership in his local, state, and national all-inclusive associations and in the special-interest association serving his particular teaching field. In answering for oneself the question as to what organizations a teacher should join, perhaps the criteria listed below will help.

Characteristics of teachers' professional organizations. The Educational Policies Commission, NEA, has identified certain characteristics that should be reflected in the purposes and policies of a teachers' professional organization.[2] These may be summarized as follows:

1. *Purposes* — The purpose of a national professional organization in the field of education is the maintenance and improvement of the educational service. In order to achieve this purpose, it is essential that there should be continuous study and research with respect to the process of education, the conditions under which the process is carried on, the results achieved, and the means of its improvement; promotion of all movements which will give stability and professional character to educational undertakings; provision

[2] National Education Association and Department of Superintendence, Educational Policies Commission. *A National Organization for Education.* Washington, D. C.: the Commission, 1937. 47 p.

which will insure the continued professional growth of those engaged in the service of education; and the maintenance of such relations with the public as will secure economic welfare, social security, and civil liberties for those who serve the public in carrying on education.

2. *Membership* — Membership in professional organizations should be voluntary.

3. *Socio-economic activities* — A professional organization should be concerned with programs calculated to improve the quality of educational service. Although avoiding partisanship on general social questions, the national professional organization should call public attention to the educational aspects and implications of existing socio-economic conditions and of proposed social, economic, or governmental changes.

4. *Protection of members* — The national professional organization should define and publicize the civic and professional rights and obligations of teachers. It should also, in certain important cases, investigate or assist state and local associations in investigating apparent infringements and engage in efforts to secure judicial rulings in defense of these rights.

5. *Branches of educational service* — The national professional organization should provide a department for each important branch of educational service. Membership in a department should require and carry with it membership in the general organization. The departments and affiliated organizations (to which latter group the requirement of individual membership may not apply) should be integrated through representation in the governing machinery of the general organization or in some other effective way.

6. *Local, state, and national membership* — Membership in any local and state or territorial organization should, so far as possible, be made co-inclusive with membership in the national organizations so that membership in one would carry membership in the others.

7. *Lay organizations* — The national professional organization should welcome the active cooperation of lay groups in measures designed to inform the public on educational matters and to improve educational conditions. In no case should it enter into organic affiliation with any lay organization which has as its primary purpose the promotion of interests outside the field of education. . . .

Scope of State Association services. Although, as pointed out previously, exclusive concern with direct economic benefits is not exactly the epitome of professional spirit, nevertheless it is a very human trait. Perhaps, therefore, a description of some of the direct, individual services which state education associations perform for their members may be helpful. . . .

In some states these individualized services take the form of cooperative buying plans which result in sizable discounts to teachers. In a sense, credit union services are in this category. One association has secured agreements with large merchandising establishments, such as department stores, food marts, service stations, etc., whereby members are granted a flat rate discount on purchases. Many state associations now provide for their members full insurance coverage — including automobile, life, health, accident, and disability insurance — at greatly reduced rates.

But, perhaps the most impressive service — impressive to the member who insists upon demonstrated benefits to the individual rather than group benefits — which state education associations perform is that of defense against unjust treatment. Several case histories depicting such services, are given below:

Case Example 1. — The Fern Bruner Case. Fern Bruner was a social studies teacher in a small town near San Francisco, from 1947–50. In 1949–50 some of the high-school students formed a student unit of United World Federalists and asked Miss Bruner to serve as advisor. Permission to do so was granted by the principal and the school board. Then a woman in the community, who believed that the United World Federalists was a subversive organization, protested the student club. The school board supported the teacher in the matter, but requested that the group not meet in the school building because of the community uproar. The woman demanded that the board fire Miss Bruner. The board refused. At this point a radio commentator in San Francisco, having received a letter from the woman accusing Miss Bruner of being a subversive, began to attack Miss Bruner on his radio program. Without any evidence other than the letter from the housewife who had been thwarted in efforts to have the teacher fired by the school board, the commentator accused Miss Bruner of being a communist.

Then the California Teachers Association entered the case. Its Tenure and Ethics Committee made a thorough investigation, cleared Miss Bruner of the ugly charges and declared her to be an outstanding teacher of exceptionally high moral character and unqualified loyalty to her country. But this did not stop the radio commentator. With no evidence, other than that mentioned above, he delivered two more broadcasts attacking the report of the CTA's Tenure and Ethics Committee and the California Teachers Association for its " whitewash " of Miss Bruner. The California Teachers Association immediately filed a libel suit in Miss Bruner's behalf against the radio commentator and the radio station over which the broadcasts were made and assumed all of the expense involved in this suit. After a dramatic trial in which the radio commentator was proved to be without any information about Miss Bruner, other than the letter, and in which he was unable to substantiate any of his charges or to show any valid grounds for having called Miss Bruner a communist, the jury found in favor of Miss Bruner and ordered the radio commentator to pay her damages in the amount of $25,000. The radio station was ordered to pay an additional $25,000 and the manager of the radio station $5,000 to Miss Bruner. The *San Francisco Chronicle* in commenting on the case, said as follows: " This case presented one uncommon and welcome aspect. The accused woman found willing and competent defenders. The California Teachers Association, having investigated and disproved the charges against Miss Bruner, came to her defense. The Association is to be commended for its intelligent and courageous conduct."

Case Example 2. — Unfair Dismissal of a Principal. A Connecticut Board of Education voted in October not to renew the contract of the principal of its high school after the current school year. The principal, who had been employed by the local schools for 16 years, was not given specific reasons for the dismissal. Connecticut's statutes do not provide for tenure or continuing contract for administrative personnel, although it does provide that a board may enter into a 3-year contract with administrators. It does not provide, as in the case with teachers, provision for public hearing in case of dismissed administrative personnel. The Connecticut Education Association established a fact finding committee to investigate the case. The only evidence of friction between the dismissed principal and the administration that the committee could find was that there were charges of untidy housekeeping in the high school and that the principal and his staff felt that their plans for a new high school building were not given proper consideration. The investigating committee reported to the Board of Directors of the Connecticut Education Association as follows: " The principal involved had served continuously in his position for 16 years; during that time the School Board never censured or warned him of unsatisfactory service. The high school faculty, upon learning of the dismissal notice, sent the principal a written expression of unanimous confidence; the bandboosters club issued a written statement protesting the Board's action; the home-school association went on record as being vigorously opposed to the Board's decision. The Board refused the discharged principal a public hearing at which he could have an opportunity to defend himself."

Failing to get any constructive action from the School Board, the CEA Board of Directors issued the following declaration: (1) that the School Board acted without regard for fair dismissal practices; (2) that all active members of the CEA employed elsewhere be notified that in its judgment acceptance of employment in the public schools of this district would be professionally inadvisable; (3) that when the School Board gives adequate assurance to its present school staff or to the CEA that it has adopted professional personnel policies consistent with accepted good practices this notice will be publicly withdrawn.[3] This action was withdrawn by the CEA Board of Directors in 1955, after the passage of a state-wide Fair Dismissal Bill by the State Legislature.

[3] Connecticut Education Association. " New Building New Principal." (How One Board of Education Rewarded 16 Years of Service.) Report of a fact-finding committee of the CEA, March 5, 1954.

Case Example 3. — Illegal Firing of Teachers. The Carver (Michigan) School Board, in March 1952, notified five tenure teachers that their contracts would not be renewed. The state tenure act provides that, " A tenure teacher is entitled to a hearing (private or public, as the teacher chooses) and is entitled to counsel." The teachers asked for a hearing within the time limit and no hearing was provided by the Board. The teachers applied to the Michigan Education Association for assistance. Legal assistance was provided and an appeal to the State Tenure Commission was filed.

The State Tenure Commission handed down a decision in favor of the teachers.

Results. The School Board failing to act on the recommendation, the State Tenure Committee filed a mandamus suit in Circuit Court to compel the School Board to reinstate the teachers. The case dragged on in the courts for several months, during which time the Michigan Education Association provided financial assistance for the teachers during the period of unemployment. The Circuit Court finally ordered the School Board to reinstate the five dismissed teachers and to pay them back salaries. After failure of the Board to observe the Court order, the case was carried to the Supreme Court which sustained the position of the Circuit Court. Thus the five teachers were restored to their positions and paid for the time that they were suspended from service. . . .[4]

What does the NEA do for me? The query, common among many teachers and especially among beginning teachers who have had no experience with their professional organizations — as was described earlier in this Section — is, " What does the NEA do for me? " This is a natural, logical question since to the teacher in Arkansas or Iowa or California the NEA, located in Washington, D.C., seems far off and more or less unrelated to the local situation. Probably all national organizations have similar difficulty in seeming real and essential to members in local communities. The foregoing descriptions of NEA services are general in nature, and although every one of them vitally affects the welfare of the individual teacher, these services are not as impressive or as discernible as some direct action or benefit the teacher sees or feels.

Thus, the following will indicate a few of the services which could or do apply to each teacher member:

Case Example 1. The NEA Legislative Division was instrumental in securing the passage by the Congress of the Mason Amendment to the Internal Revenue Act of 1954. This amendment provided a tax credit for retired teachers on the first $1,200 of income, above personal exemptions, a

[4] Michigan Education Association. " Carver School Case." *Michigan Education Journal* 31, 2:78; September 15, 1953. " The MEA Victory: Carver Teachers Reinstated." *Michigan Education Journal* 31, 8:223; September 15, 1953. " MEA Victorious in Carver Equity Case." *Michigan Education Journal* 32, 6:165–66; November 15, 1954.

credit which some other groups had long employed. This legislation means a maximum annual saving, in reduced income taxes for retired teachers, of $240, which would be the equivalent each year to the total NEA dues of a teacher for a period of 48 years.

Case Example 2. For many years one of the largest of the national mail order firms had designed and distributed to its thousands of local stores throughout the United States a window display, commemorating the opening of school in the fall, advertising school supplies. Several years ago this display included a horrible comic type of a teacher, depicting her as an ugly, mean-tempered, old " battle-ax " type — a caricature calculated to induce public contempt for all teachers. As soon as the display appeared in local store windows, calls of protest began to flow into NEA Headquarters in Washington.

On behalf of the nation's 1,170,000 teachers the NEA immediately and vigorously protested to the mail order house. The firm, though apparently shocked that anyone would protest the traditional lampooning of teachers — this to their advertising department was accepted as nothing unusual, in fact as a sort of popular pastime — quickly agreed to withdraw the offensive caricature and asked the NEA to serve in an advisory capacity thereafter in developing its annual school opening display. This is a case of remedial action in which the individual teacher alone would have been powerless.

Defending the profession and the public. Another area of NEA services which has direct implications for the individual member is that having to do with the defense of the teacher unjustly dismissed or unfairly treated and those dealing with the teacher who is allegedly guilty of unprofessional conduct or incompetent services. The one deals with the protection of the teacher, the other with protection of the public — both basic obligations of a professional organization.

If a profession, as most do, is to claim the right of self regulation, the right to set its own standards, this implies not only privileges but responsibilities. The standards it fixes must be such as not only to safeguard its members but to safeguard the interests of society as well. Specifically, the profession has an obligation to protect not only its members but to police its membership and to take disciplinary action against members found guilty of unethical practices. Therefore, a profession must maintain judicial and police machinery — machinery by which the law (code of ethics) is interpreted and machinery for investigating charges of unjust or unethical conduct. There are three agencies of the NEA charged with these functions and the nature of their separate functions is frequently not clearly understood.

The Defense Commission and the Committee on Tenure and Academic Freedom (Tenure Committee) are charged with broad responsibilities for defending members of the profession against unjust dismissal and for investigating and reporting cases, involving dismissals or threats of dismissal, which have broader threats to the quality of school services. The Ethics Committee has two broad functions: (1) to render interpretations of the Code of Ethics in abstract cases reported to it; and (2) to render decisions in case of actual hearings of persons accused of unethical conduct. In the former case these interpretations become a body of interpretive law, much as court opinions do regarding the meaning of a given law. In the second case, the decisions are referred to the NEA Executive Committee for action, which may result in expulsion of the accused from membership. In other words, the Ethics Committee serves only as a court. It carries on no investigation or execution of verdicts. The Defense Commission and Tenure Committee do carry on investigations and serve, in a sense, as the police and prosecuting attorney in cases involving alleged violations of the Code of Ethics, and as a sort of defense attorney in cases of alleged mistreatment of a member of the profession.

The work of the Defense Commission and the Tenure Committee will be described first and some case histories cited, followed by some case histories of the Ethics Committee. What are the respective responsibilities of the Defense Commission and the Tenure Committee?

In a case involving only the alleged unfair or illegal dismissal, or threat of dismissal, of a teacher, the Tenure Committee is empowered to handle this. Where dismissals or threats of dismissal involve circumstances and conditions of a broader nature — for example, attacks by groups upon the schools or political interference with the administration of the schools — the Defense Commission would be the body empowered to act for the profession. In short, cases involving only dismissals or threat of dismissals are clearly in the jurisdiction of the Tenure Committee. Cases where dismissals are incidental to school conditions of an unprofessional nature are in the jurisdiction of the Defense Commission. Thus the two — the Defense Commission and the Tenure Committee — have little difficulty in determining jurisdiction and of referral to the other when this is indicated by the facts in a given case.

Below are some case histories of actions by those bodies:

Case Example 1. — The Kelso, Washington, Case. This case illustrates how the profession, through its Defense Commission, attempts to protect its members from unjust treatment. The investigation was a joint effort of the Washington Education Association and the National Education Association. The case grew out of discontent of teachers over the handling of a special appropriation of the state legislature to supplement teachers' salaries in 1943. This was the start of a series of developments which led to steadily deteriorating relationships between the teachers and the administration. The situation finally came to a head in the spring of 1950, when it appeared that 17 teachers and five principals would be dismissed by the Board. The Kelso Education Association adopted a resolution, later endorsed by several lay organizations, requesting the WEA and the NEA to conduct an investigation. The investigating committee found that, during the controversy teachers had been intimidated, threatened, and arbitrarily treated by the administration. Seventeen teachers were asked to resign by the Board and the status of several others left in doubt, without any explanations. This was in violation of the state code of public instruction which prescribed that school personnel must be notified in writing by a specified date that their contracts will not be renewed and the reasons for such action specified.

The investigating committee recommended to the Board that: (1) assurance be given, through immediate issuance of contracts, that no teacher or principal will be discharged without just cause; (2) the superintendent of schools be removed immediately, and careful study be given to selecting a successor with high qualities of leadership and professional recognition; (3) that a survey of the Kelso school system be made by competent authorities; (4) that the School Board adopt procedures to bring about more cooperative relationships between the Board and school personnel.

The results of the investigation were that the Board accepted the recommendations of the Committee, reemployed all but three of the 22 teachers and principals involved, and dismissed the incumbent superintendent.

Case Example 2. — The Chicago Case. During the summer of 1944 the Defense Commission was requested by several lay and professional organizations in Chicago to investigate the administration of the Chicago school system. The resulting investigation centered largely on the personnel practices of the system. The investigating committee, appointed by the Commission, found " ample evidence of intimidation and punishment of capable, independent teachers who were unwilling to submit to domination, insistence upon blind loyalty to the administration rather than upon loyalty to the children and the cause of education, attempts to dominate teachers' organizations, use of transfer to punish some individuals and to intimidate others, dependence upon domination of teachers rather than upon leadership and integrity to secure teacher unity and compliance." [5]

The report condemned certain personnel practices of the administration and condemned the tie-in with the political administration of the city, and submitted a list of nine recommendations for improving the situation.[6]

Results of the investigation: Several of the Commission's recommendations have been followed and the then superintendent of Chicago schools was expelled from membership in the National Education Association for

[5] National Commission for the Defense of Democracy Through Education. " Defense Commission Completes Fruitful Decade of Service to the Profession." *Defense Bulletin,* No. 41. Washington, D. C.: National Education Association, December, 1951. p. 6.
[6] National Commission for the Defense of Democracy Through Education. *Certain Personnel Practices in the Chicago Public Schools.* Washington, D. C.: National Education Association, 1945. p. 64–66.

unethical and unprofessional conduct. The superintendent was later removed from his position.

The function of the Ethics Committee, as a judicial body, is illustrated by the case opinion given below. The Ethics Committee serves the profession as a quasi-judicial body, building up a set of interpretations, arising from actual cases, so that members of the professional organization will know what the Code means with respect to a given action or violation. Doubtless most violations of the Code of Ethics result, not from intent, but from ignorance of the meaning of the language of the Code. The growing body of interpretations of the Code by the Ethics Committee should serve to reduce the number of violations.

Ethics Committee Interpretation. *If a teacher has entered into a contract with one school district, it is improper for him to initiate or continue negotiations for a contract with another school district without the consent of the district to which he is obligated. By the same token, it is improper for a superintendent knowingly to negotiate with a teacher already under contract without the approval of the school district to which the teacher is obligated.*

Case Example. *A teacher was negotiating for a contract with two school districts, A and B, for the ensuing year. She signed a contract without a cancellation clause with District A and the superintendent thereupon notified placement bureaus that the vacancy no longer existed. Unknown to the superintendent of District A, the teacher continued negotiations with District B. Shortly before school opened she orally agreed to accept a position with District B at a higher salary. She then asked to be released from her contract with District A. At this point it was doubtful that a replacement could be secured. The superintendent of District A asks whether the conduct of the teacher was contrary to the Code.*

Committee Opinion. *It is the opinion of the Committee that on the facts presented the conduct of the teacher was contrary to Principle IV, Sections 6 and 7 of the Code.*

Ethics Committee Interpretation. *It is improper for a teacher to make remarks in public reflecting on a child's abilities and family background. However, a teacher has the right and often the duty to confer in confidence with colleagues or authorized agencies regarding a child's problems in conduct and adjustment.*

Case Example. *Teacher A discussed one of his students with Teacher B in a school hallway within the hearing of a classmate of the student in question. The teacher commented adversely on the student's mental ability and personal integrity, attributing these deficiencies to the pupil's family background. Teacher B reported the incident to the local association.*

It is the opinion of the Committee that the conduct of Teacher A was contrary to Section 2 of Principle I and Section 3 of Principle II of the Code. . . .

Under *Principles I and II* of the Code, respectively, a teacher is entrusted with the obligations of helping children to develop into " happy, useful, self-supporting citizens " and of furthering " cooperative relationships with the home." These obligations cannot be fulfilled in terms of Sections 2 and 3 when a teacher makes disparaging remarks reflecting on a child's abilities or family background in such circumstances as are herein presented. It must be presumed that in repetition such criticisms will generate malicious gossip which will get back to the student and to his parents.

The Committee recognizes that on occasion a teacher has not only the right but the duty to confer in confidence with appropriate professional colleagues or authorized agencies regarding a child's problems in conduct and adjustment. However, casual criticisms made indiscriminately, especially in the presence of other students, are clearly improper. . . .[7]

NATIONAL EDUCATION ASSOCIATION
Platform of the NEA

The Resolutions adopted by the National Education Association at its conventions over a period of one hundred years have had a profound influence on American education. Until 1931 there was a tendency to repeat each year in the Resolutions the entire policy of the Association, thereby obscuring current issues. A committee appointed in that year drew up a permanent Platform, which was adopted at the 1932 Convention. The Platform has been reviewed by each Committee on Resolutions since that time and changed in the light of new needs and purposes.

The principles, policies, and goals of the National Education Association are expressed in the Platform and Resolutions adopted annually by the Representative Assembly at the Convention of the Association. These two documents represent the culmination of the policy-making process of the National Education Association.

The Platform states the principles, policies, and goals which guide the Association.

The Resolutions supplement the Platform in two ways: by directing the officers and staff of the Association to undertake specified action and by stating the position of the Association on matters — educational in nature and national in scope — which are of current importance to the profession of education.

The Platform and Resolutions together govern the officers and staff of the Association and guide the members in their professional activities.

* * *

The National Education Association believes that the American public school is an indispensable source of national unity, common purpose, and

[7] *Ibid.* Opinion 13. p. 27–28.

equality of opportunity; that the defense and perpetuation of democracy require an educated citizenry; and, therefore, that the American system of free public education, enhanced by the traditional separation of church and state, is essential to our democratic way of life.

THE PROFESSION OF EDUCATION

A dedicated profession is essential to our system of free public education. Education, like all professions, is a service based on research, knowledge, preparation, experience, and ethical standards. Skilled, devoted teachers of moral character, dynamic personality, and high civic ideals strive to earn and hold for their profession that public confidence which all professions require to function successfully.

The task of the profession of education is to promote the growth of all the people in intellectual qualities, civic competence, international understanding, moral and spiritual values, cultural and esthetic appreciation, vocational and economic capability, conservation of human and natural resources, and constructive use of leisure time.

THE ASSOCIATION

The National Education Association, like the profession it represents, is dedicated to the American student of every age and condition. As the largest and most comprehensive organization in American education, the Association serves the student, and therefore the public, by serving its members and by cooperating with agencies which share its aims. Its program, concerned with education of every type, is designed to fulfill the need for leadership and service in education.

Only through organized action can members of the teaching profession insure their freedom to conduct independently their professional affairs. It is therefore of first importance that all persons engaged in the profession of education enjoy and exercise the right to join professional organizations. Every teacher should be a member of the National Education Association.

At the heart of a profession dedicated to the welfare of students lies respect for the human personality and for the continuing pursuit of truth. Members of the Communist party, therefore, bar themselves from the teaching profession. Communists may not join the National Education Association, nor should they be permitted to teach in American schools.

The National Education Association respects and upholds the rights of groups, including religious denominations, to maintain and finance their own schools so long as such schools meet the educational, health, and safety standards defined by the states in which they are located and so long as the American tradition of separation of church and state is vigorously and zealously safeguarded.

GOALS OF THE ASSOCIATION

The program of the National Education Association is directed toward the following goals:

1. Educational opportunity for every individual to develop his full potential for responsible and useful citizenship and for intellectual and spiritual growth.

a. In every state a system of free, effective public education extending from kindergarten through college and adult education, and adapted to all learners.

b. Adequate legal provision to safeguard the education of all students.

c. A school year of at least 180 full school days for every elementary- and secondary-school pupil who can profit from fulltime classroom instruction.

d. Class size permitting appropriate individual attention for every pupil; no basic learnings class in elementary school to exceed 25 pupils per teacher.

e. Education beyond the high school for all youth who have both the desire and the ability to benefit from it.

f. Provision for adults to participate in organized instructional programs.

g. Adequate library resources in every community.

2. Balanced educational programs to provide for the varied needs and talents of individual students and for the strength and progress of the nation.

a. Vigorous professional leadership to improve curriculum and guidance programs, to promote research, and to apply research findings to education.

b. Provision for both general and specialized education for our changing modern society.

c. Educational programs that improve both mental and physical health.

d. Continuing stress on education regarding the effects of narcotics, alcohol, and tobacco by making full use of research on these problems.

e. Educational programs that develop understanding among nations and among groups of people, including international exchange of educational leaders, teachers, and students; opportunities to learn about other peoples; and realistic teaching about the United Nations, its specialized agencies, and similar international organizations.

f. Instructional programs which teach about — but do not advocate — communism and all forms of totalitarianism.

3. The services of a professionally prepared and competent educator in every professional position.

a. In every classroom a teacher with a strong general education, depth in a special area, mastery of the knowledge and skills necessary to be a competent teacher, and zeal for continued learning.

b. The requiring of a minimum of four years of college preparation, including supervised teaching, for initial certification of beginning teachers; and a minimum of five years of college and three years of successful teaching experience required for full professional certification.

c. Development of reciprocity in teacher certification through coordination of accreditation and certification procedures, based upon standards developed by the profession and administered through the appropriate legal agencies.

d. Assumption of personal responsibility for professional growth by educators, assisted by professional associations, school systems, state departments of education, colleges, and universities.

e. Acceptance by educators of their responsibility for the standards of the profession.

f. Selection, promotion, and payment of teachers on a professional basis with no discrimination because of race, color, residence, economic or marital status, sex, religion, or political beliefs.

4. School plant, equipment, and instructional materials appropriate to the educational needs of all learners.

a. An individual desk or work-space for every pupil.

b. Safe, healthful, attractive classrooms and work areas.

c. Adequate equipment and materials available to all learners, including those in specialized programs.

d. Adequate library resources as an integral part of every school and college.

5. Effective organization, control, administration, and financial support of public education in every state.

a. In every state a qualified and adequately staffed department of education with a broad program of leadership and service to local school systems.

b. An adequately financed program of public education in every school district.

c. An adequately financed program of higher education in every state.

d. An interested, informed, and non-partisan board of education in every school district.

e. Units of school administration — reorganized if necessary — of sufficient size, resources, and enrollment to facilitate efficient and adequate programs of elementary and secondary education.

f. Intermediate units designed to serve a number of school districts on a regional basis to provide the services needed for a comprehensive program.

g. State constitutional and statutory provisions that give the voters in local school districts authority to levy the school taxes they are able to pay.

h. An equitable assessment of property and an appropriate level of tax rates to enable every school district to carry its fair share of school support.

i. A professionally prepared and competent administrative staff in every school system.

j. School attendance laws in every state which require attendance to age 18 or through the secondary school, with provision for work permits at 16 where individually desirable.

k. School athletics and health activities administered solely by school authorities.

6. A local-state-federal partnership in the financial support of public education with control of education residing in the states.

a. Tax legislation to enable every level of government to make its maximum contribution to the support of public education.

b. Substantial federal support for education leaving the control of education in the states.

c. An adequately staffed, professionally independent U. S. Office of Education with the financial support necessary for a broad program of services to educational institutions and school systems.

d. Support of public education through preferential postal rates for educational materials and reservation of broadcasting channels for educational use.

e. Participation of public education in programs of civil defense, vocational rehabilitation, and school-lunch assistance.

7. Public understanding and appreciation of the vital role of education in our American democracy.

a. Systematic effort by the profession, using all appropriate media of communication, to promote public understanding of education and to encourage wider public and parent participation in solving its problems.

b. The development of methods and materials to help teachers' associations and school officials maintain good relationships with the public.

c. The maintenance of a climate of intellectual freedom which encourages the free flow of ideas and the ablest instruction.

d. Recognition of the teacher's need and protection of his right to deal objectively with controversial issues.

8. Understanding and support of the teacher's right to participate fully in public affairs.

a. Informed participation by teachers in the consideration of all legislation that would affect the quantity or quality of education either directly or indirectly.

b. Recognition of teachers' political rights and responsibilities, including the right to seek public office.

c. Recognition of the right of all teachers to join organizations of their own choosing, except those which advocate changing the form of government of the United States by unconstitutional means.

9. Fair standards of professional welfare for teachers.

a. The development of appropriate procedures and channels through which teachers may work effectively with school boards and administrators on questions of salaries, working conditions, and school policies.

b. Salaries that provide credit for successful teaching experience; that reflect the professional skill and training required of teachers; and that are commensurate with the teacher's importance to American society.

c. Encouragement — through professional and sabbatical leaves, scholarships, salary increments, and income tax deductions for educational expenses — for teachers to maintain and improve professional competence.

d. Protection for teachers against common emergencies through such means as sick leave, medical insurance, life insurance, and credit union services.

e. A reasonable, carefully defined work load for all teachers, taking into account the demands upon them for preparation and other essential out-of-class duties.

f. Sound retirement systems that permit teachers to move from one state to another without undue penalty, and equal tax treatment of the income of retired teachers and other persons retired under similar circumstances.

g. Effective tenure laws balanced by corresponding responsibility for continuing personal and professional growth.

h. The development of effective, written personnel policies, specifying procedures for employment, promotion, and dismissal, for placement and advancement on the salary schedule, and for assignment and transfer of teachers.

10. Professional associations that evoke the active participation of all educators in working toward the highest goals for education.

a. A vigorous local education association accessible to educators in every school and affiliated with the state association and the National Education Association.

b. A strong education association in every state and territory, affiliated with the National Education Association.

c. A National Education Association that enrolls all qualified educators.

d. NEA membership goals in every state, established annually by representatives from state and national associations.

e. Unified professional dues in each state — a single fee to be collected by the local education association to cover local, state, and national dues.

f. An increasing NEA membership in all college and university faculties.

g. Improved cooperation among educators in elementary, secondary, higher, and adult education as they work in behalf of a united profession.

h. Establishment of professional qualifications and standards as prerequisites for new NEA membership.

i. Universal adoption, conscientious observance, and effective enforcement of the NEA Code of Professional Ethics.

j. Effective cooperation with the educators, organizations of other nations.

k. Active participation of more members of the profession in NEA departmental units that serve the educators' special professional interests.

l. Effective local, state, and national programs for the selective recruitment of teachers, with an extension of systematic efforts in secondary schools and colleges to guide competent young people into teaching.

m. An adequately staffed, well-equipped NEA center in the nation's capital.

n. Systematic programs for developing association leaders who are fully aware of the resources available from all units of their professional associations.

AMERICAN FEDERATION OF TEACHERS
The organization and work of the AFT

TEACHERS UNITE WITH OTHER WORKERS

Local teacher groups affiliate with organized labor. In the first quarter of this century, small groups of teachers, scattered in cities all over the country, reached out in a new direction. They joined the labor movement.

At the time this was a daring and formidable venture, for it meant a sharp break with the tradition that assigned to teachers a passive role in public affairs and restricted their sphere of activity to the care of children in the classroom. This action on the part of teachers also involved a repudiation of the notion that joining a trade union is undignified and unprofessional. Many who took this pioneering step literally risked demotion, dismissal and the disapproval of their fellow teachers. Why did they do it?

The record shows that three basic considerations prompted teachers to unite with other workers in the labor movement. One of these was the substandard economic conditions under which teachers worked in many communities. A second was the weakness of existing teacher organizations, and their failure to improve the status of teachers. The third was faith in education and belief in the crucial role that it should play in the preservation and development of our democratic way of life.

Although from the founding of the Republic our national leaders have perceived that public education was essential to the maintenance of our liberties, there have always been powerful forces which have opposed the principle of universal education, and which have fought to reduce public appropriations for the common school. Indeed, certain real estate lobbyists have even dubbed the enriched curriculum which has sought to provide each child with a chance to make the most of his potentialities a form of " sanctified squander," and they have constantly exerted pressure to restrict the school program to the " three r's " and to pay teachers less than a living wage.

These attacks on education appropriations became more severe in the years that followed the First World War. Teachers everywhere were in dire distress. Always poorly paid, their salaries now fell far behind rapidly rising costs of living. School buildings were deteriorating, and thousands of teachers were leaving the profession. In certain of our communities, the educational system, itself, threatened to break down.

From the Commission on Educational Reconstruction of the American Federation of Teachers, *Organizing the Teaching Profession*, pp. 19–21, 245–246, 253–259. Reprinted by permission of the American Federation of Teachers.

Existing teacher organizations appeared to many both within and without the educational profession to be powerless to deal with this menacing situation. A militant classroom teachers' organization, free from administrative influence, was called for; the leadership in the struggle to improve educational conditions clearly would have to develop from within the ranks of the teachers themselves. But many also perceived that teachers alone could not resist the pressure from those selfish groups which sought lower taxes at the expense of the education of the children of the great masses of the people. Thus, outstanding civic leaders recommended that teachers unite with organized labor and cooperate with the workers in a resolute effort to get more adequate support for public education.

Other influences were also at work. The war had been accompanied by a new birth of social idealism. The concept of democracy came to have a new value and significance. To many it was evident that under the life conditions of industrial America, our historic principles of human freedom and equality could retain substance only if democracy were to be interpreted in *social* and *economic* as well as in *political* terms. It was also increasingly recognized that the movement of organized labor was destined to play a crucial part in the struggle to rebuild the economic foundations of our democratic way of life. A deepened sense of the meaning of human brotherhood was also emerging. Many of the teachers in the various sections of our country who spontaneously organized into unions wished by so doing to achieve an identification with all who worked for a living. They hoped that as an organized part of the labor movement they could share with their fellow-workers in the effort to raise material and cultural standards of living, and thus make our country a better place in which to live.

The story of the American Federation of Teachers makes one thing clear. The movement to get teachers to unite with organized labor was from the beginning a grass-roots movement. It was a movement of and for teachers, and it grew out of their own felt needs — personal, professional, and social. Teachers joined labor not as a result of outside propaganda and promotion, but because they believed it provided the best promise for the satisfaction of their own life interests and aspirations. As the record shows, the national organization followed — it did not precede — the organization of locals in communities widely separated. In the history of functional organization in our great continental country, it is doubtful whether any other national body has been so continuously kept under the control of its state and local bodies as has this national federation of classroom teachers. . . .

THE LARGER ISSUES

Retrospective. This story of pioneering in education has shown that the teachers through their Federation have fought for rights for themselves and their profession and have battled even harder to make their world and the world of their pupils a better one. First, they fought for the very right to form a Federation; then, for the right to work through it — to have it as their negotiating agent. They sought higher incomes, better working conditions, and more adequate job and social security. They insisted on respect for a teacher's freedom in his personal living and in his actions as a citizen. Through the Federation they have moved on numerous occasions to end discrimination against teachers on racial and religious grounds. They have pressed consistently and doggedly to equalize educational opportunities for Americans of all ages and backgrounds, to secure a sound system of public schools free from interference by pressure groups and from harassment by anti-democratic enemies. They have successfully blocked attempts at domination or infiltration of the organization by totalitarian groups. They shared in labor's struggle for social reforms in American society. These objectives for which the Federation was striving as well as the nature of its struggles were intimately related to wider social issues and events of the era of which it was a part. In order to see the story that has been unfolded in its full significance, it needs to be examined in the context of the larger happenings of the times.

The Federation has maintained that two of its most distinctive features as a teachers' organization have been first, its emphasis on action rather than words and second, its determination to fight for its objectives while in affiliation with the ranks of democratic, organized labor. An examination of this latter insistence may furnish the clue for clarifying the motivating values of the members and leaders of the Federation.

The reading of the statements of the founders of the Federation reveals a two-fold kind of emphasis: a passionate devotion to the principles of a democratic way of living, and genuine misgivings that conditions and trends existed that threatened these principles not only for teachers but for the larger society within which they lived.

Repeated experiences through the years persuaded teachers with democratic convictions that they should form their own organization in affiliation with labor. Later experiences within the labor movement persuaded them that through such affiliation they could best further the welfare of their profession. Through their union and the larger federation with which it was affiliated they found allies who assisted them in realizing common objectives. . . .

The basic theme. Throughout this whole account there is a central theme which provides a basic meaning and unity — the struggle for simple human dignity and for the economic, social and political conditions which make it possible.

This is an ancient human goal, but the effort to attain it has been militantly supported by more and more elements of the human community as we have entered a stage of world history increasingly affected by the ideals of democracy, and by forces growing out of the scientific-technological revolution. Working people in our own country, and new groups of people in Europe, Asia, Africa, and Latin America, repressed for many years, are making efforts with increasing success to abolish conditions which degrade them. To be seen in its full significance, the work of the American Federation of Teachers has to be seen as part of this general movement in democratic and industrial society.

It was only natural that in the early years of the Federation there was an emphasis on securing higher salaries, better job security and decent working conditions. But the story of the unions shows that much more was at stake than these. Of fundamental concern was the conviction that teachers should insist on being accepted fully as citizens and persons; that they should reject with finality the indignity of being treated as the third sex or third-class citizens. Those who were active in the work of the organization in all parts of the country realized that they legitimately could expect to win acceptance as free men and women only as they themselves acted with the responsibility and courage requisite with such status.

On this particular issue there were a number of conditions and practices which had to be rejected as unworthy of acceptance. Among these were: docile acceptance of paternalism; unwarranted interference in matters involving the personal lives of teachers such as the right to marry without penalty; the right to belong or not to belong to various teachers' organizations; dictatorial administrative practices in relations with teachers and the setting of school policies; interference with teachers' rights to take part in labor or political activities.

Other kinds of conditions had to be affirmed: the recognition of the right of teachers to negotiate through their own representatives for decent working conditions; the attainment of regular procedures for democratic conference between teachers and administration so that the professional judgment of teachers would be included in consultation about matters affecting the life and program of the schools; the acceptance of the fact that teachers had personal lives and family lives of their own and had the right to make decisions in these areas as long as they observed their general responsibilities to the youth of the community; the chance to exercise freely all of their rights under the Constitution.

In a profession where it had become traditional for many teachers to accept patterns of meek subservience to authority, or to accept restrictions on their rights as persons and citizens, the very existence of the American Federation of Teachers acted as a new source of hope for those who rebelled against existing indignities and who at the same time refused to accept the alternative of leaving the profession as the only way out.

Through the program of the Federation teachers developed the habit of taking responsibility for seeking solutions to their own problems. It also had a healthy effect on the attitudes of administrators and influential elements in the community as they learned that teachers could be more than the well-meaning but slightly ridiculous figures as characterized by a common stereotype of them. They came to recognize through the program of the Federation that teachers could be self-respecting human beings who expected to be dealt with on the basis of full equality.

It is important, too, to realize that more than the welfare of the teachers was at stake in the struggles of the Federation for recognition of the rights of the teacher as a person. More and more people in all walks of life and in all parts of the world in the course of this century were slowly coming to realize that when one human being is pushed around and treated with lack of full respect, all parties tend to be demeaned in the process. Teaching is, if anything, a human enterprise. The quality of living of those engaged in it will markedly affect not only those who teach but all of the lives which they touch — the lives of their students and their parents, the families of the teachers themselves, the officials of the system, as well as other general community groups.

The effects on the lives of children living in school systems characterized by arbitrariness, unhealthy tension, and consequent low morale are many and serious and should be obvious. Perhaps the most degrading aspect is when, in such systems, the hollow form of democracy is presented to the young by practices which make them repeat the words of freedom while students and teachers live in constant and flagrant contradiction of the values of democracy. The founders of the Federation, even in the midst of World War I, sensed that the basic struggle between democracy and authoritarianism had to be decided at the level of daily living. This was a central theme in their early appeals to teachers and has continued as such to this day. The whole pattern of many an American school has developed a healthier orientation as a result of the concentration of effort in this direction by the Federation.

As a teachers' organization the Federation naturally concerned itself with questions of educational policy — questions that had to do with the types of educational programs that should be offered and the methods that should be used in promoting desirable growth of students. This was an area of heated controversy where honest differences of opinion existed. The Federation never attempted to impose a uniform philosophy and method of education on its members, but it did use its allegiance to the democratic values as a frame of reference for guiding whatever positions on educational policy which it took.

We were and are a multi-group society in an age of transition. Advances in numerous fields of inquiry constantly were bringing forth results which often had disputed import for the work of teachers and the schools. It was a period of examination, change, and critical debate. Through all of the argumentation one clear fact emerged — the great American experiment of providing available and appropriate education for all of the people was making steady and even remarkable progress. A review of the Federation's record reveals one constant concern and emphasis — that those engaged in the educational enterprise never lose sight of the central fact that the children and youth, all of them, be treated as the end for whose welfare the systems were established — and that each child be treated as having equal worth.

With these principles in mind it is clear that the Federation could not favor proposals of narrow vocationalism for some, while a limited few were gaining a liberal cultural education as preparation for leadership. The Federation never attempted to elaborate the specifics of a proper formula for the relationship between liberal and vocational education, but it did insist on the importance of both for all of the children of a democratic people. It was alert to oppose proposals which would deny experiences necessary for the full development of the person and citizen. It could do this without the authoritarian imposition of any particular theory of curriculum or methodology. The teachers and administrators of each educational unit, in cooperation with the community, were to decide on the approach appropriate for it.

The Federation did maintain that each youth had the right to a realistic understanding of the society in which he lived — this included a consideration of its strengths and weaknesses, and a searching examination of the problems and value choices with which it was confronted. This would be possible only if teachers and students could be free, responsible to take under consideration a study of the controversial issues of the times, and if the schools were free from attempts of powerful pressure groups to censor or distort.

Full equality of educational opportunity still does not exist, and the Federation has consistently backed proposals to attain this end.

The road ahead. The years covering the life of the Federation have been years involving rapid and profound changes in patterns of life for the American people. We stand at mid-century on the threshold of one of the most decisive periods in man's history. The course of events will be determined to a large degree by the policies chosen and followed by the American people.

Clearly, much will be demanded of American education as the people of the United States assume their inescapable role on the stage of world history. The teachers in our schools will have the vitally important tasks of helping to build healthy personalities motivated by generous and humane values, of cultivating habits of critical intelligence, and of developing the many skills needed in a highly complex, industrial culture. The challenge to the American people to expand and improve the quality of education for their children has been tremendous in these years. Real progress has been made in constructing buildings and providing equipment, and in developing improved programs for the education of teachers. But there are still notable gaps and inequalities in the provision of educational services. Much remains to be done.

The AFT must continue to assume a double responsibility: first to safeguard the welfare of the teacher in matters relating to salary, pension, conditions of tenure, and above all academic freedom; and secondly, to fight for a fair and comprehensive educational program for the children, the young people and the adults of the community.

The problems confronting our colleges are serious. In the next few years unprecedented numbers of students will come knocking at the doors of universities and colleges which are already full. What plans are being made to deal with these young people? The nation should not drift into a compromise solution of this problem. Already it is suggested in some quarters, that a solution lies in restriction of entry to colleges. This is justified on the grounds that universities should concentrate their resources on developing an intellectual elite by excluding the high school student of only average ability and attainment. If society wishes to ensure that all students who want and can benefit by a university education have the opportunity to do so how will the necessary expansion in institutions of higher learning be financed? Will tax-supported universities and accredited private colleges be granted tax funds based on their enrollments for needed buildings and services? Will there be a liberal system of loans and scholarships to enable qualified students to attend colleges regardless of their families' economic status? These questions should be faced immediately so that poorly planned emergency measures may be avoided through the adoption of well considered long range programs.

Civic minded teachers in our public schools as well as in our universities recognize the continuing importance of making adequate provisions for adult education in cooperation with lay organizations. Vital extension programs are a no less essential part of the responsibility of higher education than research activities or courses leading to degrees. Local public school systems, too, can play an increasingly important role in providing services for adults.

The Supreme Court ruling of 1955 implementing the 1954 decision outlawing racial segregation in the public schools places primary responsibility for hastening the process of integration on local and state school authorities. Members of the AFT in the North as well as in the South must with all other citizens accept their share of the responsibility for making the court ruling a reality.

Finally, attention will have to be given to the central issue — the survival of democracy itself. The potentialities for mass human enslavement, to a thorough and subtle extent never yet realized, are possibilities we must never lose sight of among others. George Orwell in 1984 and Aldous Huxley in Brave New World have sounded the warning. Our generation is faced with the challenge of learning to live with entirely new kinds of power and knowledge which are bound to result in the most profound economic, social, and political changes.

In the period now opening, it is clear that nothing less than the survival of democratic values in human affairs is the thing ultimately at stake. Teachers can play an important role if they recognize the importance of joining with democratic organized labor and of gaining the cooperation of enlightened elements of the middle class and other groups. The fate of democracy may be largely determined by the extent to which organized labor, farm groups and white collar middle class groups can be united in a common national movement. The kind of society we seek must be a vital and efficient democracy based on the principle of free and active participation of all men rather than one in which controlling power is permitted to center in the hands of a small economically powerful minority. Seen in this light, the work of the American Federation of Teachers has barely begun.

SECTION **3. Professional ethics**

One of the most socially significant features of professionalization is the development of the concept of *professional ethics*. Our conception of what constitutes an ethical teacher must be a serious and mature one. A simple conception of the ethical person is that he is any one who " lives by the rules." Important as " living by the rules " is, the truly ethical person is always more than this; he is a person who acts reflectively, who recognizes the complexity of human situations. In the words of Robert M. MacIver, in the first of the selections which follow, " Ethics cannot be summed up in a series of inviolate rules or commandments which can be applied everywhere and always without regard to circumstances, thought of consequences, or comprehension of the ends to be attained . . . The rules may clash with one another, and then the only way out is to look for guidance to the ideal." The truly ethical teacher, consequently, is one who is capable of using the " rules " reflectively in reaching ethical decisions in complex situations.

The ethical person is always characterized by certain moral traits. In the first place, such a person is *morally sensitive;* that is, he is aware of those situations in which the interests of others are implicated. He is, in particular, aware of the situations in which the interests of wider communities are involved. He is concerned with the general good and not only his own private good or the good of those closely associated with him. In the

second place, the ethical person is *morally intelligent;* he looks to the wide range of consequences of his actions and to the various alternatives which are available to him. He is, as we say, concerned with predicting and foreseeing probable consequences. In the third place, such a person is *morally courageous;* he is willing to stand up for what he believes to be right even at the expense of personal sacrifice. A teacher characterized by these traits, we might say, is the truly ethical teacher. But even these traits do not gainsay the extreme importance of codes of professional ethics. Such codes attempt to define the general good in terms of the specific requirements of professional functions. They do not, of course, eliminate the necessity for ethical judgment on the part of the teacher, but they do tend to make that judgment better informed than it otherwise might be.

In general, codes of professional ethics serve the interests of the public, the profession, and the individual teacher. A code of ethics serves the *public* in many ways. A professional code that is enforced assures the public that its interests and the general interest will not be sacrificed for the private interest of the professional practitioner. It further helps the public define what it may legitimately expect from the professional members who would serve them. Such a code is likewise of great benefit to the *profession*. It provides a commonly accepted base of operations upon which cooperative action can be predicated. It helps crystallize common ideals or aims toward which the profession is striving. It helps induct new members into the expectations of the profession. It provides a basis for the elimination of the unscrupulous or unethical practitioner. But the code of ethics is of equally great benefit to the *conscientious teacher* himself. It increases his moral sensitivity by alerting him to many of the situations in which the welfare of others is involved. It increases his moral intelligence by broadening the base of his own experience, by making available to him the accumulated experience of the professional group, and by alerting him to the expectations of others involved. Finally, it provides him with a moral foundation which is so essential if one is to demonstrate the quality of courage often called for.

The selections which follow go far toward explaining the nature and importance of the Code of Ethics to the teaching profession. In the first selection, Robert M. MacIver, a noted sociologist, describes the relation of such ethical codes to the public welfare. In the second selection, Cyrus C. Perry, a legal counsel for the National Education Association, discusses the particular place of professional ethics in the teaching profession. The Code of Ethics of the National Education Association, the generally accepted code of ethics of the teaching profession, and illustrative opinions of the NEA Committee on Professional Ethics based on this code, constitute the final selection. Familiarity with this code, and the rich resources it offers in directing one's professional endeavors, is indispensable to the professional teacher.

ROBERT M. MACIVER
Professional ethics and the public welfare

The spirit and method of the craft, banished from industry, finds a more permanent home in the professions. Here still prevail the long apprenticeship, the distinctive training, the small-scale unit of employment and the intrinsic — as distinct from the economic — interest alike in the process and the product of the work. The sweep of economic evolution seems at first sight to have passed the professions by. The doctor, the lawyer, the architect, the minister of religion, remain individual practitioners, or at most enter into partnerships of two or three members. Specialization takes place, but in a different way, for the specialist in the professions does not yield his autonomy. He offers his specialism directly to the public, and only indirectly to his profession. But this very autonomy is the condition under which the social process brings about another and no less significant integration. The limited " corporations " of the business world being thus ruled out, the whole profession assumes something of the aspect of a corporation. It supplements the advantage or the necessity of the small-scale, often the one-man, unit by concerted action to remove its " natural " disadvantage, that free play of uncontrolled individualism which undermines all essential standards. It achieves an integration not of form but of spirit. Of this spirit nothing is more significant than the ethical code which it creates.

Robert M. MacIver, " The Social Significance of Professional Ethics," *The Annals of the American Academy of Political and Social Science*, 297:118–124, January, 1955. Reprinted by permission of the American Academy of Political and Social Science.

There is in this respect a marked contrast between the world of business and that of the professions. It cannot be said that business has yet attained a specific code of ethics, resting on considerations broader than the sense of self-interest and supplementing the minimal requirements of the law. Such a code may be in the making, but it has not yet established itself, and there are formidable difficulties to be overcome. When we speak of business ethics, we generally mean the principles of fair play and honorable dealing which men *should* observe in business. Sharp dealing, "unfair" competition, the exaction of the pound of flesh, may be reprobated and by the decent majority condemned, but behind such an attitude there is no definite code which businessmen reinforce by their collective sense of its necessity and by their deliberate adoption of it as expressly binding upon themselves. There is no general brotherhood of businessmen from which the offender against these sentiments, who does not at the same time overtly offend against the law of the land, is extruded as unworthy of an honorable calling. There is no effective criticism which sets up a broader standard of judgment than mere success.

If we inquire why this distinction should hold between business and professional standards the social significance of the latter is set in a clearer light. It is not that business, unlike medicine or law for example, lacks those special conditions which call for a code of its own. Take, on the one hand, the matter of competitive methods. It is a vital concern of business, leading to numerous agreements of all sorts, but these are mere *ad hoc* agreements of a particular nature, not as yet deductions from a fully established principle which business, as a self-conscious whole, deliberately and universally accepts. Take, on the other hand, such a problem as that of the duty of the employer to his workpeople. Is not this a subject most apt for the introduction of a special code defining the sense of responsibility involved in that relationship? But where is such a code to be found?

The ideal of service. Something more than a common technique and a common occupation is evidently needed in order that an ethical code shall result. We might apply here the significant and much misunderstood comparison which Rousseau drew between the "will of all" and the "general will." In business we have as yet only the "will of all," the activity of businessmen, each in pursuit of his own success, not overridden though doubtless tempered by the "general will," the activity which seeks first the common interest. The latter can be realized only when the ideal of service controls the ideal of profits. We do not mean that businessmen are in fact selfish while professional men are altruistic. We mean simply that the *ideal of the unity of service* which business renders is not yet explicitly recognized and proclaimed by itself. It is otherwise with the professions. They assume an obligation and an oath of service. " A profession," says the ethical code of the American Medical Association, " has for its prime object the service it can render to humanity; reward or financial gain should be a subordinate consideration," and again it proclaims that the principles laid down for the guidance of the profession " are primarily for the good of the public." Similar statements are contained in the codes of the other distinctively organized professions. " The profession," says the proposed code of the Canadian legal profession, " is a branch of the administration of justice and not a mere money-getting occupation." Such professions as teaching, the ministry, the civil service, and social work by their very nature imply like conceptions of responsibility. They imply that while the profession is of necessity a means of livelihood or of financial reward, the devoted service which it inspires is motivated by other considerations.

In business there is one particular difficulty retarding any like development of unity and responsibility. It may safely be said that so long as within the industrial world the cleavage of interest between capital and labor, employer and employee, retains its present character, business cannot assume the aspect of a profession. This internal strife reveals a fundamental conflict of acquisitive interests within the business world and not only stresses that interest in both parties to the struggle but makes it impossible for the intrinsic " professional " interest to prevail. The professions are in general saved from that confusion. Within the profession there is not, as a rule, the situation where one group habitually employs for gain another group whose function, economic interest, and social position are entirely distinct from its own. The professions have thus been better able to adjust the particular interests of their members to their common interest and so to attain a clearer sense of their relationship to the whole community.

Once that position is attained the problem of occupational conduct takes a new form. It was stated clearly long enough ago by Plato in the *Republic*. Each " art," he pointed out, has a special good or service. " Medicine, for example, gives us health; navigation, safety at sea, and so on. . . . Medicine is not the art — or profession — of receiving pay because a man takes fees while he is engaged in healing. . . . The pay is not derived by the several ' artists ' from their respective ' arts.' But the truth is, that while the ' art ' of medicine gives health, and the ' art ' of the builder builds a house, another ' art ' attends them which is the ' art ' of pay." The ethical problem of the profession, then, is to reconcile the two " arts," or, more generally, to fulfill as completely as possible the primary service for which it stands while securing the legitimate economic interest of its members. It is the attempt to effect this reconciliation, to find the due place of the intrinsic and of the extrinsic interest, which gives a profound social significance to professional codes of ethics.

Standards common, codes distinctive. The demarcation and integration of the profession is a necessary preliminary to the establishment of the code. Each profession becomes a functional group in a society whose tendency is to organize itself less and less in terms of territory or race or hereditary status, and more and more in terms of function. Each profession thus acquires its distinctive code. It is important to observe that what is distinctive is the code rather than the standard. The different codes of racial or national groups reveal variant ethical standards, but the different codes of professional groups represent rather the deliberate application of a generally accepted social standard to particular spheres of conduct. Medical ethics do not necessarily differ in quality or level from engineering ethics, nor the ethics of law or of statesmanship from those of architecture. The false old notion that there was for that most ancient and still most imperfectly defined profession of statesmanship a peculiar code which liberated it from the ordinary ethical standards has died very hard. In truth there could be no conflict of ethics and politics, for politics could justify itself only by applying to its own peculiar situations and needs the principles which belong equally to every sphere of life.

Ethics cannot be summed up in a series of inviolate rules or commandments which can be applied everywhere and always without regard to circumstances, thought of consequences, or comprehension of the ends to be attained. What is universal is the good in view, and ethical rules are but the generally approved ways of preserving it. The rules may clash with one another, and then the only way out is to look for guidance to the ideal. The physician may have to deceive his patient in order to save his life. The lawyer, the priest, and the physician may have to observe secrecy and keep confidences under conditions where it might be the layman's duty to divulge them, for the conception of the social welfare which should induce the one to speak out may equally in the peculiar professional relationship compel the other to silence. Every profession has its own problems of conduct, in the interpretation within its own province of the common principles of ethical conduct. The medical man to whom is entrusted, under conditions which usually admit of no appeal save to his own conscience, the safeguarding of the health of his patient, with due consideration for the health of the whole community, has to depend upon a special code applicable to that situation. So with the legal profession which, for example, has to provide professional service for all litigants, irrespective of the popularity or unpopularity of the cause. So with the architect, who has to determine his responsibility alike to the client, to the contractor, to the workmen, to the " quantity surveyor," and to the community. So with the university professor, who has to uphold the necessity of academic freedom against the pressure of prejudice and the domination of controlling interests which care less for truth than for their own success. So with the journalist, in his peculiarly difficult situation as the servant of a propagandist press. So with the engineer, the surveyor, the accountant, or the technician generally, who has to maintain standards of service and of efficiency against the bias of profit making. So with the manager, the secretary, or the officer of a corporation — for here business assumes most nearly the aspect of a profession — who has to reconcile the trust imposed on him by his employers with the duty he owes to himself and to those whose services he in turn controls. Out of such situations develop the written and the unwritten codes of professional ethics.

Responsibility to the wider community. We need not assume that these codes originate from altruistic motives, nor yet condemn them because they protect the interest of the profession itself as well as the various interests which it serves. To do so would be to misunderstand the nature of any code. An ethical code is something more than the prescription of the duty of an individual towards others; in that very act it prescribes their duty towards him and makes his welfare too its aim, refuting the false disassociation of the individual and the social. But the general ethical code prescribes simply the duties of the members of a community towards one another. What gives the professional code its peculiar significance is that it prescribes also the duties of the members of a whole group towards those outside the group. It is just here that in the past ethical theory and practice alike have shown the greatest weakness. The group code has narrowed the sense of responsibility by refusing to admit the application of its principles beyond the group. Thereby it has weakened its own logic and its sanction, most notably in the case of national groups, which have refused to apply or even to relate their internal codes to the international world. The attempt of professional groups to co-ordinate their responsibilities, relating at once the individual to the group and the group itself to the wider community, marks thus an important advance.

We must, however, admit that it is in this matter, in the relation of the profession *as a whole* to the community, that professional codes are still weakest and professional ethics least effectively developed. The service to the community they clearly envisage is the service rendered by individual members of the profession to members of the public. The possibility that there may still be an inclusive professional interest — generally but not always an economic one — that at significant points is not harmonized with the community interest is nowhere adequately recognized.

The problem of professional ethics, viewed as the task of co-ordinating responsibilities, of finding, as it were, a common center for the various circles of interest, wider and narrower, is full of difficulty and far from being completely solved. The magnitude and the social significance of this task appear if we analyze on the one hand the character of the professional interest and on the other the relation of that interest to the general welfare.

Character of the professional interest. The professional interest combines a number of elements. It includes what we may term the extrinsic interest, that devoted to the economic and social status, the reputation, authority, success, and emoluments attaching to the profession as a body. It includes also the technical interest directed to the art and craft of the profession, to the maintenance and improvement of its standards of efficiency, to the quest for new and better methods and processes, and to the definition and promotion of the training considered requisite for the practice of the profession. It may also include a third interest which can be classed as cultural.

To illustrate, in the profession of teaching the technical interest in the system of imparting knowledge is one thing, and the cultural interest in the knowledge imparted quite another. Even more obvious is the case of the minister of religion, whose technique of ministration is as a rule very simple and whose main interest lies in the significance of the doctrine. The distinction is clear also in the spheres of the sciences and of the fine arts where the interest in truth or beauty may be discerned from the interest in the modes of investigation or of expression. In other professions it may be harder to identify the cultural as distinct from the technical interest, but if we interpret the term " culture " widely enough to include, for example, such objects as health and the beauty of workmanship, it may be maintained that the cultural interest belongs to every profession and is in fact one of the criteria by which to determine whether or not a given occupation is to be classed as a profession.

Now these three strands of interest are usually interwoven in the general professional interest, but sometimes they are separated and subject to the pull of opposite forces. Thus while the technical and economic interests usually go together and while, for example, the maintenance of standards usually works towards the economic advantage of the profession, these may be unfortunately disjoined. Better technique may at points be antagonistic to professional gain. The lawyer may, to take one instance, lose a source of profits by the introduction of a simpler and more efficient system of conveyancing. The architect, working on a percentage basis, may find his pecuniary advantage at variance with his professional duty to secure the best service for the least cost. Likewise, opposition may arise between the economic and the cultural interest. The teacher and the preacher may suffer loss from a whole-hearted devotion to the spirit of truth as they conceive it. The artist, the playwright, the author, may have to choose between the ideals of their art and the more lucrative devices of popularity. Finally, the technical and the cultural interest may work apart. Routine methods and processes may dominate the professional mind to the obscuration of the ends which they should serve. A notable statement of this opposition is given in the valuable investigation into professional organization in England which was published in two supplements of the *New Statesman*.[1] The investigation points to " the undisguised contempt in which both solicitors and barristers, notably those who have attained success in their profession and control its organization, hold, and have always held, not only all scholarship or academic learning of a professional kind, but also any theoretic or philosophical or scientific treatment of law."

Here, therefore, in the structure of the general professional interest we find a rich mine of ethical problems, still for the most part unworked but into which the growing ethical codes of the professions are commencing

[1] April 21 and 28, 1917.

to delve. A still greater wealth of the material for ethical reflection is revealed when we turn next to analyze the relation of the professional interest as a whole to that of the community.

Professional interest and general welfare. Every organized profession avows itself to be an association existing primarily to fulfill a definite service within the community. Some codes distinguish elaborately between the various types of obligation incumbent on the members of the profession. The lawyer, for example, is declared to have specific duties to his client, to the public, to the court or to the law, to his professional brethren, and to himself. It would occupy too much space to consider the interactions, harmonies, and potential conflicts of such various duties. Perhaps the least satisfactory reconciliation is that relating the interest of the client to the interest of the public, not merely in the consideration of the particular cases as they arise but still more in the adaptation of the service to the needs of the public as a whole as distinct from those of the individual clients. Thus the medical profession has incurred to many minds a serious liability, in spite of the devotion of its service to actual patients, by its failure for so long to apply the preventive side of medicine, in particular to suggest ways and means for the prevention of the needless loss of life and health and happiness caused by the general medical ignorance and helplessness of the poor.

In addition it must suffice to show that the conception of communal service is apt to be obscured alike by the general and by the specific bias of the profession. It is to the general bias that we should attribute such attempts to maintain a vested interest as may be found in the undue restriction of entrants to the profession — undue when determined by such professionally irrelevant considerations as high fees and expensive licenses; in the resistance to specialization, whether of tasks or of men, the former corresponding to the resistance to " dilution " in the trade union field; in the insistence on a too narrow orthodoxy, which would debar from professional practice men trained in a different school; in the unnecessary multiplication of tasks, of which a flagrant example is the English severance of barrister and solicitor. Another aspect of the general bias is found in the shuffling of responsibility under the cloak of the code. This is most marked in the public services, particularly the civil service and the army and navy — and incidentally it may be noted that the problem of professional ethics is aggravated when the profession as a whole is in the employ of the state. " An official," says Émile Faguet in one of his ruthless criticisms of officialdom,[2] " is a man whose first and almost only duty is to have no will of his own."

Danger of specific group bias. This last case brings us near to what we have called the specific bias of the profession. Each profession has a limited field, a special environment, a group psychology. Each profession tends to

---

[2] *The Dread of Responsibility* (New York: G. P. Putnam's Sons, 1914).

leave its distinctive stamp upon a man, so that it is easier in general to distinguish, say, the doctor and the priest, the teacher and the judge, the writer and the man of science, than it is to discern, outside their work, the electrician from the railwayman or the plumber from the machinist. The group environment creates a group bias. The man of law develops his respect for property at the risk of his respect for personal rights. The teacher is apt to make his teaching an overnarrow discipline. The priest is apt to underestimate the costs of the maintenance of sanctity. The diplomat may overvalue good form and neglect the penalty of exclusiveness. The civil servant may make a fetish of the principle of seniority, and the soldier may interpret morality as mere *esprit de corps*.

All this, however, is merely to say that group ethics will not by themselves suffice for the guidance of the group unless they are always related to the ethical standards of the whole community. This fact has a bearing on the question of the limits of professional self-government, though we cannot discuss that here. Professional group codes are, as a matter of fact, never isolated, and thus they are saved from the narrowness and egotism characteristic of racial group ethics. Their dangers are far more easily controlled, and their services to society, the motive underlying all codes, vastly outweigh what risks they bring. They provide a support for ethical conduct less diffused than that inspired by nationality, less exclusive than that derived from the sense of class, and less instinctive than that begotten of the family. As they grow they witness to the differentiation of community. Their growth is part of the movement by which the fulfillment of function is substituted as a social force for the tradition of birth or race, by which the activity of service supersedes the passivity of station. For all their present imperfections these codes breathe the inspiration of service instead of the inspiration of mere myth or memory. As traditional and authoritative ethics weaken in the social process, the ethics formulated in the light of function bring to the general standard of the community a continuous and creative reinforcement.

CYRUS C. PERRY
A code of ethics for educators

Two characteristics differentiate the profession of the public school teacher [1] from most other professions: the setting in which he practices and the nature of his clientele. These characteristics have affected the development and application of ethical standards in the teaching profession.

From Cyrus C. Perry, " A Code of Ethics for Public School Teachers," *The Annals of the American Academy of Political and Social Science*, 297:76–82, January, 1955. Reprinted by permission of the American Academy of Political and Social Science.

[1] The term " teacher " is used herein to mean instructional, administrative, and supervisory personnel of all types.

Unlike members of professions who practice largely as individuals and under private auspices, public school teachers practice in an institutional setting, as public employees with a common employer. As such, they are subject to supervision and direction which constitute restraints on unethical conduct not present in the case of a private practitioner. Because they are engaged in a governmental, tax-supported enterprise, the public has a direct interest in their professional standards. Probably no public service generates more interest in a community than its school system; the extent to which a community will adequately support its schools may depend upon its regard for the quality, character, and professional conduct of the teaching personnel. An adverse public judgment against a few teachers can work injury to the majority, and this in turn results in a disservice to the children.

Public school teachers, to a greater degree than private practitioners, have direct and varying ethical obligations to a multiple clientele. These obligations extend not only to the children with whom they deal but to the parents, the employing school board, and the community as a whole. In addition, as part of a common enterprise, their direct day-to-day contacts with colleagues present unique problems in professional relationships.

Early developments. Most teachers today recognize the desirability of codes of ethics applicable to their professional relationships. They are aware that codes serve as a guide in applying their particular body of professional knowledge. Until late in the nineteenth century primary emphasis in relation to ethics was placed upon a teacher's personal conduct, habits, and religious convictions. The proceedings of the early meetings of the National Education Association show concern for such standards primarily as related to the character of the teacher as a person and his ability to instruct pupils in moral and ethical principles.

In the latter half of the nineteenth century, there began to develop an awareness of the broader professional aspects of ethics. This came about partly because of the expansion of public education and the development of professional procedures of instruction and school administration. In time this broader view resulted in the formulation and adoption of codes by various teachers associations, the first being the Georgia State Teachers Association in 1896. . . .

Observance and enforcement. While various programs are under way at the national, state, and local levels to encourage observance of codes of ethics, there has been no concerted effort toward enforcement through disciplinary action. Since the adoption of the NEA Code in 1929, only one member has been removed for violating its provisions. It is not known to what extent the various state and local associations have enforced their codes through disciplinary proceedings, but it is highly unlikely that more than a few have taken such action.

The absence of a record of disciplinary action is not a serious reflection on the status of ethical practices in the profession. Undoubtedly the overwhelming number of public school teachers are fulfilling their professional obligations apart from formal code requirements. The profession is made up largely of people dedicated to their work who, because of their character and training, can be relied upon to adhere without coercion to selfimposed standards compatible with good ethical practices.

There are, of course, some teachers who fail to adhere to accepted standards. However, in connection with its program of rendering interpretative opinions, the NEA Committee on Professional Ethics has found that a substantial number of alleged violations are due to thoughtless action or to lack of knowledge of accepted professional practices. Thus an important function of the NEA Committee is education in these areas through publication of opinions construing the Code.

Leaders in the profession generally agree that national, state, and local associations look forward to the time when disciplinary action will be taken against those members whose conduct reflects adversely on the public schools. The program of the NEA Committee on Professional Ethics is designed in part to this end. It is believed that the current study program and the building up by the Committee of a body of opinions construing the Code are desirable first steps. However, the primary consideration in developing these programs on ethics is neither disciplinary action nor promotion of the teacher's individual welfare. Rather it is professional growth.

Codes of ethics are points of reference for individual teachers in developing their own standards. They also are guides to the profession in seeking to achieve its ideals of professional service. As a code is studied, analyzed, and discussed by individual teachers and groups, its implications become increasingly understood and its application to the practice of teaching raises standards in the profession generally and, in turn, the level of service to the community.

NATIONAL EDUCATION ASSOCIATION
The code of ethics of the NEA

PREAMBLE

We, the members of the National Education Association of the United States, hold these truths to be self-evident —

— that the primary purpose of education in the United States is to develop citizens who will safeguard, strengthen, and improve the democracy obtained through a representative government;

— that the achievement of effective democracy in all aspects of American life and the maintenance of our national ideals depend upon mak-

Reprinted from *Opinions of the Committee on Professional Ethics*, National Education Association, 1958, pp. 69–76.

ing acceptable educational opportunities available to all;

— that the quality of education reflects the ideals, motives, preparation, and conduct of the members of the teaching profession;

— that whoever chooses teaching as a career assumes the obligation to conduct himself in accordance with the ideals of the profession.

As a guide for the teaching profession, the members of the National Education Association have adopted this code of professional ethics. Since all teachers should be members of a united profession, the basic principles herein enumerated apply to all persons engaged in the professional aspects of education — elementary, secondary, and collegiate.

Opinions 2, 10. The term teacher as used in the Code includes school administrators.

Opinion 4. The Code has no application to members of boards of education.

Opinion 14. The official actions of a local association are the collective actions of its membership and, therefore, a local association is bound by the pertinent provisions of the Code.

PRINCIPLE I: The primary obligation of the teaching profession is to guide children, youth, and adults in the pursuit of knowledge and skills, to prepare them in the ways of democracy, and to help them to become happy, useful, self-supporting citizens. The ultimate strength of the nation lies in the social responsibility, economic competence, and moral strength of the individual American.

In fulfilling the obligations of this first principle the teacher will —

1. Deal justly and impartially with students regardless of their physical, mental, emotional, political, economic, social, racial, or religious characteristics.

2. Recognize the differences among students and seek to meet their individual needs.

3. Encourage students to formulate and work for high individual goals in the development of their physical, intellectual, creative, and spiritual endowments.

4. Aid students to develop an understanding and appreciation not only of the opportunities and benefits of American democracy but also of their obligations to it.

5. Respect the right of every student to have confidential information about himself withheld except when its release is to authorized agencies or is required by law.

6. Accept no remuneration for tutoring except in accordance with approved policies of the governing board.

Opinion 6. Tutoring for compensation, including one's own students, is proper if in accordance with policies of the board of education. In the ab-

sence of board policies, local associations should take the initiative in their formulation.

Opinion 13. *It is improper for a teacher to make remarks in public reflecting on a child's abilities and family background. However, a teacher has the right and often the duty to confer in confidence with colleagues or authorized agencies regarding a child's problems in conduct and adjustment.*

Opinion 24. *It is improper to reveal confidential information about the family background of a student who is causing difficulty in the classroom, even though the motive is to secure the cooperation of fellow students during the period of the child's adjustment.*

Opinion 27. *A director of the school band may properly give private lessons to members of the band and to students in his music classes, provided the arrangements conform to policies of the schoolboard.*

Opinion 28. *It is improper for a teacher to reveal confidential information to parents about the disabilities of children in his class.*

Opinion 37. *It is improper for a teacher deliberately to assign a grade that reflects factors irrelevant to the performance or progress of the student.*

PRINCIPLE II: The members of the teaching profession share with parents the task of shaping each student's purposes and acts toward socially acceptable ends. The effectiveness of many methods of teaching is dependent upon cooperative relationships with the home.

In fulfilling the obligations of this second principle the teacher will —

1. Respect the basic responsibility of parents for their children.
2. Seek to establish friendly and cooperative relationships with the home.
3. Help to increase the student's confidence in his own home and avoid disparaging remarks which might undermine that confidence.
4. Provide parents with information that will serve the best interests of their children, and be discreet with information received from parents.
5. Keep parents informed about the progress of their children as interpreted in terms of the purposes of the school.

Opinion 8. *The limits within which the relationship between parent and teacher is confidential have not in all respects been clearly defined by the profession.*

Opinion 13. *It is improper for a teacher to make remarks in public reflecting on a child's abilities and family background. However, a teacher has the right and often the duty to confer in confidence with colleagues or authorized agencies regarding a child's problems in conduct and adjustment.*

Opinion 24. *It is improper to reveal confidential information about the family background of a student who is causing difficulty in the classroom, even though the motive is to secure the cooperation of fellow students during the period of the child's adjustment.*

Opinion 31. *It is improper for a teacher in a report to parents to give a false impression as to a child's general adjustment in the classroom.*

Opinion 37. *It is improper for a teacher deliberately to assign a grade that reflects factors irrelevant to the performance or progress of the student.*

PRINCIPLE III: The teaching profession occupies a position of public trust involving not only the individual teacher's personal conduct, but also the interaction of the school and the community. Education is most effective when these many relationships operate in a friendly, cooperative, and constructive manner.

In fulfilling the obligations of this third principle the teacher will —

1. Adhere to any reasonable pattern of behavior accepted by the community for professional persons.

2. Perform the duties of citizenship, and participate in community activities with due consideration for his obligations to his students, his family, and himself.

3. Discuss controversial issues from an objective point of view, thereby keeping his class free from partisan opinions.

4. Recognize that the public schools belong to the people of the community, encourage lay participation in shaping the purposes of the school, and strive to keep the public informed of the educational program which is being provided.

5. Respect the community in which he is employed and be loyal to the school system, community, state, and nation.

6. Work to improve education in the community and to strengthen the community's moral, spiritual, and intellectual life.

Opinion 19. *There is no provision of the Code which governs the selection and use by a teacher of instructional materials. Good practice permits comparison of branded products, but not recommendation by a teacher of a particular brand.*

Opinion 21. *An offer by a commercial organization to pay the cost of a local association banquet on condition that it also accept as main speaker a person of the donor's selection may properly be accepted.*

Opinion 26. *Teachers may properly urge friends and acquaintances to support a school bond issue and candidates for a schoolboard who favor its passage.*

Opinion 29. *There is no provision of the Code which governs the selection and use by a teacher of instructional materials. Good practice requires that commercially sponsored materials be selected on a basis of their instructional value and that students be protected from exploitation by any special interest group.*

Opinion 30. *A teacher may properly identify and express his own point of view in the classroom, but in doing so assumes certain correlative responsibilities.*

Opinion 32. *It is improper for teachers to distribute campaign literature supporting individual candidates in a schoolboard election on school property and on school time.*

Opinion 33. *A teacher, in the exercise of her professional judgment, must decide for herself the kind and extent of her community activities.*

PRINCIPLE IV: The members of the teaching profession have inescapable obligations with respect to employment. These obligations are nearly always shared employer-employee responsibilities based upon mutual respect and good faith.

In fulfilling the obligations of this fourth principle the teacher will —

1. Conduct professional business through the proper channels.

2. Refrain from discussing confidential and official information with unauthorized persons.

3. Apply for employment on the basis of competence only, and avoid asking for a specific position known to be filled by another teacher.

4. Seek employment in a professional manner, avoiding such practices as the indiscriminate distribution of applications.

5. Refuse to accept a position when the vacancy has been created through unprofessional activity or pending controversy over professional policy or the application of unjust personnel practices and procedures.

6. Adhere to the conditions of a contract until service thereunder has been performed, the contract has been terminated by mutual consent, or the contract has otherwise been legally terminated.

7. Give and expect due notice before a change of position is to be made.

8. Be fair in all recommendations that are given concerning the work of other teachers.

9. Accept no compensation from producers of instructional supplies when one's recommendations affect the local purchase or use of such teaching aids.

10. Engage in no gainful employment, outside of his contract, where the employment affects adversely his professional status or impairs his standing with students, associates, and the community.

11. Cooperate in the development of school policies and assume one's professional obligations thereby incurred.

12. Accept one's obligation to the employing board for maintaining a professional level of service.

Opinion 1. *It is improper to seek employment by the indiscriminate circulation of mimeographed applications to schoolboards. (See Principle IV, Section 4, 1952 Code.)*

Opinion 3. *Solicitation and sale of commercial products to professional associates is looked upon with disfavor by the profession under certain circumstances. (See Principle IV, Section 10, 1952 Code.)* [1]

Opinion 4. *It is improper to accept a position made vacant by the application of unjust personnel practices and procedures.*

---

[1] This opinion was based on the 1929 Code and issued prior to the adoption of the present Code of Ethics in June 1952. The specific provisions of the 1929 Code involved are quoted in the opinion itself.

Opinion 5. The operation of a private teacher-placement agency in competition with a placement office operated by the university which employs him is inconsistent with a faculty member's obligations to the university and to his students.

Opinion 7. It is improper for teachers to consult the schoolboard regarding the dismissal of a professional associate without first presenting their views to the appropriate administrative authorities.

Opinion 9. While the right to augment teaching income by outside employment is recognized under the Code, solicitation by a teacher of parents of children in his class to purchase encyclopedias is improper.

Opinion 10. An administrator should consult with a teacher about parents' complaints before taking administrative action. He is not required to discuss parents' complaints with a teacher where no administrative action is contemplated.

Opinion 11. While there is necessarily a wide margin for individual judgment in the formulation of references, it is improper for an administrator to withhold in a reference information about unresolved, current difficulties which affect a teacher's competence.

Opinion 12. A teacher may properly resign from his position after an administrator has imposed material modifications in a contract. All the details of a teacher's duties cannot be incorporated in a contract and reasonable adjustments in teaching assignments are often necessary and desirable.

Opinion 14. A local association may properly express its views to the press on the action by a board of education against a professional colleague following rejection of its appeals by appropriate school authorities.

Opinion 15. If a teacher has entered into a contract with one school district, it is improper for him to initiate or continue negotiations for a contract with another school district without the consent of the district to which he is obligated.

Opinion 16. It is improper for a superintendent to recommend a transfer because of complaints of parents without notice to and prior consultation with the teacher and an opportunity for him to state his side of the case.

Opinion 17. If a teacher has conducted oral negotiations with a school district but has made no final commitment, he may properly conduct negotiations and accept a contract with another school district.

Opinion 18. While the right to augment teaching income is recognized under the Code, solicitation by a teacher of parents of children in his class to purchase musical instruments at discount prices is improper.

Opinion 23. An administrator may properly withhold in a letter of reference information about past difficulties which have been resolved and which do not affect a teacher's competence.

Opinion 25. It is improper for an administrator to imply in a letter of reference that he has some reservation about a teacher's competence if the teacher's record has been outstanding.

Opinion 28. It is improper for a teacher to use parents of his students as a leverage for securing an increase in salary.

Opinion 34. *It is improper for a teacher to resign to accept a new position after his contract has been automatically renewed and the board of education has refused to release him.*

Opinion 35. *In an association meeting, a teacher may properly raise a question of policy affecting all teachers alike with the official responsible for that policy.*

PRINCIPLE V: The teaching profession is distinguished from many other occupations by the uniqueness and quality of the professional relationships among all teachers. Community support and respect are influenced by the standards of teachers and their attitudes toward teaching and other teachers.

In fulfilling the obligations of this fifth principle the teacher will —

1. Deal with other members of the profession in the same manner as he himself wishes to be treated.

2. Stand by other teachers who have acted on his behalf and at his request.

3. Speak constructively of other teachers, but report honestly to responsible persons in matters involving the welfare of students, the school system, and the profession.

4. Maintain active membership in professional organizations and, through participation, strive to attain the objectives that justify such organized groups.

5. Seek to make professional growth continuous by such procedures as study, research, travel, conferences, and attendance at professional meetings.

6. Make the teaching profession so attractive in ideals and practices that sincere and able young people will want to enter it.

Opinion 2. *A teacher's refusal to cooperate in an investigation being conducted by a professional association is not contrary to the Code, but in the absence of a satisfactory explanation is a disservice to the profession. (See 1952 Code, Principle V, Section 3.)* [2]

Opinion 8. *It is not improper to report to appropriate school authorities unwarranted charges made by a parent against a professional associate.*

Opinion 11. *While there is necessarily a wide margin for individual judgment in the formulation of references, it is improper for an administrator to withhold in a reference information about unresolved, current difficulties which affect a teacher's competence.*

Opinion 20. *There is no provision in the Code which governs an administrator's use of an intercommunication system without the knowledge of the teacher, but such use can cause tension and resentment on the part of the teacher and is contrary to good personnel practices.*

---

[2] This opinion was based on the 1929 Code and issued prior to the adoption of the present Code of Ethics in June 1952. The specific provisions of the 1929 Code involved are quoted in the opinion itself.

Opinion 22. *A local association may properly report its loss of confidence in the integrity of a colleague to the school authorities provided professionally accepted procedures are followed and the report is made through proper channels.*

Opinion 23. *An administrator may properly withhold in a letter of reference information about past difficulties which have been resolved and which do not affect a teacher's competence.*

Opinion 25. *It is improper for an administrator to imply in a letter of reference that he has some reservation about a teacher's competence if the teacher's record has been outstanding.*

Opinion 36. *It is improper for a superintendent to give verbal assurance of a favorable recommendation and later issue an unfavorable recommendation. A superintendent may not properly refuse to provide a written statement of reasons for dismissal when requested in writing to do so by the persons dismissed.*

CHAPTER TWELVE BIBLIOGRAPHY

BEALE, HOWARD K., *Are American Teachers Free?* New York: Charles Scribner's Sons, 1936.

> Means of increasing freedom for the teacher are discussed in Chapter 22. The author feels that this could be best accomplished through the welding of teachers into a truly professional group. The history of professional teachers' organizations is described briefly.

COMMISSION ON TEACHER EDUCATION, *Teachers for Our Times.* Washington: American Council on Education, 1944.

> Chapter 4 is particularly pertinent. Contained within it is an analysis of some of the qualities needed by those who plan to become teachers, which include respect for personality, community-mindedness, rational behavior, skill in cooperation, increasing knowledge, skill in mediating knowledge, friendliness with children, understanding children, social understanding and behavior, good citizenship in school and society, skill in evaluation, and faith in the worth of teaching.

NATIONAL SOCIETY FOR THE STUDY OF EDUCATION, *Social Forces Influencing American Education.* Chicago: The Society, 1961.

> For a recent account of the purposes, organization, finances, leadership and effectiveness of teachers' organizations, see Chapter VIII by Lieberman entitled, "The Influence of Teachers' Organizations upon American Education."

WESLEY, EDGAR B., NEA: *The First Hundred Years.* New York: Harper & Brothers, 1957.

> Chapters 22 to 33 describe how the NEA built the professional aspects of teaching. Improvement of employment practices, salaries, and status are described. The last chapter describes the current National Education Association.

13

The Sociology of Teaching

The sociological analysis of the teacher and teaching is but one sub-part of the total field referred to as the *sociology of education*. The major parts of this field of study include (1) the relationships between the social institution of education and the other institutions of society, (2) the relationships between the community and the school, (3) the social structure within the school or school system, and (4) the effect of schooling on the behavior and personality of the participants. The preceding chapters of this book have been concerned to a considerable extent with the first of these parts. Among the topics pertaining to a study of the relationships between school and other social institutions are those of social class, social control and power structures, social change, and intercultural relations. This chapter is concerned with the remaining three parts of the sociology of education — with particular emphasis on the role of the *teacher* in community affairs, within the social framework of the school, and in interaction with the pupils.

The major importance of the sociology of education is not so much in the particular topics included in the study but in the *methodology* and *orientation* of the field. It is derived from its parent discipline of sociology. Its concern therefore is in the analysis of society so as to produce scientifically valid generalizations about social interaction. The area of education and educational matters merely is the focus of its investigations. Basically the same methods of investigation that the sociologist uses in the study of other areas of social life such as the church, the political power structure, small group interaction, and the like are also employed in the study of the educative process. A sociological frame of reference underlies the study.

The readings in this chapter deal mostly with what *is* and not with what *ought* to be. This, of course, is in keeping with the sociological point of view, which is more concerned with description and analysis than it is with prescribing normative judgments about society. Such a detached and objective point of view frequently enables the reader to get outside of himself, as it were, and view social phenomena without the distractions of personal bias or ego involvement. In presenting objective data about our social institutions the sociologist performs an exceedingly valuable service to the teacher. The professionally competent teacher is responsible for incorporating such scientific information into a consistent philosophy so as best to make the many normative judgments required of him.

SECTION 1. The teacher in the community

One of the most vexing problems facing the beginning teacher in any community is a determination of just what kind of a teacher's role is expected, tolerated, condoned, or condemned by the members of that community. Turning over in the teacher's mind may be questions such as these: Must I live in this local community or may I commute from a nearby place? Must I do all my shopping here or may I do some elsewhere? Which establishments will it be all right for me to frequent and which are considered " out of bounds " for teachers? Shall I make known or conceal my political preferences? What is the attitude of most of the parents toward " progressive " education? How much shall I allow these attitudes to influence what I do in the classroom?

The way in which individual teachers have responded to such questions has ranged from that of complete disregard for community expectations to an almost obsequious conformity to the prevailing pattern of local living. With periodic regularity one finds newspaper articles about a teacher in Community X who is being ousted from his position because of things he did in or out of the classroom that, while legal, go strongly against the role expectations that most members of the community have in regard to teachers. The initial reaction of most teachers, when they read of such occurrences in other places, is one of sympathetic concern and support for the teacher involved. Such concern often stems from a feeling of " I could very easily find myself in the same situation." Unfortunately, the issues in most such cases of dismissal are rarely clear-cut. There are frequently some complicating circumstances that basically amount to sharp differences in role perceptions and role expectations on the part of either the teacher, the administration, the school board, the parents — or all four.

On the other hand, there is disturbing evidence to indicate that many teachers are so fearful of doing anything that *may* bring displeasure that they abdicate certain roles to which they are legally and professionally entitled. A recent study by the National Education Association on the civic behavior of teachers reflects some distressing points of view that teachers have of their own civic rights and the

role that the community expects them to take in civic and political matters.[1] A representative sample of 5,602 teachers in the United States were asked their opinions about several types of civic-political activities. To the activity, " Serve as party precinct worker in pre-election activities," the responses were as follows:

Usually *do* this and think teachers *should*	3.6%
Usually *do not* do this but think teachers *should*	28.5%
Usually *do* this but think teachers *should not*	0.8%
Usually *do not* do this and think teachers *should not*	67.1%

A similar point of view was expressed in response to the activity, " In a presidential election, outside of school time, make speeches or give other services on behalf of teacher's candidate." Here a summary of the responses indicates that 23.5 per cent thought that teachers *should* do this, but 76.5 per cent thought that teachers *should not*. It would appear from these data that the efforts to prevent the denial of civic rights for teachers may well have to be supplemented by even greater efforts to prevent teachers from giving up those civic rights they now have. This study is even more alarming in view of the fact that these same teachers are supposed to develop attitudes and understanding that will prepare their pupils for *active* participation in civic affairs. Is this the kind of example to set? Presumably to counteract such a situation, the *NEA Journal* has inaugurated a regular monthly feature on the " teacher-politician." Each issue carries a picture and brief account of a teacher who is either actively engaged in politics or has been recently elected to public office.

In the following selection Jean D. Grambs deals with the wide range of

[1] " The Status of the American Public-School Teacher," *NEA Research Bulletin,* 35:1–63, February, 1957.

roles that a teacher may assume. They include roles both in the school and in the community. Note particularly the complexity of these roles and their frequent contradiction.

JEAN D. GRAMBS
The roles of the teacher

In this . . . [discussion] . . . effort will be made to identify those role-expectations of teachers held by students, parents, the community, and the school itself. Suggestions will be made relative to the extent to which the teacher's role perception produces conflict, low professional morale, and — what may be socially tragic — an institution that changes remarkably little over the decades.[1]

In analyzing the attributes desirable for candidates entering the teaching profession, a distinction has been made between "the teacher as a person and "the person as a teacher." [2] In the discussion here, we are primarily concerned with "the person as a teacher" and the way in which teaching determines how he will feel and act within the institutional framework of the public schools.

How does role behavior develop? What does the teacher do? What is the social function of teaching? When one lists all the possible roles of the teacher two main categories emerge. One category refers to the *teacher as director of learning*. This includes all those activities and concepts that are related to teaching as an *activity* or a *process*. The other category refers to the social function of teaching, the *teacher as mediator of the culture*. Under this category are included those roles that relate to the public nature of the teacher's job, the stake of society in teaching as an aspect of cultural continuity.[3]

Jean D. Grambs, "The Roles of the Teacher," Chapter 6 in Lindley J. Stiles (editor), *The Teacher's Role in American Society*. Fourteenth Yearbook of The John Dewey Society, 1957. Reprinted by permission of The John Dewey Society.

The writer wishes to acknowledge the interest and encouragement of the following colleagues who have discussed the original outline with her and in several instances have read and criticized the manuscript of this chapter: Lawrence G. Thomas, I. James Quillen, George Spindler, Joseph Axelrod, Arthur Foff, and Frederic Ferrien.

[1] There is not room here for an extended discussion of role definition. See for example: Willard Waller, *The Sociology of Teaching* (New York: Wiley & Sons, 1932), pp. 321–337; Ralph Linton, *The Cultural Background of Personality* (New York: Appleton-Century-Crofts, Inc., 1945); T. R. Sarbin, "Contributions to Role-Taking Theory, I & II," *Psychology Review*, 57:255–270 and 59:11–22. An interesting approach from clinical psychology; David C. McClelland, *Personality* (New York: The Dryden Press, 1951), pp. 289–332.

[2] L. G. Thomas, Stanford University, School of Education, mimeographed statement.

[3] See a similar division in W. B. Brookover, "The Relation of Social Factors to Teaching Ability," *Journal of Experimental Education*, 13, No. 4, June, 1945.

THE TEACHER AS DIRECTOR OF LEARNING

Any adult with a group of children acquires certain role relationships which are inherent in the situation itself: parent surrogate, source of authority, giver of affection and punishment, protector, or guide in unknown territory. The teacher, too, partakes of these generalized adult roles with respect to children, because the public school teacher is always older — the adult — in the classroom situation. But for the teacher as a teacher, there are certain more specific roles that the teaching process implies. These are considered below.[4]

1. *The teacher as judge of achievement*. One of the most pervasive elements in determining the relationship between teacher and pupil is the fact that the pupil is being judged by the teacher. Merely observing the differences in relationship and behavior between a child in a classroom situation and in a " Y " youth group sharpens the point. In the one circumstance, the child sees the adult as one who gives " A's " or " F's " and is therefore to be feared, hated, or loved, depending on the degree of success that the child can attain. In the " Y Club," on the other hand, the child views the adult primarily as a helper and adult friend.

The teacher evaluates performance, and by so doing helps to establish certain learning and behavior goals. The teacher who values obedience may tend to judge compliant students as " better," and may give them higher grades; another teacher may value the ability to argue logically; still another may value perfection in solving assigned problems, or neatness of written papers. Since there are few commonly accepted standards regarding what is to be valued and rewarded, each teacher must decide — and usually is unconscious of this process — as to which are valuable pupil achievements and which are not.

As students and parents gain insight into the role of the teacher as judge, recognize its fallibility and its power, one is not surprised to see frustration, contempt, fear, and anxiety influencing the relations of some students and parents to some teachers, as well as contentment, trust, and admiration where the teacher is a wise and beneficent judge.

2. *The teacher as a person who knows*. " Knowledge is power," said Francis Bacon. This is still a key phrase in the analysis of the role of the teacher. He stands as a gatekeeper.[5] He decides what information and skills are important and accordingly lets these selected items through to students. The knowledge that the teacher has of the community, of the children, of

---

[4] For other role categories and analyses see: Ruth Cunningham and others, *Understanding Group Behavior of Boys and Girls* (New York: Teachers College, Columbia University, 1951), pp. 141–152; Fritz Redl and William Wattenberg, *Mental Hygiene in Teaching* (New York: Harcourt, Brace and Company, 1951), pp. 235–260; Lucien B. Kinney, *Measure of a Good Teacher* (San Francisco, California Teacher's Ass'n, 1952).
[5] The concept of the " gatekeeper " function is well described in B. O. Smith, W. O. Stanley, and J. H. Shores, *Fundamentals of Curriculum Development* (Yonkers, New York: World Book Company, 1950), pp. 682–683.

the subject matter, is a vital factor in what is explored in the classroom. He selects from a vast body of material that which must be taught; he decides, also, a minimum which must be learned.

As students climb the academic ladder, their respect for the knowledge of teachers changes. The child in the primary grades views the teacher with awe and respect; the teacher knows so much! By the time the student reaches junior and senior high school he has seen that the teacher " knows " a subject field, but in the view of the student this same teacher may know woefully little about the " important " things in life. During the adolescent years academic knowledge may seem least useful. As the student proceeds to college his perspective shifts and he sees that both academic and practical knowledge can be equally important. Since most of the population does not go on to college, the citizen's view of the role of general academic knowledge is the one he took with him when he left high school — often unflattering.

3. *The teacher as one who keeps discipline.* All children expect an adult in their immediate vicinity to interfere when law and order are being violated. In the classroom the disciplinary functions of the teacher are more pervasive, and they differ in quality from those exercised by the ordinary adult with children. Behind the teacher are extensive legal and extra-legal powers. . . .

The institutionalizing of disciplinary techniques is a means of ensuring their nonpersonal quality. The discipline the teacher exercises is seen by him as a task performed for the sake of the student. If there is no discipline, students cannot learn. Therefore individuals must be controlled for their own sake.

Both the recipient and the source of disciplinary measures may develop extensive resentment of each other, out of which may come hostility and counter-attack. With a moderately skilled teacher and reasonably compliant students the conflict does not flare into the open. But it may be a source of tension even when overt hostilities are avoided. To live thus for six to eight hours a day for the working year, for a career life of twenty-five years, is bound to produce some compensatory behaviors. One observes added sharpness of manner, a cynical view of human nature — particularly in the young — and often a thinly disguised hatred of the teaching situation itself. These behaviors may result from the definition of the teacher's role as one who keeps discipline.

4. *The teacher as one who gives advice, receives confidences.* The child looks upon adults as potential helpers. Since the teacher is a constant element in the world of the child, the helper possibilities are ever present. This role has more overtones of the affectional relationship than any other.

When the teacher accepts the confidences of students, he enters the world of the young person and takes on the role of ally and protector.

As a receiver of confidences, the teacher then may find himself in opposition to parents, against whom many of the complaints of adolescents are lodged. He may also find himself in conflict with his roles as judge and disciplinarian. It is hard to assign a failing grade to a student whose intimate problems one has listened to sympathetically. The student receiving a failing grade may assume that the teacher is not *really* a friend and did not appreciate his problem. The result may be rejection of the teacher by the pupil. Teachers, to avoid such conflicts of roles, may attempt to keep a cold and impersonal barrier between themselves and their students.

The role of confidant is further complicated by factors of personal preference. The mores and values accepted implicitly by the teacher will make some students more sympathetic to him than others. Since he is not trained as a therapist or counselor, he will be able to listen objectively only to certain kinds of exploits and not others.

5. *The teacher as creator of a moral atmosphere.*[6] In the classroom the teacher identifies for the student what is right and wrong in the institutional context. As creator of a moral atmosphere, he makes it clear that cheating is wrong, that the use of obscene words is bad, or that flirting in class is in poor taste. The students expect the teacher to so identify certain acts. Many of the ideas of what is good or bad behavior are often institutional in the sense that they are external to the students and depend on institutional vigilance to be enforced. Likewise the teacher establishes what is good in terms of compliant behavior, defines " acceptable " demonstrations of initiative and " fair play." Finally the teacher establishes what is expected in interpersonal relationships. He establishes a hierarchy of groups of people.

Conflict in moral valuations may occur as a result of differences arising from social class learnings. Other conflicts between teacher concepts of " good " and " bad " groups, individuals, and behavior will derive from the philosophy of education held by a given teacher.

In recent years we have seen a tremendous expansion of the social life officially sponsored by the public school. As such activities multiply, the moral burden on the school personnel becomes greater. Teachers chaperone numerous dances, formal and informal, take students on ski trips, accompany groups for a week at the school camp, or act as sponsor for class and club parties. The etiquette of social situations, the permissible limits to juvenile exuberance, must sooner or later be established by the school authorities. It is easy to see why the community looks with special attention at the behavior of the teacher.

6. *The teacher as a member of an institution.*[7] Since we are here con-

[6] John L. Childs, *Education and Morals* (New York: Appleton-Century-Crofts, Inc., 1950); R. Bruce Raup, " The Moral Dimension in Education," *Educational Theory*, 1:35–40, May, 1951.

[7] B. O. Smith et al., *op. cit.*, pp. 635–640. Max R. Goodson and Gale E. Jensen, *Formal Organization in School Systems* (Minneapolis, Minnesota: Burgess Publishing Company, 1956). See for analysis of school as a social system and the dynamics of change in the institution.

cerned with the roles of the teacher in the *process* of teaching, we must recognize that the role of the teacher in the classroom is closely related to that he plays in the institution of which he is a part.

Each work type and work situation creates its own culture. The teacher finds his role peculiarly defined because of the nature of the school as an institution. The school establishes appropriate ways of acting on the job in terms of the other employees.

The educational process is unique as a work situation. Prior work experience does *not* fit a teacher for easy adjustment to the school work situation. The fact that there are lengthy and continuous discussions in the professional literature of education as to what constitutes a " democratic " administration-teacher relationship points to one of the contradictions inherent in the situation. Teachers, unlike other workers, do not have a well-developed sense of " the boss." Some teachers, however, do desire strong, often paternalistic, leadership from the administrators with whom they work. How can this expectation be reconciled with mature professional behavior?

The teacher's role behavior is in part determined by his position in the institutional hierarchy. One important functionary in this situation is the administrative personnel. The teacher looks to the administrator for direction. The expected relation between principal and teacher is that of one who gives orders and one who receives orders. Many teachers prefer a " strong " principal, finding it more satisfying to be told what to do than to participate in decision-making themselves. In addition, teachers consider the principal as part of the disciplinary structure of the school — one to be invoked when students defy the limited authority of the teacher.[8]

The principal's word is most powerful in the hiring and firing process. In the eyes of the teacher he is to be placated, cajoled, manipulated. The role of the teacher in relationship to the principal may undergo a change when tenure is achieved. Teachers with tenure sometimes behave as though they were trying to " get even " with administrators. The administrator has power; when the teacher has tenure he too has power — power to ignore an administrative request, to foment community criticism of the administrator, to organize cliques in the faculty who may effectively oppose administrative policies. Many administrators fear and resent older teachers whose power is reinforced by tenure, by length of service, and by outspokenness in faculty meetings. On the other hand, the principal will find that numerous teachers look upon him as a father-confessor, that he must perform a counseling and guidance function for the less mature, more dependent members of his staff.

A final word on the institutional role of the teacher: He is expected to

[8] An interesting observation on the necessity for a hierarchy of discipline authority is contained in Fritz Redl and David Wineman, *Controls from Within* (Glencoe, Illinois: The Free Press, 1953), pp. 214, 224.

be devoted to the traditions of the school, and a loyal supporter of " the way things are done at dear old Union High." School traditions are to be respected even when they go contrary to personal beliefs or good educational practice. In some systems loyalty to the school is of such importance that careers are ruined and jobs lost by seeming defalcation in devotion.

Summary. We have looked at the kind of things expected of the teacher in the *process of teaching.* The role expectations are varied and conflicting. While the teacher judges achievement, keeps discipline, establishes a moral atmosphere, at the same time he is confidant and guide, giver of advice and affection. He must have knowledge, and must know how to impart it to individuals of varying talent and interest. He has great power to promote or fail, to facilitate access to knowledge or to withhold it, to establish feelings of comradeship and acceptance, or competition and segregation based on race, intellect, finances, behavior. He is both weak and powerful in the elaborate hierarchy of the school.

These roles provide an almost bewildering assortment of possible behaviors to the teacher. Which shall he choose? How shall he choose? The *final* determinant of which of the classroom roles the teacher emphasizes and which he rejects depends on expectations of parents and the community.

THE TEACHER AS MEDIATOR OF THE CULTURE [9]

The roles of the teacher in this category come primarily from the social function of education. Each culture creates different characterizations of teachers.

The ways in which the community conceives of teachers determine to a large extent the roles he will play. The person who is identified as the " good " teacher may or may not actually be able to " teach." Administrators, guided by community opinion, may tend to select teachers on the basis of factors that have no demonstrable relationship to effective classroom instruction.[10] The teacher has, in years gone by, also experienced the cultural definition of the teacher, for as a student he developed a complicated set of attitudes and anticipations whenever he met or talked with his own teachers.

In the first section we looked at the teacher primarily from the viewpoint of the learner; now we are concerned with the view of the teacher taken by the larger community outside the school — the already schooled adults.

1. *The teacher as a member of the middle class.* The teacher is expected to demonstrate all the virtues of the middle class and avoid all of its sins. He must abide by middle-class standards of behaviors and economic beliefs.

He is considered " soft," clean, religious. Such middle-class virtues are

---

[9] See " The Freedom of the Public School Teacher " (Washington, D. C.: Research Division, National Education Association), Mimeographed, August, 1951.
[10] W. B. Brookover, *op. cit.*

closely associated with the teacher role. He is not thought of as aggressive physically, and socially does not become a competitor for community leadership. For the individual who views teaching as a pathway of upward mobility — as many do — it is essential that he disown himself from the symbols of his own class origin if it is other than middle-class.

2. *The teacher as a model for the young.* The continuous association of the teacher with young people impels the community to invoke the teacher as a standard setter. It is the wish of parents that teachers be adequate to this role. Parents actually have encouraged youngsters to use teachers as models rather than other adults. The teacher is the best and most available ally the parent has. At the same time the teacher in his role as confidant may find himself unable to maintain his neutrality and may side with the child *against* the parent; thus the parent can never be sure that the teacher will be a satisfactory surrogate for himself.

3. *The teacher as an idealist.* Because of better education and his special function as a model for the young the teacher is clearly one whose allegiance is to a better way of life than most people can live. He may be considered, therefore, not " practical." He understands theories, not reality. The role of the idealist is often negatively valued by the public. The American emphasis on material success, on being practical and hardheaded, does not provide much room for the teacher.

4. *The teacher as a pioneer in the world of ideas — the teacher as radical.* Closely related to the role of the idealist, and often scarcely distinguishable from it, is the role of the teacher as one-who-is-ahead-of-the-times.

The community thinks that the teacher may be tempted to consider new ways of doing things — revolutionary or radical. The rash of oaths for teachers in recent years is symptomatic of the fear of the teacher-as-radical.[11] The public is seeking some means of controlling the teacher, of keeping him within the bounds of conservative middle-class concepts and policies.

5. *The teacher as a person of " culture."* The teacher is frequently identified with the middle-class culture, particularly its less materialistic manifestations. One of these is an interest in art, music, literature. The teacher has been " abroad " in his education; he is cosmopolitan while the community is provincial. His interests are national and international while the average community participant is more concerned with local affairs.

As a person of " culture," he is also a cultured person. Such a role causes some to feel uneasy in the presence of teachers. As a person of " culture " he has an attractiveness especially to certain high school students. The students who like school are apt to enjoy talking about music, literature, or travel with this teacher. It is to him that they turn in seeking advice on where to go to college. On the other hand, this same evidence of " cul-

11 E. E. Reutter, *The School Administrator and Subversive Activities* (New York: Columbia University Press, 1951).

ture " may make it difficult for students without such interests to approach the teacher so identified.

There is also some ambivalence of the community toward the teacher as a person of " culture." He will be welcome in the community's " little symphony " and will be expected to stimulate boys and girls to take an interest in music and the arts; but this teacher will also be judged to be too " refined " for some circles.

6. *The teacher as participant in community affairs.* The teacher in the community is expected to be interested and helpful but not conspicuously out in front. The teacher belongs at the second layer of community life — taking minor leadership roles: teaching Sunday School; leading some youth group; contributing to charitable drives; belonging to lodges or service clubs; and supporting community-wide programs.

The teacher was once considered an important part of the community's activities and one who did not participate in them was severely criticized. Today's teacher may or may not participate. Often the teacher by his own training has an already well-developed concept of community service. Choosing to be a teacher may be one manifestation of a concept of service. Thus it is not unusual to see teachers seeking ways of becoming identified with the community and meeting community indifference or apathy.

The role as participant in community affairs is apt to be one in which the teacher wishes for more community recognition than he gets. It is less apt today to be a demand made by the community on a reluctant teacher. A *principal* or *superintendent* may move in the upper power circles of a community; the average teacher is expected to keep a more modest role.

7. *The teacher as stranger in the community.*[12] When young teachers start to hunt for a first job, they are often advised not to return to their own home town. Some of their own early teachers, still active there, may view the returning ex-student as a kid rather than a peer. Most teachers find their jobs in new communities.

It takes years of living in a new environment to feel at home in it. Often teachers do not stay long in a job, particularly the first one. The high turnover at the elementary grades means that most of these teachers leave the profession or the community after only a few years. Others who remain in the community develop their own circle of friends, usually among other teachers and individuals in allied professions or avocations. When finally they feel they can call the teaching community home they find that they are in a special part of that community — in it but not of it.

At one time the concern only of the select, " teacher " was duly entertained by the families of the local " 400." Today, in this era of mass education, the teacher is the jealous property of all. He therefore is the special concern of none.

---

[12] George Simmel, *The Sociology of George Simmel* trans. and edited by K. H. Wolff (Glencoe, Illinois: The Free Press, 1950), pp. 402–408.

The teacher, too, in a more profound sense, must be objective about the community. He must see it as both typical and unique; as a manifestation of the larger culture; and as a locality with problems and concerns of its own. As a student of community affairs for the purpose of guiding young people, the teacher's role as a stranger is a great aid; at the optimum, he behaves as the participant-observer of community processes.

8. *The teacher as the person en route.* For many teachers any given community is merely a way-point. For the men teachers, the young ones in particular, there is hope of moving up the professional ladder.

The route for many women in the educational institution is from maidenhood to marriage to home and out of the profession. The tremendous turnover of younger women teachers in the grades is one of the perennial problems of administrators. Since most of the women who enter education hope to be married, and since a good proportion of them succeed, those who remain several years either are constantly on the alert for a mate or are weighing the marriage potential of another position.

Only after a number of years does the unmarried woman teacher resign herself to her professional celibacy; often an unwilling prisoner of her job. The years of watchful waiting for a more appealing status than that of teacher leave their mark. The unmarried woman teacher comes only lately and reluctantly to accept her role in the community. She tends, even after hope for marriage is gone, to return to summer schools in far parts of the nation and to go on trips or " conducted tours " to foreign countries; [13] in the eyes of the community she is more cosmopolitan than before — in her own soul she is forever seeking a way out.

9. *The teacher as a public servant.* To whom does education belong? And then to whom does the educator belong?

One of the more controversial aspects of the teacher's role is how much control over his behavior, ideas, tenure, and technical skills should be exercised by the body politic. Of all the professions, that of the teacher is most carefully and continually under extensive and intensive public scrutiny.

In recent years with the tremendous pressure on school districts because of increased population and a building backlog, the people have been asked with monotonous regularity to vote more money for education. Thus the attention of the citizen is now continually directed towards the schools by the very nature of the present school crisis.

Happy to have a focus for both his frustrated citizenship and his personal anxieties, John Q. Public is invading the schools. He is visiting classrooms, attending school board meetings, noting the textbooks distributed to students. The teacher more than ever before is being reminded that education is a public trust and he is a servant of the public.

---

[13] How many times have we seen in the literature of travel abroad the mention of the two maiden school teachers as more or less stock characters?

This is not a particularly comfortable role. The public has many faces, many voices. To which shall the teacher respond? Can he be true to *his* concept of good teaching if this is a pattern repugnant to some power group in the community? Is the teacher or the community *right*?

Summary. The roles of the teacher as mediator of the culture are many and contradictory. The generalizations presented here must, of course, be modified in any given situation. Rural and urban emphasis will differ in terms of the expectations of teachers. Variations will exist in socio-economic class, community history, and the traditions of the school. The role behaviors defining the community's expectancies and attitudes are therefore subject to considerable individual interpretation. The factors in one situation will stress some role behaviors and be apathetic to others. But since teachers move from community to community, success requires a nimble personality that can shift and adapt role behavior according to differing community expectations and valuations.

SOME SPECIAL AREAS OF ROLE CONFLICT AND ROLE CONFUSION

" How am I supposed to know what to do? " is one of the recurrent plaints of the beginning teacher. The variety of role expectations leaves them confused and uncertain. Some of this confusion arises from the contradictory expectations met in practice.

1. *The teacher viewed by the parent.* While the parent in part shares the role expectations of the community, he also is intimately identified with his own child. The ambitions he holds for his own child may be thwarted or facilitated by the teacher. The teacher's gatekeeper function, for example, becomes most crucial to the many parents who have well-articulated ambitions for their children.

Typically, the parent presents school to the child in the terms described by the research of Stendler and Young:

. . . the school has been presented as a socializing agency. The child has been told that he must behave himself in school, must mind the teacher, must be quiet, must not interrupt, that the teacher takes the place of his mother and is the boss. In some cases, the teacher has been held over his head as a kind of veiled threat, " You'll have to change your ways when you start first grade," " Wait till the teacher sees you acting like that. You won't do it long." Most parents, however, try to present the teacher as a kind of benign socializing agent, " Be nice in school and everyone will be nice to you." " Like the teacher and she'll like you " is the gist of what some children are told.[14]

Probably the parental view of the teacher will be more positive as people who have had more positive school experiences become parents. Today's

[14] Celia B. Stendler and Norman Young, " The Beginning of Formal School Experience," in R. G. Kuhlen and G. G. Thompson, ed., *Psychological Studies of Human Development* (New York: Appleton-Century-Crofts, 1952), pp. 415–422.

school generation by and large likes and approves of school. School is less likely to be a repressive, traumatic experience. The rich offerings of the high school, particularly the emphasis on the many social and extracurricular activities, have meant that more and more youngsters stay in school. They stay because they enjoy it.

Another contribution to mutual understanding has been the development of parent-teacher conferences in the lower grades. Teachers are helped to gain insight into the parental role and parents are given aid in seeing what goes on in the school. A fine relationship can develop when teachers recognize parental needs and expectations, and are skilled in working with parents. But it is also true that many teachers fear parents and deal awkwardly with the new human relations problems.

Many parents feel keenly their own insecurity in the parental role. Children, with the sadistic wisdom of the young, have been known to invoke the teacher as the person far more adequate, lovable, and important than the parent. As Gorer says:

. . . the child can always find in the school teacher an authority who can nearly always be successfully opposed to the parents. The parents keep this acknowledged rival and superior under the closest scrutiny, demanding in her private life standards of conduct and moral rectitude far higher than those they apply to themselves or their neighbors.[15]

Parental expectations and involvements may conflict with community expectations. On the one hand, the values enunciated in verbalizations of American life drama emphasize equality and brotherhood. On the other hand, the parent may find his community unsympathetic to these goals. He will see the school as a potent social force for one side or the other.

The parent seeks and asks for the support of the school and the teacher. He considers the teacher as an ally. But the teacher, from the child's vantage point, is often thought of as champion and friend. The dilemma is a sharp one. Teachers often find their role as one of liaison between child and parent, interpreting each to the other. This kind of bridging of the generations is one of the basic contributions that teachers can make in supporting stable family situations.

The charge made by some school critics that today's education is "soft" derives in part and receives its pervasive and uncritical support from the anxieties of many people over their own success as parents. Where adults see youngsters blithely ignoring the prescriptions of the community, talking "fresh" to the helpless parent, flirting with all the dangers inherent in hot-rods and "the gang," they are inclined to look abroad for a scapegoat. Naturally some think the schools are to blame.

The teacher faces a bewildering role expectation; he feels parental pres-

[15] Geoffry Gorer, *The American People* (New York: W. W. Norton & Company, 1948), p. 99.

sure to guide and counsel the child, to take into consideration *his* peculiar personal and family needs — to make the school situation as good and friendly and successful as possible. For such efforts the teacher may find himself the target of bitter complaint. Thus, he may wonder in despair what parents do want.

2. *Differences in role expectations as a function of community, neighborhood, and region.* The roles described . . . [here] . . . are generalizations of community expectations. Like any general picture, they define areas of behavior. But within each area the specific kinds of behavior vary greatly. Different groups — ethnic, racial, socio-economic — have differing expectations of the role of the teacher. Children will bring to school different behavior patterns, which in turn pressure the teacher to become stricter, or be more permissive, to emphasize rote learning, or develop "creativity," to extend instruction in cleanliness training, or lead discussions on sex education. Movement from community to community involves often this same need to adjust role behavior. In one community the teacher may be left strictly alone. In a neighboring community he may be invited to take a Boy Scout Troop, teach a Sunday School class, or to join the American Legion. Such a shift in community role expectations can come as a distinct shock.

The gap between community expectancies and the role of the teacher provided by the teacher training institution may plunge the neophyte into a soul struggle from which he emerges cynical and defensive. He is only too apt to yield to community pressures to accept the traditional roles reserved for teachers.

The confusion as to what *are* the teacher's community roles is probably the one most accessible to resolution today because of the social forces now at work. No place is so remote in the United States that the radio cannot be heard; soon TV will be almost as available; every crossroad has its movie house. Since these media usually portray middle-class values in a middle-class urban culture one can expect a general smoothing out of social class and regional differences in role expectations. Variations among individuals or communities will of course still remain, and these will always determine which roles of the teacher will be rewarded and emphasized.

3. *The education of the teacher and role expectations of the community.* Many of the things that the community defines as "the teacher" are of the nature of myths. Generations ago it could be more truly said that the teacher was a person of "culture." He had read more and better books than others, and he valued the arts and literature above more practical and immediate pursuits. Now the teacher is rarely a real intellectual. He may be as scornful of cultural activities as his neighbors. His knowledge of the world of ideas is often narrow. Today's teacher may be thought to be a prototype of the middle class. That he is a teacher is so often accidental. Thus the teacher as a person often finds himself bewildered and just a bit disturbed when his friends in the community, as their highest form of

praise, say, " Why you aren't a bit like a teacher! " He knows he does not fit into the traditional stereotype of the teacher; but he may wonder if some expect him to be.

It becomes a professional problem when the community conserves in its role expectations of teachers a type that was real about fifty or seventy years before. At that time there were fewer schools and fewer teachers. It is probable that those persons who were drawn to teaching were, by a process of cultural selectivity, those who could fit into community expectations.

Those who enter teaching today have developed a view of teaching as *a job*. No longer are they sent out to teach after a few months or a year of normal school education. They are educated in large state colleges or universities where many vocational pursuits are analyzed, discussed, and selected. The prospective teacher also develops an idea of the *job* as a *job*. He does not normally see the educational process in its social setting. Thus the future teacher often is quite unprepared for the community's view of his role.

The educational profession is the largest numerically of all the other professional groups. It has increased numerically to take care of expanding enrollments and curricular offerings. This has meant a widening of the selective base. All kinds of jobs are now called teaching: drama coaching; football coaching; nursery school teaching; research; educational testing; counseling. This means that the teacher " type " is bound to be a misnomer. Few common qualities will be found between the head football coach and the head of the English department. Their jobs, their methods of work, their relationships with children, the community's view of them are different.

The gap between the teacher's perception of his job and that of the community has many implications. The teacher is given in his professional training an ideal of the teacher: one who is permissive, helpful, psychologically oriented in interpreting motivations, and is part of a self-respecting, socially important professional group. On the job he finds contrary expectations.[16] Trained to use the most modern insights to guide the methods he uses and to select the content that he teaches, the teacher may find that the community wants none of this. The parent is suspicious of new ways of doing things in anything as intimate and close as the education of his children. The teacher, himself educated in the community's concept of the teacher and the school, finds himself in an acute dilemma. Does he reject the teachings of the university, the authority of research and professors, and accept the usual way of doing things that the community approves? Or shall he snub the community and hold to the vision of his role as provided by his collegiate experiences?

4. *The teacher as a member of a profession.* In the hierarchy of the pro-

16 Donald McNassor, " Conflict in Teachers Who Try to Learn About Children," *California Journal of Educational Research*, 3:147–155, September, 1951.

fessions, that of public school teacher is barely above the level of the semi-professions. The teacher may be perceived as middle class in the community's social scheme, but he is barely upper-lower class in the ranking of professional groups. The individual teacher is ambivalent towards his own role. He recognizes the value and significance of his work (and he is reminded by writers and speakers of how essential is the educational enterprise), but he is treated with cool snobbery by other professional groups.[17] The value of what he does is no protection from community expectations, nor does it keep a roomful of youngsters from creating absolute bedlam if not constantly watched.

In reacting to this neither-fish-nor-fowl position the teacher may behave much like a member of a minority group. He may feel keenly his low professional status and note the "discriminatory" treatment accorded him as a public servant.

The difficulties of recruiting the top level students into the profession have been a recurrent topic of articles in the literature. The research seems to point to some kind of conditioning against teaching as a profession that occurs during the high school years. Children in the sixth grade seem positively oriented towards teachers, but this attitude undergoes a marked negative shift by the time they reach the ninth grade, and continues through high school.[18]

The profession itself further divides teachers into those who are better and those who are not so good. The institutional ladder creates status and role problems; elementary teachers are at the bottom of the heap and university teachers at the top. In order to gain status, therefore, we notice an all too human reaction — modeling behavior after those higher on the respect scale.

This lack of a clear definition of the professional role and the many imbalances that result can be seen demonstrated also in the multiplicity, competitiveness, and seeming lack of common purpose found among professional organizations. The average teacher can join a national and a state teachers' organization; he can belong to a subject matter organization with both national and state activities; he can join one of two teachers' unions; any special interests he has may involve him in the organizations of those working for the gifted child, for the retarded, for audio-visual education, ad infinitum; and he can, if chosen, be a member of one or more professional honor societies. This multiplicity of organizations is in itself not surprising in view of the many kinds of teaching jobs and the vastness of the

[17] Roger G. Barker, "Difficulties of Communication Between Psychologists and Educators," *Journal of Educational Psychology*, 416–426, September, 1942.
[18] Roderick Langston, "A Study of Attitudes Towards Teaching as a Vocation," *Journal of Teacher Education*, 2:83–87, June, 1951. See also R. W. Richey and W. H. Fox "A Study of Some Opinions of High School Students With Regard to Teachers and Teaching," *Bulletin of the School of Education*, Indiana University, 27, No. 4, July, 1951.

system. But what is disturbing to some is the conflicting view of the profession that these different organizations provide their members. Some emphasize the role of the teacher as an expert; some identify the teacher's problems with those of the working class in general; still others play up to his professional self-esteem by being highly selective in membership. And the organizations compete with each other for members and for the participation of members.

REACTIONS TO ROLE CONFLICT

The area of role conflict becomes one of the crucial issues for the teacher as a person and for those educating future teachers. When faced with role conflicts, the individual may react in several ways. He can:

1. Repudiate his role in one of several conflicting groups;
2. Play off one group against the other;
3. Stall in accepting any given role definition until the pressures subside;
4. Redefine his role so that major conflicts are eliminated;
5. Lead a double life, being a different kind of person in situations which expect different and conflicting behavior;
6. Escape from the field — resign the job or find a new one;
7. Become ill.[19]

As we observe teachers we can see these mechanisms of adjustment at work. For many teachers these devices work well, for others they fail to resolve the basic dilemma. We have noted the ways in which teachers appear dissatisfied with aspects of teaching, and it is time to consider what part role conflict plays in this unrest. By gaining insight into the nature of the conflict in any given community, school, and individual, we may be in a better position to aid the teacher in resolving at a mature level the kind of conflict he faces.

SECTION 2. The teacher in the school

Whenever a teacher is employed in a school system he enters a social situation which is highly complicated and highly structured, often filled with obstacles which stand in the way of employing his professional talents in such a manner as to make a maximum contribution to the learning of young persons. If the teacher wishes to make his maximum contribution, he must be well informed about the kind of institution within which he is expected to operate. Obviously each school has its own distinctive characteristics, its own areas of maximum freedom and maximum restraint. But despite the individual peculiarities of particular schools, the very nature of schooling in America creates certain common or general characteristics. These general characteristics are of help to the teacher in analyzing and operating successfully within *any* given school.

The importance to a teacher of un-

[19] Adapted from Jackson Toby, " Some Variables in Role Conflict Analysis," *Social Forces* 30:323–327, 1952.

derstanding the social structure of the school in which he works would appear to be obvious, and yet it has been shown, in fact, to remain often unrecognized. Studies of young teachers who leave the profession indicate that the cause of their failure, in their own eyes and in the eyes of their supervisors, are as frequently located in their inability to operate successfully within a school " system " as in their inability to handle the actual " instructional " process. There are two overriding reasons why any teacher should understand the social structure of the school in which he is teaching. In the first place, the teacher who operates with inadequate perceptions of the human dimensions of the school is apt to be ineffective in his daily operations. With the best intentions in the world, he may find his personal relations with his fellow teachers threatened or threatening. He is apt to find his own operations viewed askance. He is likely to find forces mitigating against the success of each project he undertakes. The net result tends to be a sense of frustration or disillusionment, that defeatist attitude which has so often dulled the enthusiasm and the missionary zeal with which most teachers enter upon their careers. The beginning teacher should be concerned with the social structure of the school, not only in terms of the successful operation of his daily practice, but in regard to his professional obligation to help change and improve the institution in which he works. If effective daily operation in a school is handicapped by lack of perception of the social realities of the situation, the ability to act as an effective agent of change is even more seriously limited. Here, at least, knowledge is power; and perhaps the teacher could accept no surer model than that suggested by Reinhold Niebuhr: " God grant me the grace to accept that which I cannot change, the courage to change that which I can, and the wisdom to know the difference." It is hoped that the readings in this section will suggest a useful method of analysis for acquiring the knowledge which must underlie such wisdom and such courage.

Any teacher operates both within an individual classroom and within a total school setting. Effective operation within the total school setting involves his possessing insight into a number of features of that school. A teacher must, for example, be aware of the *formal organization* of the school — its bureaucratic structure, the responsibilities of its various offices, its established channels of action and points of decision. Equally important, however, is his recognition of the *informal organization* of the school — the locus of *actual* as contrasted with *legal* power, the prestige hierarchy within the faculty and other school personnel, the informal cliques and groups (which pervade all social institutions), the patterns of deference which have developed. But it is not only organization which is important: expectations governing behavior must be recognized and evaluated. There are always formal rules and regulations — the type of regulation which is apt to be covered in teachers' handbooks and which is most easily determined. Perhaps even more important, however, are the informal expectations which govern behavior — expectations which may prescribe the " appropriate " atmosphere within the classroom, the patterns of human relations to be established with students, the canons of taste in clothing and personal habits. Analysis of the school situation must, finally, be yet more personalized: it must come to grips with the personal satisfactions and motivations of the system's personnel. It must determine which teachers find their satisfactions in warm, friendly relations with students, which look to the security of carefully delimited functions, which find pleasure in the power or authority of the positions they hold. Until such characteristics of the school system — such " social realities " — are located and identified, effective action in a school system is accidental at best. It is the purpose of the following selection by Wilbur B. Brookover to help identify such qualities in any school system. However, if any social analysis is to be complete, it must recognize that action in social institutions is not defined solely by the empirical demands of the situation: it is defined equally by the ethical demands of democracy as a way of life. Social analysis can easily lead to social manipulation if action is not guided by humane principles, chief among which must always remain the democratic injunction that no person is ever to be treated solely as a means to another's ends but is rather always deserving of consideration as an end in himself. Effective operation in a school system is not to be measured by the engineering of situations to achieve one's own ends, but by the developing of ends which are mutually shared and programs of action which are mutually acceptable.

WILBUR B. BROOKOVER
The social structure of the school

Teachers' position in the adult social structure. The position of the teacher in relation to other adults in the school society is characterized by the formal definition of his duties and privileges and by the informal clique relationships among teachers. We have already defined the position of the teacher in some respects by our analysis of the function of the school board and the administrator. The teachers' status requires that they show deference both to the administrator and to the school board.

There are instances, of course, where a teacher's position in the community may involve power greater than that of the board itself. This is illustrated by the following case.

After some years as a teacher, A became a businessman in the community in which he taught. He also was active in the councils of the leading political party. Later he again held a series of teaching positions in the school. After several years of teaching, a school trusteeship became vacant and A used his influence to get the widow of one of the leading politicians elected to this position. She soon decided on the advice of others that A should not be re-employed in the school. He was asked to resign and did so. Immediately a large number of patrons of the school expressed concern about his resignation. When pressed, he informed them that he did not resign voluntarily. Petitions were circulated and a mass meeting was arranged to demand the reinstatement of A or the resignation of the school trustee. The political leaders of the community as well as the patrons were mobilized. The person who had requested the resignation of A resigned her position in the face of the strong demands of both the patrons and politicians. A was reinstated and B replaced the widow as school trustee.

From Wilbur B. Brookover, A *Sociology of Education,* 1955, pp. 193–204. Reprinted by permission of the American Book Company.

B was the choice of the political leaders, but he was selected only after consultation with A.

This case is unusual, for few teachers have such status in the community. Generally, the superordinate position of school trustees and school
boards is unquestioned. Teachers who are asked to resign are generally expected to do so quietly. This illustrates a situation wherein a teacher occupies another position in the community which employs him.

As an employee, the teacher is vulnerable to the power of either the
board or the administrator. Because of this, a teacher may frequently be
the scapegoat for both the superordinate positions. He may have to accept
responsibility for difficulties more correctly those of the administrator or
the board. Those in authority may make it impossible for the teacher to
carry out an assignment successfully, but they seldom take the responsibility for a teacher's failure. The teacher is also frequently assigned unpleasant or impossible tasks because of the administrator's unwillingness to
tackle the work. This is illustrated by the case of a school administrator
who had for many years also been an athletic coach. When he realized
that a bad season was coming up, he turned the coaching responsibilities
over to one of the teachers. During the ensuing season, the administrator
frequently criticized the new coach and discussed his failure with the patrons. At the end of the season the decision concerning the coach's re-
employment was referred to the school board without recommendation. In
this way, the administrator was able to protect his own position at the expense of a subordinate.

There are numerous formal or officially recognized differences in teacher
positions. These vary from one school system to another. Sometimes there
are sharp differences between secondary- and elementary-school teachers in
the same building or system. The secondary-school teacher generally has
more prestige and higher status than the elementary-school teacher. The
supervising teacher's position is also one of higher status. Within the secondary school, teachers of some subjects may have a higher status. There
may be variations from community to community in this respect, but usually teachers of academic subjects such as English, mathematics, or social
studies have somewhat higher status in the system than teachers of the
vocational subjects. Yet in farming- or laboring-class districts, the agricultural or shop teacher may have higher status than academic teachers. The
same may be true of the home economics teacher's position. Although
trade or industrial arts teachers generally have lower status, they may hold
other community roles which are not available to teachers of academic
subjects.

The secondary school sometimes has a system of rank among teachers of
a given area, with a department head or similar position carrying the higher
status. Length of service in the particular school is frequently a basis for
such differentials in position. Thus in most schools the new teacher occu-

pies a position different from that of the old teacher. Some experienced teachers are sometimes disturbed by a new teacher's failure to recognize this differential. The new teacher is expected to show some deference. The following description of a small group of new teachers by a woman who had taught in the system for many years indicates something of her resentment of the newcomers and her pleasure at these teachers' failures.

This group was composed of six women teachers who were all new to our system. Together they ate lunch, rode to work, attended professional meetings, and spent most of their leisure time in one another's company. They came to only those school functions that were absolutely necessary. Always they arrived at school and left at the same time as the pupils. At faculty meetings they worked hard to push through those ideas that would make their work easier or bring them more money. The other teachers in the system tried for some time to help or to become friendly with them, but they were politely but definitely rebuffed. Only two of these girls are returning next year.[1]

The failure of this group of young teachers to show proper deference to the older teachers was definitely contrary to this teacher's image of the new teachers' position.

Informal clique relations in school faculties. The difference in positions between new and older teachers is sometimes the basis for differential clique groupings within the faculty. The six new women teachers mentioned above illustrate this type of clique formation. There are numerous other factors that become the basis for such friendship or congeniality groups. Systematic studies of the clique structure in public school faculties are not available, but the following analysis of a faculty clique structure in a small school indicates that such informal groups are significant.

This description of the clique groups in operation in a public school consists of a study of thirty teachers in their interactions.

There are several instances when the entire group meets. The teachers' club, meeting as a professional group, illustrates one such instance; their meeting as a social group would be another. It is evident in these meetings that unity and solidarity are not the rule. In such meetings one finds the clique groups functioning to their best ability to make influence felt or to show prestige.

In analyzing these cliques it is apparent that there are many determinants affecting the formation of the groups. There exists a major division on the basis of sex. The men teachers have a highly organized social clique. They meet every other Monday for the purpose of studying professional problems. This, at least, is the stated purpose of such meetings. So far, in

[1] The writer is indebted to a graduate student for the report from which this case was taken.

the seven years they have been meeting, the time has been spent playing poker. These meetings seem to result in a good feeling among the men on the faculty.

Perhaps some qualification should be made of the statement in regard to professional problems. While there is no formal discussion of such problems, there is an informal, friendly mention made of situations that exist that might cause some friction. These are usually talked about, as the evening progresses, with some good results.

There is another group of men, with almost the same members as the above group, which meets after school in the men's lounge to smoke and to talk of the day's events. The superintendent is not associated with either of these two groups, and there are two or three men on the faculty who do not ordinarily meet with the second group.

Other cliques within the men's group exist on the basis of professional interest. The coaching staff and one teacher form a clique and can be seen frequently talking together. Their conversations seem to dwell primarily on sports and the high-school's activities in relation to sports. There are other casual cliques in other subject matter fields but not nearly so consistent in their meeting. These may be made up of both men and women.

The women form their clique groups on two different levels. One is social; the other professional. On the social level there is an intermingling of high-school and grade teachers, usually on the basis of age. The older teachers, most of whom are unmarried, have occasional get-togethers in which they indulge in some bridge playing on a rather simple level. There is also a number of other women teachers, who are local residents, who have formed a clique group on the basis of their religious interests.

The three young teachers (unmarried) form a group by themselves and do not have much in common socially with the rest of the women on the staff. These three live together and are usually together at social functions which teachers are expected to attend. The remaining group, whose members are married, seems to be pretty well left out of the social activities that are carried on by the older women's group. These teachers do not seem to be a well-defined group of their own.

Within the school the women teachers in the elementary grades form a clique group and even meet after school twice a week to have coffee and to discuss the problems at hand. The high-school teachers have no such meetings but seem to stick pretty close together on academic interests. Three English teachers can usually be seen together sometime during the day and the two commercial teachers often are together. The home economics teacher seems to be more or less by herself in this situation.[2]

The following analysis of the elementary- and high-school faculties occupying different buildings also gives some idea of clique groupings.

---

[2] The writer is indebted to a graduate student for this analysis.

The following legend is used to facilitate interpreting the clique groups:

(*Elementary School*)

A — kindergarten teacher

B — first-grade teacher

C — first- and second-grade teacher

D — second- and third-grade teacher

E — third- and fourth-grade teacher

F — fourth-grade teacher

G — fifth-grade teacher

H — sixth-grade teacher

J — seventh-grade teacher

K — fifth- and seventh-grade teacher

L — kindergarten and third-grade teacher

M — fourth- and sixth-grade teacher

(*High School*)

N — music teacher

P — home economics teacher

Q — commercial teacher

R — agricultural teacher

S — industrial arts teacher

T — superintendent

U — coach

V — assistant coach

W — principal

X — literature and social science teacher

Y — librarian and language and arts teacher

Z — science and mathematics teacher

Five distinguishable cliques were the result, more or less, of common location, common levels of teaching, common problems, and common self-appraisal of ability. Further examination of the clique structure revealed a more divergent pattern. Here it was found that both in-school and out-of-school interests and activities were involved in determining the clique.

Clique Number 6 — the sport group. It consisted of T and W who were ex-coaches, U and V, and N, P, Q, K, and M, all of whom were actively interested in sports or married to men who were. This clique met regularly after all sporting events of the school for refreshments at the home of one of its members. Almost all the members were married and lived in places with sufficient facilities for entertaining the entire group. One unmarried member of the faculty, who always went with this group to all athletic events, would always excuse herself from the after-game affairs. Another member of the group, whose wife's job kept her away from the gathering, was often cited unfavorably by certain members of the group. Age may have been a factor in this group. The range was from about twenty-six to forty years.

Clique Number 7 — the younger set. It consisted of teachers K, M, P, Q, and N, plus N's wife. Members of this clique came to this school the same year, were between the ages of twenty-five and thirty, and were interwoven by many secondary likenesses. Teachers K, M, and N attended the same school as undergraduates. N, P, and Q were interested in music. All were golf enthusiasts and all were frequently invited to nonschool functions by the local populace.

Cliques Numbers 6 and 7 functioned outside the school but involved only the faculty of the school. The common factor involved was the use of leisure time.

Clique Number 8 — an in-school clique, was a subdivision of the high-school clique. It had teachers Y and X as nucleus and sometimes included Z. Teachers X and Y agreed on what was of prime importance in the high-school curriculum. They held seniority over the other teachers and believed discipline was the secret to education. Z was interested in religious education and became connected with this clique because of a common regard for religious teaching. They were the final critics for innovations of teaching techniques.

Clique Number 9 might be called the boiler-room frequenters. It consisted of all the teachers who allowed themselves to be seen going to the boiler room to smoke. Among these were teachers J, K, N, P, Q, R, S, U, and V. The superintendent, T, was a semiactive member.

Clique Number 10 consisted of U, V, T, W, and K. This group governed the athletic setup of the school. It collaborated on matters pertinent to successful athletic programs, such as keeping the proper participants eligible and keeping them out of trouble. In this clique U and V were the coaches, T and W were ex-coaches now in charge of administration, and K was the coach of the junior-high teams.

In this school system the clique structure seemed to be based on common interests. If only one factor were the basis for the clique, it was usually not a closely-knit organization. Many common interests seemed to result in more closely-knit groups. Some of the factors apparently were age, ideals, interests, and location. The number of members in any given clique seemed to have little consistent effect on the rigidity of it.[3]

In addition to the factor of length of service, which we have already discussed, these analyses illustrate the significance of other factors in the development of informal clique relationships. Among these are the age and sex of teachers. For certain types of activities, the men and women operate in separate, informal systems. Cliques sometimes cut across the sex barrier, however. This is particularly true among married teachers. The cliques involving married women sometimes included the husbands and other men teachers as well as the wives of male teachers. It is evident from these as well as other cases that teaching or some other interest is the basis for clique relationships. Men who are coaching or have fringe relationships to coaching are frequently clique associates. The illustrations also suggest that the habits of the teachers, such as smoking, drinking, and card-playing, are associated with clique relations.

Factors in clique formation. To some extent the formal positions in the faculty structure define the informal clique positions. We noted above that the elementary- and high-school teachers have somewhat different status

---

[3] The writer is indebted to a graduate student for this analysis.

and are therefore expected to behave differently. These status differentials are factors in the informal clique relationships. Some cliques cut across the elementary-secondary barrier, but others are bound by them. The subjects taught at the secondary level are also frequently factors in clique formation. Ecological factors, such as the location of schools and place of residence, are important in the friendship groups.

There are, no doubt, other factors that effect clique structure in the school faculties. It is impossible at this point to give an exhaustive analysis of these factors or to evaluate the relative importance of any one. Our purpose is to examine the existence of cliques and the range of factors associated with these informal structures. Such relationships frequently have a role in the decision-making, and influence systems operating within the faculty of any school. For practical purposes the knowledge of the clique structure and of the possible cleavages between the cliques is extremely important in faculty action. Studies of clique structure and opinion leadership in other social systems have shown the value of operating through informal group relations. Teachers are more likely to participate in school activities with enthusiasm and to attain the desired results if they can function within such friendship groups.

It is also important, however, to recognize the possibilities of cleavages and struggles for power and rewards existing among informal cliques. Many times cliques vie for favors of the school board, the administration, the students, or the patrons. Such competition may be the motivation for superior achievement, but it may also arouse destructive conflict. In connection with analysis of the clique structure of another school, an observer made the following comment:

" There were no outward signs of conflict among these cliques, but they definitely vied for the power position. Group 1 was the most powerful group. Cliques 3 and 4 combined forces in the name of youth and presented a threat to Group 1. Group 2 had long ago accepted a passive but stubborn role in the school because one or more of this group were friends with someone from another group. It was impossible for any one of the cliques to cloak itself in secrecy. This is best exemplified by a grapevine system that communicated information about the administration's doings." [4]

In this case the struggle for power tended to be vitiated because of the interlocking system of relationships among the cliques. Communication about the administration traveled from one to the other and this apparently defeated attempts to achieve greater power. Two cliques were reported to co-operate, particularly in their struggle with the most dominant or powerful of the school cliques. This and the other cases demonstrate the extensive interaction among cliques and the frequent shifting of personnel from one to another in terms of the immediate point of interest.

[4] From a term report submitted to the author.

Teacher leadership. The specific nature of leader-follower relationships among teachers is not known. Certainly, for some purposes, the formal positional relationships would define leadership to some extent. Thus, for certain activities department heads, supervisors, and other teachers having superordinate positions would function as influencers. Analysis of leadership in other groups has emphasized that leadership is not general, but rather specific in a particular situation. This means that the department-head position does not define leadership in all relations among the teachers. Leadership is now recognized as a function of the relationships among the people in particular group situations.

Research has failed to reveal any universal personality characteristics of the leader. Persons are selected for leadership roles through the interaction within the group. In many group situations, therefore, the formally or officially designated department head or principal may not be the leader. Various persons may occupy leadership positions in different situations. In faculty meetings one or two persons may be the opinion leaders; in a social gathering others may occupy the leadership positions.

Nonteaching adults. There are several other adult positions, such as custodian and school secretary. In rural schools or town systems, where students come from some distance, a staff of school bus drivers will have at least part-time or fringe positions in the school structure. Formally all these positions are subordinate to both administrators and teachers. The formal chain of command may be defined as running directly from an administrative position to the janitor, clerk, and bus drivers, but teachers generally consider their positions superordinate to those of the nonteaching adults. Generally speaking, other people in the community also place the teachers in superordinate positions. These nonteaching adults usually accept this formal definition of their positions. They recognize their subordinate position and exert little influence on decisions concerning school policy.

In some schools the informal relationships may modify the position of one of these other adults in comparison to those of teachers and administrators.

At H school, Dick, the janitor, occupied a strategic position in the school policy-making process. Dick was janitor of the school from the beginning of this consolidated school till his death, approximately twenty years later. He knew all the patrons in the small community and had been active in local political affairs. More important perhaps was his own concept of the importance and significance of his activity in the school. As in many other schools, the boiler room, the place where he lived during the winter months as well as where he did his work, became a hangout for teachers, bus drivers, and others who wished to take a smoke or otherwise get out of public view during the school day. Dick was particularly helpful to the teachers, and made special effort to make their work easier. He had all of the teachers heavily obligated to him. Early in the history of this school, the school administrator realized that Dick had given him sound advice on the organization of the school. In order to fulfill the advisor role, which he rapidly achieved, Dick sought to learn as much as he could about the work of each teacher. Through these informal relationships, Dick came to occupy a position in which he could actually decide which teachers were to be re-employed and which dismissed. Each administrator in turn depended on Dick for information from the community as well as for observations about the school. No major decision concerning teachers or policy concerning the school was made or adopted without Dick's consultation.

Although it is not typical, this case from the writer's file is cited because it illustrates the possible position that a janitor may acquire through informal relationships.

In another school the clerk acquired similar influence. Through long service to a superintendent who gradually delegated more and more work to her, she came to occupy a position very close to that of the superintendent. When the superintendent retired, the clerk was transferred to another position in the school. The new superintendent discovered that many of his official duties and functions followed the old clerk. The informal system of relationships between the clerk and teachers, other administrators, and the board was such that the duties she had performed were still expected of her as a person and not as an adjunct of the superintendent.

Similar relationships between bus drivers and patrons, on one hand, and the school board, on the other, may provide a channel of communication from the school to both the patrons and the board that completely circumvents the superintendent's office. Bus drivers have been in a position to dismiss both administrator and teachers, even though their position is officially subordinate to both.

The informal relations among these adults and other community members as well as teachers are affected by the other positions they occupy in the community. Bus drivers, clerks, and custodians are much more likely to be intimately and completely involved in the social relations of the community than are many teachers. They occupy nonteaching positions in the community. It is difficult for teachers who have not lived in the community prior to their employment to acquire a nonteaching community position. For this reason, communication flows more freely between such persons and other community members than it does between teachers and community members. The " home " teacher who has previously established nonteacher positions may have similar communications with other community members.

Generally the nonteaching adults occupy subordinate positions in the adult structure. Although school custodians, clerks, and bus drivers have such formal positions, the informal positions, as defined by their interpersonal relations in the school community, may have greater significance.

Administrators and teachers also function in a set of informal relationships, but the barriers between them and the community limit the communication that may occur in this situation. Administrators and teachers have been trained to accept and to reinforce the official definitions of their position. This is not likely to characterize the behavior of the nonprofessional adults in the school system. Some administrators attempt to define the role of all employees by similar official regulations. This is seldom accepted by the nonprofessionals as an essential aspect of school organization. Teachers frequently criticize members of these groups for using informal, nonprofessional means for achieving some end. They at least express the opinion that all school employees follow the official channels and table of organization. Clerks may occasionally acquire such attitudes, but custodians and bus drivers rarely do, in spite of the educators' efforts. . . .

CHAPTER THIRTEEN BIBLIOGRAPHY

BRIM, ORVILLE G., *Sociology and the Field of Education.* New York: Russell Sage Foundation, 1958.

> Brim's purpose in this booklet is to survey the research that has been done (mostly by sociologists) in the area of education and to channel this to the educational practitioner. Chapter VI on educators' roles and Chapter VII on students' roles are especially informative.

COOK, LLOYD A. and COOK, ELAINE F., A *Sociological Approach to Education,* third edition. New York; McGraw-Hill, 1960.

> The basic theme of this book is that schools are affected by the times. The authors illustrate this theme with case studies of schools in underdeveloped parts of the world and in the United States. The concluding chapter on " The Education of Educators " deals with professionalization, the place of liberal arts, and values.

FLEMING, C. M., *Teaching: A Psychological Analysis.* London: Methuen and Company Ltd., 1958.

> The author is sensitive to many aspects of teaching. Chapter IX is particularly interesting to the teacher-to-be who is looking ahead to the first classroom experience.

MERTON, ROBERT K., BROOM, LEONARD and COTTRELL, LEONARD S. (editors), *Sociology Today: Problems and Prospects.* New York: Basic Books, 1959.

> The chapter on " The Sociology of Education " by Neal Gross is an excellent summary of the development, present status, and possible directions of this comparatively new area of study. Gross views education as a relatively unexplored but potentially rich area for sociological investigation.

MOUSTAKAS, CLARK E., *The Alive and Growing Teacher*. New York: Philosophical Library, 1959.

> How teachers grow in understanding of themselves, others, and of education is portrayed through people who are mutually concerned about teaching problems. The book stresses how discussions with colleagues and parents can lead to greater clarification of these problems and growth in ability to solve them.

SPINDLER, GEORGE D., *The Transmission of American Culture*. Cambridge: Harvard University Press, 1959.

> This Burton lecture views the transmission of culture from the point of view of the anthropologist. Spindler analyzes two "diametrically opposed" value systems, the "traditional" and the "emergent." Many teachers, he argues, are not making a consistent adjustment to their professed values.

14

Putting Your Philosophy to Work

Putting one's philosophy to work is the very heart of good teaching. Teaching is always a very practical science, but it is practical in the most significant sense of the word. The truly *practical* is always a way of achieving what our philosophy has said is desirable in ways which that philosophy indicates are worthy. Thus any philosophy must be capable of translation into practice. As a matter of fact, a philosophy of education, on its substantive side, might suitably be defined as a set of consistent propositions which are capable of directing practice and of being tested and refined through practice. If our philosophy provides us with a set of principles which are as extensive in scope as the educational problems we confront, as reliable in action as reflective thought can make them, and sufficiently consistent with one another so that conflict and ambiguity are avoided, we may be said to have a *workable* philosophy of education. But a workable philosophy of education is of little value until it likewise becomes a *working* philosophy of education. Translating a workable philosophy into a working philosophy is the lifetime occupation of the creative teacher.

Part of a philosophy of education is always *substantive;* part is always *methodological.* The substantive dimension of a person's philosophy of education consists of his beliefs about education and values held in respect to education; the methodological dimension consists of his ways of arriving at and testing these beliefs and values. The bulk of the selections in this volume have been aimed at developing the substantive dimension of your phi-

losophy. The most important features of this substantive portion will be the educational *principles* you have developed, for principles produce dependable professional conduct. Most educational principles are social in nature; that is, they relate to man and society. Some of these social principles are *principles of value;* they are reasoned assertions as to which things are of great value and which things are of little value. Others are *principles of prediction;* they are assertions about the nature of society and the way society does in fact operate. These latter principles, usually derived from the empirical sciences, are the guides which enable us to predict the consequences of various courses of action we might take. A philosophy of education is constructed by amalgamating principles of value, which enable us to determine our ends, with principles of prediction, which enable us to plan means of achieving these ends.

While the remainder of this volume will help pull together the *substantive* parts of your philosophy of education, this chapter is primarily designed to help you formulate its methodology. In its methodological dimensions, philosophy is explicitly *a way of looking at things,* and a philosophy of education is a way of approaching, analyzing, and resolving the issues and problems which confront education and the teacher. Although there are many aspects to this way of looking at things, three stand out as deserving particular attention. The first of these is concerned with placing means and ends in a common context in which they can be conveniently related to one another and used to test one another. The second is concerned with analyzing our educational concepts and educational arguments in order to determine their intellectual stature and worth. The third is concerned with developing a method of reaching conclusions in the multitude of unresolved situations that confront both education and the teacher. It is to these three aspects of the problem of putting your philosophy to work that the three parts of this chapter are addressed.

SECTION 1. Educational ends and means

Our society seems to be bedeviled with dualisms, such as good and evil, mind and matter, thesis and antithesis, to the extent that often we try to dichotomize everything. It is natural that these same dualisms have found their way into education and that theory and practice, ideals and realities, means and ends, and philosophy and science have been placed in polar positions, often separated by a deep and wide gulf. Treated in such a fashion objectives seem to be distinct from methods, and theory is considered impractical, while practice seems substantial. In fact, the philosopher is often caricatured as the dreamer completely unrelated to the workaday world, while the practitioner is depicted as forgetting theory and really accomplishing something. Although these descriptions may have fitted some visionaries, yet philosophers have long expounded the proposition that " philosophy must bake bread."

The following readings forcefully present the proposition that ends and means cannot be separated in education and that there must be a unity between theory and practice. Every action is based upon a philosophy whether recognized or not. Whenever a student decides to take a certain class at a certain hour, it is based upon some value, which in turn is rooted in a philosophy. If the student chooses an 8 o'clock class from an inspiring teacher rather than an 11 o'clock class chosen by his closest friends, he has made this decision on a value-basis. In fact, even if he flips a coin to make the decision whether to take the course at 8 or 11 o'clock, he has made his decision on the proposition that neither the teacher nor his friends are of prime importance. He may actually feel that the teacher, friends, and class are all unimportant. The .fact remains that whatever we do or refrain from doing is rooted in a philosophy, and this in turn indicates our estimate of our values. Thus, ends and means are closely related. Goals which cannot be realized are only goals in name. Hence, democracy as an end can best be achieved by democratic, not totalitarian, means. The teacher who autocratically insists that democracy will be practiced in the classroom, whether the children want it or not, does not understand democracy. If democracy is the goal, then the method to reach this goal should also be democratic. The old saying truly applies: " Your actions speak so loudly, I cannot hear what you are saying." John Dewey and John Childs emphasize this point effectively in the first reading in this section. In a later part of their discussion they state: " A goal cannot be intelligently set forth apart from the path which leads to it." In like manner they point out that the individual cannot be separated from society. Therefore, a philosophy of education cannot deal with an individual in a vacuum, but only as he really exists, namely, as a member of society. Since education deals with people, the philosophy of education is actually general philosophy with reference to its social setting.

In the second selection John Dewey emphasizes the practicality of theory. There is no possibility of separating the philosophy of education from the science of education. Just as the philosophy of education is dependent upon a general scheme of values, so also material from all the sciences furnishes the content of the science of education. Science needs abstraction, and abstraction depends upon reflective or theoretical inquiry. Consequently, the teacher must recognize that every method which he uses, every assignment which he makes, every test question which he asks, every punishment which he metes out, and every way he treats a pupil is based upon a philosophy; and he must also realize, if he subscribes to a theory which he never practices, that he either does not accept it or does not understand it.

JOHN DEWEY and JOHN L. CHILDS
Principles underlying a philosophy of education

In previous . . . [parts of this discussion] . . . a philosophy of education has been presented. The presentation has been in terms of application and operation, not in the abstract. In this concluding . . . [part] . . . we wish to draw out the distinctively theoretical implications of the discussion and give them definite formulation. In so doing we shall try neither to present new material nor yet merely to summarize what has already been said. We shall endeavor to make explicit the ideas and principles which implicitly form the framework of our entire discussion.

In the first place there is not implied any pretension to offer *the* philosophy of education. We do not believe that there is any such thing — not in a world in which men act for opposed ends and follow divergent paths. We believe that a treatment which claims to be the exclusive and all comprehensive theory of education leads unconsciously but necessarily to a kind of insincerity; for it tends to cover up the conflicts that are highly important in practice. The statements thus far are negative. But they rest upon a positive basis.

For all education is an affair of action. Call before your mental eye any schoolroom and you see in imagination something going on, something being done. Even the schoolrooms in which silence and physical immobility are most insisted upon are still doing something. They are imposing these things as parts of a policy of action adapted to reach the ends which are prized. Instruction and discipline are modes of action. Now all truly human action involves preference. It signifies working for one end rather than for another in situations where alternatives exist. The chosen policy may be adopted on the basis of imitation and obedience to tradition, or it may be thought through and adopted on the basis of a clear view and decided choice of the ends and consequences which the policy serves. But preference for one kind of end and value is always there, because one kind of outcome rather than another is brought about as a consequence of action.

It is the business of a philosophy of education to make clear what is involved in the action which is carried on within the educational field, to transform a preference which is blind, based on custom rather than thought, into an intelligent choice — one made, that is, with consciousness of what is aimed at, the reasons why it is preferred, and the fitness of the means used. Nevertheless intelligent choice is still choice. It still involves preference for one kind of end rather than another one which might have been worked for. It involves a conviction that such and such an end is valuable, worth while, rather than another. Sincerity demands a maximum of impartiality in seeking and stating the reasons for the aims and the values which are chosen and rejected. But the scheme of education itself cannot be impartial in the sense of not involving a preference for some values over others. The obligation to be impartial is the obligation to state as clearly as possible what is chosen and why it is chosen. We have attempted to meet this obligation. We have set forth the values we believe education should strive to achieve in our own day in our own country, and we have stated the grounds of our choice. We believe that it will be helpful if those who disagree in practice, in the courses of action they are following, will also clarify and expose the grounds for their policies: in short, develop and formulate *their* philosophies of education.

So much in general. The point which most specifically follows is that some philosophy is implied in every educational measure and recommendation made as to every method of teaching and discipline. There is no possible opposition therefore between that which is termed " science " and that which is termed " philosophy " in education. For as soon as a science is actually *used*, as soon as action based upon it occurs, then values, consequences, enter in. Choice operates and produces consequences. There are, then, philosophical implications, since philosophy is a theory of values to be achieved and to be rejected. But a conflict of *philosophies*, between a philosophy and what purports to be a science, is both possible and actual. For example, the presupposition of much of the work done in the name of science is that there is no need for philosophy itself. This view itself involves a decided philosophy. It does so in at least three ways and directions. In the first place, since the only thing to which factual science *can* be applied is something already in existence, there is a virtual assumption that educational direction and progress rest upon analysis of existing practices with a view to rendering them more efficient. The underlying philosophy is that it is the function of education to transmit and reproduce existing institutions — only making them more efficient. This philosophy we deny.

In the second place, the assumption implicit in the method of much of the work referred to is that processes and functions with which education deals are isolable, because they are independent of one another. This involves the philosophical notion that character, mental life, experience, and the methods of dealing with them, are composed of separable parts and that there is no whole, no integralness in them; that what seems to be a unity is in reality nothing but an aggregate of parts. This philosophy once dominated physical science. In physics and biology its inadequacy from a scientific point of view is now realized. Yet it has been taken over by that school of educational " science " which denies the importance of a philosophy in conducting education. The ends and values which we regard as the proper ends of choice in action are consistent only with a philosophy which recognizes the basic importance of organization and patterns of integration.

The work done in the name of science (in the third place) during the recent period has been largely in connection with the *impersonal* phase of education, and has reduced personality as far as possible to impersonal terms. These terms do lend themselves most readily to factual and statistical treatment — but a non-social philosophy is implied. When it is acted upon, the implication becomes practially anti-social. It takes the individual out of the medium of associations and contexts in which he lives. It ignores social connections and bearings, and, in ignoring them, it invites that kind of educational policy which is in line with an outworn philosophy of individualism. Our philosophy, while accepting the results of authenticated scientific work, builds upon the idea that organisms, selves, characters, minds, are so intimately connected with their environments, that they can be studied and understood only in relation to them. The emphasis which is found in the previous pages upon the culture of a time and a community is, for example, one phase of this general philosophy.

We now come to the main content of our philosophy as far as that can be set forth in a brief number of explicit propositions.

I

Our position implies that philosophy of education is a branch of social philosophy and, like every social philosophy, since it requires a choice of one type of character, experience, and social institutions, involves a *moral* outlook. Education, as we conceive it, is a process of social interaction carried on in behalf of consequences which are themselves social — that is, it involves interactions between persons and includes shared values. A frequent objection to this view rests upon a misunderstanding. It asserts that this conception fails to grasp the basic value of individuality. The reverse is the case. *Social* cannot be opposed in fact or in idea to *individual*. Society *is* individuals-in-their-relations. An individual apart from social relations is a myth — or a monstrosity. If we deal with actual individuals, and not with a conceptual abstraction, our position can be also formulated in these terms: Education is the process of realization of integrated individualities. For integration can occur only in and through a medium of association. Associations are many and diverse, and some of them are hostile to the realization of a full personality, they interfere with it and prevent it.

Hence *for the sake of individual development,* education must promote some forms of association and community life and must work against others. Admit that education is concerned with a development of individual potentialities and you are committed to the conclusion that education cannot be neutral and indifferent as to the kind of social organization which exists. Individuals develop not in a remote entity called "society" at large but in connection *with one another.* The conditions of their association with one another, of their participation and communication, of their coöperation and competition, are set by legal, political, and economic arrangements. In the interest, therefore, of education — not of any preconceived "ism" or code — the fact is emphasized that education must operate in view of a deliberately preferred social order.

The criticisms made in previous pages of an individualistic philosophy do not imply depreciation of the value of individuality. On the contrary they assert that the form which the historic individualism of the eighteenth and the nineteenth centuries took is now adverse to the realization of individuality in and for *all.* It favors and supports legal and economic institutions which encourage an exaggerated and one-sided development of egoistic individuality in a privileged few, while militating against a full and fair opportunity for a normal individuality in the many.

It was implied in our introductory survey of the social demands made upon education to-day that the democratic way of life is that in which the identity of interest of the individual and the social is best realized. The democratic faith is individual in that it asserts the claims of every individual to the opportunity for realization of potentialities unhampered by birth, family status, unequal legal restriction, and external authority. By the same token it has been social in character. It has recognized that this end for individuals cannot be attained save through a particular type of political and legal institutions. Historically, conditions emphasized at first the negative phase of this principle: the overthrow of institutions that were autocratic. It is now seen that the positive side of the principle needs attention: namely, the extension of democracy to the creation of the kind of institutions that will effectively and constructively serve the development of *all* individuals. It is at once obvious that this extension affects economic, as well as legal and political, institutions.

Social arrangements are to be judged ultimately by their educative effect, by what they do in the way of liberating, organizing, integrating the capacities of men and women, boys and girls. These capacities include esthetic factors, those which lie at the basis of music, literature, painting, architecture in both production and appreciation; intellectual and scientific power and taste; capacities for friendship; and capacities for appropriation and control of natural materials and energies. It is the function of education to see to it that individuals are so trained as to be capable of entering into the heritage of these values which already exist, trained also in sensitiveness to the defects of what already exists and in ability to recreate and improve.

But neither of these ends can be adequately accomplished unless people are trained to grasp and be concerned about the effect of social institutions upon individual capacities, and this not just in general but in discriminating detail.

Philosophy has two definite factual bases, one individual, the other institutional. Each base is susceptible of scientific study. Psychology can study the matter from the side of the individual, asking how this and that environmental condition, especially in the human environment, affects the powers of this and that person; how it calls out, strengthens, furthers, or weakens and retards this and that potentiality. Since education is a process of human interactions, while physiology and other subjects may supply material, adequate educational psychology must be a *social* psychology, not an impersonal one. Also are institutions and social arrangement to be studied factually and scientifically. The study becomes *educationally* significant only when it is extended to include how this and that social condition works causally to modify the experience and affect the character and capacity of individuals who come under its influence.

II

While choice cannot be eliminated nor preference reduced to intellectual and logical entities, nevertheless concrete, positive material of experience affords the basis for making choice intelligent. The difference between intelligent and arbitrary choice is between a preference which does not know what it is about, which has not considered the meaning of what it prefers, namely, the consequences which will result from action, and one based on the preference which surveys conditions and probable results of the choice made. The social analyses and interpretations which are included in previous chapters set forth the rationale of the choice which determines our educational philosophy. We believe the reasonableness and validity of a choice can be judged by such tests as the following: (1) Does the choice depend upon a survey and interpretation which discloses existing social conditions and trends? Does it, in short, rest upon genuine and thorough observation of the moving forces of a given state of social culture? (2) Does it sense and formulate the deeper and more intangible aspirations, purposes and values, for our own educational philosophy, in our own American scene and life? [1]

In holding that the values which should determine the direction of education can be dug out of life-experience itself, we are denying by implication the position taken by some opposed types of philosophical theory. We affirm that genuine values and tenable ends and ideals are to be derived from what is found within the movement of experience. Hence we deny

[1] Criticism of the philosophy we advance is likely, therefore, to be effective according as it centers upon, first, the criteria we employ, and, second, the correctness and adequacy of the use we have made of them in interpreting and recording the social situation in which we live.

the views which assert that philosophy can derive them out of itself by excogitation, or that they can be derived from authority, human or supernatural, or from any transcendent source. Our analyses of social forces are made because of the bearing of these forces upon the choice of values and the institution of purposes.

The position we take can be maintained only by recognizing that any existing society is marked by both negative and positive values. Were there no values already experienced, there would be no material out of which to frame ends and ideals. But an end and ideal also imply something to be striven for, something therefore which is as yet non-existent. The aspect of an end which goes contrary to what exists does not come however out of the blue, or out of anything remote from actual experience. A man makes health an end because he has enjoyed it enough to know what it means and what it is to enjoy it. But he also has experienced lack of health and is aware that health is not automatic, that it has foes, and that it must therefore be pursued and cultivated. Values as they exist are often both obscure and conflicting. They neither lie on the surface nor constitute a self-coherent whole. If they did, education would be infinitely simpler than it is. The most urgent problems of current educational theory and practice grow out of the extraordinarily confused and conflicting state of values at the present time.

The conflict is practical; it involves clashes of individuals, of groups and classes. It can be resolved only where it exists, namely, in action. But action needs to be intelligent as to the values concerned, values negative and positive. Otherwise it will be more wasteful and destructive than it needs to be. Philosophy is the operation of studying the values at stake, of clearing up the understanding of them, of forming them in idea into a new integration, in which social forces will realize values in individual lives more broadly and equitably than at present. The formation of such a philosophy is instrumental rather than final. That is to say, it observes, criticizes, and integrates values in thought in order to determine and guide the action which will integrate them in fact. A philosophy based upon actual experience is so framed, in other words, as to react, through the plan of action which it projects, back into an experience which is directly realized and not merely conceived. Moreover, it is not implied that philosophy comes to completion as a preliminary and that then action takes place afterwards. There is a continuing interaction. The intellectual formulation develops from the vague to the definite through the action which it suggests and directs, and there is no end to this process. Philosophy develops as society does. It does not provide a substitute for the values which life contributes, but it does enter — vitally, if it performs its proper function — into the very social process in which values are generated and realized. A philosophy of education may thus be truly said to be general philosophy formulated with particular reference to its social office. . . .

JOHN DEWEY
The practicality of theory

EXPERIENCE AND ABSTRACTION

The history of the more mature sciences shows two characteristics. Their original problems were set by difficulties that offered themselves in the ordinary region of practical affairs. Men obtained fire by rubbing sticks together and noted how things grew warm when they pressed on each other, long before they had any theory of heat. Such everyday experiences in their seeming inconsistency with the phenomena of flame and fire finally led to the conception of heat as a mode of molecular motion. But it led to this conception only when the ordinary phenomena were reflected upon in detachment from the conditions and uses under which they exhibit themselves in practices. There is no science without abstraction, and abstraction means fundamentally that certain occurrences are removed from the dimension of familiar practical experience into that of reflective or theoretical inquiry.

To be able to get away for the time being from entanglement in the urgencies and needs of immediate practical concerns is a condition of the origin of scientific treatment in any field. Preoccupation with attaining some direct end or practical utility, always limits scientific inquiry. For it restricts the field of attention and thought, since we note only those things that are immediately connected with what we want to do or get at the moment. Science signifies that we carry our observations and thinking further afield and become interested in what happens on its own account. Theory is in the end, as has been well said, the most practical of all things, because this widening of the range of attention beyond nearby purpose and desire eventually results in the creation of wider and farther-reaching purposes and enables us to use a much wider and deeper range of conditions and means than were expressed in the observation of primitive practical purposes. For the time being, however, the formation of theories demands a resolute turning aside from the needs of practical operations previously performed.

This detachment is peculiarly hard to secure in the case of those persons who are concerned with building up the scientific content of educational practices and arts. There is a pressure for immediate results, for demonstration of a quick, short-time span of usefulness in school. There is a tendency to convert the results of statistical inquires and laboratory experiments into directions and rules for the conduct of school administration and instruction. Results tend to be directly grabbed, as it were, and put into operation by teachers. Then there is not the leisure for that slow

From John Dewey, *The Sources of a Science of Education*, pp. 16–22, 35–36, 55–60. By permission of Liveright, Publishers, New York. Copyright: 1929 by John Dewey.

and gradual independent growth of theories that is a necessary condition of the formation of a true science. The danger is peculiarly imminent in a science of education because its very recentness and novelty arouse skepticism as to its possibility and its value. The human desire to prove that the scientific mode of attack is really of value brings pressure to convert scientific conclusions into rules and standards of schoolroom practice.

It would perhaps be invidious to select examples too near to current situations. Some illustration, however, is needed to give definiteness to what has been said. I select an instance which is remote in time and crude in itself. An investigator found that girls between the ages of eleven and fourteen mature more rapidly than boys of the same age. From this fact, or presumed fact, he drew the inference that during these years boys and girls should be separated for purposes of instruction. He converted an intellectual finding into an immediate rule of school practice.

That the conversion was rash, few would deny. The reason is obvious. School administration and instruction is a much more complex operation than was the one factor contained in the scientific result. The significance of one factor for educational practice can be determined only as it is balanced with many other factors. Taken by itself, this illustration is so crude that to generalize from it might seem to furnish only a caricature. But the principle involved is of universal application. No conclusion of scientific research can be converted into an immediate rule of educational art. For there is no educational practice whatever which is not highly complex; that is to say, which does not contain many other conditions and factors than are included in the scientific finding.

Nevertheless, scientific findings are of practical utility, and the situation is wrongly interpreted when it is used to disparage the value of science in the art of education. What it militates against is the transformation of scientific findings into *rules* of action. Suppose for the moment that the finding about the different rates of maturing in boys and girls of a certain age is confirmed by continued investigation, and is to be accepted as fact. While it does not translate into a specific rule of fixed procedure, it is of some worth. The teacher who really knows this fact will have his personal attitude changed. He will be on the alert to make certain observations which would otherwise escape him; he will be enabled to interpret some facts which would otherwise be confused and misunderstood. This knowledge and understanding render his practice more intelligent, more flexible and better adapted to deal effectively with concrete phenomena of practice.

Nor does this tell the whole story. Continued investigation reveals other relevant facts. Each investigation and conclusion is special, but the tendency of an increasing number and variety of specialized results is to create new points of view and a wider field of observation. Various special findings have a cumulative effect; they reënforce and extend one another, and in time lead to the detection of principles that bind together a number of facts that are diverse and even isolated in their *prima facie* occurrence.

These connecting principles which link different phenomena together we call laws.

Facts which are so interrelated form a system, a science. The practitioner who knows the system and its laws is evidently in possession of a powerful instrument for observing and interpreting what goes on before him. This intellectual tool affects his attitudes and modes of response in what he does. Because the range of understanding is deepened and widened he can take into account remote consequences which were originally hidden from view and hence were ignored in his actions. Greater continuity is introduced; he does not isolate situations and deal with them in separation as he was compelled to do when ignorant of connecting principles. At the same time, his practical dealings become more flexible. Seeing more relations he sees more possibilities, more opportunities. He is emancipated from the need of following tradition and special precedents. His ability to judge being enriched, he has a wider range of alternatives to select from in dealing with individual situations.

WHAT SCIENCE MEANS

If we gather up these conclusions in a summary we reach the following results. In the first place, no genuine science is formed by isolated conclusions, no matter how scientifically correct the technique by which these isolated results are reached, and no matter how exact they are. Science does not emerge until these various findings are linked up together to form a relatively coherent system — that is, until they reciprocally confirm and illuminate one another, or until each gives the others added meaning. Now this development requires time, and it requires more time in the degree in which the transition from an empirical condition to a scientific one is recent and hence imperfect. . . .

Science of education not independent. Two conclusions as to the sources of educational science are now before us.

First, educational practices furnish the material that sets the problems of such a science, while sciences already developed to a fair state of maturity are the sources from which material is derived to deal intellectually with these problems. There is no more a special independent science of education than there is of bridge making. But material drawn from *other* sciences furnishes the content of educational science when it is focused on the problems that arise in education. . . .

THE PURPOSE OF THE PHILOSOPHY OF EDUCATION

It is sometimes said that philosophy is concerned with determining the ends of education while the science of education determines the means to be used. As one who is a philosopher rather than a scientist I might be inclined to welcome a statement that confers upon philosophy such an honorable position. Without a good deal of interpretation, it is, however, likely to give rise to more false than true conceptions. In this interpretation there are two important considerations.

In the first place, the notion easily gives rise to, even if it does not logically imply, a misapprehension of the relation of a philosophy of education to educational practices and direct experience in the field. In any vital
sense it is these practices which determine educational ends. Concrete educational experience is the primary source of all inquiry and reflection because it sets the problems, and tests, modifies, confirms or refutes the conclusions of intellectual investigation. The philosophy of education neither
originates nor settles ends. It occupies an intermediate and instrumental
or regulative place. Ends actually reached, consequences that actually accrue, are surveyed, and their values estimated in the light of a general
scheme of values.

But if a philosophy starts to reason out its conclusions without definite
and constant regard to the concrete experiences that define the problem
for thought, it becomes speculative in a way that justifies contempt. As far
as ends and values are concerned, the empirical material that is necessary
to keep philosophy from being fantastic in content and dogmatic in form
is supplied by the ends and values which are produced in educational
processes as these are actually executed. What a philosophy of education
can contribute is range, freedom and constructive or creative invention.
The worker in any field gets preoccupied with more immediate urgencies
and results. When one begins to extend the range, the scope, of thought,
to consider obscure collateral consequences that show themselves in a more
extensive time-span, or in reference to an enduring development, that one
begins to philosophize whether the process is given that name or not. What
is *termed* philosophy is only a more systematic and persistent performance
of this office.

What I have termed the contribution of " freedom," of liberation, is a
necessary accompaniment of this breadth of survey of actual ends or consequences. The professional practitioner in any field, from a factory to a
church and schoolhouse, is in danger of getting tied down, of getting habit-
bound, compensating for this rigidity by impulsive excursions, undertaken
according to temperament and circumstance, when routine becomes intolerable. I do not say that philosophers see life steadily and see it whole;
complete achievement in this respect is humanly impossible. But *any one*
is philosophical in the degree in which he makes a consistent effort in this
direction. The result is emancipation. When this liberation is confined
with the mind, the inner consciousness, of any one, it affords intense personal gratification, but it effects nothing and becomes specious. Its effect is
found only in operation. For a philosophy of education this operation is
found in enabling practitioners to carry on their work in a more liberal
spirit, with escape from tradition and routine and one-sided personal interests and whims.

This contribution is made by way of the third function mentioned;
namely, constructive imagination and invention. It is not enough to criticize the narrow limitations of accepted ends and values. This needful task
is but the negative side of the function of suggesting new ends, new meth-

ods, new materials. In performing this office, provision of scope of estimate and liberation of mind comes to a head. As far as the philosophy of education effects anything important, this is what it accomplishes for those who study it. Ideas are ideas, that is, suggestions for activities to be undertaken, for experiments to be tried. The proof of the pudding is in the eating. The philosophy of education not only draws its original material as to ends and value from actual experience in education, but it goes back to these experiences for testing, confirmation, modification, and the provision of further materials. This is what is meant when it is said that its work is intermediate and instrumental, not original nor final.

Our other point concerns the relations of science and philosophy with respect to means and ends. The statement as often made gives rise to misapprehension. It leads to the notion that means and ends are separate from each other, each having its own fixed province. In reality, ends that are incapable of realization are ends only in name. Ends must be framed in the light of available means. It may even be asserted that ends are only means brought to full interaction and integration. The other side of this truth is that means are fractional parts of ends. When means and ends are viewed as if they were separate, and to be dealt with by different persons who are concerned with independent provinces, there is imminent danger of two bad results.

Ends, values, become empty, verbal; too remote and isolated to have more than an emotional content. Means are taken to signify means already at hand, means accepted because they are already in common use. As far as this view prevails, the work of a science of education is reduced to the task of refining and perfecting the existing mechanism of school operations. Lack of efficiency, unnecessary waste, in the teaching of reading, writing, numbers, history, geography are detected so that they may be eliminated. More efficient methods of accomplishing the ends that already obtain are devised. This is good as far as it goes. But it overlooks a fundamental issue. How far do the existing ends, the actual consequences of current practices go, even when perfected? The important problem is devising *new* means in contradistinction to improved use of means already given. For " new means " does not signify merely new ways of accomplishing more efficiently ends already current, but means that will yield consequences, ends, that are qualitatively different. We can assign means to science and ends to philosophy only under the condition that there be persistent and unremitting interaction between the two.

SECTION **2. Analysis of educational concepts**

William James, the American philosopher, begins his famous essay on *Pragmatism* with the following anecdote:

" Some years ago, being with a camping. party in the mountains, I returned from a solitary ramble to find everyone engaged in a ferocious metaphysical dispute. The *corpus* of the dispute was a squirrel — a live squirrel supposed to be clinging to one side of a tree-trunk; while over against the tree's opposite side a human being was imagined to stand. This human witness tries to get sight of the squirrel moving rapidly around the tree, but no matter how fast he goes, the squirrel moves as fast in the opposite direction, and always keeps the tree between himself and the man, so that never a glimpse of him is caught. The resultant metaphysical problem now is this: *Does the man go around the squirrel or not?* He goes around the tree, sure enough, and the squirrel is on the tree; but does he go around the squirrel? In the unlimited leisure of the wilderness, discussion had been worn threadbare. Every one had taken sides, and was obstinate; and the numbers on both sides were even. Each side, when I appeared therefore appealed to me to make it a majority. Mindful of the scholastic adage that whenever you meet a contradiction you must make a distinction, I immediately sought and found one, as follows: 'Which party is right,' I said, ' depends on what you *practically mean* by " going round " the squirrel. If you mean passing from the north of him to the east, then to the south, then to the west, and then to the north of him again, obviously the man does go around him, for he occupies these successive positions. But if on the contrary you mean being first in front of him, then on the right of him, then behind him, then on his left, and finally in front again, it is quite as obvious that the man fails to go round him, for by the compensating movements the squirrel makes, he keeps his belly turned toward the man all the time, and his back turned away. Make the distinction, and there is no occasion for any further dispute. You are both right and both wrong according as you conceive the verb " to go round " in one practical fashion or the other.'

" . . . I tell this trivial anecdote because it is a peculiarly simple example of what I wish now to speak of as the *pragmatic method*. The pragmatic method is primarily a method of settling metaphysical dispute that otherwise might be interminable. Is the world one or many? — fated or free? — material or spiritual? — here are notions either of which may or may not hold good of the world; and disputes over such notions are unending. The pragmatic method in such cases is to try to interpret each notion by tracing its respective practical consequences. What difference would it practically make to anyone if this notion rather than that notion were true? If no practical differences can be traced, then the alternative means practically the same thing, and all dispute is idle. Whenever a dispute is serious, we ought to be able to show some practical difference that must follow from one side or the other's being right." *

It is in this spirit of eliminating arguments which are of no consequence and focusing attention on matters which are of moment (matters which make a practical difference) that modern philosophy of education works. Those who approach philosophy in this way believe it can clarify our thinking best by casting issues in language that has common meaning to all involved (or at the very least by indicating points at which language beclouds the issue), and by moving arguments from superficial manifestations of problems to the genuine, underlying point of disagreement. It may finally, they point out, help establish whether this point of disagreement is of a type amenable to investigation or proof.

As Israel Sheffler points out in the first of the selections which follows, the careful analysis of concepts and ideas has a long and hallowed tradition

* William James, *Pragmatism*, New York: Longmans, Green and Company, Inc., 1907, pp. 1–2.

in philosophy, a tradition extending back at least as far as Socrates. It must be clear in our minds that this analysis of concepts is not an end in itself; it is an instrument or means to other ends. The ultimate aim is not clarity of language but clarity of thinking. Yet without clarifying language, without carefully delimiting our concepts and defining our terms, we have as little chance of clarifying our thinking as did the disputants in William James' camping party. Contemporary philosophical analysis, which has found many of its models in the careful modes of analysis which have led to recent strides in science, is concerned with the rigorous examination of educational concepts, propositions, arguments, and theories. It would ask of educational arguments and theories such questions as the following: Are the assumptions involved made clear? Do the conclusions follow from the premises and the data? Are data which are purported to be relevant actually relevant? Are the conclusions implied in the definitions stipulated? It asks of educational concepts and propositions such questions as the following: Is this concept or proposition clear, or is it vague and/or ambiguous? Are purported differences really substantive differences or are they matters of definition? Are the concepts and propositions employed useful in terms of dealing with the problems or issues for

which they are designed, or would a different conceptual framework give greater promise of success? Are important propositions really tautologies? Are they actually capable of empirical verification? Philosophical analysis is not a game to be played where the stakes are insignificant; it is an indispensable tool to be employed in dealing with crucial issues in the field of education.

The two selections which follow are written by editors of important volumes on the role of philosophical analysis in education. The first indicates the urgency of our need " to clarify the meaning of our basic educational ideas, as of all ideas we hold important." Although the writing is rather abstruse and difficult, this selection clearly points out the fundamental directions in which modern philosophical analysts believe educational philosophy must move if it is to render its greatest service to the cause of education. The second selection, by B. Othanel Smith, illustrates one way of analyzing a key educational concept, in this case the concept of teaching itself. Until we can determine the essential characteristics of our basic educational practices and concepts, it will remain unlikely that we can fruitfully capitalize on the tremendous growth in the methodology of investigation which has accompanied the development of modern science.

ISRAEL SCHEFFLER
Philosophical analysis and education

Various activities may, with historical justification, lay claim to the honored title of " philosophy." These include, among others, e.g., logical analysis, speculative construction, culture criticism, institutional programming, and the expression of personal attitudes toward the world. It is my purpose neither to cast doubt on any of these claims nor to deny the appropriateness of any of these activities. I do, however, wish to stress the ambiguity of the general term " philosophy " and, correlatively, of the narrower term

Israel Scheffler, " Toward an Analytic Philosophy of Education," *Harvard Educational Review*, 24:223–230, Fall, 1954. Reprinted by permission.

"philosophy of education." It is certainly no striking news that the latter term is currently widely employed to mean practically anything from a well-articulated metaphysics of knowledge to the vaguest expression of attitudes toward, say, the public school system. What *is* worthy of note is that one legitimate meaning is almost consistently ignored: Philosophy of education is rarely, if ever, construed as the rigorous logical analysis of key concepts related to the practice of education. In this paper, arguing for the fruitfulness of such an approach, I shall try, *first*, to explain and illustrate the general notion of philosophy as logical analysis, and *second*, to outline the ways in which logical analysis appears to me relevant to educational problems.

The conception of philosophy as the attempt to clarify key concepts is hardly a modern invention. For the attempt, by dialectical methods, to clarify the meaning of basic notions is at least as old as Socrates. What distinguishes current analysis is, first, its greater sophistication as regards language, and the interpenetration of language and inquiry, secondly, its attempt to follow the modern example of the sciences in empirical spirit, in rigor, in attention to detail, in respect for alternatives, and in objectivity of method, and thirdly, its use of techniques of symbolic logic brought to full development only in the last fifty years. The result has been revolutionary for philosophic practice. New insights have been achieved in almost every area of traditional philosophy. The individualism so characteristic of its past has, to a marked extent, been tempered by a sense of community of investigation, unified by method rather than doctrine, and by a common search for clarity on fundamental issues. That this development represents no mere doctrinal school is evident from the fact that it comprises sharp differences of opinion within itself, as well as from the fact that a number of its early formulations have undergone orderly revision under the pressure of criticism and new discoveries. Nor can such development be considered entirely negative, for progress has been made in the settling of some older problems and the recasting of new ones, progress which is widely acknowledged by students in this domain. It is, then, this union of scientific spirit and logical method applied toward the clarification of basic ideas which characterizes current analytic philosophy.

Since critical precision rather than doctrine is the essence of such philosophy, its significance is best conveyed by an examination of concrete instances. My first illustration to this purpose is drawn from the theory of meaning, with which current analysts are perhaps predominantly concerned, and in which some of the best work has been done. I must ask you, despite its abstractness and unfamiliarity, to consider it with me in some detail, since for this philosophy detailed precision is all. Yet, I hope such consideration will afford an insight into *general* method and approach, which may emerge even more sharply against an abstract and unfamiliar setting. At a later point, of course, I shall want to suggest educational aplications. Meanwhile, it will perhaps be instructive to note how difficult is the attempt to avoid confusion even in a realm removed from the urgencies of practice, and how, even here, increasingly radical departures from common assumptions are necessitated by the quest for clarity.

Consider then, the notions of meaning and existence. Two common assumptions about these notions are: (i) That the meaningfulness of a sentence containing a singular term (i.e. a name, or descriptive phrase purporting to name a single entity) presupposes that this term actually *does* name, that is, that *there really exists* the entity purportedly referred to; failure to name removes the object of discourse and renders both the empty singular term and its context meaningless. (ii) That the existence-commitments of a theory, i.e. the entities which must exist for it to be true, are revealed by the set of singular terms which it employs. Both assumptions turn out, upon analysis, exceedingly troublesome if we want to construct a consistent and fruitful account of meaning. Let us see why this is so.

Take, for example, a definite singular descriptive phrase of the form " the such-and-such " as it appears in the sentence " The American President in 1953 plays golf." No difficulty here. The descriptive phrase, we would ordinarily say, following (i), *names* some unique entity, Mr. Eisenhower, while the sentence is a *meaningful* statement about this entity, asserting something true of it. The negation of this sentence, though false, we would declare still meaningful, as concerning the same single entity, named by the descriptive phrase in question.

Consider, now, the new sentence, " The American Emperor in 1953 plays chess," and its negation " It is not the case that the American Emperor in 1953 plays chess." Now there is, in point of fact, no entity denoted by the descriptive phrase shared by both these sentences, i.e. " The American Emperor in 1953." It plainly does us no good to declare the first sentence false, since false sentences are meaningful anyway and such a declaration would violate (i). Further, if the first sentence is false, its negation must be true, under the very same condition of failure to name by the identical descriptive phrase. So that a simple resolution to abandon (i) by taking failure to name as always implying falsity turns out impossible.

To hold on to (i) in the face of these two sentences, we must declare them both meaningless. But the consequences of such a course are plainly undesirable on two basic counts: First, it would hinge the very meaning of descriptive phrases inconveniently on fact. In general, we should prefer to keep the meaningfulness of our language independent of specific factual considerations; we want to consider our hypotheses meaningful even prior to any factual confirmation. Following the last proposal, however, we should require factual evidence of the existence and uniqueness of some appropriate named entity before we could even be confident we were *making sense* in using descriptive phrases, let alone asserting a truth by their use. Secondly, and perhaps more paradoxically, to make meaninglessness a consequence of failure to name, as our last proposal does for the two sentences under consideration, means that we cannot, within our language, even *deny* the existence of the American Emperor in 1953. For to do so, we should need to say something like " The American Emperor in 1953 does not exist," and this sentence itself turns out, by our last proposal, to be strictly meaningless.

An analogous problem arises for proper names. Suppose I deny that Zeus exists. A fairly reasonable position. Yet consider: if, in using proper names, I make sense only by talking *about* some actual entity, following (i), what in the world am I talking *about* in saying " Zeus does not exist."? In order for me to make sense, Zeus must exist, but if he does, my denial is false. Must I therefore admit, out of logical necessity, the existence of all members of the Pantheon, all characters in fiction, in short everything bearing an ostensible proper name? Furthermore, taking my denial statement as a miniature theory with one proper name (" Zeus "), it is clearly intended that, contrary to (ii), this name should be no clue to its existence-commitments, for it is intended to stand plainly committed to nothing, and certainly not to Zeus.

A well-known, and by now classic solution of the puzzle of descriptive phrases, which, in effect, abandons assumption (i) altogether for such phrases, was proposed many years ago by Bertrand Russell.[1] Briefly, Russell showed how to *eliminate* descriptive phrases in context, in favor of equivalent contexts no longer containing any phrases purporting to name unique entities, but referring quite generally to entities by means of logical variables like " something," " nothing," " everything," etc. Such elimination of contained descriptive phrases together with conservation of asserted content in effect divorces the contextual meaning from the purported naming function of such phrases altogether. For example, Russell's equivalent of our troublesome first sentence above is " something is an American Emperor in 1953 and plays chess and nothing else is an American Emperor in 1953." Though as a whole equivalent to the original, this translation provides no naming unit as a counterpart to the eliminated descriptive phrase. With this, the whole original problem disappears, there now being no difficulty in declaring this equivalent false, together with the original. But the upshot is the denial of (i) for descriptive phrases, since the original sentence is now construed as false (and its negation as true), hence perfectly meaningful, though the contained descriptive phrase fails to name. A corollary is denial of (ii) for descriptive phrases, since, if they can be significantly used without naming, they are no clue to the existential presuppositions of the theory.

A solution of the proper name puzzle was recently proposed by Pro-

[1] Russell, B. *Introduction to Mathematical Philosophy*, Ch. XVI, 2nd ed., London: Allen and Unwin, 1920.

fessor W. V. Quine,[2] who extends Russell's analysis by showing how all proper names may be construed as descriptive phrases and then eliminated as before. For our above example, we are counseled by Quine to construe "Zeus does not exist" as "The thing that is-Zeus does not exist," Russell's equivalent of which becomes "Either for each entity, it is not the case that it is-Zeus or there is more than one entity which is-Zeus." Again, since no proper name or descriptive phrase purporting to name a unique entity appears at all in this translation, there remains no difficulty in declaring it and its original meaningful, and moreover, true. One upshot is denial of (i) even where a purported *proper name* fails to name. Consequently, a second result is full denial of assumption (ii), since, for this analysis, proper names are clearly no better indicators of the existence-commitments of a theory than are its descriptive phrases, which are, for Russell, no indicators at all, as we have seen. As Quine's extension makes clear, existence-commitments are ultimately revealed solely by the use made of logical variables ("something," "each entity," etc.) when the theory is put into Russellian form. But the details of this judgment are another story.

One further problem, taken from a more familiar area, will illustrate that analysis is capable of touching our most basic notions of practice to the quick. We all talk of confirming general hypotheses by gathering relevant instances. For example, we say that a purported general law is progressively confirmed or disconfirmed by observation of its relevant instances. But consider the puzzle noted by Professor Hempel.[3] What is a confirming instance for the purported law "all ravens are black"? Clearly a raven which is black. A non-raven we would classify as clearly irrelevant altogether. Now, however, consider that our law is logically equivalent to the statement "All non-black things are non-ravens," and for this statement a confirming instance would be a non-black non-raven. But this instance we have decided was irrelevant to the first law. Shall we say that what is to be taken as an instance depends on the accident of linguistic formulation? Let us rather rule that logically equivalent sentences should be confirmed by exactly the same instances. This rule, however, is just as counter-intuitive as ever, since if a non-black non-raven is to confirm our first law, then every time I observe the sky, the sun, my typewriter, or Widener Library, I am progressively confirming the law that all ravens are black. Clearly our ordinary conceptions of what constitutes an instance are faulty somewhere, and require considerable refinement.

Enough now of general illustrations of analytic problems and methods. I have already intimated that analytic philosophers are by no means exclusively concerned with theory of meaning and philosophy of science. Indeed, much work in ethics, theory of mind, philosophy of law, aesthetics,

[2] Quine, W. V., "On What There Is," *Review of Metaphysics*, 2, 1948, and also *From a Logical Point of View*, Cambridge: Harvard University Press, 1953.
[3] Hempel, C. G. "Studies in the Logic of Confirmation," *Mind*, 54, 1945.

and theory of social science is presently under way. It is time, I think, to consider how analytic philosophy might be brought to bear on educational problems, as a legitimate and vital pursuit of philosophy of education. In analogy with applications of science to education, I suggest that we conceive of analytic applications in roughly two directions, (a) the utilization of results already achieved in the autonomous development of research, and (b) the use of acknowledged methods directly in the study of educational problems.

(a) To realize fully the extent to which the first mode of application is presently feasible, one would ideally require a detailed survey of current analysis which, as already noted, touches a wide variety of areas. Since one example must suffice, we might consider for a moment the rather fashionable proposal of Dewey,[4] Neurath,[5] and others,[6] to replace the venerable notion of truth by that of probability or verification, or analogous ideas, in view of the impossibility of complete confirmation of hypotheses. Despite its wide popularity, however, and despite the hasty conclusions drawn for practice, perhaps most analysts are agreed that such replacement would be an error, in view of Professor Tarski's semantic conception of truth.[7] For Tarski, to say that a given sentence, e.g., " the sun is shining," is true, is to say nothing more nor less than " the sun is shining." On the other hand, to say that the latter sentence is confirmed by John Doe to degree *d* at time *t* is obviously to make an independent assertion, since it may hold whether or not the sun is shining in point of fact, and vice versa. It follows that truth and confirmation are independent. As Professor Carnap has pointed out,[8] were the impossibility of complete confirmation to rule out the term " is true," it would equally rule out the term " is shining " and, indeed, every scientific term, while if partial confirmation is sufficient for retention of a term, then the term " true " is as acceptable as any. What is ruled out by the pervasiveness of probability is certainty, not truth.

A final illustration from the theory of value. It has been argued, at least since Aristotle, that the pattern of justifying beliefs relative to evidence implies that some beliefs must be certain. For if we justify some belief on evidence and this evidence on further evidence, where do we stop? We cannot continue to justify every belief relative to evidence without infinite regress. Hence, if any belief is justified, some must be known certain in themselves. Now this persuasive argument for rationalism, as recently

[4] Dewey, J. *Logic: the Theory of Inquiry*, New York, Holt, 1938.
[5] Neurath, O. *Foundations of the Social Sciences*, Chicago: University of Chicago Press, 1944.
[6] Kaufmann, F. *Methodology of the Social Sciences*, Toronto: Oxford University Press, 1944.
[7] Tarski, A. " The Semantic Conception of Truth," in *Readings in Philosophical Analysis*, ed. by H. Feigl and W. Sellars, New York: Appleton-Century-Crofts, 1949.
[8] Carnap, R. " Truth and Confirmation," in *Readings in Philosophical Analysis*, ed. Feigl and Sellars.

shown by Professor Goodman, is somewhat too extravagant.[9] In order to avoid infinite regress, we need only hold some beliefs with some initial credibility. We need attribute certainty to none. While we try to attain and preserve a maximum of initial credibility for the total mass of our beliefs, any single one is subject to withdrawal under pressure of conflict with this total mass. Recently, I have noted the possibility of extending Professor Goodman's argument to ethical justification generally.[10] For it is very widely held that in order to justify any act, goal, or choice, some at least must be held absolutely immune to withdrawal. What we need admit, it seems to me, is only that some choices or goals may have for us some degree of initial committedness, while none is immune to withdrawal. Whereas no act or choice is justifiable in isolation, every act is subject to control by all in our attempt to harmonize them by maximizing initial committedness for the mass of our behavior. If this analysis is not mistaken, then both ethical absolutism and extreme subjectivism are avoided, a corollary with important bearings on value theory and education. The analysis of justification is presently being pursued from a variety of approaches, and may prove fruitful for problems in social theory, theory of democracy, and other areas related to education.[11]

(b) The second mode of application I mentioned above consists of the direct analysis of concepts related to the practice of education. What I have already said perhaps indicates the possibilities in this area better than any catalogue I might offer. Yet it is worth noting at this point that, if obscurity surrounds such basic notions as " existence," " truth," and " confirmation," notions crucially employed and continually refined in the exact sciences, it may surely be expected to hamper the understanding of key notions tied to educational practice, notions like " disposition," " experience," " skill," " achievement," " training," " intelligence," " character," " choice," " growth." How shall we understand, to take but one example, the popular contention that growth is the goal of education? Clearly not every sort of growth is held desirable, witness growth in ignorance or brutality. Even if we eliminate obviously undesirable dispositions, shall we think of growth as simply the increase in dispositions acquired by the learner? This will not do, for a substantial part of growth consists in dropping off dispositions once mastered. We all at one time could shoot marbles pretty well but can do so no longer. Furthermore, in attempting a count of dispositions how shall we classify them? Is playing checkers one and playing

[9] Goodman, N. " Sense and Certainty," *Philosophical Review*, vol. lxi, April, 1952.
[10] Scheffler, I. " On Justification and Commitment," *Journal of Philosophy*, vol. li, March 1954.
[11] Burks, A. W. " Justification in Science," in *Academic Freedom, Logic, and Religion*, ed. M. G. White, Philadelphia, University of Pennsylvania Press, 1953. Also Feigl, H. " De Principis Non Disputandum? " in *Philosophical Analysis*, ed. M. Black, Ithaca: Cornell University Press, 1950. Also Fitch, F. B. " Justification in Science," in *Academic Freedom, Logic, and Religion,* ed. M. G. White.

chess another? If so, where do we put Chinese checkers? Finally, how shall we weight the progressive intensification of one disposition as against the multiplication of several?

Taking a new direction, we might, along lines reminiscent of Dewey, consider growth as the intensification of some master disposition, e.g. the ability to solve problems intelligently. But how is such intensification itself to be construed concretely? A simple increase in solved problems per unit time may not indicate growth if conjoined with a greater increase per unit time in perceived problems remaining unsolved. Shall we propose, then, as an appropriate indication of our meaning here, the ratio of solved problems to those perceived, per unit time? This would end in absurdity since, other things remaining equal, a decrease in perception would constitute growth, while an increase in sensitivity to problems would constitute regression. We might try a different move (as Dewey appears to in certain of his writings), and construe problems not as relative to the selectivity of a perceiver, but as somehow objectively built into the total situation. But such a move, while it is not obvious that it meets our original difficulties, clearly raises more troubles than we had to begin with: Just what is a total situation, what kind of entities are objective problems, and how do we determine their character?

Now it is important not to confuse the import of my remarks here with the widespread demand for so-called operational definitions. If this were all that is involved, it would be quite easy to define growth operationally as increase in weight as measured in milligrams, or in height as measured in centimeters, or in the average number of hairs per square centimeter of scalp.[12] Such a course would have but one drawback, i.e. it would have nothing whatever to do with our original, predefinitional concept as it figures in the educational statement in question. What is required here, it seems to me, is not the application of operationalist slogans so much as a careful analysis or explication of our original concept, aimed at the distillation of a more precise counterpart, and finally, an examination of what consequences result for educational theory from rewriting it with such newly-achieved precision, or possibly, from failure to attain additional clarity.

Nor do I here intend, by any means, to deny the possibility of a fruitful and significant clarification of the notion of growth as used in educational theory. I am pointing to what seems to me one genuine philosophic problem germane to education, calling for the use of analytic methods. And what I am urging generally is recognition of the need, by a rigorous and thorough application of such methods, to clarify the meaning of our basic educational ideas, as of all ideas we hold important. If philosophy of education accepts this task of clarification, it will be assuming not merely a famil-

---

[12] Hempel, C. G. *Fundamentals of Concept Formation in Empirical Science,* Chicago, University of Chicago Press, 1952. (Discussion of operationalism).

iar historical role, but one which is proving increasingly fruitful and stimulating in wide reaches of current philosophy, and which cannot fail to deepen our understanding of what we do when we educate.

B. OTHANEL SMITH
An application of philosophical analysis

The procedures and techniques of teaching, like those of any art, are not to be worked out by reference to ready-made ideas. Rather they are to be devised in terms of the materials and conditions at hand, and by reference to discoveries about these circumstances and what they require for the achievement of intended effects. Knowledge of what teaching is in fact is prerequisite to its systematic improvement.

We shall, therefore, attempt to give an analysis of teaching as it is. We shall begin with the most general conception, namely, that teaching consists of a succession of acts by an individual whose purpose is either to show other persons how to do something or to inform them that something is the case. The word " teaching " thus defined is used to refer to what the teacher does rather than to the behavior of the student or to what happens to him as a result of instruction. It makes no sense to say that if the student has not learned, the teacher has not taught. For learning is not stipulated as a characteristic of teaching.

It should therefore be remembered throughout this discussion that we have chosen to separate learning from teaching. We do not even use the hyphenated expression teaching-learning. For if it is intended to signify that learning is supposed to result from teaching, it is superfluous. Were the expression used to indicate that where there is learning, there is teaching, such is obviously not the case. Or if the double-barrelled expression is used to mean that teaching always results in intended learning, again such is not the case. Finally, if it is used to indicate that teaching is not teaching unless it does result in learning, the usage is arbitrary. Connecting learning and teaching verbally in this hyphenated expression serves to increase the complexity of the concept of teaching without compensating gains. So we have decided to treat teaching as teaching and learning as learning.

What teaching is. Before turning to the acts constituting teaching, we shall point out certain things which are not strictly a part of teaching but which are so closely related to it as often to be mistaken for it. These are method, skill, style, and control. By method is generally meant a particular order imposed upon teaching activities. It is a construction of how teaching ought to be done. We speak of the project method, lecture

B. Othanel Smith, " On the Anatomy of Teaching," *Journal of Teacher Education*, 7:339–346, December, 1956. Reprinted by permission. (This article is adapted from the James William Norman Lecture, delivered at the University of Florida, Gainesville, on July 2, 1956.)

method, question-answer method, and unit method. Of course, to follow any of these methods is to teach. But teaching is more than a method. And the tendency to equate the two of them has led to more than one pedagogical dogma.

When we speak of a teacher's skill we are referring to how well he performs the acts of teaching. It is sometimes said that the proficiency of a teacher is to be decided by the achievement of his students. But this way of thinking about the teacher's skillfulness is a choice among alternatives and is in no sense necessary. It is no less defensible to say that a teacher is proficient if his instruction satisfies criteria derived from pedagogical research and practical experience. In this event, the teacher might be very proficient and still some students learn little or nothing from his instruction. In the same way a physician may be very skilled and yet some of his patients may not recover. As the doctors say, the operation was a success but the patient died. Or a lawyer may display unusual skill in defending a client but still lose the case. No practitioner can rightly be held responsible for the outcome of his practice beyond adherence to the knowledge and techniques of his profession.

By style of teaching we mean the characteristic demeanor in which the teaching acts are performed. For example, a teacher may operate in a sympathetic frame of mind, or he may be aggressive toward both the students and the ideas with which he deals. A teacher may be habitually dramatic, or he may show little or no feeling at all as he teaches. Unlike skill, teaching style is personal and somewhat unique for each individual. The failure to distinguish between style of teaching and teaching itself, is one of the primary sources of the mistaken notion that teachers are born and not made.

The custodial and disciplinary duties of the teacher are frequently confused with teaching. Of course, a measure of order in the classroom is a necessary condition for instruction. But the maintenance of order is not itself instruction. In college and university classrooms the custodial and disciplinary functions of the teacher are negligible, and the distinction between these functions and instruction stands out clearly. In the public schools, however, these duties take so much of the teacher's time and energy that the line between teaching and discipline becomes blurred in his mind. At any rate, the job of housekeeping is one thing and teaching is quite another thing.

However, telling what something is not, does not tell us what it is. So let us turn to a positive description of the teaching process. If we go to the classroom, we shall see what it is that the teacher does. We shall see that what he does follows an order of events which are not of his own making, but which occur because of the very nature of the enterprise going on there. As the teacher faces a classroom group, what do we see him do? First of all he induces the students to give attention to himself. By virtue of his position, he is necessarily the central figure in the classroom, and no amount of ingratiation or sharing in activities on his part can hide the fact. While the day's disasters need not be read upon his morning face, it is still true that the first significant act of the teacher is to focus the attention of his students upon himself. When this has been accomplished, he then directs their attention to what is to be learned. He may do this in a number of ways — by telling the students what to do, by engaging them in planning what to do, or by other means. The teacher then directs the students in those activities which are designed to bring about the desired learning. Such activities may include listening to the teacher, watching him do something, trying to solve problems, practicing exercises, and so on.

These acts of the teacher are, of course, gross performances. And we shall miss the subtle, but significant aspects of his work, if we do not look at the things which the teacher does when he executes them. Throughout his performance the teacher is observing the students, diagnosing their feelings and interests, and following as best he can the progress of their understanding. He also talks, for he is called upon to explain, interpret and give directions, and these duties can be performed in no other way. Then, too, he uses all sorts of pedagogical and social sanctions to approve and disapprove, to reward and to punish, to persuade and to restrain the students at every turn in the day's work.

Signs and symbols in teaching. An analysis of these elusive aspects of teaching will take us to the heart of the teaching process. Let us see what the teacher does when he is doing these things. We see him use all sorts of signs and symbols as he diagnoses the state of the students' feelings, interests, and understandings, and likewise as he explains, interprets, and persuades. Now, the teacher cannot know the feelings and interests of his students by observation alone; for feelings and interests are not accessible to the senses. The only way he can know them is by inference. Neither a smile nor a frown is a feeling. Nor is anger a sharply spoken reply. These are external manifestations of inner states and processes. Like one who must find out the contents of a sealed box by inference from its external features, the teacher can know the inner facts about his students only by inference from visible signs. From a student's facial expression, he infers that the student does or does not want to do something. The tone of the student's voice and the expression in his eyes tell the teacher whether or not the student is angry, happy, or apprehensive. And the light in his mind shows up in the light on his face.

The fact that the deeper reactions and feelings of the student are hidden and that they are present to the teacher only by implication has been little noticed. Yet it may well be that the success of the teacher depends in large measure upon his accurate perception and understanding of such natural signs as posture, tone of voice, and facial expression. From practical experience it would seem that there is wide variation among teachers with respect to sensitivity to these cues. Some teachers of outstanding intellectual ability appear to be insensitive to what is going on around them, oblivious to the inner life of the student if not to the classroom itself until something happens to jolt them to their senses. Then it is often too late to redeem their status as teachers. Others seem to see all sorts of cues, but, knowing not what they mean, become rattled by them and thus lose control of the teaching process. Still other teachers appear to be keenly aware of every change in these natural signs and to understand their significance. They, therefore, direct their moment-to-moment behavior as teachers in terms of information coming to them by implication from the multiplicity of natural signs around them. If we could but find out how to read these natural signs accurately and how to teach prospective teachers to do so, their proficiency in the art of teaching might be better secured.

The teacher learns about his students not only from natural signs but also from their use of language. What the student says is of significance to the teacher partly because it supplies him with data by which to understand the student. Just as facial expressions and other natural signs convey by implication the feelings and thoughts of the student, so do linguistic expressions reveal the inner life to him who is able to interpret them. Suppose a student says, in response to the question of how the streams of New England differ from those of the coastal plains " I ain't sure. But is it that the rivers run slow in New England and fast in the coastal plains? Well, maybe I'm wrong. I don't know." Now what do these words tell the teacher? It all depends upon how he is tuned in and how versatile he is in changing wave lengths. These data indicate a number of things. They tell the teacher that the student is deficient in linguistic usage, hesitant in answering the question, and deficient in geographic knowledge. Other linguistic expressions of the student may indicate that he is emotionally upset, reasons fallaciously, and does not know how to explicate words.

In general, then, the symbolic expressions of the student tell us: (1) his emotional state, (2) the grammatical and linguistic errors he makes, (3) whether or not he understands something, (4) the values he holds, (5) the logical errors he makes, and (6) his factual errors. Language as a source of information about the student has, of course, been used since teaching first began. But the conceptualization of its functions should enable us to make better use of language as an instrument of instruction. For the teacher can mold his behavior intelligently to the extent that he is aware of the conditions which affect the outcome of his acts. Hence the teacher, at his best, is sensitive to this total spectrum of things which the student's linguistic expressions tell him.

Teaching as a linguistic process. The teacher not only interprets signs and symbols coming to him from the students, but he also expresses himself to his students by signs and symbols as he instructs. In fact, teaching cannot occur without the use of language. Teaching is, above all, a linguistic activity. The teacher makes assignments, gives directions, explains events and statements, interprets words and other expressions, proves propositions, justifies decisions and actions, makes promises, praises and blames students. He cannot teach without doing these things. And he cannot do any of them without using language. Can an assignment be made without language? Can anything be explained or an action justified without saying something? Can a proposition be proved or an expression interpreted without using language? To raise such questions is to indicate the way in which language is inextricably involved in the processes both of learning and of teaching. It is to show that language is at the very heart of teaching.

Let us look at some of the ways in which the teacher uses language. In the first place, he uses language to teach students how to do something. In teaching a student how to typewrite, for example, the teacher may show the student how to do it by performing the activity himself. But this will not be sufficient. The student must himself perform the activity, and he must be directed in the performance of it. So, the teacher will tell him from time to time what to do. But it is not intended that the student remember the sentences spoken by the teacher. The teacher will tell him to try so and so, don't do so and so, or you are making this movement and you should be doing thus and so. The purpose of the discourse is immediate. Its use beyond the moment may be insignificant. For once the student learns to typewrite, what the teacher told him drops out of the picture.

This sort of telling is to be found in nearly all teaching. And it is more complex than we might suppose. It entails a triple relationship in which the elements are the teacher, the student, and a third something, for example, a map, a piece of apparatus, a book, an act of either the student or the teacher. Suppose a teacher is instructing a science class by means of a demonstration. As the demonstration proceeds, the student must observe what is done and what happens. At the same time he must listen to the teacher tell what is being done, why it is being done, and so on. The student is thus in a double role of observer and listener. The teacher, too, is involved in the same way. He must pay attention to what he is doing and at the same time talk about what he is doing. But he must do even more. He must also pay attention to the entire class and choose words and ideas appropriate to the capacities of the students. This three-way intellectual performance is seldom found outside of a teaching situation. It is not an easy one to learn, and many elements of the situation escape the eye of the novice. Even the experienced teacher is seldom well enough aware of his performance to tell the beginner what to do and how to do it.

There is a second and even more significant use of language in teaching. In this instance the teacher tries to increase the student's fund of knowledge. In order to do this he explains, he defines, he justifies, he offers proof, and so on. And, as we have already said, to do these the teacher must use language. But it is a use of language which differs from that employed in the direction of an activity which a student is learning to perform. It is a discourse that expresses ideas which are to be retained, and which can be retained only as they are embodied in linguistic symbols. The teacher who explains Boyle's law by showing its logical relation to the molecular theory of matter does not do so on the assumption that what he says will be forgotten. Nor does a teacher who explains an event in human history by reference to a general proposition about the behavior of human beings intend that the students forget what he says. Of course, the teacher does not intend that the student remember the exact words or the particular sentences. But the teacher does expect the student to be able to express the ideas in his own words and to show in other verbal ways that he grasps what the teacher has said.

Since the discourse of the teacher embodies ideas to be learned, it is designed to convey ideas in accurate and succinct statements. In this sense, it is studied discourse. Unlike informal talk, its order is shaped by the nature of the task. Ideas are expressed in a sequence calculated to make them easily understood. Even the teacher's demeanor and tone of voice are affected by the nature of the task. Children recognize this fact, and when they play " school," the one who has the role of teacher adopts the voice and studied manner of the teacher.

Thus the significance of the role of language in teaching is clearly evident when we stop to think about it. Yet the plain fact is that all we know about language in this regard is a kind of unanalyzed common sense distilled from practice. It could be that when we have analyzed the language of teaching and investigated the effects of its various formulations, the art of teaching will show marked advancement.

The logic of teaching. Teaching involves logic as well as language. This is the case because reasoned discourse leads to conclusions. It begins somewhere and ends somewhere. And logic, in its deductive sense, is a way of clarifying our linguistic expressions and of ordering sentences in such a way that we can decide upon the truth of our conclusions.

Just as we have neglected the role of language in teaching, so have we disregarded logic. This neglect of logic has resulted partly from our erroneous notion that the research which dislodged faculty psychology and its theory of formal discipline also discredited the study of logic, and partly from our erroneous ideas of what logic was supposed to do for us. The overthrow of formal discipline had no bearing upon the uses of logic when properly perceived. Logic does not purport to tell us how we do in fact think. It has nothing to do with the pondering processes, whatever they are, by which ideas occur to us and by which we reach conclusions. The principles of logic describe neither thinking nor thought. Nor do they tell us how our thinking ought to proceed. They are not norms to which the thinking process should conform. Rather logic is useful to us when we scan our thinking to tell whether or not the conclusions we have reached follow necessarily from our premises, or, as in inductive thinking, to decide the probable truth of our conclusions.

Seen in this light, logic plays an important role in the process of teaching. For one thing, a statement becomes clear to us either when its key words are adequately defined or when it is fixed in the chain of sentences to which it is logically linked, or when both of these obtain. Now, teaching in its didactic sense embraces both of these performances. For, as we have already said, such teaching includes the activities of defining, explaining, justifying, proving, and the like. And these without exception are logical operations.

The fact that these activities are logical activities is seldom recognized. We have failed to recognize their logical nature because of our tendency in education to psychologize everything. In pedagogical discussion we use two sets of concepts, both of which we believe to be psychological, when in fact only one set is so. One of these sets consists of such concepts as inferring, perceiving, conceiving, generalizing, thinking, and judging. We use these in talking about psychological processes. And we are correct in doing so. Of course, there is a legitimate question as to whether there are internal processes corresponding to these names, but that question is one which we leave to the psychologists. The other set of concepts are identified by such terms as define, interpret, explain, justify, and prove. These are logical rather than psychological. They are operations which we perform with words and sentences and which we cannot perform without words and sentences. And these operations are found in the domain of logic.

For purposes of illustration we shall consider definition and explanation. It hardly need be said that a great deal of school learning consists of definitions. Our books and discussions are filled with definitions. Now in logic we are told that there are different ways of defining words. To define a word is to tell how it is to be used. We can define the word " seed " by saying that " a seed is that part of a flowering plant that holds the embryo and associated structures." What we have done is to tell the class of things to which a seed belongs, by saying that it belongs to the class of things called " parts of a flowering plant." Then we have told how a seed differs from other members of the class of things to which it belongs such as leaves, roots, and stem. Wherever the expression " part of a flowering plant which holds the embryo and associated structures" appears in our discussion we can substitute the word " seed " without changing the meaning. This is what we do when we define a word. Thus a definition represents a decision; for it lays down the rules for the use of a word. Since they are decisions, definitions are neither true nor false.

The amount of time used inefficiently in the classroom because the teacher does not know how to deal with questions involving definitions is greater, I fear, than we like to think. Classroom discussion is often snarled up by disagreements about the meaning of words, as though words somehow had meanings in the same way that dogs have fleas. Many fruitless discussions might be avoided were the teacher capable of handling definitions through a knowledge of logic and its operations.

Similarly, the logic of explanation is appropriate when the teacher is called upon to explain either statements or events, or to evaluate explanations given by students. Suppose the teacher is called upon to explain the fact that in the early morning the wind blows from the land toward the sea. What must he do? The answer is that he must try to find the premises from which the factual conclusion — the wind blows from the land toward the sea in the early morning — can be drawn. Now any number of premises may be chosen, depending upon the teacher's knowledge. But if he is trained in physics, he will reason from the general law that heated bodies expand and thus become lighter per unit of volume. It is not necessary here to follow the logical steps the teacher must take to get from the general law to the particular event to be explained. But he will go on to show that the air over the ocean becomes warmer at night than the air over the land, and that the cold, heavier air over the land then displaces the ocean air which is warmer and lighter. An explanation thus consists in showing that the fact to be explained can be taken as an instance of the general law which has been used as the explanatory principle.

Failure to understand what an explanation is leads to all sorts of entanglements in the classroom. Sometimes the discussion centers in the question of whether or not an explanation is a true one. To answer the question it is necessary that the truth of the premises be tested. But unfortunately the teacher often lacks the knowledge of logic necessary to test the truth of statements used as premises. Then, too, teachers sometimes mistake the mere recounting of events for explanation. A student is asked to tell why the French Revolution happened. So he relates events leading up to the revolution as an explanation of why the revolution occurred. Now, the mere recounting of events is not an explanation in the logical sense, for there is no general principle from which to derive the event to be explained. Sometimes, however, a student, or even a teacher, uses a general principle without making it explicit. Consequently it is subjected neither to critical appraisal nor to the test of fact. Partly for this reason, instruction in history often lacks rigor and thus fails to engage the higher mental processes of students.

Conclusion. It has been our purpose in this discussion to describe teaching, teaching as it is in fact. We have not sought to set forth any new theory of how teaching ought to be done. Rather we have analyzed teaching into some of its essential elements because it is our belief that he who would improve an art must first understand it. And the understanding of any art begins not with loose abstractions, but with systematic and painstaking anaylsis of that art.

It has been a common practice to think of teaching almost exclusively in psychological terms. This practice has too long kept us from facing the realities, the hard plain facts of teaching. I have tried to speak in terms of the facts of teaching — of what it is that we actually do when we teach. Our analysis has, perforce, been all too brief. Hence it has presented merely the bold contours and the grosser elements of the general process of instruction. Many details remain to be laid out. And since the present analysis represents an early exploration, it is to be expected that under further study and further elaboration, the present general outline will undergo changes.

Nevertheless, I believe that any candid view of teaching will throw into sharp relief most features of the teaching process that I have described. If we look frankly at teaching, I believe that we shall become aware at least of the truly linguistic and symbolic nature of the teaching process, and that the fundamental role of logical operations in teaching will become abundantly clear. If this be the case, we shall be dealing with problems that we have not recognized heretofore. And yet, it may be that through the solution of these problems the art of teaching will make its most rewarding advancement.

SECTION **3. Problem solving**

Knowledge of a problem-solving procedure is a necessity in a democratic society. Other societies, such as those that are based upon authoritarianism, reject problem-solving in many situations as unsuitable or undesirable. For problem-solving requires a commitment to intelligence and the free examination of all ideas. As Dewey and Childs have indicated in a previous selection in this chapter, mankind is now at a stage where for the first time in matters of social policy there is the possibility of more integration and consistency between thought and action. We are at the stage where social action can be consciously directed rather than left to aimless self-direction. In order for the action to be intelligently based and directed it must rest upon a method of intelligence. And since, in a democratic society, the people are the ultimate directors of their actions, the schools have an obligation to develop within the students a familiarity with and practice in the problem-solving method.

Problem-solving has been analyzed and described with varying degrees of intellectual sophistication. In the two selections that follow there is a range from relatively simple illustrations and applications to the rather complex and detailed dissection of a " complete act of reflective activity " by John Dewey.

For our purposes the essential ingredients of problem-solving may be set forth as a summary of the treatment of the " method of intelligence " found on pages 16 to 18 in Chapter 1. Briefly these include the following five elements:

1. Recognizing a felt difficulty, obstruction, or problem.
2. Clearly defining and delimiting the problem.
3. Formulating hypotheses about the problem.
4. Drawing conclusions based upon pertinent data relating to the problem.
5. Taking action in accordance with the conclusion and noting the consequences of such action.

As was indicated previously in this volume, and as Dewey points out in his writings, any series of steps describing a problem-solving procedure should not be looked upon as rigid, inflexible, and always occurring in the same sequence.

It would be a simple matter if the mere rote memorization of the steps in problem-solving insured success for the learner. Such is not the case. In practice, problem-solving is rarely a smooth and uncomplicated procedure. Probably in no other activity is it so true that " one learns best by doing." The best training in problem-solving comes not from reading *about* the process but rather accrues to those who actively *engage in* the process. The wide discrepancy between intellectual understanding and practical application is very well pointed out in an illustration provided by an educator who recently returned from an extended study of education in Far Eastern countries. He described one incident in which a university lecturer dealt for quite some time with the ideas of Thomas Malthus as they relate to population growth. The students demonstrated their understanding of the information that the lecturer had given them by very acceptable responses in class discussion and on a paper and pencil test covering the subject. But when the lecturer asked the students to apply the ideas and generalizations about the Malthusian hypothesis to their own country (which faces an acute population problem), they were unable to make any suitable applications or valid generalizations. Here was an extreme example of discontinuity between knowledge and application. In many American schools there can no doubt be found similar examples of such discontinuity.

Assuming that the classroom teach-er is interested in promoting problem-solving among his students, he will have to supplement knowledge about the process with the establishment of a proper classroom "climate." In general the kind of atmosphere that is conducive to problem-solving is one in which there is a feeling of permissiveness so that the students can delve into any areas and topics that are reasonably pertinent to the problem under investigation. There can be no sacred cows or untouchable areas. Each student's contribution should be treated with courtesy and respect even though the substance of it may be subjected to sharp criticism. And the teacher's role becomes indeed that of a director of learning rather than a fountainhead of all knowledge.

In the first of the two selections that follow, Dewey elaborates on five aspects of reflective thinking. The second selection, by Edward Hodnett, relates some very specific examples of the application of problem-solving. Although most of these examples are not directly related to classroom teaching, they are extremely useful illustrations of the need for a kind of mental dexterity and nimbleness that would stand any teacher in good stead.

JOHN DEWEY
An analysis of reflective thinking

We now have before us the material for the analysis of a complete act of reflective activity. In the preceding chapter we saw that the two limits of every unit of thinking are a perplexed, troubled, or confused situation at the beginning and a cleared-up, unified, resolved situation at the close. The first of these situations may be called *pre*-reflective. It sets the problem to be solved; out of it grows the question that reflection has to answer. In the final situation the doubt has been dispelled; the situation is *post*-reflective; there results a direct experience of mastery, satisfaction, enjoyment. Here, then, are the limits within which reflection falls.

Five phases, or aspects, of reflective thought. In between, as states of thinking, are (1) *suggestions*, in which the mind leaps forward to a possi-

From John Dewey, *How We Think*, 1933, pp. 106–118. Reprinted by permission of D. C. Heath and Company.

ble solution; (2) an intellectualization of the difficulty or perplexity that has been *felt* (directly experienced) into a *problem* to be solved, a question for which the answer must be sought; (3) the use of one suggestion after another as a leading idea, or *hypothesis*, to initiate and guide observation and other operations in collection of factual material; (4) the mental elaboration of the idea or supposition as an idea or supposition (*reasoning*, in the sense in which reasoning is a part, not the whole, of inference); and (5) testing the hypothesis by overt or imaginative action.

We shall now take up the five phases, or functions, one by one.

The first phase, suggestion. The most " natural " thing for anyone to do is to go ahead; that is to say, to *act* overtly. The disturbed and perplexed situation arrests such direct activity temporarily. The tendency to continue *acting* nevertheless persists. It is diverted and takes the form of an idea or a suggestion. The *idea* of what to do when we find ourselves " in a hole " is a substitute for direct action. It is a vicarious, anticipatory way of acting, a kind of dramatic rehearsal. Were there only one suggestion popping up, we should undoubtedly adopt it at once. But where there are two or more, they collide with one another, maintain the state of suspense, and produce further inquiry. The first suggestion in the instance recently cited was to jump the ditch, but the perception of conditions inhibited that suggestion and led to the occurrence of other ideas.

Some inhibition of *direct* action is necessary to the condition of hesitation and delay that is essential to thinking. Thought is, as it were, conduct turned in upon itself and examining its purpose and its conditions, its resources, aids, and difficulties and obstacles.

The second phase, intellectualization. We have already noted that it is artificial, so far as thinking is concerned, to start with a ready-made problem, a problem made out of whole cloth or arising out of a vacuum. In reality such a ' problem ' is simply an assigned *task*. There is not at first a situation *and* a problem, much less just a problem and no situation. There is a troubled, perplexed, trying situation, where the difficulty is, as it were, spread throughout the entire situation, infecting it as a whole. If we knew just what the difficulty was and where it lay, the job of reflection would be much easier than it is. As the saying truly goes, a question well put is half answered. In fact, we know what the problem *exactly* is simultaneously with finding a way out and getting it resolved. Problem and solution stand out *completely* at the same time. Up to that point, our grasp of the problem has been more or less vague and tentative.

A blocked suggestion leads us to reinspect the conditions that confront us. Then our uneasiness, the shock of disturbed activity, gets stated in some degree on the basis of observed conditions, of objects. The width of the ditch, the slipperiness of the banks, not the mere presence of a ditch, is the trouble. The difficulty is getting located and defined; it is becoming a true problem, something intellectual, not just an annoyance at being held up in what we are doing. The person who is suddenly blocked and troubled in what he is doing by the thought of an engagement to keep at a time that is near and a place that is distant has the suggestion of getting there at once. But in order to carry this suggestion into effect, he has to find means of transportation. In order to find them he has to note his present position and its distance from the station, the present time, and the interval at his disposal. Thus the perplexity is more precisely located: just so much ground to cover, so much time to do it in.

The word " problem " often seems too elaborate and dignified to denote what happens in minor cases of reflection. But in every case where reflective activity ensues, there is a process of *intellectualizing* what at first is merely an *emotional* quality of the whole situation. This conversion is effected by noting more definitely the conditions that constitute the trouble and cause the stoppage of action.

The third phase, the guiding idea, hypothesis. The first suggestion occurs spontaneously; it comes to mind automatically; it *springs* up; it " pops," as we have said, " into the mind "; it flashes upon us. There is no direct control of its occurrence; the idea just comes or it does not come; that is all that can be said. There is nothing *intellectual* about its occurrence. The intellectual element consists in *what we do with it,* how we use it, *after* its sudden occurrence as an idea. A controlled use of it is made possible by the state of affairs just described. In the degree in which we define the difficulty (which is effected by stating it in terms of objects), we get a better idea of the kind of solution that is needed. The facts or data set the problem before us, and insight into the problem corrects, modifies, expands the suggestion that originally occurred. In this fashion the suggestion becomes a definite supposition or, stated more technically, a *hypothesis.*

Take the case of a physician examining a patient or a mechanic inspecting a piece of complicated machinery that does not behave properly. There is something wrong, so much is sure. But how to remedy it cannot be told until it is known *what* is wrong. An untrained person is likely to make a wild guess — the suggestion — and then proceed to act upon it in a random way, hoping that by good luck the right thing will be hit upon. So some medicine that appears to have worked before or that a neighbor has recommended is tried. Or the person fusses, monkeys, with the machine, poking here and hammering there on the chance of making the right move. The trained person proceeds in a very different fashion. He *observes* with unusual care, using the methods, the techniques, that the experience of physicians and expert mechanics in general, those familiar with the structure of the organism or the machine, have shown to be helpful in detecting trouble.

The idea of the solution is thus controlled by the diagnosis that has been made. But if the case is at all complicated, the physician or mechanic does not foreclose further thought by assuming that the suggested method of remedy is certainly right. He proceeds to act upon it tentatively rather than decisively. That is, he treats it as a guiding idea, a working hypothesis, and is led by it to make more observations, to collect more facts, so as to see if the *new* material is what the hypothesis calls for. He reasons that *if* the disease is typhoid, *then* certain phenomena will be found; and he looks particularly to see if *just* these conditions are present. Thus both the first and second operations are brought under control; the sense of the problem becomes more adequate and refined and the suggestion ceases to be a *mere* possibility, becoming a *tested* and, if possible, a *measured* probability.

The fourth phase, reasoning (in the narrower sense). Observations pertain to what exists in nature. They constitute the facts, and these facts both regulate the formation of suggestions, ideas, hypotheses, and test their probable value as indications of solutions. The ideas, on the other hand, occur, as we say, in our heads, in our minds. They not only occur there, but are capable, as well, of great development there. Given a fertile suggestion occurring in an experienced, well-informed mind, that mind is capable of elaborating it until there results an idea that is quite different from the one with which the mind started.

For example, the idea of heat in the third instance in the earlier chapter was linked up with what the person already knew about heat — in his case, its expansive force — and this in turn with the contractive tendency of cold, so that the idea of expansion could be used as an explanatory idea, though the mere idea of heat would not have been of any avail. Heat was quite directly suggested by the observed conditions; water was felt to be hot. But only a mind with some prior information about heat would have reasoned that heat meant expansion, and then used the idea of expansion as a working hypothesis. In more complex cases, there are long trains of reasoning in which one idea leads up to another idea known by previous test to be related to it. The stretch of links brought to light by reasoning depends, of course, upon the store of knowledge that the mind is already in possession of. And this depends not only upon the prior experience and special education of the individual who is carrying on the inquiry, but also upon the state of culture and science of the age and place. Reasoning helps extend knowledge, while at the same time it depends upon what is already known and upon the facilities that exist for communicating knowledge and making it a public, open resource.

A physician to-day can develop, by reasoning from his knowledge, the implications of the disease that symptoms suggest to him as probable in a way that would have been impossible even a generation ago; just as, on the other hand, he can carry his observation of symptoms much farther because of improvement in clinical instruments and the technique of their use.

Reasoning has the same effect upon a suggested solution that more intimate and extensive observation has upon the original trouble. Acceptance of a suggestion in its first form is prevented by looking into it more thoroughly. Conjectures that seem plausible at first sight are often found unfit or even absurd when their full consequences are traced out. Even when reasoning out the bearings of a supposition does not lead to its rejection, it develops the idea into a form in which it is more apposite to the problem. Only when, for example, the conjecture that a pole was an index pole had been thought out in its implications could its particular applicability to the case in hand be judged. Suggestions at first seemingly remote and wild are frequently so transformed by being elaborated into what follows from them as to become apt and fruitful. The development of an idea through reasoning helps supply intervening or intermediate terms which link together into a consistent whole elements that at first seemingly conflict with each other, some leading the mind to one inference and others to an opposed one.

Mathematics as Typical Reasoning. Mathematics affords the typical example of how far can be carried the operation of relating ideas to one another, without having to depend upon the observations of the senses. In geometry we start with a few simple conceptions, line, angle, parallel, surfaces formed by lines meeting, etc., and a few principles defining equalities. Knowing something about the equality of angles made by parallel lines when they intersect a straight line, and knowing, by definition, that a perpendicular to a straight line forms two right angles, by means of a combination of these ideas we readily determine that the sum of the interior angles of a triangle is equal to two right angles. By continuing to trace the implications of theorems already demonstrated, the whole subject of plane figures is finally elaborated. The manipulation of algebraic symbols so as to establish a series of equations and other mathematical functions affords an even more striking example of what can be accomplished by developing the relation of ideas to one another.

When the hypothesis indicated by a series of scientific observations and experiments can be stated in mathematical form, that idea can be transformed to almost any extent, until it assumes a form in which a problem can be dealt with most expeditiously and effectively. Much of the accomplishment of physical science depends upon an intervening mathematical elaboration of ideas. It is not the mere presence of measurements in quantitative form that yields scientific knowledge, but that particular kind of mathematical statement which can be developed by reasoning into other and more fruitful forms — a consideration which is fatal to the claim to scientific standing of many educational measurements merely because they have a quantitative form.

The fifth phase, testing the hypothesis by action. The concluding phase is some kind of testing by overt action to give *experimental corroboration,* or *verification,* of the conjectural idea. Reasoning shows that *if* the *idea* be adopted, certain consequences follow. So far the conclusion is hypothetical or conditional. If when we look we find present all the conditions demanded by the theory, and if we find the characteristic traits called for by rival alternatives to be lacking, the tendency to believe, to accept, is almost irresistible. Sometimes direct observation furnishes corroboration, as in the case of the pole on the boat. In other cases, as in that of the bubbles, experiment is required; that is, *conditions are deliberately arranged in accord with the requirements of an idea or hypothesis to see whether the results theoretically indicated by the idea actually occur.* If it is found that the experimental results agree with the theoretical, or rationally deduced, results, and if there is reason to believe that *only* the conditions in question would yield such results, the confirmation is so strong as to induce a conclusion — at least until contrary facts shall indicate the advisability of its revision.

Of course, verification does not always follow. Sometimes consequences show failure to confirm instead of corroboration. The idea in question is refuted by the court of final appeal. But a great advantage of possession of the habit of reflective activity is that failure is not *mere* failure. It is instructive. The person who really thinks learns quite as much from his failures as from his successes. For a failure indicates to the person whose thinking has been involved in it, and who has not come to it by mere blind chance, what further observations should be made. It suggests to him what modifications should be introduced in the hypothesis upon which he has been operating. It either brings to light a new problem or helps to define and clarify the problem on which he has been engaged. Nothing shows the trained thinker better than the use he makes of his errors and mistakes. What merely annoys and discourages a person not accustomed to thinking, or what starts him out on a new course of aimless attack by mere cut-and-try methods, is a stimulus and a guide to the trained inquirer.

The sequence of the five phases is not fixed. The five phases, terminals, or functions of thought, that we have noted do not follow one another in a set order. On the contrary, each step in genuine thinking does something to perfect the formation of a suggestion and promote its change into a leading idea or directive hypothesis. It does something to promote the location and definition of the problem. Each improvement in the idea leads to new observations that yield new facts or data and help the mind judge more accurately the relevancy of facts already at hand. The elaboration of the hypothesis does not wait until the problem has been defined and adequate hypothesis has been arrived at; it may come in at any intermediate time. And as we have just seen, any particular overt test need not be final; it may be introductory to new observations and new suggestions, according to what happens in consequence of it.

There is, however, an important difference between test by overt action in practical deliberations and in scientific investigations. In the former the practical commitment involved in overt action is much more serious than in the latter. An astronomer or a chemist performs overt actions, but they are for the sake of knowledge; they serve to test and develop his conceptions and theories. In practical matters, the main result desired lies outside of knowledge. One of the great values of thinking, accordingly, is that it defers the commitment to action that is irretrievable, that, once made, cannot be revoked. Even in moral and other practical matters, therefore, a thoughtful person treats his overt deeds as experimental so far as possible; that is to say, while he cannot call them back and must stand their consequences, he gives alert attention to what they teach him about his conduct as well as to the non-intellectual consequences. He makes a problem out of consequences of conduct, looking into the causes from which they probably resulted, especially the causes that lie in his own habits and desires.

In conclusion, we point out that the five phases of reflection that have been described represent only in outline the indispensable traits of reflective thinking. In practice, two of them may telescope, some of them may be passed over hurriedly, and the burden of reaching a conclusion may fall mainly on a single phase, which will then require a seemingly disproportionate development. No set rules can be laid down on such matters. The way they are managed depends upon the intellectual tact and sensitiveness of the individual. When things have come out wrong, it is, however, a wise practice to review the methods by which the unwise decision was reached, and see where the misstep was made.

One phase may be expanded. In complicated cases some of the five phases are so extensive that they include definite subphases within themselves. In this case it is arbitrary whether the minor functions are regarded as parts or are listed as distinct phases. There is nothing especially sacred about the number five. For example, in matters of practical deliberation where the object is to decide what to do, it may be well to undertake a scrutiny of the underlying desires and motives that are operating; that is, instead of asking what ends and means will best satisfy one's wish, one may turn back to the attitudes of which the wish is the expression. It is a matter of indifference whether this search be listed as an independent problem, having its own phases, or as an additional phase in the original problem.

Reference to the future and to the past. Again, it has been suggested that reflective thinking involves a look into the future, a forecast, an anticipation, or a prediction, and that this should be listed as a sixth aspect, or phase. As a matter of fact, every intellectual suggestion or idea is anticipatory of some possible future experience, while the final solution gives a definite set toward the future. It is both a record of something accomplished and an assignment of a future method of operation. It helps set up an enduring habit of procedure. When a physician, for example, has diagnosed a case, he usually makes also a *prognosis*, a forecast of the probable future course of the disease. And not only is his treatment a verification — or the reverse — of the idea or hypothesis about the disease upon which he has proceeded, but the result also affects his treatment of future patients. In some cases, the future reference may be so important as to require special elaboration. In this case, it may be presented as an added, distinct phase. Some of the investigations of an astronomical expedition to watch an eclipse of the sun may be directly intended, for example, to get material bearing on Einstein's theory. But the theory, itself, is so important that its confirmation or refutation will give a decided turn to the future of physical science, and this consideration is likely to be uppermost in the minds of scientists.

Of equal importance is the reference to the *past* involved in reflection. Of course, suggestions are dependent in any case upon one's past experience; they do not arise out of nothing. But while sometimes we go ahead with the suggestion without stopping to go back to the original experience of which it is the fruit, at other times we go consciously over the past experience in considerable detail as part of the process of testing the value of the suggestion.

For example, it occurs to a man to invest in real estate. Then he recalls that a previous investment of this kind turned out unfortunately. He goes over the former case, comparing it bit by bit with the present, to see how far the two cases are alike or unlike. Examination of the past may be the chief and decisive factor in thought. The most valuable reference to the past is likely, however, to come at the time the conclusion is reached. We noted earlier the importance of a final survey to secure a net formulation of the exact result and of the premises upon which it logically depends. This is not only an important part of the process of *testing*, but, as was stated in the earlier discussion, is almost necessary if good habits are to be built up. Ability to *organize* knowledge consists very largely in the habit of reviewing previous facts and ideas and relating them to one another on a new basis; namely, that of the conclusion that has been reached. A certain amount of this operation is included in the testing phase that has been described. But its influence upon the attitude of students is so important that it may be well at times so to emphasize it that it becomes a definite function, or phase, on its own account.

EDWARD HODNETT
Some applications of problem solving

ALTERNATIVES

" It can't be done, chief," one of the seven vice-presidents said. " We've figured it all ways. We can't take on this contract. We haven't the capacity. We'd have to build another plant."

" How much would that cost? What other contracts could we get if we had it? Won't we need another plant soon anyway? " the president asked. The seven vice-presidents looked at their papers.

" We didn't go into that," admitted the spokesman.

" Suppose you do," the president suggested.

During one of the hurricanes that sweep the North Atlantic, a group of boatmen stood helplessly on the shore of a harbor and watched their lovely

From Edward Hodnett, *The Art of Problem Solving*, 1955, pp. 59–65. Reprinted by permission of Harper & Brothers.

sailboats and cabin cruisers drag anchor and pound to splintered wrecks on the stones of a breakwater. As his own cabin cruiser lurched toward its doom, one owner grabbed an axe and stood poised on the breakwater. As the boat quartered onto the rocks, he jumped aboard and recklessly chopped a hole in the bottom. The sea rushed in, and the cruiser sank safely in five feet of water. After the hurricane, it was raised and repaired.

What happened? All the other owners accepted one conclusion as inevitable. The anchors were not holding. The sea was far too rough for them to get to their boats and move them to safety. The boats were bound to be driven on the breakwater and dashed to pieces. All except one owner closed their minds and said in effect, " There is no alternative." The one exception accepted the inevitability of every step except the last. He saw that there was an alternative to that, and he saved a $15,000 boat.

" There is an alternative." When you are able to say that, you crack many a problem. No single form of attack cracks more. When you are faced by a problem that offers only an unpalatable solution, you do not scream. You ask, " What are the alternatives? " If you can find even one other possible solution, you have changed the problem in a fundamental way.

A brother and sister inherit a corner plot 100 feet x 100 feet. No matter which way they divide the lot, one half will be the more valuable outside corner. Is there an alternative to this unfair division? Yes. They agree to sell the piece as a whole and then divide the money evenly.

A town librarian annually warns the library board that the increase in the number of books makes the building of a new library imperative. A committee finally investigates and agrees that since the old building will hold no more books, a new one must be built at once. At this point the librarian retires, and a new one with wider experience arrives. He finds an alternative. He sees that at least a quarter of the books on the shelves are obsolete or otherwise worthless. He clears the shelves of this dead wood and saves the town the expense of a new building for several years.

A browse through the *New York Times* will yield you a sheaf of solutions by alternatives any day. Here are four examples:

Steeplejacks could not find a way to get to the top of a high water tank from which the roof had blown off. " If I cannot go up from the outside," thought Joe Curtis, " can I go up inside? " Obviously not; the tank was full of water. Joe thought that over for a while. Then he had the tank drained, got inside, built a balsam raft, and floated to the top as the tank filled again.

The police of Glen Cove, Long Island, get relief from cracking down on young hot rodders by having the Long Island Hot Rod Association meet at police headquarters and by supervising public demonstrations of hot rod cars.

Government typists had to make an X on a medical form to show whether the answer was a " yes " or " no." Since there were eight carbons, each had to be checked to make sure the X landed beside the right word. The total number of checks each day was astronomical. Then a stenographer suggested typing "yes" or "no." No checking at all was needed after that.

Inactivity is the greatest danger to the aged. Hospitals have not the equipment, time, or personnel to help old folks stay active. Aged patients often remain bedridden for the last years of their lives, although there is no medical justification for them to be. At Ullevaal Hospital in Oslo, Norway, old people are being trained by means of handrails and exercise machines to develop their muscles to perform the one hundred and fifty or two hundred acts necessary to stay active and to take care of themselves.

The alternative to going up a water tank on the outside is to go up inside.

The alternative to cracking down on young hot rodders is to befriend them and supervise their activities.

The alternative to checking every carbon to see whether or not an X is registered beside "yes" or "no" is to write "yes" or "no."

The alternative to letting old people become bedridden is to teach them how to stay active.

In 1942 and 1943 General MacArthur's staff figured it would take ten years to drive the Japanese out of the bases they had grabbed as they swept southeast across the Pacific after Pearl Harbor. At a meeting of the top brass the experts estimated that to capture Rabaul, garrisoned by 100,000 Japanese, would alone require more planes, ships, and divisions than we had — and Rabaul was only the first of a long series of powerful bases on the road to Japan.

"Well," said the General nonchalantly, "let's just say that we won't take them." Then MacArthur unfolded his strategy of by-passing the Japanese strongholds, isolating them, and letting them "die on the vine" while the Allies, hitting where the enemy was weakest, island-hopped in giant leaps toward the Japanese homeland. It was a brilliant example of successful problem attack by finding an alternative to what seemed the inevitable.

Sometimes, of course, the reverse of this situation is true. Problems sometimes do have only one reasonable solution. Then the efficient thing is not to procrastinate and suffer but to act.

Garrison was the promotion man for a publishing house. He was full of plans for selling more books and magazines. Some of his ideas were original and sound. Others were fantastic. Most were expensive. The directors of the company were conservative, penny-pinching. They vetoed most of Garrison's ideas. He grew frustrated as the years went on. Finally he chose the only reasonable solution. He moved to another publisher who wanted exactly the kind of promotional skill Garrison had. Then he was happy. He should have seen several years sooner that he had no alternative.

Doing nothing is an alternative. It means either a choice of the *status quo* with the known solution of a problem or inert acceptance of whatever solution chance or other agencies might bring. When the consequences of doing nothing seem better than the probable results of doing something, then it is the better alternative. To do nothing is therefore no way to avoid making a decision. It is a choice of alternatives.

It usually takes no brilliance to choose the lesser of two evils. But recognition that your problem is set up on this simple basis can save much time. If the situation offers a true either-or choice, then all you have to do is match the advantages and disadvantages and make your decision.

The Knowltons are building a house with a library in a wing. Either a fine oak tree will have to be sacrificed in order to have the floor of the library on the level of the living room, or to avoid cutting through the roots of the tree, the Knowltons will have to elevate the library two steps above the living room. Awkward as the steps are, the Knowltons decide to take that alternative to save the beautiful oak.

But it takes keen analysis to reduce a complex situation to a simple either-or pattern. The purchase of 885,000 square miles of Louisiana territory from Napoleon in 1803 for $15,000,000 was the greatest real-estate deal in history. It is generally considered a triumph of Yankee shrewdness. But how did this problem look to Napoleon? Napoleon had got Louisiana back from Spain in October of 1800 by a secret treaty. Jefferson had openly threatened Napoleon that French exploitation of Louisiana would lead us to look on our old friend France as our enemy and to ally ourselves with the enemy of France, Great Britain. France and England were drifting toward war. When it came, Britain's superior navy would seize Louisiana, and Napoleon would get not a cent for it. When the crafty Napoleon had cut through the maze of international diplomacy and brought his simple alternatives into view — sell Louisiana or have it seized — he had no trouble deciding to sell for $15,000,000.

Problems often boil down to the simple form of a dilemma. A dilemma presents a choice of two solutions to a problem, both of which are unsatisfactory. That is why we speak of the horns of a dilemma. Then, as just indicated, the only answer is the classic choice of the lesser of two evils.

Long ago the Greeks saw in this fact the essence of human tragedy. *Antigone* by Euripides illustrates this tragic imperfection in the solution of human problems. Polynices is killed in opposing his uncle, Creon, king of Thebes. Creon decrees that he is a traitor to the state and must lie where he is without burial rites. Antigone, Polynice's sister, is therefore faced with a problem that has no satisfactory solution. The law of the gods demands that she perform the burial rites. She chooses to defy Creon and obey the gods. For disobeying the law of the state, she dies.

When you find yourself up against what seems a dilemma, your first move is to try to crack it — prove, if possible, that it is not a true dilemma. You accomplish this in two ways. You prove that one or both of the horns are not solid — that one or both of the statements are not true. Or you prove that the either-or choice is unsound — there is at least one other more satisfactory alternative.

Consider the common dilemma mentioned in the first chapter. Your company offers you a promotion, but you will have to leave Omaha and move to Syracuse. You and your family have your roots down in Omaha. You are happy there. You do not know that you will be happy in Syracuse. But if you decline the offer, you will doubtless be passed over in the future. You may even lose ground in Omaha.

If this is a true dilemma, you have to make a choice on the lesser-evil basis. But perhaps further analysis will give you good reason for believing that you will be happy in Syracuse. Then one horn is not solid. Or perhaps discussion with your company officials will provide another alternative that appeals to you — transfer to Chicago, say.

The more choices you have, the better your solution to a problem is likely to be. As you start your attack on a problem, therefore, you keep asking, not merely, " Is there another alternative? " You ask, " How many more alternatives are there? " The difference between the fair problem solver and the first-rate one shows up here. The superior problem solver is not thrown off by three or four possible solutions, even when they are good. The presence of any number of good answers does not mean that the best has yet been turned up. Standard practice for all problem solving, then, is to list all the possible alternatives before making a decision.

Sometimes, of course, one acceptable solution is as good as another, and a search for a better one is a waste of effort. Sometimes an action on an acceptable solution is more desirable than delay to secure a much better one. Perfectionists make poor decision makers when their judgment of alternatives does not embrace these distinctions.

Figuring out alternatives and making choices among alternatives is a big part of all problem solving.

Two things you should remember:

1. Choosing among alternatives often demands courage and moral judgment as well as intelligence.

2. One alternative you should always consider — *you may be wrong.* . . .

CHAPTER FOURTEEN BIBLIOGRAPHY

BARZUN, JACQUES, *The House of Intellect.* New York: Harper and Brothers, 1959.

> Barzun makes an attack in Chapter IX on the way language is now often used to cover up error, magnify the importance of something, or increase confusion.

DEWEY, JOHN, *Experience and Nature.* Chicago: Open Court Publishing Company, 1926.

> In Chapter 10 the author describes values. He also discusses the singleness of means-consequences. He feels that philosophy must appraise values by taking cognizance of their causes and consequences. The issue

is choice, which involves alternatives. The method of intelligence is advocated.

HALL, D. M., *Dynamics of Group Action*. Danville: The Inter-state Printers and Publishers, 1957.

This book has been designed as an easy-to-read handbook for people working in groups. It is a practical attempt to help people decide what it is that they want to accomplish and how to do it. Group problem-solving is the subject of Chapter Nine.

HANSEN, KENNETH H., *Public Education in American Society*. Englewood Cliffs, N.J.: Prentice-Hall, 1956.

Chapter 14, entitled "Beware the Pronghorned Platitude," takes a number of common phrases used in education and relates the dangers behind a glib acceptance of them and also shows what a serious analysis of their meanings implies. The following phrases are some examples: "We learn by doing." "Education is life itself, not preparation for life." "We teach them how to think, not what to think."

KNELLER, GEORGE F., *Existentialism and Education*. New York: Philosophical Library, 1958.

The treatment of "the educational process" (pp. 122–141) is especially interesting. Surprisingly enough, Kneller resorts to a rather traditional concept of "learning the fundamentals" as a basis for the curriculum. Factual information should be "mastered" so as to provide the content for "uninhibited analysis and criticism."

MARITAIN, JACQUES, *Education at the Crossroads*. New Haven: Yale University Press, 1943.

Maritain criticizes a tendency to overemphasize means, develops his conception of the aim of education, and then argues against several important schools of thought regarding the ends of education — Pragmatism, Sociologism, Intellectualism, Voluntarism, and the belief that learning encompasses everything.

15

Epilogue

The material in this book is presented on the predication that it will make a difference in the professional *behavior* of the teacher. Such behavior in turn should stem from a consistent philosophy of education. The two dimensions of any philosophy are its substantive aspects and its methodology. The emphasis in the previous chapter is on methodology, whereas the remaining portions of this book are concerned with some of the substantive aspects. This concluding chapter is intended to illustrate and stress the relationship that exists — or ought to exist — between one's philosophy and one's behavior as a teacher. The critical point at which these two elements become fused is in the acts of decision-making that confront all teachers.

What are the requisites of wise decision-making? In order to provide a framework within which these requisites can be described, perhaps it would help to pose a typical situation you will very likely confront as a beginning teacher. Suppose you have to decide whether or not to take a teaching position at a given school and grade level. The following schematic diagram depicts the factors and the approximate sequence of factors that go into a reflectively formed decision.

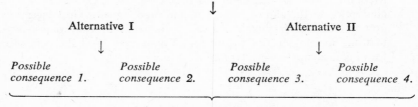

Situation requiring a decision

↓

Alternative **I**   Alternative **II**

↓   ↓

Possible   *Possible*   *Possible*   *Possible*
consequence 1.   *consequence 2.*   *consequence 3.*   *consequence 4.*

Commitments and Responsibility

↓

Subsequent reflection

An examination of the above scheme reveals that there are certain criteria that relate to the process of decision-making. In the chapter dealing with teaching as a profession, particularly in the section dealing with professional ethics (see pp. 555–572), these criteria were identified in the need on the teacher's part for (1) moral sensitivity, (2) moral intelligence, and (3) moral courage. These are not intended to be pollyanna-like platitudes. In the above scheme, for example, the teacher *must* demonstrate some degree of moral sensitivity in the mere recognition of an issue requiring a decision. He must be able to determine which issues are important and which are trivial; which merit a rather rigorous process of reflective examination, and which can be dismissed with no significant consequences, regardless of the decision reached.

Moral intelligence is especially required in identifying possible alternative choices. " Tunnel vision " is inadequate at this point. The competent teacher can envisage a wide spectrum of alternatives. The ability to come up with a perceptive and novel alternative is often the distinguishing characteristic between the imaginative and the plodding teacher. To speak of moral intelligence is not to deny the need for professional information and factual knowledge. But these become mere instruments once one has committed oneself to the moral obligation to be intelligent. Practical intelligence, therefore, becomes at heart a moral judgment. As different alternative choices are considered, each of them gives rise to various possible consequences. Again it requires intelligence to assess the alternative choices in the light of the possible consequences.

Moral courage is involved in one's commitment and responsibility and also in the subsequent reflection on the decision reached. The very decision to act in accordance with a philosophic commitment is itself an act of moral courage. Even if one were to plead philosophical amorality or nihilism he would be acting in accordance with a commitment. The opposite of a committed position is reflected in such expressions as " knowledge is power," or " ideas are weapons." Regardless of his commitment, the morally courageous person accepts the responsibility that accrues to his philosophic beliefs. If he is committed to democracy, for example, he accepts the possibility of others holding opinions at sharp variance with his. But probably the most important responsibility is the obligation for subsequent reflection on the decision reached — with the possibility of reassessing it. If a different choice has to be made, one should also accept the responsibility of acknowledging his misjudgment.

The above scheme for decision-making is not intended as a sure-fire method for resolving all issues and problems. Man is a human being, not an electronic computer. He often acts impulsively, irrationally, and inconsistently. It would be the height of naiveté not to recognize these human frailties. But an ideal is of no less value simply because we fall short of its complete attainment. It is in this spirit that the following case studies are presented. They are intended to pose situations that, although hypothetical, are representative of the kinds that every teacher will have to resolve. After the first of the three case studies, some questions will be raised concerning the requisites of decision-making. As a prospective teacher you can make your own analysis of the remaining two cases and reach what you would consider to be an appropriate decision.

CASE STUDY 1 (TOMMY)

As the three girls left his office, Betty almost in tears, Mike wondered how a simple, well-meaning teacher could find himself in a spot that required as many decisions — decisions that arose in problems which were hardly of his own making. It was certain that he would have to resolve this problem before the practice for the Christmas program went on this evening, and he almost wished he had reached a snap decision while the girls were still in his office. With only three days of rehearsals left before the program, he was really quite trapped.

Perhaps, he reflected, he should have followed Coach Allen's example and reached a hasty decision which would have settled it once and for all. But there were problems along that line, too; and he wondered what, in the long run, would be the consequence of Coach Allen's action.

Tommy, the cause of all the consternation, was one of his seventh grade youngsters and, whatever else might be said of him, one of the most unpredictable. It is sometimes difficult to know why youngsters act so unpredictably. Tommy came from a working class family in which, although the mother was working, there seemed to be few problems. Mike had had an opportunity to drive past the home on a previous occasion; and while it was in one of the less desirable parts of town, this section was by no means a slum area. Mike also knew that Tommy's older sister, Mary, had remained in school only until the tenth grade, at which time she had dropped out, with a special work permit perhaps, to secure a job in one of the local non-union garment factories.

But Tommy himself was the immediate problem. This morning, four days before the public Christmas performance, he had arrived in school with what would at least be considered a " novel " haircut. He had taken a shears and cut a swath some two inches wide running from front to back right down the center of his otherwise bushy head of hair. It was just the reverse of the old Mohawk haircut; and Mike guessed Tommy was right when he asserted, " nobody has ever seen one like this before." Tommy had since been volunteering to let any of the other boys who would do likewise join his " new club " — a prospect, Mike surmised, which was not likely to be seized enthusiastically by any of the other boys. Tommy was often viewed as a cut-up and had a certain dubious status and popularity with his class, but he was scarcely a leader into whose tracks other youngsters quickly turned.

It hadn't been long before the roof had begun to fall in on Tommy. Mrs. Radnik, his mathematics teacher, had been duly surprised but had said or done nothing about the haircut. Coach Allen, on seeing Tommy in the hall, had told him that he couldn't have any youngster like that representing the school on the basketball floor, and he needn't report for basketball practice until his hair was grown out again. And now three angry and misty-eyed young ladies had come in to tell Mike that they certainly weren't going out on the stage in front of the public to sing their Christmas anthem — with " that goof " standing there as one of the sextet. Everyone would laugh and it would be just too embarrassing! As Tommy's adviser, and as a most unwilling " director " of the Christmas program, Mike wondered what course of action he should take.

What are some of the elements in the above case that require moral sensitivity on the part of Mike, the teacher? Who else besides Tommy is involved in this situation? What are some of the considerations that Mike has to take into account with respect to the feelings of others? Does this situation even merit attention or consideration on Mike's part?

What are some possible alternative courses of action that Mike could take? What kinds of information about the nature of adolescent personalities would be helpful in identifying alternatives? How would differing conceptions of the social function of school result in different possible alternatives? What are the possible consequences attendant to each alternative?

How would Mike's commitments to democracy affect his decision? What would be some of the principles of this commitment as they relate to freedom? To individuality? To authority? What responsibility does Mike have for making his decision binding and irrevocable?

The following case is presented to enable you to make your own analysis, raise your own questions, and reflectively appraise your decision.

CASE STUDY 2 (SUE)

Sue came into Mike's office as he was in the process of trying to finish off the second sandwich of his Thursday lunch with the help of one of those cups of coffee which his thermos never seemed able to keep quite warm. She looked as ill at ease as the first day he had seen her in class, and the banter with which he had become accustomed to starting off conversations with students didn't seem to be achieving its purpose.

Sue was, Mike reflected, one of his successes since he had been a teacher at Emory Junior High School. He could easily picture how lonesome and unhappy she looked as she sat on the edge of the class that first day of school in September. Any beginning teacher with a term of psychology couldn't help spotting this kid as one who really needed help; and a lot of diligent maneuvering on his part and the part of Ellie Jones, the home economics teacher, had at last helped Sue find her place in the class. It was true that Janet, Sally, and Carol, the girls with whom she now ran around, weren't either the outstanding students in the class or the class " social lions "; but they were girls who were very much like Sue in many ways, and they seemed to enjoy school and enjoy doing satisfactory work. She had found a group of girls who had accepted her, and Mike was constantly aware of the way she had brightened up and blossomed forth since then. It took no psychologist to see that she now really liked school. And Mike recognized that he and Miss Jones weren't the only ones who had noticed the change in Sue. Bud Johnson had also obviously noticed, and Mike was vastly amused at the razzing Bud had gotten from Bill Brighten and the rest of the " basketball gang " when he had broken their self-imposed " boycott " on Emory girls and shown up at the last " hop " with Sue. Mike supposed that Sue's was a " rags to riches " story in the eyes of the rest of the girls about this time. Too bad he hadn't been able to do as much for June, who was scheduled to be sitting down in the detention room for several weeks now — and lucky that this was the worst punishment she had received — although, he supposed, it was the attitude of the other kids and not the detention room itself which was the worst part of the punishment.

But for the moment it was Sue's problems that were before him and, hesitatingly at first and then faster, were now tumbling out. She hoped he would give her his confidential advice because she didn't know what she should do. You see, she had been in the locker room when the money was taken out of Mary's locker, and she knew that June wasn't the one who had really taken it. Maybe June had taken things other times, but this time she knew it wasn't June who had taken it because she had been there and seen it all. Really, it was Janet who had noticed that the locker was open and had reached in and taken the pocketbook; and now Janet had invited their gang to go to the show with her tomorrow evening. She had tried to talk with Janet about how unfair this was for June; but after all, who cared about June — and good friends don't tattle on one another! Bud had gotten a kick out of it when she told him too; nobody else seemed to care about June. Sue guessed June wasn't the kind of a girl that others cared about. Her anxious looks down the hall revealed that she was already worried for fear that Bud or one of the girls would notice her talking to a teacher, and Mike wondered what kind of a story she was ready to tell them if they saw her sitting here and talking so earnestly with him. But he wondered more how he should advise Sue in a spot like this and what course of action he should take.

The last in this series of case studies is of a different order. It does not so much concern the teacher-pupil relationship as it does the teacher-teacher relationship, and to some extent that between the teacher and administrator. It is included as a representative example of a situation requiring professionally competent decision-making.

CASE STUDY 3 (MR. DAVIS)

Mike had just concluded a fifteen minute chat with Mr. Young, the principal, in his neatly furnished private office. He had about twenty minutes left of his free period and was heading back to the teachers' lounge for his usual cup of coffee before meeting his third hour class. He hardly noticed the custodian as he walked thoughtfully along the hallway and barely managed to return an absent-minded morning greeting.

Mr. Davis was certain to be in the lounge too, and just as certainly he would inquire about Mike's somewhat out-of-the-ordinary meeting with Mr. Young. Not that this inquiry would be made in any prying or offensive manner. Not at all. Mr. Davis was genuinely pleased and proud of the good reputation Mike had built for himself during less than two full years of teaching. After all, didn't he agree with Mr. Young to take Mike under his wing, as it were, when he came to his first teaching job here a year ago last fall? As the senior faculty member teaching English, he gave invaluable guidance and tips to Mike on scores of such items as how to fill out the student class rolls, when to get mimeographed material in, what supplementary reading books to order, and the like.

Although Mr. Davis and Mike were the best of personal friends, their viewpoints on teaching English differed frequently — and sometimes markedly. Mr. Young, of course, knew this. And this was why he had now asked Mike to serve on a curriculum revision committee that was being established by the Superintendent of Schools for their district. Mike had just accepted the appointment. After all, he reasoned, how could he respond in any other way? It wasn't that he was pressured into it. There was, however, a certain element of prestige in being asked to serve on such a committee. Besides, he really felt that the curriculum needed some long-overdue revising.

But here was the rub. The very things that Mike would like to put into the revision are contrary to the oft-repeated point of view of Mr. Davis.

And some of the things that he would like to see minimized (such as the diagramming of sentences) are the very things on which Mr. Davis prides himself. And indeed, Mr. Davis *does* a very effective teaching job in such areas.

Mike was genuinely disturbed as he approached the teachers' lounge. The last thing he wanted to do was to offend the sensitivities of a respected colleague. But he knew that he also had to be honest with himself when he began his curriculum revision work. He wondered how he could best reconcile himself to this situation.

If these case studies typify the kinds of decisions with which your philosophy of education should be able to cope, what are the characteristics of a philosophy which is worthy of your adherence? Without attempting to prescribe the *content* of any particular philosophy of education, we might mention certain criteria applicable to any sound one. Among the most urgent of the criteria to be met are the following:

1. *A philosophy of education should be relevant to the problems of teachers.* A worthy philosophy of education is one that provides principles which can be used to make the kinds of decisions and to solve the kinds of problems faced by members of the profession. The extent to which your principles were applicable in the preceding problem situations may indicate the extent to which your philosophy of education meets this initial criterion.

2. *A philosophy of education should be sufficiently comprehensive to meet the wide range of problems confronting the teacher and the schools.* The burden of the readings in this book has indicated that the problems of the teaching profession can never be encompassed by simple questions related solely to the method of presenting a given body of content to students. Teaching is a profession which in-

volves greater vision than this. Your philosophy of education will be worthy of adherence only if it leads you to, and helps you resolve, the great problems confronting this profession in a democratic society and a troubled world.

3. *A philosophy of education should be the product of a process of reflection.* Many points of view lay claim to the name " philosophy," but a genuine philosophy is always more than a set of prejudices. A prejudice is a pre-judgment — a point of view established prior to reflection and consideration of the evidence. A philosophy, on the contrary, does not come prior to reflection but is rather the product of reflection.

4. *A philosophy of education should be internally consistent.* One of the chief services a philosophy of education can render is that of enabling an individual to resolve situations which at first appear confusing or contradictory. A poorly considered philosophy can seldom serve this purpose, for rather than resolving conflicts it provides its holder with a set of inconsistent principles which merely introduce new conflicts. If principles held contradict each other, action is suspended rather than released.

5. *A philosophy of education should be consistent with the findings of empirical science.* Science and philosophy are complementary parts of the same intellectual structure. Perhaps this is nowhere more clearly revealed than in constructing a philosophy of education. The empirical findings of the behavioral sciences are indispensable tools for the teacher. The extent to which a philosophy of education is consistent with, and gives larger meaning to these findings is one measure of its ultimate worth.

6. *A philosophy of education should produce feasible solutions to practical problems.* " Life is real, life is earnest " has perhaps never been more true than for the teacher. He is faced with complex problems which demand solutions. His best intellectual resources must be at his immediate disposal in reaching these solutions. A philosophy of education which stands aloof from such problems, which would in effect deny the validity of any available course of action, is of little service to the teacher and may, in the last analysis, lead to the type of paralysis and disillusionment which would render all teaching ineffective.

7. *A philosophy of education must be subject to revision in the light of new evidence and broadened experience.* A philosophy of education should be a living, growing thing. An ideal is not the more, but rather the less helpful for never changing. Thus it is with a philosophy. One of the characteristics of a lifetime of creative teaching is the evolution of a philosophy which accompanies it. If this book has started you on the path to formulating a philosophy of education, it shall have served its purpose well. If it has led you rather to produce a " finished " philosophy, it will have ill served its purpose. Life and philosophic growth, one would hope, might be coterminous.

The final selection in this volume can be viewed in the light of these criteria for formulating and assessing a philosophy of education. Written by Laurence D. Haskew, this selection underscores the importance of building a philosophy of education and stresses the ultimate necessity of possessing a worthy philosophy if one is to be a truly successful teacher.

LAURENCE D. HASKEW
Teaching for what?

Schooling is education organized to achieve certain goals. What those goals are is determined in large measure by the teaching that takes place in schools. It is inconceivable that we can teach and not be teaching toward something. Our teaching has ends — the goals we seek to reach.

On the surface the ends may seem simple and obvious. We are teaching so Paul may know the multiplication facts or so Connie may be able to name the countries that border Yugoslavia. But we cannot be content with the surface.

Why should Paul learn the multiplication facts? Because he needs them in order to live successfully in the modern world, we say. Then we are saying in effect, that we are teaching toward enabling every person to live a successful life. But if that is the case, suppose Paul can convince us that he does not need the multiplication facts to be successful (plenty of poor multipliers seem to be very good citizens) or, more likely, suppose we convince ourselves that by making Paul learn multiplication we will be causing him to experience failure over and over and running the risk of having him lose his self-confidence completely? Which end is more important — that an individual have self-confidence or that he be able to multiply? Now we are digging deep.

Let us take another tack with Paul. When has he learned the multiplication facts? "When he can recite them if called upon," says one. "No," says another, "only when he can put them down on a written test." "I wouldn't call that learning," says a third, "because he doesn't know the facts until he can use them in solving problems that he encounters outside of school."

Here we see three decidedly different ends being sought, each under the head of "learning facts." The means we shall employ to teach Paul will depend largely upon which end we seek. If recitation of the facts is our goal, we will drill and drill on multiplication. If ability to solve practical problems is what we aim for, we will put Paul into scores of lifelike situations in which he has to use multiplication.

We should carry our illustration one step further. Calculating machines do not live very successful lives, and certainly not very satisfying ones. If we are teaching Paul to live a successful life, what else must we teach him other than arithmetical computation? Which is the real goal of our school day — to make children more competent to live successfully or to make them successful computers? If it is the latter, we may find it necessary to allot two hours daily to arithmetic. If it is the former, we may cut down on arithmetic time because we think many other learnings enter into making a life successful.

We soon discover also that we cannot catalog all the major components of living successfully under the subject fields — English, history, art, and so on — into which human knowledge has been divided. The important matters of making adjustments to other people, developing a purpose in life, and finding an antidote for selfishness do not seem to fit into school subjects very well.

Two alternatives offer themselves. We can limit our definitions of " successful living " and say we are not really concerned with all of it but just with those parts that result from learning the subjects we teach. Or we can adopt means of teaching that are calculated to develop a wide range of abilities to live. We thus choose means in terms of the ends we seek, and we choose the ends we seek in terms of — what? That is the real rub. What *does* guide us in selecting the ends for teaching?

It would be highly comforting to be able to give you a pat answer to that question, yet we doubt that you would be helped much thereby. So far no answer has proved completely satisfactory. Perhaps the really important thing is that each person work out his own philosophy of teaching goals by employing the best thinking of which he is capable. There are guides to help you do this and we will describe a few of them; but first we will show you some of the targets at which your teaching can aim. Only when you see some of the alternatives available are you ready to look for help in choosing between them.

ANALYSIS OF A GOAL FOR TEACHING

The purpose of public education in the United States is to equip each child within the limits af his capacities and interests to live successfully in a democratic social order.

This statement would be accepted readily by many educators — it has a good democratic ring. Read uncritically without too much bother over the meanings of its words and phrases, it gives the appearance of being a satisfactory target for teaching. But when we read it closely and begin to ponder its meaning and import, grave questions can be raised. We are going to dissect this statement to illustrate some of the alternatives facing the teacher in the search for ends.

For the individual or for society? Some thoughtful educators would want to reject the entire statement immediately. It puts the emphasis in the wrong place, they would say. Education is for the benefit of society, not the individual. We educate people in order that they will put group interest above personal interest. We require them to learn to read and write not for their own success but in order to become capable of managing their responsibilities as citizens. We teach them to be healthy to protect the health of all of us and to save us the cost of having to care for the sick. The statement as it reads sounds as if education is a right of the individual.

It is not. It is a duty, the performance of which is exacted by society for the privilege of living in society.

Those who champion individualism would reply that the state is the creature of the people, their servant and not their maker. The end of life is the fulfillment by each person of his capabilities and potentialities. Education should equip people to build for themselves the molds they would like to fit into rather than shaping them to fit already existing molds.

We have oversimplified these two points of focus, but they are indicative of basic ideas you will explore in your courses in philosophy, ethics, political theory, and literature. Accept our simplification for the time being and see if you can predict the answers that people holding these two views would give to the following questions:

1. How much attention should education pay to developing an appreciation for the arts (music, drama, literature, and the like)?

2. Are the extraclass activities in high school justifiable?

3. What prominence should be given to the study of history?

4. How much account should be taken of individual differences?

5. What proportion of the curriculum should be required of everyone and what proportion left elective?

6. Is there any justification for vocational education at public expense?

7. So long as what a child is doing and learning is interesting to him and is not counter to the common good, should anyone worry?

How much are the schools responsible for? Does the statement mean that public schools and teachers should tackle the whole range of things that it takes to make people successful? If so, many of our great thinkers would disagree violently, insisting that the schools should tackle only a limited part of the job — the cultivation of intellectual prowess. Some base their stand on the theory that when the intellect is cultivated everything else follows automatically.

More, however, feel that the school is not the proper agency to take over the whole task of education. " The home," they say, " is responsible for personality development, moral training, and physical health. The school has no business fooling with those matters; to do so is not only inappropriate but also weakens the home as an influential institution. The church is the agency most suitable for developing the ideals and commitments which should guide life. Business and industry are responsible for vocational education and training. Let the school concentrate on developing the tools of learning, factual knowledge of the world, and habits and attitudes of industry and reliability. Oh, they can add some citizenship training too."

Still others rest their arguments on purely practical grounds. " The school," they say, " has taken on so many things to do that it has been stretched too thin and is not doing anything well. Of course it is important that children become physically healthy, but by the time teachers get through checking for diseases, filling out records on weight and height, corresponding with parents about health defects, teaching children what to eat and how to eat, conducting them through physical exercise on the playground, and twenty or thirty other health-connected activities, they have used up their energy and a large part of the precious school day. It would be better to do a few things well than to give many things a lick and a promise."

These arguments are completely rejected by other citizens and educators whose motto is " the whole child." " We learn to live by living," they say, " and we do not live in segments. Intellectual development and social adjustment must go hand in hand because each affects the other. Some children fail to learn to read because they are emotionally disturbed or physically below par; the school would be wasting its time if it tried to teach reading with bland unconcern for emotional adjustment and physical welfare. The successful person is the balanced person, and we cannot afford to foster the acquisition of knowledge unless we can simultaneously foster the development of moral commitments and social sensitivity."

The scope for education proposed in our statement would come in for vigorous protest on still other ground. It fails even to hint that the school should attempt to affect the course of life by direct action to improve communities. In Ascension Parish, Louisiana, the schools became the agent responsible for getting houses screened, for getting deep wells dug to provide pure water, for getting all citizens inoculated against typhoid fever. As we have pointed out before, many people think this sort of thing is a legitimate and highly important role of the school. They would want any statement of the purposes of education to include " to improve through direct action the community in which the school exists."

To " equip " each child? The word " equip " would be a red flag to some educators. It carries the connotation of somebody doing something to somebody else. And they would rebel at this notion. The end of education, they would hold, is to free the individual to unfold the potentialities that are already his. They would challenge the implication that anyone can pick out goals of life for someone else.

Others would question " equip " on the grounds that it seems to call for means of education not in accord with the best theories of how humans learn. " Equip," they might say, " sounds as if the learner is a passive recipient rather than an active acquirer. We can see teachers reading this definition and getting sanction for teaching procedures that put children through a series of tasks to be done and tests to be passed, and calling that education. We contend that people are being educated only when they are participants in discovering their own needs, in planning to meet those needs, and in seeking the learning they want to acquire."

And there are other educators who would insist on retaining " equip " in the statement for exactly the reasons objected to. " The end of education is to make the individual take on the behaviors that the group has discovered to be essential," they would say. " We cannot leave the acquisition of those behaviors to chance. After all, an individual ought to be honest whether he wants to be or not, and if he won't learn to be honest on his own initiative then we have to teach him to be that way."

Equal opportunities for all? The phrase, " each child within the limits of his capacities and interests," would worry many people.

Some would see in it the notion that public education should be made available according to some hierarchy of intelligences. At periodic intervals the pupils would be tested in some way. If they showed ability, they would be allowed to go on; if not, their education at public expense would be at an end. Or perhaps the students would be separated into contingents on the basis of aptitudes. One contingent would then be educated to be tradesmen and semiskilled laborers; another would receive technical education; another, liberal arts; another, preparation for the professions.

Such a scheme has been practiced in some European countries for several decades and has been advocated in this country almost since the beginning of public education. Many modern theorists on the American educational scene apparently would welcome such an interpretation of our statement of purpose; many more would decry it, calling it undemocratic and the forerunner of a class society wherein the destiny of a man is determined by those who control his educational opportunities.

Our phrase would split educators and social theorists on another fundamental issue. It could be interpreted to mean that even in the " essential " learnings the schools would have varying standards of attainment for different children. There would be no minimum line of achievement set which each child was expected, or at least strongly urged or even compelled, to meet. Not every child would be expected to learn to write legibly, show correct language usage, or know the basic facts of American history.

With this notion many educators would strongly agree. " If the school can cause children to make progress in desirable directions, that is all we can expect; to establish and maintain minimum levels of attainment is to go contrary to child nature." Other educators and lay citizens would just as strongly disagree. They would insist that there are certain fundamentals every child simply must be made to master regardless of his own foibles and interests. If these fundamentals are not mastered, either drop the child out of the school or redouble the teaching effort until he learns them.

Then there is the question of how far the public school should go to provide equal educational opportunities for all and to develop the capacities and interests of each individual. There are many children whose capacities are severely limited by physical handicaps or other exceptional circumstances. Many children have the capacity to rise to almost any height in musical attainment, in mathematical creativity, or in group leadership.

And perhaps parents, workers, and other adults need to be studying and learning constantly if they are to cope successfully with the modern, rapidly changing world. Our statement says nothing about them and is open to criticism on that score.

To give all these people adequate educational opportunity would require extraordinary outlays of funds and many specialized services. Is it an obligation of the public school to supply the funds and services to capitalize fully on every capacity or develop the socially useful interests of each person?

What is successful living? " To live successfully " is a phrase that could be accepted by almost everyone. Some would accept it without troubling themselves much about its meaning because it is high sounding. Others would accept it because they can read into it their own definitions of successful living.

But how those definitions differ! In Marboro, sides have been taken on whether or not social dancing shall be taught in the local high school. One side contends that social dancing is necessary for successful living. The other side contends just as vigorously that abstinence from dancing is essential to living with real success.

In some parts of our country citizens have insisted that schools should teach every child of a certain ethnic background to " keep his place," while other citizens have pushed constantly for equal educational opportunity for all — two differing ideas of what constitutes successful living.

We do not apologize for placing before you the most profound philosophical, ethical, and religious problem that has faced man through the ages — the problem of what constitutes the good life. What is the end of man's life? By what scale of values shall he measure his success? Surely you have formed some answers to these questions already, but your education will serve you poorly if it does not cause you to probe even more deeply. What you eventually believe the good life to be will influence decidedly the ends for your teaching.

In your study of philosophy you will come across such terms as idealism, humanism, materialism, authoritarianism, supernaturalism, pragmatism, and rationalism. These are used to differentiate between schools of thought about the way the universe is made and how man finds his proper place in it. You will also examine many religious interpretations of the nature of God and of man and of their relationship. We shall not attempt here to introduce you to technical philosophy or religious thought but instead will try to set forth in simple, everyday terms a few representative alternative meanings for " successful living." We present them in epigrammatic form, hoping that you will ponder each and realize how it is different from every other.

Successful living is a social phenomenon; that man is successful who receives recognition, ego satisfaction, and love from those whose regard he values.

Self-realization is the key to success; that person is successful who finds gratification for the drives and potentialities he possesses.

The successful person is the one who contributes greatly to the well-being and attainment of others.

*Success is attained to the extent that man becomes master of his own
fate, able to define and solve the problems that he encounters.*

*To live successfully a man must learn that authority other than his own
can solve most of his problems better than he can; he must trust authority
and submit unworriedly to its direction.*

*Success consists in securing the means by which man's senses may be
gratified, his desires indulged, and his power established.*

*The degree of adjustment is the measure of success; the successful man
is the one who has reduced to a minimum the tension between his environment, both social and physical, and himself.*

*Successful living means adventurous living, continuous refusal to be satis-
fied with things or thoughts as they are, continuous pushing against the
bonds that restrict man's spirit.*

*A divine order of life is written into the universe and can be revealed to
us; success consists in finding this way and walking in it.*

*Earthly success flows only from spiritual success — success in establishing
close union between man's spirit and God's spirit.*

Go back over some of these statements to see what they would mean
for your teaching. For example, the first would mean that you would give
priority to teaching people to win friends, to establish leadership relations,
to develop attractive personalities, to be successful in interpersonal relationships. You would want to stimulate the development of those intellectual accomplishments that have high social worth, such as good speaking
ability, interest in popular literature and music, and business abilities. See
if you can think of one or two other matters you would emphasize and
then try the same analysis on number 2, number 3, and so on. We hope
you will see clearly at the end of this exercise that we are not dealing here
with academic abstractions but with the most practical essence of your
teaching.

In a democratic social order? Our statement commits education to one
kind of social order — the democratic. For some philosophers this would
be treason on two counts. First, it indoctrinates the child to choose one
kind of life; his free will is restricted thereby and the status quo is perpetuated. Second, it predicts the circumstances which will surround the adult,
and such prediction is downright foolish. How can we today know what
goals will dominate the social order of fifty years hence? These people
would insist that " changing " be substituted for " democratic " and that
education emphasize the tentative nature of all our current arrangements
for people living together. However, the vast majority of American educators have endorsed the notion that public education should try to support and preserve the democratic way of life.

Where we really run into trouble is at the point of agreeing on the
meaning of *democratic.* The democratic social order that was freely described and taught toward in the middle thirties would be labeled as non-

democratic and even Communistic by a large segment of our population in the mid-fifties. At any time *democratic* will mean to some the way of life we have now and to others a way of life we do not have but should strive for.

The same vigorous criticism and questioning of authority that means for some the very epitome of democracy in action seems to others dangerous and potentially subversive. The ideals of cooperation and common endeavor for the common good often collide with the ideals of competition and individualism, with both sets of ideals being labeled democratic. To some, devotion of school time to the consideration of controversial social issues is unwise and uncalled-for; to others it is an essential means of educating for democratic living. Use of democratic processes with children is " softness " and " just fiddling around," or it is " the fundamental necessity for true education," depending on who is making the judgment.

This illustrative analysis of some of the problems connected with choosing ends for teaching has not covered all the alternatives, but we hope it has served to demonstrate the nature of the problem and to arouse your interest in the true fundamentals of education.

In the midst of such differences (perhaps the most persistent symptom of democracy in action) there is no substitute for finding out all you can about the origin and development of the American concepts of education and clarifying for yourself a philosophy for teaching. Such study forms an essential part of your college preparation and of your program for continued professional development.

CRITERIA FOR CHOOSING

The educational philosophies of various thinkers have been shaped by many important influences. Perhaps looking at some of these influences will help you to decide which ones to use as criteria on which to base your own way of thinking.

Authoritative pronouncements. From time to time groups of outstanding educators have taken up the task of stating aims or purposes for education in America. Some such pronouncements have come from national agencies. Others have been issued by state committees and by local school systems. The fact that such statements exist does not prove that their purposes are the ones you should accept. The analytical exercise on pages 653–659 should serve to prevent your accepting any statement just because it sounds appropriate and should cause you to hunt for its implications. Even so, such statements can form excellent guides for your own thoughts.

The Educational Policies Commission of the United States issued in 1938 a classic statement of aims called *The Purposes of Education in American Democracy*. Note the points of view and the scope which their statement implies.

Experimental science. The rapidly accumulating body of knowledge about how people learn and the interactions between people and their environments throws much light on the means of education but relatively little on ends. The same science that makes it possible to teach respect for Jews also makes it possible to teach hatred of Jews. We possess the methodology to teach children to read critically, but whether we *should* teach them to be critical depends on our philosophy. Nevertheless, we can draw on the science of education for much guidance because it does help us in relating means — our methods and procedures of teaching — to the ends we think we should try to achieve.

Philosophy. Philosophy consists of the answers man gets when he applies his mind to puzzling out what life is about and what values are worth striving for. All of us philosophize but mostly on a strictly amateur level. Some very great minds have devoted themselves assiduously to finding the order or disorder in the universe and have come out with a variety of answers. We can follow their reasoning and find much help in ordering our own thoughts. We may not be able to learn from them the one sure path through the forest; at least we can be forewarned of forks in the path and where each leads. It is possible to earn a degree in most of our colleges with only an incidental contact with philosophy, but teachers-to-be may very well find it dangerous to deprive themselves of this kind of guidance.

Religion. Religion can help you discern values that transcend time and place, and it can also afford you the opportunity for committing yourself to a way of life built on these values. Through faith many people have gained insight into the purpose of human existence — insight which they could not have achieved by reason alone. Religious insight accounts for much of the current orientation of life and education in America.

Society's tendencies. Some people today believe that the good life is slowly and painfully being described by the human race itself. Looking back over the course of human history, they claim, we can see the race seeking certain goals, certain ways of life, evolving a certain scale of values. The struggle toward ample supplies of food, clothing, and shelter is evidence that one of the ends of life is to satisfy man's physical needs. Similarly, they trace a struggle toward what we call freedom and from this deduce freedom as an end of life.

Whether we can accept this theory or history or not, it is true that we can get considerable guidance in selecting the ends for education from what men have held to be valuable in the past. It is not wise to discard a given end or aim simply because it is traditional. A traditional end may need modification, but it can be an excellent indication of what has been considered valuable by many people under many circumstances.

The current social order. To a certain extent the schools are creatures of the social order in which they exist. We seek the end of vocational proficiency in some public schools today chiefly because our present society places great emphasis on such proficiency. As our social order in the United States has become more and more intertwined with the social order in other countries, many schools have raised to new importance the end of understanding other nations and peoples. That the current order is unsatisfactory as a single guide to the goals of education should be obvious, but it does offer clues which we can use to advantage.

Persistent problems of living. As you and I live we find ourselves confronted with problems to solve. We need to stay healthy. We have to deal with the government. We face marriage and making a home. We have to learn how to earn money and how to spend it. As we look about us we see that other people are facing almost identical problems; as we delve into history we find that the same problems have confronted our forebears. Perhaps the ends of our teaching should be to equip people to deal with the persistent problems of living. If so we can get some guidance by learning as much as we can about the nature of these problems and about the processes of problem-solving itself.

This particular guide is useful only when certain assumptions have been made; those assumptions are in themselves choices of ends for education. For example, we assume that education should help man solve his problems. But millions of people in the world believe that man's problems cannot be solved, that all he can do is rise above them to a state where hunger and quarrels with his wife and oppression by a tyrant make no difference. We also make certain assumptions about what constitutes a " solution " to a problem. Confronted with the problem of establishing satisfactory relations with others, a person could " solve " it by retreating into a daydream world of his own making. In other words, in using this guide or almost any other you will inject some values that you hold, and the question of *what* values takes you right back into the realm of philosophy or tradition.

Educational theory. A theory is an explanation of what does or will happen, carefully based on all known facts and on critical analysis of possibilities. It has not been proved to be true, but it cannot be proved to be false by what is already known. A theory is much further along the road toward truth than a guess, a speculation, or even a hypothesis. Many of our greatest advances have been made because people acted on the basis of theory; scientists achieved atomic fission, for example, by following theories not then proved. Other scientists did wonderful things with electricity, acting on a theory of the nature of electric energy which later proved to be false but which was near enough the truth to have great practical value. Education uses its share of theory. When that theory meets the definition given in the first sentence, it is a practical and useful guide to follow.

Educational theory will be extremely useful in helping you choose means for reaching desired ends. John Dewey advanced the theory that learning is most lasting when it is acquired by meeting a need the individual sees and feels. The theory stood up when tested by objective evidence and logical analysis. Miss Cotton acted on this theory by arranging with Gary to use an encyclopedia to get information about the state to which his family was moving. Thousands of other teachers have acted on this theory in other ways. Such testing of the theory has produced evidence that it is sound. Although still a theory it furnishes a useful guide to teachers in search of the best means of making learning functional.

In your career you will run into disparaging comments about educational theory. A colleague will contend that " it's fine in theory but it will not work in practice." Anything that will not work in practice is not a theory. It may be speculation, a hunch, or a doctrine; but if it is theory, it does work in practice, or it is discarded. Usually what such a remark actually means is that " I don't understand the theory well enough," or " I am not adept enough to put it into practice."

You will be told that theorists in education are flighty, unrealistic, or just plain stupid. This may be correct in regard to halfbaked formulations or well-meaning but poorly based exhortations sometimes labeled as theory. Just because something is advocated, it does not become a theory. Genuine theorists in education, such as John Dewey, Johann Herbart, Henry C. Morrison, William James, G. Stanley Hall, and Boyd H. Bode, have contributed much valuable guidance to teachers.

We have gone to great pains in this . . . [discussion] . . . to individualize the matter of ends for teaching. Actually, when Betty enters teaching she will find it unnecessary to bother her pretty little head about the ends of her teaching; others will pretty well determine the ends for her if she wants them to, or she can get by from day to day without any ends really in view. She can ride tradition in her school and keep up with the parade. That is, she will find it unnecessary to bother about ends unless she feels strongly that what she does or does not do as a teacher is tremendously important.

CHAPTER FIFTEEN BIBLIOGRAPHY

BROUDY, HARRY S., *Building a Philosophy of Education*, revised edition. Englewood Cliffs, N.J.: Prentice-Hall, 1961.

> Broudy skillfully blends the traditional and formal branches of philosophy with the educative process. He sets his discussion in the framework of educational problems and relates these to the ultimate nature of truth, goodness, and man.

KNOWLES, MALCOLM and KNOWLES, HULDA, *Introduction to Group Dynamics*. New York: Association Press, 1959.

> Since our ever-increasing interdependence involves many group undertakings and decisions, this little book may serve as a brief introduction to the study of group actions. Its annotated bibliography will be useful in locating particular areas of interest.

TAYLOR, HAROLD, *On Education and Freedom*. New York: Abelard-Schuman, 1954.

> In Chapter Four, " Philosophy and the Teacher," the youthful former president of Sarah Lawrence College deplores " the lack of a spirited and provocative philosophy in the educators themselves." Although his

remarks are mostly within the area of college teaching, they have application to teachers at all levels of instruction.

SCHEFFLER, ISRAEL, *Philosophy and Education*. Boston: Allyn and Bacon, 1958.

> This book of readings is not intended to be "practical." It uses the method of philosophical analysis in the study of educational problems. The article by R. M. Hare on "Decisions of Principle" (pp. 72–85) is especially useful in clarifying the decision-making process.

Index of Authors and Titles

DATE DUE